**W9-BZL-422**

DROIDMAKER

George Lucas and the
Digital Revolution

DROIDMAKER

George Lucas and the Digital Revolution

Michael Rubin

Triad Publishing Company   Gainesville, Florida

To report errors, please email: errata@droidmaker.com

TRADEMARKS
Throughout this book trademarked names are used. Rather than put a trademark symbol in every occurrence of a trademarked name, we state we are using the names in an editorial fashion and to the benefit of the trademark owner with no intention of infringement.

Library of Congress Cataloging-in-Publication Data

Rubin, Michael.
    Droidmaker : George Lucas and the digital revolution / Michael Rubin.-- 1st ed.
      p. cm.
    Includes bibliographical references and index.
    ISBN-13: 978-0-937404-67-6 (hardcover)
    ISBN-10: 0-937404-67-5 (hardcover)
    1. Lucas, George, 1944—Criticism and interpretation. 2. Lucasfilm, Ltd. Computer Division — History. I. Title.
    PN1998.3.L835R83 2005
    791.4302'33'092—dc22
                    2005019257

9 8 7 6 5 4 3 2 1

Printed and bound in the United States of America

Contents

author's introduction
High Magic

STAR WARS was made for kids, and the kid in everyone. In 1977 when the film released, while Lucas was celebrating his thirty-third birthday on the beach in Maui, I struggled through Central Florida's ungodly humidity, waiting in record lines to see the flick before heading off to summer camp. As a thirteen-year-old boy, I was in the target market for this film. Like so much of America, I was inexplicably drawn to those first images I had seen in *Time* magazine, to the strange names of characters and places.

That summer I was at a camp in the woods of northern Wisconsin, a thousand miles from my home. Throughout the small cabins were a black market of photographs snapped in darkened theaters—of X-wing fighters

and storm troopers—usually bartered for candy bars and Sunday cabin cleaning favors. Rumor spread of one unusually clear shot of the Millennium Falcon that went for three Bit-O-Honeys and a week of latrine duty. The camp's program director (who campers called "Starn") kept a wary eye on the illicit activities in a stern but compassionate way. Starn wasn't like other counselors. At twenty-three, he was the epitome of cool. His composure was of a Jedi master; he was deeply admired by campers and staff alike. He maintained a calm control over kids that itself became a source of camp lore; it was said he was a master of "high magic," an expression Starn himself used sometimes. If you asked him about high magic, if you were lucky you might find yourself in a long deep talk around the campfire; by morning, you were never quite sure if he admitted he was a wizard or had told you there was no such thing.

"There are things that are known and things that are not known," he'd say to his few selected protégés, "and there are things that are real and things that are not real. The important thing is that just because something is not known does not necessarily mean it is not real." Heady stuff for pre-teens.

With images of *Star Wars* fresh in our minds, we always felt a direct connection with the fantastical story through the magic of our real-life Jedi counselor. You couldn't get close enough to the warmth of that glow.

Years later, after having lost touch with those wilderness days, I was a college junior at Brown University. Crossing the green commons early in spring I came across two freshmen who were oddly familiar—former campmates. Not only were we excited to see each other, but they were—at that precise moment—on their way to meet up with a grown-up Starn, who was visiting campus that day. "Would I like to come?" Would I possibly pass up an opportunity to re-connect with the wizard of high magic himself? I wondered silently what would he really be like, far from the fire's glow and the north woods mythology. After warm hugs and a soda, we faced off in a small café for a recap of our lives. What does a charismatic legend like Starn do for a job?

"I work for George Lucas," he said.

After an afternoon of re-connection he told me he figured I'd like it at Lucasfilm, although he wasn't in a position to hire me. Maybe a summer job? Maybe an internship? With Starn as my principal reference, I began obsessively following the public face of the company: reading articles, shooting off pithy letters, making strategic phone calls to try to secure a position. Periodically there would be hope, only a month later to be dashed. This continued for eighteen months. My parents insisted I come up with a plan for a career after graduation. I insisted my schedule had to remain open. Three days before graduation I got the call that I had been waiting for. I was invited to join a new project Lucas was initiating, involving computers and Hollywood.

The Lucasfilm Computer Division was a skunkworks project that Lucas had enacted in 1979, during the making of *Empire Strikes Back*. By 1984 the advanced and secretive research in editing movies, sound, computer graphics and games had crystalized into tangible tools and products. I expected to join the graphics project (later known as Pixar), but by the time I arrived at my desk in San Rafael, California, I found I had been assigned to The Droid Works, introducing new editing and sound tools to Hollywood. I demonstrated the EditDroid and SoundDroid to directors; I trained editors in New York and Los Angeles. Eventually I became an editor myself.

The executives and managers in the company probably considered me sufficiently non-threatening and apolitical that they candidly exposed me to their tribulations. It was not uncommon for my early evenings to be spent with someone or another who was happy to rant about our company, Hollywood, and Silicon Valley. I was young enough that my social circle of underlings extended throughout the divisions of Lucasfilm and all the subgroups in the splintering Computer Division. For almost two years I experienced remarkable events first-hand, events that not only changed filmmaking but resonated through all of media technology.

By the time George Lucas began making the prequel trilogy to *Star Wars* in the late 1990s, his visions for modernizing Hollywood had become well-established practices, and the legacy of the Computer Division was widespread. Everywhere I turned were reminders of those days—Pixar movies, THX logos, epic blockbusters with computer-generated characters, immersive multi-user videogames, a host of consumer software for editing, sound and graphics—but few people I spoke with realized how much had come directly from Lucasfilm research. Because the company was privately held, because George is so secretive anyway, there were only bits of information available, much of it erroneous or exaggerated, some of it mythologized.

I decided then that I should research the story of the Computer Division—how it came to be, why a filmmaker spent a disproportionate amount of his wealth to create it, what historical events happened there, and what became of it. It would span the history of filmmaking and the history of technology. It would be comprised of the experiences of the people I had met there—the executives, the filmmakers, the scientists, the competitors, the friends—who along with George Lucas reveal this story.

Starn continued to be my good friend, my guide and advisor through my years at Lucasfilm and beyond. As Yoda said in *Episode I*, "There are always two: the master and the apprentice." Lucas had Coppola. I guess I had Starn.

But I could never get the question out of my head, "Was all that talk about magic real or just camp stuff?" It was hard to say if he ever answered. There was only one question I did recall him responding to.

"What is magic?" I asked him one evening over dinner, as my years at Lucasfilm were coming to an end.

Starn said, "Magic means 'to amaze and delight.' Of course there is magic."

If the Lucasfilm Computer Division did anything with consistency, it was to amaze and delight. High magic, I always believed, was Lucasfilm's best kept secret.

[act one]

one

The Mythology of George

[Before 1967]

George Cukor [once said], "I'm not a filmmaker. A filmmaker is like a toy-maker, and I'm a director."

Well, I am a filmmaker. I'm very much akin to a toymaker. If I wasn't a filmmaker, I'd probably be a toy-maker. I like to make things move, and I like to make them myself. Just give me the tools and I'll make the toys. I can sit forever doodling on my movie. I don't think that much about whether it's going to be a great movie or a terrible movie, or whether it's going to be a piece of art or a piece of shit.

—GEORGE LUCAS, 1974

PERHAPS the most widely held and enduring myth about George Lucas is that he is a technocrat. It's almost impossible to look at his science fiction movies—like *THX 1138* or *Star Wars*—or the achievements of Industrial Light & Magic, the special effects company he created, and not imagine the man an *übergeek*.

But ask Lucas and he'll say, "I'm not a technological guy at all; I don't like gadgets."

He writes his movies longhand on a yellow pad with a no. 2 pencil. He doesn't play videogames for fun. He doesn't even surf the Internet. Lucas enjoys a kind of Victorian pre-industrial lifestyle, a gentleman filmmaker on a private, finely crafted retreat he calls Skywalker Ranch.

"I'm just somebody who wants to make movies. You don't need to be technological to understand how to use technology."

It is ironic, then, that Lucas holds a central role in the invention and dissemination of digital media. Before he assembled the team that would become the Lucasfilm Computer Division, there had been only disparate research about computers in their application to entertainment. But his passion, capital and, most importantly, his creative priorities coalesced these scientists and set them on a parallel path—like a laser synchronizing electrons into a single wavelength of high-power light.

Something mysterious took place at his Computer Division—a series of interactions that somehow connected the archaic to the modern. In light of all they accomplished, it's difficult to imagine the work having been done by only a few dozen people in a modest building in San Rafael, California.

Lucas' research into computers was in part connected to his overarching concerns with creative autonomy. His career was ever running headlong into the issue, and so he embarked on a path to wrestle control from those who always seemed to keep it out of his reach—the studio system, executives, the filmmaking process itself. Money would eventually give him what he needed: quality, control, and independence.

His most important influence came from a dynamic relationship with one of history's great filmmakers—a true technocrat and a ferociously independent spirit—Francis Ford Coppola. The story of Lucas cannot be told without the intertwined story of Coppola. They worked together and inspired each other.

The ebb and flow of their enduring friendship has often been distorted as acrimonious. Coppola was sometimes described as Lucas' "mentor/tormentor." They are competitive, but no more than any pair of close brothers: Coppola, the older, charismatic sibling, a larger-than-life *bon vivant*—with all the passion, catastrophe, and sensuality that that implies, overshadowing Lucas, the younger, quieter, conservative one.

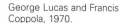

George Lucas and Francis Coppola, 1970.

"We respect each other, but at the same time we are totally different personalities," said Lucas. "He says he's too crazy and I'm not crazy enough. Francis spends every day jumping off a cliff and hoping he's going to land OK. My main interest is security."

Coppola was already a success in the years before Lucas began his career. By 1970, as he was actively assembling a film company in San Francisco, Coppola was busy announcing to the press that he someday wanted to build a "futuristic plant that would place filmmaking squarely in the technological era," possibly north of San Francisco in Marin County.

"The reason for all this stuff," Coppola said, "is to turn control of the technical side of filmmaking over to one man rather than a team of technicians. What we're attempting is to give a filmmaker the same sort of control over his creation that a painter has." When Coppola stood on stages to make those proclamations, Lucas—his lieutenant, his best friend—was close by.

Coppola catalyzed Lucas' rebellious attitudes and creative impulses. Lucas was the gifted protégé. But they also inspired one another.

"We can bounce ideas off each other because we're totally different," Lucas said in 1980. "I'm more graphics-filmmaking-editing oriented; and he's more writing and acting oriented. So we complement each other, and we trust each other. The fact that he's always doing crazy things influences me, and the fact that I'm always sort of building a foundation, plodding along, influences him. But the goals we have in mind are the same. We want to make movies and be free from the yoke of the studios."

"Francis and I were both very interested in the possibilities of the art form of cinema," said Lucas recently, "and out of that came a mutual interest in 'How do we do this? How do we break down the old system and make it easier for us to actually make movies?'"

Lucas, because of his extraordinary financial success, was able to do what Coppola could not. Beyond freeing himself from the studio system (something Coppola never fully accomplished), Lucas redefined filmmaking. By fostering the invention of new media tools, he changed the very essence of what it meant to transform imagination to the screen.

"It's like the period in the late 15th century when new painting technology, oil painting, was beginning to replace frescoes," said Lucas in 2004. "Painting frescoes was like making a movie. It took a huge group of people: experts in making plaster, in building scaffolding, in mixing colors, in applying the colors to plaster…you had to get the colored plaster to the wall quickly, and apply it in small regions before it dried.

"And then along came oil painting. The artist could mix up colors that looked the same wet or dry. The oil paintings were portable. They could be made by a much smaller group of people, or even by an individual. And most importantly, the medium gave an artist great creative flexibility—he could change his mind, work the painting, repaint areas over and over, and get a kind of malleability he simply didn't have with frescoes."

Francis Coppola and George Lucas, circa 1982.

Lucas moved filmmaking from its fresco age to its oil painting age—adding new degrees of creative flexibility previously unimaginable.

"All art is technology," said Lucas. "It's a very human endeavor. There's a certain amount of advanced intellect to master technology, whether it's scribbling on a wall or playing music. But at the same time, art is primarily the communication of emotions rather than intellect. So it's using your intellect to transfer emotions."

The introduction of digital technology to the creation of media was an advancement that would ripple through the years, far beyond the film industry, taking it somewhere that no one, not even Lucas, imagined.

To write the story of the Lucasfilm Computer Division, it becomes necessary to have a basic understanding of the company Lucasfilm. And since Lucasfilm is a privately-held corporation owned entirely by George Lucas, the various projects and divisions of the business—particularly in its earliest years—are largely a function of the interests of its founder, Lucas. And yet this story is not the biography of George Lucas. That mountain has been scaled with varying degrees of success over the past few decades. Both George the individual and Lucasfilm the company eschew any interrogation that borders on the biographical. They don't consider anything written particularly accurate, and now in his sixties, George is in no mood to start setting the record straight.

Let's start with a few known facts. George Lucas was a kid in the '50s, raised in Modesto, a middle-class agricultural town in California's central valley.

"I was as normal as you can get," he once said. "I wanted a car and hated school. I was a poor student. I lived for summer vacations and got into trouble a lot for shooting out windows with my BB gun."

Teenage Lucas and his Fiat Bianchina.

As soon as George could drive, which in Modesto meant age sixteen, he convinced his father to get him a car: a little yellow Fiat Bianchina that was more cute than sporty.

As he drifted through his high school years, George spent countless hours with his best friend, both fixing up their cars. Greasy, side-by-side, they'd mess with the engines, tweak their timing belts, and then go racing around town.

He might never have discovered film if it hadn't been for a car accident at the end of his senior year. In a twist of fate that has become the core of a Lucas myth over the decades, Lucas' seat belt inexplicably snapped and he was thrown from the car before it was mangled against a tree. Unconscious but still alive, he was badly crushed. After a long recovery, and justifiably nervous about getting behind the wheel again with his old reckless abandon, he decided to give up speed. Instead of racing cars, he started photographing them.

"I really wanted to go to art school," said Lucas, "but my father wouldn't stand for that." Soon Lucas' racing buddy introduced him to the idea of cinematography and to film school.

After graduating from high school (just barely), Lucas applied to and was rejected from both the University of Southern California (USC) and the University of California, Los Angeles (UCLA). Undaunted, he drove down to L.A. to visit racetracks and to look for a job. Through a mechanic at the track he met Haskell Wexler, not only a racing fan but also an accomplished cameraman in Hollywood. Although Wexler's early films were relatively unknown, at age forty he was on the precipice of a career explosion.[1] So there he was, engaged with this kid at the racetrack—both of them standing in the pit, both of them talking about movies.

Recalled Wexler, "I met him and I naturally liked anybody who was excited about what I did."

[1] **Haskell Wexler** (b. 1926). Cinematographer: *Who's Afraid of Virginia Woolf?* (1966), *In the Heat of the Night* (1967), *The Thomas Crown Affair* (1968), *Medium Cool* (1969), *One Flew Over the Cuckoo's Nest* (1975), *Coming Home* (1978), *Matewan* (1987), *The Secret of Roan Inish* (1994), *Silver City* (2004).

Lucas still wanted to get into USC, and Wexler was happy to put in a good word for him. "I sensed a guy who had a burning desire to explore unique visual graphics, filmic things." The fact that they both truly and deeply loved cars was their unspoken bond.

Wexler gave his friend a place to hang out and watch film being shot at his commercial film house, Dove Films. He tried to find Lucas a position on a "real" movie, but it was impossible. And the more impossible the industry made itself to young George, the more he wanted in. At one point Wexler almost got Lucas a production assistant position on a movie, only to have the Hollywood unions block him. It was incredibly frustrating.

Ultimately, George decided to go home and attend junior college. He began to study. He began to read voraciously. He refocused his lurking interests in comics, graphics, art, and painting into photography. As he was finishing school in Modesto, Lucas reapplied to USC's film department and this time was accepted.

But Lucas wasn't quick to forget how he had been treated in Hollywood.

"I just turned my back on Hollywood," he said. "I'm not interested in that anyway; I'll just go to film school and learn about film." For all the myriad reasons someone goes to film school, it was clear to George that for him, none included the prospect of going on to Hollywood to make movies.

In that era, the film industry was a closed fortress, run by the same old cigar-chomping moguls who had started it. In 1964, as Lucas entered USC, 91-year-old Adolph Zukor was still on the board of Paramount, 84-year-old Sam Goldwyn was still lingering at MGM, 72-year-old Jack Warner ran Warner Bros., and sprightly 62-year-old Darryl Zanuck was at the helm of 20th Century Fox.

As it had been for a half-century, movies were a producer's medium. Directors, like writers, actors, editors and cameramen, were all hired guns and largely interchangeable. Producers were the only ones to see a film through from story concept to theatrical debut. Their crew was all selected from rosters of qualified insiders—lists controlled by the iron grip of the unions.

And getting into the unions was nearly impossible. You had to be someone's son, or have an uncle who was a gaffer[2] or a cousin who edited. The "official" position was that you were granted admission only if you could perform some task that no one else in the union could do. Or if everyone in the union was busy and additional help was needed. The net result, of course, was that it was a closed world.

And even if you got in, there were long years of apprenticeship. Editors, for instance, had to start as "apprentice editors"—watching, getting coffee, running errands. In 1964 you needed to complete four *years* of apprenticing before you were eligible to become an "assistant editor." Assistants had a

[2] The lead electrician on a film, a member of the union of lighting professionals.

serious (though uncreative) role central to the massive organizational effort involved cutting and taping a half-million feet of celluloid into a 10,000-foot finished project. According to the Editor's Guild guidelines, after being an apprentice you had to be an assistant for four *more* years before you would be allowed to edit. And it was even harder to become a director.

There were perhaps a hundred schools in the U.S. with moviemaking as part of the curriculum. The top three were leagues beyond the rest, with full-scale programs offering bachelor's and master's degrees: New York University (NYU) in Manhattan,[3] and the largest and oldest, cross-town rivals USC and UCLA in Los Angeles.[4]

At that time, film school was blue-collar and pre-professional; a film student was the ultimate nerd. USC's film students were relegated to an old stable on the fringe of campus. UCLA's department was housed in Quonset huts left over from World War II. "All my friends thought I was crazy," recalled

[3] Where directors Martin Scorsese and Brian de Palma were film students.

[4] There was also a small program down the coast at Cal State Long Beach, attended by Steven Spielberg.

USC film students in an editing lab, 1965.

Lucas. "I lost a lot of face, because for hot-rodders, going into film was really a goofy idea."

With machines droning on all around, and equipment fixed with a wrench, some oil, a new bulb, and sometimes a solid kick, it was the kind of place where Lucas was extremely comfortable. It was somewhat analogous to his old fix-it shop experience—guys working on their cars in different stalls, helping out with each other's problems, borrowing a screwdriver from your buddy across the way—yet there were both academic and creative aspects that would be completely liberating to a born-again student and somewhat frustrated artist.

"When I went in, I just kinda ambled in. 'Well, let's see what's behind this door.' But I didn't know what in the world I was going to do with my life and where I was going, and then I stumbled into this film school and there I was, and it was like the most incredible thing I had ever witnessed in my life."

George's first course was in animation. Stringing a series of still frames culled from *Life* magazine, he delivered his first film project, a one-minute black-and-white *Look at LIFE*. Many pictures flashed by in a fraction of a second, or paused and panned for dramatic effect.

"It wasn't *movies* so much as film that moved. I was more fascinated with the medium…that real childish intrigue of 'Gosh, look at this thing…it moves.' It became a sort of obsession. I was fascinated with the mechanics of it, coming out of cars and what have you; I was fascinated with the fact that you could take real life and put it onto an image and make it move and you could manipulate it. Play with it."

What made that film particularly compelling was that he added a sound track, a flowing collage of popular music and spoken word, a seed germinated by art films Lucas had enjoyed during community college.[5] USC animation projects were almost always silent. To take the time to develop an audio track, let alone a stylistic and complex audio track, was ambitious. It won him his first student film festival prize. And seventeen other awards.

"I realized I had found myself. I loved working with film, and I was pretty good at it. So I took the bit and ran with it."

His second film, *Freiheit* ("freedom" in German) was a three-minute experiment in pictures and sound. The film depicted the suspense of one man's failed attempt to escape from East Germany. Again, like *Look at LIFE*, the film distinguished itself with a unique visual style and distinct voice collage.

"The great thing about film school," remembered Lucas, "is that it exposed me to a lot of film, and I was enthralled. That's when I got excited about film, and I just went crazy."[6]

[5] In particular, a film called *21-87* (1963), directed by Arthur Lipsett, and produced by the National Film Board of Canada.

[6] Italian director Bernardo Bertolucci once said, "The only school for the cinema is to go to the cinema, and not to waste time studying theory in film school."

Next came the three-minute *Herbie,* a surreal, sensual love poem to chrome and cars, put together with classmate Paul Golding. Set to a scratchy soundtrack of "Basin Street Blues" played by the Miles Davis Quintet, Lucas and Golding named the film for Herbie Hancock, the jazz prodigy who joined the Quintet on that album, the man they mistakenly believed was behind the piano.[7]

Lucas' final undergraduate project was an ambitious five-minute color spectacle: *1:42:08.* Channeling his passion for speed and racing into cinema, he took a dozen students (his crew) to a racetrack north of Los Angeles and shot an intense film short about a yellow sports car—not unlike his little Bianchina—making laps around a course.[8] It should be noted that students were not supposed to be making films in color. They also weren't supposed to leave the campus to shoot their projects. Lucas continually thwarted rules to execute his particular visions, perhaps revealing the lingering rebelliousness of his high school days, or maybe just the anti-authoritarian sentiment of '60s students in general.

"Everyone did it," recalled Lucas in his own defense.

Throughout film school, Lucas kept in touch with Haskell Wexler. Wexler continued trying to help the young guy, hustling to get him any job on a major Hollywood film, only to see Lucas rejected time and again by the union regulations, which were designed to keep people out. Both the incessant stonewalling by the union and the generous spirit of Haskell Wexler stayed with Lucas for years to come.

At USC, Lucas' interests evolved from animation to cinematography and finally to editing. Directing perhaps assuaged his ego, but he was always clear to point out he didn't like the activity very much. "I was introduced to film editing—the whole concept of editing—and I think ultimately that film editing was where my real talent was."

An upright Moviola—the essential machine used for editing—looked like a crazy contraption and made as much noise as a small outboard motor. At the most mechanical level, Lucas would have had a natural aptitude for the odd device: it had a pair of foot pedals on the floor for controlling the motion of the film; it also had a hand brake and a kind of clutch. Some models sported a tachometer. Watching a little screen, an editor was virtually "driving" the film. As for the creative aspect of editing, Lucas' talent was a happy discovery.

Working with film equipment was not unlike fixing an old Fiat engine. All the parts were well lubricated and finely tooled, with smooth-turning wheels and sprocketed gears—a tactile joy.

[7] The album, *Seven Steps to Heaven,* had a few tracks recorded by an interim band just prior to Hancock's joining and completing the album. The piano on "Basin Street Blues" was actually performed by English jazz pianist Victor Feldman.

[8] These yellow hot rods would show up as a reoccurring element in Lucas' films—from *American Graffiti* to *The Phantom Menace.*

The Moviola

Editing has always been a mysterious part of the filmmaking process. The general public can easily understand cameras and lights and actors, and even directing. But how the film goes from the camera to a big screen is a relative mystery. Editing was the missing link.

Once film was developed and printed, the negative was copied onto long rolls of tiny positive prints that could then be measured, moved around, and watched on all kinds of mechanical devices. In 1924 a young entrepreneur, Iwan Serrurier, had the idea to modify his unsuccessful personal film projector, called the Moviola, into a tool for the emerging film business. He removed the lens, turned the projector upside down, and built a small viewer of finely blasted glass. By the late '20s, everyone was using an "upright" Moviola; it looked like a pair of upended movie projectors, film reels locked together with a motor and gears that could be shifted from forward to reverse, and a viewer in the middle.

From an early Moviola trade advertisement.

To love editing was to embrace the Moviola. George Lucas savored it. He would sit for hours running long lengths of 16mm film through his hands, marking locations with a white china marker, strapping the film into a cutting block, and solidly chopping the bits with the hinged drop of a razor blade.

The editor's job—deciding how the film is paced or how the audience should be feeling—is frequently described as "making" the movie. Knowing where to make cuts is not an absolute science, and it can't really be taught. But if you do it often and see the results of different choices, you get a feeling for it. Like shifting gears in a manual transmission car. Who hasn't learned to drive a stick without those comical fits and starts, jerks and stalls? But somehow a driver develops a feel for easing from one gear to the next. And then you're driving. And then you're editing.

"I was an editing freak," recalled Lucas.

USC Film School,1966. *Left*: a Moviola and trim bin. *Right*: students synchronizing picture and sound tracks.

Perhaps the most important thing Lucas found in film school was a gang, a group of guys who were into making movies. Lucas was good at it; the others sensed it. It made him popular. What a wonderful feeling it must have been after years of being the outsider.

He found soulmates among his fellow USC film students, in particular John Milius,[9] Matthew Robbins,[10] and Walter Murch, who became his closest friends. Milius, a burly and outgoing fellow, introduced Lucas to the samurai films of Akira Kurosawa. Robbins and Murch arrived together from Johns Hopkins University in Baltimore and, in contrast to Lucas, were both worldly and cosmopolitan. They were different from the other students, especially Murch; he was already well versed in cinema and a virtuoso at all the department's equipment.

Walter Murch grew up mesmerized by sounds. "Maybe I heard things differently because my ears stuck out, or maybe because my ears stuck out people thought I would hear things differently, so I obliged them. It's hard to say."

In the early '50s, ten-year-old Murch persuaded his father to buy a tape recorder ("Think of all the money we'll save if we can record music from the radio instead of buying records!") and started experimenting with tape editing. Soon he was recording unusual sounds and building acoustic creations the way other kids built model planes. Later, at Johns Hopkins University, he made his first short films—silent films.

"I discovered then that editing images had emotionally the same impact for me as editing sound." At USC, he saw how both of those elements—sound and picture—could work together.

[9] **John Milius** (b. 1944). Writer: *Dirty Harry* (1971), *Magnum Force* (1973), *Apocalypse Now* (1979), *Conan the Barbarian* (1982), *Clear and Present Danger* (1994). Director: *Dillinger* (1973), *Red Dawn* (1984).

[10] **Matthew Robbins** (b. 1944). Writer: *Sugarland Express* (1974), *MacArthur* (1977), *Mimic* (1997). Director: *Corvette Summer* (1978), *Dragonslayer* (1981), *The Legend of Billie Jean* (1985), **batteries not included* (1987).

He was also still vibrating from his recent time abroad, in Italy and Paris, studying languages and art history, but soaking up something entirely different. It was 1963 and the French "New Wave" in cinema was thriving.

In the late '50s, a group of film critics for the French magazine *Cahiers du Cinema* were given a chance to become directors and put their ideas about filmmaking to the test. The *Cahiers* critics didn't like formulaic studio films; they championed a handful of American directors like Alfred Hitchcock and Howard Hawks, whom they labeled the authors, or *auteurs*, of their films.

The French critics-turned-directors, in particular Jean-Luc Godard and Francois Truffaut, took advantage of the newest filmmaking technology of the day: lightweight documentary cameras that could be handheld; faster film to capture images in low light; and smaller and more portable sound recorders. Together these technological changes allowed them to escape studio sound stages and shoot on location, where they could play, experiment, and improvise. In short: artistic freedom, personal cinema.

The New Wave was less a cohesive movement than a term the press used to describe the sudden appearance of stylistically innovative films by, in many cases, first-time directors. After sweeping in from Japan, Sweden and Italy, the wave hit France at the end of the '50s.[11] Truffaut screened his first film, *The 400 Blows*, at the Cannes Film Festival in 1959. It was an instant hit and opened a floodgate of new interest in filmmaking. That year twenty-three other French directors made their first feature films; by 1961 the number had increased to more than a hundred.

Coming from a small town, Lucas was no doubt captivated by Walter Murch's stories of cruising around Europe and North Africa on his Ducati motorcycle—a road trip he took with Matthew Robbins. Murch's feelings about editing and sound coalesced with Lucas' own attraction to the innovative juxtapositions he found in art films and the New Wave.

Through his undergraduate years, Lucas formed long-term bonds with his classmates; in addition to Murch, Milius and Robbins, his clique grew to include Howard Kazanjian, Hal Barwood, Bob Dalva, Willard Huyck, Caleb Deschanel, and others. They saw themselves as a filmmaking fraternity, hauling their cameras around campus, breaking rules, and worshipping at the altar of Orson Welles.

But back on earth, they had a different hero. Film students usually graduated and went on to work in news or education, or maybe make corporate and government films. At best they made documentaries. But there was one kid everyone knew about who had graduated from UCLA and somehow got

[11] Akira Kurosawa made *Rashamon* in 1950 and *The Hidden Fortress* in 1958; Ingmar Bergman delivered *The Seventh Seal* in 1957; Federico Fellini made *La Strada* in 1954 and *La Dolce Vita* in 1960.

a job with Warner Bros., making movies. When he directed his first feature film, *You're a Big Boy Now,* in 1966, it sent shock waves through the nation's film schools. Lucas and his group couldn't help but idolize twenty-six-year-old Francis Coppola, the only student ever to breach the impregnable walls of old Hollywood.

Said Lucas, "Every film student on the planet knew about Francis." He gave every one of them hope.

After graduating in 1966, and exempted from military service, Lucas was unsure of his next move, and took a series of jobs around L.A. One was as an assistant grip for the U.S. Information Agency (USIA), which was cranking out propaganda films as the country was heading into war.[12] Other USC students were doing odd jobs in the agency. Bob Dalva,[13] a classmate of Lucas', was assisting on a documentary about President Lyndon Johnson; it was being edited by Verna Fields. Fields was a true insider in Hollywood; she was very cool, and one of the few women in the business. She needed additional help for her Johnson documentary, and Bob Dalva recommended Lucas.

In the old days of Hollywood there were virtually no women directors or producers, and no women behind cameras. But there were women in editing. Editing—assembling the pictures together—was seen as similar to sewing. There was also an aspect to film editing that was like being a librarian, also perceived as a woman's job. In the factories that were old Hollywood studios, women sat at benches in what looked like sweatshops, editing silent movies.

When sound arrived in the '30s, that changed. Sound was somehow more technical, more electronic and, as one supposes the thinking went, required men. Soon there were few if any women working on movies at all. Editors and cameramen, directors and producers, all brought their sons on board; jobs were passed down like family heirlooms.

But by the 1960s, the pendulum began swinging back again. A number of ambitious women braved their way into the studio system. Many established male Hollywood editors took women as their assistants. (Bernardo Bertolucci's longtime editor Gabriella Cristiani once suggested that the older editors simply enjoyed working alongside young women.[14]) When the old guard later rejected working on the youth films of the '70s, their skilled assistants were ready to move into the main chair. These women began work on an impressive array of American New Wave cinema, which became known as New Hollywood.

In 1954 Verna Fields' husband, a Hollywood editor, died suddenly and she was left a single mom. Fields set up a room in her large San Fernando Valley house where she could juggle child care with editing. By 1965, with her

[12] Grips generally work for gaffers (electricians) on the set, moving and adjusting equipment, setting up props, and so forth.

[13] **Robert Dalva** (b. 1942). Editor: *The Black Stallion* (1979), *Latino* (1985), *Jumanji* (1995), *October Sky* (1999), *Jurassic Park III* (2001). Director: *The Black Stallion Returns* (1983).

[14] **Bernardo Bertolucci** (b. 1940). Director: *The Conformist* (1970), *Last Tango in Paris* (1972), *1900* (1976). *The Last Emperor* (1987), *The Sheltering Sky* (1989), *Stealing Beauty* (1996).

interest in political issues, she began editing projects for a few government agencies in the Eisenhower administration, including the USIA. While maintaining her projects with the government, she accepted a one-year position teaching film at USC.

"I had this footage of unmarked airports for a USIA film, *Journey to the Pacific*, so I hired all these kids from USC to find out where these airports were."

Fields was famous among the kids for being everyone's short Jewish aunt, a round face behind owlish glasses, inspecting the celluloid and lecturing them on threading the machine or trusting their instincts as to where to make a cut. They worked with her in her home and called her "mother cutter." They particularly loved her endless stories of editing and her "Verna-isms"—wisdom from the trenches, like "If you can't solve it, dissolve it."

Fields hired Lucas in January 1967, just as he was starting the USC graduate program in film.

The faculty at USC had been sufficiently impressed with Lucas' undergraduate films to give him a position teaching a lighting seminar for Navy film students. He taught the course at night and worked for Verna Fields at the USIA all day. She also hired a "professional" assistant (a union apprentice), Marcia Griffin, to help manage the quantities of footage and coordinate it with the film libraries in Hollywood. Marcia was buoyant and affable, a nice contrast to Lucas' rather quiet personality.

George and Marcia often worked side-by-side in Fields' home-based editing suite. They soon started dating. Even though they shared a passion for film, and for editing in particular, they had profoundly different ideologies. Marcia was committed to working her way up the union seniority ladder and into "the system"; George had little interest in the system.

For Lucas' next film project, he started with a short script by Matthew Robbins and Walter Murch about a man escaping from an underground realm and finally emerging from a manhole cover. It was called "Breakout."

Lucas refined the idea; he called the film *THX 1138: 3EB*. (He spoke of *THX* as "Thex") The story was surreal, cryptic, composed almost entirely of a man running through twisting corridors, escaping the robotic police of the dystopic future. Although USC film students didn't have access to color film, the Navy guys in the night course did. Lucas used the class he taught to execute his project. It took twelve weeks to shoot and edit.

"It's a very simple idea, and it was done that way because it was a lighting class," said Lucas. "I couldn't shoot a film; I had to shoot something very simplistic that I could put together and that would be interesting."

The photography was striking: documentary meets surveillance camera. Lucas cut the film at Verna Fields' house when he wasn't otherwise working on her Lyndon Johnson documentary. He included an unending array of visual effects. But even more impressive was the sound, a genuinely innovative acoustic tapestry. Lucas created a futuristic environment, layered from air traffic controllers' chatter and garbled public address system announcements. Lucas thrived as he assembled the components of the fifteen-minute film.

While post-producing *THX*, he made two more films for his graduate school courses. The first, *anyone lived in a pretty (how) town,* was a six-minute visual poem—Lucas and Paul Golding's interpretation of the e. e. cummings poem of the same name. Non-narrative and somewhat obscure, it had a style Lucas was very attracted to.

Finally, Lucas led his friends in making an ambitious documentary about a popular local disc jockey, Bob Hudson, called *The Emperor*. They shot for five weeks. While George directed, Paul Golding edited and handled the sound.

In the months before youth culture exploded—hippies, Woodstock, *Easy Rider*—Columbia Pictures executives decided they wanted to attract more young people to their films. They created a special project: they'd select four film school students—two each from UCLA and USC—to generate four cheap, hip, promotional documentaries for one of their movies, *Mackenna's Gold,* directed by J. Lee Thompson.[15] Students across L.A. vied for a spot. After one of his winning classmates declined the offer, Lucas accepted, and he joined the three other winners to collect the "prize": a shared station wagon, camera and lights, no supervision, and a small budget. Each student was expected to make a ten-minute 16mm film while tagging along with the cast and crew on desert locations in Utah and Arizona.

The other students produced relatively typical documentaries, choosing a subject and doing interviews; Lucas, however, took the radical approach of ignoring the film production entirely, focusing instead on the desert itself. His "documentary" was visual poetry: long shots, landscapes, abstract silhouettes of power lines, lizards. He called the short film *6.18.67,* for the date he finished shooting.

"With documentary films, I got used to shooting a ton of material and making a movie out of it in the editing room," said Lucas. "It wouldn't be challenging for me to conceptualize something and then have to follow through on it. I'd be bored to death."

On his return from the summer in Arizona, Lucas learned that USC had submitted both his and Walter Murch's names for the Samuel Warner Memorial Scholarship offered by Warner Bros. One student would be selected to work at the studio in the department of his choice for six months.

[15] Thompson was best known for *Cape Fear* (1961) but went on to do a few *Planet of the Apes* sequels.

16 The "Looney Tunes" name was a dig at Disney's early cartoons, known as "Silly Symphonies."

Lucas became enamored with the idea of hanging out in the famous Looney Tunes (Chuck Jones) animation department, looking at original cels of Bugs Bunny.[16]

Recalled Murch, "As we were going in for our final interview, we realized, naturally, that one of us was going to get it…and the other one wasn't. So we made a pact that whoever did get it would turn around and help the other if something good came along." They shook.

Lucas won.

two

Road Trip

[1967–1970]

People are hampered by money. It does not free them. It does not encourage them to go on and try new things. It makes them more conservative.

—Francis Coppola

FILM SCHOOL STUDENTS never got work as movie directors, but with luck they occasionally got a chance to write something. It was as close to a back door to Hollywood as there was for the academic crowd.

Francis Coppola's scripts from school had been impressive. Warners took notice of him after he won a prestigious screenwriting award,[1] and soon they brought him into the studio to do some book adaptations and rewrites. In short order he was offered a three-year contract, and he dropped out of the master's program at UCLA. Francis was a strong writer, a vibrant character, and a charismatic film geek.

Writing was bringing in good money for Coppola, a steady income in *the business*, but what he really wanted to do was direct. He even had an idea for a movie he wanted to make, having kicked it around since he was a kid.[2] He saved all he could with hopes of making his own movie, but by the time he'd accumulated $20,000 he realized with frustration that he'd never have enough to finance a film alone.

"So I decided I was going to risk it all on the stock market and either have enough to make a film, or have nothing. I lost it, every penny of it. In one stock."[3]

Still working for Warners, Coppola was given an important and challenging project: to develop a screenplay about WWII general George S. Patton. But after six months of research and hard work, the studio told him they were unhappy with the result, and they decided to let his contract expire at the end of its term.

[1] The Samuel Goldwyn Award, won for his script *Pilma Pilma* (chosen over his unfinished work, *The Old Grey Station Wagon*). Coppola's friend Carroll Ballard was the runner-up.

[2] He used to stick microphones around his house and listen to the voices, and he thought he could use the interesting concept in a script.

[3] Scopitone. The original video jukebox. Invented in France. Popular in Europe in the early '60s; dead by the end of the '60s.

All around Coppola, there were significant political shifts in the Hollywood power structure. Adolph Zukor had recently ceded control of Paramount to conglomerate Gulf+Western Industries. Warner Brothers' $1.6 million film *Bonnie and Clyde* was shaking up the old guard at the studio and across Hollywood.[4] It was violent (remarkably bloody gun battles). It was long (over two hours). It was completely non-formulaic. It didn't even have any box office "stars" in it.

Studio head Jack Warner didn't get it and felt out of touch with the new audiences.[5] A few weeks after screening *Bonnie and Clyde*, he announced the sale of his stake in Warner Brothers to a tiny company in New York, Seven Arts Productions.[6] It was the end of the mogul days of Hollywood.

After the buyout, anything being shot was finished and everything else was put on hold. The new regime from Seven Arts began by greenlighting two films: Sam Peckinpah's *The Wild Bunch* and a film version of the 1947 hit Broadway musical, *Finian's Rainbow*.

Coppola, still deep in debt and about to be out of work, spent $1,000 to option a popular British novel *You're a Big Boy Now,* which he hoped to develop with his old boss Roger Corman.[7]

While everything was in transition, Francis saw an opportunity for some rare time away and left for Europe with his wife Eleanor, where he worked on a lingering final Warners project. He also penned a screenplay for *You're A Big Boy Now*. When the new Warners executives realized he had written it while still technically on contract for them, they insisted they owned the movie; if it was going to be made, it would be made at their studio. Coppola, at age twenty-six, was able to negotiate a deal as both screenwriter *and* director. The impenetrable gates opened and the studio greenlighted Coppola's coming-of-age farce with an $800,000 budget.

When the film was done, aside from winning heroic stature from film students nationwide, Francis managed to get UCLA to accept the movie as his master's thesis, and they awarded him a degree. He happily returned to his old project about eavesdropping, which was beginning to crystallize after director Irvin Kershner handed him an article on surveillance and bugging; he started calling it *The Conversation*.

The new regime at Warners had locked in Fred Astaire to star in their musical *Finian's Rainbow*, but they still needed a director. Even though Coppola's contract had been terminated, and *You're A Big Boy Now* was just a modest success, Warners asked him to helm the $3.5 million project.

The film was both challenging and disillusioning for Coppola. On the one hand he was thrilled to be directing a major motion picture for a Hollywood studio. On the other hand, it was a *job*. There was little collegiate

[4] Released 1967. Directed by Arthur Penn; produced by (and starring) Warren Beatty.

[5] They drew little comfort that it cost far less than the big budget $15 million *Camelot* they were doing concurrently.

[6] The studio was for a time renamed Warner-Seven Arts, sometimes referred to as "W-7."

[7] *To option*: to pay a writer a relatively small fee for the exclusive right to turn a book or script into a movie. The alternative to having a script optioned was to sell it outright, usually for a much larger amount of money.

fun in the project. This was the big time. Recalled Coppola: "With it came the big time way of doing things: unions, budget and over budget, behind schedule, stunt men...."

Union rules obligated him to have an assistant director (the AD), and a second assistant director (2nd AD). The 2nd AD on *Finian's Rainbow*, whose job it was to run around coordinating all the elements needed for each shot, was a recent USC film school grad named Howard Kazanjian. Coppola and Kazanjian were easily the youngest people on the lot.

"Francis was the kind of director who was always changing his mind," recalled Kazanjian. "You'd show up in the morning and you'd have twenty-eight dancers ready to do a certain number, and Francis would say, 'We're not going to do that; let's do that song with Petula Clark,' and I would say, 'But Francis, we don't have the sound here, and we don't have Petula Clark here… and we have twenty-eight dancers standing around…'"

But Francis was always adamant. Kazanjian discovered that the only way to be organized enough to be Francis' 2nd AD was to go to his office at night after the shooting was completed. "We'd sit around and Francis would shoot the bull," said Kazanjian. "He'd be criticizing Hollywood, ranting about how 'I'm going to do this and that, we don't need all this equipment,' and at some point he'd say, 'Oh yeah, let's bring in the dancers fifteen minutes early,' or 'I want a crane tomorrow.' And I would stay late and see that there was a crane there in the morning."

By the summer of 1967, the Warners studio was a ghost town. The run-down animation building—known as Termite Terrace—was closed, and only one film was in production: *Finian*.

It was into this scene that scholarship-winner George Lucas found himself upon his arrival at Warners. He sat in an office they gave him, disappointed that the animation department was closed, and pretty sure that no one was going to come by and offer him a chance to direct something. After boredom overtook him, George got on the phone and called his old friend from USC, Howard Kazanjian.

"Hey, I'm here on the lot with this scholarship," Lucas said to Kazanjian. "Can I come down and visit you?"

"Sure, come on out to the backlot."

"Are you sure it's okay?"

"Sure I'm sure."

Kazanjian told Coppola he was going to bring a friend by the set, a buddy from film school. Lucas wandered across the desolate lot and found the *Finian's* production. Kazanjian introduced George to Francis, and then George settled into the shadows of the soundstage, watching the "famous" Coppola direct.

Lucas came by the next day, and the next, and the next. Howard would give him little errands, like hauling up to the editing building to get a few film frames for the cinematographer to match. And George joined Howard and Francis in their evening bull sessions.

"Francis was very open to us, said Kazanjian. "He'd say 'If either of you has any ideas, please tell me. Any suggestions at all, I would really like to hear them.'"

Coppola kept an eye on the skinny kid in jeans with an untucked button-up shirt.

"See anything interesting?" he called out.

Slowly Lucas shook his head, "Nope, not yet."

Lucas came back every day, and soon he was making suggestions about the shoot. Even though he was quiet, Lucas was also brash and self-assured; he had no compunction about telling Coppola that he was shooting a scene wrong or missing an opportunity for an interesting angle.

Coppola liked his chutzpah. Coppola liked anyone who was on his team. And Lucas, with pretty much nowhere else to go, was an amiable new fan. Like hippies at a Republican convention, the film school grads conspicuously stood out from the union guys hammering on sets or moving around lights. Lucas, in particular, was bearded like Coppola, and it bonded them as radicals. An odd couple. Coppola was large, loud, dynamic, charismatic. Lucas was skinny, pensive, and attentive.[8]

Even as the young men stood on the lot, in the very place they had always hoped to be, Lucas and Coppola found mutual dislike for the Hollywood system. Lucas expressed his hostility toward the closed unions; Coppola, who generally disliked doing *Finian's Rainbow,* found an open ear as he described the creative frustrations and obstacles he felt daily. Lucas showed Coppola his student film, *THX 1138,* and Coppola was impressed. The producer on *Mackenna's Gold* had suggested that if Lucas developed a short explanation of the story, he'd use his influence to pitch it to Columbia Pictures to see if they'd make it into a full-length film. That was the kind of thinking Coppola liked. But he urged his new friend not to venture into the shark-infested Hollywood waters alone.

They arrived at a gentlemen's agreement: Lucas would stay on as Coppola's assistant to help out with *Finian's Rainbow,* and he would get a relatively permanent position on Coppola's next film; Coppola promised to help Lucas with the screenplay for *THX.*

Where Lucas had a solid command of the filmmaker's tools and a strong visual sense for his film poems, Coppola understood opera and human drama. Where Lucas was passionate about motion and the juxtaposition of sound and image, Coppola believed strongly in the *story.*

[8] Kazanjian was with them too, but (like editor Marcia Griffin) he was already immersed in the Hollywood system: he had recently married, bought a house, and had only a couple more months to go as a 2nd AD before he satisfied the union requirements to move up to first assistant director.

George Lucas described himself as a "very anti-story, anti-character kind of guy." But his trust in Francis Coppola's intelligence and revolutionary notions made him open to Coppola's traditional concepts of story and character. Still, Lucas had to work at it.

"I'm trying to see what it's all about," said Lucas. "I'm trying to play…and I'm growing I hope."

Coppola was a disciplined writer. Lucas watched, probably in awe, as Coppola pounded out the screenplay of a project he wanted to shoot, a small personal film he called *The Rain People.*[9]

Writing came hard for George Lucas. "I'm not a good writer. It's very, very hard for me. I don't feel I have a natural talent for it—as opposed to camera, which I always could just *do*. And the same thing for editing. I've always been able to just sit down and cut. But I don't have a natural talent for writing. When I sit down I bleed on the page, and it's just awful. Writing just doesn't flow in a creative surge the way other things do."

"You have to learn to write if you're going to become a director," coached Francis.

"Oh God!" George exclaimed as he slinked off. Returning later with a draft, he handed it to Coppola…and waited.

"Well, you're right," Coppola said. " You *can't* write a script."

Finian shot over a typical twelve-week studio schedule, from the end of June to the end of September, 1967. Coppola planned to start shooting *The Rain People* as soon as he wrapped *Finian*, even though he didn't have a studio to finance or release it. He had saved a fair amount of money from his salary on *Finian*, which he was prepared to use. To get the ball rolling, he tossed in $20,000 to buy some equipment.

Coppola believed, and Lucas observed, that to catalyze these big projects it was often necessary to gamble big and start priming the pump even before the studios committed. The sheer momentum was often the only thing that kept the project alive.

"I was acting irresponsibly," said Coppola, "I was committing all my personal money, such as it was, into the film, with no guarantee that I was going to make the film."

Coppola flew a few of his friends to New York to shoot a football game he wanted to include in the movie. How narcotic it was to be in the presence of such confidence! Coppola was doing what every film school kid dreams of: coming up with an idea, writing a script, getting together with your friends and shooting it, with no one telling you what to do.

"Francis could sell ice to Eskimos," said Lucas. "He has charisma beyond logic. I can see now what kind of men the great Caesars of history were, their magnetism."

[9] Refining an older draft of *The Old Grey Station Wagon*.

Coppola got his UCLA classmate Carroll Ballard a job shooting the title sequences on *Finian's Rainbow*.[10] Lucas enjoyed merging his own circle of buddies from film school with those of Francis.

Before production started on *The Rain People*, Francis encouraged George to enter some of his films in the National Student Film Festival. The festival, which had been held only twice before, was no ticket to stardom. The 1967 winner in the prestigious drama category, an NYU student named Marty Scorsese, had done what many considered the best university movie ever. He parlayed that notoriety into a tiny budget of $24,000 to make a feature, but rumor was that not much had come of it, and now he was making TV commercials in London. Still, winning was a chance to see how your films stacked up to other kids,' and that alone made entering worthwhile.

Besides drama, there were three primary categories: documentary, experimental, and animation. George entered *6.18.67* (experimental), *The Emperor* (documentary), and *THX 1138: 3EB* (drama). When the votes were in, Lucas' pal John Milius won for best animation. *The Emperor* and *6.18.67* won honorable mentions. But in drama, *THX* took grand prize.[11]

Winning the competition got Lucas a modicum of notoriety. He and Milius, along with the other major winners at the Festival, were featured in *Time* magazine. The article ran a few stills from their films, a particularly Buddy-Hollyish portrait of Lucas directing, and a shot of Milius at a Moviola. Lucas was in full blossom—a taste of fame, a cool gang of like-minded friends, an important new supporter in Coppola, the respect from professors, and a little rebellious artistic edge.

In spite of their earlier differences, Warners professed they liked the twenty-eight-year-old Coppola and offered him $400,000 to direct another musical, *Mame*. It was more money than he had ever been offered before, but he turned it down. He wanted to do his own movie.

Somehow Coppola bluffed his way into a deal for *The Rain People*. He seeded a rumor around the Warners lot about his hot new project, apparently confirmed by his sudden disappearance to go shoot something in New York. Fearing another studio would steal their boy away, the new head of Warners signed a deal with Coppola without even seeing a script.

Coppola got Lucas a small salary to make a documentary about the project, which they treated as an "advance" for the development of *THX 1138* into a full-length feature. Francis couldn't, however, get their friend Howard Kazanjian a position on the film. Howard stayed on the lot and continued working on his union requirements, moving to the only other project at Warners, *The Wild Bunch*.

[10] **Carroll Ballard** (b. 1937). Director: *The Black Stallion* (1979), *Never Cry Wolf* (1983), *Wind* (1992), *Fly Away Home* (1996), *Duma* (2004).

[11] The panel of judges included directors Norman Jewison (*In the Heat of the Night*) and Irvin Kershner, who would later direct *Empire Strikes Back*.

The Rain People budget was set at $750,000; Coppola's salary would be $50,000—less than what he was making as a screenwriter and far below the offer he had just walked away from. Still, using his leftover savings from *Finian*, he pushed ahead, even going so far as to buy his own filmmaking equipment.

This last point was significant: though studios owned lots of cameras, lights, and editing machines, film *productions* never did. Movies were produced by small corporations that leased whatever they needed and purchased as little as possible. They rented tools, hired independent contractors (like union editors and cameramen), made their movie, then dissolved everything. Coppola was buying equipment with an eye on setting up his own studio.

In early '68, as winter made way for spring, work began on the on-the-road movie, *The Rain People.* Coppola relocated a tiny crew of two dozen people to the east coast, cramming George and everyone into six vans and heading out of New Jersey to start shooting. They planned on traveling light, from the coast to as far west as the adventure would take them. Coppola's large camper van carried his wife and kids, babysitter, and a big editing table.[12] The group chattered constantly on the CB-radios they used for figuring out where they'd go next.

Francis was finally making a movie with small lightweight cameras, just like the French New Wave directors. His team had refined other equipment as well—they improved the magazine on their Éclair cameras to hold more film, and they developed a new compact quartz light with reflective umbrellas to fully and evenly illuminate rooms.

George spent every day shooting his 16mm documentary. And every night he struggled to write a full-length draft of his student film *THX 1138*.

The production was not without its ordeals. Along with the usual issues associated with movie production, there was the badgering of the unions, in particular the Directors Guild of America (DGA), which had strict regulations about how many assistant directors were required for a studio production. While he was still in L.A. Coppola had insisted that because his film was small, like a documentary, he only needed to have one union assistant director and not two. After much debate, the union agreed. But when his production reached the east coast to start work he was summarily informed that he was now in a different jurisdiction, and he'd need to add another AD from *that* union. Coppola was fed up. The frustrations and regulations were intolerable.

He screamed at union representatives: "Unless you can get the police, the state troopers, to come and tell me to stop, there's nothing you can do. Because there's no law against making a movie. I don't need the unions. 'Cause I know

---

12 The teenage babysitter was Melissa Matheson (b.1950), who was later married to Harrison Ford. Screenwriter: *Black Stallion* (1979), *E.T.* (1982), *Kundun* (1997).

the guys who can make the picture just as well, and in some instances better, than those who are unionized."

Lucas watched silently as his documentary camera rolled, Nagra tape recorder slung over his arm.

Coppola spent weeks in conflict. "A lot of my friends who are ready to make films are watching, very carefully, to see if their films can be made within the establishment, because they'll just make it without it. There is no way any people or unions can stop them. The point is that some of the most interesting guys working, the younger guys, don't even want any part of them. And I think that's a serious danger. Because what do you do when suddenly fifteen of the best American filmmakers don't want any part of the DGA or IA!"[13]

Lucas with documentary gear on *The Rain People*.

But Francis was not always ranting in anger. He also waxed poetic in the long hours on the highway, or at the campsites along the route, about the art of filmmaking. His rants were a balance of utter self-confidence and simple self-awareness.

"The point is, I tried as honestly as I could to deal with certain themes, certain human situations, and I made a film out of it. Nobody else would ever have made that film. When I make a good film, I mean, a beautiful film—and I guess that's my ambition, to make a truly beautiful, human film—I'll know it, and then I might be very pompous about it; but I haven't yet, and I know that."

Lucas listened to Coppola's words over and over, through a microphone and headphones, on hours of tapes.

"Obviously the concept of a filmmaker is of a man who is vitally interested in every phase of filmmaking and is as interested in photography as he

[13] IA is short for IATSE, the "International Alliance of Theatrical Stage Employees, Moving Picture Technicians, Artists and Allied Crafts of the United States, Its Territories and Canada"—the labor union that oversees a range of filmmaking-related work, from the Teamsters to the Editors Guild.

is in music or in editing; although he may not do all these things himself, he works very closely with the people who do, and he is capable at doing much of this work."

It was on *The Rain People* that Coppola began to assemble what would become the core of his troupe: James Caan and Robert Duval starred in the film; Barry Malkin, a childhood friend of Coppola's, edited in the camper; Bill Butler, cinematographer.[14] And of course, George Lucas.

Deciding that they needed a set for a few important scenes (everything else had been shot *ad hoc*, on the road), they pulled into Ogallala, Nebraska. The hippyish crew turned an old shoe shop into a production office and built a soundstage in an abandoned grain warehouse. They stayed for almost two months.

While there, the zeitgeist of their New Wave notion solidified: with their new small equipment and instant studio lot, "We began to feel like Robin Hood and his band," recalled Coppola. "We really had the film-making machine in our hands and it didn't need to be in Hollywood, it could be *anywhere*."

The idea was still in the air as Coppola was invited to speak on a panel at a forum of high school English teachers in San Francisco. Busy in Nebraska, he sent Lucas in his place, both to speak and to meet a local filmmaker who was also on the panel, John Korty. Starting as a documentary filmmaker, Korty had moved to a hippie enclave north of San Francisco where, along the misty coast called Stinson Beach, he was producing his own films in the solitude of his house and adjacent barn. He had made three features in the past four years, and was perhaps the most successful independent director in the country. Korty was living the dream, and Lucas knew it as soon as he heard him speak.

Lucas and Coppola needed to see Korty's set-up. *Rain People* wrapped at the end of June, and by July 4th, Lucas and Coppola were at Korty's beach place, amazed to see his well-equipped barn/studio.

Recalled Korty: "Francis walked in and saw two arc projectors, a Steenbeck table, a three-channel sound mixing set-up, and a nice big screen, big speakers, and he said, 'My god, you've done just what we've been talking about doing.' They said this is exactly what they fantasized. They hadn't realized anyone could actually do it."

Coppola said, "He inspired us both. He was a real innovator."

As Barry Malkin worked to assemble the rough cut of *The Rain People*, Coppola headed to Europe, to try to sell the film to the British and to check out the latest film tools at Germany's Photokina trade show.[15] There he made some significant purchases for his new movie studio. "I kinda went a little

[14] **Bill Butler** (b. 1931). Cinematographer: *The Rain People* (1969), *The Conversation* (1974), *Jaws* (1975), *Bingo Long Traveling All-Stars & Motor Kings* (1976), *Grease* (1978), *Stripes* (1981), *Graffiti Bridge* (1990).

[15] Photokina: International trade show associated with photography (and film) equipment, held each year since 1950 (late Sept.) in Cologne, Germany.

crazy," said Coppola, "and bought all this stuff…and at this point I wasn't even keeping track of the money…"

Dropping almost $100,000 overnight, he picked up a number of well-made European film tools, including a professional film-editing table—the Keller editing machine, familiarly called a KEM—and a fancy audio mixing console.

"I had this notion that the new technology was going to be the magic ingredient that would enable us to succeed."

The sleek and modern KEM editing table at Zoetrope, a far cry from the Moviola.

Before coming home, he cruised up to Denmark to visit Mogens Skot-Hansen, a filmmaker and owner of a youth-oriented film company called Laterna Films, who he had long wanted to meet. Laterna produced commercials, the occasional feature, and a smattering of soft-core porn.

Laterna Films was paradise. A communal film experience. Attractive Nordic women wandering around. High-end editing and sound equipment. A gorgeous lakeside setting outside Copenhagen, complete with a large main house, long covered porches, a beach, lawns, and fields.

According to Coppola, "The many bedrooms had been transformed into editing rooms; the garage was a mixing studio; everywhere young people were working on their films, discussing their projects while eating lunch in the garden." Francis had entered his dream. He stayed for three weeks.

Upon returning to the states, he captivated the gang with tales of the trip and told Lucas that they had to get a mansion somewhere. "George and I fantasized about such a company based in a beautiful place where people could work together while they enjoyed their lives and provided inspiration and advice for one another."

Francis also returned with a name for the group. He was influenced by Laterna's large collection of antique "magic lanterns," zoetropes, and other antique optical toys that led to the development of motion pictures. Skot-Hansen had given him a zoetrope and he was moved by the gift. Coppola wanted to call his company American Zoetrope.

"We were a new generation of American filmmakers who were going to be inspired by the European style of filmmaking."

The Zoetrope

Invented in 1834, a zoetrope is a drum-like device with slots around it for viewing little images on a loop of paper. When the drum spins, the still images coalesce into a magical dance, one second long. These were, in effect, the first movies. The name zoetrope derives from the Greek roots for "life" (zoe) and "movement" (trope).

Zoetropes allowed viewers to watch all kinds of whimsical vignettes, from horses trotting, to a guy shooting a gun, in endless loops of enjoyment. William Horner invented the toy only to see it disappear from public consciousness for thirty years, re-emerging and experiencing a brief heyday into the 1870s.

In the weeks after his return Coppola was consumed with the next steps; how would American Zoetrope work? He sought feedback from everyone he trusted. Carroll Ballard, Francis' friend from UCLA, articulated the view: "There was no way one could work within [the Hollywood system]. The best chance was to get out of L.A. and find alternative financing."

Francis suggested to his wife Eleanor that they should move to Northern California. She was amenable to raising her kids away from the competitive Hollywood lifestyle, and the Bay Area seemed like a great spot. Recalled Francis, "It was a beautiful place to live and had an artistic, bohemian tradition."

Coppola was ready to escape L.A., but contrary to prevailing wisdom from Ballard, he signed a production-distribution agreement with Warners on November 19, 1968; it included an advance of $75,000 for the development of *THX*. He agreed to write and direct a remake of the 1941 comedy

Here Comes Mr. Jordan, which was going to be called *Heaven Can Wait* and would star Bill Cosby. But he was having trouble reconciling these plans with his Zoetrope agenda.

In late November, *Daily Variety* said "[After *Mr. Jordan*], Coppola plans to take off for San Francisco to establish a filmery there which he hopes will attract young filmmakers 'the way actors have gone to the Actors Studio in New York.' Coppola charges film industry unions sit like 'fat cats' and do not allow newcomers in any faster than oldsters die out or retire. He thinks it would be much healthier if teacher-student relationships could develop, with both veterans and youngsters learning from each other."

Lucas lived in a little rented house with his girlfriend Marcia, and together they edited the documentary about *The Rain People*, which he called *Filmmaker: A Diary by George Lucas*. The closing shot of *Filmmaker* said it was made at "Transamerica Sprocket Works" a fictitious company name George liked the sound of. The film was copyrighted by American Zoetrope/Lucasfilm Ltd.—the first film credit for the new, unofficial names of Francis' and George's respective companies.

Coppola's new audio equipment was expected to arrive soon from Photokina. He asked Lucas: "Do you know anybody who knows anything about sound?"

"I know just the guy; he's a genius."

In December 1968, about a year and a half after leaving USC, Walter Murch got a call from George Lucas. They talked about *Finian's Rainbow* and they talked about *The Rain People*. George, who had just finished the first draft of his theatrical *THX 1138*, told Walter about Coppola and their plans to relocate. Recalled Murch, "Francis needed somebody to do the final sound [on *Rain People*], and he asked me if I wanted to move to San Francisco and do that." Murch said yes.[16]

Barry Malkin, the *Rain People* picture editor, finished the cut in January and turned everything over to Murch, who called it "the hand-off." Malkin said, "Here it is…I'm sick of it," and went home to New York, leaving Murch to work in Lucas' old house in Benedict Canyon, alone with the film, a tape recorder, a Moviola, and a transfer machine, adding sound effects. Murch worked on the sound in relative isolation while the rest of the gang began tying up loose ends in southern California.

In February 1969, George and Marcia were married. During their honeymoon in northern California, they discovered the richness of Marin County. In no time, George and Marcia were moving to the Bay Area with Francis and Eleanor Coppola. Francis rented a big house in San Francisco's Pacific Heights; the Lucases rented a small house in the hills of Mill Valley, a suburban village in central Marin. It was a pleasant throwback to small town country living.

[16] Like Lucas, Walter Murch had been a little wayward after leaving USC. Coming in second for the Warner Scholarship was little consolation; there wasn't much work available in Hollywood for film school grads in 1967. Luckily, USC pal Matthew Robbins got a job at Encyclopedia Britannica Educational Films, and when other opportunities presented themselves, he moved on and called Murch to take over.

Walter Murch finished the sound effects in L.A., and then the Murch family packed their little house in Beachwood Canyon, including all the sound rolls from *The Rain People*, into a rent-a-truck.[17] They headed out of L.A., stopping only for lunch at Francis' house in San Francisco, and then continued across the Golden Gate, to their new home—a houseboat in Sausalito. It was a five-minute ride on Walter's motorcycle to George's house.

"Francis didn't know me," recalled Murch. "We had had one meeting lasting an hour, and three months later I came back with all of the sound mixed."

Through the end of '68 and into '69, George and Francis and some of their associates combed the Bay Area for a big Victorian house to establish their dream studio-commune. They poured through small Marin County towns like Ross, and the more secluded west coast regions like Tomales Bay (not far from Korty's barn in Stinson). But all their bids on real estate fell through, and the equipment from Europe was scheduled to arrive soon. In May 1969, John Korty found a place where they could store the post-production equipment, and conceding to the pressures of the moment, Zoetrope rented a warehouse on 827 Folsom Street in industrial San Francisco.

Exterior of the original Zoetrope headquarters, 827 Folsom Street, San Francisco.

Construction began right away on the Zoetrope warehouse; Eleanor Coppola, a graphic artist and designer, was excited about working on the space. Even in the midst of the renovations, Francis and George kept offices there. They asked Ken Miura, George's professor from USC, to help set up good quality post-production sound.

[17] When he finished the sound on *The Rain People*, Murch turned Lucas' "edit house" in Benedict Canyon over to Matthew Robbins and his wife.

Zoetrope, however, would have no shooting stages. Everyone agreed that sets were passé. "The lesson of *Easy Rider* and *Midnight Cowboy*," said Bob Dalva, "is that in five years no one is going to accept not using existing locations."

When all the new German KEM equipment arrived and was finally working, Murch started the final sound mix on *The Rain People*. But like most leading edge technologies, the new equipment was problem-prone. As Lucas described it: "We got a lot of new equipment in, and we had problems getting it working. It was cheaper because it was experimental, and nobody was using it, so we were going out on a limb."

And to complicate matters, the instructions—when there were instructions—were in German. Everything was trial and error. Still, the KEMs could shuttle film more than four times faster than a traditional Moviola, and Coppola hoped this would provide a desirable efficiency and economic advantage.

While Zoetrope boasted about their state-of-the-art tools, Coppola told the press he wanted more. "I want editing equipment that will allow a director to edit a film without rushing, in a couple of weeks. Computers can do the cutting and splicing. The director and the editor will be able to concern themselves solely with the *meaning* and composition of the juxtaposed scenes."

Lucas spoke with the *San Francisco Examiner*: "Someday, [Lucas] predicts, every ten-year old child will be able to buy a kit and shoot a movie. 'Think what this will do to our civilization. Movies will replace the pen. Everybody is going to be making movies.'"

Francis Coppola had grown up in a creative household (his father was the first flute for Toscanini's NBC orchestra). According to his biography: "Technology obsessed Francis. He adored gadgets of every description, and at the age of ten was already experimenting with sound in his home movies." He built a television from a kit when he was twelve. He was president of his high school radio club.[18]

[18] Debilitated at age nine with polio, Coppola thought for a time he'd never walk again.

His gadget-obsessions made him extremely hands-on in the setting up of his facility. When something broke on the fancy audio system, which happened more frequently than they would have liked, Coppola would sometimes drop to the floor and tinker with the insides himself. According to Murch, "You had to admire a guy who not only wrote, produced, directed, but was also able to figure out what was wrong and patch it up, which was beyond my ability even though I was the sound mixer."

Eleanor Coppola continued to renovate the warehouse. Francis dictated the technical specifications (like editing rooms with four-foot-wide doors for getting the three-foot-wide KEM editing tables in and out), but Eleanor's specialty was the hip vibe. Walk in the unassuming doorway on Folsom street and you were greeted by a flight of royal blue stairs to the main desk. A barn-red freight elevator with a purple door and orange grates slid noiselessly up and down a canary yellow shaft leading up to the projection room. Expansive exposed brick walls juxtaposed against smooth white plaster, often displaying an abstract painting, or perhaps an oversized tintype of Akira Kurosawa, Orson Welles or D.W. Griffith. A two-story Marimekko fabric as a wall-hanging tapestry. A silver espresso machine with a gold eagle on top in a central kitchen. Lounging spaces with an antique pool table, inflatable sofas from Europe, plastic furniture designed by Quasar Khanh and, of course, Lucite cases displaying zoetropes.

The hip interior of American Zoetrope, 1970, complete with Marimekko wall hanging, antique pool table, and a dog.

Lucas was getting frustrated trying to write his *THX* screenplay. Thinking it would never be done, he resumed working with John Milius, still in L.A., on their script about the war. Milius wanted to tell the story of a crazy surfing lieutenant, taking beaches by force and riding waves amid the bombs. They channeled their feelings about the insanity on the news every night into a story, which they pictured as a sort of pseudo-documentary, maybe shot on 16mm.

The market for Hollywood's product was shifting. *Daily Variety* reported that 75 percent of the movie-going audience was now under thirty years old. They were the first generation of kids brought up watching television, and their taste in movies was far different from that of their parents.

Everyone knew that *Easy Rider* had been shot for $400,000 and was likely going to gross more than $55 million. With the ability to shoot films on the road and on the cheap, the old studios were suddenly saddled with giant (empty) soundstages and hundreds of aimless high-priced employees. The news of the day was that venerable Paramount Pictures was selling its entire 52-acre Hollywood studio. Unions reported that 50 to 80 percent of their members were unemployed. Paramount, MGM, Fox and Warners all reported losses in 1969. By year-end, Warner-Seven Arts was sold again; under new management the corporate megalith was eventually renamed Warner Communications.

Soon after Warner-Seven Arts was established, it had tried to expand into the music business by purchasing Atlantic Records. But in only a few years, the new entertainment conglomerate was in trouble. Its revival would come through an unusual series of events. In 1967 a highly profitable parking-lot-and-funeral-parlor conglomerate, Kinney National Services, had decided to diversify by purchasing a pair of comic book publishers, DC and All-American Comics. Ripe with momentum, Kinney then acquired the Ashley Famous talent agency, run by the hot agent Ted Ashley. In less than two years, Kinney National expanded again; Ashley helped Kinney's CEO Steve Ross put together a deal to buy out financially troubled Warner-Seven Arts, which became Warner Communications in 1972.

There was still the problem of the *THX* script. George and Francis hired a professional writer to work on it, to no avail. Coppola suggested they take a retreat, to focus on the problem. But after a week even that was getting them nowhere. "Is there anybody else who can help you with it?" asked Coppola.

"Maybe Walter. He's strange like me and probably we could work this out together." Walter Murch had worked on the original story back at USC and was a good choice to join the project now.

"When George saw *21-87*, a lightbulb went off," said Murch.[19] "One of the things we really wanted to do in *THX* was to make a film where the sound and the picture were free-floating. Occasionally they would link up in a literal way, but there would also be long sections where the two of them would wander off, and it would stretch the audience's mind to try to figure out the connection."

Murch and Lucas began writing the screenplay for the movie, which by all accounts would be the first feature film out of American Zoetrope. In five weeks they had the script ready to go, and Lucas settled into pre-production on his film.

The feature film of *THX* was more than a longer version of the film school project. It retained the same look and feel, but Lucas and Murch had added a story and characters, both absent from the extended chase scene that was the student film. Lucas' ambition was to make a parable about his feelings for Los Angeles in the late 1960s, a kind of open cage where no one seemed to be able to escape.

The previous leadership at Warners had rejected an earlier draft of the script, but Francis took advantage of the second significant transition (in three years) to boldly resubmit it to the new executive team. Francis assured Warners that the script was done (a mild exaggeration) and production was ready to roll. Francis needed cash—a budget for this film and for the other films in development at Zoetrope. He got Warners to agree to finance the development of five scripts, including *THX 1138*.

The deal had a hook: it was only a loan. The money would have to be repaid if the films didn't deliver as promised. But Coppola was a gambling man; if even one was a hit, the expenses of all five would be covered. According to Lucas, all were "interesting, adventurous scripts."[20]

The budget set for *THX 1138* was creatively determined by Coppola: $777,777.[21] Of this, Lucas was going to get $15,000 for writing and directing. It wasn't a ton of money, but it was more than anyone had ever paid him to make a movie. At twenty-six, he'd be directing his first studio film. It would be a challenge. He had ten weeks—the same as he had had for the fifteen-minute version—to make a full-length feature film.

Lucas and Murch worked well together. Lucas focused on the "*cinema verite* film of the future" look he wanted to achieve; Murch concentrated on the musical essence of the film's ambient sounds.

Recalled Murch, "We wanted the whole picture to have an alien quality so that not only the subject matter of the film, but the film itself, would seem to be from the future. A 'foreign film,' not from some other country, but from

[19] *21-87* (1963) was the inspirational art film from the National Film Board of Canada.

[20] *The other four:* Francis' *The Conversation*, Lucas and Milius' *Apocalypse Now*, Korty's project about California and the Gold Rush, Steve Wax's film about the People's Park disaster at Santa Rita Prison Farm, and Carroll Ballard's *Vesuvia*.

[21] And 77 cents.

some future point in time." He said, "Because of this, we wanted much of the 'sound' of the film to have an ambiguous, mysterious quality, yet not without its own inner logic."

"Francis was letting me do whatever I wanted," said Lucas. "I mean, he'd make suggestions, and I'd listen to them cause he's a filmmaker and an intelligent person, but if I said 'no, I don't think that's a good idea,' I didn't have to do it."

Warners was increasingly uncomfortable with the project. Coppola insisted they wait until they saw the first cut before making demands.

"Since I planned to edit the picture myself," said Lucas, "I wanted to be able to 'make' the film in the editing. The shooting was designed for me to end up with a lot of documentary coverage so that, hopefully, I would be able to cut together a perfect performance in every case."

By the time the summer of love hit San Francisco, the summer that ended with the Woodstock concert back east, construction at Zoetrope was still going on. With all the equipment already on site, they decided try to generate a little revenue by renting it out. They also decided to outsource projects for the arriving teams of young filmmakers to work on, from commercials to government films.[22]

With the incessant hammering and dust, the editing rooms and production offices at Zoetrope were too hectic for Lucas. As shooting finished on *THX*, Lucas and Murch retreated to Lucas' Mill Valley home with 250,000 feet of film. Lucas (often assisted by his new bride) worked all day, and then Murch took over at night, doing sound. At 6 A.M., they switched back. This would continue for almost a year.

In the midst of it all, American Zoetrope was legally launched in November 1969. Coppola was the president (and sole shareholder); Lucas was vice president. Coppola had financed the business himself, spending maybe half a million dollars on the 10,000 square foot facility and renovation. There were seven editing rooms, most with fancy KEM or Steenbeck editing tables.[23] There were screening theaters and recording studios. It was cool, it was young and hip. And it was sophisticated.

On December 12, 1969, as the hippie decade was drawing to a close, Zoetrope officially opened for business. They celebrated with a party, distributing press releases across San Francisco and Hollywood, describing it as "probably the most advanced filmmaking facility under one roof in the world."

"This is a true capitalistic venture," said Coppola to the press, "designed to sustain itself and provide artistic freedom through money. I'm very conscious of survival."

[22] Korty moved the center of his filmmaking from his quiet Stinson Beach barn to the new facility. There, he developed a project he called *Have We Seen the Elephant?* about the Gold Rush and California in 1870 and 1970. In August, Lucas invited his old friend Bob Dalva up from L.A. to handle one of the training film projects for the Office of Economic Opportunity, one of two under-30-minute projects he had contracted to make. Coppola hired John Milius to work on his *Apocalypse* script, Steve Wax to develop *Santa Rita*, and Bill and Gloria Hyuck—more friends of George's from USC—to write *The Air Conditioned Dream*. Meanwhile, Francis returned to his beloved project, *The Conversation*.

Caleb Dechanel, Walter and Aggie Murch, Janet and Matthew Robbins hanging out.

Every hipster in the Bay Area and Hollywood was talking about Zoetrope; it was the epitome of cool. Herb Caen's column in the *San Francisco Chronicle* outlined a guided tour he received, describing the "mad activity" of film-making. According to Caen, "The measure of American Zoetrope's promise may be found in a note pinned to the bulletin board. It is from the celebrated Stanley Kubrick of *2001* renown, offering to film his next movie in San Francisco—at Zoetrope."

Later, the *Chronicle* would describe the scene this way: "It all seemed terribly chic and terribly sincere at the same time, with leggy blonde secretaries in crocheted miniskirts telling anxious job applicants in tattered blue jeans and Buffalo Bill hair, 'Film is where it's at.'"

Like everyone associated with American Zoetrope, Lucas was constantly enthralled by the dynamo that was Coppola. "I go out of the cage one step at a time, but Francis leaps out full force regardless of what's out there. Francis is a flamboyant character. Francis takes stuff and throws it all over and says 'We're going to Rome tomorrow,' and we *do* it. The idea behind Zoetrope is to give young people a chance. It took Francis ten years to make it…I made it in two years, now maybe someone can make it in a year."

Adding fuel to the fires of Zoetrope's enthusiasm was the Oscar nomination of *Patton* for Best Picture in 1970. The film was a big money-maker, and Coppola—vindicated by his nomination for Best Screenplay—was a force the Hollywood studios had to reckon with. In the midst of a movie studio depression in L.A., Coppola's hot Bay Area film commune was in various stages of development on perhaps nine different projects, with budgets ranging from $25,000 to $1.5 million.

[23] Steenbeck was a competing European brand to KEM, with a similar design, but a slightly different method of controlling the moving film.

By spring, Coppola was already describing Zoetrope's next phase. According to the *San Francisco Civic Light Opera* magazine, "Coppola envisions a move to an outlying area, possibly north of San Francisco to Marin County, where he would like to build a futuristic plant that would place filmmaking squarely in the technological era." The report went on to say, "Zoetrope has already employed a computer programmer to design production systems that will be implemented in the new plant. 'Systems,' Coppola says, 'that will be viable in the year 2000' and include such innovations as 'an editing room in which a director can push-button scenes that he wants to work on in any combination or sequence, electronically.'"

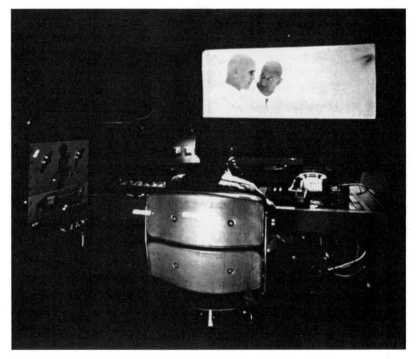

Walter Murch mixing *THX 1138* at Zoetrope's facilities.

The rough cut and mix on *THX* were done by June 1970, at least enough so that Coppola couldn't keep Warners at bay any longer. The film had been shot a year earlier and Warners hadn't seen anything of it yet. A screening was arranged in L.A. Everyone sensed it might not be well received, so Coppola suggested to Lucas that he not come with him and Milius. Lucas agreed.

Warners hated the rough cut and went ballistic. They took control of the film and began making their own changes with their own editor.

Worse still, Warners canceled their multi-picture deal with American Zoetrope; the day became known as "Black Thursday." "This is all junk," the Warner executives told the young filmmakers. "You have to pay us back the money you owe us."

It was a depressing time for everyone. Lucas felt a sense of responsibility for the debacle. Francis took the cancellation of the deal as a personal affront. The five films had no commonality except that Warners had trusted Coppola to find talent and nurture it. Now the trust was gone.

In the few months between the deal with Warners and Black Thursday, the Hollywood studios had gone full circle—from the panic surrounding *Easy Rider* to the return of normalcy they found in the 1970 hits *Airport* and *Love Story*. Both were more traditional films, and *Love Story* was even "youth oriented," so it was clear that entrusting a bunch of crazy hippies with millions of studio dollars wasn't necessary to connect with the audiences of the new decade.

"[Warners] went back to hard-core entertainment films," said Lucas. "For them it was a good decision because they made a lot of money. But they sold us completely down the river."

Zoetrope was in crisis. The teams worked hard to bring in every kind of project they could to rent the editing suites. Everyone bailed. American Zoetrope's one year rise and fall lay between *Easy Rider* and *Love Story*. As much as Coppola's company strived for independence, it still relied on capital from the Hollywood system to make movies.

John Korty got a job as a cinematographer and Marcia Lucas got a job as an assistant editor on a film by Michael Ritchie,[24] *The Candidate*, starred a young actor named Robert Redford. For the time being, Marcia was going to need to be the income earner in the Lucas family.

According to the *San Francisco Chronicle*: "Quiet once more descended on Zoetrope. 'Are they out of business?' people began whispering. Not exactly, though the proud banner that once waved above the door is now gone and the studio looks like just another electrical supply house on Folsom Street. Reality appears to have set in."

According to the terms of the deal, Coppola owed Warners hundreds of thousands of dollars that he would be paying back for the next five years.

At Francis' bleakest moment, Paramount approached him to direct a film version of Mario Puzzo's bestseller about the Mafia, *The Godfather*. Lucas urged him to do it. It would get him out of the red. It was his only real hope.

[24] **Michael Ritchie** (b.1938). Another of the expatriates from L.A. who moved north. Director: *Downhill Racer* (1969), *The Candidate* (1972), *The Bad News Bears* (1976), *Fletch* (1985), *The Golden Child* (1986).

three

The Restoration

[1970–1974]

One thing that comes out in myths is that at the bottom of the abyss comes the voice of salvation. The black moment is the moment when the real message of transformation is going to come. At the darkest moment comes the light.

—JOSEPH CAMPBELL, IN *THE POWER OF MYTH*

THE PARTY was over at American Zoetrope.

Though Coppola was in debt, he was characteristically upbeat. "It's been an interesting two and a half years. I learned how little I know about the business, but it's been a lot of fun, too. I don't regret anything."

After Black Thursday, Coppola was reluctant to take on *The Godfather*. Eventually he agreed, because it would help defray his financial problems at American Zoetrope. The deal with Paramount was for $150,000 to write and direct the film, plus 7½ percent of the net profits. Then, just as the film started shooting, *Patton* won the Academy Award for Best Picture, and Coppola shared a Best Screenplay award. It was a turning point.

"A lot of people thought, or hoped, we were close to disaster, but that can't ever be when I can go off for six months, as I just did, and earn $200,000. It's just that I finally got tired of worrying about how I was going to pay off my mortgage. I don't want to spend these years being a big daddy to everyone."

Zoetrope was humming along under the radar on Folsom Street, with Bob Dalva still using the space to create films for the Office of Economic Opportunity (OEO) and Korty doing an ABC Movie of the Week. As the OEO contract ended, Dalva set up a commercial division to keep work flowing. The Zoetrope facilities were being rented out for every Bay Area commercial, television show, and movie that came through town. Michael Ritchie booked editing bays for "Kansas City Prime" (released as *Prime Cut*). Sidney Poitier came to work on his directorial debut, *Buck and the Preacher*.

In June, Francis returned from his globetrotting *Godfather* production, hauling 500,000 feet of 35mm film—more than ninety hours of material. Paramount encouraged him to take on one of their respected union editors, an established Hollywood stalwart, William Reynolds.[1] Reynolds had already cut classic musicals (like *The Sound of Music*) and was well-versed in many genres.[2] The edit continued at Folsom Street for the next five months.

Like most of the Zoetrope team, Lucas was cut loose after Black Thursday. "I was left high and dry," he said. "*THX* had taken three years to make and I hadn't made any money. Marcia was still supporting us."

Lucas set out to establish himself on his own. He incorporated his company, which had been using the name Lucasfilm Ltd. informally for several years. He got jobs where he could; his freelance work included some second unit shooting on *The Godfather*. He tried unsuccessfully to secure the rights to *Flash Gordon*, a character he loved as a kid and was really interested in making into a movie.

> Author Alex Raymond had recently sold the rights to his Flash Gordon character to Dino DeLaurentis, a prolific Italian producer who fancied himself in the company of the New Wave Italian directors. DeLaurentis knew that Frederico Fellini, the genius who had directed classics like *La Dolce Vita*, had briefly been a comic book artist during World War II.[3] At that time, General Mussolini had stopped the importing of American movies and comic books, and Italians were trying to keep comparable materials flowing to a hungry audience. Fellini drew a few different comics for years, including Flash Gordon, and its influence on him permeated his more surreal films.

Without the rights to make Flash Gordon, Lucas started exploring his own ideas for a "space opera fantasy" as he called it. He had long mulled over the idea of updating some of his favorite genres from the serials he enjoyed as a kid. He was determined to make something commercial, anxious to revisit his successes from film school, to prove that he wasn't as cold and depressing as the *THX* film made him look.

He started working with Milius again on their Vietnam war movie. Lucas approached Gary Kurtz, another USC alum, to produce the film, and he agreed.[4] Kurtz was described as "a solemn bearded man, a Quaker, who made Lucas look like an extrovert."

[1] **William Reynolds,** (1910–1997). Editor: *Compulsion* (1959), *Tender is the Night* (1962), *Sound of Music* (1965), *Hello, Dolly* (1969), *The Godfather* (1972), *The Sting* (1973), *The Turning Point* (1977), *A Little Romance* (1979), *Heaven's Gate* (1980).

[2] Reynolds brought on an associate, Peter Zinner, to help with the massive volume of material.

[3] **Frederico Fellini** (1920–1993). Italian writer/ director: *La Strada* (1954), *La Dolce Vita* (1960), *8½* (1963), *Satyricon* (1969), *Amarcord* (1973).

[4] Kurtz had graduated a few years ahead of Lucas, and had been working—as Coppola had early on—with Roger Corman.

Early Movie Technology

In 1887, fifty-three years after the creation of the zoetrope, George Eastman invented flexible photographic film, freeing photography from the tyranny of a hooded tripod and a glass plate for every picture. It took no time for photographers to coil up long strips of this new film and expose small controlled portions to light with a shutter. But in the 1890s, flexible strips of film merged with the optical principle of the zoetrope, into a series of devices. One of the best was patented in 1891 by Thomas Edison; he called it the Kinetoscope.

In France, Auguste and Louis Lumiere were sons of a wealthy entrepreneur of photographic tools and materials. It is said that their father went to Paris in 1894, saw Edison's Kineto-scope peep shows, and told his boys, "You can do better. Try to get the image out of the box." So they did. What they invented was a small device that was both camera and projec-tor: the Cinematographe.

In the winter of 1895, the Lumieres put together a series of short films of everyday life: people leaving their father's factory, walking around gardens, playing cards, a train pulling into a station—and offered a public screening in the basement lounge of the Grand Café on the Boulevard des Capucines in Paris. The audiences were stunned: reports were that many in the room screamed and ducked for cover as the train moved toward the camera.

The Lumieres' event was considered the birth of the film business. Oddly enough, the brothers felt that the public would tire of seeing things they could see in everyday life. "The cinema is an invention without a future," said Louis.

The early history of film is replete with competing formats: different film widths, different arrangement of the sprocket holes. The success of the movie industry in some part can be attributed to the rapid standardization of the 35mm film format, with four perforations running along the side of each frame. Initially developed by Edison, 35mm film was the medium of choice for the pros;[5] 16mm film—about half as wide as the professional stan-dard—was used by students, corporations, and journalists. The smaller 8mm (and Super8) was initially created for consumers by cutting strips of 16mm film in half. As the film width decreased, the projected film image generally looked worse. Consumers got the runt of the litter.

Through the era of silent films and through World War I, rooms of workers cut neg-atives and "hot" glued the ends together between the shots by melting them. It wasn't really "editing" so much as a movie assembly line. The invention of the Movi-ola significantly improved the editors' creative control by giving them better ability to see the material they were cutting.

"Talkies" debuted with the *Jazz Singer* in 1927 although the sound (played from a kind of record) was only tenuously linked to the picture.[6] Sound was technically possible from then on, but silent films coexisted with talking films all through the 1930s and into the 1940s. As sound came on the scene, the complexity of the film assembly increased. Studios now had a roll of images and a separate roll of sound, and each had to be "massaged" independently, but still held together in a synchro-nous relationship.

[5] Called "Edison size" for a time.

[6] Walt Disney's first Mickey and Minnie Mouse anima-tion, a silent short called "Plane Crazy" accompanied the *Jazz Singer* premiere.

Editing tools changed very little over the decades. By the late '60s there was finally an alternative to the loud, clanking upright Moviola — the smooth, quiet whirr of a flatbed editing table, which Francis Coppola discovered in Europe. The reels of film were laid on plates that spun as the film threaded through centrally positioned gears and playheads. This was a sophisticated alternative—quieter and faster—although the two devices worked in about the same way, and film could easily be moved between them. Same medium, different machine. Flatbeds didn't replace Moviolas; both worked concurrently.

"Lucas is preparing another film for Zoetrope," announced a Bay Area arts magazine. "It is entitled *Apocalypse Now*, and it deals, says Coppola, 'with drugs and war, the psychedelic soldier and the end of the world.' Stroking his dark beard and pointing an index finger in emphasis, Coppola adds, 'It's like…*Heart of Darkness* set in Viet Nam.'"

Editing *The Godfather* was laborious. There were 500,000 feet of film. To add to the creative and physical demands of editing a movie, there was the data: numbers everywhere, on everything, that had to be tracked by hand and collated into volumes of notebooks. Arguably the most important numbers were the ones that ran along the edges of the negative, called "edge numbers." They were longer than phone numbers, were unique for each roll of film, and occurred once every foot. Zinner and Reynolds had a team of assistants who managed this process.

After Paramount dropped $6 million to make the movie, when the actors had gone home and the sets were put away, all anyone really had to show for their labors was the film negative. Negative was sacred. Not even assistants handled the negative. Professional handlers at the lab touched it gently with soft cotton gloves. In a very clean place. It was stored in a safe.

Editors didn't look at the negative to make decisions about what parts of this material to put together into a movie. They made a copy, a positive duplicate to look at, to mess with. No one touched the negative until everyone—the editors, the director, the studio—was sure that it was going to be cut in exactly the right place and assembled using exactly the right pieces. As with every film done for fifty years, big budget and small, Reynolds and team had a working copy of the negative—a positive print—on a roll of film, called "workprint."

Workprint included the edge numbers from the original negative. At the end of the process, after the entire workprint had been cut and assembled to perfection, a negative cutter could, very carefully, roll down through the negative to the same numeric locations and cut it to match the final creative decisions.

Reynolds and Zimmer, like virtually anyone editing film, learned to use a Moviola to cut up their workprint, but easily took to the flatbed. Rather than a foot pedal, KEM editing tables had a hand-size lever, to shuttle the rolls of film forward and backward. The images were sharp, projected from behind onto a 10-inch pane of sandblasted glass, flickering as they slowed to a crawl, as the editor inspected the subtle details of each frame.

Workprint was just a roll of silent pictures. Sound was not recorded onto the film, but centrally fed into a sophisticated reel-to-reel tape recorder called a Nagra. The Nagra had been invented in the 1950s, but it took decades for inertial Hollywood to adjust to "sprocketless" recording; by the 1970s the Nagra became established in the filmmaking industry and soon the word "Nagra" became virtually a generic term for audio recording devices for movies.[7]

To combine sound and picture, editors needed them in the same format, and that format defaulted to that of the picture: sprocketed celluloid. To create it, rolls of audiotape were embedded in rolls of clear sprocketed film called "mag," or "sprocketed mag." It could be loaded onto a Moviola or flatbed editing table and played, cut, and spliced in exactly the same way as the picture.

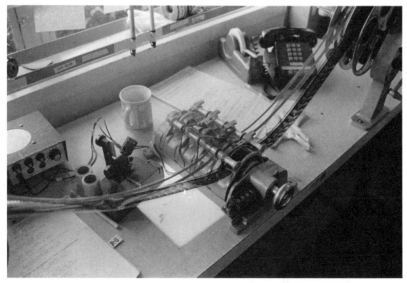

A typical synchronizing station: workprint, below, and mag, above, flow together through a film synchronizer. A cutting block, with razor blade and roll of tape, is poised to the left.

[7] The shiny silver suitcase-like box with dials and knobs was remarkably portable, rugged and reliable, and of exceptionally high fidelity. It was the sound device that, when combined with the smaller 35mm cameras and lightweight 16mm cameras of the 1950s, helped catalyze the New Wave in cinema. Manufactured by the Swiss company Kudelski, the Nagra got its name from inventor Stefan Kudelski—"nagra" is the Polish word for "it will record." The device was featured in the plot of the 1981 film, *Diva*.

Sound was always separate. If you moved the mag over the playhead when the right picture was being flashed on the small display, the picture and sound could be made to play in sync.[8] Editors would do this a hundred times a day, trying different sound-image combinations. They would cut to the sound from one shot before the picture cut occurred, following up a moment later with the corresponding picture. Juggling the relationship between pictures and sounds was as important as choosing the right picture for each moment of the movie.

Because workprint could be moved in and out of sync with its sound, it was necessary to have a simple way to identify which picture frames were supposed to go with which sounds on the audiotape. The tape didn't have any numbers. So, when the workprint arrived from the lab, the assistant editors would synchronize the sprocketed mag with the workprint and then add a new code number to the edge of both.

The result of this work was a massive wall of data that had to be methodically and carefully tracked. Assistants kept thick logbooks where they logged the edge numbers on negative and workprint, correlated them with the code numbers on workprint picture and mag sound, and added descriptions based on the scene and take numbers associated with each shot. For every frame of a movie shot, there would typically be a half dozen associated numeric codes.

Because every frame was important, decisions about where to cut a movie were meticulously derived from inspecting how each frame looked and how every detail moved. There was no guesswork. The process to cut a two-hour picture typically took four to six months.

The system for keeping track of all the numbers on workprint and mag, that eventually led to the precise cutting of original negative, was handed down from editor to editor, sacred knowledge from the brotherhood. It was not really a secret, but it was laborious, unglamorous, and critically important to master.

By November 1970, Paramount was getting impatient. They wanted *The Godfather* post-production in L.A. so they could keep closer tabs on what was happening. Reynolds moved to the Paramount lot, and in December Murch began the sound work at Goldwyn studios. Throughout 1971 the picture edit and sound mix crawled forward. It took an entire year. Eventually, the movie was cut to 2½ hours—an epic by Hollywood standards. When Paramount saw the cut, they told Coppola to make it *longer*. It released at 2:55.

[8] It was easy to slide this sync relationship around, either on purpose or by accident, by uncoupling the gears on the device.

When *The Godfather* debuted in March 1972, it was a hit. Now that it seemed his immediate financial problems were behind him, Coppola accepted a variety of jobs to support his varying creative needs. At Paramount's request, he did a rewrite of Truman Capote's script for *The Great Gatsby*. He directed a play in San Francisco, as well as an opera. And he was ready now to make *The Conversation*, a project he had started then stopped repeatedly over the years.

American Zoetrope was stable again; Francis took his first dollars from *The Godfather* and bought an impressive twenty-eight-room mansion in Pacific Heights, with breathtaking views of the Golden Gate Bridge and the San Francisco Bay. The baby blue Victorian gem had turrets, stained glass, a screening room, and an entire room dedicated to electric trains. Some friends referred to him as "FAO Coppola."

Francis filled the house with expensive furniture (Italian modern—leather and chrome), technology (a Moog synthesizer), and music (a harpsichord and a Wurlitzer jukebox full of Enrico Caruso 78s). A Warhol Mao silkscreen that had originally hung in the facility on Folsom street now hung in the living room.

While tinkering with the idea for a space fantasy, Lucas began sketching out an autobiographical story about four high school kids on the edge of adulthood. "I was getting a lot of razz from Francis and a bunch of friends who said that everyone thought I was cold and weird and why didn't I do something warm and human. I thought 'You want warm and human? I'll give you warm and human.'"

Lucas put together an outline for a rock 'n' roll movie, an exploration of his teenage experiences in Modesto. His agent pitched the story—now called *American Graffiti*—to every studio in town, where it was summarily dismissed.

With Lucas' first film a financial disaster, and only some vague ideas floating around for some new movies, his Hollywood career was looking short. Then *THX* was invited to be shown at the Cannes film festival, and though Warners had no interest in bankrolling Lucas' trip, he and Marcia decided to go anyway on the cheap, get a Eurail pass, camp out, and make it a vacation.

On their way, during a stopover in New York, Lucas seized an opportunity to pitch *Graffiti* to the studio head of United Artists (UA). Even though the studio had earlier chosen to pass on it, the executive was now impressed. By the time Lucas arrived in Europe, UA was willing to take a chance. Lucas asked Gary Kurtz to shift from *Apocalypse Now,* to producing *Graffiti*. On a roll, Lucas even pitched a crude version of his space opera. Soon, he had a two-picture deal with UA.

But the excitement was short-lived. After seeing the first draft of Lucas' *Graffiti* script, UA canceled the deal. Not ready to admit defeat, Lucas convinced his friends Gloria Katz and Willard Huyck to work on his script, to help flesh out some of the characters and add some humor. Gary Kurtz told Lucas' agent about a young executive at Universal he had worked with, who was making a slate of low-budget, youth oriented films.[10] The agent agreed to give *Graffiti* one final push.

[10] Ned Tannen, at Universal, worked with Kurtz on *Two-Lane Blacktop*, a film about two guys drag racing across the country in a '55 Chevy. The drive-in classic from director-editor Monte Hellman was also largely inspired by car culture. It seemed reasonable to introduce Tannen to the project.

Remarkably, Universal agreed to do *American Graffiti*, but only if the cast included a movie star, or at least a star producer. Lucas resisted. But then he reviewed the list of names they gave him and saw that it included Francis Coppola. Coppola was ripe with clout from *The Godfather*, which was favored to win an Oscar.

Coppola and Lucas during the *Graffiti* production.

Said Lucas, "You could see the way they were thinking: 'From the man who brought you *The Godfather*.' Anyway, Francis said sure."

While they had the opportunity, Universal also optioned Lucas' space fantasy as part of the deal.

In June 1972, Lucas began shooting *American Graffiti*, with a miniscule budget of $750,000, about the same as he had had for *THX*. Coppola supervised in name only. Busy with his own projects—which included getting *The Conversation* ready to shoot later that year—he left Lucas on his own to make the film.

Lucas and Coppola convinced cinematographer Haskell Wexler to help out with *Graffiti*, for which he flew up to Northern California each day after working on commercial projects in L.A. Lucas and Wexler finally had a chance to truly work together.

George wanted his wife Marcia to edit the movie, but Universal pushed for a more experienced professional. Lucas went to their former boss, Verna Fields, who had been growing in popularity and was now on the inside of the power structure at Universal. She had just finished cutting *What's Up Doc?* for Peter Bogdanovich, and slid *Graffiti* in before she had to hunker down on his next project, *Paper Moon*.[11] Lucas asked his old friend Walter Murch to work with him on the *Graffiti* sound, and he happily agreed.

At Lucas' urging, Coppola bought a second house in Mill Valley. The large garage was converted into editing suites. Verna Fields and Marcia edited *Graffiti* in the garage.[12] The hubbub of filmmaking around the Coppola house was more like the dream of American Zoetrope than the San Francisco Zoetrope ever was. Everyone thrived.

[11] *What's Up Doc?* (1972), Bogdanovich's follow-up to his surprise hit *The Last Picture Show* (1971). *Paper Moon* was released in 1973.

[12] Fields was only available for the first cut of the film. After she left, Murch and Lucas focused on the sound; Murch helped out with the picture cut as well.

They ran the first preview of *Graffiti* in January of 1973; Universal execs hated the movie. They didn't get it. "This movie is not fit to show an audience," they said. Arguments ensued between the studio and Coppola, who famously rose to Lucas' defense. Universal hated *Graffiti* so much they were contemplating selling it as a TV movie of the week.

Over the next many months, Lucas and his team tried to work with Universal; the film was adjusted here and there, bits were cut out. It was rescreened in March, and again in May.

"There was no reason for the cutting," said Lucas. "It was just arbitrary. You do a film like *Graffiti* or *THX*, it takes two years of your life, you get paid hardly anything at all, and you sweat blood. You write it, you slave over it, you stay up twenty-eight nights getting cold and sick. Then you put it together, and you've lived with it. It's exactly like raising a kid. You raise a kid for two or three years…and someone comes along and says 'Well, it's a very nice kid, but I think we ought to cut off one of its fingers.' So they take their little axe and chop off one of the fingers. They say 'don't worry. Nobody will notice. She'll live, everything will be all right.' But I mean, it *hurts* a great deal."

While Lucas made *Graffiti*, Coppola again worked on finishing his script for *The Conversation*. By Thanksgiving '72 he began production, which he financed himself, spending millions of his own money.[13] Francis asked Walter Murch to edit the film and also to manage the sound. Being a professional sound guy, Murch was as intimately tied to the film's themes as was Coppola.

The Conversation resonated with Coppola's excitement for, and trepidation about, technology. The film was about a professional eavesdropper, an investigator obsessed with his electronic tools. The eavesdropper eventually came to despise his equipment (which he finally destroyed) as well as his profession. Coppola once described the project as "a horror film about how this man's work affects his life, his personality."

Coppola finished shooting *The Conversation* in March 1973, and began the almost-one-year process of post-production. Walter Murch double-timed through the months of 1973, editing *The Conversation* (with an associate, Richard Chew) during the day, and mixing and remixing the sound of *American Graffiti* at night.

Soon Francis Coppola was onstage in Los Angeles to proudly pick up his Oscars for *The Godfather*. It had been nominated for eleven awards, and won three—including Best Picture. With *The Conversation* done shooting, he was already at work developing the follow-up to *The Godfather*. Royalty checks from Paramount were starting to flow.

Suitably enriched, he began a string of purchases that satisfied his sensual and luxurious tastes. First, the historic Sentinel Building in San Francisco, a classic seven-story flatiron that had survived the 1906 earthquake. He wanted the stylish edifice to be his new Zoetrope headquarters. He restored it over the coming year, and by the fall added two more properties in the North Beach neighborhood, including the Little Fox Theater. He bought a radio station, a

[13] Though he started shooting the project with Haskell Wexler, creative differences led to replacing him with Bill Butler, the assistant cameraman on *Rain People*.

magazine, a helicopter, and eventually a share of an airplane and a chain of movie theaters.

Lucas watched his friend closely. "When the idea took him to buy an airplane, he bought one for himself. I prefer miniature airplanes."

For George Lucas, the process with Universal for *Graffiti* was as infuriating as it had been with Warners for *THX*. The studio had cut about five minutes from the film as merely an exercise in power. Eventually, they selected a release date for the film.

Lucas was effectively broke. The $20,000 he had been paid to direct *Graffiti* was long gone and his debts were stacking up. "I'll just whip up that treatment, my second deal at United Artists, my little space thing," he said, "in the tradition of Flash Gordon and Buck Rogers."

Lucas took the fifteen-page outline for his "little space thing" to United Artists, but they passed. Then he took it back to Universal. They declined their option. Soon *The Star Wars* was on a desk at Twentieth Century Fox.

"It's James Bond and *2001* combined," he said. "Super fantasy, capes, swords, and laser guns and spaceships shooting at each other, and all that sort of stuff. But it's not camp. It's meant to be an exciting action adventure film."

Fox took a chance and Lucas had yet another informal deal for the movie. He was going to get $50,000 to write it, $100,000 to direct it, and they'd budget $3.5 million—more than four times the budget for his earlier two films. To get any more formal, it all would come down to the script.

After all the delays, *Graffiti* opened in August 1973. By most accounts, Universal had no confidence in the project. Much to the studio's surprise, the public loved it. Lucas was publicly vindicated. He began to get royalties and was finally able to pay off personal loans. By December his confidence had grown sufficiently that he bought first one, then two houses in San Anselmo, a small town a few minutes north of where he had been living.

The first house, which George and Marcia called "Medway," was a small Victorian with a cute garden. A few blocks away, in the old, hilly, forested part of town, they got a fixer upper, which they called "Parkway." It was a classic 1869 wood frame Victorian-style house that had been poorly remodeled by the former owner. They decided to convert it into the Lucasfilm company headquarters.

The money from *Graffiti* kept rolling in; for Lucas it was like winning the lottery. The film was breaking records. He kept the office he was given on the Universal lot, his little embassy in enemy territory, which he used when he had to show up in Hollywood.

In San Anselmo, George and Marcia built a screening room in back of the Parkway house. They turned the dining room into George's office and added some editing space downstairs. Their plan was to add offices upstairs for George's old friends Hal Barwood, Matthew Robbins, Michael Ritchie, and Carroll Ballard. It would be just like film school. It would be as much fun as they'd had at Francis' place during *Graffiti*. There was even enough room for a small support staff.

When a neighbor's house came on the market, one that overlooked their property at Parkway, they purchased that too. They could use it as temporary offices while construction at Parkway was going on.

Parkway, 1974

Aside from Lucas' bitterness with Universal for all the power games they exerted on him with *Graffiti*, it was a great period for him and his friends. Pretty much everyone was getting traction with their careers, even if it wasn't quite to the degree as Lucas.

Production on *Godfather II* began in October 1973. Between Coppola's points on *Godfather* and his executive producer slice of *Graffiti*, he was making an extraordinary amount of money. He used the windfall to refurbish his new facilities in San Francisco—the Sentinel flatiron and the Little Fox Theater.

By April 1974, even as he was still shooting *The Godfather* sequel, *The Conversation* was released to critical acclaim. While it didn't have much box office draw, the small film won the Palme d'Or at that summer's Cannes Film Festival.

By the end of summer the long shoot on *Godfather II* was complete and Francis returned to the now-completed Sentinel building offices to begin post-production. Once again, he asked Walter Murch to work on the project with him. *The Godfather II* was released for Christmas 1974 and, like its predecessor, it was an immediate hit.

Mark Berger, Francis Coppola and Walter Murch mixing *The Godfather, Part II* in 1974.

Francis picked up three more Oscars (for best picture, director, and script). He and Eleanor bought a 1,560-acre estate in Napa County, just east of Marin and an hour from their offices in San Francisco. The Coppolas had been searching for a quaint summer home where "he could make a little wine in the basement like his grandparents did." The homestead, established in 1880 as the Inglenook winery, sported a vineyard and an historic Victorian manor.[14]

While Lucas was working on *Graffiti*, Steven Spielberg (who had graduated from Cal State Long Beach a short time after George left USC) teamed up with Hal Barwood and Matthew Robbins to write a script based on one of the biggest news stories of 1969. According to the story, a woman helped her husband escape prison, kidnapped a state trooper, and led police on a 300-mile chase across Texas. They called it *The Sugarland Express*. It was Spielberg's first feature film.

Even before it was finished, Universal tipped him off to a book they had optioned: Peter Benchley's soon-to-be-released novel *Jaws*. They hadn't been able to find a director. Spielberg read the galleys and begged for the job.

Two months after the deal was inked, *Jaws* became a bestseller, climbing every "top 10" list. Spielberg started pre-production as soon as *Sugarland* wrapped and was shooting by the time it debuted. *Sugarland* was such a bomb

[14] Established by Gustave Niebaum.

that if Spielberg hadn't already been working on *Jaws*, he might never have been able to get a job for another movie.

It was in the period after *Graffiti* and before *Jaws* that Spielberg and Lucas first started socializing, seeing much of themselves in each other. Their ambitions were similar, their backgrounds compatible. George visited Steven in Martha's Vineyard that fall and watched his struggle with *Jaws*. The five-week shoot was months over schedule; there were countless technical difficulties. Lucas well understood the pressure the studio was exerting on him.

While Lucas began to work on the script for his fantasy space western, Coppola began pre-production on *Apocalypse*, Lucas' now-abandoned project that Coppola had long admired. He dived into the script, making it increasingly personal and far more epic than had ever been envisioned. It would take Coppola most of the next four years to prepare for, shoot, and deliver the massive film.

It isn't too difficult to think of these young directors as adolescents shining up their hot rods, tuning up their engines, and racing around the walnut trees, seeing who was faster. For the time being, the boys had completely succeeded at recreating the insanity, camaraderie, teamwork, and in the end, nuggie-inducing competition they had in film school.

By the end of 1974, Marcia had edited up-and-coming director Martin Scorsese's *Alice Doesn't Live Here Anymore*.[15] Verna Fields was working with Spielberg to shape up *Jaws* (in spite of the problems on the set, the material looked exciting). *American Graffiti* had brought in more than $117 million in ticket sales worldwide. Lucas' slice was about $4 million. *American Graffiti* had joined *The Sting, The Exorcist,* and *The Godfather* as one of the recent films to take in more than $100 million (not since *Gone With the Wind* in 1939 had a film made so much money). And because it was so inexpensive to make, it rapidly became acknowledged as the most profitable film in history.

[15] Like Lucas, Scorsese had won the National Student Film Festival although had a more circuitous path to a directing career. He had the good fortune to pick up the job of assistant director on a concert film about the Woodstock Peace and Music Festival. When the concert turned into a phenomenon, the documentary *Woodstock* (1970)—cut by his USC pal Thelma Schoonmaker, from 160 hours of film (65 miles of celluloid)—was an achievement. His breakout film, *Mean Streets* (1973), debuted Robert DeNiro and Harvey Keitel.

four

The Star Wars

[1975–1977]

"Many people feel that in the contemplation of nature, and in communication with other living things, they become aware of some kind of force, or something, behind this apparent mask, which we see in front of us. And they call it "god" or [whatever], depending on their particular disposition..."

—ROMAN KROITOR (VOICE OVER) IN *21-87* (1963)[1]

GEORGE LUCAS worked on his space movie all through 1974. He was hoping he could patch together one hundred pages of script from the multiple story threads and complicated relationships. The tale had already drifted through a number of odd incarnations: "The Adventures of Starkiller: Episode One of the Star Wars," "The Star Wars: From the Adventures of Luke Starkiller," and "The Story of Mace Windu." By March 1975 it was epic, like *War and Peace.*

"I took that script, cut it in half, put the first half aside and decided to write the screenplay from the second half. I was on page 170 and I thought, holy smokes, I need 100 pages, not 500. But I had these great scenes. So I took *that* story and cut it into three parts. I took the first part and said, this will be my script. No matter what happens I am going to get these three movies made."

Lucas sat down with the most action-packed section of the long story and started to refine.

He was under no delusions about the incredibly challenging business of making a successful science fiction film. Even though classic sci-fi had a long history, from *Trip to the Moon* (1902) and *Metropolis* (1927) to *The Day The Earth Stood Still* (1951), when he considered the market seriously he realized it was a niche audience and that even "successful" sci-fi movies were not expected to do much more than break even. Kubrick's *2001,* a popular success, took about two years in theaters before turning a profit. In spite

[1] *21-87,* a short film by director Arthur Lipsett, and produced by the National Film Board of Canada, affected Lucas in his earliest explorations of filmmaking, both in its construction—its unusual use of sound montage and non-synchronous pictures—and its message.

of this, Lucas worked through the summer of 1975 carving the story into a script, maintaining the vision that if he were lucky, he'd make a popular film for sci-fi fans.

The promise of the early 1970s was that an entire movie could be put on a cartridge that a consumer could stick in a machine and play. For film buffs, this was a remarkable improvement. Francis Coppola had had to build a custom theater in his house, with a projector and screen, to see the movies he wanted, impressing his friends with his inside connections to the Pacific Film Archive.[2]

Lucas had been eyeing consumer "videotape cassettes," not so much for their technology, or convenience, as for the economic opportunity they created for independent filmmakers. Videocassettes would make it easier for smaller audiences (the kind he'd obviously have with a sci-fi flick) to see his film, and for him to have some financial success even though the theatrical release might not play out well. If people believed what magazines told them, by America's bicentennial virtually all films would be available in a videotape format.

While George developed "The Star Wars," Marcia spent much of her time in Los Angeles, supervising the edit of Martin Scorsese's *Taxi Driver*.[3] During the editing of *American Graffiti*, she had transitioned, in effect, from assisting Verna Fields to replacing her. The success of *American Graffiti*, with her first Oscar nomination, plus her well regarded work on *Alice Doesn't Live Here Anymore* gave Marcia new film opportunities and the Lucas family financial relief, but most of the cash was used for basic support.

George had pitched some twenty-odd executives over the years on the *Star Wars* project. The reason they turned him down seemed to be that, as George confided to a friend, "I couldn't describe in words the thing I imagined in my head."

With the unprecedented success of *Jaws* in the summer of '75, Steven Spielberg, George's new friend, was vindicated for his somewhat out-of-control production. But Lucas couldn't fully enjoy his friend's success; he was descending into his own Hollywood nightmare. He'd just finished a second draft of *Star Wars* (another radical rewrite of the story), and it still didn't feel finished.

Lucas had a handshake deal with Twentieth Century Fox, but until the script was done and okayed by the studio, he wouldn't get a budget, and without a budget, the film was not really in the Hollywood pipeline. Once a film lost momentum in that pipeline, it could stall, fall out of favor, and ultimately get tossed into an endless turnaround from which it was not likely to recover.

[2] It's hard to imagine in this era of DVDs, but you had to be "somebody" to watch a movie that wasn't being shown (poorly) on television or wasn't still in theaters.

[3] **Marcia Lucas** (b.1945). Assistant editor: *Rain People* (1969), *THX 1138* (1971),*The Candidate* (1972); Editor: *American Graffiti* (1973), *Alice Doesn't Live Here Anymore* (1974); *Star Wars* (1977), *Return of the Jedi* (1983).Supervising editor: *Taxi Driver* (1976). Uncredited editor on *Empire Strikes Back* (1980).

Lucas knew he had to keep the project moving ahead. He had used his windfall from *Graffiti* to finance the early development of *Star Wars*, even before Fox was committed to the project. It was a risky ploy, but one he had seen work for Coppola.

The executives at Fox had a problem. They continued to have trouble imagining the story the way Lucas saw it. Recalled Gary Kurtz, "The lightsabers, in particular, are things that were tricky for the script to describe how they worked. A contemporary comedy or drama can read like a novel, and you can breeze right through it, but any science fiction film is difficult to get through because there is so much description. And *Star Wars* was no exception."

Kurtz and Lucas began looking for a graphic artist who could help the studio visualize the story. "The script was too strange," said Kurtz, "and concept art was a key thing."

A few years earlier, Lucas' USC friends Hal Barwood and Matthew Robbins had introduced him to Ralph McQuarrie, a commercial illustrator who had helped them with a space film they were developing.[4] McQuarrie had worked for Boeing, producing mechanical drawings of planes and parts, worked with CBS News making an animation of the Apollo space missions, and even had done some science fiction book covers.

Kurtz and Lucas hired McQuarrie to make four drawings. Lucas gave him wide latitude to develop the characters and images, but he was clear about what each scene and character needed to convey. In the first place, his universe wasn't sterile; it was organic—it looked dirty. Lucas wanted robots and spaceships in a real, gritty, used-car world; he called it "used space." The characters and ships had to look beaten up by time. Lucas provided a wealth of collateral materials—stacks of comic books and science fiction magazines—to illustrate the ideas.

One of the requested scenes was for an image of two robots—C-3PO and R2D2—crossing the desert of Tatooine. The C-3PO robot should be human-like, tall and slender, with the deco-elegance of Fritz Lang's robot centerpiece in *Metropolis*; and R2D2, a three-foot tri-ped with a face that (according to the third draft script) was a "mass of computer lights, surrounding a radar eye." George described the nature of the two robots as being like the bickering, comic peasants in Akira Kurosawa's *Hidden Fortress*.

Another of the images showed Darth Vader in a lightsaber duel with Skywalker. George described Vader as "someone in an airtight garment with a lot of wrapping and black bands and folds, kind of fluttering" as he moved. Vader, like the storm troopers, required a "breath mask" for passing through areas without air.

When McQuarrie delivered his concept paintings, Lucas was thrilled. It was a key moment for him, seeing those intangible internal ideas manifested

[4] Barwood and Robbins never made the film.

physically. The images helped nail the pitch to Fox, and they finally agreed to make the movie.

An early McQuarrie production frame of an X-wing fighter.

"When I made the deal to write and direct *Star Wars* at Fox, I obviously made it for nothing. All I had was a deal memo, no contract." But after *American Graffiti* was a monster hit, Lucas had new clout. Both Lucas' agent and lawyer assured him he could push for a generous salary.

"Fox thought I was going to come back and demand millions of dollars and all these gross points." Lucas had a more reckless proposal, which shocked Fox: instead of a raise, he wanted other things that were important to him. He wanted *control*.

"I'll do it for the deal memo," he told Fox, "but we haven't talked about things like merchandising rights, sequel rights."

He told them he wasn't going to cede any of the ancillary rights to his film. Profit participation—the gross points—were based on ticket sales. But ancillary rights were different and separate. These included publishing rights for novelizations, music rights for soundtracks, merchandising rights for products, and sequel rights to make and profit from any future films. Lucas had a sense about these sci-fi fans—they were zealous. They went to conventions and wore T-shirts with logos and devoured related materials like comics and books.[5]

Fans of westerns didn't do that. Fans of comedies didn't do that.

Fox agreed. They were getting him for a song.

For Lucas, the issue of creative control over his own project was more important than money. He still couldn't shake off the stupidity he had endured from the studios on both *THX 1138* and *Graffiti*. The changes the studios made in his films may or may not have mattered to audiences, but the fact that they could change them at all was unconscionable. Having

[5] The first *Star Trek* convention was held in 1972, more than two years after the television show was canceled. Thousands showed up. A year later they created a cartoon for TV.

what was called "final cut"—the legal authority to say when the film was done—was the cornerstone of this creative control.

Lucas was also adamant he needed to own his sequels. And since *Star Wars* was only one-third of the film he planned to make, he wanted to have the unilateral authority to complete what he set out to do. He didn't care if the first film was a hit or not.

The details of the ancillary rights were complicated, but in short, he had the right to make his own merchandising and licensing deals, and Fox would just get a percentage of that revenue. Fox didn't give these rights away; Lucas bartered them for much of his salary. He knew that one way or another, merchandising rights were something he planned on exploiting.

"I have a particular affection for games and toys," said Lucas. There's no doubting that I haven't grown up. All of this was a part of the film, the intention of launching toys in supermarkets, creating books and stuff. In the end, *Star Wars* is a great adventure for children."

By the time the budget was approved by Fox, it had climbed from an initial level of $3.5 million to, after some haggling, $8.5 million. Lucas had already spent $1 million of his own.

Paramount had long been rumored to be working on a *Star Trek* movie. Competition was in the air and Fox was concerned how any new product could compete with the established fanbase of *Trek*. In time, both Fox and Paramount were aiming their sci-fi films for release in time for the holidays, 1976.

Even as Lucas was pounding through drafts of the script, he and Kurtz were trying to assemble a team capable of delivering the unusual film. It had demands on both visual effects and sound that far exceeded popular films. And even if the team could have afforded experienced people from the unions (which they couldn't), any rational person would balk at the project. They needed guys from outside the system. What they needed were kids: cheap, smart, naïve, fearless.

George would have liked Walter Murch for his project, but he was unavailable.[6] So Lucas and Kurtz sent out feelers: "We need another Walter Murch," they said.

Kurtz called Ken Miura, a professor of sound at USC Film School.[7] Miura had consulted with Coppola and Lucas on the sound set-up at Zoetrope on Folsom Street. Now Kurtz asked if he knew of anyone who might be interested in collecting sounds for *Star Wars*, a film school student who would be maleable and inexpensive. Miura recommended one of his grad students who was finishing a masters that year: Ben Burtt.

Kurtz and Ben Burtt met at George's office on the Universal lot. The walls were covered with McQuarrie's production art. Kurtz pointed out the image

[6] Murch was working with director Fred Zinnemann on *Julia* (1977).

[7] Lucas, Murch and Kurtz all had taken courses from Miura at USC.

of a lightsaber duel between Darth Vader and Luke Skywalker. They talked about an early sketch of a Wookiee, with large owlish eyes.

Burtt was a good film student. When he was a kid, he did typical kid stuff, like playing sports; but where some kids collected baseball cards, Burtt collected sounds. He'd record TV shows onto a reel-to-reel ¼-inch audio tape; he'd record birds (which his bird-watching family particularly embraced); he recorded all kinds of odd things and built them into a personal sound library. He'd also shoot little Super-8 movies.

"I was very interested in movie making as a kid. I wanted to put sound on those [silent] home movies, and at the time there was really no way to do that." Burtt would create whole soundtracks for family projects, with music, effects, and even "looped" dialog—voices recorded after the movie was shot by people trying to speak lines while their lips were moving onscreen. "It was just a hobby," said Burtt.

A week after meeting Gary Kurtz, Burtt returned to the Universal office for an interview with George Lucas. George liked him at once and hired him to record the sound effects.

Kurtz got Burtt a Nagra tape recorder and some other equipment, and based out of his apartment near the USC campus, he started collecting sounds at his own pace. He often spent days wandering around the countryside with headphones on and a microphone pointed at anything that intrigued him.

"I was really sort of a PA [production assistant] on the film, a jack-of-all-trades," said Burtt. I had lots of different jobs. Recording sound one day, and the next I'd be taking Carrie Fisher to get her hair done."[8]

For a film set in an imaginary universe, everything would need sound. Lucas pushed forward with the concept that he had first seen articulated visually by McQuarrie, about the organic underpinning of this science-fiction film. Not only did space look dirty, it *sounded* dirty.

"In my first discussion with George about the film, he—and I concurred with him—wanted an 'organic' as opposed to an electronic and artificial soundtrack. Since we were going to design a visual world that had rust and dents and dirt, we wanted a sound that had squeaks and motors that might not be smooth-sounding or quiet. Therefore we wanted to draw upon raw material from the real world: real motors, real squeaky doors, real insects, that sort of thing. The basic thing in all films is to create something that sounds believable to everyone, because it's composed of familiar things that you cannot quite recognize immediately."

Lucas' acoustical "strategy" was in contrast to much of the sounds in science fiction cinema, where obscure electronic devices (like the odd-sounding Theremin) were used to cast eerie weirdness (as in *The Day the Earth Stood*

[8] He would occasionally load all the McQuarrie production schematics into his trunk (the drawings weren't considered "artwork") and haul them around Hollywood or back to Van Nuys.

Still, 1951) or where entire soundtracks were invented from state-of-the-art technology (as in *Forbidden Planet*, 1956). Lucas' universe was supposed to be familiar, not surreal.

Left: Ben Burtt tapping a powerline support wire to get the laser cannon sound. Burtt had discovered that the guywires made pretty cool sounds, but it took months to find just the right wire, with just the right tension and with wind dampeners that might change the sound. He found the perfect one on a trip to the Palmdale desert outside L.A. during Christmas 1975. *Right:* Burtt recording walruses to add to the Wookiee voice.

The visual effects of *Star Wars* were central to the success of the movie. They had to be natural, realistic, as if the film was a war documentary in outer space. At the 1964 World's Fair in New York,[9] there was a documentary that showcased the work of a young filmmaker, Douglas Trumbull.[10] When Stanley Kubrick wanted to make a film called "Journey Beyond the Stars," he didn't want it to look like a science fiction movie, he wanted it to look real. After seeing Trumbull's documentary, he knew it could be done. Trumbull became one of four special effects supervisors to create the look on Kubrick's film, which he renamed *2001: A Space Odyssey*.

Trumbull created movie spaceships that were crisp, scientific, and ripped from the pages of the NASA space program. His work evolved, and four years

[9] The fair had twin themes: "Man's Achievements in an Expanding Universe," and "A Millennium of Progress."

[10] **Douglas Trumbull** (b.1942). Director: *Silent Running* (1972), *Brainstorm* (1983). Special effects pioneer: *2001: A Space Odyssey* (1968), *Andromeda Strain* (1971), *Silent Running* (1972), *Close Encounters of the Third Kind* (1977), *Star Trek* (1979).

later he showed a more gritty vision of spaceships and computers in *Silent Running* (1972). This resonated with Lucas. Although Trumbull's machines had heart, space for him—quite realistically—was cold, slow, silent and sterile. Lucas wanted real action, like a WWII dogfight.

As *Star Wars* pre-production kicked into gear. Lucas began discussions with Trumbull, but couldn't convince him to join the ragtag team; instead he got Trumbull's talented young associate from *Silent Running*: John Dykstra. Dykstra had had valuable experience working with Trumbull, but after *Silent Running* he left Hollywood to join a city-planning organization in Berkeley, the IURD. One thing he did there was build models of buildings and cities, and then make movies to simulate what it was like to walk around in those landscapes.

Dykstra worked on these projects until their funding ran out in 1975. Then he hooked up with Trumbull again. That was when he heard Lucas was looking for effects help that involved miniature photography.

At the Institute of Urban and Regional Development (IURD), Dykstra and his engineers (Al Miller and Jerry Jeffress) had the idea of putting the camera on a dolly mover over the model cities, and connect the dolly and the camera's shutter to one of the Institute's PDP 11 computers (a "minicomputer" of the early 1970s). A PDP 11 was functionally equivalent to a 15MHz CPU with 32K of memory. Manufactured by the Digital Equipment Corporation (DEC, pronounced deck), the $10,800 device, inexpensive by the day's standards, was a new kind of machine. DEC didn't even call it a computer, rather a "programmed data processor" or PDP.

Until the PDP series, computing had been done using "batch" jobs in giant mainframe computers run by large teams, where someone would feed in a stack of punch cards and then come back the next day to see what it calculated. But the new computer had an operating system, called "RT-11," that allowed it to work in what was quaintly referred to as "real time." Using a teletype, you could enter instructions or data on the keyboard and print out information as well.

They'd film the models using a snorkel lens—a long thin barrel with a camera lens at the tip that could point straight ahead or at an angle. The assembly could be inserted into a model street and moved through any path.

By attaching the computer to the camera—and controlling the camera's position and shutter—the IURD team got the snorkel lens to produce impressive, realistic-looking tours through the miniature cities, an innovative visualization tool for civic planners. They eventually called this configuration a "motion control camera."

At six-foot-four with long hair and a beard, Dykstra looked like a rock star. While he had some film experience, and a little background in industrial design, it was his charisma that made him ideal to gather and lead a fearless team. Kurtz leased a 15,000-foot warehouse in a desolate suburb of L.A., across from the Van Nuys airport in the scorching hot San Fernando Valley. When the roll-up doors to the warehouse were thrown open, Dykstra was introduced to the enormous, dark, industrial-looking open space.

As Dykstra began figuring out how to assemble a group to bring McQuarrie's growing volume of sketches to life, Lucas, always interested in the magic of cool names, was pondering what to call them. Over the months before he had created a score of bizarre-yet-comfortable names for planets, characters, animals and objects. He was a naming machine: *Tatooine, Darth Vader, Chewbacca, evaporation farms, droids, Han Solo, Jabba the Hutt….*

Soon he was down to two options: "Rebel Arts and Technology," which he really liked, and "Industrial Light & Magic," or ILM, which became his first choice.

The two-story ILM warehouse in Van Nuys, with vines growing up the sides. Through the open roll-up door (at right) was the model shop; the upstairs windows were the Art Department.

Dykstra immediately hired Richard Edlund to become his cinematographer and the principle architect for the camera equipment that had to be created for *Star Wars*. Dennis Muren joined Edlund to handle the cinematography. Dykstra gathered a half-dozen others to make masks, paint mattes, design explosions, build models, animate miniatures and, ultimately, optically composite the elements into deliverable shots for the film.

Working on *Star Wars*, Dykstra and his team faced a barrage of technical challenges, starting with how to shoot the 360-odd effects. *2001*, which took five years to complete, had used primitive methods for shooting ships and combining miniatures with stars and other objects—doing all the work in-camera. This amounted to shooting an element, rewinding the film, and then shooting the same film again with the next element in place.

"Kubrick was a nut for getting the maximum grain quality," said Kurtz, "and he spent a long long time doing in-camera stuff. *2001* is very laconic as a film, and those shots, while they look beautiful, there is no high energy there. That's partly because of the nature of the film—that's what he wanted to achieve—but also partly because of the technical problems of achieving this."

Lucas' spaceships wouldn't be able to dogfight using the old methods. The methods Dykstra and Edlund embraced necessitated three very separate techniques. First, by connecting camera and computer, Dykstra was able to move the camera in a precise and repeatable way, so ILM could synchronize many planes of action with precision; multiple spaceships could fly on the same screen, lights and engines on the ships could be added to the images, and so on. This "motion control" made the photography of miniatures suddenly a fairly realistic replacement for shooting live action.[11]

Second, to create each separate element of an effect, motion control had to be combined with the blue screen technique—shooting objects against a solid color that could be later removed with mattes. Finally, the elements would get copied together to a new roll of film. Although some quality was lost in the process, it provided remarkable flexibility.

The unusual device that combined all the elements was called an "optical printer." It consisted of projectors, precision mirrors and lenses, and some cameras, all hooked up together. For the effects to look real, the precision of the optical printer was crucial. The old machine they picked up needed to be completely rebuilt.

Lucas was skeptical about using blue screen techniques. He had seen it tried before; the big green halo vibrating around Victor Mature in *The Robe* (1953); the misaligned shots from *The Ten Commandments* (1956) with ugly matte lines around the superimposed objects. In theory, blue screen techniques, combined with the precision of a repeatable motion control camera and a high quality optical printer, could deliver a realistic-looking space adventure. But it was hard to know if it would work.

"George is a storyteller," said Edlund, "and as far as he was concerned, we could have just run around with ships on poles and a black background…and I think that was kinda the way he thought it was going to be done back when he was writing the story. He wasn't thinking it was going to be this incredibly complicated thing."

[11] A moving camera—whether a pan, tilt, dolly, or crane shot—gives Hollywood movies that modern, sophisticated look. While relatively straightforward in live-action production, moving a camera for multi-layered effects shots was impossible before motion control.

Dykstra and Edlund recognized that one drawback of the blue screen process was the generation loss, with each subsequent image dub looking worse and worse (the more complex scenes required many dubs to create). If the final version needed to have 35mm film quality, then the starting frames had better be super-high resolution. In film, the way to higher resolution was through film frames with more area. Dykstra began exploring his options.

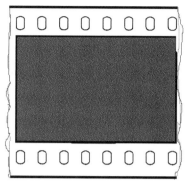

Two 35mm film frames of the same aspect ratio, but the one of the right, VistaVision, has a much larger area—providing for better resolution and easier handling.

An obvious solution was to start the process with the largest commercial film format, 70mm. This size also accommodated a physically larger frame, which slightly decreased the challenges of drawing on teeny little images. The difference between working on 35mm and 70mm film was like drawing on a big postage stamp versus drawing the same thing on a postcard. The equipment, however, was rare and extremely expensive. Films released to theaters in 70mm were generally shot in 35mm and later "up-converted" to the larger frame.

Dykstra uncovered a long abandoned camera format called VistaVision that used 35mm film (by Hollywood standards, cheap to buy and process) that could make reasonably high-resolution images. Its unique property was that the orientation of the frames on the strip of film ran lengthwise along the sprockets, as opposed to the usual stacked-up tiny rectangles. Consequently, the 35mm frames were the same shape, but had more area and thus much higher quality.

VistaVision had been Paramount Pictures' attempt to develop its own theatrical standard. Paramount first used it in Bing Crosby's *White Christmas* (1954).[12] By the end of the '50s, however, it was all but dead. ILM scrounged everywhere for VistaVision equipment—from Paramount's deep storage in L.A., to backrooms at Pinewood Studios, London.

Edlund knew of a VistaVision format optical printer that was sitting dormant. "We walked into the room to look at the machine," recalled Edlund, "and there was a camera report sitting on the machine from the last time it had been used. It was for *The Ten Commandments* (1956). They wrote up the last shot and then closed the door and no one ever went back."

In the ILM parking lot: Richard Edlund preparing to shoot the Death Star model with a high-speed VistaVision camera.

[12] Well, actually second. But no one has heard of the first film done that same year.

Making a composite image for *Star Wars* on the ILM-rebuilt optical printer originally created for Columbia's *Marooned* (1969).

By 1975, ILM had bought the printer and every piece of VistaVision equipment they could find.

Kurtz and Edlund, both technophiles, were always interested in ways computers might be useful, but in 1975 computer graphics was in its infancy. Still, in *Star Wars*, there were a half dozen or so shots *of computers* that seemed to require displays produced *by* a computer—*computer-like* graphics that were essential to the story. These included the targeting displays on the Millennium Falcon, X-wing and Tie fighters, the Death Star maps of the power generator, and the most important plot device in the film: the stolen Death Star plans that would reveal the way to blow up the ship.

Even though all of these elements could be created by traditional hand-drawn animation means—and most of them were—the one-minute animation sequence of the Death Star plans needed more. ILM put the effect out to bid from outside contractors.

Larry Cuba, a computer graphics artist, competed against a couple other burgeoning computer effects teams to propose how he could accomplish the 3-D animation. Cuba had made some pioneering films. He worked primarily in the art world, but he was beginning to think about commercial projects.

ILM was still under construction when Cuba arrived in Van Nuys to meet with Lucas. While Edlund continued to build the camera tracks, and artisans put finishing touches on the enormous Death Star surface model, Cuba threaded a Moviola with his most recent project, an art film called *Arabesque* that he had done with video artist-pioneer John Whitney Sr. (Whitney had been experimenting with films comprised of patterns of dots and lines, choreographed to music. He called them "visual music.") George watched the film on the tiny three-inch screen.

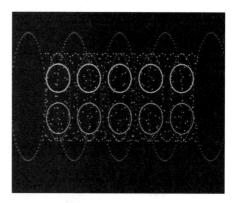

Still frame from John Whitney Sr.'s pioneering computer art piece, *Arabesque (1975)*.

"George thought that was an honor, that I had worked with Whitney," said Cuba.

Star Wars was still in pre-production, so once Cuba had the job, he had many months to figure out how to get a computer to draw the frames.

"R2 needs a voice," said Lucas to Ben Burtt, "and we need lasers that are different from what anybody else has ever done, and I don't want the engines for the spaceships to sound like rockets or jets. And this guy [Vader] is in an iron lung, so figure that one out."

When Burtt finally met with Lucas and showed him some of his ideas, Lucas was thrilled. Here was someone with Murch's passion for sound and the interest in using it to create the subtle fabric of a new environment. Recalled Gary Kurtz, "It was clear he was thinking in the right way: what ordinary things can be combined to make an extraordinary sound."

Burtt came to San Anselmo for a weekend in August 1976 to drop off all the sounds he had recorded, for someone else to deal with. He walked in with boxes of tapes—explosions, laserguns, spaceships.

"Why don't you just stay on a while," he was told.

"When I was hired, no one really gave me a plan," Burtt recalled. "They'd say 'We need a little help with something, can you come by to do it?' and whether you're going to be there a week or ten years, you just don't know."

Burtt set up the little sound lab in the basement of Parkway house—tape recorders with varispeed motors, filters, various electromechanical devices. And never left.

Star Wars had a number of audio challenges. It wasn't shot "on location." There was no real place of Tattoine where Burtt could go and record a few minutes of local sounds. The script said there's a "Wookiee," an eight-foot tall space pirate lieutenant from another planet, "a savage looking creature resembling a huge grey bushbaby monkey with fierce baboon-like fangs...a sight to behold." What the hell does that sound like?

The audio recorded on the sets in London was all but irrelevant. There were actors' muffled lines behind plastic masks, the hollow thumping of people on plywood stages, and all the rich ambience of an airport terminal. So while sound was often recorded during the shoot, most of it was only for reference. In film parlance, the movie was shot silent, "MOS" or "Mit Out Sound," a kind of residual joke from the early days of movies when Germanic directors shouted orders through megaphones. A film shot MOS was very much like an animation, which also has no intrinsic sound and must be created from a blank slate as part of the animation process.

Ben Burtt working in his makeshift sound lab downstairs in Parkway, 1977.

For all the sets, actors, props and stages used for *Star Wars* it was at its core an animated feature film. Ben Burtt decided to apply himself to the sound as he had never before.

Burtt well understood that the ideal sound for something was not always the actual sound the object made. The recorded sound of a gunshot—sounding a bit like a cap gun—was far to wimpy for Hollywood and needed to be fabricated for "realism." A laser cannon might be a violin. The sound of a jaw-crunching punch might be a pool cue whacked on a bag of lima beans. Film sound pioneers understood that sounds in film did more than enrich the environment, they often told a story and imparted emotion independent of the picture. This was what Lucas had experimented with in college; it was what Murch executed so well in *THX* and *The Godfather*, and now was the breadth of Ben Burtt's passion.

The number of distinct sounds to be included in *Star Wars* was almost inconceivable. By using the techniques of recording and mixing sounds, clever editing, modifying sounds, and combining them according to more earth-bound principles of language, Ben Burtt one-by-one invented the atmosphere of the planets and personalities for the characters.

"[Burtt] came up with this iron lung [for Darth Vader] that was a combination of other sounds," said Lucas, "and it was eerie and deeply disturbing, and I said 'That's it.'"

Film Sound

You might logically imagine that since movies record sound while they are shooting, the sound you hear in a movie is the sound that was recorded from the shoot. But that's not the case. Most sound in a movie is added later. But even knowing this, you'd probably imagine that when the actors are talking...surely that must be recorded during the photography part. Oddly enough, this is not the case either, and almost never has been.

At first, movies were silent. The stages where actors were photographed were noisy affairs. The camera itself, a big lumbering motor dragging the celluloid through the camera, sounded like an airplane taking off.

When sound was invented, it was possible to record the actors giving their lines, but it was too noisy on the set. Even when it was quiet the microphones were of such poor quality that it was unlikely a filmmaker could use the dialog as recorded; it was only as a kind of audio reference to the script. Actors would re-record their lines in a quiet studio where they could watch the movie projected while they read from the script. At first, this reading would be put on a record and played along with the movie—never really trying to pretend that the words fit exactly in everyone's mouth.

The coming of sound mandated the invention of the "sound stage," where at some level everyone tried to be quiet during the shooting, where camera motors were encased and muffled. Red lights flashed to be "quiet on the set" and the director checked with the guy listening on the headphones to see if the tape recorder was rolling and up to the correct speed before he yelled "action."

Even so, there was still a wide array of problems with the production track—from the beeping of watches to the challenge of keeping a microphone near an actor who is moving around, while not having it appear in the shot. All these conspired to make a typically poor audio track that could only be fixed, or re-created, in post-production.

Spotting *Star Wars* sound effects at a KEM flatbed editing table, Parkway, 1977.

The Wookiee voice was created from the sounds of a bear combined with small bits of walrus and other animal sounds, then formed into the tonalities of a language. According to Burtt, "You have bits and fragments of animal sounds that you have collected and put into lists: here is an affectionate sound and here is an angry sound… and they are clipped together and blended. With a Wookiee, you might end up with five or six tracks sometimes, just to get the flow of a sentence."

- The laserblasts were built from the sound of Burtt tapping a hammer on an antenna tower guy-wire, and distorting the pitch and speed.

- The hum of the lightsabers was built from the blended sounds of Burtt's television set causing electrical interference with a microphone, along with an old 35mm projector he once ran in the USC theater.

- The TIE fighter sound was constructed by mixing the squeal of a baby elephant with the sound of a car driving along a wet highway.

- The language of Jawas was a sped-up version of Zulu.

- The language spoken by bad-guy Greedo was based on Quechua, a native Peruvian dialect.

In the same way that it would be difficult to imagine watching every frame in 350,000 feet of film—more than five million individual and distinct images—it's hard to visualize the task of determining all the sounds required to fill a single frame of fantasy, and do that for every frame for the film's two-hour running time.

That fall and winter were a blast at Parkway. People would come by. Ben was downstairs like a kid in his workshop, concentrating on—among other things—the non-human voice of R2D2. Marcia was cutting the picture with Richard Chew and Paul Hirsch. On many afternoons there was volleyball or bocce on the lawn. There were always a dozen cars jamming the narrow hillside neighborhood. George and Marcia's big black and white dog, Indiana, snuggled with guests. Francis was in the Philippines, but Murch was sometimes around, as were other Bay Area filmmakers and friends.

In Van Nuys, the creation of visual effects was slow. As good a strategy as the blue screen/optical printer method seemed to be for creating dynamic shots, it was not easy. "The studio was stressing out because they didn't know who we were, other than a bunch of long-haired renegades that didn't have any screen credits," said Edlund.

Recalled Kurtz, "The opening shot of Star Wars had thirty-six different elements. We redid it so many times because of color and other problems, that by the time we got halfway through, one of the elements in the optical printer would get scratched. It's inevitable; no matter how careful you are, there is dust. So we'd have to reshoot the element, and then start over. That was one of the reasons it was so tedious."

Added Edlund, "Optical printing was a real sumo match, and we got thrown out of the ring a lot of times."

After nine months of tireless work at ILM, the production manager's voice boomed from the PA system in the warehouse, "All right you assholes, you've all just spent a million dollars. And I haven't got a single frame of film to show for it."

Lucas was increasingly frustrated by the high costs and almost invisible progress. Gary Kurtz understood the challenges involved with inventing these effects and did his best to block for Dykstra and company.

As shooting was finishing in London, Larry Cuba needed to deliver his computer animation for integration into the scenes set in the rebel base. Holed up in an icy cold lab in Chicago, Larry pushed the University's computer to

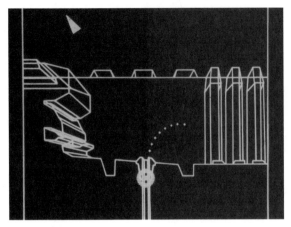

A still frame from the last part of the Death Star plans and attack sequence, generated by Larry Cuba in 1976; in its entirety 45 seconds of screen time. It was the first 3-D computer animation in a popular motion picture. The other targeting screens, while they generally looked digital, were all drawn by hand.

work long enough for him to make a frame, shoot it, draw the next frame, shoot that, and on and on.

On some of the coldest days of the year, Cuba continued to lower the thermostat on the air conditioner to keep the computer from overheating. To no avail. "I couldn't get the computer to run continuously to make the shot—it kept crashing," he said. After days of sleeping fewer than three hours each night, Cuba gave up. He turned off all the air conditioners and finally went to sleep. "When I woke up I realized the computer had run continuously throughout the night," said Cuba. "I guess it was *too* cold."

There was no local processing for the 35mm film Cuba needed for delivering the effects, so all his film was shipped to a lab in Los Angeles.

"That meant that ILM saw the effects before I did. If there was a glitch in the program, they got very confused. I'd get these calls, 'Why is part of the trench upside down?' On my screen, I couldn't see it the way they could. It was a very slow process."

In the end, his final frames were combined with a few hand-drawn touches from ILM—the little triangular ship dropping the bomb on the vent, some flashing arrows. It was the first time 3-D computer graphics were presented in a major motion picture.

Even without Cuba's computer graphics, the effects project was hell. The youthful ILM team was making it up as they went along, often unsure if anything was going to look good on film.

"These inventions were utterly necessary on a daily basis," recalled Edlund. "We had to invent ourselves out of corners we had painted ourselves into."

For George, the slog that was the production of *Star Wars* is legendary, right up there with that from *Jaws*. There were problems with the crew. Problems with the script. Disasters on the locations. Interminable days of work. Marcia worked with the editors; after the shoot in Tunisia and London, George hunkered down in L.A. with Dykstra and his team at ILM.

Finally, after New Years 1977, the entire *Star Wars* team was finally getting excited about what they were doing. Ben Burtt finished the sound editing at Parkway and took off for L.A. to work on the mix. "I felt like, if we were really lucky…we might get invited to a *Star Trek* convention," he recalled. "We could post a little table there. I thought that was the ultimate goal."

Nearly everyone at ILM thought they were working on a grade B science fiction movie until they sat in dailies and saw the final composite of the opening shot—where the big Imperial cruiser comes into frame from the top and fills the screen.

"At that point," said Jerry Jeffress, "we began to realize we were working on something special."

At Spielberg's house in Laurel Canyon, George discusses *Star Wars* with his friends. Spielberg (standing, in cap); Gary Kurtz (to his left) and Hal Barwood (sitting on railing), Brian de Palma (in profile speaking with Lucas), and editor Paul Hirsch sit with his back to the camera.

five

The Rebirth of Lucasfilm

[1977–1979]

When one man, for whatever reason, has the opportunity to lead
an extraordinary life, he has no right to keep it to himself.

—Jacques-Yves Cousteau

A FEW DAYS before the film's release, George and Marcia took off for the Kona coast of Hawaii to unwind. The couple hadn't had a real vacation together since the Cannes Film Festival after *THX* came out. That was seven years ago.

Soon they were joined by George's pals, the Hyucks, and a little later by Steven Spielberg and his girlfriend, actress Amy Irving. "We'd sit around and wait for the grosses to come in, to see what happened…" said Spielberg, "like waiting for election results."

Physically, Lucas was drained. It had been a hard slog, getting the deal with Fox, launching production around the world, and praying for a host of technologies that were required to deliver a movie even close to his vision. Emotionally, *Star Wars* had been a rollercoaster ride of highs (the motion control camera delivered great looking dogfights) and lows (the script dogged him throughout production, and the timeclock-punching British crew was, at best, annoying). His apparent heart attack near the end of the project was diagnosed as hypertension and exhaustion. By all accounts, directing the film nearly killed him.

Once it was clear that *Star Wars* wasn't going to be an embarrassment, they were all able to relax and forget themselves. By week's end George and Steven had bounced around an idea for a fun project to do together, reviving their shared excitement of the adventure serials from TV. George described his "Indiana Smith" story.

In spite of the public's interest in the movie, *Star Wars* was released modestly to thirty-two screens in the U.S. This had less to do with Fox's efforts than the theater owners' general lack of enthusiasm for science fiction. Even with its relative success in those theaters, and the buzz in the press, it still took two months before *Star Wars* reached a national audience.

Fans at the release of *Star Wars,* 1977

No one could have anticipated the fervor the film created. The movie was a bona fide blockbuster—people were seeing it again and again, often standing in line for hours. Within weeks, *Star Wars* movie posters were outselling Farrah Fawcett-Majors five to one. Before *Star Wars,* the highest grossing film of all time had been Spielberg's *Jaws* (1975); in two years ticket sales reached a staggering $121 million. By the end of 1977, only a few months after *Star Wars* national release, it had edged ahead with $127 million.

Lucas' deal with Fox was remarkable, but there was a hook: he only held the rights to *Star Wars* sequels if he started shooting in the next twenty-four months—by the summer of 1979. Lucas would have preferred to have taken a little time off, but the idea of ceding rights to every *Star Wars* sequel was unthinkable. He had begun the project with the resolve to make all three films that comprised his original story, and there was no way he was going to give that up now.

In less than two years, Lucas would have to kick off a number of significant projects simultaneously, not the least of which was actually making the next *Star Wars* movie. He would have to retain much of the key talent from the first film, he'd have to come up with a shooting script—a serious problem considering that the original script had been such a lengthy ordeal—and he'd have to make a new deal with Fox. He also had a contractual obligation to deliver a sequel to *American Graffiti*. The adventure serial project with Spielberg would have to be put on the back burner.

On the day *Star Wars* wrapped in 1977, the young artisans who built the effects workshop in Los Angeles locked the door and went on vacation. In most cases the team would have broken up, drifting along into new jobs, but television producer Glen Larsen contacted Lucasfilm and expressed interest in hiring ILM to handle a set of three television movies for ABC, called *Battlestar Galactica*.[1]

"*Galactica*," said Edlund, "kept the team together. And as much as it was a kind of rip-off of *Star Wars*, the project actually was to George's advantage. Dennis [Muren] and I often felt restricted by the kinds of shots George wanted for *Star Wars*…because we felt we could do more, far-out shots, that George didn't need…so he was limiting us. But on *Battlestar Galactica* we could do whatever we wanted; we were designing the shots, so we experimented…we got our chops together." Edlund and Muren would bring their new experiences to the next *Star Wars* film.

Lucas liked to say that he wasn't an "artist" but a "craftsman." Consequently, he had a true understanding of how hard the work was, and fully grasped the need for better and better tools. He had been loosely aware of the growing presence of computers in the world, but it wasn't until *Star Wars*, when he saw what Dykstra could do by connecting a little computer to a movie camera, that he truly realized its power to augment a filmmaker's powers. Lucas shared Coppola's vision that modern computers could be applied to aspects of the filmmaking process, in particular the editing, in such a way that the director would have more control and the entire endeavor would be more efficient.

In general, a filmmaker got a small royalty and maybe a salary or advance, for his work on a film. George Lucas was paid $15,000 to write and direct *American Graffiti*. He was paid $150,000 to write and direct *Star Wars*. But his percentage of the profits from *Star Wars* was now turning into positive cash flow, and his 60 percent of the merchandising deals was unprecedented gravy. Before *Star Wars* was released Lucasfilm had signed a licensing deal with a small toy company, Kenner Products. The fervor over the film was deafening, and the Kenner "action figures" alone were throwing off enormous volumes of cash, projected to generate about $10 million per year for Lucasfilm.

The success of *Star Wars* allowed Lucas to revisit his deal with Fox. His new-found wealth, only barely dented by a few real estate purchases, was entirely directed toward the financing of the sequel. Budgeted at $15 million,

[1] Larsen hired Ralph McQuarrie as well, to create the show's design.

a third more than what Fox spent on *Star Wars,* Lucas focused on owning outright the film he was creating; this was something that was almost unheard of in the industry, made all the more remarkable because, at $15 million, it would be the most expensive privately funded film project ever.

Any other filmmaker would need to borrow the capital to make a movie. Lucas wanted to put up the money himself. Because Lucas subsumed that risk, the deal for the *Star Wars* sequel was historic: Lucasfilm would earn 50 percent of the gross profit, increasing over time to 77 percent. Fox had to pay its own distribution costs (for film prints, advertising, and so on) and only had rights to release the film to theaters for seven years; after that the rights reverted to Lucasfilm. Lucas maintained all TV and merchandising rights.

"I had visions of R2D2 mugs and little wind-up robots," said Lucas, "but I thought that would be the end of it."

Long before the original *Star Wars* was released, Lucas had brought in an experienced publicity manager to handle merchandising; the man spent months trying to convince book publishers and comic book companies to sign onto the project.[2] He went to sci-fi conventions. He met with toy companies. His reception was at times lukewarm. After the film's release Lucasfilm was besieged with interest in licensing the *Star Wars* characters.

Up to this point, "Lucasfilm Ltd." (abbreviated LFL) was for the most part a name on an incorporation document filed in 1971, after the release of *THX.*[3] After *American Graffiti,* Lucas expanded his core team; in addition to a bookkeeper, an accountant, an agent, and a lawyer (already on hand), the company added various assistants to handle the stream of communications, requests for interviews and meetings and, of course, deals. He hired a personal assistant to keep the frenetic demands on him in check.

"I don't want to be a businessman," Lucas told *Rolling Stone.* "My ambition is to make movies, but all by myself, to shoot them, cut them, make stuff I want to, just for my own exploration, to see if I can combine images in a certain way."

Anxious to handle the onslaught of activities outside of filmmaking, Lucas knew he needed to hire an executive to run Lucasfilm, a "president" to supervise all the business aspects of his life.

"I prefer playing with camera film over becoming an entrepreneur behind a gigantic operation," said Lucas in 1977. "Tell people what they have to do, listen to their projects, approve them or disapprove them…I want to get away from all of that."

With great antipathy toward "experts" from Hollywood, Lucas searched for an executive who could facilitate the operations that were swirling.

[2] Charlie Lippincott, another classmate from USC Film School.

[3] It is not uncommon for writers in Hollywood, or other freelancers, to be advised by accountants to incorporate when it looks like they might start earning money.

Lucasfilm had had offices on the Universal Studios lot during *Graffiti*, but they'd need their own headquarters in Hollywood now, and the San Anselmo houses weren't going to suffice for the work he was planning in Marin.

"L.A. is where they make deals, do business in the classic corporate American way. They don't care about people. It's incredible the way they treat filmmakers, because they have no idea what making a movie is about. To them, the deal *is* the movie. They have no idea about the suffering, the hard work. They're not filmmakers. I don't want to have anything to do with them."

Word was out that George was looking for managerial help from outside the film business. As these things happened, Francis Coppola mentioned the search to his attorney, Barry Hirsch. Hirsch found himself standing around washing dishes after a function at his kid's school, handing wet plates to Charlie Weber, another parent. In addition to his excellent dish drying skills, Weber was a successful real estate businessman and a sometime corporate consultant. They talked shop. Weber had raised money on Wall Street and had been successful with various government housing and development projects. Standing at the sink, Hirsch realized that Weber might fill the bill.

"Do you want to meet George Lucas?" asked Hirsch.

"Who's George Lucas?" replied Weber.

Hirsch laughed: "You certainly qualify as being outside the industry!"

Weber was comfortable in a shirt and tie, a nice balance to the blue jean and plaid-shirted Lucas. At thirty-five, Weber was only a few years older than George. Weber became Lucasfilm's first president and CEO. He took over the initial merchandising and licensing deals and set up relationships with many companies. Lucasfilm was still suffering from the perceived mishandling of the first licensing arrangements. In particular, Fox had made an enormous and exceptionally lucrative sale of the rights for *Star Wars* toys to Kenner...*in perpetuity*.

Weber also took over the company's real estate tasks. At first Lucas was looking for property in the towns of eastern Marin to set up the company's offices, but land was expensive and his focus moved toward the larger agricultural properties to the west.

Weber also facilitated the purchase of an old egg warehouse in Los Angeles, which Lucasfilm intended to convert into its center of filmmaking business. The "Egg Company," as everyone referred to the low-lying red brick building, sat directly across the street from Universal Studios.

In restoring the warehouse, George and Marcia wanted to maintain its character, at least superficially. Exposed wood beams in the expansive atrium, small departments that could be built off the main common area separated with beveled glass doors that would sparkle, a central courtyard with giant plants and tables, brass fixtures everywhere. The building would be Victorian and sensible, yet solid, in contrast to the superficial world outside. "We both like the Victorian style of architecture," said Marcia Lucas. "We think it's warm and charming and inviting, and we're really comfortable in that turn of the century period."

By February 1978, from their fleet of temporary trailers assembled in a parking lot across from Universal, Lucasfilm formally announced that there would be a sequel to *Star Wars*. George also had four more twelve-page outlines for the rest of the *Star Wars* epic sitting in his office, awaiting some future time when he might develop the entire saga.

With corporate Lucasfilm growing in L.A. at the Egg Company, the Northern California filmmaking operation was being redefined as rural. The vision would solidify as Skywalker Ranch.[4] Even as real estate was examined, Lucas began outlining the buildings, the designs, and workflow he imagined there. Architectural sketches were initiated.

Weber was also building a team. His first critical hire was extracting young marketing maven Sid Ganis from Warner Brothers, to establish Lucasfilm's new marketing and publicity department. Ganis, a savvy New Yorker, charismatic and endearing, looked a bit like George. He was exactly the type of person you wanted to have supervise—if not catalyze—one of Hollywood's new marketing juggernauts.

For Lucas, delegating the business responsibilities to Weber to supervise wasn't enough. He had two films he had to produce immediately: sequels to *Star Wars* and *American Graffiti*. Gary Kurtz was already on board for the next *Star Wars* episode. Lucas asked USC pal Howard Kazanjian to handle the *Graffiti* sequel.

Lucas decided to delegate the directing aspects of the sequels as well.

"I had to direct 500 people on *Star Wars*," he said. "And I hated it."

For the *Graffiti* sequel, Kazanjian and Lucas found a writer, Bill Norton, to take on the project. Norton wanted to direct as well, and it was agreed that if his script worked he would get that chance.

Lucas had brought in one of his USC professors, independent filmmaker Irvin Kershner, to direct the next episode of *Star Wars*, now called *The Empire Strikes Back*.[5] Kershner was known for being exceptionally efficient. He was also sufficiently disconnected with Hollywood to satisfy Lucas.

At first Kershner was hesitant to direct the sequel. The burden of responsibility was almost unimaginable, since the future of Lucas' company depended entirely on its success. It wouldn't have to surpass the original, but it couldn't bomb. Because of the improved deal with Fox, the film would only have to

[4] In March 1978 Lucasfilm purchased a small property on Indian Valley Road in Marin, where the filmmaking ranch was initially envisioned.

[5] **Irvin Kershner** (b. 1923). Director: *Return of a Man Called Horse* (1976), *Eyes of Laura Mars* (1978). After producing documentaries in the 1950s, Kershner moved into television and then into film, after getting his break from Roger Corman.

do a fraction of the original to satisfy its financial goals. As long as it came in on budget.

Still debating the job, Kershner showed up in San Anselmo to speak with Lucas. There, Kershner perused the brightly colored zoning maps and architectural plans for Skywalker Ranch that covered every surface of George's office at Parkway; Lucas could hardly speak of anything else:

"There will be a main building, a big simple farmhouse. Behind that, shingled outbuildings for the filmmakers and editors. There will be another big building off to the side, sort of tucked away on a hill, where there will be a screening room, recording studio, computer center, and more editing rooms. And then, way on the other side of the property, will be the special-effects building."

Lucas hoped to create a think tank, a working environment similar to his USC film school experience, where people who were leading their fields—from writers to astronauts—would be invited to speak and mingle, stay if they needed, and catalyze the filmmakers in residence.

"It was really an extraordinary dream," said Kershner. "All the billions of dollars ever made in the film business, and no one has ever plowed it back into a library, research, bringing directors together, creating an environment where the love of films could create new dimensions."

Lucas' passion for the project, even as emoted by a relatively calm guy, impressed Kershner and closed the deal for the directing job on *Empire Strikes Back.*

Lucas was doing a fair amount of delegation, trying to focus his time on the more creative aspects of his responsibilities—developing the story and design for the *Star Wars* universe, and making sure the *Graffiti* sequel was still unique and original.

Lucas and Spielberg started pre-production on *Raiders of the Lost Ark,* the homage to movie serials they both loved. Spielberg found a witty script from a Chicago advertising copywriter, Lawrence Kasdan, and both he and George felt it was the right style for *Raiders.*[6] They hired Kasdan to write the movie.

Unfortunately, the *Empire* script wasn't moving forward as expeditiously. After the first draft was completed, screenwriter Leigh Brackett died suddenly in March '78.[7] Lucas, shaken by the loss, scrambled to finish it up himself. When Kasdan turned in his draft of *Raiders* in August, Lucas asked him to apply himself to *Empire,* shelving *Raiders* for a bit. But it was just as well. Spielberg was about to begin his big budget *1941.*[8]

More American Graffiti, as the sequel was called, got underway that same August, with Kazanjian keeping an eye on young director Bill Norton. Universal was anxious to re-release the original *American Graffiti* because of Lucas' new notoriety, but Lucas had made a deal that allowed him to put back the five

[6] **Lawrence Kasdan** (b.1949). Screenwriter/director: *Body Heat* (1981), *The Big Chill* (1983), *Silverado* (1985), *Mumford* (1999). Also writer: *Empire* (1980), *Raiders of Lost Ark* (1981), *Return of the Jedi* (1983), *The Bodyguard* (1992)

[7] **Leigh Brackett** (1915–1978). Science fiction author and film noir screenwriter: *The Big Sleep* (1946), *Rio Bravo* (1959), *The Long Goodbye* (1973).

[8] *1941*: penned by an up-and-coming pair of 26-year-old USC grads— Bob Zemeckis and Bob Gale.

minutes of material the studio cut out before its release in 1973. Universal's recutting of *Graffiti*, like Warner's hacking up *THX 1138*, was the very core of Lucas' antipathy for the studios. They were insulting to the filmmaker, and before Lucas would do anything else with his clout he would try to straighten out that kind of injustice.

Lucas hired a local film school grad, Duwayne Dunham to restore the material cut from the original *Graffiti*. Dunham and Lucas got along so well that soon he assisted George in any activity that involved film. When Lucas ran through cuts with Tina Hirsch, the editor on *More American Graffiti*, Dunham assisted.[9]

"Whenever George was in the cutting room," recalled Dunham, "I was with him. It didn't matter the show, he'd just yank me away and there we'd go." Dunham became the first editing assistant on *Empire*.

Soon Lucasfilm CEO Charlie Weber asked his close friend Bob Gindy, a real estate consultant, to help find a production space for the growing company. Gindy located a few commercial buildings in San Anselmo, in a quaint downtown area not far from Parkway and the other Lucasfilm "houses." But none was configured for the industrial nature of special effects. For that, something "greasier" was required. Gary Kurtz found the perfect location in the automotive workshops of central San Rafael, in one of the few utterly forgettable areas of picturesque Marin County. There, on Kerner Boulevard, wedged between the Richmond-San Rafael Bridge and Highway 101, Kurtz found a large car workshop that was for sale. Lucasfilm purchased the building and, after some initial remodeling, began to facilitate ILM's move to Marin. The expensive and chaotic process would take months, through the fall and into 1979.

When word came down from Weber that ILM was going to reassemble in San Rafael. Dykstra (and more than half the ILM crew) chose not to come along.[10] Consequently, the opportunity to build ILM went to Richard Edlund and Dennis Muren.

"George wanted to do everything in Marin," said Edlund, "and I said, 'There is no infrastructure up here…it's going to be difficult. We're going to have to import a lot of people.' In a sense it was like the foreign legion…that's how we kinda looked at it…we were 300 miles from the heart of the movie industry."

The unheated concrete building was a harsh environment, exacerbated by the plaster dust falling from the ceiling as workmen added a second story at the same time as the team was trying to get *Empire*'s effects put together. The sign in front of the building read "The Kerner Company."

[9] **Tina Hirsch**, Editor: *Death Race 2000* (1975), *More American Graffiti* (1979), *Airplane II* (1982), *Gremlins* (1984), *Explorers* (1985), *Dante's Peak* (1997). Hirsch started as a script supervisor and moved into editing; she was the first woman to become president of the editor's honor society, ACE. She was also *Star Wars* editor Paul Hirsch's sister-in-law.

Duwayne Dunham (b.1952). Editor; *Return of the Jedi* (1983), *Blue Velvet* (1986), *Wild At Heart* (1990); director of many television movies and series.

[10] Those who stayed, led by Dykstra, kept the workspace in Van Nuys and created a new effects company called Apogee, Inc.

"We were all very undercover," said Edlund, "because otherwise we'd have the *Star Wars* wharf rats out there, and they'd be diving into the garbage."

Concurrent with the ILM move, Lucas and Weber closed a deal for the historic Bulltail Ranch, located, ironically, off Lucas Valley Road. The road was actually named for an Irish immigrant named John Lucas, an enormous mountain man who came to Marin in 1849.[11] The 1,882-acre property cost Lucasfilm Ltd. $2.7 million; it was the ideal spot for Lucas' Skywalker Ranch development. The early estimate for the project—with a Victorian main house and library, a half-dozen associated bunkhouses, man-made lake (which could double as a reservoir for fire safety), and ultramodern post-production studio—exceeded $20 million.

As soon as the ranch was purchased, Lucas' assistant editor Duwayne Dunham grabbed his apprentice, new company runner Steve Starkey, and the two of them rented an array of high-powered lawnmowers to clear out some spaces for softball and other games.[12] Maybe a dozen company employees brought bag lunches and made themselves a picnic, as George gave walking tours, pointing out locations that might suit the various structures he envisioned.

By the end of 1978, as *Star Wars* completed its first run in theaters, ticket sales hit more than $500 million. This translated into $250 million in "rental revenue" to the studio, which gave Lucasfilm a remarkable $40 million. Plus merchandising revenues. Still, Lucas couldn't afford to finance the sequel *and* build the Ranch in its entirety.

As preparations were being made for the next *Star Wars* film, Lucas was thinking about how he would ideally like to be working. The sheer industrial nature of filmmaking was a source of frustration. The mechanical physicality of shooting and editing was not altogether unpleasant, but the impediments it put in his way—going from an idea to an image on screen—were a constant battle.

To get an idea of how complicated the process was, consider this: to make *Star Wars*, Lucas shot about 350,000 feet of film. A roll of film is 900 feet long and, when wound into a coil, about six inches in diameter. It takes two rolls—one for the picture and one for the sound, for every 10 minutes shot. So, 350,000 feet of film comes to almost 400 pairs of these little rolls. Eight hundred 1-pound spools of raw material. Hellish to organize. Slow to look through. Assembled with a razor blade and tape, almost exactly the way they'd been cut together since Edison and Lumiere invented the process.

[11] His uncle, Timothy Murphy, was an early administrator of the Mission at San Rafael, and gave his nephew access to the lands in the area of present-day Terra Linda and Lucas Valley. John Lucas built a two-story home in 1867 on his 2,340-acre property, which he called the Santa Margarita Ranch.

[12] **Steve Starkey** (b.1957). Producer; *Amazing Stories* (TV Series 1985), *Who Framed Roger Rabbit* (1988), *Death Becomes Her* (1992), *Forrest Gump* (1994), *Contact* (1997), *Cast Away* (2000), *The Polar Express* (2004).

The production of *Star Wars* relied on numerous innovations, particularly in special effects, but the filmmaking process—the tools and workflow—were as old as film itself. "Everything we did on the first *Star Wars* film, even though the film was written about as a whole new approach to visual effects, well, that was mostly hype by Fox," said Gary Kurtz, "because every single frame we did [in the film] had been done before. There wasn't anything that was really invented. We just purchased and cobbled together the equipment, because there was no money or time."

With money finally rolling into Lucasfilm, there was interest from everyone—George, Gary Kurtz, Richard Edlund, others around the company—as to where they could go beyond what they done in *Star Wars*.

"What can we do that makes this whole thing easier?" asked Kurtz.

The answer was coming. Edlund had old friend, Gary Demos, who had been frequently talking about his new computer work. "He's like the Einstein of the industry," said Edlund, "an incredibly brilliant technologist."

Demos had once worked with Dave Evans and Ivan Sutherland, the guys who invented computer graphics. Later he had teamed up with John Whitney Jr., son of the video arts pioneer, at a company called Triple-I, where they were merging computers and film. They wanted to build a digital film printer (DFP, pronounced "difip"), a computerized device that would make compositing elements a snap. Edlund was convinced these two were the leading edge.

"It took eight months to do the opening shot of *Star Wars*," said Kurtz. "[With digital compositing] you could see that overnight. Or immediately."

Whitney and Demos said the DFP could replace the analog optical film printer. With it, they would be able to scan camera negative into the digital realm, manipulate it there, add computer graphics and computer animation technology, and put it back on film with no generation loss. To ILM, that would be nirvana.

"I was pining for the digital world," said Edlund. "I could see what was possible there." The photographic process of optical line-up, the cornerstone of ILM, was complicated. "You had to fight your way through it, swashbuckling with technology to get anything that looked right."

It wasn't difficult for Edlund to convince Gary Kurtz that a digital film printer would revolutionize their effects to an enormous degree—even more, he suggested, than the computerized motion control camera. Edlund gave his nod to Triple-I, and passed the info up the chain of command.

The cost of the printer was extremely high, but Triple-I was confident that a company like Lucasfilm wouldn't balk at their groundbreaking technology simply because it was expensive. This was George Lucas, after all.

Whitney and Demos had an ulterior motive; they weren't interested in just inventing a DFP. They wanted to demonstrate their ability to replace the miniatures with computer generated 3-D models. This news wasn't particularly well-received by those at ILM, whose profession was building models, lighting them, moving them around, and photographing them.

Charlie Weber met with Gary Demos and formalized Lucasfilm's deal to get a DFP. *Empire* was in pre-production, and the deadlines were tight. Edlund and Kurtz set-up a series of milestones for Triple-I; if any were missed, it would kill the entire deal.

A still from Triple-I's X-wing fighter 3-D model test. It was never used in the films.

Lucasfilm was paving the way for ILM to stand alone as a state-of-the-art effects company. Said Kurtz, "You can do any effect you want if you have enough hours to throw at it, but in the competitive world of outside films, you didn't have that luxury, so any kind of technique, like new digital ones, that minimized the human labor involved, were explored. We were frustrated that the best shots sometimes were ruined by the photochemical process." Digital would change that.

Edlund provided Demos with some drawings of X-wing fighters and a model that could be digitized. After laborious work, Demos delivered a shot. It was dramatic and impressive, but when the computer animation played there were barely-visible artifacts, "jaggies," that ran along the edges of the spacecraft in motion.

"The shot actually worked," said Edlund, "but it didn't fit into any scenes. If it had fit into the drama, it would have been cut in."

Richard Edlund presented a report on the X-wing test. While the jaggies were small and likely wouldn't show up in the superfast clips of ships zooming by, he was fairly specific in his criticisms: the images, he felt, were too pristine. If computer images were ever going to replace photography, they had to include motion blur. It was a deal-breaker; for Lucasfilm, an image simply couldn't look computer generated.

But the larger problem for Triple-I was that their DFP was off-schedule. "We ordered some precision optical glass from Germany which was supposed to take six weeks…but after two months, then three months…" said Demos.

And as *Empire* was finally about to start production, the deal with Triple-I was terminated.

But it got Kurtz and Edlund thinking. A digital film printer would be an incredible boon for ILM. "There were several discussions," said Kurtz, "about the fact that computers appeared to be the way things were going to go in the future, even if it wasn't working then; with higher powered machinery and better software, it was clear that it *could* be working."

Maybe they should do the project in-house? George was all for it.

By the time *Empire* started shooting in March 1979, it became clear that the original budget of $15 million was not going to be enough. Fox had given Lucasfilm money in U.S. dollars, which during *Star Wars* gained about 7 percent in value as it was converted to British pounds. "It was a godsend, really," said Kurtz. "We were really struggling at the end to get the last set built."

But during *Empire* the British economy boomed, and the pound went the other way. "We lost a lot on currency exchange." New budget projections totaled $18.5 million. A few weeks into the shoot, Kurtz (the producer) and Kershner (the director) informed Lucas that the film couldn't be finished for less than $22 million. In addition, Kurtz said "we had all kinds of production problems….trouble in Norway, some of the worst blizzards in fifty years."

Lucas told *Rolling Stone*, "There were some problems. They were a little over budget, over schedule. That concerned me, because I only had so much money and I was afraid if they used it all up, we wouldn't be able to finish the movie. But I knew they were trying to do the best job they possibly could, and I thought the stuff looked terrific."

Things weren't any better at ILM.

"On *Empire* we had an endless series of problems matching snow," remembered Kurtz. "We were shooting in real snow in Norway, and we were balancing that with miniature snow and we were matching the sky backgrounds that were real with painted sky backgrounds…and there were always five or six key elements that had white in them. Just a tiny shift in the white, where it would turn yellow or turn blue, would ruin a shot. You could never predict it from day to day."

The dream of a digital film printer was high on everyone's mind.

Fraternal competition was in the air. Francis Coppola was already exploring technological solutions to filmmaking problems. He had recently installed some videotape editing systems in his San Francisco office penthouse and had hired a quirky Hungarian consultant, Zoltan Tarczy-Hornoch, to look into film image scanning. He also asked video and computer aficionado Bill Etra to help search out a scientist for graphics research.

At George's urging, Charlie Weber initiated a search for someone qualified to handle Lucasfilm's in-house research into computers and filmmaking. Weber delegated the task to his friend, real estate consultant Bob Gindy. Gindy dutifully dug in to figure it out.

Not only did the Bank of America decline to provide the additional $6 million they'd need to finish *Empire*, but by mid-July they called Charlie Weber and told him they'd no longer advance Lucas any funds until the loan was repaid in full. Lucasfilm had no more money. It wouldn't even make the upcoming payroll.

"It was one of those odd things," said Kurtz, "where there was no question [*Empire*] was going to be a big hit, so a loan didn't seem like a big risk. But it was a trying time."

Weber went to a different bank to refinance the loan—to pay off Bank of America and guarantee a new loan of $25 million. The Bank of Boston was uncomfortable with the lack of control at Lucasfilm; they strongly urged Weber to bring on a financial officer with more experience with these kinds

Workpicture and sound
cascade into a trim bin.

of transactions and lobbied for the hiring of
Robert Greber, a hot Wall Street banker.

Greber was hired as VP of Finance, and at
forty-two was the new old man in the company.
And according to him, the only person in the
rapidly growing company who didn't want to go
on to make his own movies. The bank agreed to
the loan and Lucasfilm made payroll.

With tenuous stability restored by summer,
Lucas flew to Elstree studios (near London) with
his assistant editor, Duwayne Dunham. Lucas
watched the dailies and settled in to the edit
bay there and began looking through the cuts.
The film trims, strips of celluloid sometimes a
foot long, sometimes many *many* feet long, were
clipped on hooks and draped into a cloth bag, a
trim bin. When Lucas wanted to add a moment
to the end of a shot, he'd send Dunham digging
into the bin to ferret out the needed frames.
Lucas watched the scenes, forward and backward, over and over. Then he paused and turned
to his assistant.

"Someday we'll have a digital trim bin," Lucas
announced from the silence in the room.

"A what?" Dunham replied. Lucas turned
back around and continued working the film.

[13] **Stanley Kubrick** (1928–
1999). Director: *Spartacus*
(1960), *Lolita* (1962), *Dr.
Strangelove* (1964), *2001:
A Space Odyssey* (1968), *A
Clockwork Orange* (1971),
Barry Lyndon (1975), *The
Shining* (1980), *Full Metal
Jacket* (1987), *Eyes Wide Shut*
(1999).

[14] Kubrick had just gotten
hold of artist David Lynch's
unusual film Eraserhead
(1977) and was going to
screen it at the studio theater.
Kubrick invited Lucas and
his entourage to join him.

Stanley Kubrick,[13] who had practically taken over Elstree in the late '60s during
2001: A Space Odyssey, was working at the studios again cutting *The Shining.*[14]
Lucas, Kurtz and Dunham joined Kubrick for dinner, and their conversation
swirled between their issues with Hollywood and their hopes for technology.
Kubrick was an American-expatriate, a virtual recluse, living outside London
and necessarily far from the politics in Hollywood. But he had long been interested in the growing competence of computers, and like Lucas, made films in
which he explored themes about humanity, society, and technology.

Production overages and the strong British pound combined to spiral the
budget of *Empire* upward. New projections were up to $28 million and even
the Bank of Boston wasn't going to keep making loans. Fox waited patiently
at each step, always there to offer money…for a price. They were anxious to
renegotiate their compromised deal for the film, but Lucas was uninterested

in giving them that satisfaction. It made his frustration with the production that much more acute.

Weber flew to Boston to try to renegotiate with the bank, and eventually they acquiesced. By the end of summer, *Empire* seemed to be under control. Regardless of the cash flow issues, there was a reasonable feeling that once the film was released, the problems would go away. Even if *Empire* only took in a fraction of what the original film did, loans could be repaid and business could continue at Lucasfilm.

From London, Lucas reminded Weber that the production would be wrapping up soon, and that not only would he be returning to San Anselmo with hundreds of thousands of feet of film, but that Parkway would need to be rejiggered to handle the new post-production tasks before it.

Duwayne Dunham had gone to film school at San Francisco State with an eclectic guy who he thought might be able to help out with film equipment and the odd tasks involved in managing all the materials when they returned from London. He called Jim Kessler, a tall curly-headed free thinker who was at his own career crossroads, a few weeks away from moving to Boulder and getting into passive solar power and alternative energy.

The renovated Egg Company atrium.

"Would I be interested in working for George Lucas?" Kessler wondered. "Sure. Doing what?"

"Stuff…like organization stuff." Dunham responded cryptically.

"Film stuff?"

"More operational."

"Oh, okay. Why not."

Even though Kessler figured he wasn't the first pick for the job, he followed the directions to the address he had been given and parked on the street before an old Victorian on Ancho Vista, in the hills of San Anselmo. Entering the house, he was escorted to a seat in the big empty office. *Star Wars* toys littered the edges of the room, boxed goods and stacks of paper covered tables, and tchotchkies were displayed casually on the mantle. It was an interesting room with lots to peruse. While he was looking around, the doors to Lucas' office opened.

As Jim Kessler sat facing a beleaguered Lucas, just days back from the end of production in

The Empire Strikes Back editing team: from left, Duwayne Dunham, Steve Starkey, Paul Hirsch.

London, Lucas began asking the requisite interview questions. Satisfied with the answers, he changed the tack of the conversation, growing more animated as he explained how he was going to build a filmmaker's retreat, how he was going to do these projects with computers, how he was going to make a bunch of movies every year. Over the next few hours he told Kessler about what he was going to do from that day forward for the next ten years.

"This is what I expect you to do… and this is what the company is going to do… and these are the opportunities available to you…."

Kessler was mesmerized.

"Is this something that you'd like to be involved with?" asked George, when the story was completed.

"Heck yeah," said Kessler. "Sounds great."

"Okay, you're hired."

CEO Charlie Webber found the rate of change at the company breakneck. Whatever processes worked one quarter were often insufficient a few months later. The administration, as it was, hired people incessantly. Receptionists. Electricians. Model makers. Carpenters. Photographers. Every kind of assistant. As Zoetrope finished work on their film *The Black Stallion*, Lucasfilm scooped up the talent.

Jim Kessler's job was almost like being a post-production facility manager, which was reasonable enough, except that there wasn't a post-production facility at Lucasfilm. His principle responsibility was supervising the work needed to refine Parkway from the minimal workspaces created during *Star Wars*, into a proper filmmaker's studio in time for everyone returning from London, which would happen at any time. He was going to be the administrator for the small picture and sound teams—gathering receipts and turning them into accounting, ordering (or scrounging up) equipment, and so on.

The movie had been cutting in London, concurrent with the shooting, but now the entire operation could move back to Marin, to be near George and Industrial Light & Magic's new set-up. Sound was mixed at the traditional facilities of Goldwyn, in L.A. There were no comparable facilities in Northern California for movie editing and sound work; Lucas would have to change that if he was going to distance himself from the L.A. monopoly.

Bob Gindy wasn't sure how to approach the problem of finding an expert who could revolutionize the film business by using computers, but he figured he'd start by canvassing some of the university computer science departments and see if the professors there had any information for him.

One of his first calls was to the chairman of the computer science department at Stanford, who, after hearing the pitch said, "Oh, that's very interesting, but I don't do anything like that; however I have a colleague at Carnegie Mellon University named Raj Reddy who might. Why not give him a call."

A few days later Gindy reached Raj Reddy, an assistant professor of artificial intelligence in Pittsburg. Raj said, "Oh, that's very interesting, but I don't do anything like that; however, a grad student of mine just left here a few months ago and he loves this kind of stuff. Why don't you give him a call." Gindy jotted down a name and number and hung up. The name on the sheet was Ralph Guggenheim.

At that time, there were very few people in the country, in either industry or academia, who were doing anything that might be called "computer graphics." And even fewer who had an understanding of computers *and* making movies. Ralph did. About four months after arriving at the New York Institute of Technology (NYIT) in Long Island, Ralph got the call that every young filmmaker dreams of: that George Lucas needed help.

Sitting in the NYIT labs one afternoon, Ralph answered the phone. It was Bob Gindy, from Lucasfilm.

"Hey, Marin County is a great place to live," Gindy began, "and the real estate values are fabulous; this is the place to be."

"That's great," a slightly confused Guggenheim replied, "but why are you calling me?"

"Oh I'm sorry. I'm head of development for Lucasfilm, which means, mainly, I buy real estate for George, but they've given me this assignment to build a computer research group, and the things we want to do in this group are, we want to do visual effects with computers, we'd like to be able to mix sound with computers, and we'd like to be able to edit our film with computers… we also need an accounting system here at Lucasfilm."

"Oh, that's great."

"And so we understand that you're the guy to do this, Ralph."

"How the hell did you get to me? Why me?"

"Well, I buy real estate for George, I don't know anything about this…" and he went on to explain how he had asked around Stanford, got to Carnegie Mellon, and now had found him at New York Tech.

Ralph was giddy. Sweaty. "Look, I'm honored, really," he replied as calmly as possible under the circumstances, "but I'm just fresh out of grad school. I'm working with people, however, who are doing this all the time, and I think there are some people here who you should be talking to, and we can set this up."

Gindy cut him off. "Wait wait wait, what do you mean, 'doing this all the time?'"

"Well, I work in a research lab, the New York Institute of Technology, and we do computer animation. And that's essentially what you're talking about when you ask for visual effects…in fact, the reason I'm working here is that the people I'm working with and I all agree that one day we're going to make feature films this way, and that's our driving vision, to make a feature film."

"What do you mean doing this every day? "

"Every day we're producing animation on computers…."

Gindy was stunned. Paydirt. "Wait…tell me one thing…can you create an image of a spaceship and make it fly around on the screen?"

The boys at NYIT had only two days earlier been experimenting with that effect, and it was with some irony that the Ralph told him about it.

Gindy was incredulous. "You mean to tell me I've called twenty-five places in this country, and nobody but your group is doing this? I can't believe that you're the only people doing this."

Ralph explained: "Truth be told, there *are* other people doing this, but I believe we're doing it better than anyone else… you should talk to the people I'm working with here because I think we can really help you set this up, this research thing." And Gindy was fine with that.

Ralph hung up the phone and sat in shock, in the chaotic silence of the lab, before gathering his thoughts and bolting to the office of his bosses, Ed Catmull and Alvy Ray Smith.

six

The Godfather of Electronic Cinema

[1976–1979]

Time is a plot to keep everything from happening at once.

—Seen on bathroom wall, Grateful Dead's
recording stage in San Rafael (1978)

FRANCIS COPPOLA arrived in the Philippines to begin shooting *Apocalypse Now* in February 1976. There was no way the film could be done in time for the bicentennial but United Artists execs hoped it could be done before the end of the year.

One of the early obstacles Coppola faced was the amount of time it took for him to see his filmed shots—called dailies. After film was shot in the jungle, it was shipped to Technicolor's labs in Rome (perhaps the best color labs in the world) and printed; then the positive was sent to San Francisco and transferred to ¾-inch tapes and also to small ½-inch Betamax cassettes, which were shipped back to him in the Philippines. The negative was stashed away for safekeeping. A process that happened overnight in Hollywood took about two weeks in that part of the world. Francis didn't get dailies on *Apocalypse Now*. He got "bimonthlies."

"We bought a couple of those very first Beta machines," recalled Coppola. "I had one in a little hut and I used to get these cassettes and plug them in to see [our shot film]. After a while I was lugging this Beta around. I even put one on a houseboat floating down the river and we were able to see material and make decisions about reshooting."

Thoughts of technology were never far from Coppola's mind, even when he was hunkered down in dark huts during *Apocalypse*. He would confide in Dean Tavolaris, his long-time production designer, about his dreams for improving the world: "Make a better telephone, develop a more efficient toaster, improve the style of baseball uniforms, build a beautiful little restaurant, run a revolutionary design school such as Germany's pre-war Bauhaus."

When *Apocalypse* finally finished shooting on May 21, 1977, Francis returned to San Francisco with hundreds of hours of his film transferred to submarine-sandwich-sized ¾-inch videotape cassettes. During his absence, Zoetrope had moved out of its original Folsom Street location and into the Sentinel building. In the new Zoetrope penthouse, lovingly restored by Tavoularis, Francis contracted with a freelance video company[1] to build an offline video editing suite so he could experiment with the cassettes.[2] In his new editing suite he meticulously worked the controls of the rudimentary machines. A small switcher let him introduce optical effects that would have been cost-prohibitive to try out in film.[3]

Week by week, he began to build his movie, edit the film, select the best moments. Using his videotape system, he built the complex opening sequence of layered images—Martin Sheen lying on a bed with sometimes five or six layers of helicopters, explosions, and the hotel room fan. And very long over-lapping shots, dissolving slowly from one image to the next. He roughed together the entire movie on video.

George Lucas was on a high from the release of *Star Wars*, starting to get his act together for a sequel and to set up shop in Northern California. Coppola invited him and Walter Murch to see his state-of-the art electronic editing equipment. It was clean and quiet. No assistants. No trims. Both men sat before the keyboard and monitor and typed numbers that filled the screen.

"This is a crude system," said Lucas. "You want it made for editors, not engineers. You want to be able to stop on a frame and move back and forth. You want to have all the qualities of editing and everything that we learned in film school about the art of editing."

Coppola was far more comfortable overlooking the drawbacks of videotape, but Lucas was adamant. "[Editing] has to be done on a creative and visual basis." Coppola was happy to be able to rough together a version by himself; Lucas and Murch, both of whom considered themselves film editors first, were uninterested in this kind of process.

Recalled Lucas, "It was after that I began to think about developing a [new] system that was based on editorial, not engineering principles."

When Coppola finished his editing a few months later, he gave a videotape cut of the movie to his editors with the basic instruction to "make the film look like this tape." But the videotape gave few clues for recreating those images from the million-plus feet of picture and sound. Just by looking at a shot, it would be nearly impossible to identify where it came from. The opening sequence in particular, with its extremely long overlapping shots, would be

[1] In particular, engineer Steve Calou and news cameraman/equipment designer Tony St. John, formerly of Bay Area station KRON-TV.

[2] *Offline*: a video editing setup where creative decisions are made using low-quality materials. Then, "online" editing re-creates the creative decisions with the high-quality original source material.

[3] His suite consisted of a few tape decks, a little effects switcher for dissolves and fades, a record player and audiocassette deck, an audio mixer, and a small editing controller.

easy to visualize and create in video, but extraordinarily challenging to re-assemble in film.

Film optical effects, whether simple (titles and fades), or complicated (composites of miniature spaceships and painted backgrounds), are made by describing each effect ahead of time and then building them specially, often taking days or weeks (or in the case of *Star Wars*, months). Video made it possible to experiment with mixing images and get immediate results, described as "live" or "in real time"—it was a major advantage that video had over film. But film and video don't co-exist very well. In the end, Coppola's film editors took the videotape he had created over just a few months and spent almost the entire next year struggling to assemble a comparable film version.

Francis was happy to be back in Bay Area culture. Typical of his position in the creative community, he was invited to attend a Grateful Dead concert by music promoter and Bay Area stalwart Bill Graham. In the "drums" segment of the concert, Dead members Mickey Hart and Bill Kreutzmann, calling themselves the "Rhythm Devils," began an extended percussion jam session

Walter Murch working on the mix of *Apocalypse Now*. He described his role in the film with a new screen credit: "Sound Designer."

using a host of unusual and innovative instruments. Coppola realized that the sounds would be an eerie primal accompaniment to the images in his film.

Coppola asked Hart if they would be interested in setting up a percussion session that could be integrated into the *Apocalypse* soundtrack. The ever-gregarious Coppola also invited Hart, Kreutzmann, and their bandmates to the final wrap party for *Apocalypse*. He called it "The Party." It would be a combination Easter celebration and 40th birthday party for himself, and he wanted to hold it at his Napa estate.

Eleanor Coppola asked Les Blank, a well-known documentary film-maker,[4] to shoot a 16mm film of the party.[5] "I agreed to shoot The Party mostly because I really wanted to *go* to The Party," recalled Blank.

The Party went on for two days and two nights. Amid the festivities, Francis found himself sitting around with Les.

"Why don't you come shoot the recording of the soundtrack that Mickey Hart is going to do," Francis asked. Les spoke to Mickey about setting up the details of the scoring session. Mickey didn't want 35mm film cameras because they made too much noise.

But professional video systems were not portable. Until the late '70s, using videotape meant that production had to be done by a studio with lots of air conditioning and smooth floors. But this was 1978, and there was a new solution to that problem. Sony had introduced a videotape format (superior to the Ampex or RCA 2-inch variety that had been the broadcast standard since 1956, which played on machines known as Quadruplex "monsters"). Sony's reels of 1-inch tape were more manageable and the decks were smaller. They were still as large as a narrow bookcase but were finally portable, which opened the door for a mobile production truck—and therefore location shooting.

There was only one broadcast-quality production truck in the Bay Area; it had been developed at Video Production Services (VPS), in Berkeley. VPS chief engineer Clark Higgins got a call from Les Blank, who asked him to bring a mobile unit to shoot some director scoring a movie in a warehouse in San Rafael. Higgins put together a team and headed out across the Richmond Bridge.

Arriving at the warehouse—it looked like an airplane hanger—they slowly pulled past a crew of Hells Angels, who eyed them warily. Once given the word, a roll-up door on the space was opened for them.

Inside they saw seven large video projection screens propped around the periphery, each showing the napalm climax of *Apocalypse Now*. Percussion instruments were all over the floor, in every direction, gathered in small piles or assembled into custom racks. It was a forest of instruments. In the middle of the hanger was a giant multitrack recording console. And then Higgins realized what he was going to shoot.

[4] **Les Blank** (b.1935). Independent filmmaker best known for documentary films on musicians and folk culture. Also a PhD grad of USC film school, 1967.

[5] Eleanor was working on her own documentary about the making of *Apocalypse Now*—released later as *Hearts of Darkness*.

The warehouse, called Club Front, was the Grateful Dead's workspace. The truck pulled inside and the men began to unpack four large television cameras and miles of cable to connect them to the Sony tape decks in the truck. Under the guidance of Les Blank, Higgins' crew quickly set up and began shooting the Rhythm Devils.[6] The tribal sounds were recorded by Francis' audio engineers on suspended microphones.[7]

"Francis wanted us to take the journey up river with Kurtz," said Hart. "We'd start the film and play straight through to the end, then we'd do it again. No matter where you were, you'd look up, and the cut of the film was on a screen in front of you."

The band jammed through the evening, starting after dinner and working until breakfast.[8] Throughout, Coppola was increasingly fascinated with the truck, where the video feeds from all the cameras were sent. Les Blank hadn't worked in the multicamera video format, so Coppola, who was remarkably comfortable with the technology, sat beside Clark Higgins. They watched the camera views on a series of small monitors.

"Can I work the switcher?" Francis asked Clark.

"Sure," replied the young man, and he showed Francis how to do some basic transitions and superimpositions from the live feeds.

"And I can talk to the guys and tell them to shoot something else?" Les nodded and directed Francis to the intercom switches.

"Wow, this is great," declared Coppola, giddy with the control. "I can compose the picture and talk to the cameramen…this is how movies are going to be made in the future."

The scoring session, which they referred to as "River Music," went on for days,[9] as did the video coverage of the event. When Coppola wasn't in oratory— giving the musicians tales for their motivation, or crashed out on the sofa, he spent his time in the truck with Blank and Higgins, directing the cameramen and talking about the things that were on his mind.

Coppola was still thinking about his ordeal with the ¾-inch video edit of the movie he had given to his editors. He was frustrated that it was impossible to correlate the videotape he was playing with, with the film that ultimately had to be matched up. Coppola explained to Higgins how it had taken him a few months to edit the movie on those tapes, but it took the team of editors nearly a year to conform to his image.

"Is there anything you can do to help?" he asked Higgins.

It so happened that Coppola had asked the right engineer. Higgins had been thinking about that very problem and was interested in helping Coppola. What had bedeviled Coppola's edit was not simply that the timecode numbers on the videotape could not be related to the edge numbers on the film. It was that film played at 24 frames per second, and video played at 30.

[6] The international jazz and fusion performers included Hart, Kreutzmann, Lesh, Amarantha, Errico, Hinton, Loveless, Airto Moreira, and Flora Purim.

[7] Hart badgered Coppola to use better speakers in the 70mm theaters that would be playing *Apocalypse Now*, to capture the full range of the music they were creating. Coppola was convinced, and he soon insisted that the Dead's brand of speakers (Meyer Sound) be redesigned for movie sound, and then be required for theaters to get 70mm prints of *Apocalypse Now*.

[8] "Francis was fearless, he would do anything for the work," said Hart. "That was one of the things I loved about him; if you needed it, you got it. You work all night. You work all day. You work all week. He used to walk around and say 'just make it happen, man, just make it happen!' So I made up these shirts for everyone. We wore "Make It Happen" shirts during all the sessions.

[9] Les Blank recalled shooting for a few days, rehearsals mostly, saying that the band—and in particular Brazilian Airto Moreira— was totally distracted by the video cameras; on the third day, he said, the cameras were turned off. Others present recall the shoot took all week.

[10] The process of recording the film image onto videotape using 3:2 had first been used in the late 1950s, although timecode wasn't introduced until the early 1970s. A kinescope creates a crude sort of 3:2 pulldown.

Even if you lined them up perfectly, eventually the two would drift out-of-count with each other. If you transferred one frame of film to one frame of video, the playback would speed up by 20 percent—a "Chipmunks" version of your video.

Videotape and Video Signals

A video monitor is comprised of 525 horizontal lines. To make an image, an electron beam starts at the top left corner of the screen and draws the first horizontal line. At the right edge, the beam turns off and moves quickly back to the left, skips down *two lines* and begins again. In this way every other line (the odd-numbered lines) are drawn on a video display. When the beam reaches the bottom right corner, it jumps back up to the top left again, but now draws the in between lines (the even-numbered lines). This is called "interlaced." When recorded to videotape, the signal for the odd-numbered lines comes first, in what is called "field 1" of video. Following this is field 2. One full video frame is comprised electronically of a pair of video fields. When a video camera shoots, each video frame is the union of two identical video fields.

Higgins understood that while it was not possible to get 24 frames of film to fit uniformly into 30 frames of video, there was a process that exploited the fields, 60 each second, to get around the problem. By copying every film frame to 2 and then 3 fields, the timing part of the problem could be overcome—every 4 frames of film could effectively be stretched to play over 5 physical video frames. Because of this, film could be transferred to videotape.

The name for the process was a *3:2 pulldown* and it was performed by a very expensive device called a *telecine*—a film-to-tape transfer machine. Higgins hadn't invented 3:2 pulldown; it was already widely understood in film-video circles. His concern was more how to edit the video, mindful of the fields, and somehow trace a path back to the original film. That was still a problem.

Higgins explained all this to Coppola. The only way to start on film, transfer to videotape, and still be able to get back to your original film, was to manage a database of timecodes and film edge numbers and take into consideration the way the 3:2 pulldown was performed.

"You have to start very early in the process, capturing these numbers…." Higgins began.

Coppola stroked his beard. "Do you want to work on this with me?" he asked.

The 3:2 Problem

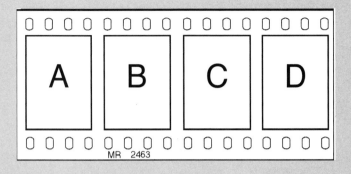

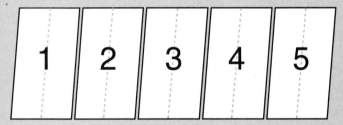

Top figure: four frames of film, which would take 4/24 (1/5) of a second to play. Below it, five frames of video, which would take 5/30 (also 1/5) of a second to play. To get film to play normally on videotape, the transfer must exploit the electronic signal that makes up a video frame—the two fields that together weave a picture.

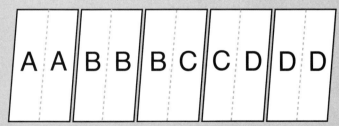

By making some transferred frames "longer" (creating a series of alternating 2 and then 3 field film frames), film and video can coexist. Even though videotape can be recorded in this unusual way, it can only be edited between frames—the frames themselves are indivisible. Thus, if choices are made about editing film using a length of videotape, there are certain phantom frames that might be included that do not translate back to a real film frame. Making creative decisions about editing film using videotape is thus highly problematic.

In April 1979, during the weeks before The Party, Francis had been asked to present the Oscar for Best Director at the 51st annual Academy Awards. Before he opened the golden envelope to give the award to Michael Cimino for *The Deer Hunter*, he stood at the podium and launched into a short diatribe.

"We're on the eve of something that's going to make the Industrial Revolution look like a small out-of-town tryout. I can see a communications revolution that's about movies and art and music and digital electronics and satellites, but above all, human talent; and it's going to make the masters of the cinema, from whom we've inherited this business, believe things that they would have thought impossible."

Even as movie stars in the audience shifted around in their seats uncomfortable at the political statement, or stared into each other's bewildered faces, Coppola gave the public a glimpse of the future. His precognisance was astonishing.

[act two]

IN THE YEARS when filmmaking radicals like George Lucas and Francis Coppola were in film school, there was another revolutionary movement afoot. It involved computers.

Computers were for code-breaking. They were for complex math problems. Like how to aim a rocket to get it to fly two hundred fifty thousand miles and land on a tiny moving target. People didn't own computers any more than they owned rockets. Luckily, a few universities and industrial-size corporations had some access to computer technology. They were usually helping the defense department with their research and development.

Beginning in the late '60s, technological innovations started making the computers faster and smaller. But a small computer is still a computer: what possible use could anybody but the government have with a computer?

Just as filmmaking had its revolutionaries in Lucas and Coppola, the computer facet of the military-industrial complex was about to be shaken up by other iconoclasts bucking the system—artists—the last thing the computer industry saw coming.

seven

The Visionary on Long Island

[Leading to 1974]

Where a calculator on the ENIAC [computer] is equipped with 18,000 vacuum tubes and weighs 30 tons, computers in the future may have only 1,000 vacuum tubes and perhaps weigh 1.5 tons.

—POPULAR MECHANICS, MARCH 1949

NO ONE WAS CLEAR on how Alexander Schure came into his money. Some said his grandfather came over from Russia, went to New York, and succeeded in the fur business. Some said he had connections to the CIA. But these were likely more colorful than accurate.

Alex was somehow connected with the American war effort in WWII, probably through his close family friend, Major Alexander deSeversky (who was known to the family as "Sasha"). deSeversky, a pioneering Russian aviator-turned-American patriot, wrote the book *Victory Through Air Power* (1942), that was turned into an important American propaganda movie by Disney. But before that, the rumor was that he may have helped the young Schure by turning over to him a warehouse of surplus military electronics equipment.

Schure was a dashing entrepreneur who shrewdly took advantage of the post-war GI Bill and started a correspondence school for vets. It may have looked like a quick-diploma factory, with ads in the back pages of comic books, but Schure sent out *real* electronic gear to the students—the surplus radios and radars from Sasha. Probably. The story is unclear. What is clear is that Schure continued to build the school, which he eventually called the New York Institute of Technology (NYIT), into a thriving business at a time when few private universities were doing well.

After launching his school in Brooklyn in 1955, he added a second campus in Manhattan. His students earned normal-sounding degrees but with an appended suffix like "technician," as in "computer science technician."[1]

[1] Or "technology" as in "video engineering technology."

In 1963 Schure purchased his first Long Island estate from the Vanderbilt-Whitney family. Shortly thereafter he began "a systematic acquisition of the land that bordered the main parcel," and joined them into the crown jewel campus for NYIT.

Old Westbury, New York, in the north-central part of Long Island, is a Gatsby-inspiring stretch of aging mansions and quaint villages, green pastures, densely wooded groves of sprawling oaks, and short drives to white sand beaches. Sixteen miles east of Manhattan, it is not far from the airfield from which Charles Lindbergh launched his momentous nonstop flight to Paris.

"I wanted to create a not-for-profit institution," said Schure, "that could have a history a hundred years from today, two hundred years if it was well managed."

Continuing to thrive off the GI Bill as Vietnam was escalating, NYIT provided a diploma for kids unable to get one anywhere else. Said one faculty member, "If you wanted a deferment, you just enrolled yourself in college." The problem was that most of the kids weren't really "college material"; they were often just trying to avoid the draft. So Schure took it upon himself to create a number of remedial academic programs for his students.

In a wave of enthusiasm, Schure decided that one way to interest students in math was to provide academic materials in comic-book form. He coaxed a New York comic book artist, Howard Spielman, to draw the math curriculum. Drawing the images led to coloring them, which led to photographing them, to turn into projectable slides. Sawyers, makers of the popular View-Master slides, wanted to work with Schure to develop the project. Schure was elated.

"Sawyers went wild about this stuff," recalled Spielman, "and then they said, 'Can you make them move?'"

Spielman built a small animation department in Brooklyn, which produced a short film, *The Development of Our Number System*. The film was entered in the New York International TV Film Festival. It won the gold medal.

Schure was born again with the win. Now he really wanted to direct animated movies. He had the money, the vision, and he was smart enough to put the pieces together.

In 1974 Alex Schure started making his first movie, an animated telling of the classic story, "Tubby the Tuba."[2] He wrote it. He produced it. He directed it. He filled one of his mansions with a hundred animators, using equipment he had purchased from the old WWI-era Max Fleischer animation studio in New York City.[3]

"All the stars were there," recalled Spielman. "Schure loved that." There was Johnny Gent, who had done animation on the old Popeye cartoons.[4]

[2] Paul Tripp, an early TV personality, created "Tubby the Tuba" as a record for kids in 1942, which he helped turn into an animated movie in 1947. He went on to host a successful kids show in the early '50s, "Mr. I. Magination" and later "Birthday House," in NYC.

[3] Max Fleischer, and his brother Joe were pioneers of cel animation. They created Betty Boop and Koko the Clown between 1919-1942 and are noted for having invented the rotoscope, for drawing cells by tracing elements of real photographs.

[4] Real name: Johnny Gentilella. He worked at Famous as an animator; he later worked for Ralph Bakshi on the film *Heavy Traffic* (1973).

Dick Van Dyke and Pearl Bailey recorded the character voices. Dozens of young artists from New York did inking and painting and camera work. It was a full-scale, real world production. Schure's infectious enthusiasm glued the project together.

As far as Schure was concerned, the process of cel animation had problems. The procedure seemed simple enough: after actors record lines from the script, line up the recording to exposure sheets and then start drawing frames on paper, copying them to transparent acrylic "cels" for coloring and photography. But a single frame was often comprised of a stack of the imperfectly clear cels. "You can't go beyond four layers before the cels start to grey down," explained Spielman. "If a character has a moving arm on layer one, and the rest of his body is on layer four, and both need to be red, then the red on top has to be a darker red to match up to the other layers lower down. It was a terrible pain."

To make matters worse, the animation process itself was slow and laborious. A professional animator like Johnny Gent would draw the characters and set up the action. But the master never drew every frame; he only drew characters at key moments of their motion, maybe every other frame, sometimes one every few frames. Fifty to 75 percent of the movie was drawn in between the key frames, usually by animators less distinguished, maybe younger—called "in-betweeners." It was rough manual labor.

Somewhat out of the blue, a 16mm film arrived on Schure's desk, sent by a computer salesman named Pete Ferentinos. It was called *Face and Hands*. Schure (owning one of the first ¾-inch videotape decks) had the film transferred to videotape and watched the video with interest. It showed animations that were created entirely, and unbelievably, by a computer.[5]

"Alex was pretty impressed with the capabilities the film showed," recalled Ferentinos.

"I thought it could solve my animation problem," Schure said.

Schure believed that the computer could eliminate the color variations that depended on position in the stack. In theory, there could be hundreds of layers. He also figured that if key frames of a character could be drawn on a computer, it might be possible to have the computer calculate the in-between frames. That would remove an enormous labor and time drain on a project. "He wanted to out-Disney Disney," said Spielman.

For his part, Schure denied any intention to go up against Disney. "Listen, I had enough on my plate." Schure contended his interest was purely to get more efficient in distributing his educational content: "Distance learning for the students not close to the university," he called it.

[5] At that time, to say a computer made an animation was about as incongruous as today saying something like a bulldozer made a cake.

"As I understood it, said Ferentinos, "Schure's grand plan was that he could produce a curriculum at NYIT in which he could train animators and use them to produce films. The films had the ability to spin off millions and millions of dollars, and the school would be the beneficiary of the profits that this great new technology could produce. He could create an annuity for the school and put it on solid financial footing. This was his vision."

Schure was overflowing with excitement, and Ferentinos, a very young salesman who knew nothing about computer graphics, realized he in was over his head.

Ferentinos worked for Dave Evans and Ivan Sutherland, two enterprising University of Utah professors who had started a company in 1968 to build specialized tools for imaging and visual simulation. The company was called, appropriately enough, Evans & Sutherland (E&S). What it did was build monstrous multimillion-dollar simulators for airplanes and ships for the Coast Guard and the Defense Department.

Ivan Sutherland, at left, with Dave Evans, December 1969.

[6] Every few years they'd add a "D" for "Defense" as in DARPA, and then remove it again later.

At the time, the Defense Department was funding fairly risky research projects at a number of universities in the country, among them MIT, Berkeley, and Utah. This was done through its Advanced Research Projects Agency, or ARPA.[6]

Through ARPA, Ivan Sutherland helped make the University of Utah (U of U) the foundation school for computers and graphics. He asked Berkeley professor Dave Evans to build a new department at the U of U in the 1960s, and then joined the team himself as a professor. Evans and Sutherland's first students included Jim Clark (interested in real-time display of information),[7] Alan Kay (developing object-oriented programming),[8] and John Warnock (exploring page-description languages),[9] all pioneers of what was called "information display," but would eventually be called the computer graphics industry.[10]

The Vector Display

When a computer made an image, it was drawn on a special screen with lines of light, known as a *vector display*. The vector display could draw pictures like connect-the-dots, creating precision etchings, and soon had the intelligence to hide the lines for the part of an object that was behind another part, which gave the illusion of a surface.[11] Evans & Sutherland delivered products, like their "Picture System," which utilized these vector displays, but they also saw the opportunity in *raster-based*, or television-type images, that could allow for shading and color—representing an incredible opportunity.

A researcher demonstrating Ivan Sutherland's Sketchpad ("A Man-Machine Graphical Communications System"), a vector drawing program for creating engineering drawings directly on a CRT display; it was his PhD thesis from MIT in 1963. This photo fails to communicate the size of the device; it extends up toward the ceiling and toward the camera, covering a wall.

Ivan Sutherland was passionate about computer imagery. "A display connected to a digital computer," said Sutherland, "gives us a chance to gain familiarity with concepts not realizable in the physical world. It is a looking glass into a mathematical wonderland."

He was so convinced in the power to draw pictures with a computer that he had tried to start his own movie company in Hollywood; he called it The

[7] Founder of Silicon Graphics and Netscape.

[8] Envisioned the first laptop PC in 1971, the "Dynabook." In 2004 Kay was awarded the Kyoto Prize (sort of a Nobel prize for computer science) for "creating the concept of modern personal computing and contributing to its realization."

[9] Founder of Adobe Systems.

[10] When there was a proposal for a network of computers using the existing national phone system, ARPAnet was established in 1969, first between UCLA and the labs at the U of U, Stanford, and UC Santa Barbara. It was the first set of links in what would become the Internet. For a time, Utah was a cornerstone of the computer universe.

[11] The "hidden surface algorithm" kept the 3-D drawing from looking like transparent objects constructed from wire mesh, instead giving them surfaces and depth. There was not one algorithm to accomplish this feat, but rather it was a generic name for a class of programs. Many U of U students developed their own special variations for the work they were doing.

Electric Picture Company. The field was so new there were few, if any, examples of computer-generated animation. He found a young engineer named Gary Demos who was interested in joining him. Sutherland invited Demos to Salt Lake City to work with him on building new hardware and coming up with ways to demonstrate the technology.

In short order, Sutherland expanded the new company to four, adding Glen Fleck[12] and John Whitney Jr., the son of the famous electronic graphics pioneer John Whitney Sr. Whitney Junior had convinced a microfilm scanning and recording company called Triple-I (for Information International, Inc.) to let him use their facilities to create some special effects for the movies. At Triple-I, Whitney Junior supervised some of the earliest 2-D computer-generated visual effects for the film *Westworld* (1973). He had a profound understanding and appreciation for the technology and for graphics, and was well-connected in Hollywood. He signed on to handle the group's marketing.

Alex Schure didn't know anything about the artfilms of John Whitney Sr., or Sketchpad, or hidden surface algorithms. But he did know a little something about animation. Back on Long Island he had scores of animators hand-drawing *Tubby*. Schure was so focused on his dream for NYIT, built on a foundation of training students and delivering profitable movies, that he was convinced he had to be first to use new technology for making animated films.

Pete Ferentinos couldn't convince his boss, Dave Evans, that Schure was for real. The graphics world in the early '70s was small and tight. The computers that E&S sold were predominately in high-security government installations, doing what they called in those days, "spook work," and Ferentinos placed his products almost exclusively in Washington and Boston. Evans told Ferentinos, "Schure doesn't have the expertise…he doesn't have the wherewithal…you're wasting your time."

But Ferentinos badgered Evans until he relented. "Okay," he said, "Ivan Sutherland is giving a seminar at the University of Colorado in Denver, and if Dr. Alexander Schure shows up, Ivan will spend two minutes with him."

"From a salesman's point of view," said Ferentinos, "this wasn't what I wanted to hear." But he invited Schure to Denver, and Schure and his wife excitedly flew out to hear E&S co-founder Sutherland speak.

Sutherland told a good story about applications in engineering, education and, of course, entertainment. He explained that with the new raster-based images, one could certainly use a computer to mechanize drawing animations and cartoons and other non-realistic images.

Schure, too, thought that backgrounds could be drawn on the computer, as well as pictures that remained essentially still. Maybe instead of drawing,

[12] Glen Fleck: an animator and engineer who had been working with designers Charles and Ray Eames. Fleck created a series of 2-minute animated shorts in the early '60s exploring mathematical principals (topology, symmetry, etc). In 1973 he edited the book *A Computer Perspective*, an illustrated essay on the origins of the first computer, based on an exhibition from IBM.

copying, and painting each cel and then photographing layers of cels to compose each frame, images could be layered in the computer and output directly to film, skipping the camera part entirely. Sutherland said it had never been done, of course, but the new technology would make it possible.

By that time, Sutherland, Demos and Whitney had all but given up on getting their film studio financed; it was an expensive and risky venture for any investor, particularly in 1974. Still, Sutherland was passionate about the vision. Though Schure was rich, he wasn't interested in financing Sutherland's project; he was, however, consumed with his own.

Recognizing Schure as a serious customer, Sutherland immediately invited the Schures to Salt Lake City, to tour the lab and to meet his partner, Dave Evans. Evans was happy to take them on a tour of University of Utah computer graphics research lab. There, he explained the changing face of graphics technology. He explained how the film *Face and Hands* was made; he said that researchers at Xerox had recently developed a way to make a raster image with something called "picture memory" and had created an image painting program for it. Schure was fascinated.

Aerial view of Xerox's research center, called PARC, in Palo Alto, California, 1970.

The Xerox Corporation was becomming increasingly famous for its research lab, which continued to develop new bits of computer technology. In the first years of the 1970s, their Palo Alto Research Center, called affectionately "PARC," was a hotbed of developments that included the first personal computer, the first window system display, Ethernet, and the laserprinter.

Alan Kay's office at PARC, where he holds an *ad hoc* meeting with visitors Steve Saunders *(center)* and digital musician Steve Savitsky *(right)*.

Researchers there had a favorite slogan, "The best way to predict the future is to invent it," and many of them did.[13]

Many of the principle staff at PARC had come directly from the graduate program at the University of Utah, under Evans and Sutherland.[14] Their research focused on the development of "personal computers," a term they coined, but as far as Xerox was concerned it was always about "the office of the future."

Dick Shoup, a researcher at PARC, began developing the first paint program for a computer in late 1972.[15] With a stylus on a digital pad, he could draw pictures that were displayed on a TV set. The painting process necessitated the invention of hardware to manage those pictures—most importantly additional "shift register" computer memory specifically designed to store data with X-Y coordinates, like a graph or an image. He called it "picture memory."

Picture memory was a dramatic shift from the way images were generally handled on vector displays. And though making an image from thousands of dots was more in line with the way film and paper images were created, it was intense for a computer to manage. The quantity of data was enormous, and the pressure it put on the CPU to draw or modify the images was almost paralyzing. At low enough resolutions, however, simple pictures could be painted with colors, something a vector display could never manage.

[13] From Alan Kay, whose full quote was: "Don't worry about what anybody else is going to do… the best way to predict the future is to invent it. Really smart people with reasonable funding can do just about anything that doesn't violate too many of Newton's Laws!" (1971)

[14] In particular, John Warnock and Alan Kay.

[15] Shoup" is pronounced like "shout," and does *not* rhyme with "soup."

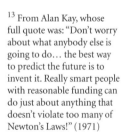

The famous "bean bag" conference room at PARC.

Using a computer to paint pixels is one of the simplest forms of 2-D computer graphics. The more pixels on the screen, the sharper-looking the image ("picture resolution"), but the more computer memory is required. The more "bits" stored for each pixel, the better the color fidelity ("color resolution"), but again, the more memory required to store the image.

A 1-bit image is black and white; a 3-bit image has eight colors—still remarkably primitive in its creative opportunities.[16] But an 8-bit image allows for 256 colors; this was about as simple as one could get and still generate a reasonably detailed image. Of course, for an image approaching the color resolution you see on television, you'd need 24-bits—more than 16 million crayons to choose from. Film is even more demanding, requiring something closer to 36-bits (almost 7 billion colors).

In the early 1970s, memory was prohibitively expensive, and the few frame buffers in existence were built to store images that could play at TV set resolution: a square image of 512 by 512 pixels on a frame buffer translated well to 480 lines, each comprised of 640 tiny colored dots in an electronic video image.[17]

Evans explained to Schure that the price of memory chips was continuing to drop; he and his students were finally able to store and display an image using a rack of newly invented RAM chips. It was still "picture memory" but everyone was now calling it a "frame buffer." E&S had produced the world's first commercial frame buffer and sold it to the University of Utah. Schure looked at it blankly.

Evans tried to explain the hardware in as simple terms as he could. The RAM chips, he said, are dedicated to hold the image that can then be represented on a screen. Each slot of RAM represents one tiny piece of the image. Lots of pieces take lots of RAM. The frame buffer makes *real* imaging possible from a computer—not just line drawings. In other words, the amount of RAM determines the quality of the images you can make.[18]

Intel co-founder and chairman Gordon Moore had once predicted that the number of transistors that could fit on a chip was going to double every year and a half. If true, RAM chips would continually be able to hold better and better images at a given price. If Schure wanted a head start, he had better get in the game soon.

E&S had no idea if their frame buffer would be commercially viable, but they were always comforted by the notion that even if picture memory never took off, the device could be used as regular computer memory. Dave Evans explained to Schure that they could build him his own 8-bit frame buffer, similar to the one they just sold to the University, for only $80,000.

[16] There were, in fact, very early computer paint experiments in 1 and 3 bits in the early '70s, at Bell Labs (Ken Knolton).

[17] A full video frame is considered to have 525 lines with 640 dots, but not all the lines hold image information.

[18] Today, the descendent of the frame buffer is the *graphics card* that is implicit in every personal computer, not an external machine connected to a computer.

An added feature of the E&S frame buffer was that you didn't have to hook it to a big expensive IBM mainframe and run it with punch cards, but rather, connect it to a "minicomputer," effectively a deskside workstation powerful enough to draw a picture, a DEC PDP-11. The PDP was a revolutionary shift toward letting engineers make a program (or a picture) on a computer, independently. Schure bought it. Evans walked him through the University of Utah laboratories; and Schure wanted one of *everything*.

There was a small catch: all this was brand new, and it would take some time to deliver some of the products he wanted. Perhaps Schure would be interested in E&S's hottest current item, the vector-based "Picture System," which would get him ready for the frame buffer? He was. And he bought dozens of other items, including a precision CRT scanner for getting images from the computer to film—which hadn't even been invented yet. He dropped just under a million dollars, entirely on impulse. He was excited beyond measure.

And then, there was the matter of how to use the stuff. Almost as an afterthought, Evans reportedly asked him, "Who's gonna run this for you?"

Schure was too focused on the big picture to have considered such mundane details. There were very few people in the world who had experience with these kinds of machines. Fewer still who had an interest in animation.

"Who would you recommend?"

"Too bad," said Evans, "the guy you want is unavailable."

"Why is that?"

"Because he's just left Utah for Boston to take a new position at an engineering company called Applicon."[19]

"Who is he?"

"Edwin…Ed Catmull. I was his PhD thesis advisor. He's a super smart guy who happens to be passionate about making movies with a computer. He's been working with the early frame buffer technology and has developed some innovative tools for image manipulation."

Catmull had at one time been prepared to be the fifth member of the Electric Picture Company once they got financing. But after Sutherland tried unsuccessfully for nine months to raise money, he finally gave up. Catmull, charged with supporting a growing family, had no choice but to go find a real job.

Schure left with the phone number for Applicon.

Catmull, it turned out, was not thrilled to be at Applicon. The thin, soft-spoken Mormon with a neat black beard had a lifelong passion for computerizing movies. At Applicon he was doing computer-aided design and manufacturing that utilized a vector display graphics system, but he was frustrated by the uncreative and uninspired work.

[19] Applicon specialized in computer-aided design (CAD), a hot new industrial use for computers in the 1970s, to facilitate technical drawings, schematics and blueprints.

Alex Schure called and made his case to Catmull. Schure wasn't a dilettante talking about making movies; he was doing it. *Tubby the Tuba* was in production. He was gearing up for a version of *Puss and Boots*. Some animators were already working on public service announcements for CBS. This distinction was critical. It wasn't just academic research—they were taking the first steps to make computer tools for real filmmaking.

The only thing giving Catmull some pause was the lack of commitment he would be showing Applicon, not only leaving a few months after arriving, but possibly taking his officemate, Malcolm Blanchard (another Utah grad), with him. The two knew each other well; Malcolm had worked on his master's degree while Ed was getting his PhD. By coincidence, Catmull found Blanchard at Applicon. Sharing an office, the duo were content, but Malcolm was more than willing to bail if Ed was able to get him a job.

Ultimately, it wasn't too hard to convince Catmull to follow the frame buffer to NYIT. As Schure reportedly said at the time, "Money has a way of changing people's minds." Catmull couldn't have cared less about money— the lure was the opportunity to make a movie. "I only hesitated long enough to make sure it was real."

ED CATMULL.

Hometown: Salt Lake City, Utah. *Family:* married, two boys. *Schools:* Univ. of Utah. *Interests:* reading, gardening, camping, cooking. *Employment history:* Boeing, TRW, Applicon, NYIT.
[From the 1982 LFL Yearbook]

eight

The Train Wreck

[1974–1977]

ARRIVING AT OLD WESTBURY in November 1974, Ed Catmull was stunned by what he found there. With winter blanketing the estates, the place was idyllic. Paths meandered between mansions, through wooded groves littered with Greek columns, spare bits of marble frieze, and working fountains.[1] He and his family moved into a small house in Glen Cove, fifteen minutes from the NYIT campus.

The first equipment started arriving almost immediately. Ed was in charge of getting everything installed in the garage of one of the mansions. Alex Schure had told him he could order any other piece of equipment that would move the project forward. Any staff he might need was his for the hiring. He had no students. No classes to teach. No timelines or deadlines.

Ed called Malcolm Blanchard, his officemate at Applicon, and offered him a job. Malcolm accepted, and arrived in January. They watched the animators at work and thought about out how they could expedite the process with computers.

For Ed Catmull, this was an opportunity to build a lab where he could pursue his dream of making animations on the computer. Frustrated with his limited drawing skills, he had spent his graduate years inventing ways to make 3-D objects with realistic-looking surfaces; objects that could be lit, staged and moved. He could "photograph" them into frames that could be put together to make a movie.

For a class project at the University of Utah, Catmull had created one of the earliest 3-D computer animations, which he called *Hand*. Working with a plaster cast of his own hand, he tediously drew triangles all over it and digitized the corner points into a computer.[2] He was able to manipulate the hand as a simple animation—rotate it, change the lighting and perspective. The fingers moved independently, controlled by changing numbers in a database, and the camera even explored inside the hand for a surreal journey.

MALCOLM BLANCHARD

Hometown: Arcata, CA.
Schools: UC Santa Cruz,
Univ. of Utah. *Interests:*
brewing, gardening.
Employment history: designing
and implementing systems
for computer-aided design
and computer animation.
[From the 1982 LFL Yearbook]

[1] Just a year earlier, Sydney Pollack had shot some exteriors there for *Three Days of the Condor*. The movie *Arthur* also used the mansion exteriors, and various nearby buildings showed up from time to time in liquor ads for Johnny Walker Black.

[2] Polygons, actually.

Ed Catmull digitizing a plaster cast of his left hand in 1972.

The process of 3-D animation involves three principle steps: *modeling*—the creation of an object in mathematical terms (usually with a mesh of lines called a "wireframe"); *animation*—moving the object (or parts of the object) around over a period of time; and *rendering*—the slow computer calculations that determine the position of objects on the screen relative to other objects, what's in front of what, how light and color affect them and, ultimately, the drawing of everything in a frame.

Of the three steps, rendering is the most complicated. It demands a huge amount of power from the computer's CPU to process the math, and it's very time consuming. Wireframes were created from webs of polygons (the smaller the better). The more polygons, the more detail in an image. The problem was that large numbers of polygons required significantly more time for the rendering. Modeling and animation were in their infancy. Though rendering was slow, by the early '70s it had advanced into "early childhood."

One of the problems that any graphics scientist had to face in the 1970s was that computer objects created in 3-D were simplistic—made up mostly of straight lines and geometric shapes. Surfaces were solid colors or simple

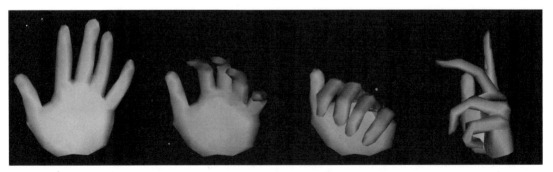

Four frames from Catmull's *Hand* (1972), one of the earliest computer generated 3-D animations. Anxious for any computer imagery available, producers used much of this material in the feature film *Futureworld* (1976).

gradations; they had no texture.[3] Since polygons are flat, computer graphic images looked inorganic. If computers were ever going to model real objects they had to deal with curves.

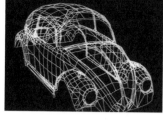

A 1970s E&S project, a 3-D model of Sutherland's Volkswagen Beetle. The wireframe at left is made by drawing lines on the body of the car, then programming them into a database. The rendered car is at right.

Another challenge of making images with a computer was that it was slow; there was no display that could immediately show the results of the mathematics being applied. After an image was rendered, it had to be output to a special film printer, delivered to the lab as a print, often days later.

It was Ed Catmull's research for his PhD dissertation that led to the smoothing out of those hard edges. Using what he called "bicubic patches," Catmull was able to define a surface by just a couple of points and a smooth curve, rather than many connected flat polygons. Because of his work, computers could efficiently render smooth curved surfaces, which in turn made drawing complex shapes possible and rendering them practical.

While Ed Catmull was creating *Hand*, his friend and classmate (another U of U grad student) Fred Parke was making *Face*. These images demonstrate faceted and smooth-shaded faces. Together, *Face and Hand* became the demonstration film for E&S, the company that made the special devices they used.

One happy consequence of Catmull's work on curved surfaces was a method to place a flat painting or photo onto a three-dimensional object. "I realized that since I had a well-defined coordinate system on my surface patches, I could map an image onto the surface."

His first experiment involved putting a picture of Mickey Mouse onto a single curved geometric shape. Soon he could put any texture onto an object, giving computer-generated elements a significantly more real-world look than could be achieved with a simple gradient of color. He called the process "texture mapping." A marble cube, for instance, could become a wooden cube simply by changing the texture mapped onto the sides. This was the second landmark aspect to his PhD dissertation.

And the third was a simplification of rendering. Taking into account how far a surface was from the viewer, he combined that information with new strategies for working with tiny pieces of picture memory. He called this the "Z-buffer."

After a few months, more of the equipment Schure ordered from E&S began to arrive; Ed and Malcolm set up the large devices in the garage behind Gerry Mansion. The '40s era pink structure was right behind the older two-story stucco mansion, now an administration building, and together they rested at the top of

[3] In addition, it was virtually impossible to calculate how an object would look when hit from more than one light source.

Ed Catmull's 1974 PhD dissertation, "A subdivision algorithm for computer display of curved surfaces" included the creation of "texture mapping." This illustration of texture mapping (the texture at left wrapped on the teapot on the right) was created by Jim Blinn, with the teapot from Martin Newell. It appeared in an academic article in 1978.

a gently sloping lawn. Ed and Malcolm divided up the large space where four shiny Dusenbergs might have once rested, with the big half housing all the racks and washing machine-sized computer hardware, and the smaller half a cozy office area with room for a few desks.

Conveniently, Alex Schure's gentlemanly comptroller had his office next door in Gerry Mansion. As the guys needed this thing or another they were directed to the kind man, who would stare blankly at their requisitions for tens of thousands of dollars of machinery he couldn't begin to understand, smile pleasantly, and sign the checks, scratching his head.

All around them were mansions filled with other Alex Schure projects. The opulent deSeversky Mansion was being transformed into a video center stocked with the latest 2-inch videotape recorders.[4] Between deSeversky and Gerry was the mansion where the frenetic activity on *Tubby the Tuba* was underway.

Concurrent with Ed Catmull finishing up his degree at the University of Utah, Dick Shoup, the inventor of picture memory at Xerox PARC, was refining SuperPaint—his 8-bit program for drawing images on the raster screen. In February 1974, Shoup invited his houseguest and former colleague, Alvy Ray Smith, to come see what he was working on. Alvy was a bear-of-a-man, a wooly long-haired Texan, who had earned and ignored a PhD in his earlier life. Shoup recognized that Alvy was a brilliant mathematician caught in the hippie anti-establishment thing. Alvy was doing bits and pieces of academic work along with pursuing his more creative ambitions. By his own admission, he was having the time of his life.

[4] Schure renamed the former Cornelius Vanderbilt Whitney estate for Major deSeversky after his death in August, 1974.

Left: The four-car garage behind Gerry Mansion, home of the computer graphics lab. *Right:* The deSeversky mansion.

Shoup showed Alvy his SuperPaint project. At that time, computers were pretty dull-looking monochromatic devices. But not this. Alvy immediately lost himself in the vivid colors coming out of the computer; he spent the entire day and into the evening drawing pictures on it. He was smitten, and he conspired with Shoup to get permission to mess around with the thing permanently.

Alvy told a friend, "The moment I first saw Dick Shoup's amazing machine, I knew how I was going to spend the rest of my life."

By summer Alvy Ray Smith had worked out a suitable relationship at PARC to work on SuperPaint, adding tools, suggesting features, and generating some of its first images. Alvy felt strongly that computer painting made possible what was, in effect, a new artform. Images could be created on computers and manipulated with mathematics. Or created entirely from mathematics alone. He moved to the San Francisco peninsula.

Alvy was not alone in his worship at the frame buffer altar. Also drawn by its glow was another artist/hippie: David DiFrancesco. David had been inspired by Lee Harrison, John Whitney Sr., and the other radical video artists of the early 1970s. Using cameras and monitors that would feed back into each other, he toyed with abstract dynamic images. He traveled to Japan and got involved with the early video art movement. It was the days of Michael Shamberg's revolutionary book *Guerrilla Television* (1971) and the more ideological *Expanded Cinema* (1970), by Gene Youngblood. David had studied film in Copenhagen for a while and was familiar with the youth culture movie studio set-up there, in particular Laterna Film.

David had contributed to such radical creative teams as "Video Grease" in Boulder—a group interested in creating art with video—and "The Ant Farm" in San Francisco. The Ant Farm became world famous for their "Cadillac Ranch"—ten vintage Cadillacs buried nose-down, rear-up in the air, along an Amarillo highway.

After winning another in a series of NEA grants, this time for the animation work he was developing, David was invited to a celebratory event at Francis Coppola's Broadway mansion, ever the creative locus in the S.F. Bay Area. There he got a chance to meet Mogen Skott-Hansen, who by then was a friend of Coppola's and a sometime guest.

In the summer of 1973, David DiFrancesco took part in a big show in Houston called "2020"—a show about "the future, as seen from the past."[5] Afterward, he returned to the Ant Farm in San Francisco. DiFrancesco's work in early videotape was motivated by a passion for art combined with a gift for and complete acceptance of technology. He was intrigued when he heard that a brainiac professor was going to demonstrate some kind of video painting program he had invented.

ALVY RAY SMITH

Hometown: Texas/New Mexico. *Family:* single, unavailable. *Schools:* Stanford. *Interests:* Chinese, makin' pictures. *Employment history:* NYU, UC Berkeley, Xerox Parc, NYIT, JPL.
[From the 1982 LFL Yearbook]

DAVID DIFRANCESCO

Hometown: New York City.
[From the 1982 LFL Yearbook]

[5] Another project funded by Stanley Marsh, the man whose patronage led to Cadillac Ranch.

David watched as Dick Shoup showed a videotaped demonstration of SuperPaint. Afterward he collared Shoup and impressed him with his understanding of SuperPaint and his experiences with another device called Scanimate. Shoup invited David down to PARC in Palo Alto to see the device for real.

David DiFrancisco was anxious to try his hand at SuperPaint. Once Alvy Ray Smith was helping at PARC, Shoup asked him to meet with David, which he avoided at first. But David was persistent. "Finally I couldn't take it any-more," said Alvy, "and I said, very reluctantly, 'OK, come down for an evening and we will jam together and see what happens.'" David and Alvy hit it off tremendously and became fast friends.

Alvy Ray Smith and David DiFrancesco flew under the radar at PARC. Alvy was an employee (hired through the backing of Alan Kay) and paid via weekly P.O.s as if he were a piece of equipment. David was an artist whose pres-ence was simply tolerated. His main support came from his NEA grants "We snuck him in so often that finally people got used to seeing him there late at night."

Where Alvy was excited by creating images on a blank canvas, David was fascinated with taking images and modifying them using the paint program. He said the process was about "putting pictures into the computer, muck-ing with them, and taking them out of the computer." The two men worked together using the frame buffer, side-by-side, experimenting every day from noon into the early hours of the morning.

"It was serial jamming. I would work on an image, then he would, then I would, then he would…it was all about altering the images with different programs to see what would arise."[6]

"We continued the nightly jamming for a long time," said Alvy.

Alvy was outspoken with everyone about the pioneering nature of what he was doing, explaining to friends and housemates how he was using one of the first frame buffers in existence. Few had ever considered drawing pictures in video, which was effectively what he was doing.

[6] PARC wasn't the only site of computer painting. Jim Blinn wrote his own paint program called "Crayon" about a year later (1974) at the University of Utah, using the E&S frame buffer.

So it was with great disbelief that Alvy, chatting up his computer anima-tion experiences to Richard, his housemate, was met with "Hey that's cool. I think my uncle does what you do!"

"Sure he does," replied Alvy condescendingly. "I know everybody in the world who's doing what I'm doing."

In the midst of David and Alvy's creative project, Xerox determined that color images had little use in the black-and-white document-processing world, and they shut down any research into images and graphics that was starting to turn toward color.

Alvy got called into his supervisor's office. "Color is not a part of the office of the future," he was told as he was laid off.

"I objected strenuously. Xerox *owned* color—all of it—and it most certainly was the future." The supervisor told Alvy it was a "corporate decision," and demanded Alvy and David remove the Xerox logo from their tapes before they left.

Alvy Ray Smith and David DiFrancesco were cut free in early 1975. Tied together by their new friendship as well as the NEA grant they were working on, the guys teamed up to develop a "plan B." Before leaving, they wrote down the brand and model of every piece of equipment in the PARC lab. They calculated that it could cost millions to set up their own workshop, something no one could get from grants alone. They needed an institution to support it.

Martin Newell's actual teapot.

Alvy and David had heard that a frame buffer was being built in Salt Lake City, at Evans & Sutherland. So they decided they needed to get themselves hired there, or at least at the University of Utah. The duo took a road trip. Alvy's big-man muscle car, a white Ford Torino (he called it his "Turin machine"[7]), was all but invisible in the white drifts of a relentless blizzard. Mountain passes. Utah in the winter.

Finally safe at the University labs, Alvy and David got a meeting with Martin Newell, a PhD candidate from the UK. Newell was growing popular in computer circles for meticulously digitizing a cheap teapot his wife picked up in a department store; he was starting to make the data widely available to researchers.[8]

Newell was so proper and straight that Alvy mistook him for a senior faculty member. His accent gave him an air of respectability. One look at the hippie artists, however, and it was clear to Newell that they would never fit into the Defense Department-funded labs growing in academia.

Newell was preparing for a trip to New York, to visit Ed Catmull's lab. He told them that he was heading out of town on a consultation trip and that he would call to discuss their options when he returned. Almost as an afterthought, Newell decided to mention the trip itself.

"Perhaps you'd be interested to learn that a madman on Long Island has just been through the lab and bought a bunch of E&S equipment, including a frame buffer, to make movies." Alvy and David could barely contain their optimism.

[7] A nerdy joke: "Torino" is Italian for "Turin," and a Turing machine is a reference to the theoretical machine defined by Alan Turing in the mid-1930s, used for early computer theory.

[8] This teapot showed up in an unusual number of computer graphic demonstrations for many decades; it now resides in the Computer History Museum. (Note: the way it looks computer-generated is slightly shorter and squished, because the data was originally recorded for the rectangular pixels of the 1974-era displays).

Newell reiterated his promise to call when he returned.

"He called," said Alvy, "an excruciating several days later."

Newell said he had been impressed with Catmull's new gig; he also knew that David and Alvy would be great assets. "If I were you guys," he said," I would jump on the next plane."

As Alvy was frantically packing for the trip to Long Island, he was ecstatic. His roommate, Richard Gilbert, listened as Alvy ranted, "An amazing thing has happened! There's this guy, who sounds like *the one*…with *the place*…that I was dreaming of, and that's where I'm going next. To work for Alexander Schure. Bye."

"Alvy," Richard announced excitedly, "I've been trying to tell you…my uncle does what you do. Alexander Schure is my uncle!"

The winter of 1975 was a bad time to take a road trip in New York. Alvy cashed in everything he had for a plane ticket. David already had a little money for just such an adventure. His dad lived in New Jersey and offered his place for the guys to crash; he also offered them his Porsche to get around in.

The day after landing, they slogged through one of the biggest snowstorms in East Coast history to eventually find the lab. The doors to the pink structure swung open to reveal a machine room that had been converted from a garage. DiFrancesco said he will never forget the look on Catmull's face: "I saw this guy at a small metal desk, and he spins around with *that look*…behind his short beard and glasses…and it was so clear his face said 'God, do I need help.'"

Alvy had expected to see a team of scientists pounding away on the incredible array of equipment they had purchased. "Two of you? That's it?" Alvy asked.

Ed's face tensed, "Yes?"

Alvy looked around the garage taking in the scene, and then back at the two men. "'Cause, I have a PhD in computer science."

Ed's face relaxed into what could best be described as a smile.

Strait-laced Ed Catmull, calm and introspective, was uncharacteristically open with the freakish-looking guys. He introduced them to the machines and Schure's plans for making movies. Executing Schure's plans was not going to be easy; Catmull couldn't be certain what needed to be done in order to be making animated movies on a computer. None of them, Schure included, had any real idea how hard this kind of project might be or how long it might take.

"Let me see if I've got this right," said David, as he and Alvy dug into some private thoughts with Ed. "You're funded by this rich fellow, or seemingly-rich fellow, who is running a school in these palatial mansions in blueblood territory no less, and you've got carte blanche as to whatever you need to get the job done?"

"That's right," said Ed.

"And what is the job?"

"The job is whatever we decide is the job."

Alvy and David were incredulous. Not wanting to believe such an implausible opportunity could be manifesting itself before them. Afraid that to accept it was to have it snatched away, like waking from a dream.

Ed was ready to hire Alvy and David immediately, but they still needed to meet Schure and show him the ¾-inch demo tapes of images they had been developing. And cross their fingers. Besides, the hippie duo weren't interested in a *job*. They only wanted Schure to let them pursue their art projects on his frame buffer.

A limo pulled up to Gerry House, and in piled Ed, Malcolm, Alvy and David, for the short but all-important hop to meet Alex at the deSeversky Mansion. Alvy and David watched in awe through smoky windows as they drifted past a gatehouse and up a winding drive past a pond and snow-covered lawn (Ed and Malcolm were accustomed to the pomp by then).

As Alvy remembers it, "We crossed the floor mosaic of the grand foyer and entered the dining room, complete with gilded mirrors, silver service and liveried waiters. 'Welcome, California!' boomed a voice from a table at the far wall. It was all very theatrical."

Schure's office was impressive. White rugs. Big fireplace. A conference room with tea and cookies. The guys had their first conversation with Schure. Schure spoke of the future, of cranking out animated movies one day.

"Our vision will speed up time, eventually deleting it," he declared. They smiled uncomfortably.

Speaking with Schure was always a source of entertainment, and Ed had forewarned Alvy and David. At first they thought Schure was crazy. But then they recognized it was just the way he was—a friendly visionary who didn't engage in a traditional conversation, one person speaking and then the other. Instead he unleashed a 90 mph barrage of words and ideas, unimpeded by the recipient's own contributions. Some referred to his language as "word salad."[9] Sometimes it was coherent and perfectly ordinary and other times it would go off into utter gibberish.

Alvy recalled, "The way you knew what you were getting through to him was, you started talking at the same time, and slowly, eventually, the words you said would start showing up in what he was saying. And that's how you knew that you had transferred the information."

Within minutes the group was piled into the limo again, heading for Alex's private residence to watch the videotapes they had brought with them.

[9] Coined by Lance Williams.

Though there were ¾-inch tape machines in many of the rooms of the house, most were in disrepair. As the group wandered the halls, looking for a working tape deck, Schure's wife Dorothy struggled to keep their pair of killer attack dogs at bay, moving the big-headed German shepherds from room to room ahead of the men and hoping they didn't get a glimpse of Alvy and David. Eventually a deck was located and the tapes were screened.

Schure liked the guys (once he shook off the long hair and hippie outfits); he felt they were the real stuff. They clearly worked hard. They had produced some solid images using this strange class of computer, and they were articulate, likable young men. Alvy was a PhD, like Ed. David, while cut from a different cloth, was a reasonably successful modern artist, although it took longer for Alex to get comfortable with him. He liked that David had been bringing in government grants. Alex hired Alvy formally, and David informally, allowing him to work with the others as he wanted, and agreeing to put him on the payroll when his grants ran out, maybe a year later.

And the guys liked Schure, his quirky conversational attributes notwithstanding. For whatever he was, he was the single person who, in DiFrancesco's words, "provided the opportunity for us to explore computer graphics *thoroughly*."

And so the team expanded to four. The Four Musketeers. Ed Catmull and Malcolm Blanchard were the family men; David DiFrancesco and Alvy Ray Smith the singles. And Alvy and Ed were the elders, at thirty-one and thirty respectively.

David and Alvy worked the schedule they had settled into from PARC days: into the lab each day by noon, until three or four in the morning. Every day. Ed and Malcolm tried to keep more normal hours. Recalled Pete Ferentinos, the salesman who became the groups' conduit to new E&S equipment, "These guys lived a very bohemian life. They didn't make any money, or very little, and just wanted to involve themselves in the technology."

Spring eventually arrived in Long Island. White peacocks sauntered around deSeversky. Bushy-tailed rabbits hopped merrily in every open field, around every tree. "I remember that *Watership Down* had been published recently," recalled Alvy later, "and we all imagined the rabbit society teaming beneath NYIT."[10]

Ed and his wife and son lived in one of the nearby small towns, squished between enormous estates, as did Malcolm and his new bride. David found a three-bedroom carriage house for rent, about a mile from the lab. Actually, it wasn't really for rent. David stopped by when he saw a classic Vincent Rapide motorcycle in the driveway. David was a collector of classic motorcycles that he

[10] Richard Adams' book came out in 1972, paperback in 1975, movie in 1978.

purchased as junk and meticulously restored, among them a Vincent Black Shadow, almost identical to this silver-tanked Rapide.[11]

A young man who introduced himself as Gordy was tinkering with his motorcycle. David and Gordy hit it off. Gordy said that no one was using the old chauffeur's quarters in the carriage house…was David interested in renting it?

In short order David was invited to meet Gordy's aunt, Justine McGrath Cushing. The carriage house was part of the McGrath estate, the retreat for Justine and her family, who might at any given time be in the Hamptons, or in Manhattan's Upper East Side.[12] The McGrath "compound" (as it was called) included a pair of stone mansions, a six-bedroom "cottage," an old carriage house, and a barn. David returned with Alvy; the two had found a home.

The carriage house on the McGrath estate—David and Alvy's residence.

Justine liked David and Alvy, and they liked her. She liked to call them "her physicists." Justine's father had provided the motor for Lindbergh's plane, the Spirit of St. Louis, and took great pride in that contribution. The field he had used as an airstrip was only a few miles from the house. A gorgeous old picture of "Father" and Charles Lindbergh graced the mantle in Justine's living room, maybe the centerpiece of the entire place.

The rooms of the carriage house sat above another four-car garage, much like the Gerry house set-up, except that instead of a lab, this space was filled with David's exotic motorcycle collection: BSA Goldstars, Vincents, Superiors. DiFrancesco repaired all of them to pristine condition. He later described the collection as "good sculpture."

Even without the promised frame buffer (under construction in Utah), it was still a time of intense work and preparation in the Lab. The E&S Picture System, despite the obvious limitations of a vector display, was good for modeling and a fair stand-in for the frame buffer.

Ed shifted his attention to how a computer might automatically add the frames between two key frames of action—the way classical animators worked. He agreed with Schure that if the computer could do the tedious "in-betweening," a huge part of the work could be sped up. Ed had already produced a crude version of the process, and now he needed to refine it for the projects at NYIT.

[11] Both 1000cc English motorcycles: the Black Shadow was for speed, the Rapide was slightly more civilized, for all-purpose riding.

[12] Justine's ex-husband, Alex Cushing, was responsible for developing Squaw Valley, a ski resort near Lake Tahoe (California).

David was becoming obsessive about getting images into a computer system and then, more importantly, getting them out in some tangible form. Looking at the images on the TV-like display was the first step to output, but scanning in and scanning out was critical.

Schure bought the group a phenomenally expensive, custom CRT film recorder—effectively a device that took the image on the TV set and, in a day or so, drew it onto a frame of film. But the printed images were noisy, messy. The device was a clone of the University of Utah's; it was probably made in a basement in Salt Lake.

"Can you get this thing running?" asked Ed.

"Sure, I'll do that," replied David.

It was about as big as his motorcycle. He decided to take the entire recorder apart and figure out how it worked. But it was a hopeless task. The thing wasn't broken; the design was flawed. Eventually he pulled Ed back to the mess in the garage.

"Look, this is never going to work. We're never going to overcome the noise. We need to get something else."

"What else is there?" There really wasn't anything else.

"I think the thing that made it so much fun," recalled David, "was that we all felt that we were on the leading edge of something that was very important."

The frame buffer eventually arrived, and the guys tag-teamed throughout the day and night to get time on it. But they were constantly impeded by a train of visitors, guests, and future competitors, who streamed through the lab and were politely shown everything going on in some detail.

"What do we have to do to stay ahead?" Schure implored the team.

Alvy talked him into ordering more frame buffers so they could display images in full color. In spite of what Xerox thought, color *was* the future. The only way a computer could make an image was with a frame buffer and the only way it could do *real* color was with three frame buffers.

In time the Lab had six frame buffers. "Enough for two of those RGB things," Schure remarked. Having 24-bit color instead of 8-bit color was more important than just making pictures more colorful. The increase in bit-depth made it possible to soften the stair-step edges —"jaggies"—in the images.

The art of getting rid of jaggies, called "anti-aliasing" involved softening lines to look realistic and, with luck, not computer-generated. Their mantra was "no jaggies." Researchers in graphics had long suggested that doing anti-aliasing would be easy, but it wasn't easy and they never did it.

Ed was adamant from the start about developing software that addressed the problem. He had a little slogan that suggested that if anyone made an image with jaggies they'd have their "ballzen shieren offen."

Eventually, others were hired to fill out the team, many from the University of Utah lab. In the summer of 1975, grad student Garland Stern came out as an intern; he moved in with Alvy and David. The following summer he returned, and having talked so much about the fun he'd had, convinced two other students to join him as interns. One of them was an old friend of Ed Catmull's, Jim Blinn.[13] Blinn spent the summer refining Ed's texture mapping work.

A summer's day in the Lab consisted of people wandering in around noon, and then getting together into cars and going out to breakfast. When they returned they would hunker down at terminals for their workday.

"There would be soft jazz playing on the stereo," recalled Blinn, "and everyone was sitting at a terminal. Every now and then someone would say 'oh wow,' and we would all get up and go over to his terminal and see the cool thing he put up on his screen, and then everyone would go back to his own terminal… and then half an hour later someone else would go 'oh wow…'"

The days drifted into night, with the programmers working until midnight or 3AM, and then it would all start again.

NYIT was better than college; it was better than a job. It was as much fun as these guys ever thought they could have in their lives. David DiFrancesco loved to scream along the estate backroads and horse paths on his Vincent Black Shadow, racing through the farms and equestrian set-ups between McGrath and the Lab. Alvy organized weekly excursions to Manhattan, for the team to attend a course on the history of animation at the New School for Social Research. For a couple bucks, anyone could pop in and attend a lecture by then-unknown instructor Leonard Maltin. Most of the engineers in the Lab were already aficionados of animation, but all enjoyed the details of the history. By the end of summer, Blinn headed back to Utah to finish his degree.[14]

Alvy was on the road often, giving lectures and demonstrating his Paint program. Returning from one trip, he was mortified to learn that Alex had sold all rights to Paint to the Ampex Corporation in California. By Christmas 1976, Alvy was at Ampex, reluctantly installing Paint on their equipment and training them to use it. He spent a month there.

In his motel room, bored, he had an idea of how to radically improve computer painting—he could redesign the software to utilize three frame buffers at one time, to paint in full RGB color. Alvy returned to NYIT and wrote "Paint3." Nowhere but NYIT would it even have been feasible to think of something like that.

After two years in Long Island, Malcolm Blanchard's wife couldn't take one more winter; as the snows returned, Malcolm left NYIT and got his old job back at Applicon. "Look me up if you guys ever go to California," he told Ed.

[13] Also Lance Williams.

[14] Then off to CalTech and the Jet Propulsion Laboratory (JPL) in sunny Pasadena, to begin to produce simulations of space probes.

Catmull wanted to revise his in-betweening software, now called "Tween," and decided the second version should be built for a more sophisticated operating system. He had heard of the work on UNIX at Bell Labs. When it became clear to him that UNIX provided great opportunities for graphics—even though very few people were using UNIX *or* doing graphics—he decided to find a UNIX wiz for his team.

To fill Malcolm's space, Ed hired a young UNIX guru from Canada, Tom Duff. Duff was a big kid, a little shy, but an excellent programmer with incredible breadth in math. "He was always a star," remarked Alvy. "But he was always astonished when someone appreciated him."

Still frustrated with the poor images from their TV scanner, David found a medical imaging company in Minnesota and adapted one of their medical imagers to the Lab's computer, thus providing a pathway to get their images on sprocketed film. This was a significant breakthrough—it didn't work all that well, but it did output to film. If you wanted to make movies with a computer, it sure seemed like being able to get the images from the computer to film was going to be important.

The Lab focused on getting higher resolution images from the small 512 by 512-pixel video size of the frame buffer. They hit on using the image from the buffer as a tiny portion of a larger image—then they could stitch together a bunch of 512-pixel squares to build a higher resolution image. They had to teach the computer how to do that, but it made reaching high-resolution feasible, at least experimentally.

Yet again, Alvy redesigned the group's paint program tools, this time creating "BigPaint," which could draw the larger picture. And then by combining the fundamentals of BigPaint (larger frames) with Paint3 (the RGB color), he made "BigPaint3"—a high-resolution 24-bit color paint system.

Alexander Schure's persona was that of the patron, the fatherly figure of NYIT; Dorothy, his wife, was the mother. And the young turks working on *Tubby* or tinkering with the computers or videotapes, they were the kids. It was a big happy family. Ever since Alvy discovered that his roommate in California was Schure's nephew, he couldn't help but call Schure "Uncle Alex," although never to his face.

Dorothy, always the great hostess, would sometimes bring the guys ice cream as they worked late in the evenings. Even if Schure hadn't been skilled at keeping his troops happy, they were happier than he could imagine—they would have worked for nothing, to do what they were doing. The estates and the freedom and the deep pockets only bathed everyone in profound hysterical happiness. It was a chance of a lifetime.

"We got to stretch the envelope in every possible way," recalled Alvy. When they showed their work at Siggraph (the annual computer graphics conference), it revealed NYIT to be the Mecca it was. In 1977, few places could compete with their innovation, putting images on a screen using a computer. Although other groups were starting to try.

"If we can get the computer on our side, we could get rid of the people," Uncle Alex could be deciphered to announce periodically.

"You can't get rid of the people," he'd be told by the team. "It doesn't work that way."

But Schure believed that somehow, when the technology was perfected, you could type something in one end of the computer, and an animated movie would magically pour out the other end. DiFrancesco joked that Alex just wanted the computers to print hundred dollar bills. "He doesn't really get it, does he?" Alvy would ask rhetorically, at least once a month.

As *Tubby* was winding down across the street, Ed continued to develop Tween, his automatic in-betweening software. Alvy pounded away on BigPaint3 and tried to teach the non-tech artists from *Tubby* to use the stylus to draw background frames. David was deeply focused on the film scanner, hardly caring what else was going on in the Lab.

New guys also contributed to the research. Garland Stern was writing software that could take a traditionally drawn cel, scan it into the computer, and paint the cel digitally using Alvy's paint tools. If he could get through the noise and aliasing problems, a massive part of the traditional "ink and paint" animation process could be automated. He called his program "Cel Paint."[15]

Jim Clark was an intense U of U engineer who joined the Lab in 1977.[16] A classmate of Catmull and a doctoral student of Ivan Sutherland, he had done his PhD work on a head-mounted computer display—it was an early version of what a decade later would be called "virtual reality." Clark never quite got along with Alexander Schure. "It was almost immediately obvious," said Alvy, "they were like two bulls in a small room, both pawing the earth." Clark applied himself to the graphics research, but his situation was tenuous at best.

The days rolled by like endless surreal adventures. For instance, one evening, David DiFrancesco and his girlfriend Maureen were disrupted from their dinner by a helicopter landing in the back garden. Apparently, David Rockefeller was there to attend a wedding at the compound. Another time, when new Lab members arrived, they got to move into Holloway House, a "single family" estate a few miles from campus, also owned by Alex. It had Corinthian columns, a long driveway, stables, a bear pit (!), and rooms for eight.

[15] He was also working on a more advanced tool to move characters on the screen for 2-D animation, something he called "BeBop."

[16] Later, he founded Silicon Graphics, Inc. (SGI) and Netscape.

Holloway House, which housed some of the graphics team. Rooms for eight, and a bear pit in back.

The Lab boys convinced animator Howard Spielman to sit for a casting of his entire body—all 450 pounds of it—so they could draw polygons all over it and eventually scan it into a computer. They never completed the project, but the life-size sculpture of Spielman stood in one of the corridors of Gerry for ages. It was the time of their lives. Too good to be true. And of course, it was.

On May 16, 1977, the team from the Lab rolled down to MGM in Manhattan for a private screening of *Tubby the Tuba*. Schure was exceptionally proud of the work. Even though it had been done conventionally, with traditional methods of animation, it was the cornerstone of his enormous vision.

But as Ed and Alvy and the other guys from the Lab were acutely aware, the movie was unwatchable. Not only were the story and performances flawed, the animation was amateurish. Lines showed. Poor shadowing. Worst of all, it was boring. One of the animators leaned over and whispered, "Oh god, I've wasted two years of my life!" Tom Duff nodded off. Alvy could barely keep his eyes propped open.

"As for me," said Catmull, "I do not fall asleep during train wrecks."

Ed's fears had been confirmed. Their benefactor had the vision, and he had the tools, but he didn't have the "goods." He didn't really know anything about making entertainment. It was much harder than it looked.[17]

[17] On the way home from the screening, driving in silence, the car came to an abrupt halt in bumper-to-bumper traffic on the Long Island Expressway; news surfaced that a commuter helicopter crashed atop the Pan Am building in Manhattan, killing four people on the heliport and a pedestrian on the street below. It was a macabre conclusion to the already bleak day.

nine

Escape from New York

[1977-1979]

LIFE AROUND THE LAB was a little less ebullient in the months following the screening.

The animators eventually moved on to their next project, a short TV film for the government called *Measure for Measure*, about converting America to the metric system. Though the film was conventionally animated, it did include some use of Garland's CelPaint, Catmull's in-betweening software Tween, and backgrounds painted on the frame buffer using Paint3.

Ed and Alvy made a series of visits to Los Angeles, to try to convince the brass at Disney to fund basic research into computerizing animation.[1] It wasn't the first time the company was on Ed's mind. While still a graduate student at Utah, he had met with some Disney technologists about applying computers to animation. Ivan Sutherland had also met with them, trying to set up an information exchange program between U of U and Disney. But it never got traction.[2]

Five years later, Disney still thought that the idea was pretty far out. It was hard to look at a single frame at low resolution, with jaggies, and imagine it could look as real as a photograph. Even if it could be done, the computer capable of managing that much digital information would have to be the size of a building. Utterly insane! If computers didn't make the process faster and cheaper, there was simply no point. Nothing proposed sounded even remotely faster or cheaper.

From time to time, Ed and Alvy would do the math on the back of a napkin over dinner or on a chalkboard in the lab. There was a lot of math involved, but it was simple: To make a picture as sharp and clear as a photograph, it would take approximately 24-bit color and big frames, maybe 2,000 by 2,000 pixels.[3] And lots of them: twenty-four frames for every second of a movie.

Even with acceptable margins of error, guessing what the market would demand as "realistic," they could see that a frame would be huge, hundreds of megabytes, and at 86,000 frames an hour, a computer would have to hold hundreds of gigabytes, maybe terabytes. And the CPU of the computer that

[1] They weren't the only ones. In the same era, computer scientists Marc Levoy and Don Greenberg also tried to convince Disney's feature animation group to incorporate computer graphics into their production process, to no avail.

[2] Disney, instead, had asked Ed if he'd be interested in working with them on the development of their Space Mountain ride at the new DisneyWorld. Ed declined, but kept the names of the people he met with at the company.

[3] This was a guess. In the mid-'70s no one had done much work to estimate how much digital resolution was in a frame of film. It could have been 3,000 or 8,000 pixels, but it was probably within the right magnitude for these long-range estimates.

could process these images would have to be tens of thousands of times faster than computers were then. Alternatively, a conventional machine could draw each frame in days or maybe weeks.

If they had to buy the computer equipment in 1977, it might cost *seventy-five billion dollars* to make a movie, which, needless to say, was unrealistic. If Moore's Law continued to be a reliable metric—and at the time this was unknown—the $75 billion price tag would cut in half every eighteen months. In three years it might cost $15 billion; in nine years only $600 million. It would take about fifteen years before the price reached dollars that would be realistic for a movie—$30 million.[4]

"The numbers were simply huge," said Alvy.

"Not being stupid," said Ed, "we knew we'd have to work on algorithms until the cost of the machines came down."

Even allowing for the general crudeness of their estimates, it appeared that the task would take at minimum a decade. Probably two. But it was never an all-or-nothing venture. Every year, computers got better and cheaper, and the images you could deliver over time would naturally get more interesting. You wouldn't have to wait ten years to see the fruits of your labor. The entire field was a movable feast, constantly changing and growing. Always exciting.

"It was never a grand development," recalled David DiFrancesco of the Lab's mission. "It was always just a series of small steps, leading, hopefully, in the right direction. You couldn't swallow the grand design in one gulp. It was impossible."

The Musketeers didn't really know how long it would take to make a movie using a computer, they didn't know what obstacles would come up technologically or economically; they knew it was going to be hard, but they all had an unspoken sense that they wanted to be wherever it was going.

[4] Not adjusting for inflation. In general, it didn't seem that a feature film could be computer generated economically until around 1992, give or take a few years.

Still frame from *Star Wars*, the briefing room scene showing Larry Cuba's 3-D animation.

Returning to Manhattan to see George Lucas' hot new film *Star Wars*, the group was amazed that it included a recognizable 3-D effect: the attack plans of the Death Star. Although it was one simple effect—an unrendered one-color vector model—seeing it was ironic in light of their ever-present passion to put 3-D onto the big screen. They watched the film a few times before heading home. *Star Wars* was great, but it only made the shortcomings of Alexander Schure all the more glaring.

Back in California, Ampex was trying to merge Alvy's Paint software with their own ideas for a television painting system. Alvy's software ran on an Evans & Sutherland frame buffer; the combination was described by one Ampex engineer as "all very expensive, very fragile, very funky." It was a working prototype of something Ampex wanted to commercialize as their AVA ("Ampex Video Art") project.

With help from NYIT, Ampex convinced CBS to try it out at the 1978 Superbowl XII. CBS hired '70s hipster artist LeRoy Neiman (famous for both his cartoons in *Playboy* magazine and his color washes of sporting events, racecars, and gymnasts) to draw pictures on the proto-AVA. As Dallas stomped on Denver, Neiman spent the afternoon sketching away on the device, making broadcasting history as the first person to draw pictures live on television, using a computer.

Ampex convinced CBS to buy a bunch of them. The head of engineering at CBS, Joe Flaherty, was a passionate supporter of new technology. Everything that the NYIT team dreamed would someday happen for Hollywood was about to start happening at lower resolutions for broadcasters. But to Ed and Alvy, this interim application of their tools on TV was merely a distraction; pushing to higher resolution was their goal. Still, the frenzy in broadcasting over graphics was interesting; it could spawn a new body of talent, and it would support their belief in the revolutionarily change before them.

Unfortunately, the product that Ampex took from NYIT was Alvy's 8-bit Paint, not his anti-aliased 24-bit Paint3. Paint produced some serious jaggies. Ampex never got to see Paint3. Their response to the problems they experienced was to start re-designing their AVA from the ground up, building on Ampex's particular expertise in broadcast video signals to avoid creating jagged lines as much as possible.

Ampex hired Rodney Stock, a hardware engineer, and Tom Porter, a software programmer, to create their new paint tool for television.

Before Alvy left Mountain View, his final act was to train someone at Ampex in the workings of his program, his old "baby." He was pleasantly impressed by Tom Porter's interest and skill. Before arriving at Ampex, Porter had been in Washington D.C., at the National Institute of Heath (NIH), helping chemists visualize molecular structures—a vast improvement over building CPK models,[5] like tinker toys with colored balls.[6] After he heard Douglas Trumbull give a talk at the new Smithsonian Air and Space Museum about the special effects in the movie *2001*, Porter was hooked on making movies instead of molecules.

"Okay," he said to his wife, "we're going to California."

When Ampex called looking for help introducing the AVA to the broadcast community, Porter pulled up stakes and headed west. CBS was hot for television graphics after the success of the Leroy Neiman Superbowl test, and after that the push was to get the product ready for release to the National Association of Broadcasters (NAB), at their annual convention in April.[7]

Rodney Stock had gone into semi-retirement after building computers when he was 30; now, a few years later, Ampex found him doing silversmithing in the Bay Area. Stock had crossed paths with the NYIT group a few times over the years, as people in the small world of computer graphics often did. He had been at Evans & Sutherland helping build their early ship and flight simulators, as well as their space shuttle simulator, and he had met the University of Utah lab students. A few years later, he took a seminar from Ed Catmull and Jim Clark at the University of California, Santa Cruz. Clark invited him to NYIT on several occasions.

"He decided I could be useful to him," said Stock. Jim Clark wanted Stock to help him with an idea he was working on—to modify some software algorithms and try to implement them in hardware.[8] Stock considered the opportunity, but ultimately passed on it.

As the leader of the Lab, Ed Catmull was continually trying to juggle his research with tasks of running a small organization. "We were trying to invent these solutions, we had no textbooks or mentors. I had to make up what I thought was the best way to organize this kind of activity. I had theories about hiring people who were self-motivated and then having a flat structure so these amazing people could do their work."

Alex Schure was getting pressure from his board of directors to show that the Graphics Lab could support itself. Catmull agreed; he felt that the technology could be commercialized at some level, maybe for broadcast graphics, maybe for TV commercials. The animators across the street from the Lab took on outside projects—for instance, they had recently made some public service announcements for CBS. It was time for the Lab to do the same.

Catmull stumbled across a resume that impressed him: Ralph Guggenheim was a young guy who had worked with computer graphics at one time and was now making films. He even had a letter of recommendation from Raj Reddy, formerly of Stanford and now a professor of artificial intelligence (AI) at Carnegie Mellon University. Catmull had absolutely no recollection

[5] *CPK model*: the best-known method for building physical models of molecules. The original method was invented in 1953 by R.B. Corey and Linus Pauling (C-P models), and then refined at NIH in 1960 by Koltun, hence CPK (Corey-Pauling-Koltun)

[6] NIH was using E&S systems to aid in molecular visualization. When E&S built the first random-access frame buffer, they sold it to the University of Utah. Then they built six more. Five ended up at NYIT. The sixth went to the NIH.

[7] NAB (pronounced as initials) is a large industry trade show, historically dominated by equipment manufacturers such as Sony, Ampex, CMX.

[8] Over time, this research became the "Geometry Engine," the core technology of Clark's start-up, Silicon Graphics. Forest Baskett moved from working with the SUN development to helping build the Geometry Engine.

of having met Guggenheim before, nor how persistent Guggenheim had been in trying to land a job at NYIT.

Two months earlier, Guggenheim had found the universe pointing him toward Long Island. Close to completing his master's degree at Carnegie Mellon, he contacted some friends (founders of the Three Rivers Computer Corporation) to see if they had any suggestions for post-graduate work. They told him that they were selling a number of their "Graphic Wonder" vector workstations to NYIT, which was using them as menu displays for a paint and animation system.

So Ralph got himself an interview with Ed Catmull, Alvy Ray Smith, and David DiFrancesco; he visited NYIT and showed them his "informational animation" projects. "I hoped they'd consider me," said Guggenheim, "though it seemed like the work didn't measure up to their standards."

Catmull didn't remember any of this. But he supported Schure's idea of starting a commercial group in the Lab, and he liked having someone on board who had written, directed, shot, lit, and edited film projects that combined live action with segments animated on computers. He only needed to await Schure's decision as to whether this was a path they should pursue. There was no telling how long that might take.

As summer drew to a close, members of the Lab prepared to attend Siggraph, the computer industry's big graphics conference. The conference was attended by the best and brightest from everywhere. They came to learn from each other. There was real openness in the graphics community and Ed encouraged his people to present papers whenever they had something to share.

At Siggraph 1978 (which had around 6,000 attendees, almost twice as many as the previous year), Ed and Alvy demonstrated one of their newest developments, which they called the "alpha channel." The alpha channel made it possible to superimpose two images, or parts of images, or multiple images.

The notion that the opacity of an object (or pixel) was as integral to the way it looked as its "color" shook up the audience, although it made immediate sense. By combining information about color and transparency, another obstacle to creating lifelike images was surmounted.

The theoretical underpinning of "alpha" was clear, but executing it was luxurious.[9] The alpha channel was created by using a *fourth* frame buffer to hold the transparency information (added to the three already in use for making a color image). Having three frame buffers for one image was rare. Having a fourth with which to experiment was completely unprecedented.

The alpha channel improved the ability of the scientists to work on anti-aliasing. Alvy proposed that the components of a pixel were now red, green, blue, and *opacity* (aka alpha)—consequently, the tools and algorithms the Lab

[9] The name "alpha" was only an internal description at first, derived from the Greek character used in the mathematics they employed.

Alvy Ray Smith (left) and Ed Emshwiller painting for the video *Sunstone* in 1979. Two of the group's five paint stations are visible. (The image on the monitor appears to float in space because the camera was jostled accidentally between the two exposures required to make the shot—lights on, to see the people; and lights off, to see the screen. "The results," said Alvy, "captured our mood perfectly.") *Sunstone* is in the collection of many museums, notably the Museum of Modern Art in New York.

researchers used all had to be adjusted for 32-bit images, one 8-bit frame buffer devoted to each of the four image components.

This remarkable observation had a practical repercussion—the already high cost of everything increased overnight by 25 percent. With a going rate of $60,000 for a frame buffer, an RGB + alpha image required $240,000 of attachments to a computer. The industry, however, was thrilled at the prospect of what a quarter of a million dollar set-up could provide.

All this equipment was starting to add up, and Schure was finally ready to start commercial graphics jobs at the Lab. Catmull had been keeping in touch with Guggenheim while he completed his master's thesis work. They connected briefly at Siggraph, and finally Catmull asked Guggenheim to join the team.[10]

Ralph arrived at the Lab in November 1978, as the group was beginning to expand from the machine-room garage into the chauffeur's quarters upstairs. Running cables up through the ceiling, they reassembled what would become their central lab with a few offices off to each side. It was a remarkably comfortable work environment. Where computer labs were often noisy, the guys had designed a space that was quiet, with the computers and the cooling fans safely removed from the terminals.

Alexander Schure was less than excited about the invention of the alpha channel or the new commercial projects and more concerned about his fading vision of NYIT as the next Walt Disney animation studio. As Japanese corporations began moving more into video and graphics, Schure became increasingly nervous about them robbing his technology and glory. Worried about betrayal, he had one of his Lab insiders peruse files on the computer—letters, emails—to report if anything unusual was going on. The associate discovered that Jim Clark was looking for a new job, possibly a teaching position at Berkeley or Stanford. He printed the letters, and Schure stormed into the Lab waving them in Clark's face.

The result was a now-infamous crashing of heads, the exact details somewhat vague, but all agreed it was a hostile confrontation that ended with Clark packing out of NYIT and heading for California. The nasty residue of the encounter permeated the graphics team.

[10] "The offer was still only verbal," said Ralph. "In fact, I only received a formal offer letter a few days after I'd started work at NYIT."

NYIT, for all its high profile at Siggraph, was not the only hotbed of graphics activity hoping to make movies. Outside the academic sphere, Gary Demos and John Whitney Jr. at Triple-I had, over the last few years, developed an impressive technological capacity with graphics in both hardware and software. In their Motion Pictures Product Group, they were designing their own custom computers and writing software for providing small elements in feature films, which they called "digital scene simulation," or for television commercials, like rotating an ABC logo or a hood ornament for Mercedes Benz. It was pioneering work.

U of U alum and former-NYIT intern Jim Blinn had even developed some software for the Triple-I minicomputers, which allowed the company to begin doing small commercial projects. Their team was betting on super-high resolution as the holy grail of graphics. Skipping the smaller DEC workstations that NYIT was invested in, Triple-I was building its own.

Catmull felt that graphics could be done at much lower resolutions than Triple-I did. High-quality images were of course important, but of greater significance, he felt, was solving issues associated with jaggies, with naturalistic motion blur, with facility for compositing an image with others, and so on. In his thinking, the perceptual factors of animation were of greater significance than raw pixel density.

This was a fundamental separation between Demos' strategy, and Catmull's. As Demos described it, "You take every aspect of what we did, and it was the other way from what they did."

Ralph Guggenheim had only been at NYIT for a few months when the call came in from Lucasfilm. Moments after hanging up with Bob Gindy, Ralph brought the news to Ed and Alvy.

"Hey guys," Ralph jovially chimed as he walked into the office where Ed and Alvy were chatting quietly. They stopped as Ralph walked in, "Guess who I just got a call from?" Ed and Alvy stared blankly at each other. "George Lucas wants to set up a research group…."

"Shut the door!" they exploded as Ralph froze in his tracks. Huddled around the desk a moment later, they wanted details, but the memory of Uncle Alex's furor with Jim Clark was still fresh in their minds. It seemed inappropriate to have a subversive conversation at the Lab.

Something was up in California. Not two hours earlier, Alvy had received an odd call from Bill Etra, a video artist/technologist who was doing some consulting for Francis Coppola. Alvy knew Etra, and he didn't take his statement that "Francis wants to set up a computer group" very seriously. He told Etra he'd think about it, although he didn't think much of the idea.

Now he thought it was unusual to hear that Lucas—also in Northern California—was fishing around too. *Star Wars* was big news, and Lucas was already a mythological figure. The idea of working for him obliterated any thoughts of going anywhere else. The team retreated through the snow to Alvy and David's rooms at the compound, got the full story, and debated how to respond.

Not wanting to leave any electronic trail for Alex to ferret out, the guys rented a typewriter and lugged it to Ed's house, off campus. They typed a letter to "Mr. George Lucas," effectively laying out what they thought was possible and when.

The first thing they insisted on was that someone from Lucasfilm come out to see their set-up. This was critical. "They had to *see* how good we had it," recalled Alvy. "We wanted to make sure their expectations were appropriate."

Back in California, Bob Gindy hung up from his call with Ralph Guggenheim, excited and optimistic; after a month of searching, he believed he was on to something. He got permission from Lucasfilm CEO Charlie Weber to go to NYIT with Richard Edlund, to see what was going on. It was a tight squeeze: ILM had just finished the move from L.A. and was preparing for *The Empire Strikes Back*. But there was a window of opportunity.

Even though it had been their idea, Ed and Alvy were nervous about having visitors; Alexander Schure was certain to know they were up to something. Still, there was no way around it, and as long as the Lucasfilm team understood the meaning of "low key" they could probably wander around unnoticed, blending in with all the other tours that ran through the Lab.

A week later, Gindy—the "suit"—arrived, looking very professional; Edlund, unfortunately, missed the news about blending in with the crowd. He arrived in jeans with an enormous bronco-busting belt buckle announcing "Star Wars" across its face. Ed and company were mortified. Their fears were unwarranted, though. No one was the wiser.

They demonstrated their work with the frame buffers and discussed what was theoretically possible with graphics and technology. Catmull was certain they could deliver the tools George Lucas needed for filmmaking. Edlund was dubious.

After the all-day meeting, Bob Gindy headed off to meet with relatives in New York. Alvy looked over at Richard Edlund and said, "So what are you doin' tonight?"

"Well, I, I don't know," replied Edlund. "I've never been in New York. What are you doing?"

"Well, I'm gonna go into Manhattan, like I usually do, and just see what happens, no particular plans. But you're certainly welcome to come with me."

The two men hauled into the city on that unseasonably warm afternoon. Recalled Alvy, "It was one of those gorgeous days when people would sit on their stoops and just watch the world go by." They spent all night playing around, just going crazy. Edlund took photographs: tall buildings, a Polish block party, a guy playing three-card monte on the street (something he had never seen before), street musicians and jazz clubs in the Village. Ear shattering performance art at The Kitchen.

They talked until the early hours of the morning, staggering back to Long Island for a short rest. Alvy was feeling comfortable with the Lucasfilm vibe. It wasn't Disney, but it was the next best thing.

Soon after, Weber met with Ed Catmull and flew him out to the Egg Company in L.A. For his part, Ed was adamant that when it came to graphics: jaggies were unacceptable, and much of his work was in trying to eliminate them. He also had been doing research into the problem of motion blur. Although Triple-I worked at remarkably high-resolutions, they hadn't explored motion blur and hadn't really solved the jaggies problems; they just made them less irritating by making the pixels smaller.

Ed impressed Charlie Weber by providing a demo reel of their work at NYIT. David had managed to scan the graphics to celluloid on their early model CRT-to-film printer. It was good that it was on film. Few in the field were delivering computer graphics on film.

Weber asked Catmull who else he would recommend for this kind of position if he himself weren't available. Ed ran through the small list of academics and industrial researchers who had experience with graphics and computers. At the top of his list was Gary Demos. There was something enticing about Catmull's simple honesty, his clarity of vision and absolute confidence in his path.

Ed Catmull got a second meeting immediately, this time with George Lucas. Flying up to Marin, he got about ten minutes of face time between shots on the ILM shooting stage. They were both about the same age, skinny, quiet, dark beards, thoughtful. Both were deep on the trail of realizing their dreams. George could sense Ed's depth and sincerity. He got the job.

"George is a practical filmmaker," said Catmull in hindsight. "He was not trying to bring in technology for its own sake, but only if it could add value."

The distinction was significant: so much computer research was simply exploring what a computer could do. Lucas knew exactly what he wanted done, and if computers could help, great. In a perfect world, the technology itself was meaningless. The priority at Lucasfilm was always technology in the service of the creativity.

After years of ruminating, Lucas' long-range vision about technology had coalesced into specific tools that needed to be invented.

The first was to create an editing system, modernizing the Moviola, surpassing the flatbed, and doing away (he hoped) with the miles of film and handwritten logbooks required to put a picture together. Picture editing was George's passion, and if nothing else, he was certain that video technology could somehow come to the aid of filmmaking. Coppola spoke of it all the time.

The second was to create a related sound system, able to integrate with the picture cut, handle the multiple tracks that comprised a movie, able to manage the dialog, the sound effects, the music—mixing and manipulating sounds, and ultimately outputting a finished track for dubbing onto a release print. Murch and Burtt would love tools for this.

The third project was to revisit Demos' plan for a digital film printer. George described it briefly. It was the reason all of this activity was getting underway.

David DiFrancesco picked Ed up at the airport in New York. "What's a digital film printer?" Ed asked, barely on the road.

"I haven't the foggiest idea," replied David.

"Well, that's what we've got to build."

"Sounds good," said David. "I can imagine it...maybe like a computerized version of an optical printer?" Ed nodded in agreement, as they continued talking on the drive back into wooded Long Island. There was a long pause in the conversation.

"How about lasers?" Ed asked cryptically, as they merged onto the Long Island Expressway. David didn't know the first thing about lasers, but he knew that pointing a camera at a CRT was a pretty poor way to make a film print from a computer.

"Lasers...." David mumbled to himself, staring out the window at the passing trees, wondering how he might go about determining how lasers could be used to scan images to film.

After several secretive trips out west, Ed gave notice to Alex; he told him he was going to work for George Lucas. Alex was disappointed. He felt the researchers in the Lab were his children, and he, the technological patriarch. Ed's notice was a sad moment of cold reality. The Lab would survive and even mature in future years, but it would never again be the same.

With Ed's impending departure, Alvy was uncomfortable remaining at New York Tech; his heart wasn't in the place anymore and felt he was misleading Alex to stick around. The team developed a plan. If it was possible, Ed would set up a lab and then he'd bring everyone on board. While Alvy and David wanted badly to join Ed at Lucasfilm, there was no assurance anything like that would happen. Ed wasn't even sure what the job would be. But it was clear that should all go well, there would be some positions open at some point. David and Alvy decided it was better to take off rather than loiter on Long Island.

Jim Blinn's desk at JPL, with the Voyager spacecraft depicted passing Jupiter, 1979. Since there was no way to show the public the real spacecraft at work, Blinn began developing realistic simulations of the spacecraft flying by planets it was actually flying by—using the Voyager's high-resolution images of the planets and mapping those images onto spheres. Martin Newell's teapot image is on the wall behind the monitors.

They didn't know if Schure would be devastated by their apparent betrayal in leaving, perhaps even bitter, litigious. He was a passionate man after all, and apparently a shrewd businessman. They all agreed that after Ed went to Lucasfilm, Alvy and David would leave too, find another job somewhere else, and if work came up from Lucasfilm, all the better. "We wanted to make sure we left cleanly, and were waiting in a holding pattern, but there was no connection between where we were going with where we had been." Alvy and David facetiously referred to this as "laundering" themselves.

Ralph Guggenheim decided to stay at NYIT, to work on the commercial projects he had started. Still, he was very interested in the possibilities at Lucasfilm. "Hey Ed," Ralph said, "call me when things are a little more set up."

Ed and his family relocated to California. Alvy and David joined Jim Blinn at Jet Propulsion Labs in Pasadena for some consulting work on his Voyager projects. Blinn was flying satellite models around; Alvy began thinking about how to create dynamic camera movement with the computer.

Alex was saddened by the loss of his bright young scientists. The Lab was growing and commercial projects were starting to come in. He was about to start pre-production on a feature film, designed entirely on the Lab's computers, a project called *The Works*. The technology was finally feeling "ready."

And so the diaspora began. As magically as the group had assembled itself in the comfortable womb of Alexander Schure, it was delivered four years later, whole and small, to the doorstep of George Lucas.

ten

Inside Wonkaland

[1979–1980]

*The best scientist is open to experience and begins with romance;
the idea that anything is possible.*

—Ray Bradbury

THE FIRST ANNUAL Droid Olympics was held late in the summer of '79 at Walter Murch's blackberry farm in Bolinas.[1] It consisted of a big potluck picnic along with a series of competitive events between "teams" (editing crews of the three or four films currently being done in the Bay Area). There was a range of events designed to show off editing and assisting skills, and there were also some events for the kids.

"The whole Bay Area community of itinerant film-workers seemed to show up," recalled Tom Scott. The biggest rivalry that summer was between Bob Dalva's group (working on Carroll Ballard's *Black Stallion*) and Walter Murch and company (from *Apocalypse Now*). The teams from Phil Kaufman's *Wanderers* and *American Graffiti II* (with Tina Hirsch and Marcia Lucas) were also serious contenders. T-shirts were made, cheers were composed, and macaroni salad augmented the hot dogs, hamburgers, and chicken on the BBQ.

For the "events," they lugged equipment—Moviolas, synchronizers, rewind tables, trim bins, film racks—out to Bolinas from the various editing rooms and set up everything on Murch's lawn.

Film editors competed in "Bobbing for Smitchies" (a timed race to find a single marked frame in a bin full of 35mm film); "Speed Rewind" (an assistant's event to see who could rewind a 1,000-foot reel onto a core the fastest); "Rack Arranging" (racing to put dozens of boxes and reels in shot order on a rack). Plus the main events: "Synchronizer Shot Put" and "Synchronizer Golf." Shot Put was a test of power; competitors would give a healthy spin to a four-gang synchronizer to

[1] The events dovetailed with Murch's birthday. Droid Olympics was held a few more times over the coming years, but disappeared by 1983.

A film splicing event from the 1979 Droid Olympics; Walter Murch *(far right)* and Marcia Lucas *(left)*.

see who could make it spin the farthest, as measured with the foot-frames counter. (Bob Dalva usually won that event on sheer strength.) Golf was sort of the opposite, a precision spin from 100 feet, to see who could make the counter spin down to precisely zero feet, zero frames in the fewest turns. "Those last few putts of less than a foot really required a deft touch," said Scott.[2]

Most of the time, however, Lucasfilm employees were focused on finishing the new *Star Wars* movie. By 1979, *Star Wars* was a well-established cultural phenomenon, with intense anticipation for its sequel. Expectations were high: *Star Wars* was going to be a hard act to follow.

The first episode, now being referred to as the *fourth* episode in the multi-picture saga, was made in Los Angeles. Special effects had been done at Industrial Light & Magic in Van Nuys; the sound was mixed at Goldwyn Studios in Hollywood. But as the second chapter began—*The Empire Strikes Back*—filmmaking activities started moving north.

The new ILM would also soon handle the first collaboration of Lucas and his friend Steven Spielberg, *Raiders of the Lost Ark*. Lucas and Spielberg were virtually unchallenged as the most successful filmmakers ever. And the announcement of their teaming up was met with appropriate awe. Spielberg had directed a couple extraordinarily popular movies—*Jaws, Close Encounters of the Third Kind*. It was hard to imagine what kind of film this dream team might produce.

Lucasfilm was like a stock that was soaring with every step it took, simply defying odds month after month. The Lucas brand became synonymous with "blockbuster," and yet the youthful company was largely ephemeral—whispered in job interviews, a name on letterhead and cards, but with no corresponding edifice or high-powered executives.

The suburban exteriors belied the frenetic pace of activity that went on inside the company's spaces in Marin. Lucasfilm was always cloaked in a kind of secrecy in all its activities. Interviews were often held away from Parkway, not even at the Bank Street apartment. When new employees were interviewed, the names "George Lucas" and "Lucasfilm" never were mentioned.

Lucasfilm was a secret club. The members of one of the hippest and most-elusive companies in the '70s were scattered throughout residential neighborhoods, industrial streets, and quaint villages in Marin County.

[2] The Droid Olympics was a big event in the social life of the Bay Area filmmaking community—with teams from not only from Lucasfilm and Zoetrope, but also Saul Zaentz Films, Korty Films, and occasionally from out-of-town productions shooting in the area.

In stark contrast to NYIT, there was no campus of any kind at Lucasfilm when Ed Catmull arrived. It was like there was no "there" there. CEO Charlie Weber was in L.A. at the Egg Company, ostensibly the LFL headquarters, but Ed was going to work in Marin, with the growing aggregation of people who made up the creative organization.

George, still in London during the shoot, told Ed he could use his office at the Parkway house while he was gone. Ed sat behind George's desk and looked around. Lucas was a cult icon. Ed got a little fluttering in his gut as he settled into Lucas' desk chair and looked through the windows at the groves of redwoods and eucalyptus. Ed had a massive project before him and he needed to be careful about how he moved forward. He tried to concentrate on the task at hand, but everything was so different here.

"When I left NYIT, I had the time to reflect on what worked and what didn't," he said later. "I realized that some of my ideas were good and some were a crock. At Lucasfilm I was determined to improve on those theories."

At NYIT, one of Ed's theories had been only to hire self-motivated people. Six years later he decided that wasn't the best approach. "First, you can't always tell if someone is highly self-motivated. Second, and more importantly, there are some brilliant people who aren't highly self-motivated but can do great things in the right structure. My responsibility was to set up a better structure."

[3] Sir Francis Drake Boulevard was one leg of a giant triangle of roads that defined central Marin: Highway 101 was the largest leg, and 4th Street/Miracle Mile was the third.

When George returned from London, Ed needed a place to work. Since Lucasfilm Ltd. was cobbled together in spaces that were found as needed, it looked as though one of Marcia's investments after *Star Wars* would solve the problem. It was a small two-story structure on Bank Street in San Anselmo, a tree-lined eddy of calm, off the more frantic river passing on Sir Francis Drake Boulevard.[3] There was a host of small antique shops on the street, leading up to Number 6, and only private residences as you moved further away from the Boulevard.

The property had one tenant downstairs and a pair of vacant apartments above. Marcia turned the apartments into offices, the center of the new Lucasfilm "Design Division." She took the larger apartment as her domain and set up an accountant and some design assistants across the hall in the studio.

Ed Catmull moved out of Parkway and joined Marcia in the apartments. As he looked over the sketches in Marcia's office, he was once again struck by the contrast between his new place of employment and his last. NYIT was an assortment of grand estates with the blueblood of wealth in every corner; the evolving aesthetic of Lucasfilm was blue jeans Victorian. "I always thought it was cool," said Catmull, "that George and Marcia had a sense of taste."

Looking up to the apartments on Bank Street.

Marcia wasn't editing in those days. While she was perhaps at her creative peak (after winning the Oscar for editing *Star Wars* and her highly regarded work with Scorsese), she was completely occupied giving her touch to the Lucasfilm aesthetic.

She had developed a taste for the work after renovating the Egg Company, with the beveled glass in the doors and Mission furniture. She had been perfectly able to execute George's Victorian tastes in every corner of the company. Now the scope of the detail had increased dramatically. There was so much to do for the quickly solidifying Ranch project that she could stay busy all day making decisions about sofas and carpets and light fixtures. The main house alone was going to be more than 50,000 feet, a combination of formal Victorian, colonial, and mission styles.

In typical George fashion, he could visualize the Ranch even if he could neither draw it nor fully describe it. In the same way he inspired the sound design or character design in his movies, he needed gifted artists to interpret his descriptions. By looking at the various results of their brainstorming, he selected the pieces to fit into his schema. The Ranch project was no different.

"I wanted to be an architect when I was a kid, because that was a way to combine my desire to do art with practical things." Lucas often said that if he hadn't been a director he would have been an architect—it was a semi-secret passion, and the Ranch gave him an incredible palette on which to ideate.

Architect's model of the Main House at Skywalker Ranch.

As the months passed, a fictional tale about Skywalker Ranch emerged, mostly from George, but also from everyone working on its design. He wasn't trying to fool anyone; it was just creative tool. It ossified into lore.

The story was about a retired sea captain who landed in the area with his wife and young kids in the 1860s. The main house was the captain's residence; built in 1869, it was a large white mansion with a deep veranda. The gatehouse and stable were built the following year and the library was added in 1910 in the craftsman style, which had become popular. In 1880 the family began to diversify into winemaking; they planted a vineyard and built a brick winery on the shores of the lake, a short distance from the main house. One of the captain's sons built a brewery behind the winery in the 1930s. As both the winery (built of brick) and the brewery (in its *moderne* style) expanded in subsequent years, the two merged into a single structure.

"The history," said Lucas, "helped everyone working on the project understand how they could have divergent styles side-by-side."

Lucas almost installed abandoned railroad tracks through the property, down the center of the winery, to explain how they used to get the big wine casks delivered, but practicality and cost dictated they get cut from the plan.

It was with only modest surprise that Ed Catmull found himself sitting at his desk on Bank Street, looking at the cover of the August 1979 issue of *Computer* magazine. It featured the Gary Demos rendering of an X-wing fighter. Triple-I had made it originally when it was vying for a role in Lucas' emerging computer research. It was incredibly detailed and really quite impressive.

Ed looked at the image, examining the boundaries between the spaceship and background, looking closely at the reflections off the too-pristine surfaces, and quickly filed it away on his shelf.

The offices and editing equipment at Parkway were supposed to be for George and his long-time filmmaker buddies,[4] but no sooner had Jim Kessler set up the equipment than a few neighbors on the quiet street began complaining about all the coming and going, the odd noises day and night, and the general feeling that someone was running a company in there.

"There would be twenty-five people who would show up for BBQ lunch and volleyball games during the week," said Duwayne Dunham, George's film assistant. "It got pretty rowdy." It wasn't zoned for anything like this. It was clear they'd need a new plan.

On Bank Street, Jim Kessler hunkered down in a nook near the copy machine, while everyone rejiggered the office configurations to make way for the teams coming back from London as well as all the new employees who seemed to be joining in one capacity or another virtually every week.

[4] Hal Barwood, Michael Ritchie, Matthew Robbins.

Gary Demos' *Star Wars* X-Wing test image, which he produced for ILM in late 1978. It was printed on the cover of *Computer* magazine in August 1979.

Bank Street was clearly going to be temporary, as even more space was needed. Lucasfilm purchased an old laundromat a few blocks away for offices, and soon began its renovation.

Forced out of filmmaking at Parkway by neighbors, Lucasfilm purchased another building for post-production, this one at 321 San Anselmo Avenue, a short jaunt from where George and Marcia were living. San Anselmo Avenue was an idyllic downtown street, with coffee shops and travel agents, a local town hall, and countless boutiques. Kessler helped orchestrate an editorial area there, somewhat mirroring the layout at Parkway. It was a homey space, with George and Duwayne upstairs with flatbeds, benches, and a bunch of Moviolas. Downstairs, Ben Burtt could build his new sound workshop for effects creation and "sound design."[5]

[5] The term "sound design" originated with Walter Murch, whose film credit on *American Graffiti* was "Montage and sound design." Murch had the credit "sound design" on *Apocalypse Now*, just as Ben Burtt later had on *Empire*. Soon thereafter, Burtt was referred to in conversation as a "sound designer" which became a new term in film.

Lucas' work schedule during *Empire* was stressful. He would meet Duwayne at the cutting room at 5:30 every morning. Sometimes 4:30. He would cut until a few minutes before 10, and then he'd drive over to ILM on Kerner and work there until 4. Then he'd turn back to San Anselmo Avenue, and reconnect with Duwayne until 6 or 6:30. He did this every day.

Apocalypse Now was finally released in August 1979. So now George could reconnect with Francis, a skinnier, world-weary Francis, who somehow managed to make a beautiful and powerful film out of the depths of his personal hell. *Apocalypse* had spiraled from a $12 million to a $31 million epic, taking years to make and almost costing him his nineteen-year marriage to Eleanor.

In the end, his marriage was intact, and he even managed to oversee the completion of *The Black Stallion*, which Carroll Ballard brought to life from Melissa Matheson's adaptation of the children's book. Both the book and the film were widely admired.

"Francis was constantly burdened that whenever he did anything it was such a big deal, a colossus, particularly out of his own making," said his associate, Thomas Brown. "He thought of himself…he *aspired* to be an amateur." The *Saturday Review* wrote, "Coppola has a natural affinity for anything outsized." Paramount Pictures chairman Barry Diller said, "Francis likes living on the brink."

With *Apocalypse Now* completed, Francis didn't pause; he was busy working on his next oversized idea. Perhaps in response to the beating his production endured in the Philippines—subject to the forces of nature, politics, and distance—he was no longer wed to the concept that a modern studio should only shoot on location and did not need sound stages. But he still felt that equipment and production should be flexible, mobile, and modern.

He hired Clark Higgins (from the Rhythm Devils shoot) and Steve Calou (who helped set up his editing suite in the Sentinel building), among others, to consult with him on ways to integrate video into his new process for filmmaking, a method he called "previsualization."

As Francis matured, so had his idea of the studio of the future; now he was using his rapidly expanding wealth and prestige from *Godfathers I and II* and *Apocalypse Now*, to build it. He began searching for sound stages in Los Angeles to buy and adapt to his filmmaking vision. He had moved away from the bucolic serenity of his earlier plans, and instead concentrated on raw technological power applied to production. He wanted a studio with the latest technology built in—sound stages, offices, and of course, a full-on state-of-the-art electronic cinema workshop.

In much the way he raved about the European flatbed editing systems in the late '60s, and the simple videotape set-up he had had in the Sentinel building in the late '70s, he now was excited about the technology that broadcasters used. He was convinced it could really help him…if he could overcome some of the obstacles that kept film and video apart.

George, knee-deep in the film process, didn't have time for theories. Making a normal film was complicated enough (and a *Star Wars* film even worse) without introducing untested equipment. He had lived through the absurdity of new and imperfectly functional equipment at Zoetrope, when they bought all those German tools. He didn't need that hassle. He was of the mind that the technology itself was unimportant; Francis loved the gadgets.

After a few years of relative separation, George and Francis were back in good form together, always friendly, always competitive. They joined forces to help Akira Kurosawa make *Kagemusha*. Lucas had heard that Kurosawa hadn't been able to get a film made in five years, even though he had won an Oscar in 1975 for Best Foreign Film.[6] Lucas went to Alan Ladd Jr. at Fox, his friend and the only studio executive to trust him to make *Star Wars*.

"Using the power I had because of the success of *Star Wars*," Lucas said, "I got Fox to put up half the money for Kurosawa to finish the film." It would serve as an advance purchase of the film rights outside of Japan. George and Francis contributed to the other half. Both men were given an Executive Producer credit, and the trio became fast friends.[7]

Through the fall of 1979, Catmull moved quietly among the teams making *The Empire Strikes Back*. He drove ten minutes from San Anselmo to Kerner Boulevard, where ILM was doing the massive, tedious motion-control work and optical line-up to make spaceships fly and miniature monsters stomp around Hoth. He walked across Sir Francis Drake and down the alleys to "downtown," where he'd grab a juice and then hurry back to watch Ben Burtt build new sounds and languages in his sound lab.

Upstairs at San Anselmo Avenue, Ed got the full impact of the archaic editing process, as rooms of celluloid hung in trim bins—cloth laundry bags that held endless piles of unraveled film rolls—while George's film assistants ran around digging up bits of this scene or that.

Ed was working seriously on his analysis of the film process. He applied himself to outlining the various ways computers might radicalize the methods, create enormous opportunities to save money and time, and ultimately give the filmmaker more control.

"I totally bought into George's notion of changing the film industry."

[6] *Dersu Uzala* (1975).

[7] *Kagemusha* went on to win the Palm D'Or at Cannes (1981), and that led to his finding a French producer for his next film, *Ran* (1985). Lucas introduced Kurosawa to Spielberg, who helped him produce *Dreams (1990)*, for which ILM did the effects.

But the technology was constantly in flux due to the rapid increases in computer power, memory, and storage. Every year, so much had changed that thinking in every field needed to be adjusted.

Catmull was finally settling in. Everyone was nice enough to him, but he still represented an oddity to the filmmakers; his bookish ways were a source of mild amusement. He was a PhD in a company with very few college-educated staff. On the downside, Ed's marriage suffered in the new locale and rapidly began to dissolve. He was characteristically stoic, and never brought his personal issues to the office. Instead, he poured himself into work, into wide-ranging plans beyond graphics, reading leading research in the fields of acoustics, broadcasting, and computers.

The truth was, Catmull knew nothing about editing and sound, and little about effects. His own passion for making animated films was not embraced at Lucasfilm the way it had been at NYIT. In some ways he was wholly unqualified for the task at hand; he would need to find experts in sound and editing.

Lucas and Catmull had agreed that, while there was a priority to the projects—first the digital film printer, then new tools for editing, then sound—Catmull would need to execute all of them simultaneously; there was really no telling when (or if) fruit would be generated from this research and development. Later, Lucas said that doing all the projects concurrently "may or may not have been the right idea."

At NYIT, only a few months earlier, Catmull could have had any staff he wanted and the best equipment by merely asking the comptroller for a purchase order. At Lucasfilm the purse was watched more closely. George was busy with a dozen major projects. His executives eyed Ed's activities cautiously, from a distance. Still, the patina of moviemaking covered the quaint spaces, the sounds and icons of *Star Wars* were in every nook, and it certainly appeared like money would never really be a problem for George Lucas.

By the end of 1979, Ed Catmull met with Lucas, Lucasfilm president/CEO Charlie Weber, and the new financial officer Bob Greber, and presented his plan for the research. The three projects would take a minimum of three years, and more than $20 million, to develop. As much as a movie. About what they thought the Ranch would cost to complete.

It was too much for Lucasfilm to stomach. Weber insisted he revise the budget. The truth as Catmull knew it was that the project would probably take much longer and cost much more. But as long as Lucasfilm wasn't up for the whole enchilada, he returned with a new budget of $10 million. The company agreed to greenlight the work.

In the history of filmmaking, no studio had ever subsidized pure research. Virtually all the significant advancements in technology that applied to the film business—from the introduction of sound to the addition of color—were done outside the studio system. When the film industry got involved, it tended to be for the purpose of stonewalling advancement.

For instance, color film had been in various states of experimentation through the 1920s. Three-color Technicolor released in the mid-1930s, and made a splash in 1939 with *The Wizard of Oz* and *Gone With The Wind*. But even then, until as late as the '60s, color was used only sporadically. This slow adoption had less to do with technology itself than with the inertia of camera operators, labs, and other unionized players, who fought any change to the industry. If it hadn't been for the competition with newly developing television, which was monochromatic, it might have taken even longer.

Lucas, separating himself further from the establishment, was going to force his will on the system by digging into his own pocket and making it happen. *Star Wars* finally put him in a position of power. Lucas continually chose to live modestly, and with the exception of his films, rarely spent money on a rich man's toys. Even luxurious Skywalker Ranch was a filmmaking center and, contrary to popular misconceptions, was never going to be his home.

With corporate approval in hand and a secure budget, Catmull called David DiFrancesco and Alvy Ray Smith, who were waiting for that moment. They had visited Ed periodically throughout the fall, taking the air shuttle from Southern California where they were "freelancing" at the Jet Propulsion Labs (JPL) in Pasadena. Jim Blinn at JPL was happy to have his friends around, and Alvy helped with some shots Jim was developing for Carl Sagan's project, *Cosmos*. Everyone knew Alvy and David were only passing time with the space guys, keeping their fingers crossed that soon they'd be able to land with Ed at Lucasfilm. (Even before they were hired, Alvy had been receiving resumes from wannabe-graphics superstars who were anticipating his ability to take them with him.)

As David finished up work, Alvy moved up to Marin County, a place that seemed eternally bathed in sunshine and blue cloudless skies. The ridge of mountains that separated the east side of the County from the bay, crowned by Mt. Tamalpais, also served to barricade out the fog and clouds. South to Sausalito, where the space between oceanside and bayside was at its smallest, it was often possible to see the fog lapping at the hilltops, spilling over in wafts of cool mist. But ten miles north, Marin was always balmy, and a pleasant change from either Long Island or Pasadena.

Within a few months the old gang was back together again. David continued his laser research for a few days a week and still hopped back to JPL as necessary. Ed was thrilled to have his friends join him at Lucasfilm.

"Ed was very, very excited," recalled Susan Anderson, Bank Street's all-purpose assistant. "I think the feeling was that they had pulled off something really great."

With Alvy and David's arrival, the space in the Bank Street apartment was even more cramped. Jim Kessler was still by the copier; Alvy worked in the kitchenette. Marcia and her assistants were preparing to move out, to the first-finished spaces at the Ranch, to more directly supervise the Skywalker development. They would all be going their separate ways very soon.

Susan Anderson wanted to move with the computer guys. "I knew I wanted to be more than a secretary," she recalled. "I knew there was opportunity in that group…it was clearly going to be huge. And I was looking forward to a chance to learn about computers."

Eventually, Susan went into Ed's office. "Listen," she began, "I really want you to know that when everyone goes their different ways, I would like to go with the computer group. Would that be okay?"

"Sure," Ed said in his characteristically mild way.

"Great," Susan said, and then walked out. A minute later she turned around and came back in. "By the way, I just want you to know that I'm pregnant. Does that make a difference?"

"No," Catmull said, completely unfazed by the news.

"Great," she said, and went back to her desk.

SUSAN ANDERSON

Hometown: North Hollywood, CA. *Family:* son Michael, born 8-22-80. *Schools:* LAVC. *Interests:* Michael & my computer children (Bespin, Dagobah, Rochester, Ewok). *Sign:* Leo. *Employment history:* KTIM Radio, Marin County; CBS Records, LA; Metromedia Television, LA.
[From the 1982 LFL Yearbook]

At ILM, veteran *Star Wars* designer Ralph McQuarrie and his associates were pounding away on *Empire*. A few of the young effects staff, recently relocated from L.A., sported T-shirts that showed Darth Vader reclining in a hot tub. On the back of the shirt it read "The Empire Lays Back."

Alvy Ray Smith popped by to see the ILM process in action, especially to watch McQuarrie paint mattes of the Cloud City above planet Bespin. McQuarrie looked drained.

"What's the matter?" asked Alvy.

"I've painted this damn city from twenty different angles and ten different times of the day. What I need is a computer."

Of all the people in the world to make this particular gripe to, McQuarrie was making it to the right guy. Alvy was supposed to be at ILM to think about the digital film printer, but he was far more interested in the painting artists. After a decade of exploring painting with a computer, he privately hoped that Lucasfilm would allow them to address the need for actual creative graphics tools.

Lucas' desire for a digital film printer required research into 2-D graphics—the coloring and layering of digital images, Alvy's expertise. This was how backgrounds could be painted, and it would be the basis for the compositing at ILM. Ed Catmull's particular interest—3-D animation—was an entirely separate world of math and objects, and not particularly within the scope of Lucas' plan. But it wasn't as simple as "yes" to 2-D and "no" to 3-D; the two overlapped in many respects.

In academic terms, the actual distinction was between disciplines called "sampling" and "geometry." 2-D was roughly analogous to *sampling*, the issues associated with fields of pixels. This was a world apart from 3-D, or more accurately, *geometry*, the issues of lines and shapes and objects.[8]

After having worked together for almost six years, Ed Catmull and Alvy Ray Smith were able to resume their well-balanced team dynamic. Ed had the calm, buttoned-up attributes, the deep understanding and far-reaching vision, and a somewhat dispassionate vantage point on the scope of the work. Alvy was ebullient and full of a charisma that excited even non-technical observers. In the microcosm of the computer team, Ed was more like Lucas, and Alvy was more like Coppola. In technology, while they never articulated it at the time, Ed was geometry and Alvy was sampling.

Sometimes it seemed as if everyone in the computer industry wanted a job with the Lucasfilm researchers. The small team were sent resumes constantly. As soon as he was situated at Bank Street, Alvy began receiving "love notes" from a scientist at Boeing. The term "notes" was perhaps misleading. Someone was sending Alvy 8×10 prints of a mountainscape, almost certainly of digital origin, with no explanation. These images caught his eye. He had never seen a computer-generated mountain look so detailed, and although it was likely the result of an application of mathematician Bernard Mandelbrot's new ideas, neither he nor Ed was sure how it had been done or who had done it.

In time they understood that the pictures came from someone making a presentation at that fall's Siggraph conference in Seattle. They both made a mental note to find out more about him. Alvy pinned one of the photos to the wall.

The Empire Strikes Back released around George's birthday in May, as was becoming a tradition. Though no one knew for sure what would happen when the film

[8] In modern terms, it is the difference between software like Adobe Photoshop, which paints pixels, and Adobe Illustrator, which draws objects that can be assigned colors. Photoshop files are image files (like JPEGs and TIFFs), and these are wholly unlike the mathematical object files from Illustrator (EPS files for example). The two file types are only barely interchangeable.

Fractalized Mt. Rainier, by Loren Carpenter, 1980.

came out, the overwhelming response wasn't much of a surprise. Once the loans were paid back, the entire executive branch gave a sigh of relief. With positive cash flow restored, Lucasfilm could comfortably give its support to the computer research projects.

Ed Catmull, like the rest of the new Lucasfilm gang, was happy to be part of the popular company. Still, the association was really only a perk; he had important things on his mind that didn't involve Darth Vader—like finding someone who could lead the editing project. It was clear to him, even with his nascent knowledge of video, that it would be years before it could really be digitized and edited in a computer. Hard discs would have to hold enormous volumes of data, a thousand times the current state-of-the-art, in order to be even remotely cost-effective.

George was prepared to be patient with the process. At the same time, he wasn't going to wait a decade; the project would need at least an interim solution. In the same way that the ILM motion control system successfully integrated a computer with more traditional camera technology, perhaps they could make a film editing tool by integrating the computer with more traditional video equipment.

Catmull knew that the computer could be made far smarter than commercial videotape editing controllers demonstrated, and that the interface could benefit from the bit-mapped graphical displays he had seen at PARC. The worst thing about videotape was its linearity. It took many minutes to wind and rewind a roll of tape, and finding a shot was tedious, even for a computer. Since it was premature to digitize the video (which would completely eliminate the issue), perhaps it would be possible to bypass many of the problems of linear videotape (and film) by utilizing an analog medium that was fast to search through, like RCA's new laser videodiscs.

Lucas had outlined his vision, but the details were sketchy: "I don't want to have a half-dozen assistants running around looking for trims. I want to be able to edit in my bedroom."

Finding trims was the bane of any editor. Sometimes they were short strips of film only one or two frames long, cut from a larger roll; but they couldn't be lost. At worst, trims would disappear forever, maybe clinging to the bottom of an editor's shoe as he wandered out to the bathroom. Longer bits might get rolled over by the wheels of a chair, damaged beyond recognition. Trims were a necessary evil of editing but had little to do with the creative act of selecting shots and carefully juxtaposing them with other shots.

With anyone else in charge, the editing project probably would have received the lion's share of the computer group's attention and resources. But Catmull couldn't help himself; he had spent his life trying to make computer animation and he had a natural sense of how to achieve progress toward that end. It wasn't that he didn't care about the editing problem; it simply wasn't his field of expertise.

Anyway, from a computer standpoint, editing was largely a database problem, of tracking edge numbers and synchronizing them with video frames. He felt that people who had experience with editing tools, in particular video editing tools, knew little about modern computers. Video people often knew even less about film. Like videogame programmers, their jobs always involved the practicality of taking affordable hardware and putting it to work right now, to get the job done.

He needed people interested in the problem but unburdened with such short-term concerns. There was virtually no academic study in video and editing in the 1970s, so his team would need to come from other disciplines.

The person who came to mind for the project was Ralph Guggenheim, a late arrival to NYIT who had fielded the original call from Lucasfilm. Ralph walked the line—with expertise in film, comfort with modern computers, and little baggage with the broadcast industry tools in use. Ed called Ralph, who was coming to the end of his time at NYIT.

"Listen," Ed said on his end of the phone, "you've made films and you've edited and you know how editors work; so how would you like to head up this editing project at Lucasfilm?"

Ralph was stunned and thrilled. "That sounds great…" he began, but he needed to voice his concerns. Unlike the other NYIT guys, he was only a casual programmer. "I'm not Mr. Algorithm when it comes to computer graphics, but editing is something I know a lot about and I could really contribute."

Ed also called Malcolm Blanchard, his long-time compatriot at the University of Utah, then Applicon, then NYIT. He was making good on his promise to call if opportunities ever arose in California.

"It's time," said Ed, and he invited Malcolm out to "interview" in Marin. Malcolm would be able to come out sometime around the 4th of July. He would move out and start work in August.

Ed also asked Ralph Guggenheim to fly out before the holiday weekend, to meet him in Los Angeles. They would go together to a company called Disco-Vision Associates (DVA) and listen to a pitch about the future of videodiscs. The company had formed in the mid-'70s as a joint project between IBM and MCA, to develop a laser videodisc for distributing movies. At a time when consumers were wrestling with VHS and Beta, DVA was trying to push their LaserVision discs, to little success.

On the way to DVA with Ralph, Ed outlined his ideas for a computerized editing system. "I've been looking at what's out there, and my feeling is that if we could tie these pieces together—a workstation with a database, a graphical interface, and some videodisc machines—we could create something right now."

RALPH GUGGENHEIM

Hometown: New Rochelle, NY. *Family:* homo habilis. *Interests:* backpacking, racquetball, birding, bedlam, mayhem. *Sign:* Cornucopia.
[From the 1982 LFL Yearbook]

The problem was always how to store the film dailies so you could quickly find the material you needed. The idea was to store them digitally. But even at low resolution a digital image was enormous; it was beyond the capacity of early 1980's hard disks to hold more than an emblematic icon of a shot, and certainly not twenty-four images for every second of material. With a state-of-the-art 10 Megabyte Winchester hard drive about the size of a dishwasher—and costing thousands of dollars—an analog medium was going to be necessary for at least a decade.

Videotapes were linear, slow to find shots and difficult to control. Videodiscs seemed the best alternative. They were analog-like videotapes, but material could be accessed quickly, with what was called "random-access." The quality was fair—better than the few-thousand-dollar Beta/VHS ½-inch tape format, but worse than the $10,000 ¾-inch tapes.

Videodiscs had their share of drawbacks: they were expensive to make, they only held thirty minutes of material (if you wanted to be able to access individual frames), and they couldn't be erased or added to. Once made, like a record album, they were permanent.

Ed was interested in striking a business relationship with DVA in which Lucasfilm would send them workprint, and they would strike videodiscs and send them back, much as a film lab develops negative and returns dailies. Ed was optimistic about videodiscs being the missing link between the well-established analog videotape and the eventual arrival of digital video.

He believed that George's editing problem could be solved if they could merge together a database—effectively the hand-written logbooks maintained by assistants—with the frames on a videodisc. Only a month earlier he had visited one of the three CMX 600s still in use. Already a decade old, the 600 was never adopted but was stylistically amazing. It could hold a few minutes of poor-quality video on racks of disks that were connected to a database of timecodes.

A brochure shot introducing the CMX 600, the first electronic "nonlinear" editing system, 1971

Ralph's interview and the DVA meetings went well, and Ed and Ralph flew north in time to join the crew for Lucasfilm's second annual 4th of July picnic.

Soon after Lucas purchased the Bulltail Ranch, a working ranch that toward the end of its career had been used as a deer hunting range, Lucas had a few friends out for a tour and a little picnic. By 1979 a few dozen employees gathered at the wild property with Marcia and George (at folding tables with red-checkered tablecloths thrown over them) for their first official company cookout. Assistant editor Duwayne Dunham, always the adventurer, flew his hot air balloon to the picnic, crashing elegantly into the golden hillside for a particularly dramatic entrance.

By July 1980, construction on the Ranch was just beginning. There were few structures on the property: an old barn and animal pen and a flimsy caretaker's house near the road. The area where the Main House and lake were going to be built had been cleared of the "deer camp," where carcasses hung in rows of refrigerators. An extraordinary quantity of cow patties were still ominously scattered like landmines in every direction.

"We had to jump around to be able to find our way to the picnic area," recalled Guggenheim. "It was very impromptu and a lot of fun, and it just seemed like this was a phenomenal group of people to be able to get the chance to work with."

At the conclusion of the long dreamlike weekend, Ralph Guggenheim flew back to Pittsburgh, where he had already committed to joining the Three Rivers Computer Corporation, a computer start-up by college friends. There, he helped prepare demonstrations of Three Rivers' hot new PERQ graphical workstation for the upcoming Siggraph conference. At the end of the summer he was ready to come to Lucasfilm.

Zoetrope was a business that perennially had ups and downs that would unnerve most business executives. In spite of occasion reorganizations, and Coppola's limited formal business experience, it remained in operation year after year. "I've been putting on shows since I was a little kid," said Coppola, referring to the puppet shows he set up for friends when Sunday morning television proved inadequately interactive, "and I always hoped people would like what they saw when they came. That's enough about business that anyone should have to consider."

In 1970, Coppola incorporated American Zoetrope. According to company paperwork, between 1970 and 1980 the company formed and reformed, merged with new entities and was renamed—at least a half-dozen times. While the post-production facility was always "American Zoetrope," his production company and a distribution company weaved in and out of names in a dance so cryptic it almost appeared comical.[9]

[9] From an in-house report: "On March 1, 1977, American Zoetrope and Coppola Cinema Seven merged into The Coppola Company (formerly known as Francis Ford Coppola Productions, Inc.), and the company name was changed to American Zoetrope. The Beggs/American Zoetrope movement into Zoetrope Studios (then known as American Zoetrope) took place on January 1, 1979. American Zoetrope's name changed to Omni Zoetrope Studios on November 27, 1979 and from Omni Zoetrope Studios to Zoetrope Studios on February 4, 1980."

Francis' wine interests catalyzed his introduction to another wine lover, Joe Flaherty, who also happened to be the man in charge of new technology for CBS. A daring and widely admired engineer, Flaherty had led CBS into working with some of the prototypical videotape editing tools in the 1970s: he led the revolution into electronic news gathering (ENG), argued for converting from 2-inch to 1-inch videotape for broadcasting, and he had seen to the development of some of CBS's own proprietary attempts at improved video editing.

Flaherty was sympathetic to Coppola's passion for moving filmmaking into video and offered CBS's enormous resources to help him. Both men could envision higher resolution video for broadcasting and filmmakers, and Francis was happy he didn't have to invent it, or pay for it, himself. Actually, it was already under development in Japan, and CBS was watching Japanese television network NHK and equipment manufacturers like Sony, with great interest.[10]

Although high-definition video was based on U.S. broadcasting research from the '50s and '60s, in the 1970s the Japanese began work on new broadcasting signals that could carry significantly more image data, for higher resolution images.

Where standard U.S. television had 525 horizontal scanned lines in a frame, NHK's high-definition television (called HDTV) produced 1125 lines. Where a TV picture was relatively square, with an aspect ratio of 4:3, HDTV was initially proposed as a little wider: 5:3.

At first HDTV was not meant to replace film, but rather to improve on television. By 1977, NHK proposed a global standard for HDTV signals—they could be watched on special high definition televisions sets and broadcast from special high definition equipment.

The American broadcast industry watched the foreign effort closely, and in 1977 the industry engineers, SMPTE, decided to create a special committee to evaluate a standard. Perhaps the biggest proponent of HDTV in the U.S. was Joseph Flaherty.

Flaherty distinguished himself by going against the general inertia of the broadcasting industry, which wanted to keep video standards fixed and immobile even in light of improving technology.[11]

"While our current system has served us well for forty years," remarked Flaherty, "continued dependence on that standard would mean that the U.S. would enter the 21st century with the lowest technical quality broadcasting system in the world. A high-definition, wide-screen presentation…is a totally new experience—as different from color television as color television is different from black-and-white television."

[10] Also Ikegami and Panasonic.

[11] Flaherty continued to be controversial. Ironically, decades later he was representing entrenched broadcasting interests and was often criticized for no longer putting the best technology first.

In March 1980, almost concurrent with Lucas' purchase of land for his film-making ranch in Marin, Zoetrope bought a classic Hollywood studio on Las Palmas Blvd., a short hop from Paramount Pictures. It was called Hollywood General Studios.[12] Dating back to the silent movie days, it had twelve sound stages spread over a ten-acre lot. When Mae West said, "Why don't you come up and see me sometime?" she was referring to her bungalow there.[13]

In its heyday the studio had been a focal point for shooting filmed television programs: in the 1950s it was home to the original episodes of *I Love Lucy* and *Burns and Allen*. George Burns still maintained an office on the lot.[14]

In the months after the release of *Apocalypse Now*, Coppola began sketching out his plans for the future—projects he wanted to facilitate at his new Hollywood studio using state-of-the-art production technologies. *Hammett, One from the Heart, The Outsiders, The Black Stallion Returns, Rumblefish* and *The Escape Artist* were all in various stages of conceptualization, with Coppola attached to each as producer, director, writer, or all three. The new Zoetrope Studios was going to be the incarnation of the modern Hollywood that he had long envisioned.

George Lucas, too, was in high gear. Lucasfilm was growing exponentially; the Ranch development had broken ground; and the computer research project was finally underway. As ever, the two friends pushed their accelerators a little harder and edged out a little more dangerously, as they raced to reinvent filmmaking, each in his own way.

[12] Three years earlier the property had been sold to a Dallas oil and gas firm, which named it the "Hollywood General" lot, and then promptly turned and sold it to Zoetrope for $6.7 million.

[13] That's only half the quotation. The actual line (to Carry Grant) goes: "Why don't you come up sometime and see me. How about Tuesday. It's amateur night." From the film *She Done Him Wrong* (1933).

[14] In the 1960s it was the site of *Green Acres, Mr. Ed, Beverly Hillbillies, Lone Ranger.* and *The Addams Family*. And in the 1970s, *Baretta* and *The Rockford Files*. The last theatrical film shot there (in the 1970s) was Warren Beatty's *Shampoo*.

eleven

Flying Free

[1980]

Discovery consists of seeing what everybody has seen and thinking what nobody has thought.

—Albert von Szent-Gyorgyi

IN APRIL 1980, Akira Kurosawa invited George and Francis to Tokyo for the premiere of *Kagemusha*. The film had performed spectacularly in Japan, becoming the most popular domestic film ever released. Only a month before, Paul Schrader, the writer of Scorsese's *Taxi Driver*, had told Francis his dream of filming the story of Japanese novelist Yukio Mishima. On the trip to Tokyo, Francis began securing the rights. It was just one more in a string of film projects that he was excited to kick into gear.[1]

By June, just after *Empire* had been released and *Raiders of the Lost Ark* began shooting, Francis hosted a "geekfest" at his Pacific Heights mansion, intended as research for a $3- to $5-million film project he wanted to do, called "Interface." He invited dozens of the brightest minds and creative innovators using computers and video; he called it his "Electronic Imagery Conference."

For three non-stop days, musician Todd Rundgren, computer artist Larry Cuba,[2] inventor Dick Shoup, and other luminaries showed their videos and participated in the big rap session. Shoup, who had built the frame buffer and computer painting system at Xerox PARC, had just formed a company to develop an affordable paint system for television and was excited about his new venture.[3]

"Interface" was going to be shot on videotape and directed by experimental filmmaker Scott Bartlett. The plan was for the movie to combine complex visual graphics from film, slides, and video with accompanying music. But Bartlett (as well as in-house Zoetrope technologists) had a number of practical questions about the look of the film, including how to synchronize the film and video with the sound, because they have different frame rates.

[1] Wim Wenders had begun shooting his film *Hammett* in February. Documentary director Martha Coolidge had been trying to develop her feature script "Photoplay" with Zoetrope, with little success. A few years later, she made the big time when her film *Valley Girl* (1983) was a minor sensation.

[2] The freelance artist who generated the only 3-D effects in *Star Wars*.

[3] Aurora Systems, co-founded with Damon Rarey. Aurora was established to compete with Ampex's AVA and the new broadcast paint system from Quantel, called PaintBox.

"Interface" screenwriter Chip Proser described the film: "It involves an individual losing all his sensory contact with the world through an accident, and being in the dark for a time…and then, through a computer tap and interface, gradually, one sense at a time, his senses are brought back on line." As the character transforms, so too would the look of the film—it would parallel Zoetrope's own transformation from film to electronic cinema. As director Bartlett said later, "Zoetrope would like to stay on the vanguard of that activity."

Francis was engrossed by the whole computer-video connection. He wasn't just the big host, but an active participant. He wanted to know what was feasible, he wanted to know where all this might lead.

But he also didn't know exactly what George's troops were up to, and he wanted to find out what that was and compare it to his own efforts. He had invited Lucas' new tech boys to the conference, but only Alvy Ray Smith showed up.

Alvy remembers that Francis was at his manic best. "He went for hours and hours talking, jumping over the seats in his home theatre, whirling pasta in the kitchen, on and on and on. I would wear out from time to time and have to sleep. I would wake up later and there would be Francis still going at it."

Coppola was fascinated by the work Alvy presented at the gathering—it included many of the still images Alvy and David DiFrancesco had made at NYIT.[4] Afterward, Alvy spoke to the group. "We at Lucasfilm are now going to start up a similar, but higher resolution, version[of what we did at NYIT]."

"When you say George is doing the same thing but in higher resolution, that's for transfer to film?" asked Francis.

Alvy responded, "The unit at NYIT was aimed at video resolution. Although it could go higher, it wasn't really tuned to go to a higher resolution. It was too slow. At Lucasfilm we're designing special equipment that will make images at film resolution. The main idea is to go to film. We're going to digitize everything that can be digitized in the film process. We're looking at video editing too."

Zoetrope was using video and computers as ways of changing the process, as a visualization tool for a movie. Lucasfilm's scientists were looking at the process of constructing sound and images, organizing them, and editing them. The two efforts overlapped significantly.

With this, the Zoetrope teams, including Francis, Clark Higgins, and Tony St. John all looked around at each other. "Hand in hand with Zoetrope research?" asked St. John.

"I don't see why not," said Alvy politically, "It seems to me that a supportive, two-pronged approach to high tech will help us both succeed."

Francis joined in, articulating the fundamental separation between his vision and George's, although they were intertwined. "I have a serious specific application," he said, referring to his desire to use video to create "Interface," as

[4] And Alvy's pre-NYIT computer-art film called VidBits.

well as the upcoming slate of Zoetrope film productions. "George has many applications. He really needs to synthesize sequences, maybe whole films. My interest is more in an electronic armature to plan films by constructing them in simulated ways, like a wind tunnel test, where I could make the whole movie before it's shot, to design the actual shooting of the production more efficiently.

"My gamble," concluded Francis, "is that the money we spend on it will be saved by the fact that we'll shoot it that much quicker. So it's an experiment that Zoetrope is doing, to start getting into more video-style production, even though right now we're wedded to film. So that when we go to all high-resolution video, we'll have the methods down."

Zoetrope was working with Sony and CBS to refine high-definition television, and Coppola believed it was the future not only of broadcasting, but of theatrical film as well.

The participants at the Electronic Imagery Conference, in Coppola's San Francisco home, June 20–22, 1980.

Thomas Brown   August Coppola   Tom Scott   Chip Proser

Tony St. John   Dick Shoup   Clark Higgins   Larry Cuba   Todd Rundgren

Francis Coppola   Bill Etra   Gian Carlo   Scott Bartlett
                                    (Gio) Coppola

Woody Vasulka   Alvy Ray Smith   Steve Calou   Peter Ivers

Responded Alvy, "I think now is the time to do that, because though it may be just a little too early in terms of the various technologies needed…now is when you've got to make the investment."

But the coordination between Lucasfilm and Zoetrope never went any further. While George was more than happy to leave Catmull and his team on their own to develop their three-year computer research project, Francis wanted tools now, he wanted them *yesterday*.

Francis remembered that he had tried to recruit Alvy Ray Smith about six months earlier, before Alvy went to Lucasfilm. Now, Francis cornered Alvy.

"All this electronic stuff that George is up to," said Francis, "it was really my idea." Alvy listened intently.

"Francis assured me that 'he was the guy,'" said Alvy, who noted their competitive natures but was comfortable with his new research position. "Sure he was a genius," reported Alvy, flattered to have "the great Coppola" speaking to him like that. "But I was never uncertain that I had made the right choice on who to go with to get this vision executed."

Although George's passion at the time was the big picture of Skywalker Ranch, he was absolutely convinced by the success of the motion control camera at ILM that computers were the way to revolutionize film. George wouldn't compare his technological interests to those of Francis, but he had an uncanny appreciation for how technology could be applied, and was in many respects more serious about the research and long-range impact than the gadget-minded Coppola.

Francis was only months away from building his new technical facility at the old Hollywood General studio, and he wanted to use it immediately on his upcoming film, *One from the Heart*. He had come up with a clever scheme, he felt, to use the film's budget to fund his experiment in using video.

George was just starting to shoot *Raiders of the Lost Ark* and was perfectly content to leave the scientists alone to do whatever it was they were going to do.

Ed Catmull was grateful that the boss didn't want any new computer tools for *Empire*. He had too much to do. Along with finding leadership for the major projects, Catmull needed to get new computers in place, networked together, and running software. Unfortunately, he was being charged with making significant decisions about computer technology at a time he was certain that everything he knew was in flux. As the '80s began, computers were going through another cataclysmic shift, away from the giant mainframes of DEC and IBM, and toward small and powerful minicomputers.

The growing possibilities of minicomputers worked in Ed's favor with regard to the various tasks he needed to address, but the pressing issue of selecting a single platform in 1980 was an impossible task. Ed was familiar with the research into minicomputers that had been going on for some time at Xerox PARC. Like many of his colleagues, he had seen the Xerox Alto, and was well aware of the direction computing was heading.

The Alto inspired many people. Andy Bechtolsheim was a student at Stanford in 1979 when he had an opportunity to be an intern at Xerox PARC, working on some of their chip designs. "I was a 'no-fee consultant,' which meant I didn't get paid, but I got to be there as much as I wanted and play around with the stuff they had."

The Xerox Alto in 1979, an in-house product at Xerox's research center, the prototype for the graphical interface and "personal computer."

What Andy got to play with was the Alto computer. One was on every desk at PARC. It was the best deal of his life. "I used the Alto every day, and by the end of the summer I couldn't imagine how anyone could work any other way. [The Alto] was obviously the right way to work with computers. But if you hadn't seen it, you wouldn't have believed it."

Xerox had invented a full computing solution—from the workstation to the network to the laserprinter.

At the computer show COMDEX, Forest Baskett and Andy Bechtolsheim saw a prototype of the MIT (Massachusetts Institute of Technology) "Nu" terminal, a device similar in many respects to the Alto. MIT wasn't trying to sell it as a product, but rather was looking for a corporation to license it.

Baskett was convinced they could achieve the same performance and functionality in a smaller, cheaper package; they went back to Stanford to work on their own Stanford University Network or "SUN" terminal. Bechtolsheim began building the proprietary CPU board for the computer, using the hot new 68000 chip from Motorola.

"Where the Alto was built from sets of chips, and proprietary parts, I wanted to build something from standard parts," said Bechtolsheim. "The SUN computer was going to be the standard-part version of the Alto." He worked his way through a number of versions before settling on a final design.

Motorola

Motorola originally had been making walkie-talkies and other electronics for the army; later, they began making integrated circuits. Although Intel was better known, and arguably had a more distinguished group of engineering designers, Motorola's CPU chips were innovative and fast. Their 6800 chips were mercilessly copied for videogames in the '70s; the new advanced 68000 chips were designed for engineers and were friendly to work with — they were the rage for the earliest minicomputers with demanding graphics. The primary competitor, the Intel processors (like the 8086), maintained backward compatibility with older models, which left them a little squirrelly to work with.

The key to the SUN was its powerful operating system, called UNIX, developed at Bell Labs and refined at UC Berkeley. Bechtolsheim wasn't the only one trying to capitalize on the new Motorola 68000 microprocessor and Berkeley's UNIX. There were dozens of companies trying to get started with these elements. But the SUN project was different. The Stanford team was going to build a computer with a graphical display, windows and icons, and they felt that UNIX needed to be improved to execute this, and not used out of the box, as it were, from Berkeley.

"No one saw the opportunity of the workstation," said Bechtolsheim. "Because UNIX is a multi-user operating system, most people simply wanted to use it on the VAX for multiple users. What they missed was the market

opportunity for single users, an early version of what became the personal computer, that actually worked."

Ed Catmull and Alvy Ray Smith needed something immediately for their computer development. At NYIT they had used a giant computer (the PDP-11) along with miscellaneous graphical peripherals, later purchasing a VAX 11/780—large, but more manageable. With no better alternatives, the VAX would still do, but Ed was certain that what they really needed was to have individual workstations for the artists. Small machines, not big iron, were the future. Ed and Alvy agreed that Bechtolsheim and the SUN guys were onto something.

JOHN SEAMONS

Hometown: Northern New Mexico. *Family:* single, and looking. *Interests:* Dan O'Neill comics, Patrick McGoohan movies, jazz, skiing, small blondes, Personal Dynamic Media. *Sign:* very Scorpio. *Employment History:* Los Alamos National Laboratory, Stanford University Computer Science Dept. *[From 1982 LFL Yearbook]*

UNIX

Bell Labs had a history of technological innovation, beginning in the 1930s. Being an arm of the phone company, they began with sound, which led to electronics, and ultimately to computers. In the 1960s, they did a project with MIT and General Electric to develop some computing tools for the massive timeshare mainframes they operated. By 1969, Bell Labs pulled out of this project and introduced their own variation, an operating system they called UNIX.[5] UNIX was a versatile system that could be made to work on a large variety of computers; it was designed for multitasking and multiple simultaneous users, the key for practical use. Multitasking allowed computers to open a file at the same time as printing a document. It was also modular, which allowed isolated parts to be modified or new parts added easily. And finally, it could handle text and some word processing. Which made it good for researchers happy to be off typewriters.

In 1973, Bell Labs begin licensing UNIX (version 6) to universities. It was expensive but made it possible for academia to begin the practical exploration of computers. Five years later they made version 7 available commercially. In 1979, the inventor of UNIX, Ken Thompson, took a year's sabbatical at the University of California at Berkeley. There he and two grad students, Bill Joy and Chuck Haley, wrote a variation of UNIX for student use.[6] Bell Labs engineers were also responsible for developing a number of key computer "languages," which were designed as central to UNIX, most importantly one called "C" (1973). These languages were the core of UNIX and the standard of modern programming.

While the proto-SUN team couldn't provide state-of-the-art hardware, they did have a smart young programmer named John Seamons, with skills in hardware as well as software. Seamons, an employee of the Stanford computer science department, had been working with Bechtolsheim on building the first SUN motherboard, which would later be called the SUN-0.

[5] The name derived from the Bell-MIT-GE predecessor MULTICS–Multiplexed Operating and Computer System. The "U" stood for "Uniplexed."

[6] Called the "Berkeley Software Distribution" or BSD.

TOM DUFF

Hometown: Toronto, Canada.
Family: single. *Schools:*
University of Waterloo,
University of Toronto.
Interests: animation,
hedonism, The Sprockets
Band. *Sign:* Elmo the
Wombat. *Employment History:*
NYIT Computer Graphics
Lab 1977-1980.

[From 1982 LFL Yearbook]

Seamons was in the process of porting UNIX to the new board when Ed asked him to help with the Lucasfilm systems. Seamons talked it over with Bechtolsheim and soon volunteered to start in the fall. Bechtolsheim liked the connection. "Lucasfilm was the ideal customer for what I was trying to build."

Back at New York Tech, Tom Duff was one of the few people left from the "gang." The plans for regrouping at Lucasfilm had been kept secret, and few in the Lab ever got wind of the underlying events. Certainly no one mentioned "getting laundered."

Soon after Catmull left, Alvy and David DiFrancesco were gone too, and Alex Schure needed to find someone he trusted to put in charge of the graphics. He settled on his son Louis, a tennis pro at a local country club. "His real love had been tennis," recalled Tom Duff. "Basically, he wasn't much fun to work for."

By December 1979, the magic at NYIT was gone and Duff took a vacation with his father, an invalid who didn't often get to travel. Duff showed his father the sites of Northern California, the redwood forests and foggy coasts, and while in Marin, took the opportunity to call up Ed Catmull to have dinner.

They met, but Catmull offered little information and less support, which gave the somewhat pessimistic Duff the sense he wasn't welcome, which wasn't the case. All Catmull was able to say was, "George is interested in spending some money on technology." Duff, a quiet sort, did his best to find out what was going on, trying to see if he could perhaps get a job. Catmull wasn't revealing anything.

When Duff returned from vacation he was, without notice, given a significant raise. "They figured something was up." It was clear NYIT thought he was being courted, and he honestly wished he were, but Catmull was making no gestures.

Schure had just lost what he considered his braintrust of Ed, Alvy, and David, and he didn't want to lose any more staff. Regardless, within two weeks, Tom Duff decided that if there were ever a chance of getting a job at Lucasfilm, he'd have to make the leap with no assurances. After finishing a long night of programming, Duff typed up his resignation, giving NYIT about six months notice that he would be leaving by the 4th of July, left it on his boss's desk, and headed home to bed.

He was awakened by his ringing phone. He answered with eyes shut.

"Hello?"

"Hello, this is Susan Anderson. Who am I speaking with? Is this Tom Duff?"

"Yeah…"

"Just a moment, I'm going to put Ed Catmull on the line."

Tom sat up in bed and tried to wake himself.

"I hear you quit your job." Tom looked over at the clock. He'd only been asleep for a few hours.

"Yeah. How did you hear that?"

"Louis called me this morning and threatened to sue me for hiring you away."

Catmull and Duff spoke for a few minutes. They agreed that if Lucasfilm was going to get sued anyway, maybe it would be okay to hire Duff at some point, although Catmull wasn't going to expect an opening in the group for a software programmer until the fall. Recalled Catmull, "While I did want people to join me, I knew that I couldn't make offers. I wasn't about to tell anybody how to exit their jobs or how to approach Lucasfilm."

"No problem, I'll be at NYIT until summer, and I'm sure I can find something to do in the interim." Duff felt that the Lucasfilm job was all but his and he only had to come up with some temporary project until an offer came through. Within two days Duff got another call, this one from the Mark Williams Company, a computer business in Chicago. They said, "I hear you're looking for work."

While Tom Duff was working at the Mark Williams Company, he thought of another person for Ed's team, his old friend from college: Bill Reeves.[7] Since Duff was planning to arrive at Lucasfilm sometime near the end of the summer, he thought Reeves should try to get a job there as well. It would be fun, he thought, for them to work together.

Reeves' job at the time was looking at angiograms. Doctors would inject dye into human hearts and then snap photos of the blood flow through the millions of large and small vessels. He put the snapshots into the computer and used graphical tools to clean up the images and make animations of the heart as it changed over time. By looking at the outlines, doctors could make their diagnoses.

As Reeves pondered where to go after getting his PhD, Tom Duff called. Reeves sent a resume´ to California and crossed his fingers. His girlfriend had just moved to Berkeley and the idea of being on the west coast was preferable to a long distance relationship.

"I was in discussions about a job with Ed Catmull when *Empire* came out," recalled Reeves. "That just pushed me over the edge. I could teach at some university, or I could go work for the guys who made *Empire*…hmmm…"

A year had passed since Alex Schure sold Alvy's paint program to the video titan Ampex for them to refine into the AVA. Tom Porter, the head of AVA

BILL REEVES

Hometown: Toronto, Canada. *Family:* married *Interests:* hiking, canoeing, hockey, Molson's & backbacon. *Schools:* University of Waterloo & University of Toronto. *Employment history:* Reeves Farm Market; Northern Telecom Ltd. [*From 1982 LFL Yearbook*]

[7] University of Toronto.

software, did impressive work refining the painting tools, and the AVA released at the spring 1980 NAB broadcasting convention.

But broadcast graphics wasn't that interesting to Porter. Far more exciting were the research and ideas presented at the relatively young Special Interest Group on Computer Graphics, or Siggraph. By the fall, like everyone interested in computers and graphics, he headed out to Seattle for the Siggraph conference. Porter was secretly hoping to meet with Alvy Ray Smith and see what new things Alvy had come up with for painting. He was sure to run into Alvy among the few hundred scientists who would likely be in attendance.

Though small, Siggraph had a dynamic history. In 1966, a Brown University professor, Andy van Dam, had petitioned the Association for Computer Machines, or ACM, to form a special interest committee (unfortunately called a "SIC") on graphics. And they said, "We don't think there's enough interest." They challenged van Dam to get a petition with thirty signatures supporting the topic.

"I had trouble finding thirty people," recalled van Dam.

But he did, and a small group met each year, which he called *SIC*graph. Attendees were mostly from large industry: manufacturers interested in CAD, previsualisation, and simulations.

By 1974, van Dam's special interest committee grew into a "group," and they changed the name to *SIG*graph. Several hundred people met at the Siggraph convention in autumn of 1976.[8]

At that time, vector graphics was the dominant culture. The frame buffer had already been developed at PARC and refined in Utah, but memory—the essence of the buffer—was expensive. The advantage of vector graphics was that you didn't need much memory and all those highly coded instructions to make images. The disadvantage, of course, was that you couldn't do shading and rendering.

There was often debate in academic circles as to whether the frame buffer allowed for "real" digital art. Vector graphics were drawn in real-time, but the frame buffer was anything but real time. The early images from frame buffers were blocky.

"What would you rather have for engineering drawings," asked van Dam, "a crisp, clean, non-jaggie line, or these very pixilated, very crude color pictures. Well, no choice there."

But no one really imagined how fast the price of memory would drop. Gordon Moore's "law" had been published in 1965, but it was less sure how long it might continue, and it would still be some years before anyone imagined the implications for computing.[9]

Between 1977 and 1979, attendance at Siggraph grew from 750 to 3,000. The 1980 conference was in Seattle, home turf of Boeing, the aircraft manufacturer. Alvy Ray Smith still had the resume´ from Loren Carpenter (a Boeing engineer

[8] Until that point the main feature was listening to academic papers on mathematics. In 1977, professor Tom DeFanti took the reins of the convention. DeFanti, as director of the Electronic Visualization Lab at the University of Illinois, had just provided the hardware and software that Larry Cuba would use to create the original computer effects in *Star Wars*. Following that, sensing the momentum in graphics, he had the idea to add a "film festival" to the conference.

[9] Moore's Law (1965): the number of transistors that will fit on an IC chip will increase exponentially over time. This was analogous to CPU power, and the theory was it would double every 18 months (actually, Moore thought every two years; he had initially made the projections through 1975).

who had stuffed it in his hand a year earlier during a Fortran conference). By now Alvy knew that Carpenter was the one sending him the mountain pictures; Alvy, certain he'd be there, was interested in looking him up at the show. Alvy had no idea there would be 7,500 people in attendance. It might be harder to find Carpenter than he thought.

Loren Carpenter had spent half a dozen years working at Boeing, using computers to facilitate the design of plane parts. Boeing's airplanes had many unusually shaped curving parts that were designed by hand, sketched on drafting tables. Carpenter would go to work early, take off in the middle of the day to take courses to finish his undergraduate, then his master's degree, then go back at night to continue working. He loved airplanes and spent some of his spare time learning to fly the new gull-winged hang gliders.

In the early '70s Boeing began to investigate using computers to clean up their drawings, removing erase marks and extraneous lines. The tradition had been to sketch the odd-shaped parts on large sheets of paper, which were used to cut aluminum forms. At the same time, engineers worked on the manufacturing of the parts, solving problems like whether a component was shaped such that a mechanic could reach inside (with the proper tool) to fix something. A computer, it was determined, might streamline this drawing and building process. There were only a few people at Boeing working on the problem, and Carpenter was one of them.

As frame buffers became available, Carpenter was vocal about the potential they might have for Boeing. Prices for frame buffers continued to drop; his boss requisitioned the $30,000 device, and Loren Carpenter had a new tool.

Carpenter began by making drawings of plane parts and eventually preliminary airplane designs. "So I'm making these pictures of airplanes and airplane parts," he recalled, "and I'm thinking I'd like to have some background on these airplane[images], because every publicity photo has a Boeing plane flying through the mountains."[10]

He needed to make a mountain that really looked like a mountain, but he was stuck trying to add enough detail using a computer with so little memory (maybe a few megabytes, and processing power under a couple megahertz).

Loren, his wife Rachel, and their young son, lived in the countryside outside of Seattle. Family evenings out often consisted of a drive into the city and a walk around town, dropping into bookshops on University Avenue. Browsing at a magazine stand, he saw the cover of *Scientific American* featuring a fractal image drawn by mathematician Bernard Mandelbrot.[11] His lips parted with a sort of silent gasp.

"I knew at once that I could apply that math to my problem," he recalled. Fractals could be used for the semi-automated computerized construction of

[10] Carpenter was experimenting with "blue sky" concepts—scenarios such as what if a plane's two wings were one above the other, or what if the wings attached at the ends—and his division generated reams of data about these kinds of theoretical craft. Carpenter would take the data and, using a frame buffer, render a reasonably realistic painting of the plane.

[11] *The Fractal Geometry of Nature*, 1978. The term "fractal" was coined by Mandelbrot.

a mountain landscape. They introduced a kind of randomness to an otherwise orderly look of geometry; the math made straight lines bumpy and pyramids mountainy. He took the magazine home.

Loren started applying fractals to his problems somewhat mystically: "I threw the problem back into my subconscious. I built a little structure of all the things I knew, leaving a little hole where the answer would go. And every once in a while, I looked into the hole to see if anything fell in. One evening when I looked, something was in there—a whole class of algorithms. Within two minutes of seeing that, I knew how to make lightning bolts, landscapes, clouds, and a host of other things that had an infinite variety of detail and scale and would also animate, because they had a consistent geometry."

Loren Carpenter had come up with a way to apply the math theories of Mandelbrot to the real-world needs in the computer.

"The first time I ran the program, a mountain popped up. I have to say, I was stunned." Mandelbrot's work generated mountains too, but the way he did them was prohibitively slow and not particularly efficient.

Loren's first tests were dramatic. The mountains grew organically and looked more real than he could have made them by drawing them. "Then I took a bunch of points and colored some rock color and some snow color and some tree color…"

The mathematical steps to build a fractal mountain, by Loren Carpenter.

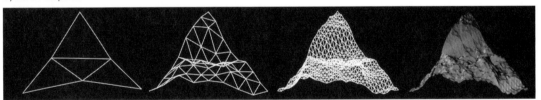

[12] When *Star Wars* released in 1977, Loren and his wife and son attended the film in Seattle. "Loren stood in the rain for four hours while we waited in the car," Rachel Carpenter recalled. "When we got into the theater, finally, there was steam coming off all the people in the audience." The couple, like everyone else in the theater, was gripped by the film. "During the part when Obi Wan is explaining the Force," said Rachel, "I just had this knowing that we would work with George somehow, sometime…"

By using simple algorithms, he got the color of the mountain to logically propagate out from the tiny triangles that comprised the shape. It took him three days to write the code and get the process working well. On the morning of the third day, Loren hurried into the office to see what the computer had generated for him the night before. There were three pictures of a mountain, the same mountain from different directions.

"It was totally stunning," thought Carpenter. "This is history here."

Loren Carpenter knew that heroes of computer graphics were swirling around at George Lucas' place—the unprecedented combination of CG and Lucas electrified the *Star Wars* fan.[12] As soon as he had images coming out of his computer, he began sending teasing notes to Alvy Ray Smith.

"But who was I, some programmer at Boeing, thinking I could go to Lucasfilm, when they could heat their building by burning all the resumés they were getting?" The key would be getting his mountain to Siggraph. He maneuvered aggressively to get a frame on the cover of the convention proceedings.

"I knew if I were ever going to have an opportunity to do real research in computer graphics, it was going to be at Lucasfilm. I didn't want to teach. I had a master's degree. I could still get a PhD, but I didn't want to teach." The growing group at Lucasfilm represented one of the few pure research locations in the world—research with no teaching responsibilities.

Ultimately, Carpenter was motivated by a similar passion as Lucas, to transfer the ideas in his head to the screen. "I wanted to see my imagination," said Loren, "And I wanted to see other people's imagination. And so in order to do that, I worked hard to give people the tools."

In spite of the quantity of great mountain images, Carpenter needed to prove that they were all views of the same mountain. He needed to show that because of the fractal geometry, no matter how close or far the camera got from the mountain, the image had the same level of detail as one would have with a "real mountain." To do this he needed to show a zoom-in on the mountain, a series of related frames that would illustrate the method.

"I had to make a movie."

Loren transferred his thrill of skirting around over the hills and sand dunes in his hang glider into a movie. "I built this landscape, came up with a little story, and laid it all out on graph paper. Then I typed a whole bunch of numbers into the computer and made some preliminary images."

It was a hard process to control. Carpenter was able to define where mountains would be, between landmark points he specified, but there was still a fair amount of randomness in the process.

"What's it going to do in between? Is it going up or down or just sort of wiggly?" he pondered. "You can't tell ahead of time unless you force it one way or the other."

It was also important, he felt, for the film to have musical accompaniment, and he had a pretty good idea of what to choose. "Flying" from the Beatles' *Magical Mystery Tour* album (1967) was one of the few pieces from the band with all four band members credited, which Loren felt was significant. It was instrumental, so it wouldn't distract from the visuals. And most important, it was the right length—he would be able to generate the 3,000-odd frames required for a two-minute demonstration. He played the album over and over against a stopwatch, noting where important music transitions were, so he could align the flight to match the cues.

Boeing put up a little money in exchange for a film credit, and they granted Loren the time to develop the project. He worked on his movie around the clock. "I would start the program at night, and it would put

Still from Loren
Carpenter's *Vol Libre.*

frames on a computer tape. Sometimes the tape would fill up and sometimes it wouldn't. Over the weekends it would always fill up so I'd go in on Saturday and change tapes." Carpenter spent more than four months on the two-minute movie.

As the various components came together, the date of the Siggraph conference was creeping up. It was unclear if he'd make it. If the lab had any problem getting the sound on the film, or if the color timing didn't work.... Any screw-up, and he'd miss his window of opportunity.[13]

A few weeks before the conference, Loren was notified that another scientist, Alan Fournier, was presenting a paper covering aspects of fractals. He read Fournier's abstract and the two met. Fournier's research focused on the mathematics; Carpenter's on the application of that math in the form of an algorithm. Fournier showed Carpenter slides of images comprised of square meshes, and Carpenter showed Fournier still frames from the unfinished movie, with triangular meshes. ("Square meshes look a lot less realistic," noted Carpenter.)

They decided to give their presentations together, with Fournier going first, and Carpenter closing. Carpenter strategically decided that it was more impressive to show his film as part of the lecture, instead of burying it in the new film/video festival that Siggraph held. He called the two-minute movie *Vol Libre,* which meant "Flying Free."

The day before the conference, the final film was ready to pick up. He had only seen the rough draft, the workprint, projected on the tiny screen of the Moviola. He had very little idea how it would look big, let alone how (or if) it all came out.

Fournier gave his talk on fractal math, and Loren gave his talk on all the different algorithms there were for generating fractals, and how some were better than others for making lightning bolts or boundaries.[14] "All pretty technical stuff," recalled Carpenter. "Then I showed the film."

He stood before the thousand engineers crammed into the conference hall, all of whom had seen the image on the cover of the conference proceedings, many of whom had a hunch something cool was going to happen. He introduced his little film that would demonstrate that these algorithms were real. The hall darkened. And the Beatles began.

[13] Even though the frames were at video resolution, 512 pixels square, Loren had trouble finding a resource that could take computer tapes, generate images, and put them on film. He found a company in Minneapolis with a high resolution CRT scanner—effectively a nice camera pointed at a nice television.

[14] Curve algorithms, point distribution algorithms, surface algorithms, and so on.

Vol Libre soared over rocky mountains with snowy peaks, banking and diving like a glider. It was utterly realistic, certainly more so than anything ever before created by a computer. After a minute there was a small interlude demonstrating some surrealistic floating objects, spheres with lightning bolts electrifying their insides. And then it ended with a climatic zooming flight through the landscape, finally coming to rest on a tiny teapot, Martin Newell's infamous creation, sitting on the mountainside.

The audience erupted. The entire hall was on their feet and hollering. They wanted to see it again. "There had never been anything like it," recalled Ed Catmull. Loren was beaming.

"There was strategy in this," said Loren, "because I knew that Ed and Alvy were going to be in the front row of the room when I was giving this talk." Everyone at Siggraph knew about Ed and Alvy and the aggregation at Lucasfilm. They were already rock stars. Ed and Alvy walked up to Loren Carpenter after the film and asked if he could start in October.

While there was no formal checklist of the components they would need to deliver for the graphical parts of Lucas' projects, Ed and Alvy were always mindful of the areas that needed significant research: (1) film input and output scanning—David DiFrancesco was working on this; (2) designing some kind of frame buffer for high resolution images; (3) animation tools; (4) new rendering tools—something Loren Carpenter had demonstrated he would be particularly gifted at; and (5) frame retouching and painting. Alvy had been doing work in this field, but since he was the team supervisor, he needed to find an active researcher. Ed and Alvy discussed their options at the hotel that evening.

There was no better place to shop for their team than at Siggraph, the world's largest grocery store for talent. The next day, walking through the corridors of the conference center, Ed Catmull bumped into Tom Porter, who stopped him in the hall for a chat. Tom Porter, the kid from Ampex, was slack-jawed and inspired by *Vol Libre*.

"Oh, you know, we saw your paint program, great work," said Catmull. "We need to do some research in frame retouching and painting at Lucasfilm. Do you want to join our group?" Porter could barely speak. "It was pure sex appeal," recalled Porter. The dream of Lucasfilm and, as he put it, "the seduction of getting to make these gorgeous images."

Like Carpenter, he answered on the spot.

LOREN CARPENTER

Hometown: Michigan/ Western Washington. *Family:* married, wife Rachel, son Tay. *Interests:* computer animation, running, reading fantasy, hiking, seeing, figuring out how things work and what they're for. *Sign:* textbook Aquarius. *Employment history:* 13 years at Boeing Computer Services, Seattle. *Other Info:* I stood in line 2½ hours in a heavy rain to see Star Wars. Somebody finally made a movie for ME!
[From 1982 LFL Yearbook]

TOM PORTER

Hometown: Lexington MA. *Family:* married to Christine Baron. *Schools:* Exeter, Penn; Stanford. *Interests:* Frisbee. *Employment history:* NIH, Ampex.
[From 1982 LFL Yearbook]

twelve

The Silverfish

[1980]

Film will never become an art form until its materials are as inexpensive as pencil and paper.

—Jean Cocteau (1889-1963)

COPPOLA ALWAYS WANTED the impossible. From everyone. New tools couldn't be built fast enough for him. "Francis would never ask 'Can it be done?'" remembered video engineer Clark Higgins. "He'd say 'This will be done.'"

Since Coppola had had extensive video editing experience with *Apocalypse Now*, he was anxious to pursue more ways video could augment his creative process. "After *Apocalypse*," said an associate, "Francis felt there had to be an easier way...some of [the filmmaking process] should be able to be handled with simulations."

In the period following his "Interface" conference, Coppola was galvanized by new technology and the bright young minds exploring it. He was now on the lookout for someone who could execute some of his notions about integrating film and video.

Word spread through the grapevine that there was such a person—facile with electronics, able to find unusual equipment from whatever odd place it was built, and able to convince the manufacturers to deliver those items on impossible schedules. Thomas Brown was a guy Francis wanted to meet. It was only a minor complication that he was working for George Lucas.

During the late '60s, while Thomas Brown was in high school in Arkansas, he played with a garage band with a questionable future. His parents desperately didn't want him in the band and promised him they'd pay for college if he'd just leave Arkansas and leave the band behind.

"I told the bass player and he said, 'Why don't you tell them you want to go to the University of Hawaii,'" recalled Brown. "If you have to break up the band, at least get a trip to Hawaii out of it." So Hawaii it was.

College introduced Brown to radio, which led to television, and then music recording. After his graduation in 1973, Brown moved to California. Eventually he landed in the seminal Record Plant in Sausalito as sort of an "assistant engineer-janitor," as he described it. Record Plant dominated the music industry in New York and Los Angeles. Taking advantage of the wave of bands spawned by the Summer of Love in San Francisco, the company had just opened a "resort" studio in the Bay Area. The Tower of Power was in studio C, Stevie Wonder was in studio A, and Sly Stone had built himself an innovative room for recording that they called "the pit."[1]

Chief engineer at the Record Plant was a tall, affable man, Tom Scott. Scott got along with Brown and found jobs for him when he could. As the Record Plant was beginning work on Fleetwood Mac's *Rumors* album, Brown left to work on a laser light show for Bill Graham's organization.[2]

The Bill Graham project was interesting, but, as Brown described it, "There was a lot of dope smoking going on while the guys were making pretty spacey laser shows." As it was winding down, Lhary Meyer (Graham's chief engineer) and Thomas Brown were itching for something else to do.[3]

"I hear George Lucas is putting together a facility in San Rafael," said Lhary, "and I'm going to apply. Do you want me to tell them about you?"

"Yea, that would be great."

Brown met with Jerry Jeffress, head of the Lucasfilm electronics department (and one of the designers of the original motion control cameras on *Star Wars*). They didn't hire him.[4]

"Well, we really like the guy," Jeffress said, "but we don't know what we could have him do."

Lhary Meyer was hired, joining the electronics department at the Industrial Light & Magic facility on Kerner Boulevard (newly re-established with people and gear from Van Nuys). *The Empire Strikes Back* was ramping up and the facility had to get operational before the film started production. There were only two other people in the department when Meyer arrived: Jeffress, from the original team in Southern California, and Kris Brown, a new guy who would be in charge of the motion control computer. In 1978 it was as close as Lucasfilm came to having a computer department.

It was this department that was partly responsible for the next generation of motion control cameras. On *Star Wars*, the motor that moved the camera head was called a "stepper motor." It moved in little jerks. It jerked forward, stopped, and jerked again. Like gears. What ILM needed was a motor that moved continuously, smoothly: a "servo" motor. A servo motor would allow the camera to move while the shutter was open, giving the stop-motion animation a more natural looking blur.

[1] The pit was a studio with no separate control room: instead, the console was placed in the middle of the musician's recording area.

[2] Up to that time, laser light shows were performed live by people moving levers that controlled the lasers, usually to the beat of music. Graham's team used an FM instrumentation deck that recorded the movement of the levers so that once performed it could be repeated precisely—a motion control system for lasers.

[3] Lhary had long stringy hippie hair, and his oddly spelled name often conjured up the mnemonic "El Harry."

[4] Brown joined Captain Beefheart's team for their Shiny Beast national concert tour. It was a bleak autumn of '78; by the time Brown was back in California, Harvey Milk and George Moscone had been murdered and Jim Jones followers had completed their Kool-Aid suicide.

While other ILM teams were having success building VistaVision cameras and assembling optical printers, the electronics department was having a dog of a time trying to get this motor right. The servo motor was a very strong little thing, capable of tremendous amounts of torque. Early prototypes were downright dangerous—occasionally they would unexpectedly "take off," nearly maiming the camera operator.

Building the equipment was challenging and time consuming. It often required getting odd parts from third-party vendors who were always putting ILM on the back burner. There were a couple of reasons ILM was routinely blown off. First of all, they were contacting companies that manufactured thousands of custom optical parts, and ILM only needed one or two of something (five was a big order).

Second, no one was allowed to tell that they were working for Lucasfilm. The company name had so much mystique that it changed everything it came in contact with. Sometimes that force made closed doors open; but other times it made prices go up. It could also catalyze an endless barrage of questions, not the least of which was where they were located.

Giving out the company's physical address was forbidden. At the time, ILM was completely unsecured. There was no gate. No fence. No security. The sign on the street read "Kerner Company." Imprinted on the front door was the nondescript "Kerner Optical Research." For years, the public had no idea precisely where Lucasfilm and ILM were. There was no telling what might happen if word spread.

In the end, ordering parts was a "treasure hunt" process. Eventually the tiny group of electronics geeks got tired of spending all their time on the phone, trying to track down some unusual part or negotiate for its speedy delivery.

"Thomas Brown loves to talk on the phone," said Meyer to Jeffress, "If we get him in here he'll get us the parts we need." It was true. So they hired him. Brown's "office" was the combo library-conference room (a room with an oak table and a phone), just past the reception desk. In a land without titles, Brown called himself the "procurement department."

Thomas Brown was able to accomplish what others couldn't. For example, ILM needed to build a three-headed optical printer for *Empire*; for that they had to have a tool called a Bridgeport Milling Machine, which would allow them to make many of their own custom tools. There was a two-year wait and ILM needed it inside the next six weeks. This is what Thomas Brown did. He made items show up.

As *Empire* was nearing completion and the work was winding down, Brown got a call in his San Francisco apartment.

"Who is it?" said Brown jokingly, in a style imitating his girlfriend's daughter, who lived with them.

"Hi. I'm Francis Coppola and I'd like to invite you to dinner." He went on to explain that he had a lot of really good ideas but people kept telling him "no." Francis said, "You have a reputation for getting people to say yes."

So Thomas Brown, with the background of a musician, who also learned how to solder cables, got into a Peugeot limo sent to his little apartment on Filbert Street. The limo then swung through Berkeley for another passenger, Dr. Zoltan Tarczy-Hornoch. Zoltan was an academic who supposedly had invented a device for measuring the speed of light. With his gleaming face peering over the cane he held before him, Zoltan quizzed Brown on all sorts of technical minutiae of which Brown had absolutely no idea. When the car arrived at Coppola's small estate in Napa, Thomas Brown met Francis Coppola for the first time.

They sat down for a big family dinner. Francis wasted no time and went directly into "Francis mode": "I bought this studio in L.A., and I want images and sound and data to flow around like hot and cold water. If you'll help me bring this vision about, I'll help you do anything you want from then on."

Brown thought to himself, "This is an offer I can't refuse."

"Zoltan," Francis said, "what do you think of this?" The bright-faced man thought for a moment and responded in his unusual accent "I've made my computations and it's do-able."

Thomas Brown resigned from Lucasfilm. "I was surrounded by the best special effects people in the world, all of whom were very nice to me," he said. "But it wasn't what I wanted to do. I felt like I had the world's finest factory job."

The day he left was the only time George Lucas ever came into his office. George poked his head into the room to see who this guy was, who was crazy enough to leave Lucasfilm and go work for Francis. "It was natural that there was this cross-pollination between Lucasfilm and Zoetrope," recalled Brown, "although George and Francis always had an unspoken thing not to raid each other's camps."

Brown began his new job by taking the bus from Filbert Street to the Zoetrope headquarters in the Sentinel Building, where he was going to set up an office. Day one: his phone rang.

"What are you doing?" said Coppola.

"Trying to set up an office," responded Brown as he stacked books on a small shelf.

"Let's go to Los Angeles."

The Peugeot limo drove up. Brown joined Coppola and his son Gio, as they headed to the airport and hopped into Nolan Bushnell's Chucky Cheese

Learjet, to which Coppola inexplicably had access. They flew to Burbank and headed for Coppola's new studio (the old Hollywood General lot, now emblazoned with the Zoetrope logo). As they walked onto the lot, they were surrounded by extras dressed as Indians and Romans, a gods-honest cliché of Hollywood played out before them with absolutely no irony—they were shooting Mel Brooks' *History of the World, Part I*. Brooksfilms had a deal with Zoetrope; in addition to the comedy, they were also working on their drama, *The Elephant Man*.

Inside one soundstage sat an Airstream trailer, which Francis had bought for one of the actors. Francis turned to Thomas: "I want to have a caravan of these Airstreams; I'm going to have my directing gear in one of them, and we'll have all the departments in the others…and we'll have this great looking caravan that goes wherever we shoot."

It was his modern incarnation of *The Rain People* experience, with its caravan of station wagons and trailers. Now he was in the big time, and the caravan deserved to be upgraded.

And so, on Thomas Brown's first day of work for Francis Coppola, he was given an assignment: to take Coppola's rag tag team of engineering consultants—known around the lot as the "video rangers"—and help them develop the equipment to go into the control-center trailer. He was made the Zoetrope executive of "ECD," which meant "electronic cinema development."

"From our first meetings," said Brown in 1981, "Coppola made me aware that what we were doing was an experiment towards a future system that would allow him to make movies that would be impossible to make without the technology we were developing. He was preparing for a time when movies would not be made on film, but on high-definition video that would ultimately surpass film in both image quality and image manipulation capabilities."

Brown described for journalists a new process for filmmaking that was closer to animation, developed by animators over decades, but never used by live-action filmmakers. Rough elements of a movie would be assembled into this form, and then slowly replaced by more and more final elements until the movie was done. At any given point in the process it would be possible to see the entire project as a patchwork quilt of pieces in development.

In spite of the similarities, Brown said that it was never thought of as a modification of the animation process. Specifically, Francis' dream was to make a film the way a sculptor makes artwork—sketching on paper, crafting a maquette, building an armature, then finally the real thing.

For Francis the corollary was starting with the story, then storyboards, then a script, then a radio play with actors, adding appropriate music and sound effects, then a soundtrack. After the soundtrack, he'd take the images from the storyboard and paste them on top of the audio. Then, as video rehearsals were held, they would replace the still images. Next, videotapes from the film cameras would be fed into Betamax machines on stage and replace the rehearsals. Then, in the end, the actual film replaced the video.

Zoetrope was in war mode. The new Zoetrope, reborn after Black Thursday, was hoping to produce six to eight films a year. By the time Thomas Brown arrived, only one film had been shot, Wim Wender's *Hammett,* but it needed a reshoot of some scenes and still had not begun post-production. To allow Coppola to focus, the project was shut down. Only two more were in the pipeline, Caleb Deschanel's *The Escape Artist*, and Coppola's own *One from the Heart*—a $15 million romantic fantasy musical.

One From the Heart was personal and intimate, like *Rain People*, but fused with a bit of the musical spectacle Francis couldn't quite impart to *Finian's Rainbow*. When Francis decided to transform his modern romance-comedy to something more surreal—he referred to it as "emotional reality"—he dropped plans of shooting on any real location. The result was that he had to build sets on every soundstage on his lot—one had 125,000 light bulbs and 10 miles of neon. The budget skyrocketed to $23 million, and Coppola had to find investors to cover the difference.

"It's like I'm at a poker table with five guys and they're all betting two or three thousand dollars a hand," said Coppola, "and I've got about eighty-seven cents in front of me. So I'm always having to take off my shirt and bet my pants. Because I want to be in the game. I want to play."

He also wanted to play with technology. "Coppola asked us to put together a room that was simply furnished and comfortable," said Thomas Brown. "He told us to put the place together as if we were under war conditions." The initial "war room" was constructed in a space over a DC power generator, a room that decades earlier had been silent film comedian Harold Lloyd's handball court. Brown brought in the small ¾-inch videotape editing set-up that Francis had built for *Apocalypse* in the Sentinel building and reconfigured it appropriately. This would have to do until the Airstream trailer was complete.

Francis anointed this "the previsualization room." Models of all the sets rested on a long green felt-covered table. Storyboards were tacked to large movable panels hanging on the walls; at a glance an entire movie was revealed. The 1,800 sketches generated by four storyboard artists were transferred to a "still store," an analog device recording to a magnetic plate. From the still store, low-resolution images of storyboards or individual frames from rehearsal videos could be called up by number and dubbed onto the videotape armature that was evolving into the movie. The room had a fantastic sound system.

The edit system in the previsualization room sat at one end of a long table that ran down the middle of the space; the models of sets (and inexplicably, a zoetrope) were at the other end. Storyboards on movable panels covered the walls.

"We went around asking companies that make this kind of stuff if they had anything that could do what Francis had in mind," said Brown. "Sometimes they had something, and sometimes they didn't. When they didn't, we went into guerrilla operation and invented it."

Francis' son, Gio, stared at the printed sign outside the chamber. It read Previsualization Facility. "There's no such thing as 'previsualization,'" he announced, "Previsualization is redundant." Everyone agreed, but the sign remained.

A key element was still missing: a way to move between film and video. The telecine machine—the device that converted 24 frames of film/second into 30 frames of video—was well established, but there was still the problem of choosing edit points on videotape and identifying a corresponding location on the film.

"We had gone to every company in the business and they always told us the same thing," recalled Brown. "They were several months away from solving the problem. We needed the solution in weeks."

Clark Higgins had been working on the problem for some time, trying to massage video and film together, trying to make sense of the intricate differences in the way they marched along. Late one evening, after staring at the problem for what seemed like days, he laid a representation on the table of a few frames of film on top of a few frames of video. Then he cut them into pieces, experimenting with edits at various points. He noticed that he could tell which video frame went with which film frame, except for video frames with timecode numbers ending in 2 or 7.

Higgins called those "ambiguous video frames," and wrote an algorithm for his new programmable calculator that would not allow edits to happen on those numbers. The software would push the edit ahead to the next video frame (that is, frames ending in 3 or 8), but the editor could override that to frames 1 or 6.

"It was an elegant way to solve a problem that no one else had been able to do," said Brown. It may have been original and clean, but it was also a kludge; not allowing an editor to select certain frames could be perceived as problematic for exacting film editors who were used to selecting the precise image on which an edit would occur. Half the battle was knowing where to cut the film, but the other half was about the editor's experience in looking at the film frame-by-frame, and the feeling of how it plays. Higgins' workaround was clever, but only a first step at integrating video in to the film world.

"The first thing we did was add up the weight of all the equipment we needed to be lugged around in the trailer," said Brown, "and found it would break the thing in two."

Already, Francis' fantasy and reality were colliding. The Airstream company did, however, make a vehicle that could support the weight: a motor home. Zoetrope ordered one. Francis asked Dean Tavoularis—the art director on a number of his films—to design the interior to be hip, cushy, high-tech, and nouveux.

At the time, video production vehicles for TV stations had the worst kind of ambience: cables dangling like vines, a small workspace for soldiering, and if they had fabric at all, it was most certainly plaid. Tavoularis came up with a modern design: dark grey interior, oak paneling, pink fabric covering the couches and control room swivel chairs, all contributing to a striking, yet solemn, space. Francis' enormous appetite for gadgets was only surpassed by his attraction to luxury.

Francis in front of the completed Image and Sound Control Airstream, 1981.

It took forever for the Airstream to arrive. Frustrated, Thomas Brown got on a plane and flew to Jackson Center, Ohio, where he found the dusty bare frame of their vehicle sitting in the assembly area. Brown took a big orange grease pencil and wrote "Zoetrope" on the front and back bumpers of the frame. Then he started bringing different workmen around and snapping their picture near it, telling them that this vehicle was being built for Francis Coppola.

"He always likes to see the people who are doing work on his stuff," Brown said. A week later it was completed.

Francis emblazoned the silver Airstream trailer with a sign: "Image and Sound Control." It was his new luxurious war room. He moved the video equipment to the trailer and added a video switcher to preview basic special effects.

"It was a next-generation system," remarked Brown. "It had a lot of capabilities that weren't possible in the previsualization room. It could keep track of timecodes and film frames…it was much more sophisticated."

Coppola was impressed with the potential of analog videodiscs. He agreed that the blisteringly fast search and scan capabilities of a disc, particularly when interfaced with his new Xerox Star computer, would make it possible to access any shot instantly. But videodisc technology was still new, storage on discs was short, and it was still impossible to record material to a disc economically. In the meantime, there was still videotape.

Storyboard images were photographed with a videocamera and edited together with the soundtrack as if they were shots from the film. But first, Francis snapped the actors' rehearsals with a Polaroid camera, to replace the storyboards. Then he'd use video shots of the rehearsals to replace the Polaroids. And so on.

Inside the Airstream, technician Murdo Laird *(left)* and Francis' son Gio get set up. Off camera to the right would sit the sound engineer.

"The whole idea," said Brown, "was not to do away with experimentation at any level. We were always going to be experimenting, but what we'd have by utilizing the Electronic Cinema concept was a more refined range of choices within which to experiment."

At any given moment in the process, it was possible to watch a rough version of the entire film. There was a projector connected to the editing system. Periodically Francis would bring the actors in and say, "This is what we're working on," and give the big picture to everyone.

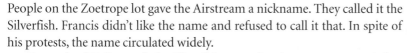

People on the Zoetrope lot gave the Airstream a nickname. They called it the Silverfish. Francis didn't like the name and refused to call it that. In spite of his protests, the name circulated widely.

To much of Hollywood, the Silverfish seemed an insane way to work, less about the future of filmmaking and more about Coppola's idiosyncratic taste for electronic toys. Actors on a set would perform with an invisible director; a scene would finish and they would stand around blankly for a moment, before a disembodied voice rang out from speakers, "That was great. One more time, please."

It took time for Coppola to evolve his use of the Airstream to fit better with the production, as he increasingly used it as an on-set office and space for preparing upcoming scenes.

Commented Thomas Brown, "Any time a new tool is created it takes a while for it to evolve into its most appropriate form and usage."

Hollywood and broadcasting trade magazines viewed Coppola's methods skeptically, or sometimes with "fierce animosity." According to *Millimeter* magazine, "The intense reaction of this volatile industry to Zoetrope's technical innovations seems as much an emotional reaction toward Coppola himself—the controversial, independent filmmaker—as it is toward the technical change."

Coppola was attracted to video and bringing modern practices to bear on the very old-fashioned state of film production. He had a tinkerer's affinity for techno-gear. Lucas, completely uninterested in gadgets, was looking for changes far more profound.

thirteen

Sound and Vision

[Late 1980]

Never before in history, before the invention of recorded sound, had people possessed the ability to manipulate sound the way they'd manipulated color or shapes. We were limited to manipulating sound in music, which is a highly abstract medium. But with recorded material you can manipulate sound effects—the sound of the world—to great effect. In the same way that painting, or looking at paintings, makes you see the world in a different way, listening to interestingly arranged sounds makes you hear differently.

—Walter Murch

TO GET AN AUDIENCE to suspend their disbelief in the artifice of cinema, Lucas understood that sound was generally more important than image. That principle was most apparent when the picture edit was rough. Good sound could make a film work; "sell the cut" is what editors liked to say. The flip side was that even with a good picture edit, garbled or poorly cut sound would make a film virtually impossible to sit through. A smooth flowing audio track was key in a movie's aesthetic success.

But that wasn't all sound could do.

Sound was the key to imbuing imaginary objects with life. Though motion was always important, sound was elemental. Animators worked to give drawings a range of dynamic movement, but it was always in combination with the richness of sounds—the voices of characters, the ambience, the music—which allowed viewers to forget they were looking at a drawing and feel they were watching a living being in a real world.

Star Wars brought this concept into sharp focus.

Star Wars had live actors in it, of course. But many of the characters were masked, either a little or a lot. Darth Vader, C-3PO, Chewbacca, and R2D2 were developed as puppets of sorts, played (actually "animated") by actors, with voices added later. Darth Vader was acted by David Prowse, voiced by James Earl Jones; C-3PO was played and voiced by Anthony Daniels, but all his lines were re-recorded as it was nearly impossible to hear clear dialog from inside his metallic suit. The voices of Chewbacca and R2D2 were carefully constructed from scores of sounds, built tediously by Ben Burtt over many months. It was sound that changed *Star Wars* from being a low-budget (or even high-budget) goofball serial into a rich and complex universe.

George Lucas had developed his feelings about sound at USC, partly from the inspiration of audio professor Ken Miura, and partly from the contagious excitement of his friend Walter Murch, who had a lifelong fascination with the medium.

Murch was always interested in sound, but his epiphany came at USC: "I only discovered film needed sound when I got there; it was a revelation to me that the sound had to be recorded separately from the image and 'cooked'— edited and mixed—before it was finished."

Murch's early experiences with sound came from the radio. Electronic music in the form of the *musique concrete* burst on the scene in post-WWII France. In 1948, Pierre Schaeffer,[1] a sound engineer and composer, took sounds—of trains, people talking, water running—recorded them onto the newly developed magnetic tapes, cut them up like bits of film, and arranged them rhythmically into tracks that played over the radio—a montage of sounds to make music. No one had ever done anything like it before; by the early '50s, it was a movement in Europe. It was a powerful influence on young Murch, who once described it as "an early, technically primitive form of sampling."

Star Wars pioneered many elements of film sound. It was one of the first films to be released in stereo. It utilized low frequency vibrations in the sound track to rattle the audience's teeth. And Ben Burtt invented countless sounds, what he called "sound design," to make the movie credible.

With sound such a significant part of his films, Lucas wanted to push control of it farther than anyone had. To find the person who could invent new computers specifically designed for audio would involve exploring the short and interwoven history of electronic music and film sound.

Forbidden Planet (1956)[2] was a landmark film—a major studio release (MGM) that involved scads of new visual effects, plus the first electronically created score and sound effects. Bebe Barron and her husband Louis had created a sound studio specifically for the film. Every device there was custom, one-of-a-kind.[3]

[1] And also Pierre Henry.

[2] *Forbidden Planet* (1956) was directed by Fred Wilcox and starred Leslie Nielsen, Walter Pidgeon and Anne Francis. It introduced one of the earliest film "droids"—a giant walking computer character, "Robbie the Robot" (the intellectual ancestor to C-3PO and R2D2). Robbie had taken more than two months to build and was comprised of 2,600 feet of electrical wiring for his flashing lights and spinning antennae. (The film also pioneered merchandising tie-ins: kids everywhere owned Robbie the Robot toys.)

[3] When the film was over, the Barrons made a few more small film scores, but nothing of the magnitude or impact of *Forbidden Planet*.

A few years later, in the early '60s, a physics professor at Cornell named Robert Moog began selling kits for transistorized Theremins.[4] A Theremin was an odd electronic device that would emanate sounds of changing intensity and frequency based on how users waved their hands around the pair of vertical and horizontal antennae. It became the classic surreal sound of science fiction films, memorable in *The Day the Earth Stood Still* (1951) and popularized in the opening music of the Beach Boys' 1966 classic *Good Vibrations*.

Building custom Theremins was Moog's hobby, as was toying with the circuits that comprised them. He developed modules that controlled voltage as it moved through a series of transistors; by turning knobs he could generate a variety of interesting sounds. The electronics squealed and moaned with vibration. It was the first synthesizer. But the modular sound synthesizer that Moog put together, like the Theremin, was analog.

Throughout the 1950s and '60s, the audio industry was a poor cousin of the technology industry. Computer research was largely driven by the military and space programs. Hard science. Hard engineering. Funding usually came from ARPA. All the musical possibilities with computers, while interesting, were usually met with a resounding "What's the point?"

Bell Labs, the research department of the phone company, looked at the analog-to-digital converter, a tool that had previously been used for instrumentation work, and wondered if the device could be applied to speech.[5] At around the same time they were developing UNIX, Bell Labs began a series of experiments with speech synthesis.[6] Their first example of pure digital speech creation was when an IBM mainframe computer "sang" the song "Daisy, Daisy, Give Me Your Answer True."[7] Constructed entirely from digitally synthesized tones, it sounded clipped and electronic.

> HAL, the computer in Kubrick's *2001: A Space Odyssey* (1968), pays tribute to that first demonstration of digital speech creation as HAL is turned off in a climactic scene. As his memory modules are slowly pulled out by Dave, HAL regresses mentally, farther and farther back in his evolution, until his final words are the "Daisy Daisy" song, the first thing he ever learned to say.

Outside of the (secretive) research at Bell Labs, there were very few places to study audio. MIT had a few courses in sound.[8] In New York, there was the Columbia-Princeton Electronic Music Center, with a room full of analog synthesizer equipment, which held concerts once in a while. But in general, audio science was not an academic subject.

[4] A long forgotten electronic curiosity, invented in the early 1920s by Russian electrical engineer Leon Theremin, from humming radio tubes.

[5] The analog-to-digital converter, developed and patented by Bernard Gordon, had a number of practical uses. For instance, he could put an electronic thermometer in a machine that changed voltage in response to temperature. The converter could turn the voltage into a number for a mainframe computer to read. It also worked the other way: the computer could produce a number that could be converted into voltage and fed to a motor; the changing number could drive the speed of the motor. There was interest in developing computer control for the motors in airplanes. A potential buyer for Gordon's invention, after a careful study of the product, predicted "there could be a market for ten of these in the world."

[6] Generated on the IBM 7094 by John Kelly and Carol Lockbaum. Accompaniment programmed by Max Mathews.

[7] The song is actually called "Daisy Bell" (1892) by Harry Dacre, and referred to as "A Bicycle Built for Two."

[8] Amir Bose was a grad student there, then professor, before he left in 1964 to start a business developing new stereo speakers that would reproduce the realism of live performances. Modern composer Elliot Carter was also a professor.

Moog's device fascinated many people; but while it made sound, it was harder to say it made music. Its sounds were challenging to control. And it could only play one note at a time. It took a certain kind of musician to explore how music could be made with it. That musician was Walter Carlos, a student at the Columbia-Princeton Center. Carlos also worked as a recording engineer, putting together his own studio complete with a number of Moog modules. He had a clear understanding of what Moog was doing, and he provided copious feedback, "Always on the back of an envelope or over the telephone," said Moog.

Carlos decided that it would be fun and interesting to use the Moog synthesizer modules to record a series of pieces by J. S. Bach, which he set out to play in his new studio. It was tedious work on the huge contraption. Carlos used an enormous state-of-the-art 16-track Ampex tape machine to overlay each line of notes, to build a polyphonic sound (like a chord).[9] The analog tubes in the Moog changed tone as they heated up. It generally took Carlos twenty minutes to set up the equipment to play one three-minute piece, and by the end of playing it once, the tune had drifted; this was a significant drawback of the analog technology. Out of tune like a cheap piano. Carlos had to stop and fiddle with the settings for another twenty minutes in order to prepare another small piece of music. Slowly, he worked through the Bach.

At the Audio Engineering Society (AES) convention in 1968, Moog surprised audiences when, at the conclusion of his presentation of how to set up a multi-track electronic music studio, he said, "I would like to play an excerpt of a record that's about to be released of some music by Bach." He started the tape deck and walked off the stage, to the back of the auditorium, to see what would happen. The last movement of Bach's Brandenburg Concerto No. 3 began to play. It was familiar like Bach, but unmistakably electronic.

"They were jumping out of their skins," Moog recalled. "These technical people were involved in so much flim-flam, so much shoddy, opportunistic stuff, and here was something that was just impeccably done and had obvious musical content and was totally innovative." The tape got a standing ovation."

When Carlos' album *Switched on Bach* came out in 1968, it was a revolution, and it heralded the dawn of electronic music. Winning three Grammy awards, it was the first classical album to be certified platinum. Moog could barely keep his synthesizers in stock. Carlos became a star.[10]

In Palo Alto, California, a Stanford music professor, John Chowning, had invented a new way to digitally synthesize sound, using a method called FM synthesis. He worked on the method with a small number of interested computer

[9] Bach polyphony is often made up of separate monophonic lines, with a chord at the end. Thus Bach works as "multiple-monophonic." In 1968, it would have been much harder to do, for instance, Debussy's "Clare de Lune."

[10] In 1967, before completing the Bach album, Walter underwent sexual reassignment surgery and legally changed his name to Wendy. Wendy Carlos became one of the first (and very few) celebrities not only to undergo a sex change operation, but to present herself and her experience to so much public scrutiny. She continued developing innovative electronic music for a number of years. After completing the soundtrack to Stanley Kubrick's dystopic film *A Clockwork Orange* (1971), however, she disappeared from the public sphere. Ten years later Wendy Carlos returned to her pioneering electronic music, the soundtrack to Disney's *Tron* (1982) and reviving her performing and input into the development of new audio technologies used in music.

and electronics students. FM synthesis was relatively inexpensive to implement on the university's mainframe. From 1966 through 1968, Chowning and his students worked to refine the method and design practical implementations, many of which they patented. The university approached a number of American manufacturers about commercializing the patents, but all passed. The computer that it required was prohibitively expensive, and no manufacturer could be convinced the situation would soon improve.[11]

While Chowning's work was financially constrained, there *was* well-funded digital audio research going on at Stanford. The defense department, while not interested in music, was happy to fund artificial intelligence (AI) projects.[12] AI research was not aimed at imitating behavior, drawing pictures, or making sounds; it was aimed at higher challenges, like *thinking*. This was hopelessly more complicated than even the best computers and software of the day could possibly deal with, even the high-end ones at the AI labs. Because of the AI subfield of speech synthesis, both MIT and Stanford had analog-to-digital converters, an essential component for research in audio, hooked up to their computers.

The Stanford AI Lab (called SAIL) hired a systems programmer from MIT: James "Andy" Moorer. A soft-spoken intellectual, Moorer had spent his life trying to make and understand sound. He was one of those electronics junkie kids of the late 1950s. A teenager in Tallahassee, Florida, when Buddy Holly hit the scene, Moorer used vacuum tubes to build a guitar amplifier. Eventually he studied electronics at MIT, but it was always sound that interested him.

After graduation there were really no jobs to be had, so he went to Stanford to see if he could help get the "intelligent" computers there to speak. After four years, Andy Moorer began working with Chowning, who became his mentor. They found other like-minded individuals, and they created a small research lab for audio, in the style of IRCAM, the new international acoustics lab in Paris.[13] They called it the Center for Computer Research in Music and Acoustics, or CCRMA (pronounced "karma"). It became the hotbed of digital theory applied to sound, and Moorer was its champion.

But even at Stanford, the idea of merging computers and music seemed abstract and futuristic. "We would walk into professors' offices and talk about computer synthesis of music," recalled Moorer, "and they would get this glassy-eyed look and sort of lean back and start talking about their piano teacher when they were ten years old and how Miss Doe was just the sweetest person ever and how they enjoyed it. They couldn't make the leap between their experience of music and what the impact of technology was going to be on music and on entertainment in general."

In 1972, Andy Moorer and his associates put together what is generally acknowledged as the first digital audio workstation; it ran on the University's

[11] A few years later, a simple digital synthesizing device with a keyboard was introduced by Allen Organ Company, which dominated the pipe and church organ market. Allen had entered into a joint venture with North American Rockwell for applying sound research that they had begun on NASA contracts in 1969. The synthesizer was designed to play only organ music. Like the pocket calculator (introduced that same year by Sharp), the Allen Digital Organ was one of the first digital consumer devices. But unlike the calculator, the digital organ did poorly in the marketplace, and it dampened the already limited consumer interest.

[12] Also at MIT.

[13] *Institut de Recherche et Coordination Acoustique/ Musique* (The Institute of Sound and Music Research and Development).

time-share mainframe. One set of instructions could take a sound and make it reverberate realistically, as if it were actually bouncing around in a small room or big auditorium. It was enormously mathematical.

Stanford tried to convince a number of audio companies to build a "reverb" machine to perform the task, which they might use in recording studios to add depth and room tone to studio recordings. As with their FM synthesis inventions, no one was interested. Recalled Moorer, "Every time we added up what you'd have to charge for the device they basically said 'get lost.'"

Moorer needed computers that were designed for handling the mathematical demands of music synthesis, and he tried his "damnedest" to convince DEC (Digital Equipment Corporation) to speed up the arithmetic in their mainframe computers. "I got a series of very snooty messages back...."

While Moorer was having no luck working with computer companies, Stanford was having no luck finding a home for the new audio patents CCRMA was churning out.

Electronic Music Reaches the Masses

[14] Jazz musician Herbie Hancock also became interested in the electronic sound and was not afraid to experiment. Hancock was a child piano prodigy, performing a Mozart piano concerto with the Chicago Symphony Orchestra when he was only 11. He graduated from college with double degrees in music and electrical engineering. After having a hit from his debut album *Takin' Off* (1963), his solo career was cut short when he was offered the chance to play with the Miles Davis Quintet, considered by many to be the greatest small jazz group of the 1960s. He took time to score the soundtrack to Antonioni's new wave landmark film, *Blow Up* (1966), which introduced him to the world of musical film scores. Hancock left the Quartet in 1968 to explore the new electronic jazz funk. In 1973, his album *Headhunters* became the first platinum jazz album.

In spite of *Switched On Bach*'s success, electronic music was still a novelty. But that changed in 1969 when the Beatles released one of the great rock albums of all time, *Abbey Road*. On hit after hit, the Brits integrated electronic sounds and analog synths. But the sounds and synths didn't call attention to themselves, and few people realized how many parts of the album were electronically produced.

It would be four more years before another popular band gave so much commitment to the electronic rock sound. That was Pink Floyd, with *Dark Side of the Moon* (1973), which incorporated many new sounds generated with modular analog synthesizers, most of which only had been experiments before then. Like *musique concrete*, they assembled interesting repeating loops that changed slowly, drifting through cycles of footsteps, airplane sounds, whatever.[14]

Abbey Road (1969), from the Beatles; *Dark Side of the Moon* (1973), from Pink Floyd.

Other bands followed the lead of exploring the unusual sounds a Moog (or other) synthesizer could make, especially when mixed into a traditional rock 'n' roll performance. One was Roxy Music, a collaborative project between art school alum Bryan Ferry and an electronic music pioneer, Brian Eno. In 1973, their band performed on the popular British musical variety show *The Old Grey Whistle Test*.[15]

Teenager Thomas Dolby was up late watching the show. "They had a pretty cool singer," Dolby recalled, "but what really got to me was the keyboard player. He wore very high stacked heels, tight trousers and elbow-length leopard-skin gloves, and stood in front of the control panel of a Moog (no keyboard) with his arms crossed and a very aloof look on his face. Occasionally he would deign to reach forward and adjust a knob slightly.

"[It] was Brian Eno, and I thought, that's all you have to do to make a ton of money and meet lots of girls! I'm gonna become a musician! I was right about the last part about becoming a musician."

Using similar tools, Donna Summer contributed to the disco explosion in her *Love to Love You Baby* album, in particular, "I Feel Love." But Summer, like Pink Floyd and the Beatles, was using the new devices to augment the more traditional instrumental performances: bass and guitar players, drummers, keyboardist.

In Germany, another band, Kraftwerk, began generating pure pop music with no band ensemble and no recognizable instruments—just four guys, each behind a synthesizer. They stood on stage like robots with dizzying light shows around them. They were the first pure electronic music band. But their following was small.

The number of electronic synthesizers sold was small and select—to experimental musicians only. Who else would spend thousands of dollars to have the opportunity to program a few notes into these time-consuming devices?

None of the manufacturers—Powertran, Crumar, Wurlitzer, Moog, Fender—was interested in (or capable of) developing a *digital* synthesizer. By 1975, somewhat in desperation, Stanford approached Yamaha (in Japan); they were thinking about using the FM synthesis in a new line of digital keyboard synthesizers. They initiated a massive development in an attempt to utilize the technology, the core of which was taking the complex software of FM synthesis and turning it into a hardware chip.[16] They produced a device called the DX-7.

At $2,000, the DX-7 was the first commercially viable digital synthesizer and every musician got one. Herbie Hancock got one of the first. Hancock joined with notorious musical architect Bill Laswell to put the synthesizer through its paces.[17] Their first collaboration, *Future Shock,* became Hancock's second platinum album. The single from that album, *Rockit*, won a Grammy and was long-implanted in the R&B and dance charts. Fittingly, *Rockit* was accompanied by a correspondingly outrageous music video, one of the early music videos for MTV, the new music television network.[18] The DX-7 went on to sell more than 200,000 units, ten times more than any synthesizer before or since.

[15] The sixteen-year run for the show made it a music group staple, with a heyday in the early '70s.

[16] It would take seven years.

[17] Along with every analog and new digital device on the market—a Fairlight CMI, a MiniMoog, rhythm machines, vocoders.

[18] The video, which won five MTV awards, was created by musicians Kevin Godley and Lol Crème, founders of the band 10CC.

Word of the brain trust forming at Lucasfilm had already spread in academic communities, to those in both imaging and sound. Ed Catmull had widely distributed an email that Lucasfilm was searching for an audio project leader. Circulating around the artificial intelligence lab at Stanford, it raised a fair amount of interest.

Scientist John Snell had been doing audio research in the Carnegie Mellon AI lab run by Raj Reddy (before coming to Stanford.) Snell was an accomplished musician, sometime lecturer at CCRMA, and founder of the *Computer Music Journal,* an academic quarterly. He had also done engineering on digital audio chips as well as composing and scoring for some short films. When Snell heard that Lucasfilm was looking around, he made a call, and then drove north to Marin for interviews.

Ed and Alvy spoke with John and were impressed both with his experience and his honesty. "They asked me who else I might recommend, and I gave them names of lots of other people," said Snell.

"What do you think of Andy Moorer," Ed asked.

Snell paused. He had been working with Moorer, one of the leading researchers at Stanford, for some time and they knew each other well. Snell had no idea that Lucasfilm had been talking with him, although it made perfect sense.

"There's no one better," Snell said. Both Ed and Alvy glanced at each other.

"Listen," Snell went on. "So-and-so is really great at software…and this other person is really great at mathematics…and this other person is a great electronics engineer. But no one brings together…no one combines all these disciplines as well as Andy Moorer."

Ed and Alvy thanked Snell for his time and interest. Soon they were driving south to Palo Alto, to visit Moorer. They found him hacking away in the shadow of the giant Stanford radio telescope near campus.[19] He had recently returned from a few years at IRCAM in Paris and was again leading the researchers at CCRMA.

Ed and Alvy were met with the kind of reception they would start to experience wherever they showed up.

"If you're here for what I think you're here for," announced Moorer, as Ed and Alvy entered his lab without saying a word, "then the answer is yes."

Like Dorothy working her way toward the Emerald City, one by one Alvy and Ed assembled a happy willing team to walk down this yellow brick road. At the computer level, digital audio and digital video had many similarities. Although audio was mathematically simpler for a computer to process, both were new amalgamations of art and technology, fields that would grow in sophistication as computer cycles and memory continued to become more

JAMES "ANDY" MOORER

Hometown: Tallahassee, FL. *Family:* married, no children (at this time). *Interests:* gourmet cooking (especially eating!), writing music. *Sign:* Sagittarius. *Employment history:* Stanford Computer Music Group, IRCAM.
[From the 1982 LFL Yearbook]

[19] At the DC Power Center, named for a real person: Donald C. Power.

available. Both were oddball fields in the military complex, in the big iron, science-fiction realm of computers. What kind of person could look at the rooms of wires, flashing lights, spinning platters, teletypes and teams of engineers, and believe that the hardware could generate art?

In one way of thinking, Andy Moorer was to audio as Ed Catmull was to graphics. The connection of the two men was the union of digital sound and picture, personified.

By the time Moorer began showing up in Marin, the engineers in the little computer group on Bank Street numbered three. Andy joined Ed, Alvy, and David in the now-overfilled apartment. Malcolm Blanchard would be showing up any day. So would a hardware guy, John Seamons. Ed's new hires, Bill Reeves and Ralph Guggenheim, would both be moving to California—into the group—imminently. Tom Duff would be there in late fall, when he finished his job in Chicago. At Siggraph they had made offers to Carpenter and Porter, who were expected to start in the new year. The group was going to need more space.

Lucasfilm had been remodeling its other commercial property for them in downtown San Anselmo, a short walk from the little apartment. An old laundromat, it was located on Tunstead Avenue, across Sir Francis Drake Blvd., behind the ever-popular Ludwig's Liquor & Smoke Shop. The space needed a fair amount of renovation to turn it into offices.

Since there was so little space on Bank Street, and Andy Moorer still had an office at Stanford, he spent most of his time there, coming north for meetings or when he needed to observe Ben Burtt and the rest of the production sound team.

Downtown San Anselmo. *Left:* Ludwig's Liquor & Smoke Shop. *Right:* The quiet neighborhood walk down Tunstead to the old laundromat.

JOHN MAX SNELL

Hometown: Chapel Hill, NC/New Orleans, LA. *Family:* single & available. *Schools:* Carnegie-Mellon University. *Interests:* Vipassana meditation, hiking, playing music, swimming. *Sign:* Leo. Employment history: Electronics engineer of large computers & signal processors; composer & musician for several short film soundtracks; founder & editor of Computer Music Journal, purchased by the MIT Press. *[From the 1982 LFL Yearbook]*

Moorer's dream was to build a digital audio signal processor, referred to as an ASP, and it finally looked like someone was going to back it. At Stanford, he had worked on an early attempt to build an ASP, a project they called "Hydra," but it never quite materialized. Now, before the end of 1980, every scientist and musician in the digital audio world —including Herbie Hancock, Brian Eno, John Cage, Wendy Carlos, Robert Moog—knew Andy Moorer was at Lucasfilm, and was going to try again.

Moorer was dealing with two primary issues: inventing the ASP, and developing an appropriate paradigm for control—an interface for making and applying sound to movies. He was going to need help and, happily, he invited John Snell.

Snell accepted immediately and joined Moorer on his periodic commutes to Lucasfilm. He was pleased to discover Ralph Guggenheim there. He and Ralph had been friends at Carnegie-Mellon; both shared a friendship with Raj Reddy in the Carnegie-Mellon AI department. And though Snell had lost track of Guggenheim through the NYIT years, they both marveled at the circuitous path each had taken to arrive at the same place.

In Marin, Moorer and Snell began to establish the hardware paradigm for the Lucasfilm ASP. Its primary function was going to be in a mixing theater, where it would handle EQ, and filters, and mix multiple tracks of audio. It would completely replace the giant analog consoles that dominated in the film and music industries.

As the cool snap of fall descended on Marin, the computer guys were ready to move into their own place at Tunstead. Walls had been inserted into the laundromat to make offices, and Lucasfilm installed beautiful worn oak desks (acquired from the public school district) topped with brass desk lamps (of hunter green glass); everything was beginning to be purchased in quantity. Still, they had but one typewriter and, oddly enough, no computers.

Although the space had been customized for the growing computer team, it was still an interim solution. It wasn't nearly big enough, and it was poorly laid out. For instance, Ralph had to walk through Alvy's office to get to his own space. The bathroom was nestled between Ralph's space and Andy Moorer's, and had two doors.

"You had to hold both doors shut when you were in there," said Moorer, "and you couldn't leave some offices if the bathroom was occupied."

According to Susan Anderson, "It was a maze. Honestly."

Ed's understated excitement grew as the team continued to assemble itself at Tunstead, like kids returning to camp for another summer of fun. Susan Anderson, as the only woman and one of the few locals, took it upon herself to acquaint many of the new arrivals to the area.

"They all seemed so young…not naïve, but *fresh*. They were really interested in everything, what was going on at the company, in the area. They were always happy to be in San Anselmo and excited to be at Lucasfilm."

As the Lucasfilm organization began to grow, Jim Kessler took charge of all activities post-production in nature, outside of the effects work at ILM. President Charlie Weber assigned him to supervise the research and development work as well. "I didn't ask for that role," said Kessler, "or seek it." In practice, Jim Kessler had little to say to Ed Catmull, who functioned largely independently of anyone but George.

George had long wanted to use the name "Transamerica Sprocket Works" in his business. He got the chance with the post-production team, calling them Sprocket Systems, or Sprockets for short. It wasn't as sexy as Industrial Light & Magic, but it had a satisfying sort of alliteration, like Lucasfilm Ltd.

Somewhat ironically, the group Kessler supervised at Sprocket Systems had itself a little alliteration: there was **D**uwayne **D**unham and **S**teve **S**tarkey on picture editing, **H**owie **H**ammerman supporting the equipment, **B**en **B**urtt doing sound, with **L**aurel **L**adevich editing sound from time to time.[20]

The computer group, formally referred to as "Sprockets Computer Services," was somewhat isolated, and operated independently from the rest of Sprockets. No one else in the company could understand anything they had to say anyway. Recalled Duwayne Dunham, "These were like two different worlds in the same environment. As soon as they started talking they'd loose me in ten seconds." Catmull ran his small team like a university department. Titles were pointless.

Catmull told the leaders of each group—Alvy, Ralph, and Andy—that they needed them to generate white papers outlining their projects. "With no computers, we had to write our papers in longhand," recalled Ralph. Rather than stumble through his illegible handwriting, he would wait until Susan went to lunch and then hop on her typewriter.

When Malcolm Blanchard got to Tunstead, he stuffed himself in a corner and started the task he was hired to do. It was a small-but-important job—get a computer to handle ILM's project-management problem, which had been straining everyone working on *Empire*.

With some basic research, he learned that when ILM did special effects, the process involved sketching out an idea, getting storyboards prepared, building one or more distinct elements (painting giant mattes, building models, sculpting masks, or combinations of these) and then, once all the parts

[20] And, inexplicably, Gary Summers assisting Burtt—messing up the whole mystical alliteration thing going on with all their names.

were ready, shooting them, and finally compositing them with the optical printer (called an "optical").

Sometimes pieces needed to be redone. Adjust a model. Reshoot the optical because of problems. At any given point in the process it was up to the effects coordinator to know how all the parts were moving along, to know the status of each required shot, and all this was managed by notes, slips of paper, scratchy marks on the storyboard pictures lining the halls of ILM. Each film ILM worked on had more and more effects shots, and each shot was getting more complicated.

At Applicon, Malcolm had learned how to build a database management system, and both he and Ed recognized this as the solution to ILM's problem. The job now was to invent this system and get it working as quickly as possible. There was no way it could be ready for *Raiders of the Lost Ark*, already in the production pipeline, but maybe for the next film after that. Malcolm was in charge of his one-man database project (which he called "Sybil"), while the rest of the team worked out the more far-reaching goals.

Next on the list for Ed, the computer researchers would need computers, ILM would need a computer for Sybil, in fact the whole company was probably going to need computers. But in 1980, there just weren't any platforms he felt comfortable with. Xerox was selling its Star system, an improved execution of the Alto. MIT had a prototype it was trying to shop around. The Three Rivers Computer Corporation was getting established to produce some kind of small workstation. And SUN was still just a twinkle in Andy Bechtolsheim's eye.

Building the digital film printer was perhaps the most significant challenge facing the group. The device on which it was based, an optical printer, consisted largely of three components: a projector, which projects two or more pieces of film; a lens system in the middle; and at the other end, a camera that records a new composite image.

As this was really just an extension of what David DiFrancesco had been doing for years, he was put in charge of building the new "projectors," which, in this case, were "scanners." What was accomplished by the lens system in the middle would need to be reinvented as some kind of digital hardware running special image manipulation software. This was the core of the graphics project and, consequently, Alvy Ray Smith's immediate problem.

DiFrancesco started immediately, figuring out how to get a high-quality image into a computer and then back onto film—settling on laser technology to laserscan in and laserprint out. There was never any question this was the technology ILM needed, although no one was certain it could be done. Triple-I had tried and apparently failed to deliver on a film printer less than a year before.

David had spent the months between NYIT and Lucasfilm learning every-thing he could about lasers, much of it from world famous engineers Gary Starkweather and Raja Balasubramanian. Starkweather was credited as the inventor of the laserprinter; DiFrancesco had known of him from his nights at Xerox. Balasubramanian was widely acknowledged as one of the foremost laser physicists in the world. (When asked what his first name was, he would wrinkle up his face as though like that wasn't a question you asked a proper Indian. "To make us happy," said Alvy, "he had us call him *Bala*.")

Laserprinting on film was different from laserprinting on paper, and it was a big step for David to get his brain around the problem. He worked very closely with the two engineers. Each had a scanning method for which he was noted—each different, each worthy of exploring as the way to get digital images to film. David's relationship with them would prove to be critical to solving the problem.

At Bank Street there had been no room to build a laser or set up computers. There was no room at Tunstead either. But Tunstead was just another waysta-tion. They purchased a VAX 11/780 (the size of a small room) from DEC, and settled on having it shipped in a few months to their new location, wherever that would be.

George Lucas was clear that the optical printer project was critical. He understood that no matter how good a computer might be at creating or compositing images, if the images couldn't be put onto film at high resolu-tion, the entire activity was pointless. DiFrancesco weighed the competing ideas about how a laser could scan. He also built a Styrofoam mock-up of a prototypical laserscanner, to start visualizing how big the thing would need to be and how to orient all the components.

The components were a different problem. Most of them would have to be custom manufactured. David started to identify the best manufacturers (usually German) for the tiny parts he'd need. Each film frame had to be held in place unerringly, and advanced with just as much precision. Even pro-fessional film cameras introduced a little wobble in their photography; this wouldn't do for the scanner. David understood how exacting every element would need to be. He found a film camera expert in Hollywood who helped him design the ultrafine controls.

A laserscanner also needed plumbing. Lasers get so hot that a cooling sys-tem would have to be built. David DiFrancesco was happy to spend his days alternating between laser science, camera mechanics, and good old-fashioned pipe work, as he mulled through the details of getting the computer image on film.

David had a unique position in the group. Although he was a technical whiz, he was not technical. He was an artist by training, not a scientist. He was never the academic that Ed, Alvy, and the others were, yet he somehow learned mountains of detail about technical things, much more than most people could master, whether it was about cars, motorcycles, cameras or, eventually, lasers.

Nowhere in the charter from George Lucas was there anything about using computers for making special effects elements. Nothing about making animated movies. He would comment from time to time that it struck him as impossible for anyone but Disney to produce an animated feature that would make any money. Still, Ed had been clear that these were important to him and central to the work they had been doing for the last decade. Ed and Alvy continued to make annual trips to meet with the technology people at Disney, to learn what they could about the state-of-the art and the process; occasionally they would meet animators. These trips didn't bother Lucas in the slightest.

Ed continued to impose on George his passion about creating and animating 3-D objects. If spaceships were going to fly around on the screen, he'd tell George that it would be from 3-D animation techniques that still needed to be invented. It wasn't in his charter, but Ed periodically titillated George with the fantasy of 3-D. It gave the group some degree of latitude in their research.

"Evolution of a Goblet," by Jim Blinn in 1980, presented a concise visual history of 3-D imaging, from the early '70s to the early '80s. *From left:* wire frame vector image; wire frame vector with hidden line removal; raster image comprised of polygons with lighting and shading; the addition of bicubic patches and smoothing; texture mapping. Blinn expanded on Catmull's texture mapping work, to develop a more realistic result that he called "bump mapping."

Jim Kessler, the team's administrator, popped into Tunstead periodically. One sunny afternoon Kessler took a leisurely walk through downtown San Anselmo; when he arrived in Alvy's office, he plopped into a chair and sat in on a conversation between Alvy, Tom Porter, David DiFrancesco, and Susan Anderson. When it was over there was a pause, as everyone looked over to Kessler, who was listening pleasantly.

"What are you doing?" asked Kessler. "What is all this?"

Tom, David, and Susan started to drift off to their desks while Alvy settled into a short course on computer graphics.

"He explained it to me in a very elementary but very understandable way," said Kessler, "and within about three minutes I totally understood what they had to accomplish, although I had no idea how they were doing it because it was all math."

Kessler pondered the explanation, about modeling and surfaces and light, and looked out the doorway toward Tom Porter, who was making some notes on the wall.

"What about water?" Kessler asked, thinking about his weekend of surfing at Ocean Beach in San Francisco. "How hard is water to do?"

Alvy smiled, like a gauntlet had been tossed on his desk.

"Water is extremely difficult because it is so random. It will take many, many, many generations and many, many, many years of software development to get it to look real."

Kessler was used to projects that took months or maybe a year. It was hard to imagine that these men were embarking on something so enormous. It bordered on frivolous.

Alvy continued, "But when that happens, when we can effectively make water look real, then by that point CG[21] will just be tools that everyone will be using, something commonplace in the industry. It will take at least ten or fifteen years."

Kessler, satisfied with his short seminar, picked himself up from the chair, skirted by Susan with a wave, and was out the front door.

While Ed Catmull was busy pulling together his team at Lucasfilm, his long-time intellectual competitor Gary Demos was at Triple-I, still pushing to get computer graphics into movies. Demos had inspired prolific novelist-turned writer/director Michael Crichton when they met during *Futureworld*.[22] While it wasn't a moneymaker, *Futureworld* had the distinction of being the first major motion picture to include a snippet of 3-D animation (Peter Fonda's head).[23] As Crichton watched the primitive CG come together in that film—it also incorporated Ed Catmull's rotating hand—Demos told Crichton, "You know, we're starting to be able to simulate actors."

So Crichton, always interested in telling stories based on new scientific realities, made up a tale he derived from that premise; he called it *Looker*. ILM briefly considered bidding on the effects in *Looker*. Catmull looked at the proposal and script and agreed with ILM that they should pass on it.

Soon, Crichton hired his friends at Triple-I—already in pre-production for Disney's *Tron*—to execute a series of computer generated effects for his sci-fi flick, starring James Coburn and featuring *Partridge Family* actress

[21] Computer graphics.

[22] **Michael Crichton** (b. 1942). Novelist/filmmaker. Screenwriter: *Andromeda Strain* (1971), *Jurassic Park* (1993). Writer/director: *Westworld* (1973), *Coma* (1978), *Looker* (1981), *Runaway* (1984).

[23] About a year ahead of Larry Cuba's sequence in *Star Wars*.

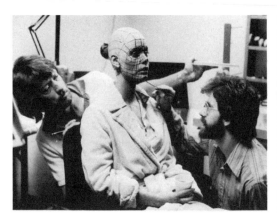 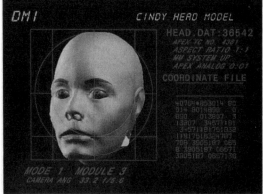

Left: Larry Malone and Art Durinski prepare actress Susan Dey for data-capture photography to use as the model for the "Cindy" database in *Looker. Right:* Still frame from *Looker,* showing 3-D model face.

Susan Dey. Demos simulated Dey's face and body, and created the "Looker effect," which recurred periodically throughout the film. When *Looker* was released in 1981, Catmull sat in the theater, comfortable with the decision not to be involved with the film, and contemplating the converging paths that he and Demos seemed to be on.

Catmull finally had the core of his three projects established, with Alvy Ray Smith running the graphics group, Andy Moorer sound, and Ralph Guggenheim on editing.

For Ralph, creating a cohesive team for the editing project would be critical to pulling off its development, but compared with the other two, he was somewhat at a disadvantage. Both Alvy and Andy were PhDs, had effectively run teams or departments, and could easily draw on vibrant academic communities to build the group they would need to execute their projects. Ralph had no associates to bring to the team; there was little existing research in the field and, worst of all, his project was a mismatched hybrid of disciplines: film, broadcasting, and electronics, as well as computers.

Unlike image or sound processing, editing had to work in real time—sequences needed to play at 24 frames per second. And you couldn't just build one digital frame, you needed thousands, millions, in order to be useful. It would be impossible to use digital video for editing for at least another decade, Ralph needed to build an analog editing tool for George. But the computers and media he'd require were still in the process of being invented.

Ed had placed Ralph on the laserdisc path, but it was proving impossible to get any laserdisc players out of DiscoVision Associates (DVA, the primary developers of the videodisc technology) with which to experiment. He needed to connect a prototypical player to a newly invented computer; exactly what kind of computer was yet another problem.

Ralph continued to wrestle with the very few commercially available graphical workstations. Because of his familiarity with Three Rivers (where he had spent the summer prior to joining Lucasfilm), he selected their new minicomputer, the PERQ (pronounced "perk").

After Ralph had been working on the editing project for a week or so, he met with George.

"We chatted a little bit about editing. I wouldn't say he had any particular words of wisdom about how he wanted it to work, although he really suggested I take a look at how their negative cutters worked, and how their editing rooms worked, so that I could understand the whole thing.

Top: A detail of the toothed wheel, showing frame numbers that line up with every four sprockets. *Bottom*: A traditional film synchronizer pulling picture and sound along together.

"I saw the same film equipment [at Lucasfilm] that I'd used in the university public relations office. They had the same synchronizers and rewinds and split reels and all that stuff. It was just as disorganized as any of the shows I had run, except they were doing everything on a bigger scale. They showed me the logbooks and how they kept their shots organized and it was just mind-boggling. What it showed me was that the most important guy in the editing room is the assistant editor."

While the editing rooms at San Anselmo Avenue (where Paul Hirsch and the boys were cutting *Empire*) may have struck Ralph as archaic, they were the norm for the industry—from the smallest commercial to the biggest film. It was Ralph's job to channel George's frustration with the industrial age equipment and apply some modern technology.

As Coppola had once pointed out, film editing was the paragon of evolution in the industrial age. Film was pulled along into a machine by a claw-arm, steadied with a pin, exposed with a flash from a shutter, then moved again, twenty-four times every second. Archaic, perhaps, but it was mechanically perfect. Videotape, on the other hand, was in its infancy. It was bound to have initial disadvantages, but it was clearly the electronic age's first steps to replacing celluloid.

Ed Catmull had sketched out a design for an editing system and presented it to Ralph when they first got together (before the 4th of July picnic). Now Ralph was working to execute it.

Ed's configuration began with a minicomputer running a database. Connected to this would be some number of videodisc recorder/players (although no one had yet invented a recorder/player and neither Ed nor Ralph was sure when or if it ever might happen). The videodisc companies told a good story, but even if they could deliver on their promise, the prices would no doubt be prohibitive for many years.

The most attractive attribute of a videodisc was the speed of cueing to any desired frame. Even at full tilt, a videotape machine might shuttle through thirty minutes of video in about four minutes. If the editor wanted to be able to watch the video as it shuttled, it would take closer to ten minutes. A disc, by contrast, could pop from the first frame to the last in a second and a half, and you could fast-forward through the entire disc while watching it in less than a minute.

A videodisc was an almost-perfect simulation of what it would be like to edit digital video. Videodiscs also supported fairly good image quality; although not quite professional standard, it was better than consumer VCRs and would certainly suffice for making creative decisions.

With the editing architecture that Ralph was considering, an editor could use the same raw video copied to two identical discs, which could then "play leapfrog" to smoothly play an edited sequence even before all the discrete shots were recorded to a videotape. With one machine alone, a shot would be played, then the sequence would pause while the disc cued up the next shot. With a pair of machines, the second one could cue up and wait for the first disc to finish playing. Over and over. Suddenly it would appear that all the individual shots were connected.

In this way, two discs of raw video could simulate the edits someone would want to make without ever needing to record to videotape—thus avoiding the tedium of videotape editing. When combined with the blisteringly fast access an editor had to any frame of material, the most laborious part of editing would virtually disappear.

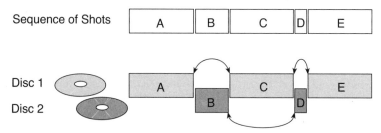

With a series of shots (A through E) cut together, they can be played back from two discs. Disc 1 plays shot A, Disc 2 plays shot B, and while B is playing, Disc 1 re-cues to play shot C, and so on.

Videodiscs

A videodisc was an analog recording on a silver platter read by a small helium/neon laser or, more commonly, an infrared diode (LED) laser. Invented in the late 1950s, by the early 1970s they were commercially introduced by two companies simultaneously: MCA in the United States and Philips in the Netherlands. Rather than face off in a format war, MCA and Philips decided to team up and standardize videodisc recording. In 1974, they announced the LaserVision format.

Within a year, Sony, Philips, and Hitachi announced their research into laser optical audio discs—*digital* audio discs. Digital made sense for sound, but it was not feasible for moving video, and no commercial research into digital video was underway. In 1977, after three years of development, the first LaserVision videodisc players were sold to the educational market. MCA teamed up with Pioneer electronics in a new joint-venture, the Universal-Pioneer Corporation, to mass-produce LaserVision videodisc players. But in spite of their efforts to avoid a format war, Magnavox introduced its own format, Magnavision. By 1980, it was clear that videodisc technology was superior to both the Beta and VHS ½-tape formats, but there was no clear standard, and the problem lingered as to how consumers could record discs. It was never satisfactorily solved.

The theoretical snag of this process involved the length of each shot and the time it sometimes took to find a shot on a disc. In the above example, if shot B was very short, say 10 frames, it would be likely that Disc 1 wouldn't have enough time to "leap," and locate the beginning of shot C. In the worst case, it took a second and a half for the laser to move from one shot to the next. A second and a half equals 45 video frames, and editors often used bits of video that were far shorter, sometimes 30 frames, sometimes 10. Two discs could not be guaranteed to be able to leapfrog through a sequence of 10 frame edits.

Ralph's plan was to use *three* discs. Three discs would work in most editing situations, for all but the fastest cuts of the shortest shots. The editing computer could show any sequence an editor wanted to see, strategize the best way to play it, schedule it, and preview it (or much of it). And if the system couldn't handle a scene because of fast cuts, there was always the option of falling back to a videotape recorder, to dump off small parts of the scene. By putting source material on videodisc, the entire process fell together. If only discs weren't so impossible to find, so expensive to record, and so inflexible to modify.

Ralph was happy to be using the PERQ for the editing system, but the other scientists were planning on working with the new VAX they had ordered. John Seamons, having left the SUN project, was busy developing a version of UNIX to run on it. As well as being comfortable with hardware, he was a UNIX expert like Tom Duff, and he was going to be a necessary component of every project. All of the scientists would need time on the VAX and eventually, it was figured, they would all need their own computers. What they really needed was a slew of individual workstations, but none of the products in the field, in particular from Seamons' old cohorts at SUN, was yet commercially viable.

A Not-So-Brief History of Microcomputers

In 1968, Robert Noyce and another engineer, Gordon Moore, founded Intel. Almost ten years earlier at Fairchild, Noyce had invented the IC (integrated circuit) chip, which allowed for the miniaturization of computers. Intel focused on making IC chip memory practical and affordable. Hundreds of these kinds of memory chips could be used, for instance, to make up the frame buffers that E&S would sell to hold an image. Intel grew its company for many years on the strength of the IC memory chip.

When a Japanese calculator company approached Intel in 1971 about designing a set of chips to run a programmable calculator, an engineer on the team decided that instead, he could design a single, general-purpose logic chip that could utilize information stored in the Intel memory chips.[24] Using the techniques they had pioneered for transistor miniaturization, Intel fit 2,300 transistors on a chip that was a fraction of an inch square—the first CPU.

[24] Ted Hoff, who later joined the Atari corporate research group under Alan Kay.

When the Japanese company ran into financial problems, Intel bought back the rights and began to mass-produce the chips. The CPU chip could manage a piece of information stored in 4 bits. The number of bits represented the largest piece of information the CPU could handle at one time. 4 bits—or 2 to the 4th power—could allow the computer to count to 16. It wasn't much. In 1972, Intel upgraded the chip to 8 bits, or 256. Still small, but it was at least functional. One 8-bit CPU chip cost $360. Two years later Intel released a more sophisticated, faster CPU, the 8080. It was ten times faster than their previous version.

A businessman in Albuquerque, New Mexico, Ed Roberts, began selling a kit of parts, (including the Intel 8080) that would allow any electronically minded hobbyist with a soldering iron, a workbench, and about a hundred hours, to make a computer. Science fiction at home! He called the computer the Altair,[25] and he got it on the cover of *Popular Electronics*. Guys went crazy for the toy. They could spend hours building it, and then hook it up to turn on and off a little light, or eventually make a teletype machine write letters. It could do little math problems. It could even be made to count. Hours of fun. Users still needed to master toggling switches on or off to give the computer a single instruction, which was part of the fun, but also slow and tedious.

In 1964 two Dartmouth faculty wrote a little computer language that made it easier to tell a CPU how to do something. They called their language BASIC; by the mid-'70s it was readily available to the public. BASIC needed to be modified for every model of CPU, and many enterprising computer scientists applied themselves to the task.

Ed Roberts wanted to provide his customers with a version of BASIC for the Altair. He found a pair of young computer geeks who said they had already built a version of BASIC for the Intel 8080. Roberts gave the kids a month to deliver their software, while he waited for new Altair kits to get set up with more memory chips, enough to hold a programming language like BASIC.

It turned out that the kids, Bill Gates and Paul Allen, had exaggerated. They hadn't *really* written BASIC for the 8080 chip—they had never even seen one. What they had was the confidence that they could do it. Paul Allen knew how to program the DEC computer at the Harvard Computer Science department. And what he did was program the DEC to do everything an Intel 8080 chip could do.

There's a thin veil between hardware and software. Usually, anything you can do in hardware can be done in software. Allen wrote an "emulator"—a computer simulation of a CPU chip. Once he had an emulator for the 8080, Bill Gates cobbled together a version of BASIC that would run on it. When Paul Allen showed up in Albuquerque with a paper tape of BASIC, it worked perfectly on the Altair. Paul Allen joined Ed Roberts' company, MITS,[26] and soon Bill Gates dropped out of Harvard and moved to Albuquerque as well.

Soon, Gates and Allen formed "Micro Soft,"[27] which owned the rights to modify BASIC to run on other newly minted microprocessors (from Intel's growing legion of competitors). They continued to license MITS to sell their BASIC as part of the Altair. MITS was also getting competitors. A couple of engineers left Intel to form Zilog, releasing the Z-80 to compete with the Intel 8080. By 1977, others had joined the fray, from Commodore with their PET computer, to Radio Shack with their TRS-80 (referred to as the "trash-80" by grumpy consumers).

[25] Named by his daughter from a location in the *Star Trek* television show.

[26] Model (or Micro) Instrumentation Telemetry Systems, Ed Roberts' electronics kits company.

[27] Presumably being a company that would make "microcomputer software." It would become one word a year later, when they trademarked the name (Nov. 1976).

In California, no sooner was the Altair on the cover of *Popular Electronics* than Steve Wozniak bought himself an Intel competitor, a supercheap CPU called the 6502 and wrote his own version of BASIC for it.[28] When Woz demonstrated the little computer he had built, his friend Steve Jobs convinced him to team up, upgrade the product, and sell it to the local microprocessor geeks at the Homebrew Computer Club. They renamed it the "Apple," far more approachable than either the robotic sounding "Zilog-80" or the science-fictiony "Altair."

In April 1976, Jobs pulled together a little money and he and Woz started Apple Computer Company. The Apple-1 was just a CPU board; the customer would build a little box to put the hardware into, and add a power supply and keyboard. Woz continued to refine it and by May 1977 was ready to ship the Apple II. It had an all-in-one design, with keyboard and computer in one attractive case; it also had an open architecture, which allowed other people to build boards that would plug into it. But best of all, you could plug it into a television set and put colors, sound, and text on the screen. Everyone wanted an Apple.

The Intel 8080, the Altair, and other "clones" could all run BASIC, but they needed an operating system on which the entire structure could be hung. The operating system is the first information that has to be fed into a computer before it can understand the higher-level complexities of a language.[29] The dominant operating system of the day was Gary Kildall's CP/M.[30] He invented CP/M in the years before the Altair was released, but it wasn't until the Altair and its clones began creating a big microcomputer market that he built a company to license CP/M, which he called Digital Research, Inc (DRI).[31]

For the next many years, virtually every computer brand ran DRI's operating system, and Microsoft's software languages, in particular, BASIC.[32] Even the Apple II had a plug-in card that allowed it to run CP/M.

By 1979, microcomputers could be found everywhere: in hobbyists' homes and some offices. There was a fair amount of rudimentary software that would allow users to type and draw a bit. The spreadsheet software VisiCalc was the original "killer app" that allowed a microcomputer to very inexpensively do something that even the DEC minicomputers couldn't do. VisiCalc was written for the Apple II, but soon was available on many microcomputers. For $2,500 or so, a business could have a turnkey system for handling the accounting and spreadsheet work they had been doing longhand (at small companies) or on mainframes with punch cards (at big companies). Even if the device did nothing else, it was a revolution.

IBM was trying again to jump into the microcomputer business after a couple of misinformed product releases. In a business deal that has become legend, Microsoft beat out DRI to provide an operating system for IBM. Microsoft didn't really have a competitor to CP/M, but they had met Tim Patterson, a young software programmer at Seattle Computer Products, who had written his own operating system for his prototype of Intel's 8086 CPU. He called it his "quick and dirty operating system" or QDOS. Seattle Computer Products sold QDOS to Microsoft for $50,000. Microsoft turned around and licensed it to IBM, renamed as MS-DOS. The brilliance of the deal was that they got IBM to agree to let them market and sell MS-DOS on their own computers as well.

[28] The MOS Technology 6502 cost around $20, versus the almost $400 Intel 8080, and in many ways it was comparable or better.

[29] The operating system allows a computer to drive a floppy disk for input or output, making it easy to move software from one computer to another. A floppy disk, although expensive, was cheaper than a teletype machine or a paper-tape feeder.

[30] "Control Program[for] Microcomputers."

[31] Kildall initially called the company "Intergalactic Digital Research" but changed the name as his business grew.

[32] Atari, Commodore, and Radio Shack actually had their own versions.

Over the previous few years, the big shift had been from the omnipresent expensive mainframes that dotted big industry, defense and academia, down to the "mini-computers." With a mini-computer, like the DEC PDP-11, there was a microchip on a board, which was the central brain, and the entire machine was relatively small.

True, it couldn't do everything a mainframe could do, but it could do a lot, and for a fraction of the size and price. For around $20,000, a fairly powerful computer could be mounted in a rack that sat in your office for your own personal use.

The new low-cost, low-power *micro*computers, available in kits for hardcore geeks, wouldn't replace a DEC anytime soon, but they represented an interesting aspect of where all this might go.

Ed and Alvy tried to put a stake in the ground for new hardware at a time when the swirling technological chaos made predictions that were, at best, only guesses. One thing was for sure: everything was getting better all the time. They were counting on it.

fourteen

Obnoxio

[1980 to 1981]

The lyf so short, the craft so long to lerne; Th'assay so hard, so sharp the conquering.

—Geoffrey Chaucer (c. 1380)

CHANGE WAS IN THE AIR, again.

Toward the end of 1980, things were getting a little lavish at the Egg Company, Lucasfilm's headquarters in Los Angeles. There was a proliferation of middle managers. The executives were driving Porsches. So were the secretaries. It just didn't feel right.

Lucas decided that it would be a good idea for company headquarters to be close to the filmmaking in Marin instead of to the market in Hollywood. Maybe it was to keep a closer eye on the business, or maybe it was Lucas' deep long-held feelings about being a Northern Californian, but one day he informed Charlie Weber that headquarters was going to be relocating.

Weber called all his division heads together at the Egg Company and read a memo from Lucas that said the offices would be closing and moving north. As soon as Weber finished reading the note, he announced his own resignation.[1]

"Shock waves ran through the place," reported *Star Wars* fan club president Ira Friedman. "People didn't know what to expect. Would they be asked to relocate *up north*? Would they even want to, if asked?" As it turned out, few of the L.A. staff was asked to make the move.

Lucas was as busy as ever getting ready for the third *Star Wars* film, now called *Revenge of the Jedi*, and was relying on Bob Greber to keep his fiscal house in order. In short order, Greber stepped into the CEO position. "It's a bit of a misnomer being CEO of Lucasfilm," he commented recently, "because George was always the CEO; he was the owner. He could listen to his board of advisors or not, and that was always his decision."

Gary Kurtz, Lucas' long-time associate, had accepted responsibility for budget problems on *Empire* but never fully regained Lucas' trust. Their

[1] Charlie Weber joined TV producers Norman Lear and Jerry Perenchio to form Embassy Communications (another in a string of Lear entertainment companies), which produced *Blade Runner* (1982). Embassy was sold to Coca-Cola in 1985.

ROBERT GREBER

Hometown: Philadelphia.
Family: wife Judith, children
Matt & Jon. Schools: Temple
University. *Sign:* Pisces.
Interests: horses, photography.
Employment history: Merrill
Lynch, Pierce, Fenner &
Smith VP/Manager, Regional
Institutional Office; lost
money for all my clients,
individuals and institutions;
then lost George's money
and to keep me from losing it
all they made me president.
[1982 LFL Yearbook]

relationship had long been drifting. More than almost anyone at Lucasfilm, Kurtz had watched Lucas evolve through the successes, through the explosive growth of the company, to a place Kurtz was no longer comfortable. When he saw Lucas' excitement over Spielberg's thrill-ride filmmaking in *Raiders*, and realized what this might mean to the next *Star Wars* film, he and Lucas parted ways. Kurtz accepted a position he felt was more challenging, producing Jim Henson's foray into non-Muppet fantasy, which would become *The Dark Crystal* (1982).

Bob Greber closed most of the offices in the Egg Company (legal department, accounting and finance, publicity), but retained the property, renting out spaces to compatible businesses and reserving some of it for Lucasfilm. Judging by how the building had been used in the past, they might still need it in the future. Lucas had periodically held screen tests for films in the large lobby. Spielberg and his producing associates had holed up in the atrium for months, casting *Raiders*. Lucasfilm marketing continued to maintain an office there, but Greber and his new CFO, Roger Faxon, moved to the new offices in Marin.

Most of the company slowly relocated into buildings on Kerner Blvd. in San Rafael, near ILM. Between ILM and the small one-story structure used for administrative offices was an empty lot. A drainage canal ran under Kerner and through the wooded space nestled between the buildings; it was mostly filled with auto run-off and other industrial slime, on its way to the bay.

Tom Smith, the division leader of ILM, stood in front of their offices talking to Jim Kessler about the area. Kessler described their interaction:

"I hear they're going to build something in this space," Kessler said.

"Oh, man, you can't let them do that," replied Smith.

"Why not?"

"It could end up a Toys R Us or something. D'ya want a toy store next door to ILM?"

The property owner already had plans for a building on the site and was only months away from starting construction when Lucasfilm purchased it.

"Mostly because we needed more space," said Kessler, "and a little bit because the idea of a Toys R Us rattled a few people."

Design began at once to generate a building for the post-production work. Unlike the rest of the Lucasfilm offices, it would have neither a Victorian look nor old world detail.

"George liked the fact that we were alone on San Anselmo Avenue, and we liked that too," recalled Lucas' assistant Duwayne Dunham. "During *Empire*, there was nobody running around, it was just us." George liked the editing suites near his home, but he didn't like crossing town to check on ILM. Having post-production next to the effects areas could be appealing. Lucas asked Dunham to work with the designers to make sure there were appropriate spaces for editorial.

The second floor was spec'd out with numerous editing room, showers, and a big kitchen. "That was the beauty of San Anselmo Avenue," said Dunham. "That was the beauty of Parkway. They were designed so we could go play tennis at lunchtime, and come back and have a place to shower, and we could eat there. These were homes, and had a homey feel to them. Fireplaces, and all that."

Lucasfilm now owned three buildings in a row along Kerner Boulevard; with the new one inserted among them, it was almost a campus. The four very different structures became known as buildings A, B, C and D. ILM occupied D, farthest from the corner. The cute little one-story stucco house hidden from the street by a row of short evergreens was B. The two-story office building with Marin-like informality, sitting on the corner and used for administration was A. The new building was C.

C Building was envisioned as a functional Northern California workspace to house a lot of creative people. Still, someday they would all move up to the Ranch.

ILM wasn't ever going to move to the Ranch. It required too much interaction with the rest of the world; it needed to be a faster hop to civilization than the winding Lucas Valley Road provided. But mostly, it employed too many people to fit within the zoning of the Ranch property. The Ranch was built on agricultural and ranch land, and was only allowed a limited number of employees per acre. Even with the large amount of acreage, the quantity of artisans at ILM would push the limits. Consequently, once the Ranch was finished, ILM would inherit most of the Kerner complex.

TOMLINSON HOLMAN

Hometown: Illinois. *Family:* single. *Interests:* cooking, movies, sailing. *Sign:* Aldebaran. *Employment history:* Univ. of Illinois Motion Picture Production Center Droid 1967–73; Advent Corporation 1973–77, Chief Engineer; Apt Corporation 1977–81, Director of Engineering.

[1982 LFL Yearbook]

Producer Howard Kazanjian went from handling *Raiders* directly into ramping up efforts for *Jedi*; he was prepared to mix the sound in L.A. at Goldwyn Sound, as Kurtz had done on *Star Wars* and *Empire*.

"It could be done for a lot less money up here," suggested Kessler. "We're designing this building anyway, so let's include a mixing theater."

Kazanjian deferred the decision to Lucas, and so Kessler made his pitch: "Why don't we do this because, if nothing else, it'll be a breakeven in cost. Anyway, we're thinking about having a technical building at the Ranch. Wouldn't it be a good idea to make our mistakes in *this* building…?" Lucas agreed that was good reasoning.

Lucas was interested in bringing in Murch's cousin, Tom Scott, to supervise the movie sound engineering needs of C Building. Kessler lobbied for someone with broader experience. After a year of searching through the professional sound community, Kessler discovered inventor Tom Holman, who had been the chief electrical engineer for Advent in the 1970s. He had been the protégé of Henry Kloss, the man responsible for popularizing "hi-fi" sound and inventor of many of the original compact and portable stereo systems.[2] After Advent, Holman founded Apt Corporation, which created the Holman preamplifier, a device that further refined the work he had done at Advent. By the late '70s Holman's name was synonymous in professional circles with the highest quality audio.

The first phase of Holman's work would be the new sound mixing environments for the dubbing stage. "Bring a new level of quality to film post-production," said George to Tom. C Building was his canvas.

As construction was coming together, it was clear that the attractive redwood C Building, even with the added theater and dubbing stage, was going to have plenty of office space. The rooms on the second floor were coming out so well that everyone wanted them. It was natural for Kessler to earmark many of them for the computer group—ostensibly working on post-production issues. For the year of construction they'd need to settle in somewhere, but eventually they would be co-habitating with the people cutting picture and mixing sound.

The company was growing larger, and while it was good for Lucasfilm, it posed some problems for Lucas.

"George is the kind of guy who likes to know everybody's name," said Duwayne Dunham. "And he didn't know everybody's name."

Editing his movies in editing rooms around computer scientists felt like too much of the wrong kind of interaction. Lucas' editing area was relocated to the first floor, along a corridor that could be locked at both ends and accessed from the side parking lot facing ILM.

"George liked that he would be able to walk back and forth [from editing to ILM] easily, and that he wouldn't have to see anybody."

Until C Building was completed, Ben Burtt's team could stay in San Anselmo, but "Sprockets Computer Services" was bursting out of the old laundromat on Tunstead. Greber soon found a couple of buildings off Commercial Blvd. in a new industrial park in the town of Ignacio, on the northern end of Marin County, where Highway 101 veered and Highway 37 broke over to Napa. (Lucas passed it occasionally on his way to Coppola's vineyard.)

"No one wanted to go at first," commented Susan Anderson, "and the space got a bad rap because everyone else was staying in San Anselmo."

They referred to the area by the name of a main artery nearby, "Bel Marin Keys," which made it sound pretty and coastal, which wasn't the case. Although the Kerner region of San Rafael was lightly industrial, the northern edge of Marin was hot, more exposed, and by comparison a bit dull. Their building was L-shaped, with a small parking lot in back by a roll-up door. The

[2] Advent was known for its audio components, but it produced the first large screen—6 feet wide—projection television invented by company founder Henry Kloss. Kloss had previously founded KLH and later co-founded Cambridge Soundworks. (It was said his brilliance at invention was not always matched by acumen at business.) Kloss had helped launch the cassette deck, and in 1968 talked Ray Dolby into developing a consumer noise reduction system, "Dolby B." It was the combination of convenience and high-fidelity as provided from the noise reduction and improved chromium dioxide tape that made the tape cassette such a remarkable success. Kloss moved into projection video, his true passion, and Holman dug deeper into acoustical research to determine how sound amplifiers could move from the traditional "tubes" toward the newer transistor variations and still maintain quality acoustics.

computer teams would fill one end of it, using the roll-up door to get large machinery inside.

Alvy Ray Smith didn't like the space. It was large. Clean, but impersonal. At least Tunstead was in a beautiful little village, as was Bank Street. Now they were getting downright Silicon Valley and it was unpleasant. Commented Anderson, "Alvy just didn't want to be away from the action."

Alvy wouldn't call the area Bel Marin Keys. The name of the town was Ignacio, but he often called it "Obnoxio."

Lucasfilm's new Skywalker Development Company hired a full-time glass designer, Eric Christensen, for all the stained glass that would be needed at the Ranch. He moved into the other end of the L-space at Bel Marin Keys and established a workshop. It was going to be a massive project, perhaps years of work for him and a number of other artisans. At the outset, it was decided that once the Ranch was completed the glass shop would continue doing commercial work (not entirely unlike the evolving plan for the computer researchers).

Sketches of ornate Victorian windows and skylights began flowing from Bel Marin Keys to George and Marcia. The scope of the project was immense. By late in 1980 the first cluster of new structures at the Ranch was almost completed, and ready for the first glass installations.

Marcia and her Design Division did their best to deliver the Lucas touch to the computer group's offices in Bel Marin Keys. Everyone appreciated the attention she gave to making the place homey and comfortable. Hunter green carpeting replaced the cheap grey weave. The offices along the main corridor behind reception were outfitted with the brass-and-green-glass desk lamps that were rapidly becoming a company staple. The building was retrofitted to include leaded glass windows to warm up a lounging area. With little exception, the scientists were very happy in their souped-up space.

A nearby warehouse was used for furniture receiving and storage; it was filled with the oak desks that were being peppered throughout Lucasfilm. Marcia instructed the guys to put Post-Its to indicate who wanted what. Ralph and Malcolm found an old elk head in the back of the storage area and put it up in their office. They called it "Lawrence Elk."[3]

Lucasfilm used one of the office areas at Bel Marin Keys for the finance department. They used another as a warehouse for Lucasfilm toys. Whenever a *Star Wars* licensee created a product, they were obligated to send a box of the item to Lucasfilm. These boxes—of Millennium Falcon lunchboxes and Darth Vader Jell-O molds, of comic books and Kenner action figures—piled up without end. Ultimately they were stored in the warehouse, periodically subjected to the covert perusal of the computer guys.

[3] But later they changed its name to "John Deer" after a John Deere tractor hat was placed on its head.

Susan Anderson was attractive and lively and everyone liked her. Outgoing and a social catalyst, she dated here and there, and she also brought her girl-friends by to meet the guys. This made her the life of their geeky parties. For the time, she enjoyed being the only girl in a male-dominated office. By the time everyone was re-situated in their new location, Catmull's divorce was behind him. The soft-spoken Catmull insulated himself so well that it was some time before anyone noticed the effect that Susan had on him.

Slowly, she drew Ed out of his quiet shell, and he began to show genuine care for her and her new son. Rumors circulated that they were seen hold-ing hands in a park in central Marin. People began noticing them standing together at gatherings. They saw Ed loosening up a little. Maybe more affable than usual.

"Think Susan had anything to do with that?" asked Alvy rhetorically. "I do." The changes were welcomed.

Lucasfilm took pride in being a big family. When job openings occurred, it was always natural for word to spread through the staff to fill the posi-tion with someone's sister, friend, or roommate.[4] At the company Christmas party in 1980, George and Marcia were honored to hand out *Empire Strikes Back* bonus checks to every employee, whether they participated directly in the film or not. The maintenance staff got checks. The security guards. The computer guys.

Susan Anderson was a single mom with a broken-down car, and still struggling to get by. "I joined Lucasfilm in November and *Empire* came out in May," she remembered, "and I still got a big enough bonus to get a new car. Lucasfilm was just a wonderful place to be."

The year before, Lucas' friends Hal Barwood and Matthew Robbins wrote a story about a dragon that was terrifying medieval peasants. Titled *Drag-onslayer*, it was being turned into a feature film by Paramount and Disney, with Robbins directing.[5] The star of the film, a dragon, was going to require serious special effects. Robbins approached ILM. It would be the division's first outside project.[6]

At first they built a giant mechanical dragon, but its movements weren't fluid enough to be realistic. A miniature would be required, but hand-ani-mating the hundreds of shots would be impractical, and besides, ILM's stop-motion technique looked unnatural.

Stop-motion animation—snapping a picture of a model, moving it, snap-ping another picture—resulted in a fake-looking film; this was true for every movie that had used the technique since *King Kong* (1933).[7] And it was pain-fully slow. If they were going to get *Dragonslayer* done on time, they needed something faster.

[4] When one of Marcia's assis-tants needed maternity leave, Marcia began asking around for references for a new assis-tant. Loren Carpenter's wife Rachel volunteered.

[5] Robbins' earlier film, *Corvette Summer* (1978) was also written by Robbins and Barwood, and starred Mark Hamill (his first project after *Star Wars*).

[6] Walter Murch agreed to work on the sound.

[7] Think Ray Harryhausen's remarkable miniatures in *The Seven Voyages of Sinbad* (1958). His famous animated skeleton sequence in *Jason and the Argonauts* (1963) took 4½ months to create.

Animator Phil Tippett came up with a plan: he attached metal rods to the dragon and moved the rods by hand; a computer connected to the rods captured the dragon's locations. Then, by playing back the program, the dragon was re-animated with fluid motion. The process was not only faster than stop-motion, there was an added benefit: models could be photographed while moving, giving miniature photography a natural blur. This innovation allowed the dragon to flap its wings (or, they anticipated, spaceships to zoom around like dog fighting airplanes) with a heightened sense of realism. Tippett called the technique "Go-Motion."

Ed Catmull watched the process with interest. Creating motion blur in 3-D computer animation was something he had been working on for years. Integrating blur would be as important to the graphics team as it was to ILM.

By early 1981, Catmull's three-pronged, three-year project had become well-defined. Alvy Ray Smith, as director of Computer Graphics Research, was charged with creating the digital film printer and its system for image compositing of the blue screen effects shots from ILM. For this he needed a hardware component—a new high-speed computer to manage the film image processing and compositing—plus lasers for the input and output of the high-resolution images.

Ralph Guggenheim, as director of Editing Research, had been working alone on the editing project before he got approval to bring in some teammates. At John Snell's suggestion, Ralph first made an offer to Dan Silva, a programmer who had a master's degree in mechanical engineering from Stanford and had gone on to work at PARC, developing their Xerox Star computer workstation.[8] Catmull had considered the Star briefly as a Lucasfilm workstation, but it was too new in its evolution. Still, Silva knew his way around minicomputer systems and had a brewing interest in graphics. The graphics team didn't have an opening, so he agreed to work with Ralph on the editing software.

The other job offer was to Clark Higgins.

Higgins was a transplant from Francis Coppola's team. He had met Alvy Ray Smith at Coppola's Interface Conference, and when Alvy called to check out his interest, he was ready for a change. He had been commuting every week to Zoetrope's Hollywood General studio in L.A., living out of a suitcase, and was not all that happy about it. Higgins was deeply passionate about helping Coppola build the "studio of the future," but he was confident the project would be steady in his absence. *One From the Heart* was on schedule in pre-production and, besides, he was an avid *Star Wars* fan.

"Clark had always been interested in extra-terrestrials," commented Thomas Brown, "and Lucasfilm was the closest thing to that he could get."

[8] The Xerox "Star" Information System, introduced in April 1981, had a bitmapped screen, windows, mouse-driven interface, and icons. It was more evolved than the system it descended from, the Alto (1972).

CLARK HIGGINS

Hometown: Seattle, WA.
Family: single. Schools:
University of Washington.
Interests: film, video, music,
skiing, and UFOs. *Sign:* Leo.
Employment history: Many
film and video related jobs:
Retina Circus Productions,
Video Production Services
(Berkeley), designer of
Zoetrope's Electronic
Cinema System.
[1982 LFL Yearbook]

"Francis," Clark began, feeling awkward about the offer. "What do you think? Should I go work at Lucasfilm?"

"Go do it," said Francis, as Clark remembers it. "Go do it because George has the money to build the editor we all want. Go do it."

Coppola's go-ahead, combined with the idea of working for George Lucas, proved too attractive. This was his dream. Clark was living in San Anselmo, just across a fence from Lucas' place at Parkway (the proximity of their homes always gave him a little charge), and he was always aware when the director-next-door made headlines. But except for occasional neighborliness, Clark didn't know George or Marcia.

Still, compared with working in Hollywood or San Francisco with Francis, Bel Marin Keys was depressing for Clark. He bristled at the differences between working for Francis and working for George.

"Working for Francis was very dynamic and very interactive. Francis is approachable by anybody. He's a visionary and it's amazing just to listen to him and hear what he's got to say.

"If you want to compare George and Francis, I'd say this. Imagine both companies want to have a baby. Lucasfilm would look into the situation and make sure the genetics were proper, and there was the right little quantum of love so it would be able to endure, and everything would be perfect. They'd go through the process and nine months later they'd have a child and they'd know exactly what it would do when it grew up, exactly where it would go to school, everything. At Francis' company, if he wanted to have a baby, he doesn't want to wait nine months. So instead of getting one woman and waiting nine months, he'll just get nine women and hope that in a month he's got it."[9]

Said Higgins, "We couldn't build the systems fast enough that he wouldn't come up with new ideas."

Lucas never came out to Bel Marin Keys to see what they were doing, so Higgins never felt part of the creative process. "We were removed from production, we weren't really allowed to interact with the films getting made on Kerner, so it was a little stale."

Lucas' team was also on a budget, completely unlike the way Francis seemed to approach his problems. If the Zoetrope team needed a top-of-the-line $15,000 Sony BVU 800 ¾-inch videotape machine, they got it. But Lucas' editing project sometimes needed to compromise, get the mid-level machine instead.

"I was blown away by what little budget we had; how they'd nickel and dime us," Higgins complained. "And all that waste of time searching out the most cost-effective thing."

But others on the team, Ralph Guggenheim in particular, didn't feel the cost-consciousness was inappropriate.

[9] Higgins attributes the observation to video expert Larry Seehorn, who also worked with both companies.

"I don't believe we had second-rate equipment," said Ralph. "My desire to stick with clunky [mid-level] decks was founded on the notion that film editors wouldn't want to spring for the fancy machines. If we could make the system work with middle-end equipment, we could keep the cost down and yet always be capable of working with higher-end equipment."

The simmering rift between Higgins and Guggenheim would linger for years.

Catmull had suggested back at Tunstead that to create a new editing system, Guggenheim would need to build it three times, throwing each out and starting again. After much internal debate, Catmull and Guggenheim agreed he should start work on the workstation with which he had the greatest familiarity, the PERQ computer from his old job at Three Rivers.

Once the PERQ arrived at Bel Marin Keys, Guggenheim and Silva loaded it with a simple database and connected the whole thing to a laserdisc player they finally received from DVA. Working on software concepts, they tried to get the PERQ to control the machine.

After ten years in video production, Higgins was the only person in the computer group with extensive real-world experience.[10] He didn't know much about sophisticated computers and programming, but he knew a lot about video machines and production environments.[11] As an engineer, Higgins had helped set up mobile video trucks and editing bays for Francis, and he participated in the design of Francis' state-of-the-art set-up. He had been helping Francis work through the complicated issues associated with transferring video (which ran at 30 frames per second) to film (which ran at 24); those concepts would need to be refined for a sophisticated film editing computer.

While the other guys worked out the architecture of the computer editor, Higgins was keeping busy overseeing video in every part of Lucasfilm—from looking at Ranch plans and Kerner blueprints, to wiring up frame buffers, to checking out loaner machines from equipment companies that the team was investigating for use with the editing project.

Andy Moorer, the director of Audio Research, was moving ahead with the design of the digital audio signal processor, the ASP. Unlike the editing project, the sound work centered on the invention of a brand new set of chips that could perform the special kinds of calculations required for digital audio. In some ways, it was comparable to the hardware work involved with the digital film printer, the project Alvy was developing.

Designing new hardware chips was a long and complex process. Once the engineer determined precisely what needed to be done, and perhaps executed the various algorithms in software, he needed to translate the software

[10] His background included a stint in 1970 with the Retina Circus—a five-person visual effects company that created some of the earliest "music video" type programming. The group was renown for psychedelic light shows during concerts in San Francisco and Seattle, and won an Emmy for their video work.

[11] Higgins' early work to create algorithms to address the film-video relationships was programmed into the new HP programmable calculators.

into fundamental logical steps that could be built with wire and chips. What might eventually become a single integrated circuit—a small dark rectangle mounted to a green plastic board—began life as a large quantity of simple chips, connected together with long strands of wire and soldered into place. This process of chip design, finding the best position of the chips on a board and the most efficient way to wire them together, was expedited by using specialized CAD software.

"In short, they needed computers and software and new tools," observed Kessler, "in order to build the computers they needed, to make the software to invent new tools."

Stanford already had a package for helping with chip design, called SUDS (Stanford University Drawing System), but Andy Moorer needed to make his own for designing the digital signal processor. After working out the details back at Tunstead, he built a new tool, which he called LUDS (LUcasfilm Drawing System), pronounced *loods* ("as in Quaaludes," smirked Andy).

LUDS was cobbled together to do exactly what Moorer needed. It wasn't particularly easy for anyone but Moorer or Snell to use. But for the complicated work on the ASP, LUDS was perfect. Most of their time was spent concentrating on the various iterations of the chips that LUDS would print out on gigantic sheets of paper. They looked like city maps, with chips in the place of buildings and wires in the place of roads. On the bottom of each page, Moorer had printed "Lucasfilm. Top Secret. Burn Before Reading."

As Moorer refined the work he had done at Stanford and IRCAM, he had a pretty good idea of what was still needed at Lucasfilm. By summer he and Snell had formed the fundamentals of the hardware design and it was time to bring on some dedicated software expertise. Soon two of the guys Moorer had known at IRCAM—Curtis Abbot and Jim Lawson—arrived, and they began to write code.

Lucas was getting caught up in Larry Kasdan's freshman directorial project, *Body Heat*. Spielberg had "discovered" Kasdan and asked him to write *Raiders*. Then Lucas pulled him onto *Empire*. Now Kasdan was anxious to direct; he had a deal with Lucas' friend Alan Ladd Jr. (now working at Warners instead of Fox) to shoot the script he had written for *Body Heat*. Much like Lucas' deal on *Graffiti*, Kasdan was only allowed to direct if he had a "name" director to "executive produce." Lucas didn't want the credit, but he was happy to sponsor Kasdan.

"He thought this overseeing business was pretty ridiculous," said Kasdan. "He thought I was perfectly capable of directing the movie and didn't even know what function an overseer served."

Through the fall and into the new year, Lucas offered his thoughts to Kasdan and popped into the editing room from time to time, but for the most part he left the new director to himself.

"Lucas made it possible to make the film with no interference at all," said Kasdan.

Lucas insisted that his name not be included on anything to do with the film. "It wasn't me making this picture; it was Larry."[12]

When *Raiders of the Lost Ark* came out in the spring, Tom Holman, Ben Burtt, and Ben's assistant Gary Summers went down to the Blumenfeld Theater in San Francisco to set up for the film's big premiere. As they walked in, the RCA service technician was just finishing the theater check-up.

"How'd it go?" Holman asked.

"Fine, fine," came the reply.

Theater sound in 1981 was largely the same as it had been in 1951. There were generally five speakers behind the screen, and typically an array of more speakers behind and alongside the audience. The dominant brand was Altec: its "Voice of the Theater" series had been delivering movie sound for most of the years that there *was* movie sound.

Something made Holman walk backstage, behind the screen, possibly because it was so easy to do in the old theater. There, he noticed the speaker cabinets were disassembled, parts were missing, woofers stolen, and the two "surround" speakers[13] installed in the closed balcony, "thus ensuring that the coverage of surround sound was highly uneven," he said.

Burtt and Holman's disappointment with finding this premium theater in such bad shape was a shock, and set Holman on a personal crusade to fix the problems in whatever ways he could.

It wasn't the first time he was made so aware of the failings in the theatrical presentation of sound. A couple of years earlier, when he had been the chief engineer at Advent, Holman went to a 70mm revival of *2001* in Boston. During the screening, he could hear that there was no right channel of sound.

"I drove back to Advent, got on the Telex machine to RCA Service Company to immediately report the problem. Weeks later I heard from the president, who said that they had checked it out and found nothing wrong."

The "state-of-the art" that Lucas wanted was not going to be hard for Holman to do, particularly after his experience in the competitive home stereo market. Up until *Star Wars*, virtually all movies were delivered with monaural sound. It wasn't that stereo couldn't be done, but most theaters were built for mono, and stereo tracks on films weren't perfectly backwards compatible.

[12] *Body Heat* (1981). Written and directed by Lawrence Kasdan. Starring William Hurt and Kathleen Turner.

Raiders was the top grossing film of 1981, with $115 million in domestic revenue. The next biggest film was *Superman II* ($65 million). *Body Heat* eventually grossed over $24 million.

[13] Altec A7s.

Traditionally, the soundtrack was divided up to play in a mix through the left, center, or right speaker behind the screen. Wider screens had an additional left and right speaker farther out, totaling five speakers pointed at the audience. The surround sound was mono, distributed evenly to the array of peripheral speakers scattered around the theater.

Gary Kurtz, producer of *Star Wars*, conspired with Dolby Labs to see that 20th Century Fox released the picture in stereo. *Star Wars* also introduced a new way for using the five screen speakers. By pushing left and right sound channels to the farthest out speakers, the pair just inside those was made available. Lucas' mixers then placed low frequency effects in those speakers, and named it the "baby boom" channel.

Human ears can hear high frequencies up to around 20,000 Hertz, and down to around 20 Hertz for very low sounds. Below that you don't *hear* the sound, but if the "volume" is "loud" enough, you can *feel* the sound. Super-low frequencies affect us emotionally, usually inducing something like fear. We feel them during earthquakes. Lucasfilm put sound effects in the baby boom channel for audiences to feel—for instance, in the opening shot of *Star Wars* where the little diplomatic ship is running from the Imperial Cruiser. It's no wonder this is one of the most memorable and ominous shots in cinematic history. It was not only cool looking, but cool *sounding*.

In 1979, Dolby Labs expanded the audio palette by creating a left and right channel to the surround track—stereo surrounds. "It was used in *Superman*," said Tom Holman, "to make him sound like he was flying over the audience." Later in the year, Francis Coppola and Walter Murch used the stereo surround track for remarkable creative and emotional effect in *Apocalypse Now*.

Although Tom Holman was supposed to be making the best recording environments he could envision, he couldn't escape the idea that good acoustics and better speakers for Lucas' theater were really only half the solution. It seemed there were more than three decades of research and advancements in speaker technology that somehow hadn't made it to the film business.

Ben Burtt's concerns about theater sound, combined with Holman's incessant griping, led Kessler to turn it around and ask Holman, "So…what do you need for good theatrical presentation?"

The question rolled around Holman's imagination for months. Kessler helped him put together a study of movie theaters. Their data showed that half of all theaters had their left and right speakers reversed. As Holman thought about what needed to be done, he realized that getting C Building completed was just the tip of the iceberg.

Alvy was focused on recruiting remarkable people to the graphics project, and he had set his sights on his old friend from NYIT, Jim Blinn. Blinn was already a respected talent and Alvy was anxious to pry him away from his work at the Jet Propulsion Labs. Luckily for Alvy, Blinn was using the same old computers he had started working on years earlier, and he was frustrated. He loved the space program, but the hot technology Alvy dangled as bait before him was successful in getting his attention.

When Blinn gave notice to JPL that he would be joining George Lucas' computer group, his boss suddenly realized the colossal nature of the loss and promised Blinn new computers if he would stay. But it was too little and too late. Blinn left for Bel Marin Keys, bringing with him another JPL graphics scientist, Pat Cole.[14] Cole was the first woman to join the team, and she and Jim were the newest programmers at Lucasfilm. Blinn was back with his old friends.

The graphics team had been using commercially available frame buffers, but they knew they were going to need something of considerably higher resolution if they were going to composite images for movies. Though they weren't sure what that actually required, they did know that off-the-shelf frame buffers didn't allow them to have enough colors, enough bit-depth, or enough resolution.

The quality of television images was (roughly) 500 lines and 500 pixels in a line. Whatever film resolution would be, it had to be easily twenty times that of television. Though people often estimated the digital resolution equivalent of film, it had never been put to the test. Theories ran from around 2,000 pixels across the frame to about 8,000. Microscopic analysis of the silver crystals in film provided some threshold, but just copying an original film negative to a positive print caused a lowering of the image resolution.

To honestly determine "film quality," real film would need to be projected in a real theater, and subjected to some rigorous analytical evaluations. So the graphics team decided to run some tests.

David DiFrancesco put together a series of films representing a variety of color and spatial computer resolutions, for the group to screen in a regular movie theater in Corte Madera, the closest "real" theater they could use. He and Alvy put an image on the screen and the boys moved around from seat to seat and shouted out from their various locations "I see it!" or "It's pretty fuzzy."

One test was like going to the eye doctor: David created an image of lines getting closer and closer together, to see how close the lines could be before the audience couldn't tell if they were seeing two lines or one.

What they realized was that no matter how high the resolution they started with—either on film negative or from the computer frame buffer—the the-

[14] Blinn agreed, however, to commute back to JPL weekly to keep things moving forward.

ater's projector was the weakest link in the chain; the almost imperceptible shaking of the film as it moved through the projector made fine lines blur.[15] Thus a rectangle of 2,000 pixels up and down by 3,000 pixels across, projected in a theater, would be indistinguishable from an image ten times as sharp.

The ILM staff was stunned at the findings; it seemed impossible that "film resolution" could be as little as 2,000 or 3,000 pixels in a line. This discovery was a bit of a relief, as it was considerably lower than anyone thought would be the goal. This new data provided the target for the hardware and software resolution they'd need.

Having an answer about resolution left them with other problems. Even at only 2,000 pixels across, there was nowhere to buy a computer frame buffer or image processor of such enormity. Evans & Sutherland wasn't interested in building it. How many people would ever need such fidelity in a computer image?

New companies offering frame buffers were springing up all the time now, starting to serve a variety of customers, from spies at the NSA to radiologists performing CAT scans. While Alvy eventually got Lucasfilm a frame buffer, he and Ed were convinced they had to find someone to build a pile of hardware to facilitate their high-end imaging needs. It would need plenty of pixel depth, and the power to handle the massive compositing operations for making a picture and writing the output to film. Alvy wrote a seven-page proposal, to convince manufacturers like DEC and Ikonas of such a product's importance. (They were still calling the tool a "difip," as coined by Triple-I. No one liked it, but it would work in the interim.)

Building the DFP was going to be challenging. The only serious interest they got was from Ikonas, the company that provided Lucasfilm's chosen frame buffer. Ikonas was one of the top manufacturers in the field.

Ikonas' co-founder, Nick England, needed more information before he could give Lucasfilm a bid for their DFP. Alvy assembled a series of thick binders that held the specifications—all difficult to decipher since Alvy's experience in hardware design was negligible. Still, with the four-inch-thick stack of paper, Alvy began working with England to refine the design.

For his part, Nick England was a little out of his element. Ikonas frame buffers were nowhere as monstrous as these specs demanded. But England knew someone he could call, who had precisely the skills to design and build Lucasfilm's machine: Rodney Stock.

Stock had been involved with computer hardware design for more than a decade, having worked on creating the earliest flight simulators with Evans & Sutherland, and he had built the hardware for Ampex's video paint system AVA (having designed the hardware side of the product that merged with Tom Porter's software). With experience in big hardware as well as creative software, Stock was the right guy to ask for advice. England extracted Stock from Ampex and lured him into some consulting on the project.

[15] Actually, after their analysis was complete, it wasn't the projector lens that was the weakest link, but rather the human eye that was the limiting factor.

"Nick couldn't show me what Alvy needed," said Stock, "unless I signed a nondisclosure agreement. But I knew it was Lucasfilm. And I knew it was big."

Cautious about his rights, Stock wouldn't sign anything and ended up getting handed a paltry dozen pages of somewhat less specific paperwork. Ikonas was offered a budget of $800,000. Could the machine be built for that? He was given less than half an hour to look it over and present his initial thoughts.

All of the other manufacturers had passed on the proposal, and Ikonas and Stock understood why. It was going to be expensive to build this custom computer. It would be huge, requiring at least a pair of six-foot-tall metal racks to hold all the boards. As part of the Siggraph community, England had known Ed and Alvy for years, even visiting with them at NYIT while he was starting Ikonas in 1978. They had checked out his small company in North Carolina on a few occasions and most recently England had dropped in on them at Tunstead.

As the old friends sat around a conference table at Lucasfilm, surrounded by lawyers intent on formalizing the complicated project, it hit a snag.

"We had assumed throughout the proposal stage that after a year or so we'd have rights to make copies of the DFP, and simply pay royalties to Lucasfilm," said England.

"That's off the table," the Lucasfilm's lawyers said.

The DFP project was a one-time only contract with no continuing rights to manufacture the systems for anybody else.

"And that really changed the deal for us," said England. "We'll spend all this time and energy and resources doing a one-of-a-kind and we won't be able to leverage the engineering investment."

Ikonas couldn't afford to do the job with the limitation. "Somewhere along the line," said England, "they decided this would be too valuable a device to let somebody else manufacture and market." In spite of the surprise change in the conditions, the teams parted amicably.

With few other options remaining, Ed and Alvy now faced having to build the monstrous contraption themselves. Alvy went back to Rodney Stock directly. This time Stock was handed the full four-inch stack, although he recalled being given the same twenty minutes.

"What I *didn't* say was 'this can't work,'" Stock said. "But it was clear to me that it would collapse with communication problems before you could even test it with images."

What Rodney Stock *did* say was that he needed more time to go through the documents. "I just can't tell in twenty minutes."

Stock contemplated the problem quickly. Lucasfilm wanted a massive image processor. It was initially described as a machine with unprecedented high color information—with 32 bits of data per pixel[16]—8 bits for each color

[16] 32 bits of data is really 24 bits of color information (16.7 million colors).

(red, green, blue) plus transparency (alpha).[17] Four processors running in parallel. Instead of getting a $5 million to $10 million Cray—a general purpose vector machine designed for things like seismic exploration and nuclear modeling—this one was to be specifically designed for printing images to film by some kind of laser scanner. Stock poured through the documents from Alvy. (Thinking about the situation, Stock later remarked, "Alvy—if nothing else—is prolific.")

Stock was particularly interested in how Alvy expected to composite various 3-D objects into a single frame, combining the objects with backgrounds, lighting them and rendering them. Anything the custom processor would eventually do in hardware would first have to be roughed out in software, and there were a large number of interesting, but untested, ideas in the spec. Maybe building the hardware was a little premature.

"Have you simulated these algorithms?" asked Stock.

"Nope," said Alvy.

"Have you built any of this stuff at all?"

"Well, no we haven't."

Stock thumbed through the pile of paper representing what he figured might be a $3 million development for a high-end device. But Lucasfilm wanted it for a fraction of that. Stock went on to outline what it would take to deliver the project. If he had to do it on a tight budget, he wanted two years. He also wanted complete control and fiscal autonomy, so he alone could decide if a dollar was going to be spent on a new engineer or a new oscilloscope. Alvy agreed.

"Listen Alvy," he said, "All I can tell you is, I will give you a machine that you'll be proud of, that will do great things, but I can't tell you it will be exactly *this* machine." Alvy nodded.

As Stock started refining the specification of the image computer, Alvy was getting tired of calling it the DFP. "Let's give this thing a name."

Alvy was certain it needed to be catchy. Everyone was competing with the raw sexy power of "Industrial Light & Magic," and the pressure for cool names was real.

Loren Carpenter was still lobbying for "Cinematrix" for either the product or the division, but couldn't get anyone to sign on. One evening, Loren, Alvy, Jim Blinn, and Rodney Stock headed out to dinner to try to work through the problem. They settled into a booth at The Country Garden, the nearest place to their offices where you could sit down and get pretty good food at any hour. It was a little noisy, but comfortable.

"Let's just name it after what it does. It makes pictures," pointed out Alvy. "But it should sound cool and scientific, like 'laser.'"

RODNEY STOCK

Hometown: Born New York City, raised East Coast. *Family:* single. Schools: Northeastern. *Interests:* folk dancing, reading, silversmithing. *Employment history:* Engineering: Ampex Video Arts (AVA); Evans & Sutherland-Flight simulators; Mobility Systems-Automated Materials Handling.

[1982 LFL Yearbook]

[17] Ed and Alvy's invention for handling information about pixel opacity.

Everyone gave nods of agreement between bites. "The 'er' at the end is good. It's a Spanish suffix that makes it a verb. Laser…pixel laser…pix**er**…"

Alvy stopped. "*Pixer?* That's pretty good."

"It sounds weird," said Loren.

"Well, something *like* pixer."

"That name will never stick," said Loren.

"Why not?"

Loren thought for a moment. "It just sounds kind of…strange. What about pix**ar**?

"That's good," said Alvy.

Jim and Rodney didn't stop eating, but their eyes registered consensus. Loren was mulling it over.

"Then it sounds a little more like 'radar,' and sort of astronomical, like 'quasar' or 'pulsar,'" Loren added.

Blinn, as an unofficial space program delegate to the meal, looked up from his soup and nodded in agreement.

Alvy was pleased. "You know, 'ar' is another Spanish verb ending," he said, in further support of his case.

"I like it. If we call it Pixar it will stick, and it sounds cool," said Loren. "This will stick."

Everyone returned to dinner, satisfied with the *ad hoc* meeting. There was some discussion of how George would feel about the name, but all felt it was worthy of the company.

The name was put to use immediately, and they were right: it was easy to say and it stuck. Rodney Stock began developing a new plan for the Pixar Image Computer (sometimes abbreviated PIC), to make it smaller, and to create a hardware component that could hook up to their existing VAX computer, which would augment its limited imaging functionality. The giant VAX could run the scanner and this PIC could run on the side, handling all the complicated processing. It was a workable solution and Rodney got to work.

Ed Catmull had developed some 3-D animation fundamentals at the University of Utah, although it was his work at NYIT that had focused on the enormous problem of creating realistic blur in animated objects. It was the motion blur in Phil Tippett's Go-Motion that was starting to make the miniature photography of models look realistic on the screen. But motion blur from a computer was mathematically complicated and not an intuitively obvious goal for engineers to develop.

Along with the insistence that his crew do away with jaggies, motion blur was Catmull's pet obsession. Even the demo materials Ed delivered to Lucasfilm showed some of his early work at trying to get spaceships to blur as they flew across the screen. But something was wrong with the approach and it often looked like it couldn't be done.

Over the next few months the specification for the Pixar device evolved. Rather than a highly specialized piece of equipment to sit between the laser scanners, perhaps it could be programmable, flexible to a variety of imaging uses.

"Once you could do the image manipulations required for special effects work in movies," recalled Ralph Guggenheim, "meaning blue screen removal, image compositing, various other image filtering techniques, who knew what other markets had big expensive images that needed some manipulations."

Though the alternative applications didn't specifically interest Ed and Alvy, they were both aware of the market value of that kind of capability…if someone was around who knew how to market it.

fifteen

Double Suicide

[1980–1982]

Audiences are becoming sophisticated enough to want first class exhibition of film. And now there is even something that can be done about it. The Lucasfilm TAP program is the first comprehensive, systematic approach to improving standards in the presentation of motion pictures. If enough of us get behind this idea we can change the standards of the industry.

—SYDNEY POLLACK, DIRECTOR. FROM AN
OPEN LETTER TO FILM EXHIBITORS, 1985.

IN SPITE OF all the computer work at Bel Marin Keys, Lucasfilm was primarily a film company, making movies, and generally concerned with improving the filmmaking process. Even though Catmull and his teams were dedicated to how computers could facilitate the work, there were ample ways to improve movies that didn't involve digital technology.

Jim Kessler had wrestled with the quality control issue on *Raiders*. They had made more 70mm prints for the film than most films ever see. Most movies are shot and released on 35mm film, about an inch and a half wide. Projectors in theaters, film equipment—everything in the system, actually—was designed for materials in this format.

If you wanted to project an image really big and sharp, you needed a format larger than 35mm; 70mm was the format of kings. Though the cost was generally prohibitive to shoot and work in 70mm, it was possible to finish the film in 35mm and then enlarge the negative to 70. The resulting projection offered an astounding theatrical experience, and epic movies were often released with a limited quantity of 70mm prints in order to dazzle audiences in New York or Los Angeles, or any of the few hundred theaters set up to handle that size.

For decades, the largest order of 70mm prints from a film lab had been ten or so. If anyone needed fifty or more prints, it was usually spread out over many months. *The Ten Commandments* was one such classic. So was *Star*

Wars. By the time Lucasfilm was shooting *Raiders of the Lost Ark*, they were ordering around eighty large format prints at a time, the largest single order ever made.

But the quality of the prints was uneven. When labs had large runs, they didn't check the prints before sending them to theaters. Lucas was irked to learn that one print of *Empire Strikes Back* arrived in San Diego with a problem. Audiences had stood in line for days in some cases, only to have the sound disappear forty minutes into the screening. It wasn't the projectionist's fault. There was no sound on the print.

"They darn near had a riot," recalled Kessler.

It was just a mistake. But it was unacceptable. "We had a distribution issue," he commented in his understated way.

Even with perfect prints, films got ruined quickly. The first time a fresh, pristine movie ran through a projector, the film got damaged. After only one viewing, more than half the prints showed visible scars—scratches, white and black specs, and breaks that were restored poorly. And after two weeks of running in theaters, the number with damage increased to three out of four, usually related to the sound track.

"The exhibitors were chewing up prints, their projectors were so badly maintained," said Kessler.

And if these problems weren't enough, the theaters themselves were in pretty poor shape. Even if they managed not to damage the expensive film prints, the theaters were often old and the projectors erratic. Kessler visited theaters running Lucasfilm movies and found screens that were unevenly illuminated by the projector bulbs, noise from adjacent movies bled into the room, and the speakers…. Of course, the speakers had been foremost in Tom Holman's mind for months.

Kessler was swirling between Lucas' determination to make the filmmaking experience better, and Holman's specific ideas for how they might do that.

"You make all these great sounds, and they're still being heard in a theater that's crappy," said Kessler. "I mean, what's the point?"

Kessler became increasingly obsessed with the theatrical film experience. His early notion had been to have employees or friends of employees go to theaters that were showing Lucas' movies, to make sure everything was okay. But casual verification wasn't going to be enough. If theaters didn't pass their test, Lucasfilm would have to offer an alternative. They'd have to help theaters change. Theaters, of course, weren't interested in changing.

"The audience doesn't care," was their general attitude.

Instead of approaching the Greber-Faxon team that ran Lucasfilm, Kessler approached George Lucas with his feelings about improving theaters, with what he called the Theater Alignment Program, or TAP.

"It'll be great for the industry. We can start with Lucasfilm prints, the way we did with *Raiders*, and maybe expand the business. We'll make money at it! It'll be a really cool thing."

"Go ahead and try it if you'd like," Kessler recalls George saying. "But I'll tell ya, you're never going to influence these people, the exhibitors; they're just stuck in their own little rut."

Lucas' discouragement didn't affect Kessler. He went on to set up meetings with film distributors and exhibitors, two groups that had a rather adversarial relationship, even though they worked hand-in-hand.

"They're symbiotic...it's a love-hate relationship," said Kessler.

His strategy was to pit them against each other. "What if we had a way of getting the goods on the exhibitors," he'd tell the distributors, "so you could really beat 'em up?"

"Yeah, that sounds great," they'd reply.

"We'll do it through this print thing. You say they're thrashing your good prints and they say they're getting lousy prints from you. So we'll give you ammunition to beat them up."

Kessler wanted to insert Lucasfilm between the two combative parties, wedging himself into a position to reveal everybody's shortcomings. No matter who lost the war, filmmakers would win—the film prints would be better managed. This was the core of TAP. But getting some control over the exhibition process, verifying the quality of the venues, still wasn't going to be enough. What they really needed was a way to improve the theaters themselves. What they needed were speakers and equipment as good as the stuff George Lucas was building for himself.

Tom Holman was responsible for this.

As Lucasfilm's chief engineer, Holman first needed to address the construction of as perfect a mixing/recording theater as could be built. For him it was an incredible opportunity to apply his long experience with how sound is heard, and the design of speakers and amplifiers. Working closely with Jim Kessler, whose observations from the *Raiders* premiere sat heavily on both their shoulders, Tom Holman attacked the problems with the excitement of an academic getting a new lab.

Holman started constructing a comprehensive system for use at Lucasfilm. He worked wonders in speaker redesigns and new room acoustic calculations. He integrated the many loudspeaker developments made by engineers since 1947, and added some of his own patented advancements. The C Building theater under construction was going to be state-of-the-art.

Around this time, Lucas was spending hours dealing with lawyers and representatives, trying to settle his disputes with the Hollywood guilds—the Directors Guild (DGA) and the Writers Guild (WGA). It was ironic that the unions that had made

ROB COOK

Hometown: Knoxville, Tennessee. *Family:* single. *Schools:* Duke University (BS Physics), Cornell Univ. (MS Computer Graphics). *Interests:* piano, reading, hiking. *Sign:* Sagittarius. *Employment history:* DEC; University of Pennsylvania
[1982 LFL Yearbook]

[1] Union rules stated that the director had to be either the last name on the screen before a movie began, or the first one seen when it ended. Irvin Kershner had agreed that George Lucas' name should be the last one seen at the beginning, but the union couldn't accept this, and they fined them both (although Lucas paid both bills).

his life so difficult as a young man now claimed him as a member. He had also allowed ILM to unionize, one of the only effects houses to be organized, in an effort to make sure his employees were well taken care of. But the unions again haunted him. Both the DGA and WGA were unhappy with the way credits were handled on *The Empire Strikes Back*.[1] By spring, George had made the bold statement of resigning from both unions in protest. *Raiders* released that summer.

In spite of Lucasfilm's ongoing graphics research, computer-generated images still looked a little like plastic. This bothered Rob Cook, a graduate student at Cornell. He thought it couldn't be simply that computer images looked plastic; there had to be something wrong with how computers understood light. Cook discovered that the way software handled reflected light—called the *light-surface interaction*—was based on using white for the bright spots in an image and its subsequent reflections.

"It turns out to be the perfect model of how light reflects off of plastic," said Cook.

But for surfaces like paper or metal, the highlight color should be something other than white. Cook wrote an academic paper on his findings and submitted it to Siggraph for publication. Siggraph, like most academic organizations, sent the paper to experts in the field to review, and the paper ended up at Lucasfilm, on Jim Blinn's desk. After reading it he knew Rob Cook was someone Alvy Ray Smith would be interested in.

"Alvy," he said, "you should look at this guy." He passed him a copy of the paper.

For his part, Jim Blinn was getting antsy. He had been spending half his time at the Jet Propulsion Lab and the rest in Marin, but he couldn't do that indefinitely. And the biggest problem was Saturn—the Voyager spacecraft was approaching Saturn, and the images it was returning were spectacular.

"I realized that my first love was really space exploration and the science, and it was time for me to commit to that, collect myself in one place. JPL was that place."

Blinn's path diverged from Ed and Alvy's for the third time, and he returned to Pasadena.

Blinn's departure left a hole in the department, and by the end of the month Alvy called Rob Cook.

"I had no idea this was coming," recalled Cook. "I was still at Cornell and just about done with my PhD, so I flew out to California and interviewed."

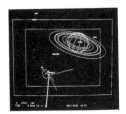

Frame from Jim Blinn's Voyager animations. Ivan Sutherland once said, "There are about a dozen great computer graphics people, and Jim Blinn is six of them."

Alvy hired Rob and by summer he joined the boys at Bel Marin Keys. Soon Rob Cook sat in Jim's old space, staring through the horizontal blinds in his office and tapping his pencil on the brass lamp on his desk, thinking about the light.

The offices at Bel Marin Keys were slow to get computers. It was frustrating at first; after all, they were the computer research group. Finally, by summer they had a pair of big VAX machines cabled to terminals around the building, and a number of dedicated graphics workstations. Bill Reeves decided that the first VAX, now the hub of a networked system of terminals on many of the scientist's desks, needed a name. He chose "Dagobah," the swamp planet that was Yoda's home in *The Empire Strikes Back*.

"It made sense," said Reeves, "because in *Empire* they referred to it as 'the Dagobah system.'"

Once the first VAX was named, it began a pattern of names from the cryptic geography of the *Star Wars* universe. The second VAX was called Bespin—the cloud city. As Malcolm Blanchard's Sybil database project for ILM evolved, he installed modems in their building on Kerner and connected them to Dagobah. It was the first remote link in what would become the Lucasfilm network.

While Reeves, along with John Seamons, had a central role in getting the place "computerized," his interests slowly drifted from hooking up computers to writing bits of code to make them work better together—device drivers—and eventually to writing software packages to allow the other engineers better access to the hardware. Reeves knew the foundations of the vector systems inside and out, and in his spare time he worked on his own graphics projects, "just to make sure the systems worked."

Throughout 1980, Coppola was busy pursuing his own visions of electronic cinema. In February 1981, after months of experimentation, rehearsal, and technological innovation, principle photography began on *One from the Heart*. On many days, Francis would sit in the Airstream and direct from there.

"When he is in the truck," said Thomas Brown, "he can play the part of the audience—a little removed from the stage itself."

Said Coppola: "I sit, I view the screen, I talk to the screen, and the screen does what I tell it to do."

Two days after filming began, Coppola invited two hundred journalists to visit the new Zoetrope studios and to witness his revolutionary filmmaking process.

"We're on the eve of a wonderful, positive new film industry…." he began.

Coppola explained his departure from shooting on location and his return to the old soundstage. Lucas had turned to the soundstage earlier, with *Star Wars.* Up until that point he was on the road, on location for his films *THX 1138* and *American Graffiti.* Lucas enjoyed the control that being on a set provided. Coppola, after the typhoons in the Philippines, came to the same conclusion.

"I want to make a very stylized love story that exists in a world all its own," Coppola explained, gesticulating wildly at the stages around them. "The characters' emotions will be reflected in the scenery. I'll be able to control the skies and manipulate things."

As much as Coppola was pioneering new territory for filmmakers, it wasn't so much invention as innovation. Journalists recognized it as a "state-of-the-art synthesis of all the new technology available to the filmmaker." His process utilized a video camera that recorded the image simultaneously with the film camera, which allowed Francis to see every take immediately, rather than have to wait a day (or more) for the film to be developed. By knowing at once if more takes were required, or if the cast and crew could move on to new shots, it was also cost-saving—it helped limit the number of takes that needed to be printed. They called the method "video assist."

Saving money was critical. As production was just getting started, the new investors Coppola had brought in to cover the $8 million budget shortfall pulled out. He had to put his real estate holdings up as collateral.

"At the end of each week we generally had a wrap party," said Thomas Brown. "Just because we never knew for sure if there was going to be another week."

To support the effort, the 400 members of the cast and crew (against the advice of their unions) unanimously agreed to postpone the payment of their salaries. Sequined showgirls on the set, like many of the crew, wore buttons that read "I believe in Francis C."

Coppola was moved to tears by the crew's trust and dedication. Everywhere he looked on the enormous faux-Vegas soundstages were reminders of the risky game of chance he insisted on playing; above his head was the hallmark of the movie's opening, an enormous Lady Luck, outlined in neon.

"If we ever had a lot of money," said Coppola to a journalist on the set, "we could be a very dangerous company."

Even as *One from the Heart* scrambled, Francis purchased the 1927 silent film *Napoleon,* by Abel Glance. Zoetrope lovingly restored the film and premiered it with a live orchestra at eight sold-out showings at Radio City Music Hall in New York. It was somewhat typical of Coppola's confidence, infectious enthusiasm, and devil-may-care flamboyance. Later that year *Napoleon* began a national tour.

While in Los Angeles that summer, Alvy Ray Smith was invited to the *One from the Heart* set, to visit the Image and Sound Control trailer and to join in a big luncheon with Francis Coppola. One stage held a detailed re-creation of downtown Las Vegas, with a fleet of lunch tables filling the middle of the faux street scene.

Alvy sat at a table with actress Teri Garr, one of the stars, and her longtime friend John Whitney Jr. *John Whitney Jr.!* Whitney was one-half of the Whitney-Demos team that built Triple-I. It was simply astonishing to Alvy how often Whitney, or his associate Gary Demos, showed up at the same watering holes as he and Ed. Whitney and Demos had been in a quiet race to develop the first computer-animated film for years, and were even at that moment working on some secret project for Disney.

"Seeing them play with one another," commented Alvy, watching Whitney joke with Garr, "made my heart sink. If John Whitney and Gary Demos were this well-connected in Hollywood, and since their Culver city company was this close to the action, did our team have a chance?"

In February, *One From the Heart* released to less than flattering reviews.

"People ask me if all this technology will make the movie any better," said Coppola. "Well, no, technology doesn't make art any better. Art depends on luck and talent. But technology changes art."

Concurrent with Zoetrope's film production, Coppola's team continued to work with CBS (Joe Flaherty), Sony, and NHK to refine what was being called a high-definition video system.

Coppola himself was already an outspoken supporter of the new format. He had even testified before a House Telecommunications Subcommittee, to debate their opposition to setting aside regions of the broadcasting spectrum for high-definition.[2]

Sony and NHK had developed high-definition camera prototypes and monitors, and when they finally produced a recorder, they invited Francis and his team to Tokyo to see it. Sony wanted to get beyond television, moving the medium toward something capable of art.[3] This fit perfectly with Zoetrope's ambitions.

People in the industry weren't using Sony's term of "high-definition video system," but rather "high-definition television." It was an exciting time—few Americans had any sense of the future of video—and for a distinguished filmmaker like Coppola to be associating himself with the project was important.

[2] December, 1981.

[3] In that vein, Morita determined that a CD should be able to record and play back his favorite opera.

But Coppola was hoping they'd move away from the idea of television and toward the world of cinema.

The evening before he was scheduled to make a presentation to Sony, Francis, his son Gio, and their technological associates went to a famous "writers" bar in Tokyo.[4] There, amid movie posters of films by Kurosawa and, inexplicably, Coppola, they engaged in a barrage of peppered vodka shots until they were suitably hammered. The next morning, at what felt like the crack of dawn, the hung-over team toured Sony's Atsugi plant, where all the equipment was made. They saw a prototype of the first CD player as well as the first professional Beta camcorder. By noon, Coppola stood before a roomful of Sony's top engineers.

"Francis gave this dazzling performance to all the designers about the type of edit systems he wanted," said Thomas Brown. "He wanted the 'everything and the kitchen sink' type edit system, as well as what he called the 'Arnold Palmer golf bag series,' which was a very compact system you could carry around with you."

Sony was pleased with their new high-definition recorder. They also had completed the first high-def video projector. "It was the first time I had seen video projection that made sense," said Brown. Commenting on the poor resolution of television in general, he added, "With any projector before, you could see the lines."

At the end of a successful trip they flew home. Sony had agreed to provide them with some test equipment to put the high-definition video through its paces. Soon more fun electronics would show up at the Zoetrope lot in L.A. As Francis and company piled into their car at the airport, someone rolled up a big joint, and in no time the stories started rolling.

Francis concocted a tale about the first class section of an airliner. The basic storyline was that a stewardess fell in love with a passenger, and what began as extra peanuts erupted into a full fledged party in the first class cabin, of which the rest of the plane was completely unaware. The party extended into the cockpit, where one of crew accidentally bumped the 'hijack' button, which was transmitted to the ground (unbeknownst to the plane crew). When they landed, SWAT teams were ready to swarm the plane.

"It's got a beginning, it's got a middle. It's got an end," Thomas Brown remembers Francis saying to him. "You and Gio can produce it. Get Dennis Hopper to write and direct it. He'll bring in everybody else."

Then he turned to his son Gio. "We'll shoot it all on videotape." Everybody was reeling. "We'll use the plane set from *One from the Heart.*" Francis had long considered the set pieces built for movies to be assets that could be used on other projects as needed.

[4] Thomas Brown and Murdo Laird, all of whom were guests of Audie Bock, their translator and Kurosawa historian.

"One of the reasons the sets were so nice," recalled Brown, "was that Francis wanted them to be able to be disassembled and put together in different ways."

In the next forty-eight hours, Thomas was out trying to raise a few thousand dollars for the project (named *Project X*); Dennis Hopper had been convinced to write it. Hopper brought in Jack Thompson to star, and suggested Jan deBont to shoot it. deBont had just arrived in the U.S. from Holland and was looking for work.

"Those guys are so poor they don't even have money for lights," Brown heard Hopper say. "He'd be perfect on our budget."

Jan deBont shot some tests with video equipment provided to Zoetrope by Ikegami and Panavision.

"It was an exciting couple of weeks," said Thomas Brown. "And another example of the way things happened around Francis. His ideas were exciting and the conviction he had in them inspired everyone."

Eventually the new loaner high-definition equipment from Sony arrived, and Zoetrope decided to produce a pair of six-minute films as a test. The first, *Six Shots*, was written and directed by Zoetropian Ron Colby; it drew upon much of the studio talent, including Teri Garr and Paul Michael Glazer (then starring in *Starsky and Hutch*).

Double Suicide was a comedy, written and directed by Bob Swarthe. The film was a short gag about a depressed guy who stands at the end of a pier about to commit suicide, when he meets a depressed mermaid who jumps on the pier to do the same. They fall in love.

The *Six Shots* production; one of the few views ever seen, reproduced in an engineering journal.

Swarthe had worked on some of the motion control effects in *Close Encounters* (1977) for Spielberg and the original *Star Trek* movie (1979) before doing some effects and the opening credits for *One from the Heart*. He convinced smash-up comedian Gallagher and character actor (and Groundlings comedienne) Edie McClurg to star in *Double Suicide*.[5]

Sony engineers were on hand to watch how their enormous prototype cameras would be used for filmmaking. They watched, mortified and scribbling notes, as Coppola's team decided the scene needed to be shot from the rafters, and so the 700 pound camera was hoisted thirty feet in the air.

"These have to be a lot smaller," the Sony team determined.

[5] McClurg was a regular on the short-lived variety TV program, *The Big Show*, which Gallagher appeared on in 1980. She achieved a following after playing Grace, the high school secretary in *Ferris Bueller's Day Off* (1986).

On 4 days in January 1982, an all-volunteer cast and crew at Zoetrope Studios in Hollywood utilized a prototype High Definition Video System to produce the following experimental programs.

The purpose of the project was to test the feasibility of shooting theatrical movies electronically and to consult in the design of equipment necessary for future electronic cinema productions.

We express our deep appreciation to those who contributed their time, energy, skills and equipment to this endeavor.

ZOETROPE STUDIOS
© 1982

Title card for a pair of six-minute original "movies" Zoetrope produced in HDTV.

"It was like putting them into real world conditions," said Brown. "Not only to see what it looks like for us to shoot video, but how does the equipment need to be modified in order to be able to shoot these cinema pieces. It was a two-way street."

"We're an end-user," said Thomas Brown in *Broadcasting* magazine. "Our interest in this is how it will help us make movies. We've always had to use equipment that was developed or designed for another purpose. Taking part in the HDTV experiment puts us in a position to influence the design of equipment, which is where we want to be."

Lucasfilm wasn't participating in Zoetrope's experiments, but George Lucas was moved by Coppola's dedication. Word was circulated that the film he was making, *Revenge of the Jedi*, would be the last picture he would shoot on celluloid. Steven Spielberg was unconvinced. He couldn't imagine working in a medium that he couldn't hold up to the light and see pictures.

CBS made a presentation to VIPs in New York and Washington in early 1982, to unveil Sony's high-definition system in the U.S. Coppola was by then considered the leading creative protagonist for the new technology.[7]

He told a gathering of engineers, "The old ways must die away and give way to new life, new technology, and new talent."

Coppola was soon in Tulsa, Oklahoma, in production on his next project, *The Outsiders* (to be followed immediately in the same location by *Rumblefish*). He relocated the Image and Sound Control van—now with a sign on the side that read "Please pretend this vehicle is not here."

The young actors on that film, including Tom Cruise, Matt Dillon, Ralph Macchio, Patrick Swayze, Rob Lowe, and Coppola's nephew Nick Cage, started teasing Francis about the trailer. By the end of the production, after incessant heckling, the name Francis disliked most, The Silverfish, was the name that stuck.

In June 1982, Francis sold the Hollywood General lot and filed Chapter 11 bankruptcy for Zoetrope. His friends knew him too well to provide financial support. It was tough love, and a low point for Coppola. One of the many lives of his company came and went. Although his entire electronic cinema division cost less than $1 million of the $23 million budget of *One from the Heart*, his theory of "electronic cinema" took much of the blame.

[7] Joseph Flaherty, from CBS, led the engineering effort. On the creative front, Coppola was joined by television producer Glen Larson, creator/producer of *McCloud* (1970), *Quincy* (1976), *Battlestar Galactica* (1978), *Buck Rogers in the 25th Century* (1979), *Magnum, PI* (1980), *The Fall Guy* (1981), *Knight Rider* (1982). Larson did a HDTV test of *The Fall Guy* in late 1981.

sixteen

One Thousand, Six Hundred and Twenty-One Frames

[1981–1982]

Geometry draws the soul toward truth.

—Plato

ALVY WAS ANXIOUS for Lucas to utilize their expertise. "We kept waiting for George to come around and ask us to be in the movies, but he never came."

Though there was one relatively small 3-D graphic in *Star Wars*, there were no computer-generated effects in *Empire*. *Raiders* wasn't using any computer effects, either. Lucas was going to start work on *Jedi* pretty soon, and it still looked like no one in the company was interested in what the Graphics Group might be able to do.

Lucasfilm was courteous to the geeks, but they were not quite family. "We got treated as a sideshow," recalled Tom Porter. "Not disrespected, but certainly not embraced." Ed and Alvy were aching to prove their viability to ILM, but the ILM people generally kept them at arms length. "There was no particular warmth there. It was sort of like 'Hey, we're busy over here. We've got *real* things to do. We've got *Raiders* and *ET* and…*major motion pictures.*'"

And while ILM kept them at bay, the clock was ticking; the computer group's three-year authorization would, in theory, come to an end at the close of 1982. Where was the digital film printer? Where was the editing system?

The company July 4th picnic was the first time many employees saw the scope of work at the Ranch. The Farm Group, a small aggregation of lovely little cottages near the entrance to the property, had been completed first. The Main House foundation had been laid out, and George, looking hip in his NASA cap (a souvenir from his associations with the Space Shuttle program) filled a time capsule with company memorabilia and buried it in a corner of the structure. Employees' kids crowded near as George inserted object after object into the large cylinder: cassettes of *American Graffiti* and *Star Wars* soundtracks, glass stars and R2 figurines, and even a bottle of 1968 Cabernet Sauvignon. Before inserting the wine item in the cylinder, George read the customized label:

> *The Story of Skywalker Ranch. In 1968, George Lucas and Francis Coppola came across country to the Bay Area to look for a spot to start a new film company. George surveyed the land around Nicasio and said, "This is it, we should build here." But Francis was taken with San Francisco, so the first studio was in the city. Years later they dissolved their partnership. George made Star Wars and with the revenues from the film he was able to build all that you see here. George's dream came true: July 4, 1981.*

On top of the frivolity of the day and the hoedown that evening, this was a milestone for George and it made everyone who shared that moment profoundly connected to his vision. George had a knack for taking ephemeral ideas and making them tangible, and the Ranch was another perfect example.

Word had been circulated since August that ILM had about 150 shots to do for *Star Trek II.* The schedule was so tight, with *Jedi* in the pipeline, that two effects producers divided up the scenes according to their particular expertise.

Ed Catmull, isolated in Bel Marin Keys, away from the rest of the action on Kerner, wanted to remind them that the computer graphics group might be able to help out. His team made 3-D models of the USS Enterprise and a Klingon warbird, and put Loren Carpenter's new rendering algorithm to its first big test. Carpenter called the program REYES, the name of a quaint west Marin town across the peninsula from Ignacio, from which he sculpted the acronym, "Renders Everything You Ever Saw."

The "mini-production" Ed delivered to ILM demonstrated the Graphics Group's ability to make high-quality images, handle many aspects of lighting and shading objects, and provide some basic painting effects. He didn't know what ILM needed, but he definitely wanted to remind them he was there. It's hard to say if it worked. No one called.

The closest the computer researchers got to being part of the filmmaking process was the incessant sound of howling wolves through the halls of Bel Marin Keys. "Over and over," said Rodney Stock. "Endlessly."

Snuggled between Rodney's and Clark Higgins' offices was a Moviola where editor Michael Chandler sat, rolling forward and backward over the footage from the film he was doing, *Never Cry Wolf.* The director, Lucas' old friend Carroll Ballard, had weaseled some space from Lucasfilm. It was good inspiration for Clark and Guggenheim, as they explored the editing process, but it drove everyone else crazy.

Ed Catmull and Susan Anderson had been dating for more than a year and were thinking about getting married. Neither of them was sure how the company would respond to their relationship; a few of their co-workers expressed doubt that it was a good idea. Regardless, they felt it was important to go to the source. Ed approached George; Susan approached Marcia. They both got the same response: "*We're* married and work together; other people can be married here and work together." Recalled Susan, "They were great about it."

The Graphics Group had been developing ideas and building tools to make photorealistic images for almost a year, but most of the team was still unversed in the day-to-day work required to make an effect for a movie. Ed knew this was critical information for them to absorb. Since Tom Porter was starting to work on the compositing aspects of imaging, which was particularly relevant to the development of the digital film printer, Ed arranged for Tom to spend some time in D Building, shadowing the ILM optical department while they finished up *Raiders* shots for Spielberg.

"Wait a minute guys, we aren't thinking the way they think," said Porter as he returned from the front lines with reconnaissance. "Every strip of film going through that machine has its own matte. They have mattes for everything. You should see what's going on over there!"

A matte was like a cookie-cutter for an image or strip of images. It allowed the part of a frame you liked to be separated from the part you didn't. Shooting models against a solid color, like blue or green, made it easier to "pull a matte," as the optical people would say. The elements of every special effect shot always included a stack of mattes, one to isolate each element. Both Ed and Alvy were well acquainted with mattes and understood their importance, but neither had taken the concept very far. Up until then, Alvy—like anyone looking to digitize the optical process—was thinking about duplicating the mattes as well as the images, and sandwiching them all together. Mattes were just another element that had to be composited.

Left: A photograph of objects includes unwanted elements and background. *Center:* To isolate the large star, a matte is "pulled," which blocks out the parts to be rejected. *Right:* When the matte and the original are optically layered, the result is a frame that includes only the large star in an empty frame.

Porter realized that mattes were so prevalent at ILM that they should be built into the very definition of an image, as elemental as the separate color channels that were combined to make a color frame. Everything the graphics team did—whether in 2-D painting, or rendering calculations, or 3-D fractal images, or all-important compositing theories—had to create, process, and store information about the matte in the alpha channel. Ed and Alvy had invented the alpha channel years earlier at NYIT, but its use was sporadic. Sometimes the fourth channel was used to store mattes for compositing images together, but often it was not. Through Porter's urging, Ed and Alvy agreed they would all embrace alpha channel mattes as a component of the image itself.

By merging the alpha information with the color channels, an image was no longer little rectangular frames with portions matted out, but rather the shape of the photographed object itself, in an unbounded field. Compositing elements was not about stacking up rectangular film frames, but adding together discrete objects—spaceships or planets for instance—and the distinction was subtle, as well as vitally important to every aspect of how they would write software, build hardware, and think about graphics.

With an alpha channel implicit in the image data *(left)*, the concept of elements in layers within frame boundaries all become moot (with frame boundaries part of the display process but not of the creation process). Areas of an image with no information essentially cease to exist, leaving the star isolated, floating in no frame whatsoever *(right)*.

If the information in the alpha channel said a part of the image was not visible, it would be possible to skip all the associated mathematical processing of that "invisible" area, saving a huge amount of computer work and making their software faster and more efficient. It also changed the very nature of the hardware requirement of the digital film printer.

"At Lucasfilm we enforced a standard, a common way that the alpha channel should be used," said Porter.

To do so required an adjustment to the painting software they were writing, and a new extension to virtually all the tools in both hardware and software that they were going to build.

"You know that renderer you just wrote?" Porter announced upon returning from ILM to Loren Carpenter's office. "I want you to go back and create it with an alpha channel."

"How do I do that?" replied Loren.

"I dunno. You just gotta spit it out to me."

Tom Duff and Tom Porter dug into the notion of compositing elements, where everything would come into a central place complete with a matte in the alpha channel. Over the coming weeks, Porter kept running into the same problem with the way a compositor would work, the language it needed to speak.

Porter was stuck with a method using Boolean math—this AND that, this OR that—which didn't seem to address what pixels in stacked frames needed to be doing. Duff broke the mental logjam; he decided that the computer mostly needed to understand the order the layers would be in, underneath an imaginary camera: this layer *above* that one, this layer *under* that, and so on.

Rodney Stock was able to hook onto Duff and Porter's breakthrough and finally get working on his part of the digital film printer. Stock had been facing a specification that required a series of specially engineered hardware boards: one for pulling mattes, one for compositing, one for painting…. The breakthroughs with alpha and matting, as well as with compositing software, was more than a pathway to build visual effects for ILM, it was a simulation of how dedicated hardware would need to work—it was the missing cornerstone to the hardware development he had been waiting for.

Historically, it had been "one guy, one computer, one image." By standardizing the tools—the color space, the ways image files were stored and processed—the Lucasfilm group was making it possible to work on images as a team. But a team needed a big project to conquer, to test their mettle and their tools, and to refine their focus. They were a team without a game.

When ILM started work on the *Star Trek II* movie, there were still a few shots that the staff couldn't quite wrap their arms around.[1] In particular, there were shots that included elements associated with futuristic computers.

"Maybe the computer people would have some ideas."

They called Alvy Ray Smith, who made the haul through torrential rains to ILM on Kerner, always a fun adventure for any purpose. In the little glass conference room behind the reception desk, Jim Veilleux, the effects coordinator, began to outline a few shots he wasn't sure how to approach: a few seconds of a molecule transforming from a crystalline structure to a DNA-like helix; a few more seconds of some security clearance device that included a voice recognition sequence for Captain Kirk; some related frames with a retina scan; and finally, a potentially big sequence—a demonstration of the "Genesis Effect," which Veilleux outlined as best he could.

The script said: "And then the planet transforms…" followed by "EFX sequence here." Alvy recalled that the shot was described to him as "A rock in an aquarium that somehow got covered with green growths."

[1] *Star Trek II: The Wrath of Khan*, directed by Nicholas Meyer. Meyer (b. 1945) went on to direct the TV movie *The Day After* and films, including *Volunteers* (1985), *Star Trek VI: The Undiscovered Country* (1991). He also wrote the screenplay for *The Seven Percent Solution* (1976), *Time After Time* (1979), *Star Trek IV* (1986), and *Fatal Attraction* (1987).

"Do you know what can be done with computer graphics?" asked Alvy. Veilleux shook his head. So Alvy explained a few things about the state of the art. He talked about resolution and rendering.

When Veilleux described a simple zoom in on the planet, Alvy knew they could move much more dynamically than that. He had done some work in 1980 to help Jim Blinn fly Voyager models around Jupiter.[2] He knew he could create an imaginary camera that could move with a velocity that the motion control cameras at ILM could not. "If you simulate your physics well," said Alvy, "you get the right effect."

The resolution ILM needed was likely to be an issue. The deadline was in March. Computer effects at film resolution would make the project impossible to complete on schedule. Even if it were possible to have software that could handle thousands of pixels of resolution, it would take months to build, and hours to render every frame. They weren't even exactly sure how big film resolution was, although their early tests showed it to be in the 2,000 to 4,000 pixel range.

"We cannot work at film resolution," Alvy announced. "Is that going to be a problem?"

"No problem," Veilleux replied. All the effects were supposed to show up on monitors onboard the Enterprise, so nothing needed to be really photorealistic.

"Okay. I'm going to go back and put some stuff together for you and come back here with some ideas about what we can do," concluded Alvy. And he was off, as he described it, "jazzed to the gills."

For how many years had they been dreaming of this? Alvy recognized the shot as their big break. *A major film.* If they couldn't get George's attention before, maybe this would do the trick. Alvy stayed up all night scribbling his ideas for frames of the movie on green engineering paper. He only drew what he was confident they could deliver.

The next day Alvy called a hurried lunch meeting with Veilleux. He played videotaped examples of the kinds of things the team could produce, he showed some JPL Voyager animations, and they talked about the various shots. Alvy was concerned about overtaxing the engineers, great scientists perhaps, but not really tested on production deadlines with demanding high-end clients.

After a couple meetings with Ed Catmull and Jim Veilleux, Alvy whittled the roster of shots from four to one, the longest and most dramatic one, the Genesis demo. They could create a few seconds to help with the retina shot perhaps, but that was secondary. Alvy passed the rest of the scientific shots to an expert in molecular modeling, a professor of biochemistry at UCSF.[3]

[2] Voyager was at that very moment swinging by Saturn, and Jim Blinn's computer animation of it was frequently shown on national television.

[3] Dr. Robert Langridge, professor at the University of California, San Francisco. His DNA image led to a stunning mandala-like axis-on view of DNA that was featured on the cover of *Science* magazine in December, 1983.

Alvy pitched ILM on his six-panel storyboard, and he had a few suggestions that intrigued them. The Genesis probe, the missile fired at the dead planet, could be like, well, a sperm, and the dead planet, an egg. After impact, there could be this planetary splitting, like an egg cleaving and differentiating, but at a global and explosive scale, until the living planet was "born." Alvy was hot for the idea, but it was a bit edgy for everyone else. Maybe they could keep the sperm-missile, but not be so obvious with the planet part.

Alvy described the shots they could use of a JPL-like space flyby, of growing fractal mountains. At some point the surface of the dead planet would emerge from some kind of "chaos" and be a living, water-and-vegetation-covered Earth. His best description of the chaos was the red swirling spot that stormed on Jupiter. For the moment, it would have to do.

Alvy returned to Bel Marin Keys with the news. They were going to deliver 1,621 frames of animation. One thousand six hundred and twenty-one frames equals sixty-seven and a half seconds.

"This is a sixty-second commercial to George Lucas," said Alvy to the team, "to show him what he's got."

 The storyboards were just the starting place for their sixty-second piece; there was still indecision about how much or how little graphical complexity to commit to. They could certainly use Loren's fractals for the landscape, *Vol Libre*-like, but should they create the planet as a 3-D model or just a sphere with a painting of a planet texture mapped to the surface? There was no such thing as "scanning" in a texture; could a non-technical matte painter from ILM use their computerized paint system to make a picture? Could they figure this out and execute the effect on schedule? And what, exactly, would they do for the "chaos"?

It was important to Alvy that the effects support the story, and not eclipse it. "No gratuitous 3-D graphics," he told the team in their first production meeting. "This is our chance to tell George Lucas what it is we do."

Even after a year and a half, Alvy hadn't spent a great deal of time with Lucas—no one had—but after attending a few screenings with the boss, he felt he understood him a little bit, at least how he watched a movie.

"He watches the camera," Alvy said. "He's fully aware of what the cameraman is doing." Alvy was adamant that the effect they generated needed to have a camera shot in it that no human camera operator could ever have done.

Loren built his fractal mountains and worked on the task of designing the flight path of the camera with a real-time geometric modeling program that Reeves had put together. He also took it upon himself to figure out the star fields.

Creating star fields, it turned out, was not as simple as it looked. When the L.A.-based ILM team was working on *Star Wars*, they had tried for months to develop realistic star fields for space. But no matter what they tried, everything looked fake. Finally, they realized that only real space looked real.

By the time Loren needed to invent star fields, he built on this observation. Using the Yale Bright Star Catalog, which had data for the 9,100 stars visible from earth with a magnitude of 6.6 or brighter, he converted the data to 3-D maps and assigned actual colors and brightness to stars based on distance. Then he and Alvy sat around looking at stars and debating where the Genesis planet might be.[4]

Tom Porter had written some software that could draw organic soft-edged lines, and Alvy asked him to try it for the exploding volcanoes, an integral part of the ensuing chaos. But painting and compositing the objects together distracted Porter. Bill Reeves had some ideas for building on that work, so Reeves made an uncharacteristic move from working on the vector displays to the raster system, from black-and-white to full color.

Up until this time, objects were modeled in computers as geometric shapes, with surfaces you could cover with colors or with paintings called texture maps. You could write code to light the object, shade the object, and make it look pretty realistic. But many objects had no surfaces. An explosion. Fire. Smoke. You couldn't describe any of these with simple surface geometry, and the problem came up again and again.

What Porter had been exploring, and what Reeves pushed further, was the idea that ephemeral objects like fire and clouds could be drawn with thousands of tiny components that moved in proscribed ways. The components didn't really have surfaces to map or color, but if you made enough of them and gave them attributes such as direction, speed, color, and transparency, they had an organic feel to them. The transparency part was critically important—you had to see some objects moving behind other objects—which was a change from the intense work done to hide surfaces behind other surfaces in 3-D modeling.

Reeves looked at fire and fireworks and decided that each "particle" of the fire started hot—bright yellow—and as it moved upward like an artillery shell, arching into the darkness, it cooled and its color changed from yellow to red, and eventually went clear. To make a fire, he added more and more of these little ballistic objects, eventually about 10,000 per frame, blurring together, printed on top of each other. Together the particles formed a kind of moving volume.

"Bill was dealing with the 3-D particles themselves," recalled Porter, "and how to control them. The breakthrough was that particles could be used to visualize 3-D objects, which until this point had only been made of flat polygons and curved patches." If you program enough moving dots with the right rules about moving, color, and transparency, the result looks a lot like fire.

[4] Recalled Alvy, "Loren had the notion of choosing a location in a part of the heavens that would place recognizable constellations in the background." From Epsilon Indi, one of the five nearest stars to Earth where there is some hope there could be life, the Big Dipper would be visible in a form not too distorted from our vantage point on Earth. More interesting, perhaps, was that from Epsilon Indi, the Big Dipper would have one more visible star, our sun. Loren went to an atlas and, liking the connection to Epsilon Indi, found the *Indus* River. There he found the name "Keti Bandar," a city on the mouth of the river at the Indian Ocean. That became their name for the planet.

Recalled Alvy, "He animated a few preliminary fires, which were very beautiful and inspirational."

Although Tom had been working on related issues, Bill invented the techniques for *Star Trek*. When the time came to write a paper about it, Alvy urged him to come up with a good name. After some brainstorming, Reeves called it a "particle system." Could he adapt it? Make an explosion?

ILM did not want the 3-D modeling for the planet, but the projectile being fired; the "Genesis Probe" would work as a tiny 3-D element.[5] They decided to leave it in its "sperm shape." Because it was so small on the screen, and visible for so short a time, it didn't matter.

As they continued to develop ideas, Alvy was still unsure what to do about the "chaos." In time, he and ILM decided to abandon the volcano idea and focus on the cool wave of fire that Bill was able to make. They turned it into an expanding ring of fire, like a prairie fire, which would expand from the impact point of the missile-probe and engulf the planet. They decided to use the fire to transition from the growing mountains to evolving life on the surface.

The team continued to dance their way through the various obstacles they encountered. Tom Porter, Tom Duff, and Loren Carpenter worked independently or in continually shifting dyads, moving from the star field generation problems to the compositing problems to the texture-mapping problems. Ed Catmull even joined in to apply his expertise at motion blur, to help the crew get the effect done on schedule. Alvy ran interference, directing the shot, refining the look, selling it to ILM, continually refocusing everyone on the ultimate goal: to get George hooked.

Rob Cook had spent months working with Loren on parts of his REYES renderer. The program was actually a number of bundled-together smaller programs that created the images—one figured out what surfaces were hidden, another did shading, and so on. As Rob and Loren tested out REYES, there was always one part that was a bottleneck.

"The slowest part was the shading," said Cook, "so I tackled that and rewrote it, and then the hiding part was the slowest, and Loren rewrote that, and then the shading was slowest again."

In the friendly spirit of competitiveness, they continued to try to outperform each other. "'Ah, take that! Take that!' We went back and forth three or four times, and really enjoyed it," said Cook.

Cook was also working on a texture-mapping program, which would be an all-purpose tool for applying truer surfaces to objects. But that task was too ambitious for the real-world production deadline *Star Trek* put them on; it was exactly the kind of issue that Alvy was working to avoid. In the spirit of practicality Tom Duff came up with a shortcut to wrap a planet around a sphere. Activity was frenetic. There was little room for error.

[5] Modeled by Pat Cole.

"It was really exciting," remembered Pat Cole. "We were on a roll and we knew we were doing something special. There was a real feeling that we were all in this together, that it was worth the all-nighters, worth the catnaps on the floor. But it was very stressful…very stressful…"

One way they alleviated stress was with music. There were a lot of musicians in the group. Andy Moorer played banjo. Charlie Keagle, the hardware technician who was assembling the first ASP, played horns with The Band on *The Last Waltz*.[6] Another technician, Annie Arbogast, had a punkish band on the side.

In early December, a band of the jazz musicians including Tom Duff[7] began slinking onto the C Building dubbing stage in the late evenings to rehearse. No one had said they couldn't do it, and for musicians it was a performance space of unusual quality. During the day, ILM had been shooting some blue screen shots from *Poltergeist*. They had built a scaffolding and placed a miniature of a door high above the stage. In one scene a monster comes screaming out of a closet door. This was the door. Between sets Duff decided to climb up the scaffolding to snoop around. That's when he fell.

Duff was lucky the fall didn't kill him, but it shattered his arm badly; he needed a metal plate and it involved a scary-looking scar. Alvy was nervous about the schedule. The injured Duff's coding was slowed only slightly. He still managed to jerry-rig the texture mapping software in time. Catmull handled the requisite hand-slapping and spent time smoothing ruffled feathers in the administration.

Next door to the graphics team, getting their first thrilling taste of a production deadline, Ralph Guggenheim, Dan Silva, and Clark Higgins were just completing the first draft of their editing system—which they called the "Dodo" (later described as "extinct before it was even hatched"). Now they were ready to throw it out and start again. The Dodo had timecode on the PERQ display and three screens. It only controlled two machines. The next version would need a database and interface.

Malcolm Blanchard finished his database project, Sybil, in time for ILM to use it on *Star Trek 2*. Sybil could track the work and archive it, print film and lab labels, and generate camera and shot reports and effects element sheets. For the effects teams it was an absolute godsend and became the cornerstone of their project management.

Now he was ready for another project. Since the Sybil database represented a significant portion of the structure needed in the editing system, Malcolm stripped off the front-end designed for ILM and began to reconfigure it as a tool for editing data.

[6] *The Last Waltz*, the concert film of the final 1976 performance of The Band, documented one of the great musical teams of all time. The film was directed by Martin Scorsese and released in 1978.

[7] Rob Poor (bass), Dan Silva (keyboard), Charlie Keagle (sax), Mike MacKenzie (percussion).

As work ramped up, Ralph Guggenheim felt something amiss with team-mate Dan Silva. "Dan did a lot of great work on the Dodo, but as that phase of the project drew to a close, it was clear that his attention and desire was drifting to Alvy's insanely interesting Graphics Group, where his real passion lay." Unfortunately, there was no position available for him there, and Guggenheim felt that it would be hard to keep Silva motivated in the edit group as they moved into the next phase.

Ultimately Silva left the group and returned to Xerox, much to Clark Higgins' chagrin. Ralph Guggenheim and Malcolm Blanchard were a tight duo, officemates at Bel Marin Keys as they had been at Tunstead. Clark Higgins and Dan Silva were their counterparts. Losing Silva offset the balance Higgins enjoyed; he spitefully wondered aloud whether Silva's departure had any connection to space and budget being freed up to make room for Malcolm in their group. It didn't.

Loren began rendering the fractal mountains by Christmas but everyone was concerned there wouldn't be enough time to render the entire sequence by the deadline. Their pair of VAX computers crunched day and night during the holidays, to generate a demo for ILM by the first of the year.

They settled on a strategy: instead of trying to render the entire mountain sequence at one time, they'd render every 8th frame, which was called "rendering on eights." About a week later, when it finished the pass, they'd check it out and then render every 4th frame ("on fours"). The idea was that if they ran out of time, the final sequence would be a little jumpy but still complete—it was, after all, supposed to look like a computer simulation. With luck they'd make it to "twos" and eventually to every frame.

When Loren finished the fours, he noticed a problem. As the mountains were growing, the camera flying low over the surface ran into a mountain ridge. No one saw it on eights. But impact was certain on fours.

It was too late to change the animation path or mountainscape; the entire sequence would need to be re-rendered. Loren had to create a canyon at the impact location so the camera could pass through. But the mountains weren't hand-drawn; they were calculated by the modeling software. Changing them wasn't as easy as erasing a peak; it wasn't a picture so much as a program. With few options available, Loren hacked his way into his own digital landscape, confronting the enormity of data representing all the points on the screen—every peak, every color.

He spent a week messing around with the numbers until he found the mountain where the camera needed to pass. Then it was easy. Typing a few numbers, he changed the elevation of the peak from a mile up to a mile down. Instant valley. Well, sort of instant. He told the mountains, as it were, about the path of the camera. Then had the mountain check to see if there was a collision of altitudes. If there was, it drew the mountain to a height just below the camera. Although no one liked the flat bottom to the valley, it was on screen for a fraction of a second. It was the only feasible solution.

Record floods in San Anselmo, captured by photographer Kent Reno.

Outside, Marin was experiencing torrential winter rains, and they were getting worse. The team was supposed to move into C Building in the new year, but the weather (as well as work on the *Star Trek* project) was interfering with packing, and the building wasn't quite finished yet.

Most of the rain gauges in the county overflowed during the storms, and so there never were any reliable figures as to how bad it got. Seventy-pound manhole covers bobbed in the rising waters from the Bay. There was flooding in San Anselmo, Ross, Kentfield, and Larkspur.

In the street outside the offices in Bel Marin Keys, standing water was less than a foot below the concrete floor on which the big VAX computers rested. The team rushed in one rainy morning after Christmas, scouring the complex for any 2 × 4s they could use to raise the computers. While a dozen guys rocked the heavy VAX computers back and forth, others slid blocks of wood under them, hopefully buying them another day of flood protection; the move to Kerner would have to be accelerated.

No one slept much that night. Some of the guys couldn't even go home since the roads were flooded. They watched the rising water warily. The post-production teams in San Anselmo were also scrambling from the floodwaters, preparing to move into C Building at the same time as the computer guys.

Jim Kessler had facilitated the divvying up of C Building spaces for the two factions: Ben Burtt and his team taking the custom audio rooms and, of course, the big movie-theater-sized mixing stage, and the computer group moving into the small upstairs rooms and the odd spaces downstairs among the audio rooms. The geeks were going to be happy to be back in a civilized location.

A covered balcony connected all the outside rooms that faced the one-story finance department in B Building. The whole right side of the building was set aside for George's picture cutting.

Moving to Kerner was like coming home. By January 11, 1982, the computer guys were finally enveloped in the Lucasfilm "campus"—a few buildings along an industrial avenue in San Rafael.

Unlike most academic or even corporate campuses, it was completely without identity. There was no signage. No gate. No guards. No central gathering area (with the exception of perhaps Unknown Jerome's cookie factory out back). It was an interior organization, hidden from the outside world by a misleadingly bland façade.

The idea was to not attract the particularly zealous *Star Wars* fans—there were already 150,000 in the fan club—and it helped to bond employees. It was as if everyone who worked there was a member of a secret club. Much like a Hollywood studio, a wink and a nod and you could walk right by the front desk at ILM without a word; a moment of hesitation and outsiders would be captured, sequestered, banished. But no one came around. Lucasfilm was invisible.

David DiFrancesco was generally off by himself in a room, or on the downstairs porch by the canal, tweaking the lasers. The laser scanner wasn't ready for prime time, but he had set up two competing technologies for generating a super high-resolution image on film, which he ran day and night. He called his devices RIS/ROS—raster input scanner, raster output scanner—to remind everyone this was really two machines, not one. Since the lasers wouldn't be ready any time soon, for *Star Trek* he would have to rig up some kind of 35mm studio camera to shoot each frame off a high-resolution monitor to deliver the effects to ILM.

The group had grown considerably since Ed first holed up in George's office. About twenty-five computer group employees now worked in C Building. Most of them were the scientists, and mostly men.[8]

Jim Kessler poses at the front entrance to C Building: Sprocket Systems, 1983.

[8] A new administrative assistant arrived soon after C Building was finished, Dorothy Land, the third woman to join the group.

C Building was occupied by Sprocket Systems, and was now Jim Kessler's domain in much the way that D—Industrial Light & Magic—was Tom Smith's domain. Little fiefdoms within the Lucas kingdom. Kessler and Smith and the other division managers ran things pretty much the way they wanted, reporting weekly to new president Greber on budget and whatnot.

Since George was perpetually busy with films—either *Raiders* or the next *Star Wars*—and the million and one decisions about the Ranch, he decided to set up a small "board" for his company. If Lucasfilm were a public company this might have been a Board of Directors, but in a company with only one shareholder, they were simply consultants who, George hoped, would be candid with him and bring to bear a high degree of fiscal sophistication. Greber, and CFO Faxon, ran Lucasfilm conservatively, and not knowing much about film in general, kept an eye on the bottom line while not providing any particular direction to the division heads. Something that division heads particularly enjoyed.

Kessler often felt that management did not want the staff to be entrepreneurial, but to just handle the work that filtered down from George. Sometimes work would come in from Lucas' friends, such as Spielberg, but neither the sound guys nor the effects teams were officially contractors for hire, even if that was an eventual plan. For his part, Kessler was nervous about how they'd stay employed when George wasn't making *Star Wars* or *Indiana Jones* films.

Kessler contacted John Korty in Mill Valley. Korty had been working on his animated film *Twice Upon a Time*, and it was getting close to the time when audio work would be required.

Korty had come to George with a story and a new animation technique he had developed, called Lumage (for luminous images). "The images were cut out and lit from below," explained Korty, "which gave them a special glow."

George connected Korty to Alan Ladd Jr., who financed the project. George had little involvement with the film (although he had been a big fan of animation since USC), but was still listed as the executive producer. The movie was a fantastical tale, right up George's alley. Promotional materials described it as "An evil outfit called the Murkworks, led by a devilish character called Synonamess Botch, wants to replace the world's sweet dreams with nightmares, which are delivered as bomb-like eardrops by a platoon of winged creatures resembling a cross between vultures and pterodactyls."

Kessler had been worried that the first project they put into the new audio facilities on Kerner would be *Jedi*. "Let us do the mix," he suggested to Korty. "It will give our new mixing theater a shakedown. We'll give you a really good deal and it'll be great." Korty had been planning on doing the mix in Los Angeles, but agreed.

Not everyone was excited about the outside work. A number of the sound team disliked bringing outsiders into their custom facility (and they were paid whether George was working on a movie or not). But Kessler prevailed and *Twice Upon a Time* broke in the new building as well as paved the way for other outside projects at Sprockets.

The Sprockets theater was a marvel. Visitors to C Building from Hollywood and from theater exhibitor companies were stunned by the audio. "They wanted that sound in their new facilities," said Tom Holman, "because it was clearly better."

Ben Burtt and Tom Holman take a moment in the Sprockets dubbing theater in C Building, site of the original THX speaker installation.

Having the computer team so close to Sprockets and ILM changed the chemistry of the workgroups, and it didn't take long for cross-pollination to begin. Sprockets parked an unused Moviola in a dark corner of the conference room; it was an interesting art object for the computer scientists. A couple of the younger ILM staff came by C Building and enjoyed looking over the shoulders of Loren Carpenter and others, at the cool pictures their new neighbors were producing. One of these guys had an Apple II computer for fun (he was the "computer expert" at ILM), but the computers in C Building were far more sexy.

Matte painting was a special artform at ILM. In the great tradition of movie special effects, artists took oil paints and worked directly on enormous glass sheets, leaving dark spaces through which motion pictures could be inserted.

If the painting was right and the match-up between live action and painting perfect, an audience never noticed the combination. Though it would seem to be about realism, the best matte painters achieved something closer to impressionism, knowing just how much detail to add and when to fudge and let the audience do the rest.

Once Tom Porter had a working version of his paint program, he invited the ILM matte artists[9] over to play with the software in much the same way Alvy and David had enjoyed the first frame buffer and paint software at Xerox. Chris Evans used the tool to make an earth-like painting of the finished Genesis planet, which they could wrap around a sphere.

The rendering was painfully slow. The computer generated some frames in as little as five minutes, but others—like fractal mountains or particle systems of fire—demanded five hours, even at video resolution. One thousand, six hundred and twenty-one frames. The fractal mountains alone took a month of full-time rendering.

While the software team worked on the Genesis Effect, the hardware team was still hammering out specialized hardware to speed up the rendering of the graphics. In the meantime, Alvy's team did modeling with an Evans & Sutherland Picture System, and rendering on their DEC VAX computers. If the new hardware could be built, they expected to render an image two or even three orders of magnitude faster. An increase in speed of a hundred to a thousand times would be essential as the length of the animations they wanted to create got longer and the images got more realistic (and thus more complicated).

As the deadline approached that March, the Graphics Group held short screenings of various parts of the shot for ILM, to refine some problems they still needed to overcome. Steven Spielberg, who was working next door with ILM, finishing up the effects on *E.T.*, sat in on their dailies one afternoon and was utterly blown away by what he saw. George's friends Hal Barwood and Matthew Robbins, who were on Kerner visiting their old pal Spielberg, encouraged him to talk to Catmull after the screening and get a tour of the Graphics Group. They called over Tom Porter to see if he'd give him a demo of the paint system.

Spielberg sat at the same workstation that Chris Evans had used to paint the planet, and played and played with the pen and tablet, zooming in on pixels and blurring them. He asked a lot of questions. Tom Porter remembered the discussion well:

"When will you guys be able to make a ninety-minute movie at film resolution?"

"It might be awhile," Porter told him. (At the rate they were going, it could be a decade away.)

[9] Mike Pangrazio, Chris Evans, and Frank Ordaz.

Steven Spielberg, like most people, had never seen a graphics workstation before. He invited Hal Barwood to watch over his shoulder as Porter gave him basic instructions, "Click here…press that button…draw here…"

Spielberg was elated. Even though the concept had been invented a decade earlier, it was a rare experience even for someone like him. With a grin on his face, Steven turned to face Porter and proclaimed, "What a great time to be alive!"

By the end of March, the final elements of the Genesis Effect were completed and delivered to ILM and to their clients at Paramount.

Paramount loved it. The resolution was so good that Veilleux asked the software team to raise the contrast, to increase the "video-look" of the images by intensifying the scan lines of the monitor. It pained them to do it, but there was never really any choice. Alvy was very pleased with the camera work in the shot. It was dramatic. The camera moved and twisted and continually reoriented the audience as it flew around the planet.

By late May 1982, there were company memos circulating at Lucasfilm for everyone to pick a time and place for their private screenings at the larger Marin theaters. *Star Trek* was about to come out, and *E.T.* a week later. There were wrap parties in the evenings. Contract employees finished up and the permanent staff began to take off for vacations.

After the employee screening of *Star Trek II: The Wrath of Kahn*, Alvy sat in his office contemplating the months of work. Then a head poked in his door. It was George Lucas. Alvy looked up in amazement. The graphics team had accomplished a great deal on a production deadline. They refined fractals. Invented particle systems and a paint system. Improved texture mapping and compositing. Even created star fields.

George said, "Great camera shot," and then disappeared. Alvy sat back in his chair, and behind his bushy beard, his face opened up into an enormous grin.

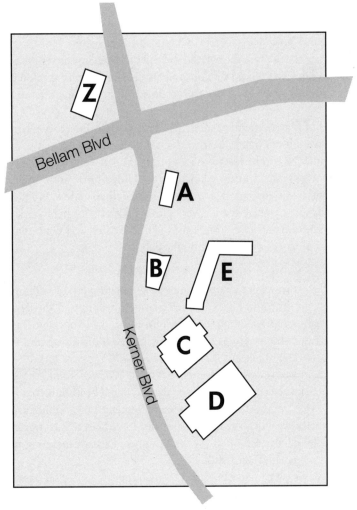

Diagram of "The Kerner Company," the complex of Lucasfilm buildings hidden in plain sight along Kerner Blvd. in San Rafael.

seventeen

Queen's Rules

[1982–1983]

Whether the pitcher hits the stone or the stone hits the pitcher, it goes ill with the pitcher.

—Don Quixote by Miguel de Cervantes

THERE WERE A HANDFUL of unwritten rules of conduct at Lucasfilm. Low down in the ranks of the organization, they passed between co-workers. George couldn't possibly have known about them. The rules were nothing unusual—just professional behavior expected of professionals.

No autographs, for instance.

There were far too many visits from stars and famous directors to allow the employees to gawk at the guests. (Or even co-workers, many of whom were reasonably well-known. Even by 1982, it seemed like every other office had an Oscar sitting on a bookshelf next to some *Star Wars* toy.) Rumors circulated of one wayward (and short-lived) employee accosting James Earl Jones, who was recording his Darth Vader lines and who was wholly displeased with the behavior.

In the months after the Genesis Effect, the Graphics Group seemed to be demonstrating their tools to all sorts of "George's friends." Steven Spielberg was at Kerner with some frequency. So were Barwood and Robbins, and Michael Ritchie. Martin Scorsese came by to look around. Sydney Pollack dropped in with Sylvester Stallone.[1] Tours for dignitaries were a part of every week.

"George was clearly proud to bring his buddies by," figured Tom Porter, "which was a nice sort of feedback for us."

When Akira Kurosawa was in California for the American premiere of *Kagemusha*, he visited Francis and, later, George. George gave him a tour of the Kerner facility and showed off the miniatures at ILM and other technology at the company. "We were all terribly excited to introduce the great Kurosawa to computer graphics," said Alvy.[2]

[1] Stallone brought with him a small entourage of starlets who stood around him as Porter gave a demonstration of his paint system. Taking a stylus, Sly proceeded to scribble madly on a tablet, something that appeared to onlookers like a horse, but not a very good one. With a grunt of finality he dropped the stylus, reared back, and announced, "Look! Italian stallion!" which was met with the high-pitched shrieks of joy from his coterie, "Oh Sly!!"

[2] When Kurosawa entered the darkened computer lab for his demonstration, a computer workstation was along one wall, and in a far corner sat an idle Moviola. Kurosawa stood close to the computer as Loren Carpenter gave him an overview of their work. During the demonstration, however, Kurosawa wandered over to the abandoned Moviola and touched it gently, wistfully. "He never said a word," said Alvy.

Kurosawa inspects models at ILM, flanked by Richard Edlund *(left)* and Lucas *(right)*.

Another rule: *No photographs.*

It wasn't just George who didn't enjoy a camera being pointed at him within the confines of his own organization. It was as if the entire company emanated a vibe of "no pictures." Everything that everyone did was exciting…and secret.

Security around the films was legendary. The element of surprise was central to the release of a multimillion-dollar movie. Scripts were coded, and few at ILM ever saw more than a few pages of anything. Scripts and signs and T-shirts for *Jedi* were code-named with a fictitious film "Blue Harvest," and company employees wore their "Blue Harvest" shirts proudly.[3]

[3] With the tag line, "Horror Beyond Imagination."

Walter Cronkite visiting ILM. *Left:* With Lucas. *Right:* Cronkite, Lucas, Edlund, Kurtz.

Probably the most important of the unspoken Lucasfilm rules: *No chatting it up with George.*

It was rare to see George wandering around Kerner, but if he was there, it was a *faux pas* to approach him. Of course, if George spoke to you, you were expected to have a conversation, usually about what you were working on.

"Queen's rules," as Andy Moorer once described it.[4]

The separation intensified the mystique even for those who worked around him. "We were so disconnected from George it was ridiculous," groused Clark Higgins, who was far more comfortable with Coppola's gregariousness and manner of sharing ideas with everyone nearby.

"It seemed to me that the company was carefully designed to protect [Lucas]," said Malcolm Blanchard, "to keep the rest of the world away so he could do what he wanted...that's his personality, a shy guy who likes to make films."[5]

Ralph Guggenheim standing at a flatbed film-to-video transfer machine.

Phase two of the editing system was accelerated after Guggenheim and team were settled into C Building. They had learned a lot from their PERQ experience with the Dodo, but it was clear that the platform wasn't going to be sufficient for their needs. But there was another option, and the team had been eyeing it for months.

[4] Director Bernardo Bertolucci once described meeting Queen Elizabeth: "They give you a book of how to behave around the queen. I remember it said in some cases to refer to her as 'ma'am'—rhymes with 'spam.' It always set up an odd association for me."

[5] Another rule: Be wary of hiring anyone who tells you "I'd do *anything* to work at Lucasfilm."

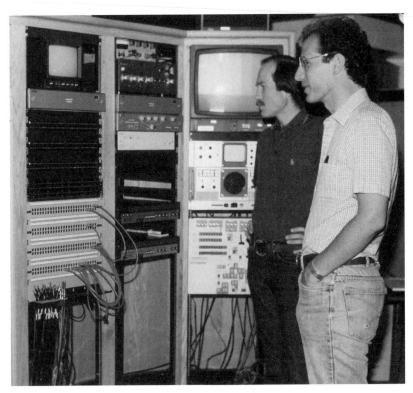

Malcolm and Ralph pondering the equipment in the C Building video machine room.

The project John Seamons left when he joined Lucasfilm was a graphical workstation from Stanford: the SUN. In the interim, Seamons' associate Andy Bechtolsheim had raised venture capital and was ready to produce his first product: the SUN-1. It was small and it ran on UNIX, both of which made everyone in the Computer Division very comfortable. They could write their code in the hip language C instead of the less powerful Pascal that was used by the PERQ. And it would handle the simultaneous control of external devices better than the PERQ.

Andy Moorer (who knew of the project from his time at Stanford) and the other project leaders felt the SUN would be a solid platform to build around. Seamons had a prototype of the hardware: it was time to put it to the test.

"When SUN got funded in February 1982, I had already starting building workstations," said Andy Bechtolsheim, "I hand-built the first twenty or thirty at Stanford. We started shipping product in May 1982, and Lucasfilm got most of the first units." At the time, and for many years, Lucasfilm was the largest OEM client for SUN products. Lucasfilm installed the workstations companywide. The hardware team immediately established an infrastructure of networked SUN computers. They called it "Yodanet."

The founders of Sun Microsystems in 1982. *From left:* Vinod Khosla, Bill Joy, Andy Bechtolsheim, Scott McNealy.

Yodanet provided every employee with access to email and, more importantly, company communications, bulletin boards, and messaging. When the fan club had excess posters, everyone got an email. When someone saw a house for sale in a great neighborhood or when new VistaVision T-shirts from ILM were getting printed, everyone knew immediately.

The machine room upstairs in C Building in early 1983. Central is the DEC 11/780s (aka, the VAX) called Dagobah, filling about five cabinets. Off camera to the right is the VAX 11/750 called Bespin. Twenty pound 50MB or 100MB hard disk packs dot the washing machine-sized disk drives that are connected to the computers. The entire room represents fewer than one or two gigabytes of storage.

As they phased out the VAXes for the new SUNs, Seamons transferred the files and the identities of the computers to the new platform. They still had the VAX's names—Dagobah, Bespin, Kessel, Endor, Tatooine—but the SUNs arrived in such quantity, the guys ran out of Lucasfilmy names. The first few were C-3PO and R2D2, of course, followed by Lando. But in no time Nellybell was running the prototype sound processor, and Jedit the video editing system. Lightnin controlled the laser film scanner and dozens more were workstations for the engineers.

David DiFrancesco's work on the laser scanner and printer moved into high gear once he established a space in C Building where he could build the "floating" concrete slab on which to construct the precision lasers— this would render them immune to subtle vibrations. The year before he had criss-crossed the country to meet with laser experts in a half-dozen industries, from Photo Electronics Corporation in Florida to Kodak in New York, CBS Labs in California, Goodyear Tire and Rubber in Arizona….

And now he had two laser systems, each one representing a different theory about the best way to achieve the fine resolution their device would require. As *Jedi* was underway, David gave his machines their first trial, printing a still image of a blue screen shot for ILM. Both machines succeeded; both were able to make a single image, but this was still a long way from producing a long series of frames with the resolution and accuracy Lucasfilm demanded.

David DiFrancesco standing amidst the two laser recorders he built, prior to running the first production through the system—and before there was a computer built to handle the images.

With the phase one Dodo behind them, and the key to the next phase identified as both the integration of a database and a graphical front-end with the SUN, Ralph Guggenheim asked Malcolm Blanchard to join the editing project fully. Blanchard phased out of his work for ILM; now he would spend his time between designing data structures for Sybil to support the editing system and, eventually, designing a user interface for editors.

"I don't know really what the interface should look like," said Blanchard.

"Check with Jim Kessler. Maybe you can go downstairs watch some of the editing on *Jedi*."

Lucas' schedule on *Jedi* was similar to *Empire*: he'd show up to edit at the crack of dawn, work until afternoon; then he'd slip over to ILM, returning a few hours later to work until early evening. Blanchard quickly got permission to sit in on his process.[6] Lucas was particularly interested in the development of the editing system, and so he was pleased to have Blanchard observe him while he labored in the archaic, tedious machinations of editing. He hoped this would be the last time he had to use strips of film to make a movie.

Upon entering C Building, instead of going left and upstairs past the mixing theater to his office, Blanchard entered the cordoned-off right side of the building used for editorial. George Lucas hardly ever used the front door, choosing instead to enter Sprockets or ILM from the hidden parking lot.

Lucas said little as he sat before a flatbed editing table in the darkened room, his white cloth gloves sliding smoothly over the spinning plates of film. Duwayne Dunham dutifully stood behind him, fetching trims from the bales of film strips hanging in the back of the room and in the room next door. Blanchard slipped in behind them. He sat quietly, watching Lucas cut: his hands going back and forth, back and forth, getting another piece of film, cutting it in, threading it up, back and forth....

"So I'm sitting there and realizing that, while this is all very cool, all the interesting stuff is going on in George's head. Just watching an editor doesn't really tell you a lot about the process." After an hour, Blanchard stopped taking notes. He couldn't think of anything to write down. Images moved forward and backward, over and over, in minute steps, tediously.

"After about two hours of this, I'm thinking there are people out in the world who would give body parts to be sitting where I am, watching George Lucas cut his latest *Star Wars* movie...and I am bored out of my friggin' head. All I can think of is, Please let me out of this room!"

By the summer of 1982, after almost two years of work, Andy Moorer and his cohorts finally completed the first working prototype of the audio computer, the ASP. The massive ASP consisted of eight oversized boards assembled

[6] Lucas allowed only a small handful of people to visit him in the *Jedi* cutting rooms. Dunham recalled that one was Steve Jobs.

entirely by hand, requiring more than 3,000 IC chips. It represented a number of significant engineering breakthroughs.

Most computer companies would execute a plan this ambitious with dozens of engineers. Andy had done it with a team of four—two on hardware and two on software.

A typical section of a professional audio mixing console, with eight slices (running vertically at left) and a column of master controls along the right side. A full console often consists of sixty or more slices.

The interface to the ASP was a separate issue. John Snell had met repeatedly with Ben Burtt and the rest of the Sprockets sound team. They all felt that the audio computer had to look and work pretty much like the traditional tools they knew. A mixing console, the device the ASP ostensibly replaced, was enormous, like a banquet table, covered with columns of sliders, knobs and buttons, called "slices," repeated over and over, covering it completely. Each slice controlled a single track of sound that played back the mag holding one bit of dialog, or music, or effects.

As scenes played on a large screen, engineers "rode" the console, adjusting the volume of thunder, for instance, or the EQ of Luke's voice, until all the elements for the scene were in balance.[7] Once all the components sounded good, they'd get mixed down to fewer tracks (a "mix down") in small sets. Eventually there would be three tracks—dialog, music, and sound effects—that went into a final mix.

It was all very linear. If a mixer discovered that Yoda's voice was hard to hear against the background thunder, lowering the volume of the *mixed* dialog track would lower the volume of *all* the sound together; in many circumstances a fix would require going back to earlier mix downs, and practically starting again. The process, like optical line-up at ILM, demanded a digital alternative that would free the team from generation loss and the inflexibility associated with building tracks linearly.

Andy Moorer interviewed the members of the Lucasfilm sound department about their tools. "It's really odd when you're trying to revolutionize the industry," he recalled, "because if you just go and ask someone what they want, they'll show you what they've got and say, Give me this exact same thing, only better."

Sound engineers liked their big consoles. They could keep fingers on multiple sliders at the same time, tweak a knob here and there, and always know where every setting was. Though Ben wanted the flexibility that digital processing and random access might provide, it couldn't be at the cost of changing the interface.

John Snell had long been interested in the physical interface of computers for music. He had made sketches and early prototypes at Carnegie-Mellon in

[7] EQ = equalization. A balancing of the relative "volume" of the various frequencies (e.g., bass, treble) of a given sound.

the early '70s, and he was beginning to experiment with what became known as "touch screens."

"I thought of it as a real-time interface to the computer," said Snell, "for touching and working with data. Musicians and mixers really like to use their fingers and hands, and computers had been exclusively typewriter-oriented machines."

Snell wanted a computer interface that would allow the mixer to have all ten fingers on the screen at one time and could sense different amounts of pressure. But when he circulated the idea at Sprockets, he was met with an inordinate amount of resistance.

The Sprockets' mixing consoles were made from the highest quality sliders and knobs; for a digital version, they wanted the same control surface—the same buttons, the same knobs, the same sliders—connected to the ASP. Any computer scientist could immediately look at a professional mixing console and recognize the sheer redundancy involved—it was wasteful and archaic. Making not only the insides digital, but the interface too, could be remarkably efficient and cost-effective.

"We felt that you could use one knob or slider and have the software change its function," said Snell, "and a console could be built with perhaps eight sliders, or twelve, but not a hundred. [The old console design] simply wasn't practical."

John Snell's interface for the digital audio console, version two (1981). The audio function of every slider, knob, push-button, and LED display was programmable. Its companion graphical interface with a touchscreen eventually became the primary interface for editing and mixing.

It also wasn't affordable. With a limited budget, Moorer was convinced that resources should go into the processing, not the knobs and push-buttons. While the processing hardware continued to evolve, the interface hardware continued to get debated just as it had been in 1981, and throughout 1982.

C Building was intended to be a huge space for picture and sound post-production and the three computer projects, but it was filled to overflowing soon after everyone moved in. In addition to computer scientists, the support staff was increasing. A variety of technicians had been added to the team, primarily to help with the building of the Pixar image computer (PIC), but also with the technological support for the new Lucasfilm computer network.

Tom Porter, kicking back in the third floor lounge in C Building.

Almost everyone was doubled up in every available space. Employees grumbled periodically about who had how many windows in his office, yet they still worked day and night, engrossed in new developments.

"There were always space wars on Kerner," said Susan Anderson. "Everybody needed space; the place was growing fast and sharing the building was hard."

"People were working way too much," recalled Bob Greber. "I'd walk into buildings and ask people to go home. I'd say 'It's Saturday, what are you doing here? We're not open today.' But people loved the work they were doing."

Greber could often get the Sprockets guys or ILM artists to head home, but rarely the computer scientists. "They worked very peculiar hours and I think they loved the idea that they were a little different."

Annie Arbogast was one of the technicians. With her energetic bleached-blond curls, silver bangles and broad smile, she radiated a rockstar demeanor; she was far hipper than the typical tech employee. When Annie heard that ILM was looking to tweak the scratch track for the puppets who sang a musical number in Jabba the Hutt's sordid little throne room, she was immediately galvanized. The sequence had an instrumental track but it needed alien lyrics. She wrote a song she called "Laptinek" (using a toy she had that could make unusual word sounds as inspiration). George heard Annie's scratch track each time he reviewed the scene, and soon he was enjoying it, enough so that he opted to keep Arbogast's song in the film, on the lips of Sy Snootles in *Episode VI*.[8]

Bob Greber was right: it always seemed that no matter what someone did at Lucasfilm, what they really wanted was to be in the movies.

Susan Anderson's responsibilities were growing (though she was holed up in what was basically a storage closet on the second floor). One was the overseeing of new terminals as they arrived on every employee's desk.

The computers were hard for staff to operate. UNIX-based. Flashing login prompts and long command strings to print. Anderson moved throughout the company getting each department—administration, marketing, Sprockets—into the digital age.

When George's computer arrived, it was placed in his editing room and he took the screen login name, The Boss. "He used it for one thing," said Dunham, "and one thing only: who is making the cookie run to Unknown Jerome's. That was it. People would call up and say, 'Who's The Boss,' and I'd say, 'Who do you think it is?'"

"When we got to Bel Marin Keys, the guys literally had to move the typewriter off my desk and put a computer terminal in its place," recalled Anderson. "A year later, I was doing that for everybody at Lucasfilm."

There were two segregated cultures within the company: the filmmakers and the computer geeks. Before, they were separated by geography. Now they co-existed on Kerner.

Anderson continued: "I went over to ILM and sat down with these [film makers] and said, 'Okay everyone, let's log on.'"

"Sometimes it was very complicated having conversations with those [computer] guys," said Duwayne Dunham. "I'm serious. Sometimes George and I would talk about it. It was hard to communicate. As soon as they would start talking it was like 'this is over my head.'"

With the creation of a Lucasfilm campus, George encouraged the growing spirit of familial empowerment at the company. For instance, Ralph Guggenheim created a course he called "Introduction to Computer Programming" for the non-technical employees. "The first few classes were just general information about what made computers tick and were widely attended," he recalled. "Then we proceeded to teach some introductory Pascal (a popular computer language at the time) and had the few who stuck it out write a simple program or two."

One employee was Craig Good, part of the janitorial staff. Craig not only made it through the course, but soon advanced to become a computer systems technician and a valuable member of the division.[9]

[8] Word was that composer John Williams, who was scoring the third film, was lobbying for his daughter to write the piece.

[9] Another member of the janitorial staff who excelled in the course was Jenny Fulle. In 2005, Fulle became Executive VP of production at Sony Pictures Imageworks.

In the same collegiate spirit, ILM's matte painting department began holding live drawing classes in the evenings. They'd get a model to stand around in their studio with half-finished matte paintings of forests and docking bays and planets. "If you were interested in hanging around inside ILM or just wanted to spend an otherwise dull evening with some artists and a naked woman, it was a great activity," reported one attendee.

As email and company-wide memos became part of the culture, more of these diversions were fit into the hectic weekly schedules.

The Graphics Group took to wearing T-shirts that had the international "forbidden" sign—a circle with a red line through it—over a set of stair-like "jaggies." Jaggies were still the bane of computer graphics on raster displays.

"Unfortunately, and erroneously, some people equate this look with computer graphics," wrote Alvy in an *American Cinematographer* article about the *Star Trek* effects. "It is like assuming the flicker of early movies is the nature of film."

No jaggies were going to be allowed at Lucasfilm. Ed and Alvy put that law into effect. "Don't write software that doesn't take care of jaggies; it won't be accepted." While the rule emanated from their deepest sensibilities, it also served to differentiate them from other graphics teams working toward a full-length computer-generated movie: in particular, Whitney and Demos at Triple-I.

Summer 1982. *From left:* Ed Catmull, Alvy Ray Smith, Loren Carpenter. Note Alvy's "No Jaggies" T-shirt.

The Wrath of Kahn was released on June 6, 1982.

While Alvy's team was working on the Genesis Effect in 1981, Triple-I spent the year focused on a different project. A young animation director named Steven Lisberger had written a story about a man being sucked into a computer.[10] It was called *Tron,* and in 1980 Disney agreed to make the live-action movie. The effects supervisor was Harrison Ellenshaw, a long-time Disney matte painter who had supervised the mattes in both *Star Wars* and *Empire* for Lucasfilm.[11]

Most of the story was set inside a PC; consequently the movie required 1,000 special effects shots, about fifteen minutes of them using computer-generated imagery. The majority of the "computer effects" were done without computers, but rather by rotoscoping—drawing on film frames by hand. Still, *Tron* had more computer effects than any film before it, and since the film was really *about* computers, it gave the impression of being one giant computer-generated effect.

Reported the leading special effects magazine of the day, "*Tron* signals the emergence of the Walt Disney organization from the black hole of formula filmmaking which has characterized the studio since the death of its founder."

But before the effects were created, John Whitney and Gary Demos had a falling out with management at Triple-I, and left to start their own company. Triple-I subsequently did a few shots for *Tron*, but three other computer animation teams were enlisted by Disney to complete the effects.[12]

Tron came out July 9, 1982.

And while *Tron* was a cult sensation, spawning videogames (of course) and lunchboxes, the film was a disappointment at the box office. Many in the computer industry felt its failure negatively impacted the role graphics could play in the movies. Though the computer effects were not to blame (and were arguably the high points of the movie), the belief was widely held that the short-sighted Hollywood establishment would see computer effects as box-office poison.

Catmull disagreed with that observation. "The studios didn't pay any attention to *Tron* because they only pay attention to successes. The only setback was that of a wasted opportunity."

Computer development had been going on for two years and, even allowing for some delays in getting started, it was moving too quickly through its budget. Lucasfilm executives Bob Greber and Roger Faxon wondered if anything really commercial was going on. They attempted to figure this out through meetings with Ed Catmull and the various project leaders, but the answers were too obscured by computer talk.

[10] Written in 1976: at the time, Pong was still fun and Atari was growing.

[11] *Harrison Ellenshaw* (b. 1945). Visual effects producer. Matte painter on *The Shagy D.A.* (1976), *Star Wars* (1977), *Pete's Dragon* (1977), *The Black Hole* (1979), *The Empire Strikes Back* (1980); Visual effects supervisor or producer on *Tron* (1982), *Captain Eo* (1986), *Dick Tracy* (1990), *Ghost* (1990). Also, the son of matte painting pioneer, Peter Ellenshaw.

[12] Robert Abel and Associates, the Mathematics Applications Group, Inc. (MAGI), and Digital Effects. MAGI provided most of the effects in the film.

BOB DORIS

Hometown: Woonsocket, RI. *Family:* single. *Schools:* Harvard. *Interests:* cooking, reading, organ. *Sign:* Libra. *Employment history:* Boston Consulting Group.
[1982 LFL Yearbook]

They wanted to hear from an MBA. They decided that they needed somebody on the inside who could speak business and explain to them what, if any, opportunities existed. For their part, Ed and Alvy wanted to get someone else on the payroll who could market their stuff and eventually find people who would buy it, so they could focus on development.

The person they found was Bob Doris, a young MBA with a law degree, both from Harvard. They all interviewed him. He was a star at the famous Boston Consulting Group, which Lucasfilm administration liked. He was a really smart "suit" with an interest in technology, which the computer scientists liked.

They hired him. But it wasn't clear to Doris exactly what he was supposed to do. For some time, it wasn't even clear whether Doris worked for Catmull or vice versa. They just started working together.

When Whitney and Demos left Triple I, they started a new company, Digital Productions (DP). So certain that the jaggie problem could be solved by using massive quantities of pixels, they bought a $4 million Cray supercomputer to use for rendering. (The Cray didn't eliminate jaggies but it made them much smaller.) They scoffed at Lucasfilm's smaller VAX (and new SUN) set-up for processing images.

It was hard not to be just a little jealous of DP's hardware, but the prevailing thought around Lucasfilm was that it was overkill, like a hundred-foot ruler, big and impressive but not practical.

But here was Gary Demos, with a new lab, with all the kinds of equipment one would need for filmmaking—rendering software, film scanners, that kind of thing—and clearly some big money behind him. Were Ed and Alvy missing something?

Having made the sale to DP, Cray Research was persistent in its pitch to Lucasfilm; they sensed deep pockets and recognized the massive needs of the computer graphics team. Salesmen would wine and dine Ed and Alvy, show off their hot installations, and offer up bits of free render time. As Cray pressed, Ed and Alvy had little more than a visceral sense that it was the wrong direction for them.

With Bob Doris on board, they had a sophisticated business guy to help them see once and for all if it made any financial sense. As soon as Digital Productions came online, curiosity got the best of him, and Ed Catmull called

Gary Demos *(left)* and John Whitney, Jr. pose before their new Cray at Digital Productions.

up Gary Demos to arrange a visit to their new digs in L.A. He took Bob Doris with him.

"I think they wanted to show off," said Doris. "And I think they were flattered to have Catmull visit."

Bob Doris asked Demos detailed questions about their organization. On the plane ride back, Bob ran the numbers. To make a fully rendered computer animation running 100 minutes, on a budget of around $10 million, the film couldn't cost more than around $1,600 per second. Doris estimated that Digital Productions, using their Cray, would make animations costing ten times that amount. According to Doris' calculations, the only kind of project DP could afford to make would be television commercials. Because commercials were the most expensive films made per second, computer animation could be a cost-effective alternative.

Cray's sales pitch addressed this concern: the expense of the supercomputer could be offset by running two businesses concurrently—the animation business, and a business to rent out Cray "cycles" when the machine wasn't in use. All kinds of industries could use them, from industrial research to the national weather predictors.

Bob and Ed agreed that in spite of Digital Productions' impressive set-up, it couldn't work for Lucasfilm. "We felt getting a Cray computer would blow our wad," said Catmull.

Gary Demos and John Whitney, Jr. were always lingering in Ed and Alvy's periphery. First at Triple-I, knocking at Lucasfilm's door, and again at Digital Productions. And yet they were never business competitors.

"There really wasn't a business there," said Catmull. "We were intellectual competitors. Both Lucasfilm and DP were driven to develop computer graphics to the point that they could be used in movies."

But Catmull and Demos had different belief systems and different priorities. Catmull had continued his active participation in the academic community. He encouraged everyone on his team to publish papers. The connection to Siggraph, which helped Lucasfilm find talent, was in marked contrast to Digital Production, which didn't play an active role in that world. Another difference was that Catmull did not want to jump into production too soon.

"I believed that we were so far away from practical solutions that we were far better off participating in this small but stimulating community. It is not enough to be driven, you must be really smart about your resources. We knew this was a marathon, not a sprint."

After Bob Doris arrived at Lucasfilm, there was a change in the way the scientists were viewed by the company. Before Doris, Ed's group had worked under Jim Kessler, as part of Sprockets Computer Services. After Doris, the group became its own division, like Sprockets, like ILM. Now that they were a division, they needed a name and logo.

"We had a hell of a time with names," recalled Alvy. "We wanted a sexy name like Industrial Light & Magic, but we couldn't get two people to agree on one. We had these naming contests…we had hundreds of names. George even threw in a couple, but everybody hated them."

Loren proposed "Cinematrix"—it could be said two ways, either CIN-EMAtrix or CINEmatrix, and it was interesting both ways. But it was argued that it was too heady and people would find it confusing. In the end, unable to resolve their differences, they simply referred to themselves as the "Computer Division." Comprised of the graphics project, the editing project and the sound project, the Computer Division was finally on political par with the other major pillars of Lucasfilm. They had achieved a new legitimacy.

The official logo of the new division, circa 1983.

For the most part, Ed Catmull was happy to have someone running interference with the executives. But Doris' arrival also signaled the end of the glory days of pure research, when there were no customers, no demands. Now they had someone looking for products. With target markets. And eventually, with release dates.

Always present was the knowledge that computer research at Lucasfilm had only been chartered for three years and that period was rapidly drawing to a close.

The issues of making a high-resolution image continued to sit on the shoulders of the graphics team. If they were going to build a computer, if they were going to write software, they had to figure out what it needed to do. As computers got better, scientists were able to make more sophisticated and detailed images. But they needed to be proactive. Where was all of this going?

Most of the researchers worked with intense focus on the tasks at hand, with little eye on the politics, little focus on the horizon. As the Marin summer drifted on, Rob Cook sat in Loren Carpenter's office, looking out at the green and gold slopes of Mt. Tamalpais. Cook recalled their discussion:

"We've got this fractal technology. We've got a way to shade the polygons," began Rob. "Ed is working on texture mapping and stuff, but we've got to put this stuff together. How detailed an image do we need."

Loren stared out the window for a moment, across the building tops of San Rafael, toward the horizon, toward the mountain.

"I want to make a picture of that."

Rob looked behind him, at the details of the scene. Of the thin sway of the telephone lines, of the minute shades of green in the mountain. Of the concrete in the street.

"What's the most efficient way, using geometry, of making it?" asked Rob.

"I don't know. How many surfaces are out there? How many polygons are out there?"

The basic premise, particle systems notwithstanding, was that everything needed surfaces for the photons of light to hit, to bounce off of or reflect back from. Every surface needed to be calculated, formed from smaller polygons, and every lighting calculation was dependent on the quantity of those surfaces.

"I want a level of detail where if I'm standing here with a 35mm movie camera and I take a picture of that, the information content of the image is identical to what comes out of a computer."

After making *Vol Libre* and working on the Genesis Effect, Loren had a rough idea of what it might take, and they were nowhere near able to do it. *Vol Libre* had maybe 100,000 polygons.[13]

Ed joined the meeting and the three of them worked through the math. Multiplying color samples and figuring in screen resolution and adjusting planes, they debated and scribbled through the afternoon.

And then it just appeared. The number. The place their computer and their images somehow had to go. If they were ever going to create photorealistic images, their computers had to manage eighty million polygons.

Eighty *million*.

Early 3-D graphics (like Catmull's *Hand*) had been executed with a few *thousand* polygons. By the time *Tron* and *Kahn* were created, graphics still had only around 100,000 polygons. Now they were looking at two orders of magnitude greater complexity.[14]

By setting their sights on eighty million polygons, it changed their entire way of thinking. It was clear that that was too many to draw. "It seemed sort of crazy at the time," recalled Cook.

But Catmull liked the challenge. It forced them to rethink the process. They needed to create ways for the computer to add detail somewhat automatically. Realistic models would have to get built from simple objects that merged over

[13] Polygons relate to the construction of a scene; pixels relate to the translation of the scene to a screen. There isn't a direct correlation between the number of pixels on film and the number of polygons needed to generate a realistic-looking scene. They not only didn't know how many polygons they'd need, they still didn't know how many pixels they'd need either.

[14] That's like having a car that goes 60mph when you're zooming down the highway and needing to drive closer to 50,000mph. (The speed of sound is around 760mph.)

and over into more complex objects—a "hierarchical modeling scheme." They also needed to figure out how to light a scene with so many surfaces—with so many mathematical calculations it would cripple any computer.

It was the vision of eighty million polygons that made the graphics team at the Lucasfilm Computer Division different from any other graphics group in the world. Instead of solving their problems with monstrous Cray horsepower, a sledgehammer, they were going to solve it with better math. They were aiming so high and so far that no one could imagine what a world like that might mean.

Almost twenty discrete number values would have to be stored for every surface. Rob and Loren figured they could texture-map the polygons with a color, or transparency, or scratches, maybe five or six texture channels, each one in red, green and blue. "If we can do all this, then we can make an image that looks as good as film."

This would not have been possible on the VAX still sitting in their lab, but even if it had, it would have taken somewhere on the order of a week or two to render every frame. And since no frame buffers were large enough to hold that many pixels, each frame would have to be broken down into tiles, and put back together before scanning to film. It was insane.

"So, let's make a frame," suggested Loren.

Siggraph would be coming up later in the year. Presenting an image of the quality they described would be a suitable goal.

Rob Cook sat in his office and stared at the assortment of objects sitting on his desk. A block of wood. A series of napkin rings he had been collecting from Pier 1, made of brass, steel, copper. He held the wood block in his hand and watched the light from the window reflect off the surface. It was incredibly detailed, with veins of grain in various shades of brown, and scrapes and nicks in the surface from his incessant toying with it. He had been thinking about light and reflection since Cornell, and he needed to develop new lighting models to replace the hopelessly primitive existing concepts. He began to develop an idea for lighting; he called it "programmable shading." It would require a new language, which he decided to call "Shade Trees."

Alvy loved the idea. "Making shading into a language was a genius move," he recalled.

George was impressed enough with the computer graphics in *Wrath of Kahn* to agree to use some in *Revenge of the Jedi*. Months earlier, ILM effects supervisor Dennis Muren had come by Bel Marin Keys to see if he could get help with the effects. While *Jedi* was early in pre-production, he wanted to previsualize a scene in which an imperial speeder bike (a motorcycle-like vehicle) zooms through a forest, dodging trees and going over stumps. White knuckle fast. Muren hoped he could test out the shot with a computer-generated forest that he could drive his camera through in real time. But early tests didn't work well; Muren wanted to get the trees closer together and the camera moving faster and faster.

"There was no way we could get control in real time moving at those speeds," said Tom Duff. By the time the Computer Division was in C Building, Muren had mocked up his tests in more traditional analog ways, using Clark Higgins' expertise at video.

That was at the end of '81. Almost a year later, Dennis Muren was back at Catmull's door, hoping that the Computer Division could automate the tedious rotoscoping required to make the lightsabers in the movie. ILM teams had tried different methods over the years, even wrapping reflective tape on sticks, but the deceptively simple-looking effect was a challenge. Ultimately, artists had had to draw each saber glow by hand, each frame, one after another, for every duel. It seemed that a computer that could paint frames, the kind of thing Catmull's boys put together, could help.

Tom Duff and Bill Reeves tried for weeks to use the computer to make lightsabers that were as good as the rotoscoped versions, but ultimately all the tests were rejected.

In the end, the only effect that ILM needed that was appropriate for the Computer Division was a simple animated line drawing of a forcefield radiating out of the planet Endor, surrounding the Death Star, during Admiral Ackbar's presentation to the troops. A few spheres made of vector graphics and some other geometric-looking details. The effect would not require any of their recently

The state of development at Skywalker Ranch. The Main House *(center)* is mostly completed, although the dome is not yet on the library *(back left corner of the Main House)*, and the "solarium" (to contain a darkroom and some offices for the library) is just getting framed. The Brook House *(bottom left)* is almost done.

developed painting and rendering skills, and it was not particularly impressive from a computer standpoint.

But there was an aspect to the effect that was new. The models, easy to generate on the vector-based Picture System, needed to be moved with control. No one had any production tools to animate a 3-D model, and so Tom Duff decided to rough together the fundamentals of an animation system.

He had begun thinking about this when Dennis Muren had him moving the camera through the forest of Endor with the speeder bikes. Now, he and Reeves had developed a new tool. As they tried to generate the effect, they wrote and rewrote the code, improving it each time. They shot the special effect off the screen of the vector display (three times, once for each color required); it was composited in traditional (and painful) ways at ILM.

"The effect wasn't so groundbreaking," commented Duff, "as the tools used to do it."

The animation system was central to the toolkit the Graphics Group was developing, and over the coming months it would continue to be refined.

Bob Doris was pouring over an analysis of the computer market: what was happening and where it was likely to be over the next decade. There was lots of opportunity. But it spanned a wide range of industries.

The PIC, for a time called the "Pixar 2-D Frame Buffer," could not only generate film-quality effects, but it could be useful in any field that had very, *very* large images to manipulate.

The digital audio signal processor would revolutionize film sound, and the de-noising technology could be used to repair old damaged recordings or to ferret out voices from a noisy forensic wiretap.

The editing computer was designed to track film edge numbers and to cut movies, but it might have a larger market for commercials and corporate videos, which demanded the purchase of far more editing tools than Hollywood. Given enough time, Doris thought professional editing tools might be affordable for consumers, the largest market.

Under Doris' management, it might be possible to turn the Computer Division into a profit center for the company.

Sprockets and ILM were principally in-house teams working on George's films, keeping themselves busy when George didn't need them, but available when he did. Sprockets was mixing and editing *Jedi*, and they had just completed a mix on John Korty's animated feature *Twice Upon a Time*. ILM was trying to establish itself as an independent company. They had just finished doing 45 shots for Spielberg's *E.T.* and *Poltergeist*, although they were pretty busy now with 500 composite shots for *Jedi*, the most ambitious project they had ever attempted, with 25 percent more shots than *Empire*. The graphics guys had impressed George when they developed the Genesis Effect for *Star Trek II*, much to the surprise of the rest of the teams at ILM.

The risk involved with developing and using cutting-edge technology was palpable. On one hand it represented an association with the shiny entrepreneurial world of high technology. On the other, it was far afield from Lucas' innate core competency, producing entertainment. It didn't help that Francis Coppola had taken Zoetrope into bankruptcy not that long before, and Lucas was aware that Coppola's technological ambitions on *One from the Heart* may have been partially to blame.

Bob Doris had a lot to sort through.

The 1982 Christmas party, another in the growing list of exceptional Lucasfilm events, was held in the Garden Court of the Sheraton Palace Hotel. Huey Lewis entertained. The highlight was Steven Spielberg's 35th birthday, celebrated with a simple cake adorned with 18-inch candles. By year's end it looked like the gray clouds from the summer were gone and Lucasfilm was once again a juggernaut of youthful success and enthusiasm.

The computer guys were slowly transitioning their projects from research into product development. It was difficult to organize the scientists into a commercial venture, harder than anyone thought. "You don't turn a switch," said Bob Doris. More technicians were hired to support the work. More administrative help. More design engineers and draftsmen. A new laser scientist to work with David DiFrancesco. The Computer Division was beginning to represent a significant proportion of the film company to which it was attached.

At the 1982 NATO (National Association of Theater Owners) convention in Miami, Jim Kessler and Tom Holman presented the plan they had been developing, to help improve movie presentation. *Jedi* was going to be their first project.

"We decided to provide a service for every theater showing *Jedi*," said the director of Lucasfilm's Theater Operations group. "We wanted the film to be seen in the way it was intended to be seen."

In the months leading up to the *Jedi* release, they sent out mailings to more than a thousand movie theaters, providing minimum recommended standards for projectors and sound. They also hired two dozen field service technicians to visit all 70mm theaters to align the projectors and teach them how to do it, and they provided a toll-free number for emergency questions.[15]

[15] By summer 1983, the 800 number was in constant use. There were about 150 70mm prints of *Jedi*. Lucasfilm staff reviewed every one.

Other studios began to pay TAP (Lucasfilm's Theater Alignment Program) to maintain quality over their own blockbuster releases. These included *Indy II* (with an astonishing 250 large format prints) and *Star Trek III*.

Lucas was pleased with the program. Jim Kessler recalled it this way: "I remember driving to take George water skiing in the Petaluma river, you know…he never water skis…and George says to me, 'You know Jim, I was wrong. I was wrong about the TAP thing. You did exactly what you said you were going to do…and remember how I said changing the industry was going to be like spitting into the wind…well, *you must have been standing down wind!*"

With the Theater Alignment Program starting to take form, the next logical step was to work on the problem of sound. Most movie theaters were still saddled with old speakers with monaural sound. Dolby Labs had developed stereo sound that could be encoded optically on the film, a significant breakthrough. But just because films were recorded and mixed in stereo didn't mean that audiences would hear them that way. The cost of a mono sound system in a theater was under $5,000. A new stereo set-up might run $15,000.

Whether stereo or mono, the theaters often still hooked up the equipment incorrectly, or didn't tune it for the room where it played. Consequently, film dialog was too often muddied. People in the audience would frequently whisper "What did he say?" to the person sitting next to them. Contrary to the public's perception, the problem wasn't that the volume was too low; it was more often that the acoustics were poor.

Kessler wanted to sell them on the new system that Tom Holman had invented. The Lucasfilm theater in C Building sported Holman's speaker system. It was obvious to everyone involved that it would be ideal if theaters played movies on the same speakers that Lucasfilm used while mixing them.

"Visitors to C Building from Hollywood and from theater exhibitor [companies] all wanted it for their new facilities," said Holman, "as it was clearly better."

But Lucasfilm wasn't ready to start selling it. Kessler didn't care. He was working on packaging it as a generic loudspeaker system, and not just for films by Lucas or Spielberg. And he pondered what to call it.

"Administration would be very concerned about using the Lucas name on the product for a variety of reasons, not the least of which is that it would probably alienate many theater owners."

"It's gotta sound cool, high-tech, and I wanted a way to credit Tom Holman, the inventor," said Kessler. Doodling around, "I just wrote the initials for Tom Holman Crossover on my desk one day."

"Crossover" was a reference to the way the speakers divide the treble and bass for ideal acoustics. Traditionally, the crossover is done passively, in a loudspeaker. Holman had designed an electronic crossover. Kessler wrote "crossover" with an X, as in "X-over." He smiled as he recognized the letters THX from George's film *THX 1138*.

"George always seemed to like them, and had used them as a private joke on a license plate on Harrison Ford's roadster in *American Graffiti*." Kessler liked that the name was both very "Lucas" and still not immediately identifiable as Lucas.

"THX, that's perfect!"

So Kessler rushed down the stairs and into the cool dark mixing theater beneath him, where Lucas was sleeping on the couch during another marathon *Jedi* mixing session. Lucas woke up and watched in silence as Kessler waved the paper around and ranted about how perfect the name would be.

"Great" was all he said, and that was the end of it.

Said Holman, "People have been asking the question for years: what does THX stand for? And this was exactly Kessler's marketing intent: keep 'em asking question after question, and they're talking about you!"

It was also going to be important to give theaters some tag to put in front of films playing in a THX theater. One image was lodged in Kessler's mind: the Mark IV logo that was hammered onto the wall at the end of the '50s TV show *Dragnet*.[16] It had a gritty and unmistakable sound with each hammer strike. That's what THX needed. Kessler sketched a simple THX trailer with three static cards and a fade-up on the THX logo at the end.

"This was being done under the radar," said Kessler. "Can you imagine me going to [the CFO], or to George, and asking for permission to hire an ad agency?"

At first, Kessler found little support from executives in the company, but managed to receive the blessing of marketing VP Sid Ganis. "I didn't dare show anyone anything until it was finished," recalled Kessler.[17]

Kessler found Andy Moorer in the second floor kitchen when he pitched him on his vision for a THX logo. He'd handle the image part through an outside animation company, but wondered if the ASP could generate a cool sound.

"It's gotta swirl around and it should be like this really big one dynamic thing," Kessler explained, "and make sure we all get the stereo high range and low range."

Being a musician and composer himself, Moorer was excited to have a musical project. He agreed to meet with the animator to go over the storyboards and then score to that.

"We need a theme for this...something really really big, that comes out of nowhere," thought Moorer. He looked at the timings on the storyboards. The piece would be thirty-five seconds long. The animation would start in black, and then get lighter, and then the big THX logo would fade in after so many seconds.

[16] Mark IV was Jack Webb's production company. *Dragnet* was a groundbreaking "realistic" police show from 1951–1959.

[17] Kessler and Ganis coordinated with Lucasfilm VP of Business Affairs Bob Beitcher, having joined the company in the summer of 1982, believed in the project and helped Kessler put together the trailer and greased the political wheels at LFL. Beitcher left Lucasfilm in 1986 to become the managing director of Jim Henson Productions. After having executive positions at Paramount and CFI, he became the president/CEO of Panavision in 2003.

Moorer retreated to the prototype ASP he had built. It was the only device of its kind in the world. But even the hot new MIDI format wouldn't allow him to do what he was thinking. He envisioned a power chord that would emerge from a cluster of sounds. He built a single note from thirty-two voices of synthesized sounds. Moorer called the sound "Deep Note."

Thirty-two simultaneous voices of sound from a synthesizer in real time would be a computational challenge, even by modern standards. Moorer programmed the computer to generate a cluster of sounds between 200 and 400 Hertz that sort of "wandered up and down," but soon resolved into a big carefully planned chord based on a note of 150 Hertz, a little below D.

The exact trajectories of the "wandering" sounds were created randomly by the ASP, so every time Moorer ran the program, the score was slightly different. He ran off several versions and presented them to interested parties. Eventually, everyone settled on one with a loud tone that went up and then straight down to the very bottom. He created a 6-track tape of the sound.

A week later, the original tape got misplaced and he was asked to make another copy. "So I came back in, ran off the score again, and everybody said, 'That's not the same one,' and I said, 'Uh oh, we're in trouble now.'"

Because of the slight element of randomness in the generator, every time Andy ran the Deep Note program, the output was a little different. In time, he managed to recover the original random number that was used as the seed and regenerate the favored version.

When the THX logo animation arrived at the mixing theater, to be synchronized with Deep Note, the timings in the picture didn't match those from the storyboard. Though this was a typical real-world problem, it was precisely the kind of scenario the ASP was being designed to address. Andy casually returned to his console, pulled up the program, tweaked the numbers, and ran off another score. In five minutes he was triumphantly back at the theater with a new version that synchronized perfectly with the images.[18]

Kessler worked out the minimum requirements for installing THX sound into a theater. The most unusual feature of the system, perhaps, was the need for specific room acoustics. Controlling reverberation time, background noise level, freedom from ambient noise, reflections, and so on, it became the first time anyone had ever tried to mass produce room acoustics. It was an unusual business proposition: it wasn't enough for a theater to want to buy into THX, they actually had to *qualify*.

No typical profit-motivated manufacturer would limit its sales opportunities so dramatically. In addition, considering the frustration that Dolby Labs and other companies had had over the ongoing maintenance of their installations, Lucasfilm decided to lease the THX Sound System, with long-term

[18] Possibly one of the most recognizable sound logos ever, and certainly the most recognizable piece of completely digitally synthesized music. It plays more than 4,000 times every day.

agreements that could be revoked by Lucasfilm for non-compliance to quality standards.

Kessler transitioned from the management of Sprockets to running the newest division at the company: THX/TAP.[19]

Alvy was modestly satisfied that the Computer Division was playing a role in *Jedi*, but the work was barely stretching their capabilities. He decided, at the same time, to focus the team on the issues of high-resolution images. Cat-mull had thrown down the gauntlet with the goal of eighty million polygon images, and now Rob Cook was interested in making one high-resolution picture, perhaps the highest quality image ever generated by a computer.

Alvy Ray Smith, 1983

"I just started working on it, and then people started joining in," said Cook. "Alvy really supported the effort."

Rob Cook ended up with a design that incorporated all their skills—a scenic mountain road, winding around hills and along a big bay. Throughout the spring of 1983 team members worked on their respective expertise:

Loren Carpenter used his fractals to generate mountains, rocks, and water.

Cook textured and shaded a road, hills, fence, and double rainbow. He added shadows and reflections.

Bill Reeves used his particle system to make grass.

Alvy rendered forsythia plants along the fence using his "cellular autom-ata" methods.

Newcomer David Salesin, a recent grad from Brown University, helped add ripples in the puddles.

The group used Reeves' modeling software and Porter's compositing software. They also used their old REYES rendering software, now handling a 4,000 by 4,000 pixel image. Nothing that big had ever been done, and no computer could handle it alone. The picture had to be broken down into smaller chunks so the frame buffers could process it, only later reas-sembled.

The image, which they started calling "The Road to Point Reyes," was intended to look like a location in western Marin, also giving a nod to the REYES renderer they invented. It was jokingly referred to as a one-frame movie, primarily because it carried a list of credits that was longer than many short films.

[19] Eventually known as the Theatre Operations Division.

"The Road to Pt. Reyes," completed April 1983. The graphics team referred to the image as "a one-frame movie."

The demand for a graphics computer was ever-present. One scene in *Revenge of the Jedi* had sixty-two separate picture elements combined in one frame. It required 500 passes through the old optical printer. Commented Alvy, "That's a lot of multiple exposures, and if you make a mistake, you have to start over." These were serious practical issues that the Pixar computer would address.

Everything Bob Doris saw in the Computer Division pointed him toward an inescapable and unprecedented conclusion, and it was time to make his report to George. Actually, what he had to say was big. His meeting had to include executives Greber and Faxon, and the Lucasfilm board of advisors as well.[20]

"I think the Computer Division, and the editing project in particular, needs an outside partner," he began. "We need someone with manufacturing expertise in the video industry, delivering product to market, with sales and support. Lucasfilm isn't that kind of company."

The assembled group listened to his suggestion. "We also need a partner with cash, to continue supporting the development of the products."

[20] Lucas maintained a small group of outside advisors, a "board," made up of lawyers, corporate operations and financial experts, to run things by once in a while and to give him perspective.

George didn't want to relinquish control of development, but the board advised him that the research group could become a black hole in the long run. Lucasfilm reluctantly agreed to let Bob Doris find a partner for the editing project.

The audio research team, while smaller than graphics research, were active participants in the academic digital audio community. Somewhat parallel with Siggraph for graphics was the Audio Engineering Society (AES). Andy Moorer frequently reviewed journal articles and kept current with the state-of-the art and with new talent in the field. When the first prototype of the ASP was finally completed and debugged, Andy presented papers on his and his teams' findings at the 1983 AES conference, and he announced what Lucasfilm intended to do next.

Andy Moorer with the first prototype of the ASP, 1983.

At the end of his presentation, a distinguished audio researcher walked up to Moorer. He launched into a short diatribe about the insanity of the effort, and was relentless in his criticism of him and the ASP.

"Either you are a genius," he said, "or your balls are bigger than your brains." Andy turned to him with his puckish smile and replied, "I like to think that both are true."

Francis Coppola and his team at American Zoetrope were invited to Italy to give a talk about electronic cinema, and Thomas Brown suggested that Clark Higgins do the same about the research at Lucasfilm.

"At presentations like this," said Clark, "people want to see something… particularly when many people in the Italian audience won't speak English." Clark helped Zoetrope put together a thirty-minute video on their *One from the Heart* previsualization process, and it dawned on him that if he went it would be lousy to get upstaged by Zoetrope.

So Clark decided to go. Since Lucasfilm wouldn't "send" him, he put in for vacation to take the trip (his first in two years). Ralph Guggenheim wasn't pleased. It wasn't Clark's project to speak about. And the idea of Clark stopping work on the editing project when every day counted was more than irksome. Clark didn't care.

In preparation for his talk, he asked all over the company if he could shoot some video of internal projects. Bypassing Ralph, he got the okay to shoot a little video of the Computer Division's projects. "No screens," he was told.

So Clark Higgins got a videocamera and shot Andy Moorer working on the audio signal processor, and got a few shots of editing with laserdiscs. He called over to Jim Kessler and Ben Burtt to see if he could shoot the giant mixing console in the C Building theater ("Mix C") that Ben was using. All was okay.

Pushing through the double set of silent padded doors of Mix C, Clark found Ben working on the console, putting together the final mix for *Revenge of the Jedi*. Clark quickly and inconspicuously shot his material and started to leave without ever noticing Lucas sitting in the darkened room.

When Clark returned from his shoot, Ralph was livid. This was a *faux pas*, as far as he was concerned, and the last straw with his loose cannon employee. Officially, there was nothing wrong with Clark's shoot in Mix C. Clark had done little more than irritate his boss, Ralph.

The video shoot and the invitation to Italy were just two of the little Clark-things that needled Ralph. But there were other transgressions. A few months earlier at the company Christmas party, there was another typical Clark event. Clark had been interested in the UFO accounts of Billy Meier,[21] a Swiss citizen. Meier had some of the most celebrated photographs of spaceships and had numerous accounts of the human-like beings from the Pleiades who had watched Earthlings for millennia. When Meier contributed to a comprehensive book about the topic, Clark took the opportunity to send Lucas a copy in the inner-office mail. When Clark heard that Steven Spielberg was in D Building, he tried to get him a copy of the book, too.

"Steven and I had discussed Billy Meier at the 1982 Christmas party," said Clark. "It came up as he was talking about his experiences of showing *E.T.* to President Reagan at the White House."

[21] Real name: Eduard Albert Meier-Zafiriou.

Word of that odd little episode, along with other tales of Clark's mischief, was summer fodder in other Lucasfilm divisions.

In the battle resulting from their irreconcilable differences, Clark couldn't win. He was good at what he did, but his outspoken candor and general disregard for protocol—combined with his extraterrestrial idiosyncrasies—worked against him. Stories of Higgins' activities exaggerated and spread.

Soon Clark got called into Ed Catmull's office. Bob Doris was there. So was Ralph. "We've been thinking about this for awhile," said Ralph, "and I think we're going to have to let you go."

Clark was stunned. Afterward, the president of Lucasfilm, Bob Greber, invited him to lunch to discuss the turn of events. Greber was supportive. Clark recalled their conversation:

"Listen, you've been helping us a lot, you've done a ton in all areas, but Ralph says he can't work with you anymore and he's the head of the project, so…you're the one who has to leave."

A few days later Ed found himself chatting with George. While it was uncommon to talk to Lucas about the intricacies of the employees, Ed decided to mention it.

"You know, we let Clark Higgins go."

George let this sink in for a moment. Ed remembers George's response. He said, "It's about time."[22]

Lucasfilm was beginning to change. While it was still a big family, it had grown dramatically over recent years, adding enough management and mythology that politics was an increasing factor, particularly among the computer people, who never quite fit into the film business. New bosses arrived and wondered if the behavior of their subordinates was appropriate; there was a growing intolerance for people who didn't accept the norms. This was the adolescence, of sorts, for the organization, starting to feel its body, its maturity, its history.

There was a new propriety. It became the next Queen's Rule.

[22] Eventually Clark Higgins returned to Lucasfilm. In 2005, Higgins often consulted with ILM as a video expert.

[act three]

eighteen

A Hole in the Desert

[1982–1983]

One of the most difficult tasks men can perform, however much others may despise it, is the invention of good games. And it cannot be done by men out of touch with their instinctive values.

—CARL GUSTAV JUNG (1875-1961)

AS *STAR WARS* was still hitting theaters, Atari, the "wondercompany" that had started the videogame craze with *PONG*, ran out of money. Founder Nolan Bushnell had badly miscalculated how long and hard the road would be to stay up with the rapidly changing technology.

Only a few years earlier, when Atari was still a hot company, Bushnell was riding the wave: "We treated programmers like mini-gods. We gave the best ones private offices. Then we put a hot tub in the engineering building. We hired the best-looking secretaries we could find for that department. Atari beer busts—the all-night parties we'd throw to celebrate revenue goals—had already become legend. Were there planning sessions where we smoked pot? Absolutely. Did we have some incredibly crazy parties? "Probably true. Was the company probably the hardest-working company in the world? Probably true as well."

Bushnell had been working on a secret project called "Stella," which involved making a custom chip and combining it with a graphics display, sound synthesizer and an adaptor for the TV set.[1] The most radical feature was that it would run from cartridges, making Stella an open platform able to play a never-ending variety of games.

In spite of its potential, Stella development was constantly confronting bad news. The game market appeared to be in decline. And to make matters worse, Fairchild Semiconductor (the company that invented the semiconductor) had just developed a cartridge-based system they called their Video Entertainment System, or VES, and they were about to be first to market. If Atari wanted to minimize the damage, they needed to reach consumers quickly.

[1] The chip was based on the MOS Technology 6507.

For the manufacturing and distribution of Stella, Atari needed millions of dollars, which Nolan Bushnell couldn't seem to find anywhere. He tried to raise money from Disney. Then from MCA. He reached out to investors. He was running out of options.

One day Manny Gerard, a Warner Communications executive, got a call from an investment broker: "Would you be interested in a technology-based entertainment company, growing rapidly?"

The notion of a programmable videogame blew him away. In a day, Gerard was on the phone with Bushnell. "It wasn't a game company," said Gerard. "It was an entertainment company. It seemed to me like a business we should be in." Bushnell liked the synergy with Warner's films and music. Gerard soon visited Atari in Silicon Valley, to see a demonstration of the Stella prototype. When he returned to Warner's he penned a short memo: "I've seen the future and it's called Stella."

After discussing the matter with Warner boss Steve Ross—a big gambler at heart—Gerard got the green light. Still, Gerard was concerned about giving the young engineers so much money. "There'd be no way to motivate them," he worried. "I have to keep them tied up." Warner purchased Atari for $28 million; but it was a deal carefully constructed to keep the core engineers on board.[2] When it was done, Nolan received about a million dollars in cash and an unsecured note for another eleven million. If Atari ever died, the note was worthless.

And so Stella was funded and headed into production.

At the time Warner acquired Atari, it was a remarkably unstructured company. "Smoke dope, chase women," quipped Gerard.

Gerard soon became frustrated with Bushnell, who was scarcely seen after he and his associate Joe Keenan were paid off. "You can't disappear and walk in six months later and say, 'Let's do this.'" Bushnell felt that Gerard was trying to take his company away from him. They clashed often.

As the Consumer Electronics Show (CES) approached, Atari looked for a release name for Stella. They chose Video Computer System, or VCS.

Fairchild responded by changing the name of their VES to Channel F. Channel F released with twenty-one available cartridges, but graphics were poor and the games were universally detested. One reviewer wrote that the entertainment value in the racing game was like "losing a toe in an industrial accident."

By the end of 1977, Atari had sold 250,000 consoles, fewer than they had hoped. But they had launched with no advertisements, no press. Some of the VCS games were incredibly good, but a few were problematic. Reports were that the chess game, for instance, blanked the screen while it thought about its move—sometimes for hours.

[2] After paying off the outside investors, the deal stipulated that around 10% of the price was in cash, and the balance in Atari debt. There was also a bonus program, giving engineers 15% of the after-tax profit, but the earlier years had never had much profit and the old guard hardly considered that a perk.

It was no wonder that customers weren't buying—from Atari *or* Fairchild. Not only were the games imperfect, people were still burned out from *PONG*, and were uninterested in dropping another $200 for yet another toy that would likely be in the closet in six months. Many people still had their five-year-old Magnavox Odyssey consoles—the product that preceded Atari but never quite captured the market's imagination—collecting dust.

Another problem for Atari was that Apple Computer had just been formed to sell a home microcomputer, and even more products were competing for the same geeky dollar. There was Altair's classic computer kit. There were new inexpensive "personal" computers from Commodore and Radio Shack.

After Warner spent more than a hundred million dollars developing the VCS, Bushnell showed up at an executive meeting in New York three weeks before Christmas and announced, "It's over for the VCS. We've saturated the market. Sell off the inventory and let's get out of here. We're going to get killed!" He seemed irrational.

Warner CEO Steve Ross was nervous at the pronouncement. The next morning he called Gerard into his office, who recalled him saying, "Look, the guy I bought this company from just told me I'm fucked. What's going on here?"

Gerard suggested that there was no point in responding until after the holiday numbers were counted. "In twenty-three days we'll know one way or the other. I think it's going to be a hit. If I'm wrong, we're fucked anyway, and if I'm right, we're going to have a very big year."

Were games dead?

By the end of 1978, Atari had sold 550,000 units, clearing out every game on the shelves of every store in the United States. Unhappy with Bushnell, Gerard hired Ray "The Czar" Kassar as president of Atari's new "consumer division."

"Ray," explained Gerard, "brought discipline to the table."

Kassar wanted to go in the direction of Apple and Commodore and sell one- or two-thousand-dollar microcomputers. Bushnell wanted to focus on the few-hundred-dollar console market, and build a better console.

"Guys, we have to do things the way I want, or I'm out of here," announced Bushnell.

"Nolan, you're out of here," Gerard responded.

Ray Kassar, in his dark imported three-piece suits and flashing cufflinks, took over as CEO of Atari. Though not much taller than anyone around him, he carried himself regally, his silver hair neatly trimmed and always impeccable. No sooner was Bushnell out the door than massive changes swept over the company. Security was ratcheted up. It was no longer easy to wander around and visit friends in other parts of the campus. There was more internal paperwork. Discipline and dress codes were enforced. There were layoffs. People who weren't fired were quitting.

Focus shifted away from research and toward marketing and sales. The company created a home computer division and kept employees segregated from the guys in home games. They announced the Atari 400 and Atari 800 personal computers at the January 1979 CES show. The Atari marketing engine made the bold move to advertise the VCS year-round and introduce new games year-round, and not just in the holiday season.

The programmers at Atari didn't like the corporate environment. Word on the street was that Kassar had called them "high-strung prima donnas." More people quit.

Early Activision games. *Left:* Dragster. *Right:* Fishing Derby.

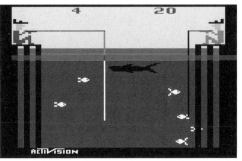

[3] Vector graphics harkened back to the original computer game invented in the '60s at MIT, *SpaceWars!,* played at 2AM by computer scientists on industrial strength DEC computers.

[4] *Lunar Lander* was designed by Jack Burness; programmed by Rich Moore; vector graphics by Howard Delman. *Asteroids* was designed by Lyle Rains; programmed by Ed Logg; sound and vector graphics by Howard Delman.

[5] Fairchild couldn't compete and quit the business (and soon closed up all operations in California), and the hundreds of thousands of VCS consoles in homes plugged into Atari's new pipeline of games.

In the summer of 1979, *Space Invaders* reached America and changed the face of arcades and public videogame consciousness. It was impossible to walk into a pizza place or sub shop without being confronted by the electronic thumping of the game. *Space Invaders* had been released two years earlier by Taito, an electronics company in Japan. There, the game was so popular that entire arcades were opened exclusively for it, rumored to have caused a nationwide shortage of "yen" coins until the mint quadrupled the supply.

After that, Atari's coin-op developments accelerated and in August they produced the first arcade game with vector graphics, *Lunar Lander.* Vector graphics were sharper and crisper than the jaggie raster graphics in *Space Invaders.*[3]

By November 1979, Atari released a second game with vector graphics, *Asteroids.*[4] It became a major hit and in just a few months dethroned *Space Invaders* as the king of the arcades. In time, Atari sold 56,000 *Asteroids* machines to arcades.

Meanwhile, Atari programmers were hard at work developing dozens of titles that only worked on the VCS. And consumers were buying them. By the end of 1979, only a year after Bushnell left Atari, the VCS was the hottest Christmas gift on the market, with sales of over a million units. Atari negotiated for the exclusive U.S. rights to distribute *Space Invaders* on the VCS; it released in January 1980. Its success catapulted the VCS and Atari into the economic stratosphere. Videogame fever encased America.[5]

At Atari, game designers got little public credit. They received royalties for successful arcade games, but nothing from the home game versions. Four disgruntled programmers left the company and formed Activision, to compete with Atari in developing titles for the VCS platform. They produced some of the first innovative games for the VCS, and proved the system could support more interesting games than Atari itself was creating. Atari sued them, claiming they were violating non-disclosure agreements.[6]

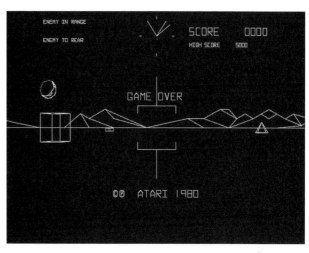

Screen from Atari's *Battlezone,* the first videogame with 3-D graphics.

Meanwhile, Atari's arcade group came out with another smash, *Battlezone,* using the vector graphics they were getting good at producing, and providing the first game with 3-D graphics.[7] It gave the player a point of view over a highly geometric wireframe landscape, very much like a military tank simulator.[8]

By the end of 1980, Atari had made hundreds of millions in profit, which represented more than a third of Warner Communications' annual income. Many believed Atari to be the fastest growing company in the history of America. The party had begun.

"It was a gusher," reported Gerard. "When Atari popped, it was a gusher. $345 million in operating income. Unbelievable."

The firehose of cash allowed Atari to develop one of the largest research divisions in Silicon Valley. It acquired Cyan Engineering, the think tank from Grass Valley, California that produced Stella. Cyan had a reputation for creating innovations "from glue and bailing wire." Their productivity was astonishing. When Atari execs flew up to Grass Valley to visit the research team, their plane was met by two guys in jeans with enormous bushy beards.[9] "They look like the Smith Brothers," Gerard's wife commented, referring to the icons from the cough drop box.

In time, Atari moved everyone to Silicon Valley. They hired Alan Kay, the father of the "personal computer" (from Xerox PARC) to become their chief scientist. Kay was given an unlimited budget to follow two directives: from Gerard, to take risk, and from Kassar, to dream. They had dozens of secret projects.

Alan Kay had expected to be able to do whatever kind of research interested him, usually referred to as "blue sky research," but Atari quickly wanted

[6] Activision prevailed two years later.

[7] By Howard Delman, Roger Hector, and Ed Rotberg.

[8] Around 15,000 were sold. Atari produced a modified version for the U.S. army.

[9] Steve Mayer and Ron Milner.

more concrete development. Almost from the get-go, there was contention about the scope of their projects. As a result, Kay was often absent from the lab, either spending his time on the road or back at MIT. The lab ebbed and flowed between periods of organization and disorientation.

Manny Gerard was a hero at Warner Brothers; the Atari division propped up the communications giant. But it was swerving out of control.

"From $75 million, to $432 million, to a billion-one…. It's very hard to manage growth that fast," said Gerard later, "especially when the culture you're starting out with—and I'm only slightly exaggerating—is a bunch of guys smoking dope."

Stories of Atari's opulence were rampant. For instance, at the CES show, Atari served catered meals with thirty-thousand-dollar mounds of chilled shrimp. And whenever Kassar arrived at the Atari campus from the airport, the parking lot was cleared of cars; a helicopter would land, pick up Kassar, and deliver him to a limo that would drive him the few hundred feet to the building's entrance.

The Atari execs built themselves a hall of expensive office suites that was called "mahogany row." They ate together in a corporate dining room, with its chef imported from a New York restaurant (rank and file employees never saw the fabled dining room). At a time when Silicon Valley companies were still cubicles and pocket-protectors, Kassar's Atari was like Hollywood. Lavish. Staggering.

"I say this for myself and for everybody involved—massive success breeds arrogance," commented Gerard in hindsight. "I don't give a shit who you are. I don't care what you say. It just does. That was one of the problems." During Atari's explosive growth phase, whenever they had an executive who wasn't working out, they'd just assign him to something new, something they'd call a "special project." Eventually there were special projects all over the place.

"At that time," recalled Atari researcher Doug Crockford, "we were already a deeply sick company, but an extremely successful one. Still, there was no external feedback about how sick we really were. That was the context when we were trying to do this [advanced videogame] research."

By 1981, the arcade videogame world was reaching a feverpitch—it was impossible for anyone to imagine it continuing, and yet it grew month after month.

Atari released *Tempest*, the original vector display game, with color—a new feature. But all else was eclipsed by a game from Japan, *Pac-Man*. Distributed in the U.S. by Midway, the pinball giant, *Pac-Man* became a cultural phenomenon. The yellow character, originally called "Puck-Man" from the Japanese *paku-paku* meaning "to eat," not only dominated in arcades, it was soon found on lunchboxes, board games, and hundreds of other products.[10]

Home games were not met with the same obsession as arcade games, but they made money. In spite of poor graphics and controls, the market had grown to just over a billion dollars in 1981 and two billion in 1982. In both years Atari dominated the field, selling more than five million VCS units. Atari now delivered half of Warner's revenues and two-thirds of its earnings.[11] After just a few short years Atari was a brand name with significant value. Some of the billboards in the movie *Blade Runner*, set in 2019, even sported Atari logos.

When Atari licensed *Pac-Man* for release on the VCS and manufactured twelve million cartridges, Wall Street analysts predicted $200 million in sales.[12] There were only about ten million VCS units in consumers' homes; Atari had expected that not only would every VCS owner buy the game, but that new consoles would be sold on the strength of the game alone.

But VCS *Pac-Man* had poor graphics, poor sound, and gameplay that was totally unlike the successful arcade original. After the 1981 Christmas season, an impressive seven million cartridges of *Pac-Man* had been sold. But many were returned, joining the unsold millions in a warehouse in Texas. Atari's reputation as a game leader was tarnished and the company badly needed to follow up with a hit.

Everyone at Atari knew that something was happening in Marin. Manny Gerard and Ray Kassar felt they needed to learn more about the research Lucasfilm was doing. At their request, Bob Greber invited them up to San Rafael.

The Atari brass couldn't get a tour of ILM (the building was on tight pre-*Jedi* security). About the only thing Greber could show Atari was some of their earlier work with fractals and ray tracing.[13] "They had their socks blown off," recalled Greber.

As the group toured the offices in C Building, they were met with the most realistic images anyone had ever seen on a computer display. "Those are computer generated?" asked the execs incredulously. "Unbelievable!"

"These guys have terrific technology," thought Gerard, "and we ought to be in business with them."

But George was not convinced; he thought it might be a distraction. Greber lobbied for the plan. Games were big money, and it seemed crazy not to get into that action. Ultimately, Lucas conceded, as long as Atari funded the project. By June 1982, Bob Greber announced a deal.

[10] It was followed up with arcade game sequels, *Ms. Pac-Man* in 1981 and *Super Pac-Man* in 1982.

[11] At the time, Atari home computers represented 40% of the PC market.

[12] Atari guarded its *Pac-Man* property closely. They sued, and won, against Magnavox for their Odyssey 2 game called *K.C. Munchkin*. It was a fairly obvious rip-off of their game, albeit one with far more impressive design.

[13] Scenes from the "Genesis Effect" were just finishing, but were completely off-limits.

"The venture is the first of its kind between a videogame and home computer maker like Atari and a movie company," reported the *Wall Street Journal*. Other movie studios and game developers quickly followed suit. There was simply too much money to be made to ignore it.[14]

Lucasfilm licensed Atari to produce an arcade game of *Raiders of the Lost Ark*.[15] But when it came to home games, the distinctions between arcade games and toys played at home got a little gray.

In the months before *Star Wars* was released in 1977, Fox and Lucasfilm had agreed to an exclusive license with a small toy company, Kenner Products.[16] Their deal was broad, for "toys and games." It was for a lot of money, and at the time was considered "a precedent-shattering master toy license." It stood as the principle income-generating deal in Lucasfilm's pocket—more than from books; more than from lunch boxes.

Kenner interpreted "games" to include board games that could be delivered by sister company Parker Brothers.[17] There was no reason for Lucasfilm to argue. There was probably no better partner than Parker Brothers, owners of some of the most popular board games of all time: Monopoly, Risk, and Clue.

It took time for Parker Brothers to fully realize the value of its deal with Lucasfilm. They had exclusive rights to develop games from the *Star Wars* series, and while they didn't know much about the relatively new world of video games, they were determined to learn. Parker Brothers quickly released a game called *Empire Strikes Back* (played on the Atari VCS), one of the top ten sellers that year, and a tribute to the intense value of the *Star Wars* brand in the videogame market. They also started work on another game, *Star Wars: Jedi Arena*.

There was concern at Lucasfilm about the overlap of the "toys" rights held by Kenner, "games" rights held Parker Brothers, and the oddly evolving world of videogames—particularly in arcades. Was a videogame a toy? After some assuaging of concerns and a bit of bartering, Parker Brothers relinquished some of their exclusivity, and Atari was given license to produce an arcade version of *Star Wars*.

They rapidly modified the design and graphics of *Battlezone* to represent Luke Skywalker's point of view out of his X-wing fighter while attacking the Death Star in the climactic scene of the original movie. The vector graphics, though now in color, were similar to the state-of-the-art vector graphics Larry Cuba had used for the simulation of Skywalker's attack pathway, back in 1977. The sit-down cockpit style of the game and immersive action made it popular. Parker Brothers continued to generate home games for the Atari platforms using the intellectual property from *Star Wars*.

[14] In 2004, the videogame market (software and hardware) was estimated at $21 billion.

[15] It was released in the fall of 1982.

[16] Kenner was best known as the creator of Play-Doh and Spirograph, but had a hit with their 1975 license of the *Six Million Dollar Man* in the new world of "action figures."

[17] Parker Brothers was purchased by General Mills in 1968, a few months after General Mills acquired Kenner.

But the games from Parker Brothers and Atari were licensing deals, not entirely different from lunchboxes or posters. Lucasfilm had, after all, some of the greatest computer minds in the world all gathered together in Marin. It seemed natural to the Atari executives to apply that talent to games.

Atari had a letter of intent to fund a $1+ million Lucasfilm development effort for new and innovative games. These new games would be, according to Greber, "a completely different new type of home entertainment product."

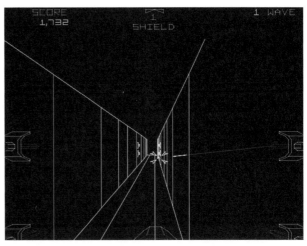

The *Star Wars* arcade game from Atari.

Ray Kassar was quoted in the *Wall Street Journal*: "Lucasfilm is a highly talented, creative bunch, and they know how to use technology to entertain." Lucasfilm's position, as reported by Greber, was that they intended to "dramatically affect the evolution of the electronic entertainment industry."

Alan Kay and some of his top Atari researchers, were invited to Lucasfilm to visit the computer labs. "I was really impressed," recalled Doug Crockford, one of the engineers. "It was the smartest, most focused R&D operation I had ever seen. We were not nearly as well organized."

All this mutual adoration was wonderful and exciting, except that the brilliant Lucasfilm computer scientists in Bel Marin Keys knew nothing about videogames. It was with a little shock that Greber informed Catmull that he should start putting together a videogame effort within his group.

In the late summer of 1982, Ed Catmull found Peter Langston at a blue-chip Wall Street law firm. Peter had joined the firm as the in-house UNIX guru.[18]

Langston was an unlikely member of the legal team. While at Reed College in Portland in the late '60s, he had been in the folk-rock band Entropy Service. (He had studied chemistry but wasn't all that interested in it.) After graduation, he stayed in Portland to play with the band, which was fun; they were performing at all the best spots in town.

Unlike most liberal arts colleges in the '60s, Reed had a computer center. Langston needed a job, and found one managing the center. In the process, he taught himself something about computers. For him it was a short step to begin writing computer games. Within a year he had built a range of unusual games.[19] Most significantly, he created a global simulation "game" he called *Empire*, done with strings of text commands and data in tables.

[18] Langston was hired at Davis-Polk after one of the partners thought that instead of buying massive IBM mainframes to track casework and organize client information, they should try a new minicomputer.

[19] His creations ranged from intricate simulations of artificial worlds to a dog-fight-in-space game called "Star Dreck," a parody of the television show.

Empire players controlled variables of population, military, technology, energy, infrastructure and, of course, money. It was a real-time game in which people—usually other computer science students in the lab—managed nations, "kind of like *Risk*," said Langston. Like the board game, it was played with multiple human players simultaneously. "My approach to programming is intuitive," said Langston. "I don't approach game design as a conscious problem."

> The *Hackers Dictionary* defines "Empire" as "any of a family of military simulations derived from a game written by Peter Langston many years ago. Modern 'Empire' is a real-time wargame played over the Internet by up to 120 players. Typical games last from 24 hours (blitz) to a couple of months (long term). The amount of sleep you can get while playing is a function of the rate at which updates occur and the number of co-rulers of your country."

PETER LANGSTON

Hometown: NYC. *Interests:* playing games, playing music, playing computers, playing art, playing around. *Sign:* multiple Aquarius with a Libra moon; you come here often? *Employment history:* Consumer's Union; Dance Notation Bureau; Robert Joffrey; Yelping Hill Assoc.; Cheshire Academy kitchen crew; Peter, Paul & Fink; Reed College Computer Center; Portland Zoo Electric Band; National Science Foundation; Puddle City; Evergreen State College; Entropy Service; Smithsonian Astrophysical Observatory; Harvard Science Center; Metropolitan Opry; Davis Polk & Wardwell. In that order.

[1984 LFL Yearbook]

When Entropy Service hit the local glass ceiling, the band decided to move to Boston. Langston secured a UNIX computer account at Harvard University. (In 1974, Harvard was trying to get its university email system working with the new computers as it joined the new-and-growing Internet.) In short time, he developed "Peter's Post," the mail server at Harvard, and he continued developing games on the University's facilities. By then, *Empire* had a life of its own, drifting through academic institutions, all the while getting refined by the people at each lab.

Langston had become a bona fide UNIX genius. His reputation at Harvard helped him get drafted by law firms, first in Boston, then in New York, all trying to get computerized. He always made a condition of his employment that he'd get to spend some time on their computer working on his games. No one ever seemed to mind.

When Catmull found Langston at Davis-Polk, a prestigious Wall Street law firm, he had already heard that Langston was a star. Catmull told Langston that Lucasfilm was starting a new division.

"We want to look at ways of using high tech stuff outside of the film industry," Catmull told him. "It looks like games are going to be a big part of that."

Langston went to California to look around. But he enjoyed New York. He really didn't have to work that hard, he had plenty of time to play music, and the Lucas project sounded like a big undertaking. Ultimately, the romance of working with George Lucas was overshadowed by the romance of being a fun-loving, highly-paid UNIX whiz kid. Langston declined the offer.

"Well, we really think you're the person," Catmull said, in the ensuing conversations. "How about this: we'll fly you back to New York every two weeks. Half a month here, half a month there."

"Eventually I said yes," recalled Langston. "Who was I to say no?" So Peter moved to Marin. There was excitement being associated with Lucas. "It was always interesting to go into a video [or] equipment store in Marin and be treated like a kid; and then when they found out you worked for Lucasfilm, they'd want to lend you stuff. George was magic. That was the fun part."

Peter Langston, with his fluorescent-light-induced pale skin and long brown hair pulled back into a ponytail, was not a typical game developer. *American Film* magazine referred to him as a "jazz" programmer, a guy who just sat at a keyboard and improvised.

Langston understood that Atari wanted a bit of the Lucasfilm magic. "That magic," he said later, "consisted of two parts: an uncompromising attention to detail (leading to a sense of involvement and realism even in the most unrealistic of situations) and the use of high-tech tools to make possible the creation of formerly impossible sequences and images."

Langston's job, as Catmull had described it, involved games, but it was broader than that. George Lucas was interested in "interactive entertainment"; games were really only the smallest part of his fascination with the Atari project—he was curious if there was potential in using those interactive tools for education. He had a fascination as well for the interface between people and machines.

With Atari's capital, Langston needed to find games developers who weren't the typical type starting to grow in Silicon Valley. He wanted "boy wonders" in terms of technical ability and who were, in his words, "a little bit visionary." Because he cared little about being a manager, he wanted a self-motivated team, "I wanted co-workers rather than employees."

And so Peter Langston set up in a little office upstairs in C Building, down the hall from Alvy and the guys working on high-resolution graphics, above Andy who was trying to build a digital audio signal processor, around the corner and below Ralph who was trying to get the editing system to accurately control a laserdisc player.

Peter Langston arrived at Lucasfilm the same day as Bob Doris. While Langston made himself at home, Doris tagged along with Greber and Faxon, attending discussions relating to the computer group. They handed Doris the letter of intent they had worked out with Atari and asked him to finalize whatever was required. He spent time with Catmull trying to get his head around the projects they were developing, the obstacles they still faced, his realistic impressions of who else might want these devices and when something—*anything*—might be able to generate some revenue.

Within the week, Langston began scouring the hills for the kinds of programmers he needed. Everyone in C Building handed over suggestions of people they had met, or worked with, or gone to school with. He started discussions with a few prospects and planned to meet others at that fall's Siggraph conference.

Atari proudly announced their new relationship at the Consumer Electronics Show (CES) in Chicago. In the late '60s the CES was where new TV sets and stereo systems were debuted by electronics manufacturers; by 1982, it was going Hollywood. Not only was Lucasfilm entering the game business, but so was Paramount, Fox, and MCA.

Steven Spielberg told the *Hollywood Reporter* that videogames were his favorite form of entertainment. "I play at the end of every day to unwind," he said.

Though videogames were a dominant force at CES, the vibe on videodiscs was strong, both in connection with videogames and as a stand-alone format to deliver entertainment. Philips—which marketed the Magnavox and Sylvania disc players—had a major presence at the show. The *Hollywood Reporter* quoted one industry analyst: "History will show that the five breakthrough developments of 20th century electronics were audio recording, radio, TV, computers, and the videodisc."

The Lucasfilm graphics guys were proud of their contribution to *Star Trek II*, but they didn't have time to develop any presentations about it for the 1982 Siggraph conference in Boston. They did, however, spend time there chatting with an affable guy named David Fox, who was writing a book about computer graphics. *Computer Animation Primer* was going to include a large section on state-of-the-art computer animation, including illustrations from *Star Trek II* and Loren Carpenter's *Vol Libre*.[20]

David Fox had worked as a counselor, and he deeply believed that games were an interesting way to teach people about themselves. In 1977, David and his wife Annie founded the Marin Computer Center, a non-profit community access space where locals could drop in and learn about the wonders of technology for a few bucks an hour.[21]

As a freelancer, Fox had done game conversions for software publishers. He had also designed one original game, *Mix and Match Muppets,* for Sesame Place, a theme park from the Children's Television Workshop.

When Fox heard through the Marin grapevine that a games group was forming at Lucasfilm, he quickly reached Peter Langston. Fox pointed out that the second half of his soon-to-be-released book included a tutorial for novices on how to make reasonably sophisticated animation on the Atari 800. He had admittedly done only a tiny bit of game design, but he was enthusiastic, accomplished, and clearly self-motivated to work on the Atari platform, expertise Langston would need. And he was local. Peter hired him.

[20] The book was published later in 1982.

[21] Using one of dozens of microcomputers on-site.

On his arrival, Fox settled into C Building offices already filled with teams working on graphics and hardware. He doubled up with Loren Carpenter, a videogame fan who had enjoyed his time with Fox at Siggraph.

Carpenter, who was still reveling over the success of his fractal software that made the *Star Trek* "Genesis Effect" possible, found himself in a lull. He had been working on a refined renderer, a new REYES package, with Rob Cook, but the version needed "massive reworking," and that was best done by one person alone rather than a team.

Within hours, Loren and David were brainstorming. Loren was interested in how games were built. David immediately immersed himself into the company culture and began wondering aloud if there was overlap between the high-end research and home computers.

"I wish we could have those cool fractal landscapes generated in a game," Fox said, as the two of them gazed into their respective terminals.

"I don't see why you can't," replied Loren pleasantly.

David looked up. "Because we're using a 6502 CPU with about 1.79MHz and 48K of RAM. Not a VAX. How would you ever do the math that quickly?"

"I think it could be done, even at pretty low resolutions." Loren turned and looked out the window. "I wonder what it would look like?"

Loren went home and pondered the question for the weekend. When he returned he announced that it struck him as possible. The "3-D" landscape might look a little like cardboard cutouts of mountains, but it could work.

Within days, Loren and David outlined a little game that capitalized on their fractal mountains. David produced a typical Lucasfilm white paper on the game's development.

"Rebel Rescue," as he began referring to the idea, was this: "The player is operating a high-speed X-wing-like craft. The object is to fly over rugged terrain while trying to locate a missing Rebel pilot and his downed plane on an enemy-infested planet. The point of view is from the cockpit. To create the sense of moving over the terrain, horizontal fractal lines will be used."

The new employee had many questions, including whether he could even use the word "rebel" since it sounded like a *Star Wars* term and might result in licensing problems. He asked in one report "I know we can't use *Star Wars* characters, but can we use *Star Wars* places? Vehicles? Weapons?"

Peter Langston was still searching for new members for his team. A rather interesting candidate came via Tom Duff. While "laundering" himself between NYIT and Lucasfilm, Duff had spent time at a software company called Mark Williams, outside of Chicago. A co-worker, Dave Levine, a serious and often somber engineer, was doing UNIX-like programming but pining for something more interesting. When Duff heard that Langston was searching for game developers, he remembered Levine and gave him a call.

DAVID FOX

Hometown: Los Angeles, but escaped to No. Cal. before permanently damaged. *Family:* happily married to Annie, 3½ year old daughter Jessica. *Schools:* UCLA, Cal State Univ. Sonoma. *Interests:* Science-fiction, bike riding, good films, good music, chocolate. *Sign:* Capricorn. *Employment history:* 1977 co-founded with Annie the Marin Computer Center, the first public access microcomputer center. Co-authored 3 books, *Pascal Primer, Armchair Basic* & *Computer Animation Primer. Other info:* Wants to create an "interactive amusement park" where the rides are convincingly real.
[1983 LFL Yearbook]

DAVID LEVINE

Hometown: Chicago. *Family:* symbiont. *Schools:* intuition. *Interests:* music making, ice skating, flying, reality control, debauchery. *Sign:* detour. *Employment history:* Itty Bitty Machine Co.; Gimix, Inc.; Mark Williams Co. *Other info:* Taught Yoda everything he knows.

[1983 LFL Yearbook]

Years earlier, Levine had developed a custom frame buffer—probably the first—for high quality black-and-white graphics on the dominant microcomputers of the day: the Altair and the original IBM PS/1. In spite of the various technical odd jobs he held over the following years, his interests remained in computer software and, in particular, simulations.

"I had been writing reactive, interactive things on computers for a few years," he recalled. The job at Mark Williams—a systems job—was a bit of a fluke. But even there, Levine wrote games for fun, much as Langston had, for the engineers to play on the VAX.

Langston, not particularly interested in the managerial aspects of his job, was hiring slowly and cautiously. He decided to wait and see how David Fox worked out before hiring anyone else. Dave Levine wanted the job, and moved from Chicago to San Francisco in hopes that the bold step would lead somewhere. Still, it took months of persuasion to get Peter to hire him.

By October, Peter finally called. Dave moved into a bed and breakfast in San Rafael called the Panama Hotel, and there he met another engineer—David Salesin—who had just graduated from Brown University's computer science department and already had a reputation as a gifted mathematician. Salesin would be joining the graphics group as Levine joined games.[22]

Langston was trying to build a department with visionaries and academics, purposely avoiding experienced game programmers. "I think I turned away more good people than I should have," he figured. But the people he was after, solid computer scientists, viewed his projects cautiously.

"It's funny, often the people I went after—if they had any sort of standing in the computer community—were very nervous about a job associated with the word *games* in it. A number of people who would've been great, and I think would've really distinguished themselves, were afraid to be involved in something that seemed to be so frivolous."

It took time for Langston to be able to describe the projects "so it sounded," as he put it, like "a legitimate enterprise." The people who were ready to sign on were already a little rebellious. Neither David Fox nor Dave Levine cared about legitimacy—Fox, the idealist, because he had such a positive attitude about everything; and Levine, the iconoclast, because he couldn't care less about what others thought.

Games and computer graphics were at that time two extremes on a digital continuum. Games started at one end, with the most common, affordable computer hardware available, and then made as good an experience as possible by using the smallest number of computations, the fewest bits. The games programmers were sometimes called "bit hackers," a derogatory term. Everything on the screen had to be drawn and redrawn in real time. The faster

[22] The Panama Hotel had been a brothel in the early part of the century, and retained its quaint funkiness, lush courtyards, and romantic balconies. "We regularly put up visitors and prospective employees there," said Ralph Guggenheim, "because we liked the non-conformist feel of the place." It had a bar and good restaurant and quickly became a favorite watering hole and lunch spot for the software teams on Kerner, a few minutes away.

that things could regenerate on the screen (which usually meant poor detail), the more action to the game.

At the other end was high-end computer graphics, realistic looking imagery using the most sophisticated kinds of mathematics, the most powerful computers, and often taking hours or days to generate frames. Alvy Ray Smith and Ed Catmull had what amounted to a solemn blood oath when they formed the graphics group that they'd never let a jaggie out the front door. Videogames were all about jaggies.

"The best graphics to come out of a game," Alvy later said, "were the worst graphics ever to come out of Lucasfilm."

The Lucasfilm research library in E Building.

When it didn't seem like another engineer could fit into the offices in C Building, the games guys moved into the spacious rooms in yet another addition to the Lucasfilm campus: E Building, next door. No more doubling up on space, now everyone had his own office. While E Building was only a few feet from where they had been, it was segregated from the rest of the Computer Division. Bob Doris felt the move served a number of practical functions, not the least of which was to keep the projects from distracting each other.

"We didn't want the games guys messing around with computer graphics, and we didn't want the graphics group getting too involved with games," recalled Doris. "It was a big temptation."

E Building was lightly industrial, only slightly modified from when the structure had been part of some sort of retail strip mall. The far end of the building was still filled with the Lucasfilm research library—hundreds of books and magazines that the departments in ILM used to help visualize scenes.[23] The library was scheduled for relocation to the Ranch when it was completed, but for the time being it was at one end of E Building. Games was on the other end.

Once Games was moved into E Building, Atari shipped over some arcade videogames on the back of a flatbed truck. The guys were excited to see Atari's new *Star Wars* game, mimicking the climactic scene from the movie where Luke is racing down the Death Star corridor trying to shoot the vent and blow the thing up.

[23] When a matte painter wanted to know what the mountains looked like on the west side of the Andes, for example, the librarians could locate a dozen issues of *National Geographic*, or an old mountaineering guide handbook, and deliver them to ILM.

Peter Langston, exploring the details of the Atari service manual, found a setting whereby the game graphics and spaceship speed could be frozen (still allowing for normal targeting and shooting) whenever a certain pair of wires were crossed. While it was difficult to enter this mode (you had to keep getting into the cabinet to reset the jumper on the chip), once it was turned on it was impossible to miss a target or get hit by enemy fire.

Langston ran a wire from deep inside the console to the front panel by the coin slots, and attached a big red videogame button to the front, to access the mode. A week later, someone added a label above the button. It read "The Force." Flying along at hundreds of miles per hour, if you panicked, you hit The Force and you were on top of the game. Press the button again and you're back flying. It was a favorite of the employees who came around to play in E Building's mini-arcade.

No one ever saw Lucas there, but Spielberg frequently came to play. He was next door on the C Building stage, shooting some blue screen elements for *Indiana Jones and the Temple of Doom*. He quickly discovered the *Star Wars* game. In no time he was addicted, and asked that the machine be set up near the stage so he could play it there. When there was any break from the shooting, Spielberg would be hidden in the *Star Wars* cockpit, slamming the fire button, dodging the obstacles, and when all else failed, smashing The Force button.

When *Indiana Jones* wrapped, Steven was apparently disappointed to be leaving the *Star Wars* game behind. No sooner was he back in L.A. than he had someone in his office call over to Atari, asking for his own *Star Wars* game. It was shipped out immediately. Word of ensuing events spread like wildfire throughout the games group: it was late afternoon in Atari's offices in Sunnyvale when the call from Spielberg came in.

"Where the hell is my Force Button?!!"

"What are you talking about?" came the nervous voice on the other end of the line.

"The Force Button! I can't play without The Force."

Dave Levine wanted to pursue a game that brought real-world physics to bear upon the players. "I wanted something that players would find fully immersive." Levine believed that for a game to be great the playing field needed to be level, giving opponents equal equipment and letting it be fought purely on skill. He designed *Ballblazer*.

In his game, two ships are floating above a checkerboard-like field, each trying to throw a sphere (held by a tractor-beam) through a goal. What made *Ballblazer* unique was that both players would have simultaneous first person views of each other. Key to Levine's vision was that it wasn't man versus machine, but rather a two-player game.

"Then it becomes a social interaction—the computer is a neutral concurrent medium of interaction between two people. You do not play against the computer or test your skills against a program, but you have an opportunity to play against another person."

In addition, the universe they played in would have all the physics of the real world, with inertia and mass and friction. "I've always wanted to build a device that allowed people to play with invisible forces, such as magnetic fields," said Levine. No one was sure if the Atari could deliver this experience in real time.

By late fall, everyone was doing a lot hacking around with their projects; Levine was figuring out the physics of his world, and Fox was still developing "Rebel Rescue." Finally they got some Atari equipment to experiment with. They were supposed to be designing for the VCS, but they all knew a more advanced machine was in the pipeline from Atari, built with the same innards as the Atari 800 home computer.

"It's the age-old problem," said Levine. "Design for the platform with the huge installed base and try to push the state of the art, or forge new territory for the more capable new platform but with a small user base and smaller market."

David Fox grabbed Peter Langston and they wrestled up a spare Atari 800 computer and a couple of ring-bound volumes on programming the 6502 chip. Loren Carpenter went home again. Three days later he came in to the office beaming.

"I want to show you something," he said to Fox, who pulled his chair over to Loren's computer. He had done it. He had recreated, in primitive form, the fractal generation of mountains, just as he had done in *Vol Libre*, just as he did as an element in the Genesis Effect, but in real time.

"I was curious to see how much of a fractal I could get out of that thing," he said. "You needed to be able to fly around, which meant turn and bank, and you needed to be able to pitch up and down and change elevation." The resolution was pretty poor, but it was better than anything ever seen out of the Atari 800.

"The hard part isn't necessarily the fractal generation of the surface," Loren said, "so much as doing the hidden surface work in real time."

It was remarkable that it could be done at all. Fox pulled Langston and Levine into the office and showed them the real time 3-D mountains that Loren had them flying over.

"Think we have a game?" asked Fox.

"Absolutely." Langston replied.

The small games group was gaining in their comfort with the Atari, and all agreed that the new, more powerful computer was the platform to use.

Fox knew well the issue of taking games written for one platform and porting them to another platform. It was always a pain. Together they strategized that the holy grail of game design would be to write a game at a very high level of code with no regard for the computer it would eventually be played on, and then plug it in to a magical compiler that would rejigger all the parts and rewrite them to fit whatever game device was required.

The guys spent months wrestling with the idea.

After *Star Wars* there were about a half dozen Lucasfilm employees. By the end of 1982, a majority of the 350 employees were new. Adding the ILM and production staff working on *Jedi* and other films, there were more than 600. With so much frenetic indoor activity, the company worked at getting everyone outdoors. There were maybe nine softball teams that played near the Ranch construction (including the "EEE Wacks," and the "Force Fielders"). Umpteen volleyball teams.[24] Whale watching and river rafting trips. A new thirty-foot sloop, christened "Seawalker," was purchased; employees could take it out of the harbor at Corte Madera and sail around the Golden Gate Bridge, assuming George or his friends weren't using it.

Lucasfilm couldn't know how deep the problems were at Atari. The company showed unprecedented profits rolling in on their income statement. Sure, there were corresponding expenditures, but it truly appeared that Atari was on top of the world and could do no wrong.

In late summer, Atari managed to buy the rights to *E.T.* from MCA-Universal and Steven Spielberg for $25 million.[25] They planned to release it as a game on the VCS (now renamed the VCS 2600) in time for the Christmas 1982 buying season. The plan was to follow quickly with an arcade version.

But there were major problems with the game, and they weren't all the game designers' fault. The VCS 2600 had been engineered to have a lifespan of a year or two, and now it was going on five. Moreover, the programmers had been told to develop and produce the game in about six weeks; much of it was based on code from another game, so all they had to do was rework graphics and gameplay.[26] But its graphics were embarrassing. Gameplay was frustrating. In the end, the *E.T.* game on the 2600 was described by many as the *worst videogame of all time*.

If this wasn't bad enough, Atari was deflecting rage at a third-party 2600 game called *Custer's Revenge,* which showed General Custer running from arrows and getting points for raping an Indian woman tied to a pole.[27] Hundreds picketed at its debut in New York.

And then, to make matters worse, before the end of the year the company was embroiled in a scandal. On December 7, 1982, at 2:41 PM, Ray Kassar sold

[24] "I still have my volleyball trophy from the year that we were first," recalled Langston. "I also have my softball trophy from the team that George and I were on. George played second base and I played first; we never got a double-play but we kept trying."

[25] Where it might have cost around a million to develop a new game.

[26] The object was to help E.T. find all the parts of his phone and get home, accomplished by jumping into pits and then, if no FBI agents were around, slowly *slowly* climbing out.

[27] Developed by Mystique/American Multiple Images. Mystique released two more X-rated games, *Beat 'Em, Eat 'Em* and *Bachelor Party*. They closed operations soon after the release of Bachelor Party.

5,000 shares of his stock in Warner Communications. At 3:04 Warner Communications made its fourth quarter earnings announcement, revealing to the world the scope of the missed expectations at Atari.[28] Warners stock dropped 33 percent in one day. The following week Kassar and another Atari executive found they were under investigation for insider trading. By the end of 1982, Atari had hit the wall; Warner stock was in the toilet.[29]

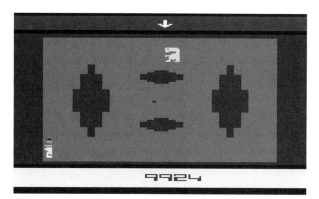

Atari's *E.T.* videogame.

Greber and the senior executives at Lucasfilm were shocked by the news from Atari, but relatively unscathed. "We had a right-of-first refusal deal with them," recalled Greber. If Atari wasn't going to be around to distribute Lucasfilm's games, someone else would.

The home games market, once dominated (and thus standardized) by the Atari 2600 format, was fragmenting rapidly. Atari updated the VCS 2600 and named it the 5200. The 5200 would come out with its own arcade hit of *Galaxian* and the megastar *Pac-Man*. Of course, the success of the VCS 2600, with 70 percent of the market, directly competed with the 5200. Atari's new cartridges were not going to be compatible with the older machines. Atari's biggest new competitor was Atari.

Mattel tossed its hat into the ring by introducing a game unit called Intellivision. A distant second to Atari, they represented 15 percent of the market.

And then Coleco released ColecoVision. Their strategy was based on offering home versions of all the arcade hits they could acquire, including *Donkey Kong, Zaxxon,* and *Turbo.*

Already wrestling with more than five million unsold or returned *Pac-Man* cartridges, Atari added *E.T.* cartridges to the pile and arranged to have them all taken to the desert outside of Alamogordo, New Mexico and buried. That spring, fourteen trailer trucks hauled the contraband to a giant landfill pit. To keep people from digging them up, the IRS insisted they pour concrete over the top. Ostensibly destroying "defective product," they buried their problem and moved on to other, more pressing issues.

By the spring of '83, Bob Doris had a pretty good feeling for what was happening in the Computer Division, and one place where he didn't like what was happening was in Games. It just didn't feel like Peter Langston was managing the project. Even though there were games under development, progress was slow and unfocused and it seemed like Peter was at fault. On the other hand,

[28] Instead of the 50 percent increase in sales projected, they reported 5 percent.

[29] Imagic, a spinout of disgruntled Atari engineers in the vein of Activision, had set up shop in Los Gatos in the summer of 1981. By 1982, they had solid profits on projected $50 million in sales and were gunning for an IPO (initial public offering). They were in the midst of their IPO roadshow when the Warner announcement hit, virtually eviscerating the golden games market and wiping out interest in their offering.

Peter never wanted to manage the games projects and felt he had made this clear to Ed when he was hired. If things weren't being well managed, well, that was too bad.

By the time Peter hired his third teammate, Charlie "the dragon" Kellner, Bob Doris had taken it upon himself to instill some discipline in the group. They began to have regular project meetings and decided to focus entirely on *Rebel Rescue* and *Ballblazer*, and abandon the dreamy idea of a master game compiler.

"[A master game compiler] was a blue sky notion," said Bob Doris, "that would have been great if it could have been done. Of course it couldn't be done, and never really has been done." Dave Levine reluctantly agreed. "It was an idea…but soon we had to give it up."

For the next few months considerable progress was made on both fronts and the first pair of games took shape.

Charlie Kellner, a sci-fi fanatic, had been one of the early employees at Apple computer. He was known as a brilliant Apple II programmer, and a multi-talented perfectionist. While he was in the education department at Apple, he designed a music synthesizer and wrote a classic bowling videogame for the Apple II. Like Dave Levine, Kellner believed that immersive computer simulations were important, particularly for education.

"After all," Kellner said, "a physics lab is nothing more than a simulation, and this can be done on a computer." In 1982, Kellner moved to a new Apple project called the Macintosh, developing the "boot beep," the famous start-up sound of the Mac, before moving on.

"When I heard that George Lucas was starting a game division…that was it."

David Fox really enjoyed the fact that *Rescue* was an exciting game that didn't have the typical guns-shooting-at-aliens thing happening. Players were pilots, flying their rescue ship down along the planet to pick up other pilots downed by enemy fire. It was tricky maneuvering, but the Atari 5200 came with an analog joystick that offered 360 degrees of rotation, far better than the up-down-left-right constraints of the digital joystick on the 2600.[30]

Dave Levine and David Fox were prepared for a visit from George Lucas. George wasn't a game player, but he had an uncanny sense for entertainment and knew the value of a compelling storyline.

Lucas and Levine saw differently on *Ballblazer*. Being deeply into the subplots and storylines of the games, George didn't like the pair of somewhat identical ships—referred to as "rotofoils"—as the characters.

[30] The same joystick was also shipped with the Atari 800 computer.

"He wanted some kind of fancified alien craft," recalled Levine, "that had different personalities. Not unreasonable at all, but for me it was absolutely essential that the game be a virtual sport—with everything identical mechanically—mind against mind, skill against skill. This was my agenda at the time."

George begrudgingly accepted the young programmer's wishes, and moved on to visit David Fox. Fox demonstrated the *Rescue* game, flying around, picking up pilots. Lucas was impressed with the graphics the tiny computer was able to generate. After a minute his face registered something amiss. Fox recalls their discussion:

"Where's the fire button?"

"What?" replied Fox.

"Where's the fire button?" repeated Lucas. Fox looked at the game and back at George, and pursed his lips.

"Well, there is no fire button. To destroy the enemy, you have to get them to follow close behind you, then you head toward a mountain and swerve at the last second. They'll then crash into the mountain. In the game, all the guns were removed to make room for more pilots."

"Is there no shooting because of game play reasons or philosophical reasons?" George asked, turning to David, who looked him in the eye and thought about how to reply.

"Well, um, I guess it's more philosophical."

"Great," replied George. "Put in a fire button. I want to shoot at things."

David Fox testing his prototype of "Rebel Rescue."

Lucas made a story suggestion to make the game more interesting: why not have some of the pilots be aliens in disguise. That way, instead of just flying around picking up pilots and avoiding getting shot, there was dramatic tension when a pilot ran up to the ship. If it was an alien you'd have about a second to hit your shield to zap him. David was jazzed and made some notes.

And like most interactions between George and his troops, he was gone almost as quickly as he had arrived.

Langston got to exercise his musical talents on the games, on *Ballblazer* in particular, building on his background in a range of music, from jazz to rock to folk. This was the kind of thing Langston loved. He and Levine agreed that a jazzy score would augment the dynamic game.

"One game reviewer, an eminent jazz player, said the score sounded like John Coltrane did it," commented Langston. "I think that's my best compliment so far."

"Peter's primary focus is on fun," commented Levine. "To him fun is serious business. It's something I always admired about him."

The games programmers packing in to Millipede while Ed Catmull checks his watch—a comic scene staged for the company yearbook, but not far from a typical event.

In May 1983, Lucasfilm was finishing the release details for *Revenge of the Jedi*. The company was generally dominated by feelings of goodwill and excitement. Over the prior months everyone in the production divisions, in the licensing groups, in the fan club, even in the Skywalker Ranch development group, had been working feverishly to prepare for the final episode of the trilogy. Now that it was almost done, the future of Lucasfilm was bright even if it was still a little vague.

What would happen at the company after the films were done?

Everyone knew that George was looking forward to a break. He'd been working virtually nonstop on the *Star Wars* films since 1975. The Ranch wasn't done so he could refocus his attention on its completion, which would be possible once there was money from the final film.

Even as the *Jedi* company screening and wrap party were being orchestrated from George's office, Bob Doris was orchestrating his own little party. Early prototypes of the first two games were ready to show to the anxious brass at Atari. Ray Kassar (still onboard in spite of securities allegations) and Manny Gerard needed these games to be hot, and Doris was looking forward to displaying the radical work Langston and the boys had generated.

The demonstrations were as good as could be expected of prototype software. Manny Gerard liked *Ballblazer*. "Wow, this is really amazing," he said, playing the two-person point-of-view game. He was less thrilled about *Rebel Rescue;* it was not as exciting a game concept, but it was stylish, the graphics were interesting, and it was certainly innovative.

"These are really great!" Gerard announced at the end, and everyone breathed a sigh of relief. The engineers were beaming.

"Well, I came up with some ideas for packaging treatment…" began Bob, when he was interrupted by Manny.

"Whoa, they may have told you. I'm a particular maven with this stuff."

Though Atari was technically responsible for product packaging, the Lucasfilm team took it upon themselves to come up with some ideas they liked. Doris had taken the liberty of having Chris Werner, a production artist at the company, mock up some boxes.[31] Each was unique, but all were solid white with various forms of embossed lettering.

"I asked George to come look at the options before the meeting," said Doris, "because the worst thing for us would be to show this to Atari and not have had George see it first." George came by for a few minutes, looked things over, and picked one of the white boxes. George didn't have any training in marketing, but he always had confidence in what he liked.

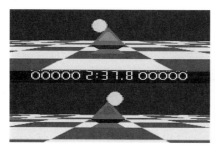

Screen shots of *Ballblazer (left)* and *Rebel Rescue (right).*

[31] Director of Creative Services at Lucasfilm, beginning in 1982.

Bob Doris lined up the product boxes for the group to look at after the games demonstrations. Gerard, picking up the white box, began to launch into Bob Doris. Doris recalled the events of that meeting with clarity:

"I think this is terrible!" Gerard announced defiantly. "This won't work. There is no way we can go to market with this sort of stuff." And in a moment all the other Atari execs chimed in with comparable criticisms, about how it would get smudged and show fingerprints. (According to the lore of consumer marketing, an all-white package is a bad idea.)

"Holy shit," Doris thought, "what have I gotten myself into…"

"Well, I like it," said a quiet voice in the back.

No one saw the sleight man in jeans wander into the room and take a position by himself in the corner.

Everyone spun around to see who had crossed swords with Gerard.

"I like it white. I think we ought to use *that* one," pointing at a box, said the man.

It was George. Gerard looked him over and took a breath.

George continued in his quiet way, "I think it looks better."

And being the consummate businessman he was, Gerard backpedaled. "Well, *you* know consumer marketing." Doris and the rest of the Lucasfilm team exhaled quietly, and the festivities returned to their earlier level of ebullience.

For the time being, the box would be white.

nineteen

Non-Stop Coffeepots

[1983–1984]

RETURN OF THE JEDI opened in theaters on May 25, 1983. Just a month earlier, George decided that the words "Jedi" and "Revenge" were mutually exclusive. There was no Lucasfilm announcement. They just started calling the movie by the new name. Fox wasn't thrilled with the last minute change—posters had been printed, advertising was well underway.[1] "Fox has little say," said a publicity spokesman for the studio. "It's a Lucasfilm decision."

By the time *Jedi* was released, a number of theaters were using Lucasfilm's THX Sound System. Warner Brothers, in Hollywood, was the first studio to buy it for its dubbing stage. "Its installation broke the chicken-and-egg hegemony that had dominated theater loudspeaker installations," commented Tom Holman, inventor of the system and chief engineer at Sprockets. The theater chain General Cinema also joined the club, upgrading three theaters with THX.

Two weeks before the nationwide opening, the employees of Lucasfilm got to see the film at the Coronet Theater in San Francisco, most for the first time.[2] The unbearable anticipation for the final installment of the *Star Wars* trilogy, an event that was reaching a fever pitch for the general public, was of perhaps even greater intensity for the people who made the film.

No matter what you did at the company—whether it was creating some kind of effect or sound, or typing up the deal memo from the legal department—you were connected to the movie. The computer scientists, like the contractors building the Ranch, were reasonably distanced from the production itself, and yet no one could be part of Lucasfilm and not feel the energy from the film. At the opening moment of *Jedi*, as the lights dimmed and company logo twinkled across the big screen, the audience had an uncontrollable emotional release. Goosebumps. Tears. Grins.

The film was (obviously) well received. The long credit roll that for a non-employee was considered interminable, turned into a joyous party at the theater punctuated with spontaneous applause and shrieks. Bill Reeves and Tom Duff were credited for their "computer graphics," to the appreciation of the rest of the Computer Division.

[1] Actually, the film had originally been called "Return of the Jedi" when Lucas opted for a harder edge for the title; the name change was a switch back to where it started.

[2] There was a simultaneous screening in Corte Madera, to accommodate the Marin-ites.

Afterward, buses hauled everyone to Ghirardelli Square for a company-wide wrap party at Maxwell's Plum Restaurant. Except for Carrie Fisher, the actors were absent. The employees were the stars—the happy, lucky family of Lucas. Glasses were raised to George and Marcia.

The elation from the film, which would normally have lasted months beyond the company screening, was cut short by the news that George and Marcia were getting divorced. While few in the company knew them one-on-one, close enough to be aware of their personal issues, everyone generally thought of them as the "mom and pop" of the business. George was the famous father; Marcia had the personal touch that seemed to warm everything.

"They were a team. If he was black she was white, and vice versa. It was a well-balanced thing," recalled Jim Kessler. "Independently, they were kind of like balls with unweighted sides so they spun out in goofy ways."

The fallout from the divorce was serious. Lucasfilm was worth between $50 and $100 million, depending on how one looked at the value of the movies and the revenue forecasts from the various licensees. There were big variables in any estimates: lots of building still to do at Skywalker Ranch, and an unknown value to the computer research going on. There was also a significant amount of cash. In a common-law state like California, a divorcing couple simply splits the marital assets. Rather than divide control of the company, Marcia and George agreed that he'd keep the company and she'd take the cash, a pretty even split in 1983.[3]

Few at Lucasfilm had a clear idea of what would get George's attention in the coming months. The trilogy was done. Indiana Jones films would keep most people busy. George was looking forward to finishing the Ranch and handling the thousands of things he had been putting off since the 1970s.

"He started racing cars again," recalled Jim Kessler.

By the middle of summer, in the post-*Star Wars*, post-George-and-Marcia era, the company was starting to reorient itself. It occurred to Bob Doris that the researchers were nowhere near completing the video editing and digital sound mixing projects. While he believed that George had been clear in his charter for the Computer Division—that editing and sound were top priorities—Bob felt that resources were disproportionately moving toward Ed Catmull's pet project: the graphics computer. Ed was aware of this too.

"I think Ed's greatest fear," said Doris, "was that at some point somebody higher up—George in particular—was going to say, 'Wait a minute, the stuff you were supposed to build, you haven't built.' And it was becoming pretty clear that this was a problem."

The Ranch was moving along. The group of bungalows around the Main House was framed and roofed. Design was beginning on the technological centerpiece of the Ranch, an enormous structure that was called, simply, the "Tech Building." A short bike ride down the road from the Main House,

[3] Some of this she took immediately and the balance she accepted as a note, payable over a number of years.

the Tech Building was where all the mechanical aspects of filmmaking at the Ranch would be done.

The fictional history of Skywalker Ranch always included a bit about how the old winery, built by one of the sea captain's sons, expanded mid-century and collided with the smaller brewery toward the hillside (to explain the sudden change of architectural styles within the building and it's T-shaped structure). The "old winery" was going to be renovated into an Art Deco center for digital filmmaking.

With no soundstages and no production, the Ranch was going to be a retreat for writers (doing pre-production), picture editors, and sound mixers (handling post). Francis Coppola's old declaration about "images, sound, and data flowing around like hot and cold water" was going to be manifested in a three-story building of brick, stone, and wood, designed like a winery, on the shores of "Lake Ewok."

Tom Holman had succeeded beyond everyone's expectations in his execution of C Building; he produced some of the most remarkable filmmaking workspaces ever, and, in the process, launched the TAP/THX projects. After testing out numerous ideas on Kerner, Holman transitioned into working full time on the engineering specifications for the 750,000 square foot Tech Building.

Before the design could be codified, Holman had to know precisely how it would be used, and what kind of equipment was going to be housed there. The questions had been lingering for years, but now they were in black and white, and the subject of weekly meetings. The Tech Building turned the entire focus of Sprockets mixers, engineers and, of greater consequence, Lucasfilm management, toward the Computer Division.

When would this new digital equipment be ready? How much commitment should be made to new tools and how much of the old machinery needed to have a home at the Ranch? The idea was to do away with all the archaic rolls of film, dubbers loaded with sprocketed mag, and on and on. Digital equipment would necessitate an entirely different environment of air conditioning, power, cabling, and more. The building was underway. Answers were needed immediately.

Questions about equipment led to larger issues about the Computer Division itself. *What was their relationship to the rest of the company? Would there be permanent space for them in the Tech Building? What kind of personnel would make the transition to the Ranch?*

With *Jedi* done, a lot of people at the company had more time to look around and take stock of what was going on, to try to come up with some answers. Bob Greber and Roger Faxon had been the principle leadership before, but now George was around a lot more.

To answer the questions for himself, Ben Burtt began to take an active interest in the research projects, especially the picture and sound tools. Most of the Sprockets team really couldn't be bothered with the R&D efforts, but Ben was genuinely curious and personally committed. He gave feedback on the prototypes without being asked, in addition to the more formal feedback sessions with scientists and filmmakers that the company often conducted around big conference room tables.

Once the Pixar Image Computer was named, it put pressure on everyone else to be clever. For the editing system, Clark Higgins had always called it the Competitor—short for "computer editor"—but no one really considered it a real product name. The initial prototype was called the Dodo, since it was intended to go extinct. But none of these was a market-ready name.

George had an idea. The computers they were developing were like the droids in his movies. R2D2—the friendly little all-purpose helper, technically savvy, always can-do—was a great archetype for the products; even C-3PO, intergalactic translator and mediator of "human-cyborg relations"[4] was a nice image for the approachable interface on technology they advanced. Bob Doris liked the association as well, and in short time, the editing project became known as the EdDroid.

Early marketing concept sketch for the EdDroid.

[4] From *Star Wars* Episode IV.

To fill the void created by the absence of Clark Higgins, Ralph Guggenheim found Steve Schwartz, the chief engineer of Excalibur Video, a post-production facility in Los Angeles. "Steve brought a lot of expertise in the day-to-day workings of video facilities," said Guggenheim. But more important was Ralph's feeling that Schwartz "got" the Lucasfilm vision of what editing could be. Schwartz was an ideal fit for the small team.

The EdDroid didn't really edit yet, but Steve Schwartz looked past that detail. While an editor typically looked at a monitor, his or her hands were on a physical device of some kind, to shuttle through the material, to select frames on which to make cuts. A film-style editing tool needed to have a film-style editing control surface, but videotape editing tools had a number of advantages. Schwartz assembled a box with an array of choices: knobs, shuttles, track-balls and mice, and a dozen kinds of buttons and switches. Now they just needed to put a film editor in front of all this to get an impression.

After Jim Kessler talked it over with the picture cutters at Sprockets, he decided that Duwayne Dunham should put the machine through some tests. Duwayne had set up a 16mm camera at the Ranch and had been shooting time-lapse material of the Main House's construction.

It was going to be a present for George. But when George discovered the surprise, plans shifted to presenting it to the employees at that summer's picnic. There was no time to get expensive videodiscs made, so he was going to use the Droid to edit videotape.

The morning Duwayne was due to start working, Ralph got a call.

"He's where? In the hospital?!"

Schwartz, listening in, slumped into a chair next to Ralph's desk. Everyone knew Duwayne was an avid sportsman. Skiing. Ballooning. Now he had torn his Achilles tendon in an early morning tennis match with ILMer Nilo Rodis and he was in a cast from toe to hip, making it impossible for him to sit in a chair.

Would it be possible to reconfigure the editing system, Duwayne wondered, so he could edit while reclined on a sofa, his leg up on a cushion? Steve Schwartz redesigned the human interface to accommodate him.

A selection of buttons and knobs was placed on the editing control pad, referred to as the "Pastry Cart"—a small box tethered to the SUN via a thick cable. From the Pastry Cart an editor could do almost everything; little on the keyboard was required. Schwartz lengthened the cable to reach the sofa. Schwartz was pleased with the retrofit. The team was nervous in anticipation of Duwayne's reaction to their work. Ralph decided to handle the training.

But Duwayne hated just about everything about the machine. He didn't like the way it worked. He didn't like any of the control surface choices. "Well, *hate* is a strong word," said Duwayne, "But it did not work. You couldn't actually cut two frames together." It was such a disaster it was as if he said, "Tear it up and start completely over, guys, cause it's all wrong."

"There was a philosophical difference between what they were trying to do and what we needed it to do," said Duwayne. "In film, every single frame is accounted for and is very important. Because of the 3:2 pulldown [the way film is transferred to video], an odd apparition is created in video, phantom frames that don't exist on the film."

It was impossible to get a videotape to play only "real" film frames, although videodiscs could, in fact, be recorded to look just like film. Duwayne was convinced the computer scientists wanted to disregard his fundamental concerns. "What they seemed to be saying to me was 'what's a frame or two here and there.' To a film editor, it's everything."

His tidal wave of negativity hit the team. Ralph, who was always positive and upbeat, held his frustration in check, but it was hard to conceal. "Being incapacitated with post-surgical pain and learning to use a computer for the first time," said Ralph diplomatically, "was a fatal combination."

Everyone assumed the news of the debacle went directly through Sprockets and right to George. But no one heard a word.

With the Droid debut already circled on the calendar, Ralph Guggenheim needed another software engineer on the editing team, someone who had production experience developing professional editing tools, who had worked with real time operating systems, the problems of videotape machines, and who understood the intricacies of timecode. The vibe around the Computer Division was increasingly about being prepared for commercial products, and it was an aspect of technology that only Steve Schwartz had much experience with.

Malcolm and Ralph decided to make a visit to the world leader in videotape editing products, CMX. The company occupied a nondescript box in sun-baked Santa Clara, an hour south of Marin, in the most industrial part of already-industrial Silicon Valley. Having been formed in 1970, CMX not only dominated the industry, it had invented it.

The road to CMX began in the early days of radio broadcasting. The pioneering efforts of crooner Bing Crosby led to the formation of Ampex, which produced the first commercial audio tape recorders in 1948. After a few years Ampex (and Crosby) moved into videotape recording research, and in 1956 produced the first VTR. Over the next fourteen years there was wide experimentation with videotape and ways it might be edited. Finally the broadcasting giant CBS, a large consumer of VTRs, combined forces with the magnetic medium experts at Memorex to launch CMX (which stood for CBS, Memorex, eXperimental) to develop videotape editing systems.[5] Their first product capitalized on a newly developed technology called "timecode," which gave an electronic number to every frame on a tape.

[5] Formed by Adrian Ettlinger—the inventor of the CMX 600—and Bill Connelly (both from CBS), and Bill Butler and Ken Taylor (both from Memorex). Butler became the company's general manager.

CMX introduced a two-machine system, the "nonlinear" CMX 600 and the "linear" CMX 200. Ironically, the creative (but expensive) 600 did not catch on. But the videotape-controlling 200 was a hit.[6] And where nonlinear editing just wasn't practical, the linear style caught on.

Nonlinear Editing and the CMX 600

The CMX 600 was a seminal tool for editing. It was comprised of a computer terminal connected to a stack of removable disk platters, each holding about five minutes of material.

Videotape was shot in a studio on high-quality 2-inch reels, then dubbed to the magnetic disks in the CMX 600's disk stack.[7] With six $30,000 disk drives working in concert, the 600 could locate any frame in under a second (from about thirty minutes of dailies). Because the edits were not being recorded to (linear) videotape, the 600 gave an editor some of the experience of cutting film, a "nonlinear" editing style that was highly desirable.

The timecode numbers from the original 2-inch tape were duplicated to the magnetic dubs; consequently, all decisions made on the CMX 600 could be saved numerically. When the editing was done, the editor could print out a punched paper tape encoded with a list of timecodes for each shot in the proper order.

Then the second part of the system, the CMX 200, took over. The editor input the list of cut shots and the 200 reconstituted it linearly—one shot after another from beginning to end—on a master 2-inch videotape that would eventually be broadcast over the airwaves. By 1971, CMX was selling the combination 600/200 for $500,000. In April of that year, it was demonstrated at the CBS stockholders' meeting. Before the end of the year, CBS Television had used the prototype system on a movie-for-television called *Sand Castles*.

Over its first decade, CMX introduced a series of breakthroughs that established them as the market leader. Most significant of these was standardizing the format for timecode editing information, the edit decision list (EDL); this allowed lower quality video to be used for making creative decisions ("offline editing") while the expensive high-quality video was only brought in at the end ("online editing"). The style of editing advanced by CMX became the standard for videotape editing for the next twenty-five years.

[6] Only five CMX 600s were built. Improvements to the CMX 200 rapidly led to the CMX 300, beginning a lineage of products that continued for decades.

[7] The half-resolution images on the disk were black and white and of poor quality (very grainy); they looked far worse than 16mm film, arguably worse than 8mm. But this was just working material to help with making decisions, like a film workprint; few besides editors or producers ever saw them.

The CMX 600 in action, 1970; the images are stored out of frame to the right. The light pen used for control rests on the console.

Throughout the '70s, CMX continued to expand, effectively dominating as the sole manufacturer of videotape editing tools for professionals and broadcasters. At the same time there was also worldwide activity in the development of videotape formats and standards. Videodiscs were introduced in 1976 and within a year there were competing formats, LaserVision and MagnaVision. Consumers were besieged with a host of technologies.

Neither the analog videodiscs nor the concurrently-announced digital audio discs were recordable. For recording, nothing beat the economics of tape. Sony announced their new high-quality ½-inch videotape format, called Beta, just ahead of Panasonic's slightly inferior image format, called VHS. Neither of these new formats competed with the broadcaster's 2-inch tape format (or even the ¾-inch Umatic), but both were comparable to the images and sounds consumers were used to receiving on televisions.

Videodiscs had the unique ability for random access—hopping from spot to spot quickly and easily—and were far more resistant to wear-and-tear. Because their images were of slightly better quality than those on tape, marketing was targeted to the discerning movie fan. But consumers were adamant that they wanted to record shows from the air and found the high cost and inability to record insurmountable obstacles. With videodiscs ruled out, a virtual marketing slugfest erupted between the two remaining formats—Beta and VHS.

During Lucasfilm's visit to CMX, Ralph and Malcolm met Rob Lay, the designer of two of CMX's most advanced editing controllers. Lay had graduated from Rice University as a student of avante garde filmmaking and computing. He was like Ralph in that respect, a fan of Ricky Leacock and interested in the blending of technology and art. Rob Lay was schooled in the vision that video artist-pioneers had espoused in the 1970s.

"We needed to put film in the hands of the people as a democratization of the medium," said Lay. "We needed to make editing systems that the people could use to write like a pen, make a word processor for video."

Lay was the missing link between the computer and film sensibilities of Ralph, and the professional video sensibilities of Clark Higgins or Steve Schwartz.

Lay had been inspired by Coppola's 1981 essays on how new technology liberated filmmakers. "For me," said Lay, "there was definitely an editing problem. I had been making films all along. Super 8 cameras were dirt cheap. Film stock was dirt cheap, but the immediate problem was always editing."

In early 1980, Lay had proposed to CMX a complete reworking of their established 3400 editing project, which he called the 3400 Plus. It utilized every bit of new technology available at the time.

"We needed maximum power, so we were looking at all these motherboards that had just come out, and the latest chips," recalled Lay. "It was a strange time and everything was very expensive…."

The 3400 Plus utilized new CPUs and a database management system, and though it was still a videotape editing system, it began to push the boundaries of interface and functionality. CMX took the 3400 Plus prototype to the 1983 NAB conference, and feeling the impending success of the product, pulled young Rob Lay from the leadership and replaced him with an experienced product manager, leaving Lay disgruntled. When Ralph approached him at CMX, Lay was more than receptive.

ROB LAY

Hometown: Houston, TX. *Family:* Single (Annapurna, 5; Artical, 1). *Schools:* Rice University. *Interests:* mountain climbing, windsurfing, racquetball, running, tennis, film watching and filmmaking. *Experience:* Media Center, CMX Systems. *[1984 LFL Yearbook]*

If Lucasfilm needed a dose of reality, then CMX was nothing but reality. No significant forward momentum could occur because they had incessant demands from the enormous installed base of CMX products in the field.

"There was always huge pressure to get product released and there were all kinds of corners that were getting cut. The vision was just getting compromised right and left," said Lay of his years at CMX.

Lay couldn't experiment with better computers because their cost was too high to pass on to customers; all development had to be done on the existing low-cost processors and a weak-but-real-time operating system.

Ralph pitched Rob hard. "We have this core thing that nobody else has. It's the way editing should be!" Rob recalls him saying. Ralph explained the vision of the graphical interface, of leapfrogging videodiscs, of integrating effects into the editing—something that couldn't be done with traditional video editing except by triggering outside devices.

Rob was excited. "Lucasfilm had that mystique," he said. "They were so smart…they had it all figured out…."

"My interest was in being closer to the blending of filmmaker and machine," he recalled later. "Lucasfilm certainly appeared to be right there making films, and less of the 'let's build this commercial product.' It was always 'let's make it work first, and then maybe it could be commercialized.' I liked that process."

But it was a siren song, as Rob soon found out.

When Bob Doris went back to Lucas and Greber to suggest that they needed a manufacturing partner for the soon-to-be completed prototype for the EdDroid, they finally agreed. And with the major trade show for editing products less than a year away, they needed to move quickly. They needed a company that knew how to build a market-ready product for the video industry, one with a fairly large balance sheet of cash, and one with a good brand name in the business. Ideally their partner would be privately held, like Lucasfilm, and relatively profitable.

The obvious choice was CMX. But CMX had lost market share over the years and by 1983 was in poor financial shape. It was obvious that some big company would acquire them soon and they'd be a poor supporter of the work still ahead for Lucasfilm.

Interactive Systems Company (ISC) was created in 1978 by Dave Bargan, a disgruntled CMX engineer, and Jack Callaway, an enterprising video hardware engineer specializing in machine controllers. ISC was looking to build high-end editing equipment to compete with CMX; by 1983 they had succeeded in eroding CMX's market lead.

Grass Valley Group (GVG) was a long-time manufacturer of production switchers and routing equipment—electronic boxes that fit into the flow of video around an editing bay or post-production set-up.

Bob Doris seriously considered partnering with one of these companies. ISC was growing quickly, but it didn't have a long track record. GVG was established, but had little experience with editing systems.[8] Doris and Guggenheim weighed the merits of each alternative. Both were rejected.

Their last option was Convergence. Convergence manufactured editing tools for the low-end market. They made editing equipment for corporate and industrial needs, but were never a player in the big leagues. If broadcasting was sports, industrial video would be "semi-pro." Still, they had a very successful editing tool called the ECS-90, which was used in tens of thousands of post-production facilities worldwide, and best of all, they had a large horde of cash.

"We had always taken the point of view that a successful editing system would have to be relatively inexpensive, just like a KEM [flatbed editing table]," commented Ralph. "Choosing Convergence as a partner was a combination of a company with the business strengths we sought, who also knew how to make equipment inexpensively." The ECS-90 was a robust workhorse and that was precisely what Lucasfilm needed to deliver to film editors.

Bob Doris met with Convergence president Gary Beeson and they hashed out the details of a joint-venture agreement. The new company would be half owned by each company, with Convergence providing capital and the manufacturing, marketing and distribution, and Lucasfilm providing the R&D, the patents, and of course, the brand. The unnamed joint venture was officially launched in September 1983 to produce Lucas' EdDroid.

They had twenty-six weeks to get everything ready.

Rob Lay begin working at Lucasfilm in October 1983, just weeks after the deal with Convergence was executed. The day Rob arrived Ralph Guggenheim sat him down in the machine room of C Building and showed him what they had been developing.

"What we realized," Ralph began to reveal, "was that the way to do editing systems is to build them around a database management system."

Lay sat silently. "This was the big secret?" he thought. His 3400 Plus project at CMX, which he had been slaving over for ages, and which debuted at

8 Incidentally, in 1984 the Grass Valley Group merged with ISC.

NAB earlier that year, was based on a database. And while Lucasfilm's project was being done on a SUN workstation, it still didn't have any kind of graphical interface—just columns of numbers like the old CMX systems.

Lay was blown away. He had been certain the Lucasfilm project was further along than this, and yet here he sat, six months from debut, looking at an engineering lab of equipment. Steve Schwartz agreed with him and brought in some editors to look at the state of the Droid.

After a short demonstration, one of them turned to Rob Lay and said, "This is all you have?"

Lay nodded grimly. The editor continued, looking into the screen of timecodes. "This is a disaster. You guys can't show this."

Rob Lay was deflated. But there was a silver lining. Lucasfilm believed in the project, and everyone in the division was gunning for NAB. There was money available, Ralph Guggenheim and Malcolm Blanchard were smart computer scientists, and ultimately, George Lucas was solidly behind the work.

Even though no new *Star Wars* films were in the works after *Return of the Jedi* was released, Lucasfilm still retained its long-standing magical vibe. Throughout the fall of 1983 Kerner was a hotbed of activity. ILM was starting to work on shots for two new films, *Raiders II* and *Star Trek III*. Kessler's THX/TAP Division was already generating more revenue than it was costing. Two large national theater chains had installed Lucasfilm's THX loudspeaker system in new theaters and were retrofitting old ones.

The fan club—managed as part of the marketing effort—had moved into A Building. The club had been launched when two very lucky *Star Wars* fans became company employees and soon corralled some 150,000 fans from around the world, generated a newsletter ("Bantha Tracks"), and generally interacted with the teeming masses insatiable for news from George. Emails popped up whenever surplus *Revenge* posters or Indy T-shirts were available for employees. Employees were some of the biggest fans.

Rob Lay and Ralph Guggenheim wandered over to D Building for a rare ILM open house, to show off all the models and props built for *Jedi*. They started talking about the user interface; they were each passionate about the problem. Rob insisted a graphical display was necessary; Ralph agreed, but felt it was a distraction and they needed to get the core product functional.

Rob Lay, bypassing Ralph's hesitation, teamed up with Malcolm Blanchard, who had been doing the preliminary work on the interface; he begged Malcolm to push the effort forward faster. Malcolm had been experimenting with the SUN's capabilities for drawing a graphical user interface (UI), and had come up with some ideas.

Most noteworthy was something that had come up after George's friend Bob Dalva spent some time trying to make the system work. Dalva was an editor, and he had many editing questions for the computer scientists: "How do you do a sound overlap with this thing?"

Malcolm didn't know what he was talking about. A sound overlap was an edit in sound that didn't happen at the same moment as the edit in picture. Dalva grabbed a sheet of paper and sketched out a track of workprint, a track of sound, and showed where the edits fell in relation to each other. The drawing made it easy to understand. Malcolm added this to the interface. He called it a timeline.[9] On the SUN it was a horizontal bar across the screen representing the strip of film, one track of picture and two of sound, as if they were running through a synchronizer.

"It was an idea that was floating around out there," said Lay, "but no one had done it in real life. I had made a presentation about one to CMX a few years earlier, and I think I'd read something about a design somewhere. But we were doing it."

"We long considered timeline editing a goal for the project," said Ralph. "Any reluctance I had was simply due to the enormous number of features we were trying to add in an orderly fashion."

In keeping with the filmmaker's metaphor, the timeline began on the right side of the screen—the way film did on a flatbed editing table. The thick picture track rested on the bottom and a pair of sound tracks lay above, again like a film bench. Also in keeping with the film editor's metaphor, there was a workspace in the center of the screen that acted as a cutting block, where source material could be chopped up before sticking it into the growing timeline.

When Dalva returned a month later to try the system again, he was pleased. Rob Lay loved the interface.

Once again, a schism was forming between Guggenheim and his video expert, this time Steven Schwartz; Rob Lay began to float between them as a sort of buffer. While Lay and Schwartz had spent years in the professional broadcast industry (Lay building systems and Schwartz using them), they worried privately that Ralph didn't have enough experience to guide this type of project.

"It could have been the perfect marriage," said Lay. "You needed someone who wasn't immersed in the industry to see beyond it."

And in some ways it was—Ralph Guggenheim recognized that UNIX was the future. But as Steve Schwartz repeated endlessly, UNIX was not a real-time operating system and it made the operating of an editing system troubled to its very core. In the real world of video production, machines needed to start

[9] A few crude timelines had been seen in editing tools before, usually ASCII characters aligned to form square shots. The Droid introduced the concept in its modern incarnation, bitmapped graphics, with synchronized tracks running along indefinitely, able to be selected and manipulated on the screen.

and stop instantly, with button pushes, and the intervening computation of the SUN computer made the system feel sluggish.

By early 1984, the product was coming along quickly. Guggenheim brought in a new programmer, Andy Cohen, to help them complete the prototype. The team of five pounded out software as the weeks passed; the debut of the product was closing fast.

Writing code was generally slow and frustrating. The Computer Division had a few SUNs, but mostly software engineers worked on terminals connected to one of the handful of VAXs, which was generally the norm for computing in the early '80s.

"The secretaries and the programmers were on the same machines," recalled Lay. "You'd sit there at the terminal, but as more people were on the system, vying for the same CPU cycles, everything slowed down to a crawl. You'd sit there waiting for the cursor to move, going crazy."

Then, more frequently than anyone would have liked, the machines would crash. Not just a system crash, which required rebooting, but a corrupted hard disk. No matter how often you saved your work, there was nothing that could save you from the death of the disk.

"When the damn machine would crash," said Lay, "fifty people would loose work. The guys in the systems group were the most stressed people in the world. Non-stop coffeepots."

When the system was overloaded, running slow, there would always be groans emanating from open doors in C Building. When the system crashed, there would be a palpable cry of anguish coming simultaneously from many offices: the graphics project, editing, audio…. Bleary-eyed scientists would stumble from their desks and into the halls to commiserate.

Andy Cohen, Malcolm Blanchard, and Rob Lay sit around the EdDroid prototype, 1984.

The editing guys were running at full tilt to hit their deadline, dredging up every inner vesicle of innovation each had to provide. "I was sleeping on the floor, mostly under my desk," said Lay. "But I enjoyed that cowboy lifestyle."

As they got closer to their goal, it became more real—they were creating a film-editing tool that was completely unprecedented.

But they were all uncomfortable with the name. Convergence was getting ready to manufacturer a nameplate for the machine, and as the design was being hammered out, along with the supporting marketing materials, EdDroid was not working for them. Overnight, in virtually the same way *Revenge of the Jedi* became "Return," EdDroid was renamed the EditDroid.

The EditDroid consisted of software running on a SUN-1 computer and connected via an Ethernet cable to a black box that controlled the outlying video peripherals: laserdisc players from Pioneer and videotape decks from Sony. A few times a year Ed Catmull and Ralph Guggenheim would get in Pioneer's face about the promised affordable, recordable videodiscs. "They're coming, they're coming," Pioneer promised. But only months away from NAB, new disc player/recorders were nowhere in sight.

Bob Doris told Ralph that the Lucasfilm powers-that-be were making an industrial design expert available to the EditDroid, to turn the components of the system into a cohesive and very Lucasfilm-y product. Ralph was happy to take advantage of it.

"Lucas really wanted a big screen feel," said Rob Lay. "Editing in the theater: that was the vision. He was really behind having the biggest screen possible." Lucas was also emphatic that controls and surfaces had to be minimal. As Lay recalled it, "The image was king."

A cool perk at Lucasfilm was that it had creative designers on staff. Soon, Nilo Rodis-Jamero, one of the rising stars at ILM, began to apply himself to the EditDroid product design. Nilo had designed and built some *Empire* props, costumes, and Boba Fett's ship, and later took a leading role on *Poltergeist*.

A Polaroid of the EditDroid under development.

"He really understood the look of machinery that had personality," remarked Steve Schwartz.

Once Nilo's early sketches were approved, he began working with another industrial designer, Pete Ronzoni. Ronzoni had designed some of the space pilot helmets in the *Star Wars* films and was a successful fabricator. Ronzoni and Rodis formed a small company—R2—for handling the project. They were excited to deliver a futuristic editing system that was appropriate for the Lucasfilm brand. They sent sketches to the Droid team for periodic review. The machine was going to be very sexy.

The Pastry Cart was redesigned in black, with a central KEM-style shuttle knob and an assortment of buttons with red LED labels along the left side, trackball on the right. The contraption was renamed the TouchPad. The long cable from Duwayne's early sessions remained, so editors could push back from the screen to work. The Droid demoed well, but until recordable disks were readily available it would likely be prohibitively expensive to use on a large production.

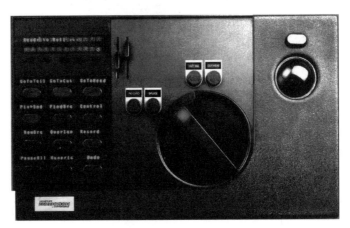

The production-ready TouchPad controller for the EditDroid.

For testing and demonstrations, the editing team had been given some outtakes from *More American Graffiti*. "Ralph," Steve Schwartz begged, "we need some kick-ass demo footage for NAB. We need *Star Wars*."

Guggenheim knew that asking for material from the *Star Wars* films, particular for a public showing, was generally frowned upon, and he didn't like being shoved into an uncomfortable position.

"George won't go for that," Ralph argued, a convenient enough rebuttal. *Graffiti* footage would be a better demonstration of an editing system than a bunch of special effects shots, most created with an optical printer. But Schwartz was determined.

When George came by C Building for a meeting with Ralph, he stopped to see the new EditDroid design. The team called it the "Death Star" console. It had almost nothing on the desk but the TouchPad—which Duwayne had despised—with an enormous rear-projection video display behind the smoked Plexiglas façade.

George dropped his lunchbag on the console and looked at it, satisfied. "It holds a tunafish sandwich," he joked.

Steve Schwartz was nearby and laughed at Lucas' remark. "You like working for a guy like that. He breaks the ice and gets you to chuckle." Schwartz always felt that Lucas was misjudged as aloof.

"You couldn't ask for a better guy to work for. A straight shooter. I thought he was very approachable."

George toyed with the new control panel on the EditDroid. "This looks real great," he said.

Picking up a small television remote control from a chair he said, "You know, I really just want to point at the image. I want to do it with this remote. Can it be as easy as a TV remote?"

Editing traditionally, as George was used to, was fairly simple. But instructing a computer to do that work took a number of buttons—tasks were too complex to be done just by pointing. Ralph agreed that it would have been slick to have a minimal laser-type device to control things.

George sat down at the black desk that curved around him, and gingerly clicked on a shot with the trackball. The videodisc instantly cued to the chosen frame; that would have taken an assistant many minutes using film. He took the KEM knob in hand and turned it to the first magnetic detent; the disc began to play. It almost felt like film.

Next he turned the shuttle to the "stop" position. Nothing happened. The disc kept rolling. He looked at Ralph. Ralph looked at the computer, then over to Rob Lay. The computer was frozen. Everyone tried not to look panicked.

Schwartz recalled what happened next. Oblivious to the system crash, George turned to Ralph, "What you need is something with great picture and sound to put on it."

Schwartz saw his opportunity to join in the fray. "George, do *you* know where we can find some material with great picture and sound?"

George took the bait. "Well, we have some stuff in the warehouse…and we're doing *Indiana Jones* downstairs…I'll get Michael Kahn up here…maybe there are some outtakes…you can grab anything you want."

Schwartz was beaming, although Ralph was irritated with him for bringing it up. It went okay, but it just as easily could have backfired.

Within a week, Steven Spielberg popped upstairs for a quick look at George's new editing invention. He stood before the Death Star console, and with a satisfied sort of "humph," disappeared into C Building to continue working on *Indy II*. Before long, Spielberg's editor, Michael Kahn, came upstairs to see the Droid for himself.

Kahn had been cutting film since the late 1960s, and after editing a film for Irvin Kershner, got a job cutting young Spielberg's *Close Encounters of the Third Kind* (1977), thus beginning their close working relationship.[10]

Kahn was busy with *Indy*, but returned for a few hours every day that week to give any feedback he could. He was impressed that on one day he could make a suggestion, and it would be integrated into the system in time for his return the next day.

[10] **Michael Kahn** (b. 1935). Editor: *Close Encounters of the Third Kind* (1977), *Eyes of Laura Mars* (1978), *1941* (1979), *Raiders of the Lost Ark* (1981), *Poltergeist* (1982), *Indiana Jones and the Temple of Doom* (1984), *The Color Purple* (1985), *Fatal Attraction* (1987), *Empire of the Sun* (1988), *Indiana Jones and the Last Crusade* (1989), *Hook* (1991), *Schindler's List* (1993), *Jurassic Park* (1993), *Saving Private Ryan* (1998), *Minority Report* (2002).

"At that point it was hard to edit anything on the Droid," recalled Rob Lay, "but [Kahn] would look at the screen and make comments about how it was designed, and how the process worked."

"When he saw the degree to which we were revising and improving the system around his ideas," said Guggenheim, "he became even more excited about the process." Before Kahn's tour of duty was completed, the EditDroid sported a new button on the interface, a feature he was confident would improve usability. It was referred to for months as the "Michael Kahn button."[11]

Inexplicably, Steve Schwartz was given license to pour through the outtakes of *Return of the Jedi* to find suitable demo material for the EditDroid. He found an impressive X-wing fighter scene that he knew would attract crowds, and he also settled on perhaps the only "talking heads" scene in the action packed film, with Yoda talking to Luke Skywalker. A talking head scene (as a basic back-and-forth conversation is sometimes referred to), even if it tended to be a bit dull, was essential to demonstrate basic editing functionality. With luck, the story and characters would make up for any shortcomings with the "wow" factor.

As the vision for Skywalker Ranch took form, it was implicit that beneath the pastoral Victorian façade, its underlying engine would be high-tech and digital. It was not just a coincidence that the computer research was initiated concurrently with the physical development of the Ranch—both were the interwoven components of George's vision for Northern California filmmaking.

Most of the artisans building the Ranch had never worked on anything of that scale before. For woodcrafters and glassmakers, as for filmmakers and computer scientists, all the projects at the Ranch were ambitious and unprecedented—this was their art, after all, their passion. An enormous stained glass dome over his library. Entire houses constructed with a jewelry-box precision. And Lucas, a craftsman like them, was their biggest fan and patron.

[11] Later renamed "slide cut," it allowed an editor to take a transition and slide it around—adding frames to one side of the transition while taking away the same number from the other side. This is a particularly important feature if an editor is creating an overlap, where the picture cut occurs slightly before (or after) the sound cut. Kahn was famous for his overlaps. On Apple's Final Cut Pro, the feature is known as a "roll trim."

There was an initial understanding between George Lucas and Ed Catmull that the results of their work might lead to commercial products, presumably for the professional industry. That far-off idea in 1979 was good enough to get their research rolling. If the tools made by the Computer Division worked for Lucas' particular needs, then they could probably be sold to Hollywood. But it's important to recognize that the products weren't being designed with the *market* in mind.

It was a recurring way of thinking at Lucasfilm: build a mixing theater, a stained glass shop, an editing system, make them great, and then see who wants to rent/buy the stuff when it was done. It's the way artists think: create what you want; sales are completely separate (and sometimes moderately distasteful). Business people look to serve a definable market, and design product that can be manufactured affordably, shipped efficiently, repaired easily, and updated methodically.

While Lucas inspired the computer scientists, Bob Doris cautiously eyed the business. Meeting with Andy Moorer, they reviewed what had been accomplished on the ASP project over 1982, and most importantly, what it would cost to mass-produce. After analysis, they determined the ASP was completely unaffordable, even for the highest-end of the audio industry, which at least valued sizzle and novelty. Moorer needed to rebuild this ASP so it would cost less. So Moorer and his team came to work the next day and started again.

Having a working prototype of the ASP (regardless of how they might reinvent the hardware) gave them an opportunity to start writing audio software to run on it. It was, after all, only a sound processor; one still had to ask it to do something.

What was Ben Burtt doing these days that was laborious, that perhaps the ASP could help with? What tasks were particularly well suited to being computerized?

Moorer set up a meeting with Ben Burtt. First, he wanted to show Ben a little program he had put together, for the ASP to play some Bach.

"It was quite nice, quite beautiful," said Ben. "And I ribbed him a little saying that, yes, the ASP can produce music, pure tones, musical things, but what I want is a pick-up truck exploding and going down a hill, and that was too complicated a sound to create. We still had to go out and record things like that."

Andy Moorer in the sound pit, testing audio sliders, fall 1983.

Andy urged Ben to think about what kind of acoustical problems he was having. He didn't need to think long.

"Ben Burtt said the biggest bottleneck was the spatializing of sounds; it was his biggest time sink," recalled Andy. Ben needed fine control over the room size around a sound, a magic knob that would adjust the spatial environment so he could immediately hear how a sound could be varied.

His traditional method was slow and tedious, with tape decks and amplifiers. And creating flybys! All those objects—space ships, motorcycles, airplanes—that had to be made to sound like they were moving fast by an imaginary microphone. He needed a Doppler shift that could be added to a sound.

Andy provided a solution. "We put a box in his little mixing room in the basement of C Building, connected through the wall to the sound pit, where the ASP resided." He wrote Ben a basic set of programs that would allow the box to input a sound, fly it around at a desired speed, and output it.

Andy then asked if there was anything else; anything at all. An idea crossed Ben's mind. One thing that had been dogging him was the sound of arrows being shot at Indiana Jones. Ben was starting to work on *Indy II* and once again faced the problem of having a credible sound for an arrow. Not just any arrow would do. He wanted the exact arrow sound he remembered from a movie he had seen as a kid, *The Adventures of Robin Hood* (1938).

Ben had tried unsuccessfully for years to record an arrow with the sound from the movie. "I knew that real arrows didn't sound like that, real arrows have a swishing sound."

Not only is an arrow pretty quiet, it's only near the microphone for a millisecond. Ben was certain they'd faked it for *Robin Hood*, but he never could create any sound that he liked as much. "I thought maybe it was a violin or something; it was almost a musical sound."

[12] Actually, it was slightly more involved. Burtt and Moorer's acoustic analysis showed that the sound could be generated from a real arrow with a particular cut of its feathers.

Burtt gave the classic film to Andy Moorer. With the ASP and various tools, Andy synthesized the sound of the arrow. He showed Burtt how it was made of certain waves and fundamental frequencies and harmonics. Admitted Ben, "He had imitated it very well."[12]

Said Andy: "All the arrows in the *Temple of Doom* were done on the ASP."

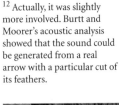

Blue screen elements from *Indiana Jones and the Temple of Doom*, showing a particularly "arrow-intense" scene. It was the first real production test of the ASP.

twenty

These Aren't the Droids You're Looking For

[1984]

Even more important...is the way complex systems seem to strike a balance between the need for order and the imperative to change. Complex systems tend to locate themselves at a place we call 'the edge of chaos.' We imagine the edge of chaos as a place where there is enough innovation to keep a living system vibrant, and enough stability to keep it from collapsing into anarchy. It is a zone of conflict and upheaval, where the old and the new are constantly at war.

—Ian Malcolm, in *The Lost World* (1995)

BY EARLY 1984, Bob Greber and Roger Faxon were lame ducks at Lucasfilm. With the *Star Wars* trilogy done, George was back at the helm, no longer an absentee landlord. The divorce, for all the emotional turmoil it created, left him more focused on work.

Before *Jedi* wrapped, George would meet with his president for a few hours each week. "I told him what we were doing," commented Greber, "and he was either pleased, or not."

But after *Jedi*, George became a fixture on campus. He would walk around Kerner, look over the shoulders of ILM staff or sit in on sessions at Sprockets. Obviously, there was now a management problem: the company had two bosses. Lucas and Greber spoke about the situation and agreed there should be only one boss at the company.

Recalled Greber with a smile, "The only problem was that we agreed it should be him, and not me." They decided that Greber should stay on for another six months or so, and then transition to the company's board of advisors.

Bob Doris and Ed Catmull were a little nervous with the interregnum at Lucasfilm. Lucas enjoyed having solid financial advice—a CFO—and he would eventually be looking for someone. It could be reasonably assumed that a new CFO would get to work on saving the company money (or perhaps try to increase revenues by commercializing things rapidly); either way, the Computer Division would be high on the list of things to be "fixed."

Soon after his arrival at Lucasfilm, Bob Doris realized that the Computer Division needed to be an independent company. The computer teams didn't fit in at Lucasfilm. Leaving the fold held little emotional tug for either Doris or Catmull, who were less enchanted with the Lucasfilm aura than many of their cohorts, and singularly interested in pursuing their particular passions. Catmull wanted to make computer animated movies. Doris wanted to deliver tools to what he was certain was a large and growing market.

Lucasfilm research could produce prototypes and new technology, but it wasn't going to do for the manufacturing, sales, and support that would invariably be required of a new equipment company.

"George looked at the products the way he looked at films," said Doris. "A film is a one-off product. Once you put your heart into creating it, it can be licensed and relicensed in numerous ways. George wanted to license all the cool technology that they had developed, but he had no interest in being the manufacturer."

After New Years 1984, the entire Computer Division was in high gear. There was no president at Lucasfilm, although there was no lack of excitement. The Games Group was putting the finishing touches on their first two games for Atari, *Ballblazer* and *Rebel Rescue*, and Steve Arnold had joined as their new leader. The audio team was finally expanding, as Michael Hawley arrived from Yale to work on software, Peter Nye to attack the user interface, and Jeff Borish to help with the new hardware. And the Graphics Group was putting together their first animation project. A Disney animator, John Lasseter, had just begun consulting with the team and was starting to design characters. And the Edit-Droid, just a few months from its debut at NAB, was finally taking form.

Before 1984, the NAB broadcasters convention was a small, salon-type show with small equipment demonstrations in small hotels. By 1984 it had grown to almost 40,000 industry attendees (from about 5,000 attendees in 1976). Before, there had been no glamour to the equipment demonstrations, but that was about to change.

When the EditDroid was unveiled at the Lucasfilm booth, it shook the very foundation of broadcaster technology. It fed the appetite of those looking for something besides a typical videotape recorder and keyboard. The

The digital audio software team in the pit, February 1984. *From left:* Andy Moorer, Peter Nye, Curtis Abbot, Bernard Mont-Reynaud.

sleek, black Death Star console curved around the editor, who looked into a large, high-quality image created by a rear-projection video system. The marketing team had assembled a demo tape to play before each demonstration; it began with the unmistakable *Star Wars* theme music. Each hour, as the demo was about to start, crowds would push up to the stage, causing chaos in the aisles, overflowing onto the carpeting of other manufacturer's booths.

Over and over, the EditDroid demonstrator went through the architecture of the product. *"On the right, you'll see a graphical display with data about raw material, and a workspace and timeline where the edited sequence is constructed. The system tries to keep you from staring at data any more than you need to. Big, and central, is the display of your cut material, where you can watch your work instantly after you make changes. On the left is a smaller display for watching the raw footage, the source material, that you select from the data display with a trackball. Point and click, and any shot pops up here instantly."*

A SUN workstation provided the graphical display, with a database linking the original film to a set of videodiscs of raw material. As the cursor moved over the various regions of the UI, it changed from a little logbook icon over the source material, a scissors icon in the editing part of the screen, and a

Cover image from the EditDroid brochure, 1984.

tiny Darth Vader mask in the control band that ran along the bottom.

Many people had never seen a bit-mapped graphical computer display. It was the stuff of the U.S. military, or maybe high-end industry like Xerox PARC.[1] Now men who owned radio and TV stations around the United States, attendees in cheap sport coats and many with little bow ties, crowded around with old technology hippies who knew a lot about electronics, and stared at the Lucas magic brought to bear on their industry.

It was as if they were peering into the future, maybe through a window at a World's Fair Pavilion of Tomorrow.

Lucasfilm had transferred the raw material from *The Return of the Jedi* to videodisc, which added spice to the demonstrations. It was the Yoda death scene with Luke Skywalker, set in the Dagobah swamps, and people couldn't watch it enough. "People weren't even looking at the editing system, they just wanted to see *Star Wars*," reported one attendee.

It would have been a perfect moment if Lucasfilm had been alone with their computer based film-style editor. But echoing in the halls of NAB were the dying words of Yoda, "There…is…another…Skywalker…."

[1] Only a month earlier, the world was shaken with the announcement of Apple's Macintosh computer in a commercial shown during the Superbowl, and soon known as the "1984" spot. Apple was about to introduce the bit-mapped display to the general public.

[2] Very fun to play with. Ron Barker's avocation was interfaces; he was a skilled remote control helicopter pilot. "I don't want to edit with a keyboard," Schuler recalled Barker saying. "You can't fly a helicopter with a keyboard." So he developed the highly tactile machine, somewhat resembling a Moviola.

There was another product being introduced at NAB—a direct competitor to the EditDroid—and it was literally around the corner from Lucasfilm's booth. It was called the Montage Picture Processor; it had been developed by an English entrepreneur, Ron Barker, in collaboration with video engineer Chester "Chet" Schuler. It wasn't as high-tech as the EditDroid, and it wasn't as revolutionary as the EditDroid. But it was perfectly evolutionary—a non-linear videotape-based system. Not using videodiscs, it wasn't quite as sexy, but it made up for it in practicality.

[3] Small picture labels were considered superfluous on a videodisc-based system, since pointing at any shot instantly retrieved the original footage; for a videotape-based system, which took some time to cue, it was a godsend.

The Montage used a custom microcomputer that controlled a set of seventeen Betamax machines. It had no graphical interface, but cleverly used a series of small video monitors and a pair of hand-size knobs that both selected and shuttled video.[2] It also had a digital frame grabber that took a black-and-white snapshot of important frames of video. That way, the editor had reference images of the material even without shuttling the tape decks around.[3]

Though the Montage was developed independently of the EditDroid, farther from Hollywood than even Lucasfilm, Ron Barker was aware of its development. In 1981, Barker had visited American Zoetrope to witness the video experiments in the Silverfish and Coppola's previsualization system. Thomas Brown at Zoetrope had suggested he visit Clark Higgins at Lucasfilm. The editing system at the time was pretty basic, but even so, the team only showed Barker the first incarnation—the Dodo—and kept the second version under wraps. Barker disappeared and hooked up with an engineer he had known, Chet Schuler.

In a spare bedroom in Barker's home in Weston, Massachusetts, Schuler and Barker began experimenting. Barker convinced a local investor to part with $50,000 to seed the project, to get a business plan written. Central to their editing product was a frame grabber—they wanted digital snapshots of video frames, to aid the editor in finding material and to decrease the pain of shutting videotapes around looking for something. The entrepreneurs experimented for six months until it was a good enough proof of concept that the men raised their first round of professional capital, $1.5 million from Prudential Insurance.[4]

Where videodiscs moved so quickly that only a few were needed for any piece of video, videotapes were longer and slower, and thus required more copies to preview edited sequences without recording; hence the bank of Beta machines.

Unlike the EditDroid booth, the Montage booth was closed off—a carnival tent with a funhouse inside. With smoky Plexiglas windows, attendees could almost make out the device, but it left anyone passing by both curious and frustrated. You had to be a VIP to sit before the machine. Its secrecy in plain sight added to the mystique.

Sony employee Ken Yas stood in the crowd watching the EditDroid demonstration, "It was genuinely hard to get close," he recalled, then he talked his way in to see the Montage.

"You felt privileged to even be in that environment," recalled Yas. "These two companies were different from each other, yet radically different from every other thing at the convention."

For the first time, NAB had captured an element of glamour. Crowds stood around the two booths, unsure what they were showing, but certain *something* was happening. It wasn't just the new editing systems that were magical. The crowd was interested in the people at the controls. The demonstrators were stars in their

Cover of the Montage brochure, 1984.

[4] November 1982. If they could deliver a prototype in one year, Prudential would come in for additional financing.

own right. ("How did you get this job?") "No NAB since has captured the innocence of that moment," said Yas.

Montage was presenting something very different from the EditDroid. It was not a concept demonstration. Months earlier a Montage had been sold to a post-production facility in New York and was cutting small projects. "We were showing our first real product," said Schuler. "The EditDroid was just smoke and mirrors."

Schuler was right; the Droid was only barely functional in its debut and it would be a rush to get the product to the same degree of usability as its new competitor. The Montage was a creative approach to editing, but no less expensive than the EditDroid. Barker started working with an enormously charismatic salesman, Craig Sexton, who was getting Montages placed all over Hollywood.

Clark Higgins saw the Montage demo at NAB and reconnected with Ron Barker after the show. He joined the fledgling operation to help them figure out the film-video interface. Higgins transferred much of his education about the importance of sound to the then largely visual editing system. "Francis always said a movie is 65 percent audio," recalled Higgins.

The new EditDroid team just after NAB. George Lucas is seated center, Ben Burtt to the right, and Ralph Guggenheim just behind George. *Standing, left to right:* Andy Cohen, Rob Lay, Kate Smith-Greenfield, John Lynch (all software designers), David Blomgren (tech writer), Steve Schwartz (video), Pete Ronzoni (industrial design).

After NAB, the Droid team was exhausted. Employees drifted back from Vegas, the EditDroid was shipped to Marin, and Rob Lay took off for three weeks of mountain climbing in Washington. From an engineering standpoint, the project was in hiatus.

Production had just begun for Walter Murch's pet project, *Return to Oz*. Murch had written the treatment in 1981, a sequel of sorts to *The Wizard of Oz*, and had intrigued Disney with the live-action fantasy. Of all Murch's highly regarded accomplishments, he was not often thought of as a writer. And yet he had co-written *THX 1138* with Lucas, and had even penned the original screenplay of *The Black Stallion* with Carroll Ballard and Gill Dennis. Murch re-teamed with Gill Dennis to write *Oz*.

But the other thing Murch hadn't yet tried was directing. Shooting began in London, with ten-year-old Fairuza Balk in the starring role. When the film ran into budget problems, Disney put Murch in a corner and Murch turned to Lucas for support. Lucas began commuting to London to help out, to oversee production, but insisted on taking no salary and no screen credit.

"I told Walter I didn't want to be officially involved because *Return to Oz* would then be viewed as *my* picture, not his."

In May, George Lucas and Steven Spielberg came to L.A. to immortalize their handprints at Mann's Chinese Theater. Upon his return, Lucas met with Bob Doris and Ed Catmull to discuss their new proposal: they wanted Lucas to spin off the entire Computer Division as an independent company.

"Let us build a business out of this," Doris pitched. Lucas was resistant.

"Why can't you do this as part of Lucasfilm? Why does it have to be spun out?" Doris recalled him saying.

Doris and Catmull couldn't convince Lucas of the need. Instead of creating a new company, Lucas authorized an expanded budget for the division. Doris and Catmull made a case about the oddness the geeks represented at the film company, but Lucas wouldn't hear it. The company would get a new building on Kerner for them.

When word got back to the research teams (through the grapevine) that Doris and Catmull had gone to George to spin out the group, it was not met with a universally positive response. The project leaders didn't like that their fate was being discussed without their knowledge.

Alvy in particular wasn't interested in leaving the movie company. At that moment he was up to his eyeballs in the most advanced computer-generated movie ever made—even if it was just short animation to demonstrate the Pixar computer to Siggraph audiences. To spin out of Lucasfilm would take them away from the magic of moviemaking. They'd be little more than a Silicon Valley start-up. Alvy wanted the Graphics Group to have no part of Doris' plan.

"There was always a political earthquake happening underneath us," said Rob Lay.

This represented the first schism within the "old" division—graphics cleaved off intellectually from editing and sound (Games was always sort of

The entire Computer Division—graphics, editing, sound, games, tech writers, administration, computer support staff—at its peak, posing for a group shot on the side of C Building. Summer 1984.

on their own). But the members of the four projects—the researchers, the administrative assistants, the systems programmers, the technical writers— now numbering seventy, would only hear rumblings of the political situation. But they were all so engrossed in their various activities that they trusted that it would all be handled with their best interests at heart.

Convergence, Lucasfilm's partner in the EditDroid project, was handling all sales and marketing. Deborah Harter, a midlevel employee at Convergence, saw the Droid as an opportunity and rose to lead marketing for the new joint venture. Richard Moscarella placed the first few Droids in Hollywood at one of the preeminent post-production facilities in town, Complete Post. Even before the Droids arrived (and certainly before they really worked) Complete Post hired a cabinetmaker to build a custom desk and room for the Droid equipment. A wooden console sat in the middle of a room awaiting the arrival of the fancy new hardware.

"It was the ugliest god-awful antique-looking thing," said Rob Lay. "It looked like a big piano…so people were calling it the OrganDroid."

Deborah Harter soon hired Ken Yas as the EditDroid product specialist. Yas had spent years at Sony, introducing video to the filmmakers at the American Film Institute (AFI), and he was already acquainted with the team from Convergence.[5] Harter, Moscarella and Yas opened offices at Lucasfilm's old L.A. headquarters, The Egg Company.

The ASP prototype sat in the basement of C Building. While Andy and his team worked on the low-cost version, he was always anxious to solve some filmmaker's problem with his new hardware. Luck, as they say, is the union of preparation and opportunity. And the opportunity came from Berkeley.

Milos Forman was across the Richmond Bridge, about half an hour away, mixing *Amadeus* at Fantasy Films.[6] *Amadeus*, a movie about Mozart, was a period piece shot in eastern Europe. There was a scene in the movie (the asylum scene) where the performances of Salieri and Mozart were excellent but the audio recording was not. To hear the dialog, they had to turn up the volume, but doing so raised the background noise level too, which buried the actor's voices in static.

Forman's sound engineers, Mark Berger and Tom Scott, knew that Lucas' teams were pioneering new technology for exactly this kind of problem.[7] They brought the tapes over to Andy Moorer and asked if his ASP could help.

"Yes," said Andy, happy to have a chance to once again explore the world of noise reduction. (Back at Stanford he had a graduate student, John Strawn, who had worked on the experimental project to denoise the famous Karen Silkwood tapes. The results were marginally useful; the de-noising process introduced a fair amount of odd distortions into the recordings.)

"The only thing is," said Tom Scott," we are in the middle of production, and have to figure out if we can use these tracks or need to come up with another plan."

"Another plan" meant ADR—automatic dialog replacement. There is nothing "automatic" about ADR. Actors stand in a theater and try to fit their own lines into their mouths as the film is projected on screen. ADR is used for a substantial amount of the dialog in Hollywood films—very little dialog comes from recording on location, and only a little more comes from shots from controlled studio sets. In spite of industry dependence on ADR, it is tedious and most directors feel it never fully recaptures the emotion from that original moment on-camera. The ability to clean up a production track using a computer would be momentous. It would save performances otherwise ruined by the sound of an airplane overhead, or a carpenter's hammer

[5] The AFI project was Sony's new initiative to get video in the hands of corporations and filmmakers. Yas traveled around the country giving seminars, " a sort of outreach program." In the pre-VCR era few individuals, let alone corporate types, had any experience with videotape. Yas' success in launching in-house video departments at Xerox and IBM helped him land at the AFI in Hollywood, where he gained respect for Convergence's low-cost, and yet innovative, offline editing tools.

[6] Fantasy, owned by multi-faceted producer Saul Zaentz, was the third leg of the Bay Area filmmaking community, along with Zoetrope and Lucasfilm. Zaentz purchased Fantasy Records in 1967, and in 1968 scored a hit with Creedence Clearwater Revival. In 1975 Zaentz produced Milos Forman's *One Flew Over the Cuckoo's Nest*. The string of independent films to come from Zaentz includes *Blue Velvet, The Mosquito Coast, The Right Stuff, The English Patient, Crumb,* and *Fly Away Home.*

[7] Tom Scott had worked with Zoetrope here and there over the years, having been introduced by his cousin, Walter Murch. His expertise in sound engineering was well known around the San Francisco Bay Area for both music and film.

on some distant stage. To surgically change a word in an actor's mouth. Andy was excited by what he was certain he could do to a piece of sound.

"How much time do I have?" Andy asked, looking forward to the challenge. "About a week."

Andy smiled and left with the tapes, unsure what he could do but deeply interested in trying. Tom Scott and Mark Berger would likely be happy with any amount of the production sound that could be saved.

Andy immediately digitized the tapes into the ASP. Then he excised small samples of pure noise and had the computer analyze them—getting, in essence, a fingerprint of the background noise. Then the pure noise was subtracted from the dialog tracks, leaving the human voices intact. It took some work to filter out the right amount of noise—too much sounded artificial, too little and the voices weren't clear.

"About half of the tapes they brought me we were able to clean up," said Moorer. *Amadeus* was the first feature film to utilize their new noise reduction technology.

It was growing clear to Bob Doris that the research scientists at the Computer Division were having trouble serving two masters. All their projects had begun simply, to devise new tools for Lucasfilm, for George. But now there was a growing need for the things they were making to be viable commercially as well.

In-house products can be quirky: the hardware needn't be reproducible or easy to manufacture, and the software might solve immediate problems but not a range of problems. Doris decided to leave the researchers alone, and construct a second team that would be focused on taking the prototype work and developing commercial products. He called this the Commercial Products Group, and their first trial would be to take Andy Moorer's in-house LUDS systems—for designing hardware—and make it a bona fide product. They changed the LUDS name to CADdroid.

CADdroid was perfectly emblematic of the tools being invented at Lucasfilm. It was a production tool, and since it worked for them, the thinking went, it would probably work for a larger market.

Moorer had designed the software for himself; it did exactly what he needed it to do and it did it well, though it worked in a way that was not particularly user-friendly. It was not graphical, which made it non-intuitive. Michael O'Brien, the engineer signed on to lead the project, revised the interface. He also explored the full range of features it required, to satisfy a range of potential customers.

As excellent as LUDS had been in-house, it was highly flawed as a product—it required an inordinate (and potentially disproportionate) amount of work to make saleable. The issues surrounding CADdroid were not entirely different from the issues every Computer Division tool would face.

A few weeks after NAB, Ralph Guggenheim told a few people he was looking to change directions, to join his old NYIT friends in the Graphics Group. He felt he had delivered what he had promised: the prototype of the Edit-Droid. By summer he still hadn't selected his replacement to lead the Edit-Droid team. Who could turn the concept demonstration into a real product? Rob Lay became the director of the project.

The first thing Lay had to address was the problematic hardware coming from Convergence. It was the hardware that controlled external machines: the disc players, the videotape recorders, the effects switcher. None of it worked. Lay and Guggenheim (in transition) flew down to Irvine.

"How are we going to make this fuckin' thing work?" Lay shot into the engineering team in Irvine.

Convergence had hired some outside consultants to try to figure out what was wrong, to little positive effect. So Lay and Guggenheim met with Convergence president Gary Beeson and his engineering management.

"Everybody sat around and looked at each other wondering what we could do," said Lay. "And finally I said I could just move down here until it's done."

And so he did. In November, Rob Lay rented a station wagon, loaded it to the gills with computer equipment and his white husky, Anapurna, and drove down I-5 to Irvine, to work with Convergence.

The black box that controlled the video peripherals became known as the "Planet," and that was, of course, connected to the SUN. Inside the Planet were interface cards—each its own 68000 computer—connected to an external video machine. You could tell when the Planet was healthy by the pulsing of a series of red LEDs on the front edge. Even with the smoked-black glass door closed, the LEDs strobed back and forth in an eerie retro-computer way.

The Convergence engineers had never built a device as demanding. Lay rode herd on them week after week, trying to get them to finish the machine control.

"I'm trying to manage these guys...but I'm on the outside," said Lay. "I'm a middle-manager to start with, and I didn't even work for Convergence, so it was hard to get them to follow me. Besides, these guys were showing up hungover, having been up all night chasing women or something, and stoned, and it wasn't going anywhere."

After seven weeks of culture clashing, Lay packed it in. "This isn't going to happen at Convergence." He decided he needed to get the hardware back from Convergence and hire his own programmers.

By the time Lay arrived back at Kerner, the EditDroid project had moved into a new building at 3301 Bellam Blvd, catty-corner from A Building. It was called Z Building. They finally had a home.

twenty-one

My Breakfast with Andre

[1983–1984]

It's kind of fun to do the impossible.

—Walt Disney

ED CATMULL AND ALVY RAY SMITH visited the Disney studios every year from the end of the 1970s to the early 1980s. As kids, both had been inspired by Disney. They had every expectation that it was the place that would lead the charge into the future. That's where the great animators were, after all. "[Our] first couple of visits were more in the order of adulation," said Alvy.

Over those years, the two of them had witnessed the fallout from the end of the mogul era at Disney, much as Lucas and Coppola experienced at Warners. After Walt Disney died in 1966, the studio went into shock. Plans that Walt had been developing, like the theme park in Florida, continued to move forward, but the pioneering spirit was gone.

Even though the vast majority of animated features in the U.S. had come from the Disney studio, it appeared that Disney management was content to rest on those laurels. The "Nine Old Men" of Disney—the animators who had led the teams on such Disney classics as *Pinocchio* (1940), *Fantasia* (1940), *Dumbo* (1941) and *Bambi* (1942)—were still the principal animators at the studio. From the 1950s through 1970s, virtually no new animators were brought on board. No one was being schooled in the methods and the secrets.

Walt's older brother and business partner Roy Oliver Disney, oversaw the company until his death in 1972. Roy had completed Walt Disney World in Florida, his brother's dream, but he hadn't been nearly as successful as Walt in the movie business. After Roy Oliver's death, a regime of executives took over, trying to harvest the golden eggs and juggle political infighting with Walt's relatives, without killing the goose.

The hippie years presented some innovation to the field of animation, but not at Disney.[1] By 1973, with an enormous amount of catching up to do, Disney

[1] Notably *Yellow Submarine* (1968) and *Fritz the Cat* (1972).

347

started to recruit new talent—Don Bluth, in particular, who was being groomed to be the leader of what they hoped would be the "Nine *Young* Men."[2]

"One of the questions that's never been answered is what took them so long?" commented animation historian Charles Solomon. "They had the best animators in the world, but they also had to be aware that these people were aging."

Disney continued to roll out mostly uninspired feature animations: *The Aristocats* (1970), *Robin Hood* (1973), *Pete's Dragon* (1977). There were occasional bright spots, like *The Rescuers* (1977), but by and large animators did what they wanted, on no rigid schedule. When films were done, the studio simply released them. The young Disney artists were increasingly frustrated.

Ron Miller, an ex-pro football star who married Walt's daughter, was made head of Disney's films in 1976.[3] Miller had spent the prior decade involved with the producing of many of the Disney television projects and the occasional live action film.

"He simply didn't have the vision the job required," commented Solomon. "A pleasant enough fellow, but he just wasn't the man to replace Walt."

When John Lasseter was a kid, he was fascinated by animation. "I loved cartoons. I would get up at the crack of dawn on Saturday, get my bowl of cereal, and watch cartoons from when they started until *Bowling for Dollars* came on." In high school he discovered that people could make cartoons for a living. "It never dawned on me that you could do this for a career."

His senior year of high school, he began writing to the Disney studio looking for guidance or maybe work. They wrote back, telling him that they were starting a special character animation program at the California Institute of the Arts (known as CalArts). Disney, badly needing new talent, had developed the program as a feeder to their animation department. Lasseter decided that was where he would go. For the next several years, many of Disney's new artists came from CalArts.

John Lasseter's junior year animation project, *The Lady and the Lamp*, won a 1979 Student Academy Award.[4] He was galvanized by the success and created a small furor when he won a second Student Oscar the following year for a senior project he called *Nitemare*. Like his classmates, notably Brad Bird, Tim Burton and Henry Selick,[5] Lasseter was trained in the CalArts/Disney style, on how to design characters in the classic tradition. He was thrilled when he was finally offered a job to become part of the great history of Disney animation.

The Friday before John Lasseter arrived at Disney, Don Bluth left, taking with him more than a dozen other animators and assistants—about half of the animation department of Disney. The studio was floundering.

[2] **Don Bluth** (b. 1937). American animator. *The Small One* (1978), *Secret of NIMH* (1982), *An American Tale* (1986), *Land Before Time* (1988), *Anastasia* (1997), *Titan AE* (2000); also the arcade videogame *Dragon's Lair* (1983).

[3] In 1980, Miller was promoted to president and COO.

[4] Student Academy Awards for university student films were initiated in 1974.

[5] **Tim Burton** (b. 1958). Director: *Pee-wee's Big Adventure* (1985), *Beetlejuice* (1988), *Batman* (1981), *Edward Scissorhands* (1990), *Ed Wood* (1994), *Mars Attacks!* (1996), *Planet of the Apes* (2001), *Big Fish* (2003), *Charlie and the Chocolate Factory* (2005).

Henry Selick (b. 1958). Director: *The Nightmare Before Christmas* (1993), *James and the Giant Peach* (1996).

Brad Bird got a break directing *Family Dog*, an animated episode of Amazing Stories, which led to his writing material for Matthew Robbins' film *batteries not included* (1987). He went on to direct some Simpsons episodes and eventually animated features: *The Iron Giant* (1999), *The Incredibles* (2004).

"Here I was thrilled to be at Disney," recalled Lasseter, "and everyone was moping around."

The animators who remained after Bluth's departure struggled with the projects on the table. "I was always feeling that animation had reached a plateau with *101 Dalmatians* [1961]," commented Lasseter. "Somehow, I felt that the films after that, while they had wonderful moments and characters, overall were just the same old thing."

In 1980, Disney was working on *Tron*, the most forward-thinking movie it had embarked upon in years. Involving state-of-the-art computer graphics, it was based on the very hot world of videogames. A pair of Disney animators prepared storyboards for the computer scenes, and that connection gave Lasseter an opportunity to see a scene in development. The "Light Cycle" sequence captivated him.[6]

"It absolutely blew me away! A little door in my mind opened up. I looked at it and said, 'This is it! This is the future!'"

Walt Disney had always pushed his animations to have dimensionality. He had pioneered a technology in which layers of painted glass sheets moved independently in the front of the camera, to increase visual depth and complexity. Called the multi-plane camera, it was almost two stories high and could handle up to five layers (with a number of technicians required per layer).[7] It was expensive to use and difficult to experiment with. Still, if Disney thought the shot was important enough—such as the opening scene of *Pinocchio*—he could use it to give drawings a heightened sense of perspective. In effect, the shots were "2½-D."

But the camera could only pan and zoom around the artwork. Lasseter could see that a computer could surpass the multi-plane camera and would allow it to move *into* the art and around objects. He felt that "it was totally in the spirit of Disney."

One of the remaining animators from the *new* old guard that produced Don Bluth was Glen Keane.[8] By the time Lasseter arrived, Keane was practically a studio elder, having graduated from CalArts in 1974. Keane had been trained by some of the "Old Men," in particular Ollie Johnston.

John Lasseter ran into Keane's office and began ranting about the possibilities of computers. "Disney was hiring these four outside consultants to develop the effects in *Tron*, but when the film was over, all that knowledge would not be at Disney."

[6] Created by MAGI (the Mathematics Applications Group, Inc.). Disney animators Jerry Rees and Bill Kroyer designed the scenes.

[7] The technicians who ran it joked that it was so huge it could only be run at night because turning it on might take down the Burbank power grid.

[8] **Glen Keane** (b.1954). American animator. Responsible for such leading Disney characters as Ariel (*The Little Mermaid*), Beast (*Beauty and the Beast*), Aladdin (*Aladdin*), Pocahontas, and Tarzan. Glen is the son of Bil Keane, creator of the newspaper comic "Family Circus."

He argued that it was important for the company to retain some of that new information, and Disney management agreed. Keane and Lasseter both felt that the technology could make it possible to have dynamic backgrounds for the characters, but that the characters themselves would still be hand-drawn in traditional ways, using the computer only to aid in their positioning. Keane helped Lasseter convince management to test their theory in conjunction with one of the computer companies working on *Tron*.

Keane and Lasseter began a 30-second piece based on *Where the Wild Things Are*, the classic children's story by Maurice Sendak.[9] Lasseter worked on developing the background "set" of a stairway that the character Max would run down, chasing his dog around the room. Keane drew Max and used the computer to facilitate the positioning of the characters.

"It was exciting," said Lasseter. "Look at the advancement in the art form. Look at the beauty of it," he told his bosses. But they weren't interested. Disney only wanted computers to the degree that they made a project faster or less expensive.

Tim Burton was also at Disney during this period, having joined from CalArts just before John Lasseter. He pitched them about doing a thirty-minute animation for the Disney Channel, in the vein of *How the Grinch Stole Christmas* and the Charlie Brown specials, shows he had loved as a kid. He called his project "The Nightmare Before Christmas," and he presented his poem of that title with accompanying sketches; but it was too edgy for the studio and they rejected it.

A detail of naturalistic plant growth—"cellular automata"—from Alvy Ray Smith's *white.sands*, April 1983.

Between jobs on traditional Disney projects, he did a short called *Vincent*, a tribute to horror film maestro Vincent Price, in what would become his characteristic dark humor and stop-motion animation style.

Disney was fostering new talent, yet rejecting their projects. They nixed Sendak. They buried *Vincent*, not even submitting it for the animated short category at the Academy Awards (which many think it would have won). The young animators were frustrated.

Lasseter had another project he wanted to do; he wanted to adapt a story called "The Brave Little Toaster," using computers to generate lush forest "sets" for his characters to move through.

He interviewed all the major computer animation groups in the country, including the teams that worked on *Tron* and the guys at Lucasfilm. Flying up to Marin, John met with Ed Catmull and Alvy Ray Smith. Alvy wanted to do the project. He was anxious to undertake a showcase piece of animation.

[9] Also coordinated with MAGI.

Recalled Tom Porter, "Alvy was ready to take on the world."

Alvy was a specialist in making computer-generated plants. His pioneering work in "cellular automata" showed that he didn't need to draw every part; his software provided naturalistic growth, and he could provide bushes and plants wherever they were needed (such as he did along the highway in "The Road to Pt. Reyes"). Making a forest would be fun.

But Lucasfilm wasn't in a position to take on that kind of work, and while Lasseter made a solid impression on Ed and Alvy, he went back to Disney empty-handed. The Graphics Group had a number of major issues still on their plate before they could start taking on outside projects. That was before *Star Trek II* and the Genesis Effect.

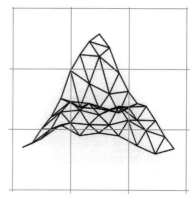

3-D model (*left*) is a web of polygons. To place that image on a screen, the model must get translated to a 2-D grid of pixels (*right*). Each pixel may have a fraction, or one, or many polygons "behind" it, and yet may have only one color value assigned. The challenge was how to determine what value to give each pixel. (Adapted from a model by L. Carpenter)

No matter how good the modeling and lighting, no matter how detailed the objects, getting the scene on a frame—rendering it—always seemed to introduce the stair-stepped artifact called jaggies. Everyone who came to Lucasfilm understood that this was a central hurdle. Rob Cook spent most of 1982 and early 1983 focused on the problem. It was a moral imperative.

To appreciate his problem, recall that computer modeling creates 3-D objects from webs of polygons. Textures can be applied to those surfaces. Computer "lights" can be shined on those surfaces. More and more polygons make more realistic looking but more complex objects.

Putting an image on a screen of pixels requires translating a 3-D scene onto a flat surface. While they seem related, there is a difference between 3-D model detail (the complexity corresponding to millions of polygons) and the "resolution" of an image, described by the number of pixels on a screen. Moving from one realm to the other is a logic puzzle that could have been ripped from the back pages of *Scientific American*.

If one pixel neatly corresponded to one polygon, it would be simpler to guess its color, but there are usually many polygons behind every pixel, and often fractions of many polygons. As objects get more realistic, the number of polygons within each pixel increases, which intensifies the problem. As more realistic lighting models are used, with more realistic surface characteristics, the problem gets even more complicated.

The puzzle was to come up with a mathematical equation that could predict what any given pixel should look like. The errors produced the jaggies. In technical terms, Rob was working on a "sampling problem." How could he accurately sample complex scenery in order to create images without jaggies?

Catmull had pioneered a way to do it during his PhD research: *area sampling*. This meant adding up all the colors of all the polygons visible from any pixel and averaging them to get a single color. Area sampling was not widely used. Loren's first version of the REYES renderer used it; but even as he tried to make it better and better at reducing the jaggie problem, it could not address their other problem: motion blur.

If "no jaggies" was their religion, and "eighty million polygons" their mandate, then "motion blur" was the Holy Grail.

A film camera had motion blur because the camera shutter was open for a brief moment, and real objects in the real world are sometimes moving during that moment. If computer graphics were ever going to look realistic, it was important to be able to duplicate this effect. Not only was the lack of motion blur the hallmark of fake-looking graphics, but the stop-motion animation style they were effectively utilizing always played back with a sort of stutter. ILM had nailed the problem with their Go-Motion technique during *Dragonslayer*.

"Without motion blur," said Catmull, "we could never be in the movies. It was as simple as that. Our success depended on finding a solution and we were very clear on it."

The Graphics Group badly needed a breakthrough.

Rob Cook was working on the more common approach called *point sampling*. Point sampling selected a few rays of light, as few as one per pixel, and used those values to estimate the color of the whole pixel. "Point sampling," said Tom Porter, "seemed somehow based on faith…on probabilities."

To determine the color of each pixel using point sampling, the computer would look at an imaginary light beam moving backwards—from the viewer's eye, through the pixel, to the 3-D object (comprised of those polygons), and ultimately to the light source. It would take into consideration the surface, its composition, color, reflectivity, and translucence, and crunch on those to choose a color. Ed Catmull thought that point sampling was a doomed technique.

"If we're going to do cinema-quality images," Ed told Cook, "we have to look at the whole area. We can't look at points."

Point sampling had historically been rejected as too simplistic for quality imagery. Perhaps Catmull was right; Cook found it hard to find any theoretical underpinnings to the strategy. There was just no reason to think it would work.[10]

Even though his early experiments produced images that were bad, full of jaggies, Rob Cook was undaunted. He tried to sample the colors from a number of light beams in and around each pixel, and sort of average them. That was a little better. Through 1982, Rob tried variations on this theme. He used more samples. He used fewer samples. He broke up each pixel with an imaginary grid, and started sampling from the middle of each little square.

Said Cook, "It was the conventional wisdom that point sampling aliased and there was nothing you could do about it."

More samples required substantially longer rendering times; if Cook could solve this with fewer samples he'd have been very pleased with himself. For no good reason, he was certain he was on the path to a solution. Catmull didn't agree. Point sampling left vast regions of the image that were never considered.

Catmull was determined to come up with a more elegant method, one that addressed motion blur. The search for a solution turned into a friendly competition, with Ed Catmull working on one method and Rob Cook working on the other. Said Catmull, "I found the competition invigorating."

While Cook spent his days in the "3-D room" trying to break through the anti-aliasing problem, and Catmull worked on his competing theories, Loren Carpenter was concerned with general problems of rendering surfaces. Tom Duff and Bill Reeves were next door, trying to build an interactive tool for modeling shapes and objects. Tom Porter was another door down the hall, focused on his paint system and how to composite high-resolution images.

"I walked by those guys," said Ben Burtt, "and was always thinking, 'I wonder what they are really doing?' They're fun guys, and they had their little project, but it had nothing to do with the movies we were making."

As Rodney Stock sat on the third floor of C Building with his head in his plans, he couldn't concentrate. He had revised his ideas about the Pixar Image Computer, which was turning into a massive and elaborate machine. He knew it was being developed uniquely for ILM but he couldn't escape his background in building commercial products.

"I wanted it reproducible. I felt strongly that it should be modular and scalable."

Heading downstairs, he stumbled into an *ad hoc* meeting in the hallway: Loren, Ed, Alvy, and Rob Cook were debating the sampling problems. Point sampling evenly across a grid made for terrible jaggies. He stood quietly by.

[10] Tom Porter made a bet with Tom Duff that point sampling would take over the world. Duff couldn't imagine that that was possible.

"I wasn't a PhD, like most of these guys. I'm not a research person. Hell, I just have a high school background, so I just listened."

But Stock had a good handle on the software computations that graphics required, a necessary component of hardware design. He had come to Lucasfilm with strong ideas about software, even if he didn't have the skills to execute them himself. Before the meeting was over, he found his voice.

"Listen, I think that instead of sampling regularly, try dithering the sample points." The gang looked at him blankly, so he continued.

"Why don't you break up the grid by taking point samples from random squares from within the grid instead of all of them. I think it's a really good idea."

Stock was worried that Ed would be thinking, "Why isn't Rodney upstairs working on his hardware." Finally Ed said, "Well, okay, Rob, why don't you try it out."

Every few months, when Rodney Stock ran into Rob Cook, he'd ask if he'd tried the dithering. Rob still hadn't—there were just too many other far more logical paths to go down first. But Stock was persistent, and eventually Cook sat down and gave his radical suggestion a try. Surprisingly, it was an elegant idea. And it sort of worked. It started reducing the jaggies. It looked promising.

Cook started pursuing the idea of randomness in the sampling. Instead of selecting points evenly across a grid, why not throw darts at the pixel and sample there? Rob tried it, and it worked, mostly—the worst the jaggies went away, but the visual noise it introduced was unbearable. He tried more darts; he tried fewer.[11] But the random point distributions were *too* random. Sometimes the points were too close together.[12] A successful sampling method couldn't allow for even a rare case of patterns.[13]

The point sampling experiments seemed to be moving in the right direction, but everyone still had the ominous sense that there was no reason for it to work. Then, as if to respond to the late night anguish and endless frustration, the universe provided a gentle nod of support at the precise moment it was most needed. In the July 23rd issue of *Science* magazine, Alvy came across an article about the monkey retina.[14] The article showed how the rod and cone cells in the back of a monkey's eye were distributed in patterns generally like those Cook was using in his point sampling. He realized he was seeing something essential for Rob Cook's problem. Alvy dropped the magazine on Cook's desk with a coy smile.

Said Cook, "[The cells looked] remarkably like my own distribution of sampling points: random, but not quite random." He had found wonderful scientific evidence supporting his formerly outrageous ideas.

"Here we are, toying with sampling techniques," said Tom Porter, "and along comes an article about the real world that evolution has produced

[11] Cook even tried a dither pattern discovered by Benjamin Franklin, that Catmull had found in his research.

[12] While it was statistically unlikely, even random card dealing could lead to four aces in a row.

[13] This was not unlike the problem pollsters have in gathering data. Pollsters don't have to ask everyone in the country who they're going to vote for. They're able to take a not-quite-random sample of people, and from that data extrapolate with reasonable accuracy the total election.

[14] *Science*, July 23, 1983: "Spectral consequences of photoreceptor sampling in the rhesus retina," by J. Yellott.

monkey retinas that capture images in this same fashion! What's the chance of that? Apprehensions disappeared! Confidence zoomed!"

In short order, Cook found a number of diverse academic fields of study—information theory, nuclear physics, mammalian physiology—that all utilized this principle, none of which referenced any of the others. It was called the Monte Carlo technique (named for the casino) and it demonstrated how samples could be random but not too random.

Rob Cook realized that point sampling would always have some kind of implicit artifact, in the same way a poll always has some margin of error, but the artifact didn't have to be show up as jaggies. Instead it could be manifested as noise—which might be a better problem to have than those nasty stair-steps. The human eye, after all, is exceptionally well tuned to see edges and lines, which makes jaggies that much more pernicious. Noise, on the other hand, is routinely disguised in the human visual system. This was clearly the right direction to go.

> Visual artifacts in a digital image can be manifested in one of two ways: as jaggies or as noise.
>
> In still images, jaggies along the edge of an object look like sharp L-shape transitions, making the edge look jagged. In moving images, jaggies look like ants crawling along the edges of objects, as the L-shape transition moves.
>
> Noise, on the other hand, looks like salt-and-pepper speckles in fields of gray. In moving images, noise looks like static, the "white noise" or "snow" you might see on a TV set.

From the summer and into the fall of 1983, Rob Cook and Ed Catmull continued to make progress on the jaggies. Catmull had some success with his area sampling solutions as well, but none was particularly elegant. "We were trying to trump each other on a weekly basis."

Cook had decided that for each pixel, sixteen samples had to be taken from random spots around it. This provided a pretty good-looking image, but it was a big number crunching problem. Tom Porter watched as Cook wrestled with the jaggies, the noise, and the math.

Staring at the random point samples at each pixel, Porter made a casual suggestion: "What would happen if you distribute the samples randomly in time as well as spatially?"

In animation, if an object is moving, its position will be slightly different both before and after any given frame. That would create an interesting kind of artifact, Porter figured. They thought in silence for maybe ten seconds, maybe a minute. Porter didn't need to say the words, but he did anyway.

"Wouldn't that solve the motion blur problem?" The implications dawned on them both explosively.

Cook anxiously adjusted his sampling solutions to address the new idea. The initial thought was that for each of the sixteen pixel locations he wanted to sample, he would try grabbing the visual information randomly in time. This required 256 samples instead of 16. It required intensive calculations and took forever to process.

"Rob," Porter said, "what if you just used *one* time sample at each of the sixteen locations inside the pixel, but made each one fall at a different time?"

That would mean a fraction of the computation time, and that was good. But it would possibly create other visual effects, and they were not sure how that would look. Rob Cook tried it on some gray polygons. It seemed to work beautifully.

The long-standing problem of motion blur, the element that professionals long felt kept computer graphics out of feature films, had been solved in four logical steps. From point sampling…to sampling randomly…to sampling not exactly randomly…to sampling not exactly randomly in time as well as in space. The information in a single frame of animation was related to the information in previous and subsequent frames.

Cook's point sampling solution was elegant; he called it "stochastic sampling," referring to the randomish pattern of samples. It seemed to solve a host of problems. When applied to the curvature of an imaginary lens, it created photographic looking depth-of-field in the image.

"What about fuzzy shadows? What about penumbras? What about translucency?" Each time they applied the new concept, they were met with remarkable results. It really was like the Holy Grail.

"Oh my god," said Cook, "this is *all* these things." It was a happy accident. It was also based on a fixed number of samples—sixteen—and therefore largely independent of the complexity of the scene: eighty million polygons would be no more of a problem than one. In the end, Ed Catmull was never bothered that he lost their "competition."

"Okay," thought Cook, "we've been messing with this for a year…it's time to start writing this into the rendering program."

But Loren needed a break, and was mentally distracted with the arrival of the Games Group to the division. He and David Fox had been playing with some applications of his fractal engine, and he decided to change his focus and leave Cook to the new code in the renderer.

The original rendering code had been named REYES. Now they were scrapping that first incarnation and starting again, combining the old ingenuity from Loren and utilizing their new knowledge of how to sample a scene and generate a photo-realistic image. Cook called the new renderer REYES…again.

"We probably should have called it something different," figured Cook. "But really, it was just like an internal name." Rob worked on the new REYES throughout the fall, and by the end of the year the code was just about ready to render something. Rob generated some little test patterns while he debugged.

After three years, a handful of still images, and the relatively simple "Genesis Effect," Alvy was ready to apply their tools to what was called *character animation*, to make the computer generated forms come to life with personality.

Earlier, Bill Reeves and Tom Duff had written an animation program, refining the foundation that Duff had pulled together during the *Star Trek II* scene.[15] "We wanted to test our system, but we weren't really a production group," said Reeves. They tried to get some help from ILM, but ILM was dismissive. "They were friendly to us, but we weren't really relevant."

Alvy was going to need to approach this from another direction.

Ed and Alvy continued to go back to Disney each year, exchanging ideas with the technologists, meeting animators, interviewing all of them about the process and production. "We *knew* we could solve their problems and save them money," said Alvy.

In the fall of 1983, on their annual pilgrimage, they decided to visit their old acquaintance, John Lasseter, in the animation building. Lasseter, still a round-faced kid with glasses, invited them to check out what was going on in the department. Last they had heard he was trying to put "The Brave Little Toaster" together, but that repeatedly hit snags.

Lasseter was different from the other Disney animators. Where most retreated the moment Alvy began to discuss computers, Lasseter was immediately excited by everything Alvy said. He wanted to hear all about their progress and anything Ed and Alvy could tell him about Lucasfilm.

They all shared a love for animation, and as soon as John realized how profound this was, he led the pair deep into the studio's Ink and Paint building, down the stairs, to an area called the Morgue. Here, in a relatively unsecured area, Disney studios kept all the cels and artwork from all their films. John pushed open the door and flipped on the light, revealing a basement full of shelves, file cabinets, and flat drawers.

He turned to the guys: "What do you want to see?"

"You're kidding," said Alvy.

"What do you want to see?" John repeated with confidence.

[15] With Eben Ostby and Sam Leffler.

"Oh God, how about Dancing Hippos from *Fantasia* by…what's his name…Preston Blair…Preston Blair's Dancing Hippos." Alvy had studied up on 2-D animation back at Xerox and had been inspired by Preston Blair's classic workbook, *Cartoon Animation*. Blair illustrated the basic tools of animation: squash, stretch, anticipation, exaggeration. He taught the basic walk cycle, the run cycle, the classic bouncing ball. Alvy was a major fan.

"Okay," said John, and he walked over to a chart, scanned it for a moment, then pulled out a folder from a bookshelf, opened it…and there were Preston Blair's original drawings of the Dancing Hippos.

John flipped through the short stack to make them animate. "I'm in heaven," thought Alvy. Ed left Alvy with John, elbow deep in the history of animation. "What do you want to see now?" asked Lasseter, and the two of them spent the rest of the afternoon pulling out scenes…from *Fantasia*… from *Dumbo*…reminiscing about the movies, getting to know each other.

Alvy returned to Marin reinvigorated with a vision of character animation. He wanted to center the software and algorithm development efforts on an achievable goal. They had all accomplished an enormous amount for *Star Trek II*. Anyway, coming up with a short animated movie would be fun. As Alvy mentioned in a company report, "It was a chance to do a small piece of production, which the members of the Graphics Department tend to find stimulating."

Alvy convened his department to discuss a project. It was going to be very simple. An android would wake up in the woods, get up, turn around, see a beautiful scene, and be happy at seeing it. The goal was, in Alvy's report, "to render a showable sequence of 3-D articulated animation, with edits, in a rich setting." It needed to show the best of what they were able to do. It was strictly an in-house project for demonstration purposes.

According to Alvy, "The piece was meant to be symbolic: a computer-animated 3-D character wakes up and sees the world." He started calling the android "Andre," and the name stuck.

Alvy was inspired and soon produced a set of nine crude storyboard frames. He envisioned Andre waking up, looking around, and smiling. And then Andre could run through the forest and out to a cliff overlooking a rich fractal canyon. It wasn't much of a story. But it would demonstrate their capabilities and would give them a chance to work on character animation.

They tried to come up with names. Initially favored was "Androids Awake." Louis Malle's film, *My Dinner with Andre*, had been released a few years earlier, a heady artfilm, but the team admired it.[16] Soon they were all jokingly referring to their film as "My Breakfast with Andre."

[16] *My Dinner with Andre* (1981). Directed by Louis Malle; written by and starring Andre Gregory and Wallace Shawn.

In November, as pre-production meetings continued on Alvy's android flick, Ed Catmull was invited to speak at an animation conference in Long Beach, on the Queen Mary ocean liner. The Queen Mary had been taken out of circulation years earlier and was permanently moored in the giant harbor, about an hour south of Hollywood.

John Lasseter had ruffled enough feathers at Disney, pushing "The Brave Little Toaster," that he was being laid off between projects, although he was still heading to Long Beach for the conference. Lasseter heard Catmull speak and the two of them chatted briefly after the lecture. The gears in Catmull's mind began to turn. Ed needed to check in with his partner at Kerner.

"Hey Ed?" said Alvy, "What's going on?"

Ed briefly recounted a few details of the day. They talked about the status of *My Breakfast with Andre* and then Ed said rather calmly. "Guess what. I just saw John Lasseter, and…he's not at Disney anymore."

"Ed, get off the phone and hire him. Now!"

"Yeah. I know. That's a good idea. Just making sure you agreed."

Ed walked back to the conference and found John sitting in another seminar. He waved him down. "Would you be interested in doing a little consulting for us, maybe a month or so, designing an android for an animation we're putting together?"

Lasseter was receptive. Lucasfilm wasn't Disney, which was both good and bad. He had seen *Star Wars* when he was at CalArts and it was a landmark experience.

"I couldn't believe that this movie, almost a comic strip, could be so immersive, so expressive, that it could have that profound an impact on everyone who saw it. A lot of us from CalArts thought we should go and do special effects, but it only made me want to see if I could create that same degree of impact from an animation."

John Lasseter came up to visit Kerner and meet with the team. They all got along fabulously, like old friends, like mutual fans; then all too soon he returned to L.A., to make sketches of the android. They told him the character needed to be built from geometric objects, and he began exploring all the possibilities this created. The old Mickey Mouse animations, done by Walt himself, were also very geometric; they inspired Lasseter to push the character as far from a robot as he could.

"I didn't really want to do an android," said Lasseter. "Lucasfilm already had the Droids and I didn't want it to look like that." So he began sculpting a more clown-like android. He drew dozens of sketches and sent them north.

"I didn't know if they'd like the non-android direction I was taking things."

Ed and Alvy were thrilled. "This is fantastic."

Tom Porter tried to be patient, but the new REYES renderer still wasn't completed and he really wanted to render a complex image with motion blur, to prove the idea worked. All the test images had gone well. Alvy's animation project was going to put the software to the test but maybe it would be a good idea to try it out first. Even though the new REYES wasn't ready, Rob Cook gave Porter a part of the new motion blur code and he inserted it into a crude amalgam of ray-tracing software that he and Tom Duff scrounged up.

Porter modeled some cue balls on a pool table—basic spheres, pretty simple really. It was only one frame, but in the rendering he applied their new understanding of anti-aliasing and motion blur. Loren tweaked the pool table surface with some randomness to look real.[17]

Lasseter suggested some graphics for the reflections and painted a fictitious room around the scene: he included a guy walking in front of a window, to reflect in the small curved surfaces. Tom numbered the balls to mark the year and ran a "quick" version of the image at video resolution, to see how the effect was working. The balls appeared to have been captured while moving. It looked like a photograph, from the neon beer sign reflected in the balls themselves to the streak the cue ball made after striking the others.

Tom Porter sitting before his workstation. *Opposite page:* Details from "1984."

[17] In early December, John Lasseter, Tom Porter, and Rob Cook went to a pool hall in Novato to get some reference photographs of reflections off pool balls and to look at typical pool table ambience.

With all the components in place, Tom Porter started rendering the image at high-resolution on the pair of VAX computers in C Building. It took three weeks to complete the image, through Christmas and New Years 1984, more than 290 hours of raw CPU time. The magazine *Science 84* accepted the image for its cover with the headline, "This Picture is a Fake." It was the most realistic computer-generated image yet made.

Ed and Alvy knew they needed to hire John Lasseter permanently. But it would be impossible to bring him to Lucasfilm and give him a title like "animator." Animators were only possible at ILM, not at the Computer Division. After some discussion, they all settled on "interface designer."

During his research for "The Brave Little Toaster," John had studied the state-of-the-art in computers. He had watched all the films that had been presented at Siggraph conferences and read the papers. By February 1, 1984, John moved full-time into the hot seat on the Lucasfilm animation project.

"I walked in the door of C Building and immediately realized that everyone I met—Catmull, Smith, Porter, Cook, Carpenter—were the people who had been responsible for all the phenomenal work I had studied. Catmull had brought together the top people. Almost everyone had a PhD. How was I going to animate alongside these guys? I couldn't write a line of computer code."

JOHN LASSETER

Hometown: Whittier, CA
(yes, that's Richard Nixon's
hometown too). *Family:* dad,
mom, big brother, twin sister
and don't ask me how it feels
to be a twin, because I've
always been one and I don't
know anything different,
so there. *Schools:* Play Acre's
Nursery School, Jon Gnagy's
How to Draw (Channel 5-
Saturday Morning), CalArts.
Sign: Neon. *Interests:* powder
skiing, packed-powder
skiing, hard-packed skiing,
rock skiing (in that order),
drive long distances to go
skiing (I'm from L.A.), the
Jetsons, wind-up toys, taking
hikes in the woods of Marin,
hugging trees. *Employment
history:* driving trucks and
delivering Chevrolet parts
for my dad, Disneyland
(sweeping up spilled
popcorn and ice cream
wrappers, ride operator on
the Jungle Cruise), Disney
Studio, Richard Williams
Animation, Disney. *Other
Info:* very single, call collect.
[1984 LFL Yearbook]

[18] The TV had a position of
prominence among the toys
at the foot of John's bed; they
showed up later in *Toy Story
2* (1996) and *The Incredibles*
(2005).

[19] Edmund Dulac always
tried to paint with a soft edge
to allow for registration
errors when the illustrations
were reproduced in print.

It was clear that John wasn't going to write code. But he was going to sit with the scientists and explain exactly what their code needed to do.

"It was very ying yang," said Lasseter. "I'd push them to write code that could perform something I needed, and then I'd see what they could do with their code and it would inspire me to new things we could try." Through their back and forth, the project developed and their trust in Lasseter grew.

John was adamant that he couldn't animate a character to be very expressive if he could only work with basic geometric shapes. Andre's torso, initially a sphere capped by a cone, could be moved by sliding the cone on the sphere, but that was too sterile a movement. The typical transformations of a sphere were mathematical and geometric—scale, stretch, skew—and none was the kind of manipulation he needed. John wanted *squeeze*. John wanted *bend*. Spheres needed to be more like water balloons than balls.

Ed Catmull removed himself from management long enough to help out with the modeling of the characters. "I don't normally get involved in actual production," recalled Ed, "but every once in a while I get my hand in and do a little something." Ed understood the problems John articulated and developed a model for a new primitive shape that could be more expressive, a teardrop shape that could bend.

"It was the first time computer models were able to be manipulated in that way," said John, describing the smooth interface of the models with subtle artistic controls, "and it changed everything."

Lasseter moved north and found an apartment in the Haight-Ashbury district of San Francisco, moving in with David Salesin, the new graphics scientist who had arrived a few months earlier. As two of the youngest guys on the team, they quickly bonded, in and out of work. Lasseter moved his collection of wind-up toys to his room, adding an old 1957 Philco television set he found at the Sausalito flea market.[18] They had parties at their pad in the Haight (John's hand-drawn invitations were always admired). They worked closely to improve software for Andre; Salesin added modeling tools for making eyelids and lips.

The main setting of *Andre* was a forest in autumn. Though Alvy was the plant-growing expert, he ceded that territory to Bill Reeves, since they both agreed that a forest was better grown using his new particle system. It turned out that his particle system wasn't just for fires or smoke; fields of grass and forests of trees had remarkably similar properties. Reeves began researching the ways trees looked, flipping through countless *New Mexico* magazines that Alvy delivered, and another pile of Lasseter's *Arizona Highways*. Alvy dragged the group to the Mt. Tamalpais watershed in the hills behind Fairfax, so everyone could explore a particularly lovely spot where wild irises were in bloom.

"The way they'd approach the issue of leaf color was to take a leaf, put it under a color microscope, and grab the real color of the leaf," said Lasseter. "I told them that they're missing something basic. Leaves could be any color, depending on the light. They'd look one way in bright sun, differently on a hazy day. A tree might even look purple." Once understood, it was not a hard concept for Rob Cook to incorporate into the computer.

All along, Loren and Rob had been striving for something approaching "reality," to make the images look photographic. John was trying to get them to recognize that there was a caveat, that sometimes it was important to look unreal, but in realistic ways. It allowed an animator to have a style. The computer was a brush. They needed to make software that could handle non-real lighting schemes.

John Lasseter took Rob Cook and the rest of the production team to the Palace of Fine Arts in San Francisco to see an exhibit of Maxfield Parrish's painted illustrations. Although Parrish was associated with Howard Pyle and J.C. Leyendecker (and later Norman Rockwell), he had developed innovative painting technologies in the early 1900s. At that time, the three color process was emerging in the printing industry, and Parrish began experimenting with the best painting techniques to accommodate the new printing methods.[19] By mixing cyan (off-blue), magenta (off-red) and yellow, printers created an enormous range of color. Parrish made his paintings in three translucent colors over a white board (with some opaque colors applied on the surface), suggesting the play of light *through* the layers of clear varnish he used to separate his colored layers.

When viewed under proper light, the paintings appeared to glow, more like a projected image than a painting on canvas. After seeing the exhibition, the team visited a San Francisco restaurant that featured an original Parrish behind the bar. It only took a moment for Lasseter and Cook, standing before "The Garden of Allah," to feel the radiance of light that had been captured.[20]

Lasseter's storyboard sketches for *Andre and Wally B.*

[20] George Lucas also had deep admiration for the classic commercial artists like Leyendecker, Parrish, and Rockwell. Much of the artwork that hangs in Skywalker Ranch is of this genre; the original painting "Garden of Allah" by Parrish hangs in a featured location above the fireplace in the Ranch library.

"It's not real," pointed out Lasseter, "but it's really cool."

"I get it," said Cook.

Back in C Building, Bill Reeves built a forest of 46,254 trees, all of them different. "Maybe that was overkill," figured Reeves. "We could have gotten away with far fewer."

Lasseter played with Andre and, as part of his process, created a second character, smaller, more dynamic: a fat bee. The bee had a nasty streak. With Rob Cook's new lighting techniques in mind, Lasseter put a big, shiny, stainless steel stinger on the bee, thinking it might be good motivation for the storyline. Everyone got a kick out of the bee. If the joke was "My Breakfast with Andre," then the second character had to be Wally. Their working title became *Andre and Wally B.*

John drew up a new storyboard, revising and tightening Alvy's original script. The panels decorated the walls of the conference room in C Building, their production war room. He added pastel color pages for backgrounds and inspiration. Lasseter and Reeves spent weeks hashing out camera shots, lighting, tree and rock placement.

"Lasseter was down the hall from me," recalled Ben Burtt. "The animator kid with all the toys on his desk. I thought [their work] was fascinating, the idea that they could create an entire environment in the computer. I remember feeling in awe; I wasn't much of a visionary and I didn't think this was going to become part of feature filmmaking. I saw it as, 'This is going to be amazing for animation.' Like George Pal's PuppetToons."

Even though the *Andre and Wally B.* story was now roughed together, the issue of character animation still remained. More to the point: how can an animator with few computer skills access the various software tools for modeling needed to build a character and move him around?

The animation room in C Building.

Ed Catmull *(left)* and Alvy Ray Smith reviewing the storyboards on their first character animation project, *Andre and Wally B.*

[21] Once the animation tools started coming together, Lasseter invited two of Disney's "Nine Old Men," Frank Thomas and Ollie Johnston, up to visit the production.

"I told them that if they were making tools for animators," said Lasseter, "then the interface would have to be interactive and responsive, and couldn't be like writing code."

Tom Duff was as excited about making the tools as Lasseter was about using them. Maybe the ruse was true—John really *was* there to do interface design. Each day, as Lasseter tried the animation system, he'd make suggestions for improvement and Duff would hack away for a while and return with a better tool.

"For instance, computer scientists always start numbering from zero," said Duff, "but animators start with frame one." Duff called his animation program "Motion Doctor," and he designed it to be easily extensible, that is, simple to augment with better tools as they were developed.[21]

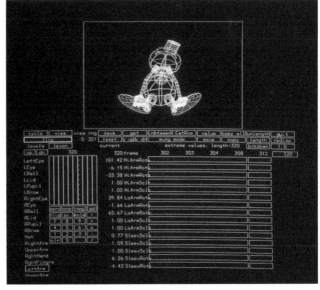

A glimpse of the new animation tool invented for the project, called Motion Doctor. Andre sits on the screen in wireframe, with tools to move his various body parts lined up below.

As the Graphics Group excitedly advanced the pioneering short film forward, Ed met with George. He decided to be as candid as possible: "I want the group to do animated films." George didn't react. He just sat quietly and listened as Ed articulated his passion.

The next day Bob Greber showed up at Ed's office, in what would be one of his final official acts as Lucasfilm president: he reported that George didn't want to do animated films.

The message, and the way it was delivered, helped Ed see that the writing was on the wall. Lucas was often concise, but sending Greber indicated that he knew this was bad news, news he didn't want to have to deliver to his long-time associate. At some point, and Ed really wasn't sure when, the glory days at Lucasfilm would have to come to an end.

As spring made way for cloudless summer, production on *Andre and Wally* was in full swing (officially it was not an animation project but a demonstration of their technological capabilities). The Pixar hardware was moving along quickly too—it would still be a race for Rodney Stock and crew to have it ready for its debut at Siggraph '84.[22] Even thought there were three other research teams buzzing through C Building, the computer graphics lab was always a good spot for anyone tired of writing code and looking for some place interesting to hang out for a few minutes.

[22] Another hardware engineer, Mark Leather, joined the team late in 1983 to expedite the completion.

Bill Reeves *(left)* and David Salesin.

Tom Smith, the long-time leader of ILM, stepped down as general manager to produce the upcoming Ewoks television movie, directed by Lucas' old friend John Korty. Warren Franklin, who had been at ILM since *Empire*, took

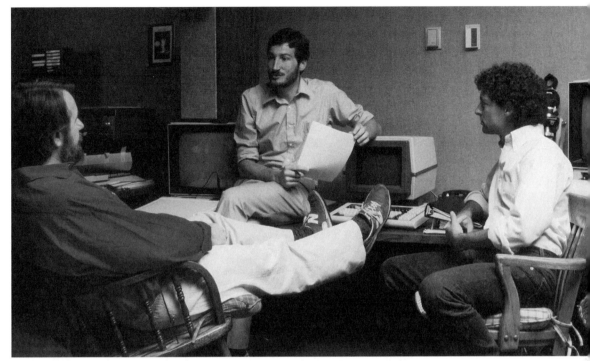

From left: Alvy, Porter and Salesin.

over for Tom. The special effects group in D Building was busy with *Indy II*, *The Neverending Story*, and *Star Trek III*, and they barely noticed the animation next door.

Tom Duff finished his animation tool, Motion Doctor, confident it was solid and productive. Comfortable with that closure, he decided that after eight years with Ed and Alvy, he wanted to do something different, to work on the Cray supercomputer. Duff told Alvy he had an opportunity to join Bell Labs. For years, Bell Labs had been "The Place to Work," the most far out research spot in the world.

A small group gathered in the lounge to see Tom off to his new job. Eben Ostby, who had joined the team in 1983, moved into Tom's position. Eben, like David Salesin, had come from Brown University's computer science department, under the tutelage of Siggraph pioneer Andy Van Dam. There was a growing Brown group in B Building, as the one-story office next door to C started filling with the computer team's overflowing growth.[23]

As more and more new members of Lucasfilm came from east coast colleges, they began aggregating socially, most often at Salesin and Lasseter's apartment. The growing computer-mathematics clique often spent Sunday mornings in San Francisco's Chinatown, meeting in groups of five or ten for dim sum.

[23] In the spring, Bob Drebin and Ronen Barzel came on board, in preparation for the completion of the Pixar Image Computer. Drebin was working on the interface and tools associated with compositing on the computer. Kate Smith-Greenfield, another of the "Brown Mafia," arrived a little later and was trying to get the EditDroid production ready after its debut at NAB.

Brown University alums, *(from left):* Bob Drebin, David Salesin, and Ronen Barzel.

With things so busy on Kerner, few employees got to see what was happening out on Lucas Valley Road. Everyone saw the phrase "Skywalker Development Company" on T-shirts and in company phone rosters, but the project itself was as hidden away from the staff as it was from the public.

Skywalker Ranch was an enormous development project, in high production mode for almost four years non-stop. Woodworking and glassmaking shops created hundreds of custom elements. The glass team built more than 150 unique light fixtures for the Main House alone, from sconces to large period lamps and chandeliers.

After years of work and millions of dollars, Skywalker Ranch was going to be the centerpiece of the Lucas universe. The Main House was easily the centerpiece of the Ranch. And the stained glass dome was arguably the centerpiece of the Main House. The team of stained glass artisans took six months to build the 19-foot dome. It was comprised of 400 sheets of glass, finely sculpted into 49 separate panels. They finished the dome in April, but it took until July for the heavy and fragile panes to be lowered into place.

B Building on Kerner.

With the dome installed, the library took on a new look. The warm redwood and sensuous curves and details were continuously bathed in the amber light from the dome. Books from Hollywood studios' abandoned research libraries were purchased and began to fill the shelves. The spiral staircase led to the upper balcony with a door into George's inner office. This was *his* library.

The library at the Main House under construction. The hole in the ceiling is the eventual location for the stained glass dome.

At the 4th of July picnic, 1984, yearbooks were handed out. "This is the year for the Graphics Project to bring several projects to completion," began the page on the Computer Division. "In particular, the Pixar Compositing Station should be completely assembled this summer. A transfer of this technology to ILM will occur when the alignment, calibration, color correction, and reliability tests are complete."

David DiFrancesco had recently produced some of the first stills from the laser scanner, but now he spent every day testing it. "Lots of tests," he said. "Tons of tests. And tons and tons and tons."

David was honing the technique, balancing whether or not one technology was going to be better than another at running long test pieces. He'd observe them in the theatre, he'd get critiques from people he was trying to interface with at ILM. "Not too much from the industry at large, but a few. Disney was present sometimes. They were interested in what we were doing."

Looking up at the installed dome in the Ranch library.

From left: Don Conway (laser technician), David DiFrancesco, and Tom Noggle (interface engineer) stand around a device they built (an optical Fourier transform projector) to test the resolution of the laser film recorder.

Everyone knew that the slowest part of making *Andre and Wally B.* would be the rendering. It was going to be brutal. Even with only two minutes of animation, it would take every resource they could find.[24] Bill Reeves began using all five VAX computers at Lucasfilm; not only Dagobah and Bespin, which were theirs to play with, but also Kessel, Endor, and Tattoine—the backbone of the Games Group, the finance department, and ILM, respectively. These machines were needed primarily for rendering the backgrounds. It wasn't enough.

Bill had a friend at MIT working on its experimental Project Athena.[25] They had ten VAXs, and they donated time to Reeves, who used them for rendering the massively complex forest in the opening trucking shot. It still wasn't enough.

Finally, Rob Cook and Loren Carpenter decided to go to the mountain, to Cray Research in Minnesota, manufacturer of the fastest supercomputer available—the Cray XMP. The Cray got so hot that specially balanced fluids ran in its cooling pipes, liquids akin to those used to support human body organ transplants. The Cray was built into the center of a large open room—a kind of futuristic altar, with a separate control room nearby.

For years, Cray Research had been trying to convince Ed and Alvy to buy one of the beasts; but with a multi-million dollar price tag, they could not figure out how it could make financial sense. And besides, though it was fast, it was not necessarily fast at precisely the kind of mathematics they needed.

[24] Looking backward at Moore's Law: 20 years ago computers were 10,000 times slower than they are today. Or, to reverse it, imagine a computer today, transported to 1984—it would cost 10,000 times as much, or about $10-$20 million, about the same as a Cray supercomputer.

[25] MIT began a five-year research program in May 1983 to explore integrating computer technology into the curriculum; their network of computers was donated by IBM and DEC.

For the money, it would need to be much faster than the VAX. But at the 11th hour on *Andre and Wally B*, the loan of two CPU Cray XMP-2s would do just fine. Sort of.

The Cray, being the industrial monster it was, was programmed through a language called Fortran. All the graphics code Lucasfilm had produced was written in a language called C. Cray had a buggy program that could translate from Fortran to C with a compiler that the Lucasfilm team was welcome to mess around with. So even before the machine could help them, Rob and Loren had to debug their massive C compiler.

Weeks were spent in Minnesota, squeezing their software onto the Cray, crunching frames as quickly as they could, extracting the data and merging it with the rest of the elements.

Back in San Rafael, Alvy Ray Smith was trying to complete the soundtrack for *Andre and Wally B*.[26] Not really sure where to turn, and with no actual budget for the "demonstration," Alvy ran into Ben Burtt in the Sprockets lobby. Ben had recently finished the soundwork on *Indy II*.

"Much to my surprise, Ben said that he had nothing creative to do for a week or two," recalled Alvy, "and besides, he was rather intrigued by the weird project upstairs." Jim Kessler figured it would be fine to use the facilities for the small effort. Lasseter produced the pencil tests for the animation, which Alvy got shot onto film for Burtt to work with.

It was a race against the clock. Siggraph was only a week away and the film was still incomplete. Rob and Loren slept little, each taking short naps while the machine flashed its lights or while the other pulled his hair out wrestling output. Soon Cray donated another machine, the faster four-processor Cray XMP-4. They were using all six Cray CPUs at 100 percent capacity, even pushing founder Seymour Cray off his terminal at one point to try to complete the rendering. It was going to be close.

The film scanner was still incomplete when the time came to get the rendered frames onto film. David DiFrancesco rigged up a film camera synchronized to the CRT display. It sat in the graphics lab on a tripod with a piece of paper taped to it that said, "Do not touch." Frame by frame, the images appeared on the monitor in the darkened room and were photographed onto film.

[26] Andy Moorer, busy completing a new element for the ASP, provided some simple digital effects.

The darkened graphics lab, illuminated by the camera flash, with Rob Cook *(at left)* pulling frames onto the display, Alvy *(center)* watching the images, and David DiFrancesco supervising the shoot.

The classic Mitchell camera shooting the animation off the computer display, one frame at a time.

Where many research groups and graphics teams in the industry were enormously secretive about their work, the Lucasfilm Graphics Group was not.

"We always encouraged the team to publish all their new ideas, whenever possible," recalled Alvy. "It's hard to get a paper accepted at Siggraph. The majority get rejected, so getting one in is a big deal."

The Lucasfilm graphics team had *seven* papers accepted to the 1984 proceedings. It was some kind of record. Ed gave a presentation, as did Alvy. Reeves introduced his particle systems, and Tom Porter and crew explained the guts of the hardware they had invented—the CHAP.[27] Rob Cook explained his principles of light and color and gave a second talk with Tom Porter and Loren Carpenter on rendering. Tom gave a third talk on compositing and their alpha channel concepts.[28] The prototype of the Pixar Image Computer was going to be shown privately, although Alvy talked about the machine and its capabilities.

While there was remarkable development going on in graphics all over—in academia (Cornell), in business (Digital Productions)—it was as if the small team threw away the rules and reinvented the entire field. The Lucasfilm scientists were superstars.

Lucasfilm reigned at Siggraph. Many members of the Computer Division attended in their Lucasfilm shirts. "Having a badge that said 'Lucasfilm' made me a sort of an instant celebrity," said games designer Noah Falstein. "I sometimes forgot to mention that I wasn't in the Graphics Group."

[27] "The Channel Processor-CHAP" by Adam Levinthal and Tom Porter; the CHAP was the brain of the Pixar computer.

[28] "Shade Trees" by Rob Cook. "Distributed Ray Tracing" by Rob Cook, Tom Porter, and Loren Carpenter. "Compositing Digital Images" by Tom Porter and Tom Duff.

Siggraph was not only a conference and video/film festival; there was also an exhibit floor complete with booths from all the major equipment manufacturers. Evans & Sutherland. Ikonas. Cray. And a small booth from the new SUN computer company.

Lucasfilm, in a hotel suite, was showing specially invited guests the first Pixar computer. "It was finished hours before the show opened," said Drebin. "We were up all night making it do stuff."

Getting in to see the machine was like getting one of Wonka's golden tickets. Tom Porter wandered the show floor and found people from academia or industry who might be potential customers for the product.

"I think half the people up in the room were from the CIA," recalled Porter.

For the first day of the show, the SUN booth was deserted. Few had heard of the new workstation and no one was paying them much attention. When Alvy spoke at his seminar, he raved about the SUN, the platform the Pixar was connected to. Within hours, the SUN booth was overrun.

A few days before the conference, George Lucas decided to attend the debut of *Andre*, and headed out to Minneapolis. He had begun dating Linda Ronstadt, the famous singer, and her schedule allowed her to accompany him.

On the opening night of the conference, George, Linda, Ed, and Alvy arrived at the convention center in a limousine. They were sneaked into the auditorium after the lights were dimmed for the films.

As *Andre and Wally B.* played, the audience was captivated. It was light years beyond the kinds of images the scientists had produced or even seen before. (Siggraph reels traditionally consisted of TV commercial promos, hideous art crap sometimes lovingly created by pretty good artists with pretty crude tools, and rendering demos produced for, and by, engineers with nominal aesthetic sensibilities.)

Andre and Wally B. incorporated the just-announced principle of motion blur; it had characters and a storyline, albeit a skimpy one; and it created the kind of sensation that changed an entire industry overnight. The audience exploded at its conclusion. The Lucasfilm team was beaming.

"People there *know* when they're seeing something new and great," said Alvy.[29] "I was of course thrilled," he continued, "because I was the director of this piece and because George Lucas was there. He was finally seeing what he had."

The film had been an ambitious task. As a demonstration of their superior technology and advanced thinking, it was perfect. But it wasn't a particularly great movie. While the press acknowledged that the technology was groundbreaking, it was still judged against traditional films and came up short.

[29] The film was so captivating that few in the audience even realized that a couple scenes toward the end were only partially rendered line-drawn characters over the completed backgrounds. Siggraph normally had a policy about not screening unfinished works, but for *Andre*, let it slide.

Still frame from *Andre and Wally B.* Wally's wings demonstrate the motion blur in animation. The particle system trees and grass are visible in the background.

The *Toronto Globe* said, "The eerie effect of this blend of man and machine is neither as rich as classic animation nor as realistic as many of the live action special effects which Lucasfilm itself…has already produced." The reviewer went on to say, "The film comes across rather like a sleek puppet show. Finding a technical means to inject vitality into these characters is going to be one of Lucasfilm's biggest challenges."

The ninety-second project, if budgeted out like a movie, might have cost half a million dollars, although it would have been hard to quantify the work in traditional ways. At the Lucasfilm party after the film, George was complimentary to the guys. But those close to him recall he was somewhat displeased. Why would anyone go through the trouble to make a project so graphically interesting and not tell an interesting story? It was an expensive technology demonstration and it was a lousy film, and it likely reinforced his ideas that no one but him should be making movies at Lucasfilm.[30]

[30] Lasseter went back to Disney, thinking he might be in development on *Brave Little Toaster*. But he learned that *Toaster* had been permanently shelved and so he quit. Lasseter started at Lucasfilm permanently in October.

The Pixar computer was born on July 22, 1984. It was alive, but just barely. A number of news articles had come out during the year, teasing the industry that something was cooking at Lucasfilm and everyone wanted to see what it was. Very little software had been completed in time for the demonstrations in the Siggraph suite, and perhaps the most it showed image-wise, other than color bars, were still frames from "The Road to Pt. Reyes" and Porter's "1984." As a manager of the effort, Tom Porter mingled with interested parties, painting a tale of what the remarkable, high-resolution imaging and compositing workstation would soon be able to do.

Back on Kerner, Bob Drebin settled into designing the compositing product that ILM would need. ILM would also have to do high-resolution painting. All the image painting software ever created to that point—like Alvy's Paint3 or BigPaint3—treated an image as a sheet of paper to be colored. With the idea that an image's matte was a fundamental part of the image, it was theoretically possible to make a single image that was actually itself a set of stacked image layers. The ability to paint a frame in layers gave an artist a number of remarkable abilities.

While hardware was Mark Leather's specialty, this idea of painting in layers intrigued him. It seemed like a good idea to write some software to give it a try, and he figured he knew enough to do that.

On a Friday afternoon, he and Bob Drebin sat in Yu Shang, the Chinese restaurant and sushi bar across the street from C Building, and discussed the issues with writing code for the Pixar computer. The system was very new and very crude. This made it exceptionally hard to write software to do anything, very slow to figure out how to structure, very buggy. There was no "desktop" or even remotely approachable interface. The computer sat in Leather's office next to a large high-resolution monitor; the computer was covered with UNIX windows and numbers; the video monitor was black.

On Monday morning, Drebin wandered into Leather's office and noticed a detailed painting of a Barbie doll on the computer screen, and an open book beside the computer: *You Can Draw Barbie*. Beside the screen image was what appeared to be a set of image tools.

"It looked like Leather had scanned an image from this Barbie book and left it on the screen," said Drebin, "except it wasn't really possible to scan an image back then. I thought it was a practical joke. Here was this perfect image, and on the sides and bottom of the screen were buttons of a paint system, like he had mocked up the screen…but it would have been hard to mock up a screen back then. I moved the cursor and clicked a button and things changed on the screen."

Leather had actually written and designed a new painting program and used it to paint its first image, Barbie. Mark called the software LayerPaint, and in no time it was the standard painting tool throughout the division. It worked at film resolution. It was a tool that ILM might finally be able to use.

At Disney, the tide was changing. In 1984 a hostile takeover was attempted, trumped when Roy E. Disney managed to purchase a controlling interest in the company. By September, Ron Miller had resigned (tactfully described as "under fire") and was replaced by a new executive team. Disney brought in a CEO, Michael Eisner, from Paramount, and a president, Frank Wells, from Warner Brothers.[31]

The new executive team was close to killing feature animation altogether. They'd explored moving their animation to Taiwan to lower expenses, but the idea was canned—they'd never be able to keep control of quality.

The technical management, the guys who had been meeting with Ed and Alvy over the years, had long supported the introduction of computers to solve many of the production issues. As early as 1978, Ed had shown them proof that a computer could subsume the ink and paint part of the traditional cel process.[32] Now, six years later, Disney was finally interested in discussing the opportunities with Lucasfilm. Eisner had ushered in a new Disney era, "of innovation, prosperity, and high executive salaries."

Disney was deeply wed to the idea of humans drawing and painting cels in the grand tradition. They were afraid a computer would "take away the magic." But they couldn't escape the gripping expenses.

Ed and Alvy began a long series of developmental meetings with the studio on how they might execute such a bold plan as eliminating inking and painting. It wasn't a radical introduction of 3-D animation, as Lucasfilm had been quietly exploring, but rather the slow computerization of the traditional 2-D process. Even as John Lasseter had been animating away in 3-D using MotionDoctor, Alvy was outlining a new tool for Disney, a "computer-aided production system," or CAPS.[33]

CAPS would computerize Disney's ink and paint. Instead of having artists draw on paper, clean up the drawings on paper, copy the finished drawings to clear acetate, and then paint the acetates one-by-one by hand, they would scan the drawings into the Pixar, and paint and composite them there.

Alvy carefully laid out the entire development plan. "My proposal, based on very detailed flow charts of how their house worked, explained how a sequence of special purpose stations would be designed, using the Pixar Image Computer as hardware, and special software written to implement the special purpose."

Disney and Lucasfilm went through many rounds of modification. While Disney execs were enamored of the concept, they were extremely worried that Lucasfilm would somehow use the technology against them.

During the epic negotiations between the computer graphics project and Disney, Alvy and Loren Carpenter began some unusual meetings to explore a new project with a Japanese publisher. The company was interested in developing an animated film of the classic mythological character known as "Monkey."

"We had enough technology," recalled Carpenter," that we thought we might be able to make a TV show, or special, or something…we weren't sure."

[31] Roy joined forces with Stanley Gold and was supported through an alliance with Texas billionaire Bass brothers. A full accounting of this tale is detailed in *Storming the Magic Kingdom,* by John Taylor.

[32] Catmull had shown Garland Stern's "Cel Paint" package prototype at NYIT, which made it clear the process worked; they used it on *Measure for Measure* and some other Lab projects.

[33] They also contemplated the impact this would have on their side business of selling original cels to animation collectors. CAPS would eliminate original cels.

Monkey was an institution in Japan. There was a comic book of *Monkey*, and there were also about a hundred stories of Monkey. "Kind of like the Arabian Nights," said Carpenter.[34]

The publisher and Alvy wondered whether it would work to introduce the characters to Western audiences.[35]

Ralph Guggenheim was also involved with early *Monkey* meetings because it was a potential feature film editing project. "Very few people at the time were thinking about doing a CG feature film," said Guggenheim. *Monkey*, Alvy felt, would be another venture to showcase the team's expertise at computer graphics.

Just before Halloween, everyone took a short break from CAPS and *Monkey* as Alvy and his long-time girlfriend Zu got married on Bainbridge Island off the coast of Seattle. Ed Catmull was his best man.

Work on both *Monkey* and CAPS then continued for most of the following year. *Monkey* would never come to fruition. But CAPS would change everything about their relationship with Disney.

Most of the graphics team posing after Siggraph '84. *Left to right:* Loren Carpenter, Bill Reeves, Ed Catmull, Alvy Ray Smith, Rob Cook, John Lasseter, Eben Ostby, David Salesin, Craig Good, Sam Lefler.

[34] Monkey was a mythological creature, a bit of a god, a bit of a trickster, in monkey headed-human form. He could pull a hair from his head and turn it into an iron staff, or toss hairs and create additional copies of himself. The story of *Monkey* arose about the time Buddhism came to Japan, via India and China in the first few centuries BC.

[35] Not entirely unlike the *Power Rangers* characters and series, introduced a few years later.

twenty-two

Playing Games

[1984]

It's misleading to suppose there's any basic difference between education and entertainment. This distinction merely relieves people of the responsibility of looking into the matter. It's like setting up a distinction between didactic and lyric poetry on the ground that one teaches, the other pleases. However, it's always been true that whatever pleases teaches more effectively.

—Marshall McLuhan, in Explorations #7, Classroom Without Walls, 1957

SOON AFTER *JEDI* was released, Peter Langston received authorization to expand the small Games Group. There was a short list of prospects, but none of them seemed to fit the team. Finally, before the 1983 holidays, Peter found a designer/artist and a couple of programmers he was interested in hiring.

Noah Falstein had just been laid off from an established videogame company and was excited to move to California.[1] "I remember being stunned that Lucasfilm was developing games," said Falstein. "They hadn't released any yet…but I was thinking that this was the coolest possible thing in the world." Langston liked Noah, but the group was unsure how he'd fit in.

"They were reluctant to hire me because I was the first person they were going to hire who had actually worked in the games industry," Noah said. "I think they were afraid I would contaminate their purity with old-fashioned ideas from the way videogames had been done before." Noah had to convince them that, at twenty-four years old, he still had some good ideas left. Langston wasn't sure.

Peter was, however, able to commit to Gary Winnick, who was not a programmer, but a commercial artist who had interest in animation and film. "When computers came along, I bought an Atari and started fooling around with it." Soon he was working at Atari, helping with game art design. Winnick had freelanced for Lucasfilm on artwork for the first couple games they had developed with Atari—in particular, creating the "Jaggie Monster" for *Rebel Rescue.*[2] After the success of that collaboration, Langston was comfortable

[1] Falstein's resume said he had worked at Milton Bradley, making some Atari VCS games, and at Williams Electronics, the designer of many popular arcade videogames such as *Joust* and *Defender.*

His college thesis was a videogame called "Koronis Strike: A Computer Simulation Game of Mining and Combat in the Asteroid Belt."

[2] George Lucas particularly liked Winnick's "Jaggie Monster" when he reviewed the prototype of *Rescue.*

GARY WINNICK

Hometown: Santa Cruz, CA.
Family: single. *Schools:* Santa
Cruz High, Cabrillo College,
Monterey Peninsula College.
Interests: hiking, painting,
animations, film. *Sign:*
Scorpio. *Employment history:*
Manager of Lenz Arts, Santa
Cruz; Animator with Home
Computer Division of Atari.
[1984 LFL Yearbook]

offering him a full-time position. Winnick's boyish demeanor meshed nicely with the small team.

While Langston mulled over his new staff, Ed Catmull and Bob Doris were mulling over theirs. Doris felt that Peter Langston was either unable or uninterested in managing the group, but he had too much to do to handle it himself.

"At a certain point," recalled Doris, "Ed and I got very nervous because we knew that if we didn't have something out the door that would be acceptable to Atari, in the proper timeframe, it would be a real big black-eye." They wanted to change the direction from the slow, almost pure research attitude they seemed to possess, to something more proactive, more market-driven.

Doris hired a headhunting firm to find an executive who didn't fit the traditional profile. It would take someone with an unusual combination of traits to spearhead an effort in the growing games industry, and who was at least a little sensitive to George's interests in interactivity and education.

The name that was returned to Doris' desk was Steve Arnold.

Lucasfilm Games Group Jan 1984. *From left:* Kellner *(standing)*, Levine *(sitting)*, Langston, Fox, Carpenter, Winnick.

Among the young talent that Atari had been sucking up in the heyday summer of 1982 was an idealistic grad student from Indiana, Steve Arnold. With a PhD in psychology, Steve had dreamed of building an experimental school near his hometown and was interested in ways technology might be integrated into childhood development.

Atari, then maybe the hottest company in the world, asked Steve to give a seminar to their home computer division about software for kids; it went so well that the president of the division asked him to join the company as a product manager of "blue sky products," to help ideate far-reaching concepts that didn't fit within any of the company's established categories.

It seemed like a good opportunity to get out of Indiana for a while and learn something about business before starting his own. "I was convinced that personal computers were going to change the way kids learned how to think, and I wanted to figure out what that was all about."

Atari hit the wall at the end of 1982. The company owned exclusive licenses to a number of hot arcade games, which they were developing for their own Atari platforms, but demand for their hardware was dropping off, and consequently software demand dropped too. The company was losing as much as perhaps $100 million per month.

By April 1983, one Atari executive recognized that there might be an opportunity in those arcade game licenses, if only the company could break a few rules.[3] He created a "skunkworks" project, completely secret to everyone in the company as well as in the industry, and he asked Steve Arnold to lead it. It was called AtariSoft.

"It was an act of desperation," recalled Arnold, "that we turned into an act of radical creativity." Everything about AtariSoft flew in the face of established Atari management. With a core of perhaps a dozen staff, they set out to produce thirty-nine games for five different platforms by Christmas.[4]

Atari fired Ray Kassar in the fall of 1983, and replaced him with the calm and efficient James Morgan, a former big tobacco executive. Warner Communications continued to put a best face forward.

In spite of industry-wide losses of $1.5 billion, Atari announced to *Business Week*, "We are going to reignite the consumer's love affair with video games." Even as the rest of Atari was on the ropes, AtariSoft succeeded, and in five months revenues went from zero to $70 million. Atari promoted Arnold to the vice president of marketing of Atari products.

"It was clear to me that the company didn't have a clue where it was going, that it was unlikely to survive," said Arnold, "so I resigned."

Just as Steve Arnold was about to head back to Indiana to work on his experimental school, Lucasfilm's headhunter contacted him. Bob Doris wanted someone with some experience in games, but also someone who could ride herd on the adolescent-types who were videogames developers.

Steve Arnold fit the profile. Before Atari, before his PhD, he was the program director at a boys' camp in upstate Wisconsin. Running the activities of dozens of pre-adolescent kids as they canoed across lakes and played games in the woods more than qualified him for the job.

STEVE ARNOLD

Hometown: Indianapolis, IN (The Heartland). *Family:* extended. *Schools:* Macalester College, BA, CIIS, MA, PhD. *Interests:* water skiing, white water canoeing, psychology, high magic, sci-fi, pizza. *Sign:* Virgo. *Employment history:* Private practice consulting and family/child psychotherapy; Atari. *Other Info:* lunatic prophesies for the coming weird times…
[1984 LFL Yearbook]

[3] Fred Simon, a mid-level executive and Steve Arnold's supervisor.

[4] Actually, they produced thirty-six games; three were dropped from the plan.

NOAH FALSTEIN

Hometown: Chicago. *Family:* Shem, Ham and Japeth. *Schools:* Hampshire College, Amherst MA, senior project was a computer game. *Interests:* science fiction, games, homemade ice cream, Gilbert & Sullivan, champagne. *Sign:* Beware the Dogma. *Employment history:* Milton Bradley, Williams Electronics. *Other Info:* Disciple of Hedon.
[1984 LFL Yearbook]

In January 1984, the Games Group suddenly expanded. Steve Arnold arrived at Kerner at almost the same moment as Gary Winnick.

And just as when Bob Doris joined the company two years earlier, it was unclear exactly who Steve reported to. Titles were never given much weight at Lucasfilm. Bob Doris was the manager of the Computer Division, and Ed Catmull was maybe the "director." Steve Arnold became manager of the Games Group, but Peter Langston was the "team leader." In spite of the vague nature of their origins, within a few weeks everyone was collaborating pleasantly, all focused on completing the task they were hired for, to develop new games.

After years of being called "Rebel Rescue" (and sometimes "Behind Jaggie Lines")[5] the release name of David Fox's game became *Rescue on Fractalus!* It was time to add more staff, and so Langston decided to bring in Noah Falstein. Upon his arrival, Falstein immediately began helping out with the odd jobs required to push *Rescue* and Levine's *Ballblazer* out the door.

Unfortunately, those two games would not be ready for release by the CES show later that January, and the painful decision was made to hold them until the summer CES show. The six-month delay would be enough to finish the game testing and produce new packaging and good manuals.

Peter Langston had no particular agenda for Winnick and Falstein, but he anticipated that once current projects were done, the new team would begin work on new ones.

"I puttered around a bit," recalled Noah, "and came up with a few ideas, but it was always pretty informal." What Noah wanted to do was to use the fractal generator that had been created for *Fractalus.*

"I was blown away by the two games, *Fractalus* in particular, because of its science-fiction theme."

Noah suggested a game in which instead of flying over the fractal landscape—an effect that looked good but wasn't much of a navigational challenge—it might be interesting to drive through it.

"One of the things that bothered me a bit about *Fractalus* was that the mountains in the distance sort of popped into view instantly, and it seemed to me that there might be a better way to fade them in, from fog and mist." He got to work on developing a new science-fiction game.

The Lucasfilm media engine was revving up. Winnick involved himself with the cover art for the two games that were finally getting ready for market. The all-white boxes were scrapped; the hip games demanded suitably Lucasfilmy packaging. The scope of the artwork was completely out-of-scale with the project: the packaging was being produced like a feature film.

[5] A subtle dig at the graphics group, who continued to parade around Kerner in their "No Jaggies" T-shirts.

The company screening of *Indiana Jones and the Temple of Doom* in May, 1984, was a pleasant perk for the Computer Division, all of whom received blue-jean jackets for the film.

Winnick worked with both Daves (Fox and Levine) to develop the concept art, and then spent time in D Building as ILM model makers constructed miniature props for the photographs. They built an actual rotofoil—the craft in *Ballblazer*—and a cockpit for the Valkyrie fighter in *Fractalus*. Costumers designed a space suit for David Fox to wear for the shoot. ILM composited the elements for the covers as well as for packaging and manuals. The entire Games team posed as haggard Valkyrie pilots for the back of the *Fractalus* box. Atari paid perhaps thirty grand for the effort.

Detail of the cover art on *Rescue on Fractalus!*, with the games team dressed as weary Valkyrie pilots. *From left:* Kellner, Carpenter, Levine, Langston, Falstein, Winnick.

"At the time, I believe this was the most expensive game packaging ever produced," figured Winnick.

In May, the third of Langston's new teammates arrived in E Building: Chip Morningstar. Morningstar had just left a long run on Ted Nelson's famous Xanadu project, the idealistic computer plan to invent "a magic place of literary memory."[6]

Nelson had coined the term (and concept) of hypertext, which fit into his larger vision of hypergrams (branching pictures), hypermaps (with transparent overlays), and branching movies. Recalled Morningstar, "Few people could actually work with Ted for more than a day or two without becoming clinically insane."[7] He was happy to be in the relative calm of Lucasfilm.

Everyone in the Games Group had the exact same title, "designer/programmer," except Morningstar, who was hired as a "software toolsmith." Morningstar was a Unix wizard who, like Langston, could refine the low-level

[6] Xanadu had been in various stages of development for a decade. Nelson initially intended to allow writers using computers to revise, compare, and undo their work easily, something that was unknown at the time.

[7] A small team ran the project in Ann Arbor and eventually California, while Ted Nelson remained on the fringes, in Pennsylvania and Texas, often with little interaction. Xanadu never reached fruition, but many of the core ideas found their way into the modern Internet.

CHIP MORNINGSTAR

Hometown: Various places.
Family: Wife, Janice; 4 cats.
Schools: HS drop out; BS
Computer Engineering, U of
Michigan. *Experience:* U of
MI Space Physics Research
Lab; Environmental Research
Institute of Michigan;
Project Xanadu. *Interests:*
Model trains, science fiction,
reading, computers, space
development, high-tech
prognostication.
[1986 LFL Yearbook]

code required to make the programming compile properly and efficiently. He had originally been interested in joining the Graphics Group, but Games was looking for help just as he was leaving Xanadu. He settled into an office with Noah Falstein and started helping everyone pull themselves together for the coming week's big trip to the CES show.

Warner Communications spent the first quarter of 1984 searching for a way out from under Atari, which had lost half a billion dollars in the prior year. Rumors of a sale circulated for months, usually focused on N.V. Philips, the Netherlands-based electronics concern. Industry analysts, facing the certain end of the videogame era, were watching the ascent of the home computer.

As the Lucasfilm games debut approached, Atari teams were busily testing them. Typical home games of the era were slow, 2-D, visually bland, and with nominal storylines. By all accounts, gameplay on *Rescue on Fractalus!* was fast and visually dynamic, and the back-story fun and rich. *Ballblazer*, too, was widely admired.

Because of some internal software developed by the testing teams, and a device they called a "super drive," Atari's engineers were able to duplicate games in spite of copy protection installed on the disks, and do it in a matter of seconds. While there was no World Wide Web in 1984, there was an Internet used by academic and industrial computer facilities.[8] But it wasn't the Internet that was to blame for circulated copies; it was pure "sneaker net."

The piracy crippled Lucasfilm's efforts. Copies of the prototypes circulated from game tester to game tester, to best-friend, to avid fan, until anyone with an Atari 800 computer had an illegal copy and had played it voraciously. By the summer of 1984, the games had not been released. But they were available at flea markets nationwide.

[8] Morningstar showed some of the games guys how they could use the company network to email friends around the world. Email was still relatively new for most people in 1984, but *Byte* magazine regularly published maps of the main Internet hubs, and if you knew the path of computers, a savvy user could email just about anywhere. "I remember being excited that an email arrived from a friend in Massachusetts," said Noah, "just a few hours after being sent."

In spite of internal problems, Atari defiantly showed up at the summer CES convention in Chicago. Their slogan at the show was "*June 3, 1984: The Day the Future Began.*" It was seen on T-shirts throughout the convention.

Atari hosted a major shindig at the Westin Hotel, showing off a long list of new technologies. They announced their MindLink System, which let users play games without conventional hand controllers, picking up impulses from wires connected to a player's forehead ("a high tech headband" said their press release). They announced new computers and new educational software. And finally, they announced the release of *Ballblazer* and *Fractalus*, the games from "Atari-Lucasfilm."

The Lucasfilm presentation caused a stir. In spite of the ongoing piracy, many spectators had not seen the games. After viewing the demonstrations, they assumed the group was cheating—there was no way the little personal computer could be producing those point-of-view graphics and such dynamic gameplay in real time. Some people looked under tables and behind curtains to find hidden videodisc players. But there were none.

Both Atari and Lucasfilm knew that releasing the games quickly might stem the tide of piracy, as they were rapidly approaching the "final" debut. Upon returning from Chicago, the Davids began the detailed process of tying up loose ends.

Fruitless.

Ten days later, the day before Lucasfilm's annual 4th of July picnic at the Skywalker Ranch site, Warner Communications announced the sale of Atari to Jack Tramiel, the founder of Commodore Computers.[9] Atari staff recognized the sweeping changes that Tramiel would likely bring, and panicked. Stories circulated about employees grabbing their computers and files and pouring out the back doors of buildings, even as the fleet of white Rolls Royce limousines carrying Tramiel and his sons were rolling up to Atari's main building.

The conquering army had arrived. Tramiel was as colorful and flamboyant as Kassar had been. Commodore, the company Tramiel started twenty-five years earlier and mysteriously left six months ago, was now going to be his competition. In the first days after his arrival, more than half the Atari workforce in Silicon Valley (more than 500 people) was terminated, although only a few years earlier the company had peaked with about 6,000. "Tramiel," reported an Atari spokesman, "dislikes large corporate structures."

The programmers at Lucasfilm were stunned. "There was a general sense of horror," recalled Noah Falstein, "and we were all wondering if they'd come up with new T-shirts that said 'July 3, 1984: The Day The Future Ended.'"

Atari was gone. All its assets had been acquired by the Tramel Corporation,[10] but the terms of the distribution agreement with Lucasfilm said it could not be legally transferred. Thus, Lucasfilm was in the interesting position of having its partner eviscerated but being left rather unscathed itself. According to Bob Doris, "It was sad for a minute, then it was simply, 'Let's find a new distributor for our cool new games; let's port them to whatever the most popular platforms are.'"

But while management was calm, the programmers were frustrated. David Fox and Dave Levine were helpless to stop the growing volume of pirated copies leaking out, and once again were unable to get the real games distributed.

An hour south of Lucasfilm, the old Atari campus was in a state of pandemonium. Security guards were trying to stem the tide of looting that seemed to be exploding in every direction. As the remaining staff left work at the end

---

[9] Tramiel paid $240 million for the beleaguered company—$140 million in senior debt and another $100 million in subordinated debt.

[10] Now spelled phonetically to avoid irritating mispronunciations.

of the day, often with their personal computers in tow, guards had difficulty discerning what was allowed to walk out the front door. Without much to go on, the guards were rumored to have stopped employees from leaving with their Atari brand computers, but let employees leave with their Apple IIs and IBM PCs.[11]

Peter Langston, 1984.

The two Lucasfilm games were playable, but they weren't really finished. Bob Doris and Steve Arnold met with Jack Tramiel soon after the transition was completed. But it was clear that Jack's focus was in a completely different direction.

Steve reported back to his troops on the meeting, perhaps the most interesting anecdote being that Tramiel looked and spoke like Jabba the Hutt. Within a day there were two photos taped to Steve's door: a still from *Return of the Jedi* showing Jabba the Hutt next to a clipping of Tramiel from *Time* magazine. Someone had added the caption: "The Hutt Brothers: Jabba, Jack." Steve took it down soon thereafter, as prudence got the better of him.

The piracy had taken the wind out of the sails of the products—anyone with an Atari 800 computer already had them. And Atari, for its part, was in no position to take over the distribution. *Rescue on Fractalus!* and *Ballblazer* were completely embroiled in the legal morass of the Atari debacle; Lucasfilm's only real option was not to sell the games. At least until a new distribution partner could be found.

[11] There was a large safe in the engineering building where Atari kept the master ROMs of all the games. But the key was nowhere to be found. The movers couldn't move the thing, and so it sat. Weeks later the remaining staff discovered a key taped to the underside of a desk and eventually tried it on the safe. It worked. The engineers debated whether they should tell anyone they had found the key or just take the ROMs and sell them to Atari's gaming competitors. Eventually, they left the safe open and before long, management came by and took the contents to another place.

As Steve Arnold ramped up his leadership role, Peter Langston, the founder of the games project, continued to phase himself out. The teammates, uncomfortably caught up in politics beyond their interest, had ample time to ideate their next creative steps.

In one of his final leadership acts, Langston encouraged the programmers to play *Empire*, the game he had invented years earlier—but not as a pastime; this was serious. "It was specifically for the purpose of getting us to think about alternative modalities of game design," recalled Morningstar.

The games guys—Chip Morningstar, Noah Falstein, David Fox, Charlie Kellner, and Dave Levine—began an intense month of experimental playthrough of the game. *Empire*, still considered a benchmark in the industry, was a text based, multi-player game, a sophisticated variation on the board game *Risk*. It was played by typing commands into a terminal and seeing the results of the aggregate decisions made by all the players at the end of the turn. It was also an enormous time suck.

The essential question Langston wanted them to focus on was this: precisely what was fun about the game, and what was a limitation to their enjoyment. One of the problems with *Empire*, they decided, was that every game seemed to follow the same evolution: exploration, resource buildup, consolidation, nuclear annihilation. Even though there was the potential for rich interaction from having real human beings as players, the same pattern always unfolded because there really wasn't much else people could do. The game was closed-ended in this sense.

"We thought it might be more interesting if the world was much bigger and the player goals more open-ended," said Morningstar.

By fall Peter had moved on, but the game continued.

Steve Arnold, as manager of the group, worked with Bob Doris to come up with a new distribution deal for their games. After reviewing the handful of options, they settled on Epyx, one of the top game software companies in 1984. They worked out an agreement for *Fractalus*, *Ballblazer*, and Lucasfilm's next two games, which were already in development. Following the January's CES show, Lucasfilm announced a one-year distribution deal with Epyx.

As the initial games finally started to roll out from the company, the famous Lucasfilm marketing engine was applied in force to the new projects, and articles on the projects appeared everywhere. Commented Steve Arnold, "We are trying to bring together some of the excitement and challenge and mystery of a good film or book with the action of a good sports event or game."

Charlie Kellner, after finishing up his low-level software work on the first two games, really hoped to design his own. Steve Arnold agreed and soon Kellner began architecture on a fantasy game he called *The Eidolon*. Like Noah's game, it capitalized on the fractal engine. Like the other games in development, it had an interface from the player's point of view. The game concept was fantastical: the Eidolon itself was a globe with a single seat on the inside.

As Steve Arnold described it, "A scientist has mysteriously disappeared from an abandoned Victorian mansion, leaving behind a device, which you discover and can use to propel yourself into an unseen world."

The user wasn't exploring space, but innerspace—an adventure set in the player's mind—exploring cavernous mind tunnels replete with trolls and dragons, and "guardians of the id," as company literature explained it.

One of the principal technological advancements of *The Eidolon* was software that scaled the characters on the screen—characters grew larger as they approached the player, and shrunk as they ambled farther away. *Ballblazer* had used scaling to make the rotofoil grow and shrink as it moved closer or farther, but that was for an unchanging geometric object. *Eidolon* was scaling a moving character. This dynamic improved the simulation of depth and, ultimately, the enjoyment of the game.

Winnick made a concept sketch of a player in the *Eidolon*, which soon was posted to the wall of E Building as inspiration.

Left: Winnick's drawing of the "real" Eidelon. *Right:* Charlie Kellner, 1984.

Noah Falstein was working away on his new adventure game. Set in the year 2049, Noah's premise was that players traveled to a distant planet to salvage superior weapons technology from abandoned space ships. Players drove tanks through the fractal landscape and sent out robots to acquire whatever equipment they could from inside alien ships, while they battled various futuristic life forms and flying saucers.[12]

"You play the part of a wily techno-scavenger with a trusty science-droid, nosing around the universe, looking for old technologies left over from past civilizations," said Steve Arnold.

Steve called the boys into his office for an impromptu meeting. The five of them plopped down in all available nooks. "We need to come up with a name for Noah's tank game," he said. "I can't keep meeting with Epyx and calling the thing 'Noah's Tank Game.'"

[12] As Steve Arnold described it: "You come across the fabled Koronis Rift, used millennia ago as a weapons testing ground by the Ancients, a consortium of highly evolved aliens."

Noah Falstein, 1984.

The team murmured in agreement. In spite of everyone's respect for Noah, his working title of "Tanks A Lot" was rejected outright. Without any better ideas for a name, Noah decided to borrow from his old college project. He dubbed the new game *Koronis Rift*, although the similarities with his thesis pretty much ended with the name.

 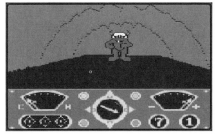

The second pair of Lucasfilm games: *Koronis Rift* (left) and *The Eidolon*. Both utilized first-person vantage points from spacecraft, and a refined low-bit-rate fractal engine for the landscape.

Corporate shakeups were the news across Hollywood. Barry Diller left Paramount and moved to Fox. Michael Eisner and Jeffrey Katzenberg left Paramount for Disney, ending the reign of Ron Miller at the studio. Fox owner Marvin Davis sold half the company to businessman Rupert Murdoch.

After a year of running Lucasfilm himself, and with headhunters unable to find a new executive to take over, George asked his board of advisors for options. He was still largely distrusting of business executives, and objected even more to professional Hollywood studio types. He was thinking more in the direction of a sharp and fearless leader, maybe an astronaut. Many on his advisory board tossed their hats in the ring. Lucas was skeptical.

Lucasfilm was a hard company to run. While it looked a little like a movie studio, and had the assets of a Fortune 500 company, it was still just a family business, and now after the divorce it had but one shareholder. George really didn't want to be the company president himself, but he also didn't want to have a company president do anything that he wasn't going to approve of.

Bob Doris saw the impending change of administration as a key moment to be proactive. As he and Ed Catmull had done six months earlier, they approached George directly, now with a modified proposal. This time they suggested dividing the Computer Division into two parts: the Graphics Group on one side and the Editing and Sound Groups merged together on the other. The Games Group would remain as part of Lucasfilm, producing branded entertainment. George was receptive.

Lucasfilm already had a partnership established with Convergence to manufacture key components of the EditDroid editing system. Now Doris was suggesting that relationship be expanded, and that Lucasfilm partner with Convergence to make an independent new company. A name was suggested, and George liked it: The Droid Works.[13] Bob Doris was authorized to pursue the spin-off.

An early draft of The Droid Works logo.

The EditDroid had debuted the previous spring, 1984, at Convergence's booth at NAB. The Droid Works could build on that momentum at the next NAB show, announcing the new company. With The Droid Works well on its way to establishing itself as a "real business," particularly with Bob Doris at the helm, George could focus on more pressing issues, like finding the new executive.

Lucas wasn't sure how his company was doing after his year at the helm but he knew revenue had been in flux, and he wanted an experienced manager to get control of the dozen projects spinning in every direction.

Long-time advisor Doug Norby, a former CFO, volunteered to be the third president of the company. George accepted. Norby had been on the small board of advisors since 1981 and was intimately familiar with the operations of the company as well as the issues facing Lucas.

[13] Reminiscent of George's *Transamerica Sprocket Works.*

With Bob Doris preparing to cleave the editing and sound projects from the corporate body, and the graphics and games groups becoming viewed as their own discrete entities, Doug Norby began his analysis of the situation.

It was clear the Games Group was different from the Graphics Group in several important ways. First of all, it was small and relatively inexpensive, and didn't demand a lot of management's attention. Second, because Atari had financed its beginnings, it didn't have a history as a major cost center. Third, whereas the Graphics Group (like the other development projects) were principally concerned with building tools to create entertainment products, the Games Group's mission was to create entertainment products directly. This made it seem a lot closer to Lucasfilm's core business. Finally, George's intuition was that interactive entertainment was going to be an important part of the business somewhere off in the future, so it was probably a good idea to cultivate a native understanding of the medium in-house, in preparation for the distant day when the technology was mature.

Lucasfilm held what was billed as an all-company meeting on the big ILM soundstage, to introduce the employees to the new president. Folding chairs were set up in rows, with a pair of long folding tables in the front of the room. As Norby and the other executives eyed the tables facing the crowd, they didn't want to sit down.

"We would have looked like the Politburo or something," said Norby. Instead, Norby convinced George and the others to sit *on* the tables, more informally. George wanted to stand in the back, but Norby urged him to join them in front.

Norby politely announced his excitement about the opportunity they all shared, mentioned his long time on the Lucasfilm advisory board, and outlined his vision for the hard tasks ahead. The Editing, Sound, and Graphics groups, while they were in place on Kerner, were not included in the audience, but Games was in attendance along with Sprockets, ILM, and the rest.

Lucas then started describing the sweeping changes that Norby would be executing. Doug Crockford recalled Lucas' telling them that it was time for the company to act like a business and not just a bunch of uninvited guests at his house, eating his food and spending his money.

There was not a single profitable division within the company; if it hadn't been for the licensing revenues, there would be very little income to offset the large expenses.

Norby then took over. He was friendly but steely. He said that Lucas had been supporting the company long enough; it was time for the company to begin to support him. It was going to be a serious reorientation.

Noah Falstein also recalled George's speech: "This company has gotten too diversified. We're going to concentrate on movies, doing special effects for movies, doing sound for movies, making movies themselves…it's all going to be about movies!"

DOUG NORBY

Hometown: Grass Valley, CA. *Family:* lots. *Schools:* Grass Valley High, Harvard. *Employment history:* McKinsey, Fairchild, Itel, Syntex. *Interests:* IJ interviews; what George means by "Great."
[1986 LFL Yearbook]

The news was well received by everyone except the short row of guys from Games. "We were sort of looking at each other kinda horrified," recalled Falstein, until George said, "and we'll do game stuff too." There was a groan from a few people sitting around ILM. "I think they were hoping to get rid of us," Falstein said.

Lucas, ever the storyteller, proceeded to describe the Games Group as, what he called, "The Lost Patrol." The story became a parable the games guys retold often:

"Nobody knew for sure where they were or what they were doing," George said, "but they were somewhere *out there*; every now and again somebody might see their flag on the horizon. In some far off day they would return home, bringing news of distant lands and wonders beyond imagining."

So the Games Group was not spun off along with the rest, but instead became its own business unit within the company: the Lucasfilm Games Division.

twenty-three

Rendezvous with Reality

[1985]

RAY: *"Personally I liked the University: they gave us money and facilities, we didn't have to produce anything. You've never been out of college. You don't know what it is like out there. I've worked in the private sector, they expect results."*

PETER: *"For whatever reasons, Ray, call it fate, call it luck, call it karma. I believe that everything happens for a reason. I believe that we were destined to get thrown out of this dump."*

RAY: *"For what purpose?"*

PETER: *"To go into business for ourselves."*

> —RAY STANTZ (DAN AYKROYD) SPEAKING
> TO PETER VENKMAN (BILL MURRAY) IN
> *GHOSTBUSTERS* (1984)

ONE REASON Doug Norby was tapped as the new Lucasfilm president was that he had had experience as a turn-around artist in tricky waters. Trickiest in the Lucasfilm waters, as Norby discovered, was the cash flow problem.

Following the release of *Jedi* in May 1983, *Star Wars* products were widely licensed, and they produced an ongoing flow of revenue. The Kenner toy deal alone had been providing almost $20 million per year. But in 1984, Kenner was preparing for a separation from General Mills (its parent company) and had packed its distribution pipeline with product to boost how the company looked on paper.

"When I got [to Lucasfilm]," said Norby, "there were twenty-two weeks of toys in that pipeline." The net effect was that sales appeared higher before the spin-off and virtually collapsed afterwards, while retailers were saddled with an enormous inventory of products.

While George's divorce was going to be a cash strain on the company, it was not unexpected. What came as a surprise was that revenue from the licenses had virtually dried up. Without new films, fewer kids were demanding *Star Wars* lunch boxes or action figures. The decrease in market interest combined with the Kenner spin-off led to a sudden and cataclysmic drop in cash.

As soon as Norby took office, he was faced with the shortfall. Estimates were that there were perhaps twenty weeks of cash left in the company. Recalled Norby, "We just couldn't afford to fund this stuff." "This stuff" was, among other things, the Computer Division. Lucas had been on a long crusade to transform the film industry, to get it to adopt more advanced technology. "It was an ambitious and very noble pursuit," said Norby. But expensive.

Lucas was looking down the gauntlet of many frightening circumstances. Though he didn't like the idea of radical change at the company, he trusted Norby, who had performed these sorts of turnarounds at technology companies before.

"Do what you have to do," Norby recalls being told by Lucas, "and I'm just going to stay out of it."

There were only three ways to address the problems: cut spending, increase revenues, or get outside money. Norby was working on all fronts.

"There were people problems in the company, fairly severe ones," recalled Norby. "Lucasfilm had been running itself. The inmates were running the institution, and they were fighting amongst themselves. We not only had to address the cash problems, we had to do a cultural change."

The most important change for the new president was to get Lucasfilm to transition into a stand-alone business, to move from dependence on George to independence. "It's a huge mindshift for the people. And to get them through it with anything like morale left was quite a challenge."

The new administration looked over the company critically. Much of the primary work at the Ranch was done, and yet the vast workforce of the Skywalker Development Company—the painters and builders, the glassworkers and landscapers—still hung around, charging the time to whatever building was in progress in a rather cavalier fashion. Norby felt the teams were taking advantage of Lucas and closed down the entire effort. There was still work to be done, but it could be completed later, when finances were under control.

Industrial Light & Magic, long famous in the public's consciousness, was losing money, not because something had changed, but because nothing had. The division was never a self-supporting business—it was the group who executed George's special effects. Though well respected, ILM essentially had only three clients: George Lucas, Steven Spielberg, and the *Star Trek* franchise. When one of those three was not making a movie, ILM had periods of no work. And while many of the staff were freelancers hired for a particular film—causing the division to ebb and flow in size from season to season—the overhead and fixed staff were considerable.

Since its formation, ILM never needed to look for work—work found them. Norby insisted the division reorient, and set up a small marketing department dedicated to Hollywood business. ILM bristled at what they felt was groveling for jobs. But faced with the alternative of more layoffs, they set up an office at The Egg Company and began developing relationships with other filmmakers and outside studios.

Said Norby, "A lot of people were resisting this rendezvous with reality."

Another tactic of Norby's was to move ILM from a kind of "organized chaos" of people working on the various aspects of the process, to a matrix borrowed from the aerospace industry, with supervisors and producers moving each project through the departments, adhering more tightly to budgets and schedules. The problem at ILM had long been the tension between art and craft on one hand, and business and production on the other.

"We got the division to be a whole lot more efficient and predictable," recalled Norby.

Once that predictability was in place, ILM began the internal analysis to know precisely what it cost to make a matte painting, for instance, or to build a model. With this information the division was able to bid for projects. The fixed-price bids, now based on extensive knowledge of the costs of effects, allowed the division to build in a profit margin.

"That's what really got us growing," said Norby, "because the producer down in Hollywood loved to have one part of his budget that he could rely on."

Doug Norby also approached Marcia Lucas to see if they could adjust the divorce settlement to be less impactful on the company, which she was amenable to. "We owed her a big chunk of money, and it was going to be due in one lump sum." She agreed to a payout over ten years.[1]

Finally, Norby began scratching around for outside money. He looked everywhere. No bank would loan Lucasfilm cash. (George was unwilling to divulge the financial statements any institution would require for such a transaction.) Maybe if Lucasfilm made another *Star Wars* movie the finances might revive? Norby gingerly ran the suggestion by George. But he was burned out. Norby recalled him saying "I just can't do it; you're on your own."

Norby next came up with a plan to sell off a small part of Lucasfilm to private investors. "Would George have been okay with that?" he wondered in hindsight. "Probably not. But it was either that or go down the tubes."

[1] The company was solid enough by 1989 that it paid off the settlement in full, on the original schedule, after less than five years.

He began discussions with the Bass Brothers of Texas, billionaires from oil investments throughout the '70s and early '80s. They visited the company and toured the facilities, "kicking the tires," as one employee put it. Only months earlier they had taken a 25 percent stake in troubled Disney.[2] "[They] wanted too much of the company for too little money," recalled Norby, and discussions broke down.

In time, Norby identified a Japanese bank that was prepared to provide a line of credit to the company based on the Lucasfilm name alone. LFL didn't need the money yet, but this would give them latitude to keep moving ahead on plans.

Norby executed the first significant layoffs Lucasfilm had ever seen. He felt he had little option but to cut the number of employees in half. Many of them had been part of the "family" since the original films, and morale sank.

It was the post-*Star Wars* era, and the company had to become re-focused. Why anyone expected to be kept at a movie company no longer making movies came as a shock to Doug Norby and his new CFO, Doug Johnson. The two men, known as "the Dougs," accepted the brunt of employee ill-will at the strategy chosen to keep the company afloat.

"It didn't look like I was going to be able to do it at first," recalled Norby. "There just weren't enough strings to grab to pull out of that accelerating dive.[3]

The Dougs—or the "Dweebs," as they were malevolently referred to— were widely disliked by the employees, who saw them as hatchet men with no sensitivity to the Lucas dream. There was a tendency for employees to imagine that when things happened they didn't like, it was because George didn't know about it.

"If George only knew the truth, things would be different," staff would murmur in the corridors of Kerner. People at the company were unwilling to believe that Lucas was capable of doing anything wrong or nasty.

According to Bob Doris, "It's a George thing. He's successful at creating a myth for himself. I'm sure the Dougs weren't doing anything more or less than George wanted them to do."

Rumors circulated that they had plans to fire everyone at the Computer Division and sell off the equipment for scrap.

"That wasn't the case," said Norby. "Our plan was to sell the divisions as businesses; we weren't trying to fire everyone and sell equipment. We thought we could make more money if we sold them intact. You get more money if you can sell the division *and* the people, and I was hoping to sell them for a lot of money."

Norby asked a venture capitalist-friend of his to look over his restructuring work at the company and offer an opinion. "You've got two good things here," he was told, "ILM and Games."

[2] Richard Rainwater, who was largely responsible for cutting the deals for the Bass family, was itching to move out on his own. He had built the Bass Brothers empire from $50 million in 1970 to almost $5 billion.

[3] Lucasfilm company joke: Q. How many Lucasfilm employees does it take to screw in a light bulb? A. None. We outsource that now.

Norby and the Itel Story

In the years before Lucasfilm, Norby had been the CFO at a far different company called Itel. Itel was in the IBM mainframe computer rental business, founded in 1968. For a long time you couldn't buy an IBM mainframe; you could only lease one. This not only made owning a computer easier on customers, but it gave IBM a steady revenue stream and made it that much harder for a competing company to get into an IBM installation. Eventually the Justice Department determined this to be a monopoly, and the government broke it up.[4]

Itel found a market opportunity: borrow money from banks, buy the equipment from IBM, and then turn around and lease it at a significant discount to the same customers that IBM already had. Enormously profitable, and Itel grew like crazy. Within nine months of their formation they went public. Doug Norby was among the founders.

There are two kinds of leases that Itel used, and each differed widely with regard to how tax was paid. One could be canceled. One could not. If the lease couldn't be canceled, you could report all the revenue the moment the contract was signed. With cancelable leases you reported your revenues month by month.

This meant that Itel could book millions in profit as they were making deals, much of it years before the money actually came in.[5] Itel used the profits to diversify, getting into the shipping container business and short line railroads, tankers, and jet aircraft.[6] They were achieving more than 40 percent growth every year, year after year. "We were selling maybe twenty or thirty computers a month," said Norby. Itel had offices all over the world. Eventually, Norby left Itel and joined Fairchild Electronics.

In the early 1970s IBM got wise to what was going on and it did two things: it slashed lease prices, and it began to introduce new models.

Overnight, Itel revenues collapsed. "In December we [leased] twenty computers, in January, seven, and it was down from there." Customers canceled their leases in droves and switched back to IBM, leaving Itel in an awkward position. It couldn't cut costs fast enough to keep up with the revenue drop. Old equipment began coming back. These were now considered almost worthless, below the value on the balance sheets, and thus had to be written off.

The banks that had lent Itel money wanted to know what was happening. They were confused by the company's balance sheet, and stared blankly at the computer leasing division's weird financial statement and warehouse of used equipment. The banks needed someone on the inside to help them untangle the web of financial confusion. They set their sights on Doug Norby, the old CFO.

At the banks' behest, Norby was drafted from Fairchild with the hope he could unravel the confusion and restructure the enormity of loans.

Norby found that while many leases were reported as non-cancelable, and the paper profits had been taken, many customers had surreptitiously been given side letters that allowed them out of their deals. What this meant was that Itel should not have taken profits on all the leases, and their reporting for a number of years needed to be cleaned up. There was no internal information about who or how many lessors had the side letters, and so the scope of the problem was difficult to assess. This was the Enron scandal of its day.

[4] IBM made so much money from the monopoly that they dragged out the legal arguments for years, which cost less. The Justice Department finally issued a consent decree, which forced the company to sell certain pieces of equipment on the open market, although it was allowed to continue with the leases.

[5] These leases were often sold to other financial institutions to generate cash. Even though they were amassing large debt to the financial institutions of California, their balance sheet looked solid.

[6] At its height, Itel owned about 70,000 railcars.

Itel stock collapsed and the government's Security and Exchange Commission (SEC) began investigations into their accounting practices. Doug Norby, the CFO, helped them dig through the web to uncover the details of the problem.

"I was brought in because the banks were scared," said Norby. "They sent in other CFOs, but the president wouldn't accept them. I was the only one he'd accept." Norby cooperated with the authorities and helped them pierce the smokescreen; his work helped get convictions against some of his former partners.

Norby himself was never implicated in wrongdoing; on the contrary, by his extraordinary manipulations of the bleak situation, he was able to revive the company, find its value and recapitalize it. By the end of the lengthy SEC investigation (1979), Norby was exonerated by the Justice department. Soon after, *Fortune* magazine pictured him picking through the wreckage of Itel, in charge of reviving whatever was salvageable for the company's shareholders. He was anointed by the business magazine as a "turn-around artist."

Lucasfilm's board saw the article and felt that, in light of the challenges on Lucasfilm's financial plate, he might be a valuable addition to their team. To many Lucasfilm employees, however, Norby's background was murky at best. While the Itel debacle was well behind him by the time he was working with Lucas, rumors about the historical events were used to fuel distrust. There was an ugly patina associated with Itel, and employees at a company undergoing downsizing were quick to latch onto that.

It was beginning to dawn on Ed and Alvy that whether the Division invented new tools or not, it was clear that *someone* would be inventing them soon, and Lucas would be able to pick and choose the components he liked. Other companies were trying to develop nonlinear editing systems, other companies were pushing digital audio, other people were doing research into computer graphics.

While there was a modicum of ego involved, the inspiration for Lucas' research division was only to *have* new tools, not necessarily to invent them. Lucas never had any interest in being in the equipment manufacturing business. His company was about ideas and entertainment. Games fit that profile. But the tools invented by the Computer Division, as cool as they might be, did not.

With Doris largely preoccupied, Ed Catmull and Alvy Ray Smith thought it fell to them to find a way out of their tenuous predicament. "It was clear Lucas had to let us go," recalled Alvy. He and Ed conspired quietly.

[7] Silicon Graphics, or SGI, founded in 1982 by Jim Clark to capitalize on his innovation, the "geometry engine," a chip that accelerated graphics computations. SGI went public in 1986.

Alvy had already been chatting with their old friend from New York Tech, Jim Clark, for inspiration. Clark himself had become fed up with engineering jobs and had just a few years earlier started Silicon Graphics to make workstations for the emerging world of industrial graphics.[7] Now Silicon Graphics was burning through millions in venture capital and gearing up for an IPO; Clark was a font of wisdom.

"How come you're still working for *the Man*," Alvy recalls Clark saying. Jim Clark was a born entrepreneur and was thriving in the strange atmosphere of incessant struggle and opportunity he had created for himself. "It's not that hard; you can learn it all in less than a year."

Ed and Alvy were certain the team they had assembled was the best thing ever to happen to computer graphics. It was like an all-star rock band, like an Olympic team. They fit together; they were creative and ambitious and coordinated. They had a single purpose and drove toward it like conquistadores, relentless singularity of goal—to make an animated movie entirely on a computer.[8] The team had been growing steadily and without pause since the 1970s. Alvy said it would be "a sin" to break up the talent.

They also knew with certainty that Norby had to protect Lucasfilm. Although Lucas had spent millions to develop new digital machines to advance filmmaking, and he was passionate about their effort, he no longer had the luxury to continue funding them.

As Ed and Alvy pondered their fate in this new universe, it was clear that the arrival of Doug Norby was the coming of their antichrist. The day of reckoning would soon be upon them, and it would be foolish to let the company's administrators determine their fate.

"Lucas doesn't know what to do with us," Alvy said under his breath; it was like blasphemy. "The Dougs are going to fire us if we don't turn this into a company. Let's start a company."

"Yeah, good idea," Catmull admitted. And not knowing much about starting a company, he and Alvy snuck out to the bookstore at Larkspur Landing, a few minutes from Kerner. Alvy plopped down with *Buy Low, Sell High, Collect Early and Pay Late*, and began flipping pages. Ed was staring blankly at books on reading financial statements. By the time they headed back, they had each found two books on "how to start a business" and decided to begin their self-education.

Meanwhile, Graphics continued operating with full knowledge that the sword of Damocles was hanging overhead. Bob Doris had spoken to Ed about spinning off numerous times over the prior year. Though Bob had to deal with the Dougs frequently (because Lucasfilm held a majority interest in The Droid Works), he had little formal contact with Ed or Alvy after TDW was split off. But Bob managed to meet with Ed often enough to relay his new experiences of working with Lucasfilm, and he coached him on ways the Graphics Group might want to re-invent themselves.

After Siggraph 1984, Tom Porter found himself filling a gap in Pixar marketing, trying to reinvent himself away from software. Up to this point the entire

[8] The members of the team they left at NYIT in 1979 started trying to create a full-length feature film entirely in 3-D computer graphics, and had been working continuously on the project since then. Called *The Works*, written by their fellow scientist Lance Williams, the project was shut down in 1986 before completion.

Computer Division's marketing was being handled by Mary Sauer, a diminutive vortex of energy who Doris drafted from Wharton. But as the graphics project was moving to market more slowly than the pair of post-production tools, Sauer shifted her focus from Pixar to Droids, which left Porter to supervise their preliminary marketing efforts.

"I wasn't really a marketing person, but when Ed needed to show potential customers or investors what we were doing, I was a good choice. Anyway, I was happy to put on a coat and tie every other day."

After sorting through the response cards from the conference, Porter spent some time fishing around in each plausible marketplace for the Pixar, to see what businesses were out there and what they were doing. He poked into anything he could find about how a graphical system could be used outside of movies. "The special property of the Pixar was that it could handle very large resolution images," said Bob Drebin. "So, who had large images?"

Porter contacted representatives from a range of industries. Geophysics. Automotive design. Medical imaging. Scientific visualization. They all used images in their work.

Medical imaging, in particular, caught Porter's imagination, and after a bit of research he was on the phone with an engineer from Siemens. Porter wasn't sure how Siemens created medical images, or what they did with them, but they were a large industrial player in the imaging field. Representatives from Siemens looked over the new Pixar demonstration video, then they sent over a digital tape from one of their CAT scan machines.[9]

"Here," they said, "if you want to try stuff, see what you can do with these."

No one in the Graphics Group knew much about medical technology, and they weren't given any direction, so Porter handed the material off to Bob Drebin, who at least had studied biology in college. He started to think about what he was seeing.

"When you have a tool," said Drebin, "you start to think your tool can solve every problem. You start to map all your problems into your tool. The Pixar was a compositing tool, so I wondered if we could treat each of the CAT scans as a series of layers."

Drebin began to stack the individual human slices of information as if they were elements in an optical line-up from ILM. The images were all gray-scale, with the various shades of grey representing something about the density, he imagined, of the scanned human patient. It looked like a woman's hip, although from the slices, it was pretty hard to recognize it as much of anything.

[9] *CAT scan*: Computed Axial Tomography was invented in 1972, introduced in 1974. Widely available in 1980. The inventors won a Nobel prize in 1979. Name later changed to CT scan.

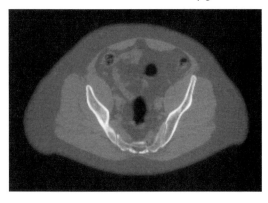

Drebin layered the slices, but immediately ran into simple problems. "How do you come up with an alpha value for each layer? What is transparent and what is opaque?" Instead of letting all the layers simply flatten out, he maintained their separation in much the way the scans were taken, about 4mm apart. Then he made up some arbitrary rules about color and transparency.

"Let's make this bright area—probably bone—pretty opaque. And this outside area that is really dark in the CAT scan and looks like it might be fat, let's make that transparent green; and this middle area, maybe other tissue, how about translucent red."

So he rendered the stack and did a composite. It was a 3-D pelvis. It came out pretty well.

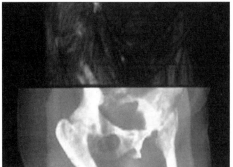

"We just assumed that once we did it, this must be how everyone had been doing medical imaging," said Drebin. "We really had no idea what was going on in the field." Drebin made a series of cool images and then contacted a few people in the medical imaging community to come look at what he had done.

"Is this new?" Drebin asked the gathered physicians.

"Yes," he was told, but it was controversial.

Lucasfilm's 3-D rendering of a pelvis, from CAT scan data *(opposite page)*. Drebin refined the established concept of the "voxel" (short for volume element), a sort of 3-D pixel.

There were already a few competing methods of human visualization using 3-D and CAT scans. But the alternatives were manually created with a mouse or extremely blocky and hard to visualize. What Drebin had produced looked like a three-dimensional image, and it looked very natural. Where there were dots on the CAT scan that looked like artifacts of the process, the Pixar model revealed it to be a fine mesh of veins. There were ample details that couldn't be seen on a CAT scan slice nor revealed by the competing methods of visualization in play in the medical community.

"People flipped out when they saw this stuff."

As part of the Lucasfilm marketing effort, they produced a series of remarkable images, which ended up being printed in a glowing article about the Computer Division that came out in *Business Week* in April 1985: "A Better Kind of Image from the Wizards of Hollywood."

That's when Drebin got the call.

The doctor on the other end of the line was loud and intense. "I'm sorry, but that's my pelvis; you can't use my pelvis, not without permission!"

Drebin was stunned. He hadn't really thought much about the picture itself, or where it had come from. Dr. Elliot Fishman, radiologist at Johns Hopkins in Maryland, had taken the CAT scans with their Siemens machine a year earlier. But in 2-D or 3-D, he recognized his patient's pelvis.

"But things took off from there," recalled Drebin.

Fishman, prone to enthusiasm, wasn't really mad. What he wanted was to understand how the image was created. He had been working on the cutting edge of 3-D visualization of CAT scans for a few years and he fully appreciated the importance of what he was seeing.

Most radiologists argued that the 3-D rendering, while cool looking, had little medical value. There was little, they said, that trained radiologists could see in a 3-D model that they couldn't see in the 2-D slice. It might be good for less-trained physicians, but for experts in the field, this was just bells and whistles.

Fishman disagreed, and had been trying to make the case that the 3-D scan had value. Drebin agreed to work with Fishman in refining their techniques and determining if the new method was indeed significant. In short order, Drebin was in Maryland, getting his head scanned.

While Norby was preoccupied with keeping Lucasfilm afloat, Bob Doris' attention moved from the Computer Division as a whole to the specifics of ratcheting up the Droid Works venture with Convergence. Convergence CEO Gary Beeson was anxious to use the Lucasfilm brand to help his successful second-tier video equipment manufacturing company move into the big time and compete with such industry stalwarts as CMX.

CMX had recently stumbled from their domination of the editing business with an ill-timed foray into direct broadcast satellites. Their misstep proved an opportunity for other companies, such as the Grass Valley Group (GVG) to make pushes into the high-end broadcast tools market. Doris was able to construct an agreement with Beeson, with Lucasfilm retaining a two-thirds interest in The Droid Works, giving Convergence a one-third stake. Convergence would supply cash, manufacturing know-how, sales and support; Lucasfilm would supply research and brand.

The Droid Works planned to have the EditDroid again at the 1985 NAB show, this time in a newly branded "TDW" booth. This would also be the opportunity to debut the SoundDroid prototype, with hopes of taking some big orders and shipping product before the end of the year. The Graphics team had debuted their Pixar Image Computer privately in a suite at Siggraph 1984, and now, concurrent with the Droid folks going to NAB, the Graphics team was going to take the Pixar public at the big National Computer Graphics Association (NCGA) conference. After almost five years, the three primary projects of the Computer Division were emerging, in various forms of completion, ready to face the all-new issues of the marketplace.

Left: Malcolm Blanchard rehearses the script at the first public showing of the Pixar Image Computer, while Tom Porter (at left) works on the script and Bob Drebin (at right) tweaks the software, in the hours before the opening of NCGA 1985. *Right:* The original Pixar signage, displaying only the Pixar name and the Lucasfilm logo.

"From a product standpoint," said Norby, referring to the Graphics Group, "they were going down a blind alley."

"Expectations were way ahead of reality," said Bob Doris. "Handling the Computer Division was something in which you could never win. It didn't matter in what dimension you measured expectations—on a straight-up business basis, what George was thinking, what Ed or I was thinking—in every dimension our expectations were out of line. Norby knew this. He was the consummate corporate gamesplayer."

Norby made his CFO Doug Johnson the point man on everything associated with the disposition of the Computer Division. Then he distanced himself from the situation. "Doug Johnson handled those [corporate acquisition] tasks because, in the first place, I'm not that great a negotiator," said Norby.

At any rate, Norby had far more pressing problems than the disposition of the divisions. "This was a peripheral problem," said Norby. There was the overarching cash flow issue. But his constant battle was the cultural one. "Cultural change is the hardest thing in business."

Johnson looked over the Graphics Group, and after his analysis of the products and market, determined that it should be valued at $35 million. Neither Ed nor Alvy was certain how he arrived at the number, but with that figure in hand, the Dougs began looking for anyone who might be interested in a prototype high-resolution image processing computer that alone would sell for $100,000 (it would cost five times more for a turnkey graphics solution) and for which the group had a small wave of advance interest.

Alan Kay, a friend of Alvy and David DiFrancesco from Xerox PARC (and fellow U of U alum with Catmull), was a close friend of Steven Jobs, and had just become an "Apple Fellow" in 1984. Jobs was still running Apple, although there was trouble there. Trying to ignore his board of directors, Jobs was looking around at the landscape of the industry. He was deeply interested in graphics and Kay suggested he meet with Alvy and the Lucasfilm Graphics Group to see what they were up to.

Soon, Ed and Alvy were invited to Steve Job's place in Woodside, a nearly empty 25,000-square-foot hacienda outside of Palo Alto. There was no furniture in the house, just a black grand piano and a German motorcycle in the living room. Jobs recognized them as a bunch of really smart guys who knew a lot about graphics and who always needed a lot of computer power.

They had lunch (salad with little edible flowers in it), then went out on his lawn, where he pitched them on what he wanted: to take the whole group and make a new computer company. Ed and Alvy declined. They wanted to run their own company.

"It was early in the spin-off process," recalled Catmull, "so we declined, but on good terms…we just went our separate ways."

The Dougs assured Ed and Alvy that they would handle the buyout and not to concern themselves with it. Alvy took this as an insult, but Doug Johnson insisted, "We're the business guys; you're the technical guys. You leave everything to us because you don't know what you're doing and we do."

"The reason they were instructed not to negotiate," said Norby, "was that they were the employees and George was the owner. It really wasn't theirs to sell. I thought that was a reasonable position."

The group was placed on a platter for the investment community to scrutinize. Most professional venture capitalists had trouble with its valuation as a business. Lucasfilm initially wanted $15 million for their stock, plus the group would require another $15 million of new cash to get moving. What concerned professionals the most was that Lucasfilm wasn't simply looking for investment, but looking to sell some of its stake in the company.

Explained Bob Doris: "If you're a VC and someone comes along with a business idea and says, 'Do you want to invest in this?' and you say, 'Sure—how much?' and they say, '$10 million,' and you say, "Sure, I'll put in $10 million," and they say, "No, we want $10 million for our stake," VCs will generally back away." And so they did.

Alvy was skeptical of the Dougs' ability to sell the graphics project. "They kept trying to fire all our people," he recalled, "thinking that it was the technology that people were buying, not the talent."

Norby disagreed. "I knew that the only thing in the Graphics Group was the talent." He was certain that the Pixar Image Computer was ill-conceived and overpriced.

"I knew it was going to be hard to sell, because the product concept was not viable. It was costing way too much."

The Lucasfilm administrators had been eyeing the rise of SGI and felt that it was offering comparable technology for a fraction of the cost of the Imaging Computer. But the SGI computers were fundamentally different, and actually somewhat compatible. All Lucasfilm saw was the ever-decreasing cost of this technology and the hundreds of thousands they were asking for their product. Anyway, just as with The Droid Works a year earlier, George was sure that he had no interest in being in the equipment manufacturing business.

By spring 1985, the Dougs had abandoned the VC route and started focusing on corporate buyers. Soon they came up with a few interested parties. First was Philips, the Dutch electronics giant and one of the largest companies in the world. Second was Siemens in Germany, manufacturer of the CAT scan equipment that seemed to have a natural fit with the Pixar, and which had expressed interest in either marketing the device or investing outright. Hallmark, the greeting card company, was also interested. There were some nibbles from industrial printing companies like Hell and Crossfield, but those dried up. And finally there was General Motors.

Philips (like Siemens, which soon backed away) was largely interested in the Pixar computer for it's medical applications. Medical imaging was estimated to be a $50 million market, and the Pixar, it seemed, might help capture a sizable share of that. GM saw the Pixar computer as a key component of advanced automotive design. In June, Alvy and Ed toured the GM Advanced Concepts Center, looking at their process for car design and auto simulation. By the end of the month, Hallmark had dropped out, and it was down to two.

Lucasfilm wanted a deal that got the division off its plate and yet continued to keep it somewhat under its control. Instead of selling the group outright, the deal was for Lucasfilm to have two partners. That way, while they couldn't be a majority owner, they could at least be an equal with two other minority owners.

They wanted both EDS (a new division of General Motors) and Philips to each give up $10 million for their one-third slice. This would effectively repay LFL for its initial Computer Division investment; Lucasfilm also wanted rights to existing and any yet-to-be-developed technology the new company would produce. General Motors and Philips were both interested. At General Motors, for capital acquisitions their VPs had to approve it; for deals dealing with computers, the EDS guys had to approve it.

EDS was run by a quirky billionaire named Ross Perot. It was a time when Perot had been openly critical of the General Motors management and they were increasingly involved in open warfare. Negotiations with Lucasfilm dragged on into the fall. Every time cash flow projections were revised, the parties had to revisit the valuation.

Ed and Alvy struggled to protect the rest of the Graphics Group from the vagaries of the negotiations. Steven Spielberg was producing an adventure called *Young Sherlock Holmes*, directed by rising star Barry Levinson[10] and written by Spielberg's young anointed protégé Chris Columbus.[11]

In the new film there was a scene: *a priest enters a church and one of the stained glass windows—the figure of a knight—breaks out from the frame and begins to walk into the room, sword drawn, to kill the priest.* It's an hallucination in the movie, but the intention was it should look absolutely real. *The knight chases the priest out of the church and into the street.* The stained glass knight needed to be transparent, and flat. You had to see through him at some angles, clear to the background of the church. It would be almost impossible to execute the effect with miniatures or models. If it could be done at all, effects supervisor Dennis Muren figured, it would take the computer.

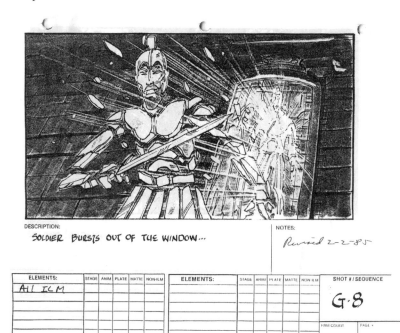

[10] **Barry Levinson** (b. 1942). American director: *Diner* (1982), *The Natural* (1984), *Tin Men* (1987), *Rain Man* (1988), *Avalon* (1990), *Wag the Dog* (1997); screenwriter on TV and movies, including *Silent Movie* (1976), *High Anxiety* (1978).

[11] **Chris Columbus** (b. 1958). American writer: *Gremlins* (1984), *Goonies* (1985), *Young Sherlock Holmes* (1985); director: *Adventures in Babysitting* (1987), *Heartbreak Hotel* (1988), *Home Alone* (1990), *Mrs. Doubtfire* (1993), *Harry Potter/Sorcerer's Stone* (2001), *Harry Potter/Chamber of Secrets* (2002).

DESCRIPTION: SOLDIER BURSTS OUT OF THE WINDOW...

NOTES: Revised 2-2-85

A page of the ILM storyboard for the Stained Glass Man.

All the tests up to this point had been successful and it was time to use the Pixar Image Computer, the new graphics and rendering software, and David's laserscanner and laserprinter on a film effect. It would be the proof of concept for everything they had been doing for Lucas since 1980. If they could pull this off, it would be the first time a computer effect was integrated with live action.

Warren Franklin, the general manager of ILM, asked Ed to recommend some guys to handle the imaging computer and develop computer graphics specifically for their needs. None of the existing Graphics Group was really interested in getting out of R&D and into effects production. While Bill Reeves, Eben Ostby, and John Lasseter began preparing for the effect, Ed and Alvy began searching for someone to run ILM's new small computer group—a liason between the researchers and the traditional effects teams.

George Joblove had been following the work at NYIT while he was a student at Cornell, studying computer graphics. He watched in awe as Catmull and company left New York for Lucasfilm in 1980 ("It sounded like the hot ticket at the time") and soon he and another Cornell student, Doug Kay, headed out to California to look for work.

GEORGE JOBLOVE

Hometown: New York City. *Family:* Just Kay and me here. Her family is 9000 miles southwest, mine 3000 miles east. *Interests:* Sensory stimulation and intellectual stimulation. *Schools:* Cornell, and more Cornell. *Employment history:* John Deere; Marks & Marks; Joblove/Kay.
[1986 LFL Yearbook]

Joblove and Kay met television graphics pioneer Harry Marks, who had executed some of the first on-air computer graphics for the networks, in particular ABC. Marks was a graphics designer but had an appreciation for the visual style and simulated camera moves that computer-generated imagery could deliver; he was unafraid of new technology and deeply passionate about exploring new territory. He started a company called Novocom to produce on-air promotions, and he hired Joblove and Kay.

Television programs and commercials were all shot, edited, and delivered on film, and so on-air graphics generally had to be made for film as well. "So we became logo pilots," Joblove snickered, "for two years."

When Marks changed directions, as he did periodically throughout his career, Joblove and Kay were cut loose. They got a loan and started their own TV graphics company (set up in a space at Novocom); they were among the earliest groups dedicated to computer graphics in production.

When Ed Catmull reached George Joblove at the end of 1984, he explained the opportunities at ILM.

"I really think you should interview with them," Catmull implored Joblove.

"That's really nice, and we both appreciate it, but you know, we just got our own little company going and we have barely been doing this for two

DOUG KAY

Hometown: Queens, NY.
Family: Beth & I are the only Californians, the rest of our family is in the northeast, but they like to visit. *Interests:* Reading, tennis, movies. *Schools:* Cornell Univ (BS. MS). *Employment history:* Marks & Marks; Joblove/Kay. *[1986 LFL Yearbook]*

years, and we kind of feel like being our own bosses, so thanks very much, but we really like what we're doing."

Ed hung up, dumbfounded. He couldn't remember the last time someone he wanted to bring into the team rejected the idea. It gnawed on him. He called Joblove back.

"Are you crazy?" he unleashed.[12] "Just come for an interview. Just come up and at least talk to them."

Joblove and Kay flew up to the Bay Area and drove out to Kerner. After meeting with Warren Franklin, they figured that maybe they were out of their minds to pass on the opportunity. Industrial Light & Magic was, in fact, the top of the heap and they were going to have unprecedented opportunities under that banner. "They ended up making us an offer, and we accepted it."

George Joblove and Doug Kay joined Lucasfilm around the same time as Norby took over as president. With all the layoffs, it was an odd time to on Kerner, but they were somewhat protected; Lucasfilm was changing its priorities. Putting the Pixar to use at ILM was a priority.

As Joblove and Kay were learning the ropes, Muren supervised the complicated effect, and the Graphics Group began to put together the pieces. David DiFrancesco scanned in the background film images for reference. After consulting with Eric Christiansen, the artist responsible for much of the stained glass at Skywalker Ranch, ILM matte artist Chris Evans painted the character using the computer team's old paint system (the new LayerPaint wasn't quite production-ready). Eben Ostby modeled the stained glass man and Lasseter animated his movements using the animation system initiated by Tom Duff and refined by Ostby and Reeves.[13] Soon Joblove and Kay became the interface between ILM and the Graphics Group.

The Pixar computer was used to composite the animation with the backgrounds. Crossing their fingers, Lucasfilm rendered the complex images back onto film using the laserprinter.[14] The process worked. The system worked. Even though the film was released in 1985 and soon disappeared, the Stained Glass Man became a historic moment in film technology.

By 1985, with the arrival of computers, there was both excitement and fear at ILM. Dennis Muren had been skeptical of the computer's ability to match the quality they routinely achieved, but his confidence was growing.

[12] Commented Catmull, "Actually, I had another adjective before 'crazy' for emphasis, but I wouldn't want that in print."

[13] Also, Bill Reeves and David Salesin did the shading.

[14] The resolution at that point was high, but they determined not as high as the original film, so ultimately they rendered the effect against a black background before scanning to film. ILM composited the elements in their traditional, more comfortable way.

In September, George Lucas told the *Wall Street Journal*, "The movie business turns out to be a miniscule market compared to others we now find ourselves involved with." Referring to the Pixar Image Computer, he went on to say, "It's like we designed this very sophisticated race car capable of doing all sorts of amazing and complex feats on the race track and then come to find out that a huge segment of the population wants to use it to commute to work."

A production still of the Stained Glass Man in the film *Young Sherlock Holmes*.

The only other company interviewed for the *WSJ* was Gary Demos and John Whitney Jr.'s Digital Productions. DP was still hyping its $10 million Cray, trying to keep it busy with whatever graphical work was out there, while Lucas was helping position his Graphics Group for its sale. The Pixar sold for about one-fiftieth the price of a Cray, and could do as much, if not more. DP scoffed at the notion.

There was a chasm between C Building and D Building, and it was wider than the diminutive parking lot. It was a cultural chasm. While the Computer Division felt the friendly disinterest of ILM, ILM felt the defiant independence of the Computer Division.

Observed Joblove, "[ILM could see] that the Graphics Group wanted to go off by themselves without a lot of interaction. I think the perception was 'don't bother us, we're going to do this, and when we're done you're going to love it and it will be great.'"

These feelings always had to be combined with the general attitude people had around computers—that this device was going to change the world. And a lot of people were fearful for their jobs.

Ed and Alvy bumped into Steven Jobs at the 1985 Siggraph conference in San Francisco. Since they had last seen Jobs, he had been removed as CEO by his board of directors, and instead handed the largely ceremonial chairman position. Although he held more than $100 million in Apple stock, he was largely out of the company he had so passionately started. Ed and Alvy weren't sure what the lesson of that experience was.

Lucasfilm was there with T-shirts and a booth showing off its remarkable product, the Pixar Image Computer (although the Dougs forbade them to deliver any goods until the spin-off was completed). The booth was swamped with fans. To those attending the conference, Lucasfilm already represented a bunch of rock stars; for them to have a product was doubly exciting.

Orders for the Pixar Image Computer were beginning to accumulate, but ship dates were "To Be Determined." Catmull dug around to see if Steve Jobs was still interested in the group. "Too expensive," he said. "I'm more in the $10 to $15 million range, and it sounds like Lucasfilm is more than double that," Jobs told Catmull. "If the price drops, let me know."

When Siggraph was over and everyone was back in Marin, Tom Porter poured through his hundred or so cards of prospective customers and began to collate them into groups. The Pixar, after all, was just a piece of hardware that made big images and could process them quickly. For every market that might be interested in the functionality, there would need to be dedicated application software made for the purpose. Every industry would need its own. Having so much opportunity was also a problem.

As Ed and Alvy dealt with investors, circulating their business plan, the feedback they were getting was that the plan was too unfocused.

"While the equipment looked interesting," said Porter, "it was fairly pricey. And while we had nibbles in many different markets, it was unclear that we had the software crew necessary to support going into five or six directions: the high resolution print business, the rendering business, the medical imaging business, the defense department image analysis business. Each one needs its own application development, its own special software."

Left: The stylish Pixar booth at Siggraph 1985, featuring the new Pixar logo that John Lasseter created. *Right:* John Seamons demonstrates the Pixar.

The pressure was on Ed and Alvy to decide which way to push the development.

Periodically, Steven Jobs spoke with Ed and Alvy. Jobs lingered on the periphery of the Lucasfilm negotiations, curious to see if their "outrageous" valuation was going to get real, to see if GM or Philips would really close the deal. But it was only morbid curiosity. By September he was ideating his own next big thing; he assembled the core team that would become NeXT computers. Lawsuits with Apple exploded. Jobs resigned. Everything was in motion.

Doug Norby had to conclude the Graphics Group sale immediately, or simply close it up. His back was against the wall, and it didn't leave Lucasfilm in a very good bargaining position. While Lucasfilm tried to negotiate from a position of strength, anyone close to the story was aware that they weren't going to continue to fund the venture. The high price they demanded may have been a defensible valuation, but the truth was, the Dougs were bluffing.

In November, after months of painful debate, they reached their final stages of negotiations. Each component of the partnership—Lucasfilm, EDS, Philips, and of course Ed and Alvy—met at the penthouse of the Philips offices in New York to close the deal. Philips was perched above 42nd Street, looking out over the rooftop of Grand Central Station. The young turks representing EDS made sure everyone understood that no matter how good the talks went, it wasn't a deal until Ed Catmull and Alvy Ray Smith shook hands with either Ross Perot, or his second in command, Mort Meyerson.

"Just wanted to tell you up front," the young men in sharp suits informed all gathered, "they could come in and blow off the deal at the last minute."

This didn't come as a shock. Before leaving town Ed and Alvy had breakfast with Scott McNealy, CEO of SUN. Having watched SUN evolve from day one, they appreciated Scott's ability to build the business. He had had some dealings with EDS and gave them a word of caution about Perot. Alvy recalled their conversation:

"I just want to warn you guys," McNealy began, "we had a deal that was all but the handshake done. I got in a room with Perot at O'Hare airport as we were both passing through town and he said, 'Are you married?' 'No.' 'Are you from California?' 'Yes.' He looked at my beard, and left. The deal was off."

Both Ed and Alvy had beards and wondered if they should shave. They didn't. "I can't overemphasize this," McNeely urged. The story echoed in their ears as they left for New York.

The representative from Philips, Frank Low, was the oldest man in the room; neatly assembled in a classic-styled European suit, he was gentle and kind. He took Ed and Alvy under his wing during the discussions. He recognized that they were raw beginners in this business world, and he took some pride in guiding them through the negotiations. For months of discussions, and now in a final all-day session, he sat quietly, scribbling notes on 3 × 5 index cards.

Philips made it clear that their interest was in the talent, not simply the technology. Lucasfilm, Alvy felt, didn't seem to understand the concept. In the days before the meeting, Doug Johnson had urged Ed and Alvy to reduce the staff at the division, to justify a lower price tag. They resisted. Management hammered on the issue. Neither he nor Alvy could convince them of their point of view.

An hour before GM arrived for the second day of debate, Alvy exploded at Doug Johnson. "I can't believe the largest company in the world is about to walk in here for a meeting and you are talking about firing our talent rather than preparing strategy for the meeting!" The outburst was received in utter silence, perhaps due to the harshness of the accusation or maybe just because Alvy rarely lost his cool so violently. The other attendees began to arrive and the painfully important day commenced.

"It was one of the most tense meetings I've ever been to in my life," said Alvy. "My head was throbbing with pain. There was so much going on and the stress was so high."

Frank Low, the old gentleman from Philips, after days of virtual silence, sat up, looked at his index cards, and proceeded to unwind his litany of problems with Lucasfilm's position. He had his arguments in a row. He was methodical and calculating. "He cut them off at the knees," recalled Alvy.

There was a coffee break and Alvy wandered over to him and said "Frank, that was beautiful."

Frank turned to him quietly and said, "It's like a ballet, isn't it?"

The teams reconvened; it was the make-or-break moment. Gordy Davidson,[15] the lawyer representing the graphics guys, realized that negotiations were about to stall. EDS and Lucasfilm were at an impasse.

"I watched Gordy reach down inside himself, in the heat of battle, and eek out a slight rewording of the arguments on the table," said Alvy, "and break the logjam."

Alvy leaned over to Ed, "That's the art of these guys…that's what we pay for."

At the end, everybody was nodding "yes." Maybe ten heads bobbing up and down looking around the table at each other. It was a done deal. All that was left was the handshake.[16]

[15] An attorney with a master's degree in electrical engineering, he went on to become the chairman of Fenwick and West, a large legal firm in Palo Alto.

[16] Perot founded Electronic Data Systems (EDS) in 1962 and sold it to General Motors in 1984 for $2.5 billion.

Killing time, Loren devised a liquid nitrogen-powered rocket and a group headed out behind Kerner to launch it. *From left to right, standing:* Craig Good, Loren Carpenter, Rachel Carpenter, Bruce Young, John Seamons, Mark Leather, Jeff Mock. *Front row:* David Johansen, Neftali Alvarez, Lane Molpus.

The next morning, on November 21, 1985, General Motors held a Board of Directors meeting to address, among other things, the $5.2 billion purchase of Hughes Aircraft. Perot was vocal that it was a mistake for GM to spend that money; he attacked CEO Roger Smith and the entire GM Board of Directors, assailing them with public criticism. He later told *Business Week* that "revitalizing General Motors is like teaching an elephant to tap dance."

It was suddenly clear that GM was never going to approve a deal that EDS endorsed. "We had EDS at the table," Norby recalled, "but we didn't have General Motors on the table. We didn't know that until the very end."

As November turned to December, EDS drifted away. And with that, the deal was off.

Lucasfilm had no fallback position. They had played hard, bluffed big, but in the end had nowhere to go when EDS went away. Philips was still interested in the company, but couldn't justify taking the whole thing themselves, even if Lucasfilm would have permitted it. Lucas couldn't have been pleased with the collapse of the deal. As 1985 was drawing to a close, the Dougs were flummoxed to find an alternative.

Bob Drebin *(left)* and Mark Leather working out a demonstration of the Pixar Image Computer's medical visualization features at the RSNA conference around Thanksgiving, 1985.

As the holidays approached, Steve Jobs reached Doug Norby and pitched him. He offered fundamentally the same thing he had offered earlier in the year. This time Norby was receptive and invited Jobs up to hammer out a deal.

Jobs called Lucasfilm as he was driving north on the 280. In the days before, he had offered $5 million. Now, as he was on the road to meet with Doug and he smelled blood, he started pushing for a better deal.

"I'm only coming up if you lower the price," Norby recalls him saying. "So I hung up on him." About an hour later, unsure what would happen next, Norby was notified that Steve Jobs had arrived.

Norby wanted this to be over. The task of selling off the graphics research had been Doug Johnson's responsibility since he arrived at Lucasfilm. Norby had promised himself that the Graphics Group would be sold or closed by year's end. Jobs knew that Lucasfilm wasn't in much of a bargaining position.

"He knew we were desperate," said Norby.

In addition to the sale of the graphics hardware, the Graphics Group wanted all rights to the short films and projects they had done to demonstrate their capabilities. They wanted "The Road to Pt. Reyes." They wanted *Andre and Wally B.* And they wanted the project, currently in production, that John called *Luxo Jr.* Lucasfilm agreed to joint ownership of the old productions. Lucasfilm wanted to get the technical developments the group would create, for some years to come, and wanted them to help set up ILM to continue with graphic research, but on a production-by-production basis.

The scientists and Jobs accepted.

Jobs was concerned about competing with Lucasfilm at some point, which was perhaps the biggest potential snag. After long hours on the phone the two parties came to an agreement. Purchasing the hardware company was a good-but-risky deal for Jobs and badly needed closure for Lucasfilm.

Soon after everyone was back from the New Year's holiday, Ed and Alvy went to George to say goodbye. The deal was all but done. George was somber but encouraging. "I think he was disappointed that we couldn't stay on at the company," observed Alvy, "maybe a little irked that someone else might get credit for what he had created." That same evening there was a little party at Steve Job's place, a celebration.

On January 30, 1986, Lucasfilm and Jobs formalized the documents, and the Graphics Group in its entirety—people, hardware and software, films and history—became its own company, sold by Lucasfilm and purchased by Steve Jobs and "the employees," of which there were forty. Signed by Ed Catmull and Alvy Ray Smith.[17]

They called the new company Pixar.

[17] Documenets were signed on the 30th, and the closing was on Feb. 3, 1986.

LUCASFILM LTD

INTER-OFFICE MEMO

To: All Employees

From: Doug Norby *Doug*

Date: February 7, 1986

Re: Pixar

As you have probably heard, Pixar, the Computer Graphics Division
of Lucasfilm Ltd., has just been sold to Steven Jobs. Jobs will
have the majority interest in the firm, and Pixar employees will
own the remaining shares. Ed Catmull and Alvy Ray Smith will
join Jobs on the Pixar board of directors.

George originally formed the Computer Division and Pixar in 1979
to bring high technology to the film industry. Although Pixar
has been sold, the company will continue to use the Pixar Image
Computer and other technologies to produce computer animation for
films through ILM, and for home entertainment through the Games
Group.

We originally funded Pixar to create images for our movies. The
most recent example of the success of the endeavor is the
"Stained Glass" sequence in YOUNG SHERLOCK HOLMES, a combination
of Pixar and ILM skills. During the development of Pixar, we
discovered that it had many additional commercial benefits, such
as medical imaging, seismic imaging, graphic arts, remote
sensing, etc. We decided to sell Pixar to Jobs so that these
different markets can be commercially pursued. Our company
retains the rights to all technology developed to date by Pixar
so that we will continue to use it in making movies and video
games.

Please join me in wishing good luck to our Pixar colleagues in
pursuing their new endeavor.

twenty-four

Stay Small, Be the Best, Don't Lose Any Money

[1985]

You are in a twisty maze of passageways, all alike.

—Ominous message from the game
Adventure, by Will Crowther.

AFTER DOUG NORBY ARRIVED, all the company divisions were expected to become self-sufficient. This included the little games group, squirreled away from the chaos swirling around the Computer Division, ever keeping their heads down. While Norby played no leadership role in the direction of Games, it was obvious that the era of research was on the wane; the forward-thinking work on game interactivity now needed to be balanced with a market-driven practicality.

Norby wasn't alone in his hands-off approach to the group. Although George Lucas received weekly reports from all department heads, he mostly left Games to its own devices. When he did have advice for Steve Arnold it was pretty simple: "Stay small, be the best, and don't lose any money." This became a mantra for the boys.

Corporate R&D is generally about investing in research with some future expectation of a return on that investment. But Lucasfilm's Games Group was established the other way around, like a licensing deal, with outside money from Atari. Under Norby, that strategy was expanded—outside partnerships were a great way to finance research projects in the dangerously undercapitalized company.

That degree of risk aversion would have killed most companies. But Lucasfilm existed in a strange kind of bubble that made it different from other companies, especially those in the computer games industry. Because of the phenomenal success of the *Star Wars* and *Indiana Jones* franchises, as well as the reputation of the Computer Division, the company had enormous brand clout. In much the same way that Lucasfilm drove a ball-crushing deal to get Paramount to finance *Raiders of the Lost Ark*, Chip Morningstar said that "the expectation was that people would pay us to do things, and then we would take a share of the profits of whatever resulted."

Companies were lining up to make deals with the Lucasfilm Games Division. Steve Arnold began meeting with not only games distribution companies, but a variety of other organizations that wanted to tap into the brand sex appeal and technological savvy Lucasfilm possessed: RCA, Apple, Philips, IBM, the National Geographic Society, Fujitsu, to name just a few.

Games kept pretty much to themselves in E Building, sequestered from the graphics, editing, and sound projects, although staff from all over the company popped in to play *Centipede, Indiana Jones,* or *Star Wars* in the Atari arcade. In late 1984, the group moved across Bellam Boulevard to Z Building, the newest member of the Kerner complex, where they joined The Droid Works.[1] The arcade went with them.

Games took over the ground floor while The Droid Works filled in above. There was free movement up and down the connecting staircases, but few made the journey. A tenant occupied the top floor, a chiropractor who no one ever saw or heard, and yet his oversized sign clung to the windows along the third floor.

As soon as the Games Division was situated in Z Building, they started to form sub-groups. Most of the team worked on games production, but George Lucas had made it clear he wasn't particularly into videogames. While he was always interested in making *successful* videogames, and having the Games Division operate profitably, he was far more curious about the kinds of inter-activity that games represented, methodology that could be applied to either entertainment (as in games) or education. Steve Arnold's own interests were also in education, and the ability of the division to explore new learning models became his pet project.

Lucas had also become convinced that videogames and movies would someday merge in many respects, evolving into a new form of interactive entertainment as the technology got more sophisticated. The two would have overlapping kinds of user experiences, with increasingly similar image and sound fidelity, and most importantly, similar elements used in their creation and tools used for their production. Steve Arnold was given free reign to explore multimedia in all its evolving forms.

As Steve described it, "How can we invent new storytelling that makes it more fun to play these games, without really inventing new technology?"

[1] Kerner lobbies and offices were decorated with artwork from the films: ILM had big matte paintings of Endor and Hoth; Administration had the "real" Yoda under a glass dome sitting near reception; Z Building was mostly decorated with movie posters, nicely framed.

The Games Division operated very low on the radar, with small profits (or in some quarters, small losses). Lucasfilm continued to support the development of the first couple of Epyx games while Steve Arnold got his bearings.

By the end of 1984, Steve set up a multimedia group to focus on special educational projects, the beginning of what he called "Lucasfilm Learning." Central to these projects was Douglas Crockford, who had spent several years working for Atari corporate research (the team set up in early 1982 by Alan Kay). His job focused on all aspects of interactive entertainment: music, computer graphics, and games.

When Tramiel took over Atari and closed the research group, Crockford became a free agent. Steve Arnold interviewed him soon after, but Doug wasn't interested in what looked like a short-term project. After a few months of looking around, Crockford found a disquieting trend.

"Nobody was interested in what I had been doing at Atari; it was like I had been on vacation for two years." He took what he called a "serious job" with National Semiconductor, but knew immediately it was the wrong direction.

A month later, he called Lucasfilm back. "Steve, I made a terrible mistake…."

Doug Crockford slid into an office with artist Gary Winnick and began fishing around for work, since it wasn't particularly clear what he'd be doing.

"I was going to be in the games group," he said, "so I figured I'd be doing something about the technology behind games." He began by helping to get projects in process out the door; he wrote the theme song for Noah's game. It would be months before the right partner came along to galvanize Crockford's interactive interests.

DOUG CROCKFORD

Hometown: Buffalo, MN. *Family:* Daughter, Jane. *Schools:* SF State U. Experience: There and back again, and lived to tell the tale. *Interests:* Dog and pony shows.
[1986 LFL Yearbook]

Lucasfilm Ltd. was creating a new Production Division, with plans to produce five films per year. The Ranch had been designed to support this flow, and the little cottages that surrounded the Main House—the Carriage House, the Brook House, and the others—were intended to house the team on each film as it passed from pre-production to post. It was expected that when the Tech Building came online the following year, projects would move through the facility using the time-and-money-saving tools that The Droid Works was developing—the EditDroid and the SoundDroid.

The Production Division's first production was *Labyrinth*, a film co-produced by Jim Henson's company, directed by Henson, and staring David Bowie and Jennifer Connelly, in her debut starring role.

Lucas had been working with Gloria Katz and Willard Huyck on one of his pet projects, *Radioland Murders*, for a long time.[2] The Huycks were George's old friends who had saved the *American Graffiti* script and who had risen to his support many times over the years. A few years earlier, Lucas mentioned how much he enjoyed the noirish *Howard the Duck* comic books. "I think you

[2] Gloria and Willard were married. Though they had different last names, they were often referred to as "the Huycks."

guys would really like this because you have a weird sense of humor," Lucas said, as he passed a few issues over to them. They were indeed interested, but the rights were unattainable. In 1984, the rights surfaced and Willard called Lucas, "Listen. We can do *Howard*."

It would become the next project at the Division.[3]

Universal was interested in the film—they had noted the success of *Ghostbusters* (1984*)*—and pushed the Huycks to make a comedy-fantasy rather than the small realistic film noir they had envisioned.

"Actually, the story was much more like *Roger Rabbit* (1988)," said Willard. Lucas wanted to help the Huycks bring their film to the screen; he became a sponsor, much as he had been on Kasdan's *Body Heat*, although this time Lucasfilm was going to work on the effects, the sound, and would attach its name to the project. If anyone could bring a comic book to life, Lucasfilm could.

Production was also creating two half-hour animated Saturday morning programs; one based on Lucas' "ever-lovable" Droids, R2D2 and C-3PO, and a second based on the Ewoks. Two live-action specials were also planned, also based on the Ewoks. Tom Smith stepped down from the management of ILM to produce the first Ewok special, a two-hour television movie, with John Korty set up to direct.

Lucas used his market clout to help other friends get their projects executed. Lucasfilm didn't have the capital to finance films, but Lucas could do for Walter Murch, Haskell Wexler, and Paul Schrader[4] exactly what Coppola did for him on *THX 1138* and *Graffiti*—lend his name.

Every division across the Kerner landscape was busy with its own frenetic deadlines. ILM was looking for the right moment to begin utilizing the barely-tested power of the Pixar Image Computer on a production deadline. Ed and Alvy declared the Pixar was ready. Dennis Muren at ILM kept its capabilities in mind as he reviewed each effect shot from every film, wondering what would be the right moment to test it out.

They were preparing to crank through an unprecedented slate of films: *Starman, Cocoon, Back to the Future, Goonies, Explorers, Young Sherlock Holmes,* and just a little further down the pipeline was *Howard the Duck, The Golden Child,* and *Star Trek IV*. And if that wasn't enough, ILM was in discussions to execute two unusual projects for Disney—the simulator ride film *Star Tours,* and the 3-D 70mm Michael Jackson music video, *Captain Eo.*

Walter Murch agreed to spend some time at Kerner editing *Captain Eo.* While doing a music video didn't have any special appeal for him, the project was technically innovative, and that *was* something he liked. *Captain Eo* was not only being shot in 70mm—relatively unusual—and edited in 70mm—a little more unusual—but it was shot with a special 3-D camera that had two

[3] In early 1986 Lucas hired a new vice-president for the Production Division, Charlie Maguire. Maguire was a cuddly bulldog from Hollywood who had risen from associate producer to producer in the '60s and '70s; his movies included *Shampoo* and *Heaven Can Wait*.

[4] **Paul Schrader** (b. 1946). Writer: *Taxi Driver* (1976), *Blue Collar* (1978), *American Gigolo* (1980), *Raging Bull* (1980), *Mishima* (1985), *Mosquito Coast* (1986), *Last Temptation of Christ* (1988); Director: *Mishima, Auto Focus* (2002).

lenses and two magazines of 70mm film. With a left eye reel and a right eye reel, the film had to be edited in unusual ways. Murch worked on *Eo* at Sprockets, even as other old friends were coming and going from the facility.

With The Droid Works across the street now, C Building was left to Sprockets and to the Graphics Group. Like ILM, Sprockets was jammed with outside sound work—*The Legend of Billie Jean, Fletch, Mishima, Latino, Cocoon* and the Imax film, *The Dream is Alive*.[5]

Throughout 1985, there were company screenings in Corte Madera and in C Building, new T-shirts, and a constant flow of Hollywood personalities on Kerner to get their head molded with plaster, shoot some blue screen effect, or re-record some line of dialog: Lea Thompson, River Phoenix, Eddie Murphy, Leonard Nimoy....

There was tremendous job opportunity in the cash-starved company as it tried to expand. Lucasfilm had a tradition of hiring locals as well as promoting from within. Lori and Kim Nelson, sisters who were receptionists at ILM, moved into the optical department and then to effects supervision. Craig Good started with the janitorial staff and eventually wrote software and supervised post-production with the Graphics Group. Jim Kessler, who started by setting up the editing tables at Parkway, ran Sprockets and then the THX program. Every division was full of secretaries who were making films, assistants who had eventually replaced their bosses, and managers who moved into company executive suites. It was an honorable tradition within the company and it added to the familial vibe that was part of Lucasfilm culture.

An employee's length of time with the company was a badge of respect— anyone who had been there before *Jedi*, pretty cool; before *Empire*, amazing; before *Star Wars*, a bwana. The company yearbook, another nod to the youthful and familial organization, was handed out at the 4th of July picnic every summer since 1982. Along with reports on each division, party, film production and company expedition, the roster of employee photos and captions typically announced "At Lucasfilm since..."

Noah Falstein was looking for someone to port the existing Lucasfilm games to the Commodore 64. He found Ron Gilbert, a college dropout with a gift for videogames. Gilbert had already been moving games to the C64 when the company he worked for went out of business; Noah brought him in to start working on a C64 version of *Koronis Rift*. Steve Arnold liked him because he was not only incredibly talented but pleasantly inexpensive to hire; Noah liked him because he was darkly funny and a remarkably good programmer.

[5] Jim Kessler also agreed to have Sprockets do a small test project for an automobile manufacturer, to have some of his more junior guys try to invent more expressive car sounds that would alert the driver to various internal states: a variety of beeps and chirps that would be made when the car door was left ajar, when a light was on, when the trunk was unlatched.

RON GILBERT

Hometown: La Grande, OR.
Schools: Eastern Oregon State
College. *Experience:* Human
Engineered Software.
Favorite Book: The Body
Language of Sex, Power and
Aggression. *Interests:* cooking
with sushi, barbequed steak
tartar, searching for the
perfect bimbi.
[From 1985 & 1987 LFL Yearbooks]

As the games developers continued to amass in Z Building, Steve Arnold began to implement new protocols for game design. Rather than have some of the team design while others did programming or porting, everyone was encouraged to come up with new ideas and present them to the entire group for critical discussion.

"You could always plan on a couple game designs, little one-pagers, crossing your desk every week. From somebody. It was so creatively energizing," recalled Gilbert. "It wasn't like someone said, 'Hey, I really want to make this game'; it was like, 'Oh, I had a really dumb idea in the shower today, so I'm going to write it up as a one-pager.' People would pass it around, you'd read it; it was just neat. And so I did that."

Gilbert was inspired mostly by the text adventure games he had played, the kind where he typed a command such as "walk east" or "grab sword" and the computer would parse the text, figure out the verb and the object, and then return some new fact or your status.

Zork was typical of the classic text adventure game. "[Adventure games] were kinda frustrating," remarked Gilbert with his typical sardonic wit, "because I don't like to read. But then I saw a quasi-graphic text adventure game called *King's Quest*. It was an odd and novel mix of text strings—players still typed instructions—but there was a little graphical character on the screen who responded to the commands. Something clicked in my head. The first thing I wanted to do was get rid of the text part."

Ron's first one-pager was just such an adventure game. He called it "I Was a Teenage Lobot."[6] It amused the team. "Pure gold," he said with a smirk. It was never developed.[7] And like most of the game proposals circulated, it ended up in Steve Arnold's ideas file.

The Games Group was working on two fronts. Traditional computer games (home games), were developed by small teams and funded either from the groups' internal budget, or as development deals (the way most movies are done), with money coming from an outside partner. The second front was educational in nature, multimedia in format. These were almost always funded from the outside. Steve Arnold kept the fires going in all directions.

In the design of games, it was a rule that the group was absolutely forbidden from using the company's film properties, especially *Star Wars*. That was viewed as the same thing as spending Lucasfilm money, since these properties were, in effect, money in the bank. When Atari wanted to make a *Star Wars* game, they had to pay a hefty license fee, and so Lucasfilm made money no matter how well or how poorly their game did. If Lucasfilm had chosen to make a *Star Wars* game itself, then it would have been taking all the risk.

---

[6] It took place in a world where robotics was secretly discovered to be a dead-end innovation. Rather than scrap it, malevolent scientists captured people, gave them lobotomies, and inserted them into robot shells, pretending they were machines.

[7] Neither was his follow-up, "Electric Croquet."

A few times each month, companies would knock on Steve Arnold's door, looking to do business with him. Sometimes they had a specific project in mind, but more often they just had a vague idea or two and probably thought it would be cool to visit Lucasfilm—see the movie production facilities, maybe get a glimpse of George or some other famous person (the role of glamour can't be overstated). In the course of schmoozing with these folks, Steve would make a judgment as to whether they were serious prospects, and if so, he'd grab a couple of ideas from the file where he kept all the game proposals his team had developed. If one of these seemed related to what the prospective partner was interested in, Steve would connect his staff with the partner and they'd all have a meeting.

One of the companies that came knocking was RCA Labs, from Princeton, New Jersey. RCA was developing a compressed digital video and audio system for delivery with their new compact disc format, and they wanted a new entertainment platform based on it. Steve Arnold dropped this on Doug Crockford, and in short order Doug began hopping to New Jersey to initiate the project.

Chip Morningstar and Noah Falstein shared an office in the plush new Z Building. Chip worked on software tools while Noah pounded away on *Koronis Rift*. They were both interested in the generation of more powerful personal computers (based on the Motorola 68000 16-bit processor) that were springing up; these included Apple's newly released Macintosh,[8] the soon-to-ship Amiga, and the highly anticipated experimental format from Philips called CD-I. The labs upstairs at The Droid Works were focused on the computational power of the 68000 CPU, but Noah and Chip were more interested in the increasing number of consumers with modems.

Consumer technology, it seemed, had matured to where it seemed feasible to connect a modem and utilize a network. Noah and Chip came up with a pair of proposals: one they called *Lucasnet* (an early version of a games portal), and one they called the *Lucasfilm Games Alliance* (an early version of a MMORPG).[9] The Lucasnet proposal began:

> *"Picture, if you will, a network, an intricate web of knots and threads spanning thousands of miles. The knots are machines, made of silicon, metal and plastic. The threads are metal wires. It is a computer network. The machines are computers, sitting in homes, schools, and offices across the continent. The wires are telephone lines, tying the hundreds upon hundreds of individual processors into a single, unified whole. At each of these machines sit people. People of all kinds and all ages…they experience the signs and sounds of that which exists only in the wholeness of the web, and in their own minds."*

[8] Launched with the famous 1984 commercial during that years' Superbowl.

[9] Massively Multiplayer Online Role-Playing Games, which then looked in concept a lot like what *Star Wars Galaxies* turned out to be, 20 years later.

Included were a series of innovative game goals: to be open-ended, to be low-cost to play, to distribute the processing to the home machine, and to support different levels of player interest and ability.

The proposal went through the usual process of discussion and revision, got expanded (and retitled *Lucasfilm's Universe*), and then found its way into Steve Arnold's idea file along with the rest.

"And that was the last of it," recalled Chip, "aside from periodic bouts of wistful speculation about just what a fun project it would be if only we could find somebody to fund it."

Then Clive Smith came along.

In 1985, the Commodore 64 was the king of consumer-level machines and Commodore International was riding high, though competition from Apple and IBM was on the rise.[10] Clive Smith, the vice president for strategic planning, joined Commodore as Tramiel was exiting. Among his first initiatives was the purchasing of personal computer maker, Amiga.

The talent behind the first Amiga computer—code-named Lorraine—were the same folks who had developed the Atari 2600, 400 and 800.[11] Silicon Valley rumor was that Amiga had been set up as a separate company because it was impossible to get anything done within Atari's dysfunctional confines; but once the machine was ready, Atari would buy back in. It was also rumored that when Tramiel purchased Atari, he had incorrectly thought that he was getting some part of Amiga as well. He was unhappy to learn this was not the case and instigated bitter competition and occasional lawsuits.

Every year, Commodore came up with some accessory to sell to its Commodore 64 owners. One year it was inexpensive printers, another year floppy disk drives, and in 1985 it was going to be a cheap 300-baud modem.

As part of this initiative, Smith had Commodore make a large investment in an up-and-coming, consumer-oriented online services company called Quantum Computer Services, which ran a service called QuantumLink (Q-Link, for short). At the time, QuantumLink was designed exclusively for the Commodore 64. Q-Link was launched as an early bulletin board service (BBS), but included a graphical interface on top of basic messaging and games.[12]

Clive Smith was one of the unsolicited knocks on Steve Arnold's door. Smith was shopping for two kinds of projects: things that could leverage modems plus an online service, and things that could leverage the Amiga. Miraculously, out of the file came two solid ideas: first, the *Lucasfilm's Universe* proposal, and second, one of David Fox's proposals for an Amiga-based space game that he called "The Starbound Saga." Fox's "interactive entertainment experience"[13] had a multi-part story that would run through game episodes.

[10] The Commodore 64 came with 1MHz 8-bit CPU and 64K of memory (about half of which was busy with the screen buffer). A personal computer in 2006 is approximately 20,000 times faster, has 80,000 times as much memory, three million times as much disk space, and has a network connection about 5,000 times faster. There's also a separate special purpose processor for rendering 3-D graphics onto the screen.

[11] In particular, Jay Miner.

[12] The company initially offered a service that foreshadowed online software delivery. Using a device that plugged into the Atari 2600 and a telephone line, the service downloaded games on a pay-per-play basis. Unfortunately, it was launched just as the first wave of home video gaming was coming to an end, and the company transformed itself into Quantum Computer Services in 1985.

[13] A term not widely used at that time.

"Steve grabbed David and me, and off to the conference room we went to meet with Clive," said Chip Morningstar. "We made our pitch, and Clive loved both proposals." However, they experienced very different fates.

Commodore wanted Lucasfilm to develop Fox's "Starbound" for them, but their concept of the deal, according to Morningstar, "seemed to consist of us developing the game and them being thrilled."

While the Amiga game was unable to get traction, the work with Quantum Computer Services continued to move forward. Clive made the initial introductions to Quantum in the summer of 1985. In spite of Commodore's large ownership position, Quantum functioned independently and it had considerably more of an entrepreneurial attitude than Commodore did. With a promising plan, Steve Arnold asked Chip Morningstar to prepare a pitch.

"I started thinking about open-ended virtual worlds, though we didn't have the vocabulary to talk about it then (which made the whole process much more difficult), and the design immediately started moving away from the kind of "outer space/conquer the galaxy" kind of fantasy that Noah and I had originally discussed. It was clear that a lot of the experience QuantumLink was delivering to its customers lay purely in the social dimension—people interacting with other people."

Chip wanted to appeal to people outside the hard-core gamer demographic, which at that time was still primarily adolescent males, and try instead to appeal to the more mainstream, non-gamer population who used Q-Link. So the design became much more generic. Said Morningstar, "We ended up with a world that looked kind of funky and suburban, rather than something based on science fiction."

Chip Morningstar, 1985

At the same time, Quantum also contracted with a company called P.F. Magic to develop some games that users could play on the Internet.[14] The result was a set of home "gambling" games called *Rabbit Jack's Casino*.

The Commodore and QuantumLink people were visibly enthusiastic about the prospect of working with Lucasfilm; but as Chip explained the details of his project, most faces went blank. Chip wanted to make a virtual world where many players could have characters they controlled. He coined the term "avatars" for these online personalities. Nobody really had a clue what he was talking about when he tried to explain what the thing was supposed to be.

"Actually," said Chip, "most of the people at Lucasfilm pretty much didn't have a clue either."

At Steve's suggestion, Chip wrote a number of "day in the life" scenarios, to help people who had never seen anything like this imagine what the experience might be like, and Gary Winnick drew lots of storyboards to visualize them.

QuantumLink was the first major online service that was tailored for the consumer market. Although other services got some of their paying user-hours from consumers, the customers they really cared about were businesses, which they viewed as more serious and more profitable.

In 1985 Quantum had about 50,000 subscribers; their main competitors were CompuServe, GEnie, and Trintex.[15] Modems were slow—300 baud with high-end users at 1200—and allowed for little more than small strings of text to flow over the phone lines. People did messaging. There were some community forums.

The 800-pound gorilla in this industry was CompuServe, which in 1985 charged a hefty $20.00/hour during "prime time" (basically, during normal business hours) and $12.00/hour "off peak" (evenings and weekends). In contrast, QuantumLink charged $3.60/hour on evenings and weekends and wasn't available during the workday.

All summer, Lucasfilm was beginning to enjoy the fruits of everyone's labor. There were company screenings of Walter Murch's directorial debut, *Return to Oz*, screenings of Robert Zemeckis and Bob Gale's *Back to the Future* (produced by Spielberg), and the smaller film, *Explorers*, directed by Joe Dante (who had just done *Gremlins* with Spielberg) and for which ILM did the effects.

Steven Spielberg was on the cover of *Time* magazine (George, Francis, and Michael Jackson were also in a short *Time* blurb on *Captain Eo*). Even the

[14] "P.F. Magic" reportedly stood for "Pure Fucking Magic," the brainchild of ex-Atari programmer Rob Fulop. Fulop started P.F. Magic after leaving iMagic in the games crash of 1984. It was later purchased by Ubi-Soft, which in 2000 acquired the publishing rights for the *Myst* series of adventure games.

[15] Trintex: a joint venture in 1984 of CBS, IBM and Sears. In 1986, CBS dropped out, and the venture launched Prodigy—a more graphically-oriented online service—in 1988.

Computer Division's Graphics Group was featured in *Time* after their impressive showing at the summer Siggraph conference in San Francisco. ILM hosted an open house showcasing all the models and matte paintings they had completed over the last season, especially all the sets and costumes for the second Ewoks television movie.

On July 27, Lucasfilm announced that the Main House, the centerpiece of Skywalker Ranch, was completed. There was still considerable landscaping ahead, and the other buildings were still being finished, but George's new offices and the company's top executive headquarters were ready for its debut. Employees throughout the company could sign up (with *one* member of their immediate family) for a tour of the spectacular structure.

    The company memo rather ominously read: "This will be the only opportunity for Lucasfilm employees and for those who contributed so much to the design and construction of the Ranch to see the Main House before it is completed. There will be no tours once it is occupied."[16]

    As the Ranch was nearing occupancy, the Marin *Independent Journal* ran a week-long series of front-page features on Lucasfilm. It had been two years since the release of *Return of the Jedi*, and the general public was increasingly curious about what Lucas was up to.

[16] Which wasn't actually true: years later employees often took their families and very good friends to the Ranch and had lunch and a little wander through the Main House.

The Old Gang. *From left:* Lucas, Dalva, Robbins, Barwood, and Murch, in the newly finished Ranch solarium, adjacent to the library.

By mid-year, Doug Crockford was still developing his project with RCA, which he called "CompressoVision."[17] He was often back east and typically on his own. RCA saw the new entertainment concept as "interactive movies" and Lucasfilm seemed an ideal partner. But like the rest of the entertainment and technology world, RCA had little idea what an interactive movie was. The prevailing wisdom was that it would be somehow just like a videogame, but on a big screen or something. Crockford knew that their thinking was not feasible.

In the fall, RCA announced a conference to be held in New Jersey at year's end. Crockford planned to use the event to demonstrate that a movie and a videogame are fundamentally not similar, in spite of whatever creative elements they share. In a video game, you get blown up from time to time, and just start again or get another "life." A movie is passive, where the audience is taken on a ride created by the filmmaker.

"I wanted to show them in cinematic terms what the consequences of that were. That once you got that invested in the characters and situation, it's intolerable to get blown up."

He got a laserdisc of *Star Wars*, and with the EditDroid and the in-house Droid expert, re-cut scenes of the movie so that periodically, when Luke Skywalker was in danger, he'd get blown up.

One of the short clips he made from *Star Wars* looked like this:

> *R2D2 and C-3PO enter an escape pod. The Imperial bad guys watch the pod drift off.*
>
> *"Hold your fire. There are no life forms. It must have short circuited…."*
>
> *New dialog: "Oops."*
>
> *A Turbo Laser fires. The escape pod falls towards Tatooine, then explodes, hit by the laser blast.*
>
> *The end credits and music begins. "Written and directed by George Lucas."*

"A lot of my work," said Crockford, "was dealing with the conflict between predestination and free will. Giving you just enough free will that you feel like you're participating, and getting the depth of participation without allowing you to screw up the story."

Crockford flew to Princeton with Steve Arnold to make the presentation. While Crockford outlined his ideas about interactive movies and showed the re-cut *Star Wars* for dramatic effect, Steve Arnold got a stack of messages that Lucasfilm headquarters was trying to reach him. Something about the negotiations with Steve Jobs for Pixar.

[17] RCA's product was called "CDAV," Compressed Digital Audio/Video. RCA first showed it at Microsoft's CD-ROM conference in Seattle, 1987. By then the name had changed to DVI (Digital Video Interactive). Crockford described the event: "They showed a video of a woman waterskiing. It got a huge reaction for two reasons. First, the nerds had not seen video coming off of a CD before, and that was a big deal. Second, the color fidelity wasn't very good, so the skiier's suit seemed to disappear." The DVI technology was sold to Intel in 1988.

There had been a small snag in the discussions, and Lucasfilm CFO Doug Johnson needed Steve to try to work things out. Apparently Jobs was concerned about Lucasfilm competing with some of Pixar's potential markets—ILM in special effects and the Games Division in interactive entertainment. Johnson told Arnold that if he wanted to save his business, he had to get involved.

Sitting on the phone with Doug, he spent the first evening of the conference in a hotel room, brainstorming ways to describe their business for Jobs in such a way as to ameliorate his concerns. In the evenings Steve and Crockford would discuss the Jobs situation and work on the wording of various sentences from the contract.

"At one point," recalled Crockford, "I described our group as 'purveyors of fine slogans and buzzwords,' which Steve Arnold liked." Arnold worked through the days and in the end, Jobs relented; the Games Division was spared any fallout from the Pixar sale.

The presentation at RCA was a landmark in the growing connection between movies and games. But RCA decided to shut down the project even before it began. Videodiscs were not succeeding in the consumer market as they had anticipated, and after decades of accumulating corporate problems, they were struggling. Soon after the termination, RCA was purchased by General Electric, and then sold again to the European electronics conglomerate, Thompson.[18]

The Lucasfilm *Universe* project with Commodore and Quantum was still moving happily forward, and it seemed likely that Lucasfilm would close on the deal to start development. The project was renamed (again); it was now called *MicroCosm*.[19] Finally, in early October, Steve Arnold and Chip Morningstar flew out to Virginia for a big nail-it-all-down meeting with Quantum. The teams assembled in a big conference room: Steve Arnold, Chip Morningstar, Clive Smith from Commodore, and some of Quantum's business and legal folks, notably their CEO, Jim Kimsey, and their head of marketing, Steve Case.

"The meeting was supposed to be a formality," said Chip, "where management on both sides blesses the deal, they shake hands, and off we go." All that remained was for the business people to agree to the terms and for the lawyers to work out the details of the contract.

But this didn't happen. There was a clash of corporate cultures, between lawyers mostly, and by the end of the first day the deal was virtually dead. After an informal dinner between the players—sans lawyers—they resuscitated the plan and came to a handshake agreement. The next day the Lucasfilm team returned to California.

[18] With only Zenith left from the old dominating TV companies, it was the beginning of the end of American-based television manufacturers.

[19] A nice play on words, as the personal computers of the day were still often referred to as "micro-computers"–the same root as Gate's MicroSoft.

"Once we returned to Marin, Lucasfilm's lawyers got into the act," recalled Morningstar. "One thing I could always say with supreme confidence while working at Lucasfilm was this: *my lawyer can beat up your lawyer*. Lucasfilm doesn't have lawyers, it has legal ninjas—demons and wizards of the bar, each one utterly lacking in mercy."

Lucasfilm's lawyers contacted Quantum's lawyers, and a contract started taking shape. They worked on the contract through October. And through November. And through December.

It didn't help that the lawyers discovered a trademark issue with the name *MicroCosm*. Steve Arnold met with Chip and the group and they began to brainstorm yet again, for the fourth and, they hoped, final title for the project. They settled on *Habitat*.

In early 1986, there was a big debut party for *Habitat*, held at the classic "me-decade" club, the Palladium, in New York City. After a press conference to announce the new product, Lucasfilm set up a dozen demo stations around the dance floor where conference attendees could play at the private reception. As the evening went on, the doors to the club were thrown open to the public—as Chip described them, "mostly over-moneyed, style-conscious, deeply superficial young fashionistas." As the dancing began, it became increasingly difficult to give demonstrations, and the computer geeks stood out in stark contrast to the Wallstreeters who filled the club.

"It was quite an anomaly to have this essentially hip nightclub where people dressed in black…and then all these computer geeks showing off their multiplayer computer games," said Steve Arnold. "It was a little bit of a mismatch between PR positioning and target audience."

A frame from Lucasfilm's *Habitat*, the prototype of the first MMORPG.

When Lucasfilm and Quantum did their first beta test for *Habitat*, they had 500 disks, 500 players. The audience went nuts for the game; they loved the compelling and immersive world. Much to Quantum's joy, users spent hours online, rooting around and mingling. Analysis showed that the test audience amounted to one percent of the total traffic on Quantum's network for one month (this was more significant than *Rabbit Jack's Casino*, where the estimated 15,000 people who frequently played the game accounted for about three percent).

But what began as joy turned sour; Quantum decided that *Habitat* was *too* popular, and too load-heavy. If the test scaled up, 15,000 *Habitat* players would subsume 30 percent of the computer's capabilities, ten times as demanding as Quantum's next best game. Their system would quickly max out.

In spite of what appeared to be a hugely successful demonstration, Quantum decided not to roll it out as a commercial service. They reported that their server software wasn't very efficient, and it would take on the order of months to try to improve it. In its current form, the game would wreak havoc with their pricing methods; they would loose money on every hour of *Habitat* they delivered.

Chip Morningstar was skeptical. "Quantum's protestations about the inefficiency of the server software were a bit disingenuous. Actually, the server was pretty efficient and what performance issues that it had were easily addressed. Their problem was that they were scared of the marketing risk and of the support and administration costs that might be involved."

Said Steve Arnold, "It would have been a huge success—in terms of customer acceptance, customer adoption, but for Quantum, they felt it would have been a disaster in terms of economics."

In 1989, Quantum changed its name to America Online.

twenty-five

Into the Twilight Zone

[1985]

There's a wide difference between completing an invention and putting the manufactured article on the market.

—Thomas Edison

THE LUCASFILM COMPUTER DIVISION was no more. Pixar was its own business. Games had become a unique division at Lucasfilm. The post-production tools were now embodied in a start-up company, The Droid Works (TDW). With little fanfare, a remarkable era was over.

The Droid Works staff was conflicted. On one hand there was the excitement of being part of something new, something growing. The opportunity was huge. No Lucasfilm division had ever spun off before, and the pedigree seemed to anoint them with guaranteed success.

The employees of TDW immediately signed up for a stock option plan, one of the perks Bob Doris insisted be part of the deal. Employees at Lucasfilm-proper eyed the situation with envy: the Droid workers got to participate in the success of the company! If LFL employees were able to have stock in the films, they would be rich many times over. It didn't seem fair. Lucasfilm staff got T-shirts and generous bonuses after each *Star Wars* film release, but those were now over—it seemed like The Droid Works got the better end of the deal.

On the other hand, they were no longer part of the "family." Their email was suddenly separated from Lucasfilm's. Announcements sent "to the company" didn't seem to make it to the second floor of Z Building. There was rumor that TDW employees wouldn't get invited to the company picnic, Christmas party, or even be in the yearbook. There was separation anxiety.

And yet, they were still on Kerner, looking out their windows at A Building or the same hills they used to see from C. It was easy to hook up with friends for sushi at Yu Shang or grab a sandwich at La Croissant. The old Computer Division still gathered for soccer in the fields behind Kerner, or ultimate Frisbee face-off on weekends in Golden Gate Park. But something intangible had shifted.

Rob Lay and Andy Moorer got to be "vice presidents" of The Droid Works, which seemed like a promotion from their role as Lucasfilm "managers." Bob Doris was the president and CEO of the new company, and he had great ambitions for the venture. And even though TDW was independent, Gary Beeson from Convergence (the strategic partner in the company) and Doug Johnson from Lucasfilm, were both on the board of directors.

Before the EditDroid debut at NAB, there had been only the boring establishment—film cut on Moviolas and video cut with CMX-style keyboards. Doris knew that the EditDroid was revolutionary, and that their primary obstacle was the fundamental inertia of the film and television industries. After NAB, Bob Doris became acutely aware of the competition—something that had previously held little importance. But with the Montage working in New York (and arriving in Los Angeles any day), maybe he needed to rethink the battlefronts.

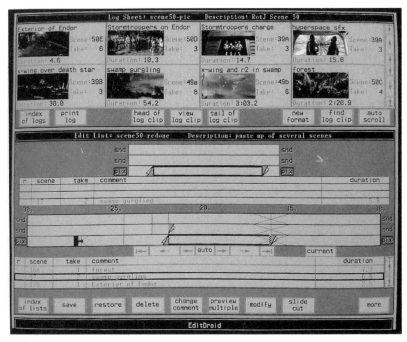

The initial EditDroid SUN display, with a mock-up of the "Trim Bin" option in the top Log Window. The timeline for editing ran from right to left, which film editors using flatbed editing tables found familiar, and the picture track ran beneath two sound tracks, the way film runs through a synchronizer. The cursor is a small pair of scissors in the Edit Window, which changes into a log book in the Log Window. At the very bottom of the screen, in the Control Window, the cursor changes into a Darth Vader head.

One of the first responses to the Montage was envy at their really cool little black-and-white frames; each frame represented one snippet of film. Bob met with Rob Lay to see if a feature like that would be feasible for the Droid.

With the addition of a little frame grabber, small digital pictures could be captured. A new field could be added to the database for each clip, and there could be a picture label on the SUN display if the interface was formatted for it. But the SUN could go one better; an upcoming feature to the SUN-2 was a high-resolution color display. While it was an expensive upgrade, the color display would allow small, sharp, color thumbnails to represent the source clips—better than the low-res b&w monitors on the Montage.

Doris wanted it available at once and the development team set out to prototype the feature. Lucas would finally have the digital trim bin he always envisioned. It became known as the "Trim Bin" option.

The digital audio group had moved to Z Building with everyone else, but the ASP itself stayed in the sound pit in C Building. To go to work, Andy or John would walk across Bellam, skirt along the front of A Building, then weave back behind B Building through the narrow line of parked cars, then through an open gate protecting pedestrians from an odd little creek, and then in the back downstairs door of C, past David DiFrancesco jiggering with a big laser near the doorway. The sound pit and Ben Burtt's sound lab were down there.

Burtt used the prototype machine to its fullest on the projects he was doing. "He took the morning shift up until noon and then we would take it over at noon," said Moorer.

As Bob Doris looked around at the technological landscape, he wanted to form the ASP into some tools that he knew had definite markets. Andy was long prepared for Bob to start applying commercial pressures.

"It was what he was hired to do," said Andy. "It was a natural evolution. I thought it was time."

Andy Moorer in his Z Building office.

Along with delivering a lower-cost version of the ASP, software development was starting to get aligned in a couple of directions. First there would be a sound editing and mixing product.

John Snell had implemented the touch-screen interface, even with the quiet disapproval of Sprockets engineers, and had rigged up a "throw-away" prototype of an 8-slider box, "to make sure everything was working," said Snell. With the ongoing pressure to commercialize everything that was being developed, the prototype was demonstrated publicly—first as a concept demonstration, and then in conjunction with the sales pitch for the EditDroid.

Rows of dubbers—audio recorders and players—connected to the Sprockets mixing theater. Reels of mag are loaded up on each machine, and mixed down to successively fewer reels, until there are stereo pairs for dialog, music and effects. As many as thirty or forty at a time might be employed on big film sound mixes.

If the ASP team was going to be reinventing the way movies were mixed, they had better know something about it. So Ben Burtt invited the whole group to a little lesson he set up. Sprockets loaded up all the sound tracks for the last reel of *Return of the Jedi*, and the computer geeks had a day to mix the end of the movie. There were 72 tracks—72 reels of 35mm sprocketed mag spread around the big theater in C Building—loaded up on dubbers, enormous analog refrigerator-like columns holding a big reel of film and connected to the mixing console in the middle of the screening room.

Moorer and Snell and Jim Lawson immediately grasped the subtle problems associated with finding sounds, listening to them in different ways, and adjusting tracks.

"The sound of a grizzly bear on a track is all chopped up. It seems impossible to use," recalled Moorer, "how [the Sprockets] guys can tell what it will sound like combined and faded together with another track, where the odd jump cuts don't disrupt the effect...is unbelievable."

The problem with digitizing the theatrical mixing environment was most acutely one of storage. The 72 tracks, each ten minutes long, represented a huge volume of digital audio,[1] to play in concert, to mix in real time, to add complex mathematical distortions to adjust EQ or filtering. At the time, the largest hard disk in the company was a washtub-size 350MB drive. Most computers were lucky if they had a 40MB drive. The SUNs shipped with 20MB. To be of immediate use to Sprockets, the ASP would have to tackle a smaller part of the process.

Andy went back to Ben: "What's another big problem you have to work through, that doesn't need to play so much sound simultaneously, or instantaneously."

The ASP, even as specified, was only expected to handle playing eight tracks simultaneously, which was considered reasonable and professional, although not aspirational. And at this point, it wasn't even playing eight, only four. Four tracks. What is four tracks enough for?

"Effects spotting," said Burtt. Effects spotting meant watching a film and noting where and what kind of sound effects would be necessary.

Collecting sound effects that would be potentially useful in a scene was insanely tedious. Lucasfilm had a remarkable sound "library"—hundreds and hundreds of ¼-inch tape reels of short bursts of acoustic gems. With each numbered and listed in a thick printed catalog: "Tape 142. 1983 Plymouth Horizon—door slam, trunk slam, start engine cold, rev engine, horn honk series; 1982 Mercedes—drive by, door slam, rev engine, seat belt beep." There were tapes of cars, tapes of animals, tapes of machinery, tapes of weather.

The library of recorded sounds that Burtt had amassed over years sat on shelves and shelves, logged before there was timecode on audiotapes, found only by tedious searching and playing. While most sounds were recorded by Ben himself, audio assistants who had arrived during *Empire* were able to take on small projects to capture specific sounds.

The library had grown to be one of the most comprehensive and well-organized collections in the film business. Being able to instantly access and try out individual sounds from the library was advantageous. Andy Moorer was certain he could provide a digital tool that would change effects spotting.

Bob Doris wasn't thrilled with Convergence's contributions; the feeling was growing that he had selected a highly flawed business partner. Slowly, Lucasfilm began to retract from its dependence on them, first pulling back engineering and, later, parts of sales and marketing. Gary Beeson, president of Convergence, quietly receded into the background. Sales director Richard Moscarella was frustrated by the slow development process, "I have nothing to sell," he told Ken Yas, and soon left Convergence entirely. Deborah Harter remained to coordinate sales and marketing, supported by Yas.

Everyone in The Droid Works, but most acutely Bob Doris, had been anticipating the arrival of lower cost videodisc replication. The disc companies had been promising it for years, and it was beginning to look like they were not only substantively off their projections, but maybe unable to deliver

[1] Twelve hours of sound, or about 7GB to store digitally.

at all. Cheap recordable discs were the cornerstone of the EditDroid's viability, and not having them was starting to become its most significant drawback.

Videodiscs teetered on the brink of market acceptance and respectability—providing better quality images and markedly superior user-experience than any tape format.[2] Still, consumers (and editors) needed to be able to record them at will. And the arduous process to make discs forced the EditDroid into the unfortunate category of high-end curiosity, as it struggled to achieve practicality.

What the EditDroid needed was an advocate—someone to coax it along and foster its development. The *doula* should have been Lucasfilm: either George himself or an editor from Sprockets who was passionate about the device. But that didn't happen, and the Droid remained an outcast. Support would have to come from the last place the company would want to go for product TLC: Hollywood.

While Northern California was the headquarters and the site of development, Los Angeles was the largest cohesive market for the product. Only movies and television could afford a $200,000 editing system for film. Unfortunately, movies and television weren't the kinds of projects that purchased equipment, especially an expensive tool like an EditDroid. For that, a third party would have to put up the money, buy and support the device, and rent it out. There were businesses that did this; they were called post-production facilities.

In 1984, about 80 percent of all television programming was shot on film, cut on film, and transferred to videotape only when it was finished. TV show production was simply a diminutive version of feature film production. Post facilities made their business out of the other 20 percent—material shot on video, edited and mixed in video.[3] If they could come up with a way to get TV shows shot on film, to edit on *video*, it would revolutionize their industry.

Film editors rejected videotape editing. It was seen as technical and uncreative.

The advent of the EditDroid and other film-style video tools represented a remarkable opportunity for post facilities. If film editors adopted these products…there was no telling how much new business could be created. Still, everyone in Hollywood production already knew the time-tested process of making a movie or TV show. There was never a question about who did what, or how much should be paid for it. It was a well-oiled machine.

Post facilities were up for the challenge, but the studios had almost no interest in modernity. Changing the process would be nothing short of missionary work.

Through no small effort on Moscarella's and Harter's part, the first five EditDroids were placed in three of the most important post-production facilities in Hollywood, beta sites for the new product: Unitel Video, Complete Post, and Pacific Video.[4]

[2] In 1984, The Criterion Collection was launched, a business providing classic movies on videodisc for film buffs. The discs included special features and commentary, common on DVDs today but nonexistent in the videotape distribution of movies for consumers then.

[3] Primarily news, sitcoms, soap operas, talk shows, and a few music videos.

[4] *Beta site*: a real-world test location for a new technology product, just preceding a wide release.

Post-Production Facilities

In the late 1970s a new industry began to grow in Hollywood. As more television productions were being created independent of the networks, and later sold to them (or the arriving cable channels), a new market began to grow. The idea was to take advantage of the complicated and expensive video broadcasting tools that the smaller production companies didn't have.

Pioneering businesses such as Vidtronics and Compact Video purchased high-priced video equipment for editing, for transferring film to tape, and for doing video effects, and rented the package to television shows by the hour, usually with a skilled technician or craftsman at the helm of each device. Eventually, even broadcasters and film studios began to utilize the services, as they outsourced some or all of their own projects. The facilities were very close with producers, networks and studios, who might spend many hundreds of dollars per hour for this work.

By the early 1980s, there was an even greater proliferation of competing "post houses," as they were called. Teams of engineers or salespeople would abandon one facility, raise capital, and start their own. Some offered boutique services, such as handling only new music video clients (who were arriving with the creation of MTV)— providing comfortable enclaves for rock stars and their rock-star editors or effects creators. Others specialized in creating sound, or in transferring finished films to video for release on cassettes.

Post houses were recognized for having their own unique look-and-feel, deeply dedicated clients, and usually very customized devices invented by the staff engineers for one-of-a-kind results. It was a high-ticket, often cutthroat industry, built on relationships and new technology. Post houses were constantly testing new bleeding-edge tools or partnering with equipment manufacturers, to get one-up on the competition.

Unitel, though established on the Paramount Studios lot, was not exclusive to Paramount's projects.[5] They liked the EditDroid and tried to convince shows to try out the new system, but beyond cursory interest they couldn't get traction. Unitel management was incessantly badgering the Droid workers: "Is George using it yet?" which was traditionally met with the non-answer, "He's not making any movies right now."

Complete Post had developed a niche handling multi-camera situation comedies. These shows were often shot on film, but unlike episodic dramas, which were made like little movies (with one camera on the set), sitcoms utilized three cameras simultaneously. Sometimes they were shot on videotape, but the high-end shows still used film. Complete Post transferred the film to videotape and then ganged a bunch of videotape machines together and edited in the traditional CMX linear way.

"They saw the EditDroid as an offline tool, a creative editing tool," said Ken Yas, "and they wanted to replace their CMX linear systems."

[5] Because they had no parking inside the walls of the lot, and were hidden deep in the multi-acre walled city, the hike to their front door kept many clients away.

But Complete Post was pressuring Lucasfilm to add features to the system that would allow it to handle multi-camera productions. This was a very specific kind of editing process that was wholly different from the kinds of functions required to edit movies and most television shows.

Down the street from Complete Post was a new facility called LaserEdit, which had worked with the only company in operation developing videodisc recorders and specialty players: the Optical Disc Corporation (ODC).[6] LaserEdit wanted ODC to develop proprietary two-headed videodisc players for use with an otherwise traditional editing system.[7] Complete hoped that the Droid, being videodisc-based, would help them reclaim that territory. "Some effort was made in that direction," said Yas, "but it was a complete waste of time."

The third beta site was Pacific Video, run by Emory Cohen. Cohen had a vision of the post facility of the future, and it displaced the role of the photochemical laboratory, which was the technological underpinning of Hollywood. He called it "The Electronic Lab" and he saw these new nonlinear editing tools as the cornerstone of that effort.

"Something came out of the Pacific Video experience that did not come out of Unitel or Complete Post," said Ken Yas, "and it was an application, an actual putting of the Droid to work on a TV show."

Pacific Video, like all the top post-production facilities, was a high-end service organization. If a client wanted something special, they did their best to provide. While the new breed of electronic editing systems all fit into the process Pacific Video embraced, they actually cared little which product a studio wanted them to use. "Choosing an editing system is a very personal thing," said Leon Silverman, VP of marketing at Pacific Video. "If a customer wanted an EditDroid, we got them an EditDroid. If they wanted a Montage, we got them a Montage."

The beauty of Pacific Video's Electronic Lab was that they translated the entire video workflow into film terminology and priced it in film-like ways. Studios didn't rent an editing system by the hour, but rather by the week; raw material was referred to as "dailies" and priced by the foot rather than by the hour of transfer time. Film people could understand, finally, videotape post-production. The new editing systems were not forced into an existing flow, but were sculpted into a new kind of electronic post-production process that no one had dared try before.

Lorimar Telepictures—a major television production company and an important client at Pacific Video—found itself in the unique position of having different episodic programs choosing to try different editing systems: *Falcon's Crest* editors wanted to use the Montage; *Knott's Landing* editors were interested in the EditDroid. As long as the shows were delivered on time and on budget, Matthew Knox—the VP of post-production at Lorimar— approved the use of the unusual products.

[6] DiscoVision Associates (DVA), the venture between MCA and IBM, was shut down in 1982 and most parts were sold to former partner Pioneer Electronics. DVA remained as a small company holding the rights to all the laserdisc-related patents. Members of the DVA development team joined forces to start a company to develop a recordable videodisc. They called it ODC.

[7] LaserEdit called their special in-house product the Spectra system, and although it was a linear, keyboard-controlled method of working, the raw material was transferred to videodisc, which made finding shots and cueing edits very fast. It was finely tuned for editing sitcoms and was starting to erode Complete Post's domination of that market.

While the EditDroid and Montage slugged it out, scratching at the door of Hollywood feature films, there was a third competitor floating around Hollywood, an inelegant looking product called the Ediflex. The Ediflex was not new; it had been invented by broadcast engineer Adrian Ettlinger in 1980. Ettlinger, with white hair and goatee and looking like Colonel Sanders' brother, garnered industry-wide respect for his early work on the development of timecode. Then, he was one of four people credited as founders of CMX—the joint venture of CBS and Memorex.

Ettlinger was the senior designer of the CMX 600, unchallenged as the first "nonlinear" editing system, with black-and-white images stored on platters of magnetic discs.[8]

The Ediflex had a different interface style from either the Montage or the EditDroid. Assistants would take the script of the show, number every single line, and identify where that line could be found in every scene and take. It was called the "Script Mimic" and it allowed editors to rapidly see the delivery of any given line at every angle, in every shot. It worked best for the relatively formulaic editing found in many weekly television shows. The lion's share of the work was subsumed by the assistant creating the mimic, and not by the editor. For scenes with little script, like certain kinds of action, it was less impressive. The most non-formulaic projects found the Ediflex to be the least appropriate tool.

Isolated prototypes of the Ediflex had been rented over the prior year; it was efficient and stable. By coincidence, Pacific Video provided an Ediflex for the first season of the Disney Channel's *Still the Beaver*[9]—creating a three-way contest for its nonlinear systems. Manufacturers feared that it was a winner-take-all competition. But that wasn't the case; it turned out the difference between systems was largely one of style and editor's preference. As long as a product worked, it had a life in Hollywood.

"There was excitement in the editorial community," Silverman said, "that there really could be a better way. They were concerned, obviously, that the technology was very immature, and prone to mechanical or computer failures, but as immature as they were, they were better tools than scissors and tape."

The editors on the Lorimar shows, all in their 60s, were the most venerable of the Hollywood television establishment. Some had been cutting shows since TV was created. Few had used a VCR, let alone a computer. All of them needed to be trained in using tools that, for the most part, had never been real-world tested. The two editors on *Knott's Landing*—Mort Tubor and Bob Phillips—were initially petrified by the alien EditDroid.

"They wouldn't do a keystroke without an approval from me in the room," said Yas. "Augie Hess and I sat there through the entire season, to make sure nothing went wrong."

[8] The 600 was abandoned but led to the invention of linear online and offline editing systems. Ettlinger eventually left CMX. In the late 1970s, he worked again with CBS and its partner Sony to make a new kind of experimental editing system for television programs. Ettlinger utilized a light pen on a special screen to control a small stack of Sony Betamax machines. Only two CBS-Sony systems were ever built, but they were used on television programs throughout the early '80s. Later, he improved on it, this time using Panasonic's VHS format but keeping the light pen control screen. Ettlinger called his first version the ED-80 (for the year he developed it); in 1984 it was renamed the Ediflex.

[9] In 1983, CBS made a TV movie, a sequel to the 1950s-era program *Leave It to Beaver*, which they called *Still the Beaver*. In 1985, Disney Channel picked up the series, and ran it for one season before selling it to TBS.

Every system had full time "babysitters," as they privately referred to themselves, to sit alongside the professional editors on the projects. The job was complicated. It involved being a system trainer, but it also included a fair degree of technical support—coordinating problems with the engineers—none of which were in L.A. Most problems had to be addressed at once, in the hailstorm of panic that surrounded something going wrong.

"It's lost my edits!"

"It's not playing back the cut the way I cut it—I know I deleted that head turn!"

"The stop button doesn't stop anything!"

Mort Tubor got a nosebleed one day while working, and alarm rippled through the ranks. "We thought the machine gave him a stroke," said one of the field service engineers. But eventually the old editors learned how to use the new machines, and the new software revisions seemed to address at least the most debilitating of problems.

The projects at Pacific Video, dramatic TV shows, were more forgiving than feature films because they didn't need to manipulate negative to match the computerized edit. The shows were all shot on film, but they were delivered to the broadcasters on 1-inch tape. Thus all the nasty complications that were created when trying to move from video to film could be avoided. Once the original negative was duplicated to videotape (using a telecine machine), it could be put away forever.

It looked like these new electronic film editing systems were going to work after all and eventually save producers a fair amount of money.

But two things happened to conspire against that plan. The first had to do with the highly lucrative international market for television shows. A Lorimar executive who happened to be in London caught glimpse of *Dallas,* their crown jewel, on TV. It looked terrible. The image quality was embarrassing.

TV in the U.S. is encoded in a standard called NTSC—525 lines of video in each frame, playing 30 frames every second. Many nations (particularly in Europe) use a different standard, called PAL—625 lines of video playing 25 frames per second.[10] It was always okay to transfer a finished project from film to video (PAL or NTSC) but lousy to transfer from NTSC video directly to PAL. If you wanted to release your television show overseas, you had start with a cut negative.

But the second factor, the *coup de grace,* came from the growing fear of the future, what the broadcasters called high-definition television (HDTV). For years Coppola and Zoetrope had been vocal about pushing the new format forward. By 1984, word of HDTV experiments were beginning to surface, and the rumbling was growing louder. It was clear that HDTV was going to be of much higher resolution than either NTSC or PAL. For producers, the only

[10] Experts agree that PAL is a superior looking format. Developed for color television in Europe after WWII, it had the benefit of coming second. Created in the U.S. before the war, NTSC had to work on b&w sets and then get modified later to play in both b&w and color.

way to save the value of your television show in the high-definition future was to have it stored on film, and not on the much lower resolution NTSC video master tape.

If these electronic nonlinear systems were going to be useful, they had to be equally adept at cutting videotape and cutting film. None of the new products had proven it could accurately cut negative. As if technical matters weren't enough, there was also the issue of price. A Moviola could be purchased for $11,000, or rented for about $65 per week. The Droid Works was selling a full EditDroid system for more than $200,000. Post-production facilities were renting the electronic film editing systems for around $2,500 per week. The Moviola was an industry standard that was going to be hard to displace.

In February 1985, the Montage Company ran out of money. Interscope Investments, a film company, came up with $5 million to take over the business. Now, flush with new cash, Montage was now revived as part of a filmmaking organization, for which only The Droid Works previously had bragging rights. Interscope bought out founder Ron Barker and installed new management.

Interscope Investments

Interscope was co-founded by Marshall Fields heir Ted Fields. Fields' path to moguldom, and eventual investment in Montage, was an odd one.

In 1979, producer Peter Samuelson teamed up with actor Donald Sutherland to make a handful of movies in Canada, including *A Man, A Woman, and a Bank* (1979).[11] When Canadian tax-shelter laws changed, half the financing on the film vaporized, and Samuelson scrambled for a new partner.

Samuelson wrote to 25-year-old Ted Fields, then embroiled in forcing the sale of his family's assets: 10 percent of the Marshall Fields business, measuring in the hundreds of millions of dollars.[12] Ted met with Samuelson and agreed to put up the missing investment. Soon, Ted Fields was in the movie business.

The project worked out well for them both, and in 1981 Fields proposed they go into business together, with Fields' capital and Samuelson's film know-how. With record executive Jimmy Iovine, Fields created Interscope Communications and Samuelson ran the film division.

The story is told of Ted Fields having lunch with Peter Bart, the president of Lorimar Film Company and a sometime mogul,[13] who tells Fields a story his daughter devised. The story became *Revenge of the Nerds* (1984), which was the first project for Interscope and Peter Samuelson. Samuelson helped Interscope buy Panavision, the movie camera company, from Warner Communications for $40 million. He also facilitated Interscope's investment in Montage.

[11] Co-starring Brooke Adams and Paul Mazursky.

[12] 90% of Marshall Fields was sold to company management in 1917, and today is a division of Target.

[13] As VP of production at Paramount in the early '70s, Peter Bart was largely responsible for getting Francis Coppola to take on *The Godfather*.

The EditDroid was being outfitted with software updates on a weekly basis. With the product finally stable, George asked his friend and editor, Bob Dalva, who was between projects, to spend some time on it and give feedback to the development team. Dalva was in discussions with Haskell Wexler about editing his upcoming project, *Latino*, his semi-fictional account of the political turmoil in Nicaragua. *Latino* was just one of the independent films that Lucas was sponsoring in one form or another that year.

"On the one hand I'm doing these huge productions," said Lucas, "and at the same time I'm helping on these little productions for my friends."

Across the street in C Building, Walter Murch's *Return to Oz* was done, so he stuck around to do the editing on Coppola's *Captain Eo*, starring Michael Jackson.

Coppola and Jackson dropped in for an EditDroid demonstration. As Rob Lay began explaining the system, Coppola pushed him aside and took the controls himself, asking questions as he ran into dead ends. Michael Jackson sat behind them, peering at the screen over the large Coppola, occasionally uttering a bit of praise.

Murch also spent time analyzing the EditDroid. For a time there was hope he might use the Droid to cut *Eo*, but everyone at Sprockets agreed it wasn't ready to cut film.

Sprockets was also mixing Paul Schrader's small personal project, *Mishima*, a co-production of Zoetrope Studios and Lucasfilm. George had given Schrader some script comments early on, and had visited the shoot in Japan at one point. Lucas had persuaded Warner Brothers to finance half the film, and both George and Francis had a very light touch in the project, staying true to their vision of allowing filmmakers to make their own films.

Before Peter Nye arrived to the audio project, the ASP was controlled by a command-line interface, much like MS-DOS, and a small box of knobs that John Snell had built for Ben Burtt. The new SoundDroid interface featured Snell's touchscreen and a novel by-product of the digital audio: a waveform of the sound. Where it was thick the sound was loud, and where it was thin the sound was quiet.

The visual representation made it radically easier to identify words, sounds, musical cues and pauses that all aided in editing. That task was formerly performed by "rock-and-rolling" over a bit of tape, back and forth, until the editor was confident he was in the quietest part of a sound.

The visual waveform had been demonstrated originally in a program called "S" (for "sound") that Andy Moorer developed at Stanford in 1970. As he was imagining its use for music, the display ran horizontally, left to right. Peter Nye, a computer-music student of Moorer's, implemented the paradigm on the SoundDroid for a film-oriented system, which traditionally viewed tracks running vertically, from top to bottom. The Droid Works trademarked the feature as "See the Sound."

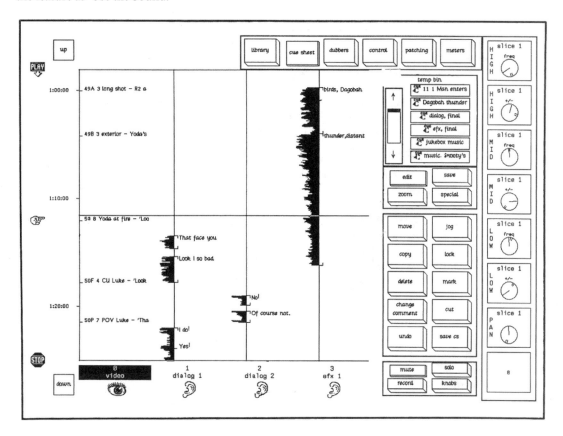

Demonstrations of the SoundDroid started with a short journey from Z Building, through the Lucasfilm campus, and over to the back door of C. There, downstairs, guests entered the sound pit, the acoustically silent chamber that sat dark and silent as people filed in. It was always cold in the pit. Most people were astonished that the room had so little echo; it was as if it sucked the sound out of your ears and left a conspicuous hole of silence.

When Peter Nye gave a demonstration of the machine, he always began by turning on the computer. Guests sat and watched the SUN display go through its various initialization routines, but once the SoundDroid software kicked in, the screen went dark, the room got silent, and then the slow, intense swirling of sound began to radiate from speakers all around.

The start-up tone of the computer was not a little gong, like on the Macintosh, but Deep Note, the sound logo of the THX system. At the time

The main display of the SoundDroid, called the "Cue Sheet." The interface ran on a touchscreen, and let users "grab" a sound cue with their finger and drag it around the screen to new or different tracks. There was also an associated eight-slider control surface with automated sliders and a small array of knobs.

no one had ever heard the sound logo, and the effect in that small, acoustically perfect room was overwhelming. As Deep Note resolved into its final
chord you couldn't help but have a tear in the corner of your eye, the hair still
standing straight on your neck. No movie theater could recreate the experience of hearing that sound in the pit. Once a demonstration began like that,
everything else was gravy.

And the gravy was pretty good, too. Novices were stunned. Professionals
thrilled. SoundDroid allowed a user to go to a digital library of effects, grab
one, and drop it on a track running vertically on the Cue Sheet. There you
could slide it around, up and down in time, or over to another track. There
were handles on the edges of each sound, so it could be shortened or lengthened into endless loops as desired. By using the tools on the right side of the
screen, any given sound (or entire tracks) could be augmented with professional audio controls, including EQ, pan, and an enormous variety of filters.
All the tracks were slaved to a videotape with the corresponding picture and
a pointing finger—the "now line" showed where you were scrolling through
the project.

As usual, scene 50 from *Return of the Jedi* was the principle demo material.
Peter Nye would show off by dropping thunder and bird sounds behind the
establishing shot of Yoda's hut on Dagobah, and then drop the volume of
those sounds down on the cut to the inside of the hut as Yoda approached
Luke Skywalker, and the sound of the fire crackled in the foreground.

"That face you make," says Yoda. "Look I so bad to young eyes?"

"No, no…master Yoda" protests Luke.

"I do…yes, I do…" Yoda walks for a moment then turns around. "Sick
have I become. Old and weak."

Luke watches Yoda.

"When 900 years old you are, look as good you will not, hmmm?"

Even if the employees couldn't watch it one more time, visitors never got
tired of that scene. More than one sale was made of the unfinished product
based on its psychic proximity to Yoda.

With no shipping date scheduled, deposits on the SoundDroid began
coming in, from high-end musicians and established film production companies. At some point, Bob Doris stopped taking deposits and began leaning
on Andy Moorer to finish the low-cost version of the ASP. Andy brought in
a few more engineers from the ranks of his ex-students at IRCAM and Stanford, and the team that had remained tight and virtually unchanged since
1981 grew from four to seven.

Of the few places that had purchased EditDroids, including the National
Film board of Canada (for producing some documentary segments) and
Soundworks Digital Studios in New York (trying it for Bruce Springsteen

music videos, with only marginal luck), the most unusual was a small outfit in the San Fernando Valley outside L.A. It was called Marsh International.

Marsh was run by David Marsh, a tall curly-headed '70s caricature of the porn industry with too few buttons on his shirt, revealing dangling gold medallions. Neither Bob Doris nor Mary Sauer, sort of east coast preppies, realized at first what his small production company actually produced. And when they did, they had trouble reconciling the potential content of his laser-discs with the fact that Marsh ran what he described as the "busiest Droid in Southern California." Marsh, although admittedly a pornographer, was unhappy with that aspect of his past. The Droid Works field service staff felt he was using the advanced technology in EditDroid to try to escape history with upscale, mainstream projects.

"His hands were soiled," Ken Yas reported after speaking with Marsh one day, "and he just didn't want to bear that burden any longer."

The project he purported to be doing most of the time was a film of his own creation, *The Lords of Magick*, a film no one ever fully understood and which never seemed to approach completion. He said it was about two sorcerer brothers in tenth century England who show up in modern day California.

Marsh built an EditDroid emporium in his converted warehouse, turning the black Death Star console creamy white with teak wood trim. Somewhat like his *Miami Vice* suits. Marsh was a happy customer although he was mysterious enough—and his projects were hidden away sufficiently—that little news of David Marsh found its way to the reports Bob made to Lucasfilm executives.[14]

Competition among the new "nonlinear" editing products in Hollywood was intense. Camps set up quickly; some post facilities had products with which they had expertise; certain editors were particularly skilled at one product over another, and endorsed it whenever possible. Virtually every nonlinear editing tool ever built was busy, rented by the various post facilities in Hollywood for full TV seasons (26 episodes) at a time. Short of a catastrophic political snafu with a producer or network, once the season started, three editing systems were rented for the three groups of editors who tag-teamed through the season.

In the competitive Hollywood environment, there were two pathways for moving the EditDroid ahead of the Montage or Ediflex. The first was to train more editors. Editors were generally afraid of the new technology, and often rightfully so. Post facilities held free training to help the established roster of film editors—the ones who routinely cut TV programs—get comfortable with their products. The film union in Hollywood, IATSE local 776, worked

[14] *The Lords of Magick* was released in 1989 with David Marsh listed as co-writer, director, producer, editor, and senior computer animator. Marsh wrote and directed one more film in 1995 called *Stormswept*, a sort of psycho/slasher/soft-core party movie.

with the various manufacturers to establish organized training. But everything moved slowly.

Perhaps the best break the new electronic tools got was the dreaded Hollywood Writer's Guild strike in 1985.[15] As the weeks of the strike continued, shows stopped being made, and editors, anxiously wondering when they'd work again, used the time to try out the new products and take classes. Over the strike's duration, hundreds of union editors were trained on one or more of the new tools. By the time TV production started again, many were finally interested in trying the products.

The second pathway was to entice editors to use the EditDroid for more *TV pilots*. A pilot was a single test episode for a new show. If the network liked the pilot, they purchased it and put in an order for either half or a full TV season. The post-facilities vied for the pilots, because if a pilot was purchased, the facility usually wound up with an enormous new stream of business. Shows ordinarily wouldn't switch editing tools (or facilities) mid-season, or even between seasons, but if a show was canceled a new show replaced it, and that represented a lucrative opportunity.

Through the combination of training during the strike, and the enormous number of pilots trying out new systems, by the fall of 1985 the broadcasting industry was starting to get serious about the EditDroid, the Montage, and the Ediflex. Where TV editors ventured, feature film editors would eventually follow.

Even as the EditDroid made its first inroads in Hollywood, the future of videodiscs was still murky. Lucasfilm wasn't alone in its anticipation of videodiscs saving everyone from analog tape.

Nicholas Negroponte, described by a journalist as "academe's number one videodisc visionary" and Jerome Wiesner, president emeritus of MIT,[16] had been searching for funding to complete their $21 million Arts and Media Technology Center at MIT. They gave a series of presentations to Hollywood executives all through the early '80s.[17] But Hollywood wasn't biting.

"The studios aren't interested in this sort of thing," said a Fox executive. "They don't care. They're resistant to change and are not interested in hardware."

Three years later, the MIT Architecture Machine Group (ArcMac) officially merged with a few other multi-disciplinary groups and became the MIT Media Lab. In 1985, the first true Media Lab grads were beginning to look for projects; some of them had been doing the most interesting research in laserdiscs and computers that anyone had seen. In spite of the interminable delays, videodiscs were still the cornerstone to the success (or failure) of the EditDroid.

Rob Lay began absorbing key MIT talent into his EditDroid project, beginning with recent Media Lab alum Ken Carson.

[15] The strike was principally about royalties to TV and film writers for videocassette sales, which the studios were trying to cut back.

[16] And former science advisor to President Kennedy.

[17] One, called "Dataland," was described as "a collection of futuristic wonders contained in a high-tech room on the MIT campus." Dataland demonstrated voice-activated computers controlling large screen video. Another demo, "Movie Maps," was a computer-controlled videodisc that gave users an interactive drive through Aspen, Colorado.

"I had been doing the usual videodisc, stereo vision, 3-D display sorts of things when I took a course with the Film and Video group, which got me interested in how to apply ArcMac's computer technology to video editing," recalled Carson. "Video was so cool, running at 30 frames per second, as opposed to computer graphics that would update a frame every couple of seconds—if you were lucky."

The 1985 television season heralded a slate of creepy anthology shows, in particular a new *Alfred Hitchcock Presents* and Steven Spielberg's *Amazing Stories*. In that vein, producer Phil DeGuerre wanted to revive the classic '60s science fiction show *The Twilight Zone*. (DeGuerre had made it big in Hollywood after his series *Simon and Simon* went into syndication.)

Anthology shows of this type were ideal for the new breed of electronic nonlinear film editing tools. The projects were shot on film, like movies, but relatively little film was used since each episode was short—an advantage because it cut down on the number of expensive videodiscs needed (or videotapes, for the Droid competitors). Each episode was usually helmed by a Hollywood movie director taking a stab at bite-sized TV; using a "film-style" system would be particularly appealing.

In the fall, Unitel decided to try a single segment from the first season of *The Twilight Zone* on the EditDroid. Titled "Nightcrawlers," it was directed by *Exorcist* director William Friedkin.[18] With Droid expert Augie Hess at editor Gary Blair's side, the project went smoothly enough that the second season was committed to the EditDroid.

Craig Sexton tried in vain to get the Spielberg show on the EditDroid as well. The project was arguably as "right" for the product as any. Lucasfilm's connections should have helped. Lucas' friend Spielberg was the executive producer, and Steven Starkey, Lucas' old film assistant and Sprockets fixture, was an associate producer.

The roster of *Amazing Stories* directors read like a Hollywood Who's Who: Joe Dante, Brad Bird, Danny DeVito, Clint Eastwood, Tim Hutton, Irvin Kershner, Marty Scorsese, Robert Zemeckis, Matthew Robbins. A good experience on the EditDroid for their TV segment would reasonably lead any one of them to trying it out on their next films.

"They never came around," said Yas. They cut on film.

The directors who moved through the *Twilight Zone* were also impressive, and though not quite of the status of the *Amazing Stories* team, many were introduced to nonlinear editing for the first time on their segments.[19]

At the Mill Valley Film Festival in September, a host of Bay Area filmmakers made presentations at a forum on the art and craft of film editing. Marcia Lucas was there with scenes from *Return of the Jedi* she had made compelling in spite of incomplete footage, in particular Yoda's death scene. Bob Dalva

[18] Episode 1.11, aired Oct 18, 1985.

[19] One director was Martha Coolidge. She directed *Valley Girl* (1983), *Real Genius* (1985), *Rambling Rose* (1991), and *Lost in Yonkers* (1993). A few years earlier she had tried to develop a film project with Zoetrope. *Ramblng Rose* (1993) made technological history by being the first high-end feature film cut on the Avid, edited by Steve Cohen.

showed some work from *Latino*, which was still in post-production at Sprockets. Michael Chandler showed some of his work from cutting *Amadeus* and his most current work on *Mishima*.

Droid Works employees sat in the crowded theater, energized by the presentations. But they were also reminded how far they were drifting from their love of movies and editing. Their time was consumed with supporting a product that was having difficulty finding a home.

The number of electronic projects in Hollywood was growing, and The Droid Works' sales and support needs increased. To keep the Droids operational, more field service engineers were added.[20] Field service was in a constant battle with Sales and Manufacturing over spare parts. The only way to keep the existing Droids alive was to have ample parts available, so that when a control board died suddenly, a working board could be quickly swapped in, the dead one sent to San Rafael for repair. But each component of the system was handmade. And expensive.

As Manufacturing in San Rafael churned out parts, the field service guys wanted them in L.A. But Sales wanted the parts to make more Droids. More Droids for more sales. The battle raged on. There were never enough spare parts. Customers were always screaming about some deadline being missed because of a hung computer. Headquarters in San Rafael was blissfully isolated from the ruckus in L.A.

Production in Marin was beginning to ramp up on *Howard the Duck*. A memo was circulated around the company that they were still trying to cast a voice for the little duck, and any interested employee was welcome to try out. Soon, the movie's stars began arriving in Marin, getting ready for the shoot. Over the years, actors and films came through ILM and Kerner, but they were usually shot in other places. But *Howard the Duck*, referred to by the company as *HTD*, was shooting in Marin, sometimes on the streets around Kerner after hours.

Lea Thompson was a relatively new star in 1985, hot on the heels of her role in *Back to the Future*. Her co-star, the tall geek Tim Robbins, had had only bit parts up to that point, but he was intelligent and funny and excited about the opportunity. At 27, in spite of his large frame, baby-faced Robbins looked and acted as youthful as his co-stars.[21]

Lucas still wasn't ready to use the EditDroid himself. The Droid Works sales force, anxious for respectability, finally convinced someone else to try it for a feature film. Crown Pictures International was making a direct-to-video, low-budget feature film called *The Patriot*, directed by Frank Harris. It was

[20] John Newlander and Jeff Taylor.

[21] Robbins arrived in Marin with John Cusack. Nineteen-year-old Cusack had starred in recent youth hits, *The Sure Thing* (where he met Robbins) and *The Journey of Natty Gann*, and was booked to do at least two more films before the year ended. Robbins and Cusack had just completed an insane sophomoric road trip to Nashville, interviewing star-struck teenagers and Elvis fans along the way to the gates of Graceland. Pulling into Marin with hundreds of hours of video and a fair amount of marijuana, they wondered if they could shanghai an EditDroid after-hours to cull their road trip footage to something more manageable. They worked on this until *HTD* production began and Cusack left for his next film.

an action film about terrorists who intercept some nuclear weapons. Harris gave his editor, Rick Westover, the opportunity to cut the film any way he wanted, as long as the project remained on schedule and on its incredibly tight budget.

The goal of marketing was to entice the high-end filmmakers who could afford the product and validate its use. Until that happened, sales had little choice but to comb the low end, the people who were willing to try anything to save money. Manufacturers hungry to test out dangerously untested products would practically give away editing time, brokered through willing post-production facilities, and complete with ample customer support from the engineers who invented the thing—all this made the tools attractive to hyper-low-budget projects.[22]

Westover was no stranger to the direct-to-video path for films, but he still didn't realize he was going to be the first guy to use this product on a feature film. "I saw a demonstration with footage from *Return of the Jedi*," said Westover. "And assumed. When I realized I was the pioneer, that's when paranoia set deep in my heart. I haven't been that paranoid since I was a hippie in the '60s."

Through the vigilance of Augie Hess and Ken Yas, Westover completed the film and had a relatively positive experience. He said his work was "frame perfect," a reflection of the accuracy between the video he cut and the film negative that was made to match. He also reported that his editing time was shortened by weeks.

But the EditDroid missed the opportunity to be first to cut a major feature film. Months earlier, Andrew Mondshein had taken the leap using the Montage on Sidney Lumet's film, *Power*. It was not only the first feature film to go electronic, it was a higher profile film from a mainstream director. "I knew I was a guinea pig," said Mondshein.

By the time the EditDroid was cutting *The Patriot*, Mondshein was already getting ready to use a Montage on a second major motion picture, Susan Seidelman's *Making Mr. Right*.[23]

It was a lead that The Droid Works would never overcome.

[22] The first features to try the new nonlinear editing tools were usually films consumers never heard of. The historic moment for a new product was not the first film cut, but rather the first *big budget* or high profile project—it could make or break a new tool.

[23] *Making Mr. Right* (1987) starred John Malkovich.

twenty six

Esoteric unto Occult

[1986]

The point of life is to fail at greater and greater things.

—Ranier Maria Rilke

WITH PIXAR GONE, Doug Norby and Doug Johnson focused their attention on the slow progress at The Droid Works. Bob Doris had made his initial sales projections based on the response from the Droid's debut at NAB '84. Interest was high. But after the first deliveries, numerous problems had to be addressed, and sales plateaued.

The Friday after signing the Pixar deal with Steven Jobs, Doug Johnson arrived in Z Building to see Bob Doris. Not finding him in his office, Johnson began milling around the lobby. Finally he ran into Doris who was exploring the company, as he often did, in his socks. Doris was surprised to see the executive in the halls unannounced. Johnson looked Bob Doris up and down, and with no sign of humor, told him to put his shoes on.

That was Bob Doris' last day at the company.

Doug Johnson took the interim position of CEO while he and Norby began to figure out what to do. Bob Doris called over to Ed Catmull in A Building, now free following the Pixar sale, to tell him of his unceremonious end. Commented Ed in his quietly ironic way, "So they took it out on you."

Earlier that year the *Wall Street Journal* had reported that if Lucas didn't have a major financial success soon, "he would have trouble keeping his empire afloat." The fact was, Lucasfilm *was* struggling daily to stay afloat.

To address the radical shortfalls in cash. Norby continued what he hoped would be a short streamlining of the company. The Fan Club,[1] art departments, photo library, licensing, and publishing were all slashed. The *Marin Independent Journal* announced, "Lucasfilm zaps payroll in company shakeup." Morale was down across the board.

Lucas was relieved to have Norby at the helm, dealing with the daily operation of the company after a long year of doing much of that himself. Now he

[1] The Star Wars Fan Club had for three years been run by überfan Maureen Garrett. Her assistant, Jok Church, stayed on to move the remaining Fan Club materials to the Ranch. Feeling the ongoing shift in the company, Jok pitched Lucasfilm on an idea for a kids science television show with R2D2 and C-3PO. It was called "Here's How." Interested at first, LFL soon balked. Eventually Jok left and turned the idea into a syndicated comic strip, *You Can, With Beakman and Jax*. In 1991 the strip was turned into the popular kids science program *Beakman's World*. The show ran for many seasons, first on PBS then on CBS.

could focus on his primary interests: getting the Ranch fully operational and supporting the film projects he was shepherding.

One film was *Willow,* a fantasy tale that he thought might be another franchise, like *Star Wars.* Lucas had decided that the story, built on his interest in mythology, should be directed by Ron Howard, the kid he cast in *American Graffiti* who had grown into the successful director of *Splash (1984).* The second film was *Tucker,* the story of Preston Tucker, the ingenious automotive maverick. *Tucker* was Francis Coppola's pet project and had been in various states of development for a decade.[2] The script captured Coppola's fascination with technology; Lucas was attracted to the story about cars. They both enjoyed the tale of a small guy, a man outside the system, trying to succeed against the odds.

The luscious redwood library in the Main House was inaugurated by becoming the backdrop for a Bill Moyers special, a series of interviews with George's spiritual mentor Joseph Campbell. In 1949 Campbell had written the popular book, *Hero with a Thousand Faces*—his first work—which had been an important influence on Lucas as he was developing the *Star Wars* universe and plots. After a number of years, they became friends.[3]

[2] There was also *Powaqqatsi,* a sequel to Godfrey Reggio's visually striking and innovative film *Koyaanisquatsi* (which Francis had executive produced). George wasn't involved until Francis ran into financial problems and needed some assistance.

John Thompson, EditDroid engineer, looking for bugs; in Z Building.

A metamorphosis of Lucasfilm was underway. Sid Ganis, the company's highly respected marketing chief for many years, left in March to become president of Worldwide Marketing at Paramount. Almost simultaneously, Mary Sauer, The Droid Works VP of marketing, handed in her resignation. With Doris ousted, Sauer's interest in sticking around and dealing with the Lucasfilm executives was pretty low.

Bob Doris and Mary Sauer had been the business leaders. With both of them gone, there wasn't anyone driving the ship. Mary wouldn't be packing for another few months; she was only staying to help with the transition, but exactly what she'd be transitioning to was unclear.

The spring was filled with swanky demonstrations of the EditDroid and SoundDroid prototypes. The Grateful Dead, locals in the San Rafael scene, drifted in occasionally. Jerry Garcia sat at the EditDroid console with his band scattered around the room watching him edit a scene from *The Twilight Zone* TV show, a program for which Mickey Hart had done the music.[4]

Star demos continued into the summer. Stevie Wonder. Barbara Streisand. Norman Jewison. Terry Gilliam. George's friends as well as many successful directors visited Kerner to get their hands on the EditDroid and to get a sense of where the state-of-the-art was in 1986. But the high-profile demonstrations belied the instability throughout the company.

It wasn't only The Droid Works that was suffering; so was its primary competitor, Montage, which had already been formed and reformed over the last few years. In March, Interscope announced that the Montage Computer Corporation would be liquidated; this was a little ironic because the Montage was arguably the market leader, with twenty-nine systems in the field.

Alan Alda had started editing *Sweet Liberty* on the Montage. "Sometimes new things that are so valuable are still slow to catch on because they are frightening," he said. "I vacillate between being absolutely certain this is the future, and hoping so." The system was also in the planning stages for cutting Susan Seidelman's *Making Mr. Right*, and possibly Stanley Kubrick's *Full Metal Jacket*.

The Montage Picture Processor was far more successful in its head-to-head competition with the EditDroid, but Montage had gone out of business twice in just a few years. In a sense, the EditDroid never felt as "real" as its competition, but never failed to excite spectators and galvanize the imagination for what the future had in store. Unfortunately for The Droid Works, this rarely converted to sales.

After months of searching, Droid Works chairman Doug Johnson announced a new president had been found. Bill Butler had fifteen years earlier been the first president (and one of the co-founders) of CMX. He was

[3] Moyers was producing a six-part PBS show, *The Power of Myth*, introducing the public to Campbell's encyclopedic knowledge for world cultures and comparative mythology. Eventually the show would be turned into a book. George Lucas and Linda Ronstadt accompanied Joseph Campbell to the National Arts Club in 1985, where he received the Gold Medal of Honor in Literature. Campbell died suddenly in 1987, just before the debut of his PBS special. When Campbell died, *Newsweek* said, "Campbell has become one of the rarest of intellectuals in American life: a serious thinker who has been embraced by the popular culture."

[4] The Dead had a number of odd connections to the Lucas research. In particular, Betsy Cohen, an audio scientist who had studied with Andy Moorer at Stanford, was close friends with Bobby Weir, and kept the Dead apprised on the state-of-the-art in digital sound. Bob Bralove helped introduce Stevie Wonder to digital audio (and brought him to experiment with the Droids), and later worked with the Dead.

respected as having "turn-around" experience and a familiarity with both the broadcast industry and technology companies.

Butler was cool and steely, unlike the jovial and talkative Bob Doris. He always had a sort of windblown, just off the yacht, look to him. Even as he was evaluating how to restructure the aggregation he had been handed, he was figuring out how to book time on Lucasfilm's company sloop, Seawalker.

Steve Martin's company, Aspen Film Society, had been one of the first production companies interested in the Droids. Aspen's president, Bill McEuen—producer of 1985's *Pee Wee's Big Adventure*—had put a deposit down on both an EditDroid and a SoundDroid and had been waiting patiently for a year for the products to get finished.[5] McEuen liked the Droids. But TDW had had his deposit since April and now he was ready for some serious tire kicking. McEuen had a project he wanted to do electronically, and so he began to step up the pressure on TDW.

Paul Golding—George's USC colleague on *Herbie* (1966)[6]—was working with Aspen Film. He was ready to direct his first feature film; he had a script called *Pulse* that he described as a "high-tech thriller." It had some special sound and visual effects that Sprockets was going to help with.

Bill McEuen had been friends with Sprockets engineer Tom Scott from their music days, and both were excited about the project. The budget of $6 million didn't leave much room for a $2,500 per week editing system, but it wasn't only the cost that scared Golding; he wasn't convinced that it worked. His demo of the system was plagued with an Ethernet problem that made the computer appear sluggish. But the worst part was the negative vibe he picked up around Sprockets.

Golding told Mary Sauer, "When it's good enough for George, it will be good enough for me." The Droid Works marketing department scrambled to make the project happen, but the obstacles were too great. Sauer turned the project over to Bill Butler, which was the equivalent of killing it altogether.[7]

Andy Moorer settled into the new administration, kept a low profile, and tried to finish up projects that were long underway. To be practical, The Droid Works began looking for products that could be extracted relatively quickly from the overarching SoundDroid. The first logical result was called Sound-Droid Spotter, a stand-alone sound effects spotting station that utilized the database on the SUN with basic processing tools.

The SoundDroid was too big, too general, and too expensive. There were several smaller markets that a scaled-back version of the technology would more readily be able to address. Effects spotting was one. Noise reduction was

[5] Aspen Film: one of the earliest companies to do so—in April 1985. McEuen, a skilled producer, was also the longtime manager of the Nitty Gritty Dirt Band, and he was a big fan of new technology. He had teamed up with Steve Martin in 1976, producing a few projects before hitting paydirt with *The Jerk* (1979). With its success, he began work with Paul Reubens, aka Pee Wee Herman.

[6] Also: *The Emperor* (1967) and *anyone lived in a pretty (how) town* (1967).

[7] In November 1986, Aspen Film Society demanded that their deposits be returned. *Pulse*, written and directed by Paul Golding, cut on film, released in 1988.

another. Specialized synthesis was a third. It would take years before the costs of storage and processing would make a digital post-production workstation viable for movie sound.

After the sale of Pixar to Steve Jobs, the group was still located in their old offices in C Building, and a rash of new activity began. All the Pixar Image Computer sales that had been amassing over the prior year were finally able to be filled; the hardware team was frenetically building computers and shipping them all over the country. As they began to grow and more of Lucasfilm moved to the Ranch, Pixar expanded into available spaces on Kerner.

John Lasseter had been working on a new animation project with an eye on releasing it at the 1986 Siggraph. He had long enjoyed messing around with the metal desk lamp in his office, moving it around in interesting ways; he had even proposed doing a short film based on bringing the lamp to life. Such a project not only had the advantage of being simpler than *Andre and Wally B.* in terms of visual complexity—there would be no forests, no ambient sunlight, no "sets" to speak of—it also benefited from the animation tools having more than a year longer to develop.

Finally, the metallic lamps would do little to stress out Rob Cook's notions of realistic surfaces—it wasn't like trying to computer-generate a human face or hair or water...a desk lamp was a mechanical contraption, so looking metallic was an asset. Since the story was about a pair of Luxo lamps, the animation would demonstrate much of their experience in dynamic lighting. There was still a fair among of work to do developing soft shadows. David Salesin began addressing the problem.

The SoundDroid Spotter— for facilitating the addition of a digital library of sound effects to films and TV. *Left*: Detail from the display. *Right*: The system before its industry debut.

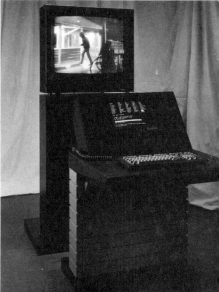

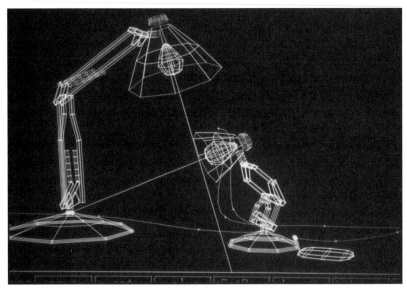

A wireframe model during *Luxo Jr.* production.

[8] Butler and Doug Johnson believed they could cut the monthly rent in half and improve efficiencies by moving everyone into a single building. Six of the company's thirty-six employees were tapped to be part of a new facility committee. The distraction added to the collapsing company resolve.

[9] Ron Gilbert and Gary Winnick continued refining the juvenile adventure game that Ron called *Maniac Mansion*. *Maniac Mansion* didn't involve the visual sophistication of the 3-D simulation games, but Gilbert didn't want to make a game about speed and dexterity; he wanted to make an absurd, darkly humorous puzzle. And he wanted to make it easier to play than the adventure games of the day.

Technically speaking, Pixar was independent of Lucasfilm; since Pixar was no longer part of the "family," they weren't getting invited to company screenings and didn't get emails about T-shirts or the summer picnic. In all their excitement, few cared.

Morale at The Droid Works, on the other hand, sank to an all-time low. As one employee put it, "Everyone is very nervous, distrusting, pessimistic, and anticipating…something."

The new president was regarded as a hatchet man, and no one trusted his cool demeanor and methodical accounting of company assets—both physical and human. In June, Butler announced that the company would have to find new offices—Z Building was simply too expensive. "We are currently spending $36,000 per month on facilities," Butler told the company in a memo. "In addition, we are spread over three separate buildings."[8]

Further adding to the separation anxiety, The Droid Works employees watched the pack-up and move of the Games Division into the Gate House at Skywalker Ranch.[9]

Being cut off from the pulse of the mother had taken its toll on the staff that had been with Lucasfilm for years. As an attempt to slow down the daily erosion of enthusiasm, Norby agreed to invite The Droid Works back to the Lucasfilm 4th of July picnic and to include them in the LFL yearbook.

Many staff members enjoyed the magic that was theirs by association; it soothed the scars of stumbling on their own. While some in administration or accounting cared little, the simple act of being invited to screenings, getting a holiday turkey or new T-shirt, was often enough to make the challenges of the work bearable.

The second season of *The Twilight Zone* was underway at the old CBS Radford lot in Studio City—renamed the MTM lot, when Mary Tyler Moore's company acquired the bungalows, soundstages, and backlot.[10] It was a quaint studio, friendly by Hollywood standards, and full of history. *Gunsmoke* had shot on the dusty backlot streets decades earlier. The old *Gilligan's Island* lagoon sat dry, like a skateboard park, with piles of palm trees stacked along its edges. The big productions now were *St. Elsewhere, Remington Steele,* and *Hill Street Blues,* all shooting daily.

On the CBS-MTM lot, a look at the side of the façade that is the entrance to *St.Elsewhere's* hospital, 1986.

    The two-story cutting building, a tile roofed Spanish bungalow, was busy with Moviolas clattering away on each of the shows. Except for the two rooms with EditDroids. Those rooms were quiet. Calm. Not fancy, but not piled with celluloid either. Guest directors drifted in to work with the editing staff, an editor and assistant manning each Droid. Three episodes were in progress at any time; the third editor didn't use an EditDroid, but rather an old CBS-Sony system that sat in the next room. The CBS-Sony system was technologically quaint, but it was reliable and effectively free, so it was used.
    Lucasfilm was finishing the slate of smaller films and joint projects they had been working on. Haskell Wexler completed *Latino.* George's involvement was largely supportive, as it had been on *Mishima* and *Oz.* He had given his advice on both the script and on the editing, but his major contribution

[10] Before moving on to NBC, Grant Tinker, Moore's business partner and ex-husband, had offices in the little administration building right behind the front gate. Producers Bruce Paltrow and Steven Bochco later became fixtures on the lot, which tended to have a small-town, friendly ambience, especially when compared to the larger studio lots.

Film editor Greg Wong cutting an episode of *The Twilight Zone* on an EditDroid. (Many clients chose not to use the sleek looking Death Star console, and instead created a make shift configuration of monitors and telephones, with the TouchPad in the center.)

was adding his name so as to facilitate a distribution deal for the small films. Audiences were unenthusiastic.

For *Howard the Duck's* debut weekend,[11] George waited on the beach in Hawaii for the news. But *Howard* wasn't *Star Wars*. Its first weekend in the box office was dismal. And it got worse the second weekend. In the first ten days, absolutely critical in the Hollywood system, *Howard the Duck* took in less than $11 million. It was being compared to *Heaven's Gate* as one of the most spectacular bombs in the industry. It was not a great time for such lousy news.

"They're all interesting movies," said Lucas, "movies that I cared about and wanted to see made one way or another. Some of them were small failures, some of them were huge failures, and some were extremely nice movies. But in most of the interviews with me, even within the company, they're passed right over as though they never existed. But those movies may be closer to what I am than *Star Wars*."

The drive along Lucas Valley Road to the Ranch was long and twisty, and after a while, the thrill of being there waned. The plans for a company recreation center were shelved. There was no place to eat outside of the dining room in the Main House. If you didn't want the organic and fresh foods George had made each day, it was a twenty-minute drive to the next possible eatery. Unlike Kerner, there was no way to hop out and run your errands at lunchtime. Still, inside the gate at Skywalker Ranch, even in its half-finished state, the aura and magic were there.

The massive Tech Building was supposed to have been completed by summer. In anticipation of this, Norby hired two Toms to run Sprockets and execute the move to the Tech Building. Tom Kobayashi had run major Hollywood sound facilities. The other Tom was a familiar face around Lucasfilm, Tom Scott. Scott recalled Norby hiring him and saying "the whole place will be entirely digital. The only requirement for the facility is excellence. Money will not be a problem. There is no need to ever make a profit."[12] Said Scott: "I thought I had found Nirvana."

But with the tools not finished (and unclear when they might be production-ready) and cash tight at the company, Lucasfilm had a challenging decision: how to finish the building. *Should it be a digital-only facility, as had been specified, or would it need to have analog mixing consoles and rooms for film?*

---

[11] August 1, 1986.

[12] For the record, Doug Norby is positive he didn't tell them there was no need to make a profit.

Tom Holman had done such a good job designing the technology in C Building that the Tech Building was a natural next step for him. The THX sound system was a *bona fide* revolution and secured his place in film history. Still, the monstrous building plagued them all. The completion of the facility fell to the three Toms. It was difficult to tell Norby when that might happen.

The Tech Building under construction. Development slowed as it neared completion and the first generation of digital post-production tools—from Lucasfilm or elsewhere—was not quite ready, 1987.

Toms Scott and Kobayashi were effectively representatives of The Droid Works' largest client, and they were placed on the TDW board of directors. Their role was to help "translate" the technology for the Lucasfilm executives. But the economics and features of the Droids kept them from replacing the established workflow at Sprockets. Filmmaking continued at Lucasfilm, but the report was that the Droids were not ready. "[The post-production needs of] *Tucker* and *Willow*…conspired against the continuation of The Droid Works," said Scott.

Bill Butler began hatching a plan to unload the Droids. Hunting for a strategic partner for the Droid technology—either a financing partner or someone to purchase the technology outright, Bill Butler settled on his old friends at Bosch and BTS, the companies he had worked with in the years prior to joining Lucasfilm.[13]

BTS liked the EditDroid. They had many products for broadcasters but were looking for "an editing solution" to fit into their flow. Though the Edit-Droid had problems, it might complete the picture. But BTS wasn't interested in the SoundDroid.

To find a home for Lucasfilm's audio tools, arguably far superior technologically than the editing machine, Butler approached leading audio

[13] In the years after founding CMX, Butler had been consulting for German technology giant Bosch. Bosch was a partner in a Salt Lake City operation called TeleMation that manufactured sophisticated televisions for professionals, and in January 1981, Butler became its president. A year later they renamed it Fernseh (German for television). Butler restructured and streamlined Fernseh, increasing sales, developing international markets, and cutting a third of the employees. He left in the fall of 1983, but his relationship with Bosch was solid. When Butler heard that Bosch and Philips teamed up to develop broadcast equipment in a new venture they called Broadcast Television Systems (BTS), he felt they'd be a good recipient of Droid technology.

equipment companies, including British professional manufacturers Neve and AMS. While there was some digital audiotape recording making headway into the audio business, digital processing was something more, and adopted slowly. The old analog process, like film editing, was both well-established and completely understood.

Butler was busy negotiating on both fronts—with Bosch for the Edit-Droid and with the British companies for the SoundDroid. Throughout the fall he worked the process, and was candid that money for The Droid Works would run out in December. Butler told his staff that he had found external capital interest, "joint venture" interest, although it seemed more likely that he'd structure an all-out sale.

Tom Scott, in charge of finding the right equipment for the Tech Building, was becoming and expert on the Droids. Ultimately, a decision had to be made, and he chose highly respected analog SSL consoles for the Lucasfilm mixing theater instead of the SoundDroid. Scott said that the decision to put analog equipment in half of the building was a bit of a disappointment to Lucas. The unofficial comment about this from Lucasfilm was, "We need engines that run." The phrase echoed through The Droid Works for months.

The engineers at TDW were shifted from EditDroid support, to entirely rethinking the product. Entering a new mode of planning, they devised "Trio," a single workstation that would handle editing, sound, and graphics. While development was underway, Butler wanted assurances it would be ready for sale at NAB 1987. Rob Lay privately felt it would take at least a year longer than that.

The Sunday *New York Times* on October 16th ran a full-page feature, "Film Editing Goes Electronic." It began: "A new generation of electronic editing systems is edging its way into movie-making."

While the story described the status of the EditDroid, the Montage and the Ediflex, the story's most significant aspect was the observation that this

Left: Ken Carson and Michael O'Brien work out the technical specs on the Trio. *Right*: John Thompson.

Augie Hess and Ken Yas debrief following an EditDroid demonstration at The Egg Company. The rack of laserdisc players is on the right.

equipment wouldn't be good enough to edit television on videotape without having the ability to cut film to match. In other words, the most important reason a studio would cut negative for a TV show was for the possible future of high definition video.

According to the *Times*, there were fifteen Droids in the field, thirty-two Montages and twenty-five Ediflexes. New competitors were starting up all around them, although all were just small variations on the basic analog theme. Everyone knew that soon, some product would catch on like wildfire.

The Droid was still waiting for the moment when videodisc recording would be cheap and easy. Until the cost of a disc was a few dollars, rather than $100 or so, the product's future would be short. Indication was that it would still be a decade before a computer could store digital video at a quality comparable to a videodisc, for the same or less money. Better tools would be needed long before then.

By fall, everyone in The Droid Works was skittish. Research continued moving ahead, but the market pressures forced development into eternal catch-up. The L.A.-based sales force was stymied. No end user was going to put down a $150,000 deposit before a series of basic questions were adequately answered, questions product manager Ken Yas was certain were unanswerable.

"We heard it all the time: Are you going out of business? What is happening with SoundDroid? Why isn't George using it?"

Ken vented by shooting a sarcastic email to the L.A. staff providing answers he could never say to potential clients. "Yes, we *are* going out of business; there is no SoundDroid—it's too expensive and, anyway, it's esoteric unto occult; and George has become a Rosicrucian Adept and doesn't care any more…so *when do you want to take delivery*?"

Ken Yas—frustrated by the utter disconnect he felt between Hollywood and San Rafael—was itching to leave The Droid Works. Besides, he didn't want to be an equipment manufacturer. He wanted to be the end user. He wanted to be the client. The filmmaker. Yas had made a series of entertaining videos long before most people had ever seen video, back in his Sony-AFI days. And now he was anxious to be able to use the tools he was selling.

A week later, Yas sent Bill Butler his resignation. He was leaving to start a film unit at a successful videotape post-production facility in Hollywood, The Post Group. It wasn't filmmaking exactly, but it definitely moved him a step closer. Said Yas at the time, "To invent tools for this industry is nothing short of missionary work."

Before Thanksgiving, The Droid Works was slimmed down to fewer than thirty employees, maybe half the size it was a year earlier. Bill Butler called a company meeting to announce that Lucasfilm had agreed to fund the Trio project for eighteen months, although there was wide disbelief in his report.

"The Droid Works is in the toilet," employees murmured in the halls of Z Building. At least half the remaining staff was prepared to leave at any moment. Besides a weekly paycheck, the only reason there wasn't a full-on mutiny at the meeting was that people were calculating whether they wanted to stick around for the Lucasfilm Christmas party, to which they were inexplicably re-invited.

"I've never seen anything like it," wrote one employee in a private journal. "Bad morale isn't even the best way to describe it. *Misery* is perhaps a better word. Collective sadness."

Everyone knew that Lucasfilm was ramping up its production division, with *Indy III*, *Tucker*, and *Willow* all in the pipeline. Anyone with an interest in film was eyeing internal positions that might open up with the company—as a way to transition from the sinking Droid Works ship.

On December 19, 1986, Bill Butler informed key staff that the EditDroid had been invited by BTS to the U.S. Film Festival. A small team including Rob Lay and Ken Carson prepared to go, but were understandably skittish about going anywhere when it was almost certain the company was undergoing radical transformations.

"We aren't going anywhere on a plane without a roundtrip ticket in hand," they said, "and accommodations paid for in advance."

There was little expectation that the company would be around when they returned. Even with the festival invite, BTS was waffling on a deal. Bill Butler sent an email to the team leaders, "There is no reason whatsoever to interpret this current situation as being either favorable or unfavorable."

The writing was on the wall. One employee commented that Z Building was starting to look like a morgue.

On January 22, the Droid team arrived in Park City. The nine-year-old U.S. Film Festival was about to become the Sundance Film Festival; but in 1987 it was still a quiet gathering on the snowy main drag of Park City.[14]

The EditDroid was set up in a large room (a converted bowling alley near the famous Egyptian Theater) along with some equipment from BTS—their telecine machine and a graphical animation computer that allowed users to perform simple 3-D graphics. It was all very high-tech and impressive, and VIPs from the festival toured through the space. Bosch promoted the venue announcing "Film and Video: They do work together," and had introductions and workshops every hour for three days.

The key cast and crew of the big films at the festival—*Beyond Therapy*, *Stacking*, *Square Dance*— all signed up for EditDroid demonstrations. A petite fifteen-year old Winona Ryder sat through scene 50 from *Return of the Jedi*.[15] So did Robert Redford. It was all very impressive, although any questions about the future availability of the product were met with evasive replies and knowing glances among the team.

In the midst of the star-studded demonstrations, on January 23, Lucasfilm issued a press release that announced that The Droid Works was being closed. According to the announcement they were going to "cease commercial manufacturing and marketing of the EditDroid and SoundDroid and continue research and development of electronic editing systems under Sprocket Systems." Said Doug Norby, "We feel that additional supporting technology needs to become available before pursuing marketing efforts."

Apparently Butler's negotiations with BTS had fallen apart, and the EditDroid and its small team in Park City were free agents, left at the festival to hustle for future work, promote their own technological interests, and just have a good time.[16] Which they did.

The close of The Droid Works made headlines in *The Hollywood Reporter*: "Hollywood Ponders Droid Works Demise." Ken Yas said in the article, "You need to understand the full range of implications—economic, political, and social—that would revolve around trying to change the way editors do things. Without that wisdom and insight, the company was doomed to fail."

[14] It wasn't officially renamed until 1991. The premiere of Steven Soderbergh's *sex, lies and videotape* in 1989 put the festival on the map, and Quentin Tarantino's directorial debut, *Reservoir Dogs*, in 1992 secured its place in the industry.

[15] With a part in *Square Dance*, it was the year before her breakout role in *Beetlejuice*.

[16] Rob Lay and his team conspired to pitch BTS on their own next generation nonlinear editing system. Lay had heard that Apple was planning to release new higher power Macintosh computers in 1987, code-named "Paris." He thought they could build a low-cost product for the Mac. "We formulated a plan to get Lucasfilm to license us the source code of the Droid," said Lay. But Bosch wasn't open to the alternative. Eventually, the group disbanded.

Ken Carson sent his compatriots an email that read, "What a long strange trip it's been." And with that, the disaspora was complete—the breeze had taken the spores from Lucasfilm and scattered them to just about everywhere.

epilogue

Return and *Revenge*

[1987–2005]

LUCAS MADE the *Star Wars* saga to finance his dream. That dream, like Coppola's and so many of the radical filmmakers from the 1970s, was to overturn Hollywood. To make films outside the "system."

Coppola's execution of this was American Zoetrope. Lucas' was Skywalker Ranch. Both were fueled by modern technology that they'd buy if they could, and invent if they had to. Money gave Lucas an advantage few else would ever have. In addition to escaping the system, he used that money to fund years of pure research into new technologies producing a wide range of results.

The projects that made up the Lucasfilm Computer Division all experienced radically different fates in the years following 1987. Games and THX stayed on at Lucasfilm. A few Pixar Image Computers remained at Lucasfilm as well, installed in Industrial Light & Magic, their powers rippling through the films they'd create. The computer researchers realigned with their respective industries, and their technological work was born again in new forms.

On these last few pages is a short navigation through the legacy of the Lucasfilm projects.

The Editing Project

The closing of The Droid Works was not the end of the "droid" vision. Lucasfilm pulled the EditDroid back into the deep recesses of Sprockets, in the back rooms of the Tech Building at the Ranch, and gave a small team of new video engineers a few more years to try to refine the product, stabilize it, and get it functional for cutting negative accurately. Lucasfilm bought itself time and a new calm.

Only twenty-four EditDroids were ever manufactured. The product that was its principal competitor, the Montage Picture Processor, had faired only slightly better. While more than twice as many Montages were built, the company went out of business twice over the period of the EditDroid, and declared bankruptcy in 1986.[1]

[1] Montage was bought at auction for $700,000 by New York attorney Simon Haberman, who recognized the value in the Hollywood rental market. Haberman continued to develop the product to compete with the analog nonlinear systems.

In 1988 the first all-digital video editing systems were built in east coast isolation. Avid founder Bill Warner showed a prototype of his Avid/1 at NAB 1988 in a hotel room. It ran on the Apollo graphics workstation and played video at only 15fps without audio.[2] Among the feedback he got was to move to the Apple Macintosh platform. Apple was also interested in seeing the Avid run on its hardware.[3]

In 1989 the Lucasfilm editDROID was re-released (same name, different capitalization). Coinciding with the corporate reorganization of Lucasfilm, the editDROID came out of in-house seclusion and was starting to get some use in Hollywood. Lucasfilm opened a Los Angeles branch of LucasArts Entertainment, which, among other things, rented the few editDROIDs that had been built (eighteen new systems, with twelve more under construction).

Oliver Stone and his editor David Brenner were early to give it a shot on *The Doors* (1990), but it would be a few more years before there was any real interest. Competing analog products continued to get introduced, with features improving, and prices dropping on system purchase and rental.

Prototypes of the EMC2 and the Avid (now on a Macintosh) were shown at the NAB convention in the spring of '89. As the price per gigabyte of storage continued to decline, the more useful it made a digital editing system: it could store more raw film to work on, and it would present its stored film with increasingly better resolutions.[4]

The next few years represented the most painful transition—the digital editing tools were not yet very good and still very expensive, but the nonlinear analog tools were clearly going to be dinosaurs, and thus a hard sell. Montage quickly realized that the highest value in its business was not from the editing rental market, but rather from the copious patents secured by the systems' inventors.[5]

By 1992 Coppola's friend Carroll Ballard had used the new editDROID for scenes on *Wind*, with his editor Michael Chandler (who had cut *Amadeus*). John McTiernan, hot off *The Hunt for Red October,* tried the Droid on his follow-up film, *Medicine Man.* And young upstart director Steven Soderbergh, after the rush from *sex, lies and videotape*, opted to edit his film *Kafka* on the Droid. The system was starting to hold its own.[6] But digital arrived faster than anyone had expected. For years it would be so inferior to analog that few professionals would touch it, but that didn't stop the teeming masses in corporate and small town America who were thrilled to get their hands on the manipulative power of digital media.

Besides Avid and EMC2, which had already taken a shot at performing the rigorous demands of feature films (albeit very low-budget films),[7] a third digital product also came out in this period, the Lightworks, from a team in London. The co-founder of Lightworks wanted to build a system that was both simple to use and more playful than traditional systems.[8]

[2] Avid's founder, Bill Warner had previously been a marketing manager at Apollo computer, where he experienced difficulty in making demonstration editing reels on linear videotape. The initial competitor to the Avid was the EMC2 (from Editing Machines Corp.), developed concurrently by Bill Ferster in Washington, D.C .

[3] Apple showed Warner the in-house EconoDroid that the Lucasfilm Games Division had built for them, to prepare material for interactive presentation.

[4] In 1991 Apple announced a new file format: QuickTime. The debut of QuickTime coincided with Adobe's release of a new consumer editing product: Premiere. Adobe had purchased software called "ReelTime" the prior year. Randy Ubillos, the product's inventor, had developed it largely as a demonstration tool for new video digitizing cards that were being produced by his employer, SuperMac.

[5] The Montage originated the use of digital picture labels to represent clips of film, and the value of enforcing these patents was a coup for owner Simon Haberman. Soon, Montage was collecting fees from every digital editing system on the market…and eventually Microsoft and Adobe.

Rather than a KEM-style shuttle knob—as was central to the edit-DROID—the Lightworks featured a Steinbeck-style controller, a small shuttle lever with very fine control over the material. Unlike the EMC2 and Avid, where editors preferred to use a typewriter keyboard—the Lightworks was entirely focused on the high-end, high-profile markets.

In 1992, virtually no Hollywood feature films were cut digitally, but 1993 became a year of radical transition; digital tools reached a break-point economically—storing the hours of film required could now be managed on available disk drives; and functionality—the tools now had all the features required to edit and conform film accurately, without crashing.[9] Dozens of film editors tried the Avid and the Lightworks. In February, Avid went public, positioning itself as the market leader in the burgeoning field of digital editing.

Both Doug Norby and Steve Arnold attended NAB in April 1993 and saw the unprecedented explosion of lean software companies, new video formats, and intense interest in digital nonlinear editing.

"Did you see the Avid?" Steve Arnold asked Norby upon returning to the Ranch.

"Yea, I know…I know…we're hosed." Norby replied.

J&R film company, the owner of Moviola, began the slow phase-out of their Moviola rental business, and began to acquire digital nonlinear editing systems to rent; these included all the editDROID inventory from Lucasfilm. The upright Moviola had been the staple of editors for almost seventy-five years. No more would ever be made.

With Lucasfilm no longer selling editing systems, the only remaining issue was to capitalize on the patents and technology they had invented over the years, to find them a home. Norby began investigating both Lightworks and Avid as potential strategic partners. George said he liked the Lightworks, but found it too similar to the editDROID.

He felt that editing picture couldn't exist without a digital solution for editing and mixing sound, and Lightworks didn't have it. Avid did. Avid had just purchased Digidesign, a leading digital audio software company. Lucasfilm critically evaluated both products and both companies.

"Lightworks was like us," commented Lucas, "a bunch of editors who said 'Let's just build a really great system,' whereas Avid was a corporation that said 'We're out to make money,' and so they had thought about it completely differently."

In 1994 Lucasfilm struck a deal with Avid, selling them all the underlying Droid technology and allowing them to wear the crown as official inheritor

[6] During this time, both the Montage and Ediflex were being improved. Use of nonlinear systems was growing, but still small: each TV season more high profile projects gave them a try, from CBS's massive miniseries *Lonesome Dove* to Kubrick's theatrical film *Full Metal Jacket*. At Clark Higgins' urging, Francis Coppola decided to try the Montage on *Godfather III*.

[7] Notable was Sam Raimi's cheap thriller, *Army of Darkness*, which cut on the PC-based EMC2.

[8] Paul Bamborough, co-founder of Solid State Logic, a leading audio console manufacturer.

[9] *Lost In Yonkers, The Fugitive, True Lies, Mrs. Doubtfire,* and *Speed* were all successfully completed and released.

of the Lucas editing legacy. That year, while the technology was still relatively new and untested, dozens of the biggest names in filmmaking were dipping their toes into the digital nonlinear water. Not entirely unrelated, the industry gave the products its ultimate blessing—both the Avid and the Lightworks received Academy Awards for technical achievement.

By 1995, the list of directors who had committed to digital nonlinear editing tools included James Cameron, Mike Nichols, Peter Bogdanovich, Oliver Stone, Chris Columbus, Alan Pakula, William Friedkin, Barry Levinson, Robert Altman, Quentin Tarantino, Lawrence Kasdan, Clint Eastwood, Sydney Pollack, Brian DePalma, Norman Jewison and Danny DeVito.[10]

At the 1995 NAB trade show, Avid showed a prototype of an AvidDroid—an Avid run by a very editDROID-like controller. But the product was more marketing grandstanding than technological marriage, and it soon disappeared.[11] But Avid continued to grow. Where they had a little hotel room in 1988, Avid now dominated the tradeshow floor.[12] And Lucasfilm was finally, and completely, out of the equipment manufacturing business.

Mel Gibson had used the Lightworks on his film *Braveheart*, which won Best Picture in 1996, though editor Steve Rosenblum failed to win an Oscar. A year later, in 1997, an Avid was used on the film that won both Best Picture and Best Editing—*The English Patient*, cut by Walter Murch, produced by Bay Area independent filmmaker Saul Zaentz. Considering how competitive Lucas and Coppola had been over the decades, and with each of them taking sides, as it were, in the nonlinear arena (George with the EditDroid and eventually Francis with the Montage), it was a fitting moment understood by very few. Perfect the award should go to Murch, their close friend and collaborator. While the technology came from neither camp, the moment was a tribute to them both.

The success of Avid changed all editing. The company was smart enough to acquire venture capital, giving it a cash position unprecedented among manufacturers of competing products. Not since the Moviola in film, and CMX twenty years earlier in video, had a company so dominated the tools of the editing industry. But there was always room for improvement.

Commented Lucas, "I think the Avid is way too complicated for its own good."

The price of storage and CPU cycles continued to drop along the predicted lines of Moore's Law, and soon digital video editing was no longer the hegemony of the studios and broadcasters. The trends that allowed Avid to wipe out CMX would come to haunt it ten years further down the road. Apple recognized the coming affordability, and launched an all-out assault on the

[10] Spielberg's conspicuous absence was largely due to his editor Michael Kahn's passion for celluloid.

[11] More importantly that year, Avid continued with corporate acquisitions. After the purchase of Digidesign, it acquired high-end paint and compositing system companies, Parallax Software and Elastic Reality.

[12] Both Avid and Lightworks shared the 1994 Scientific and Engineering Academy Award.

market leader. The product Final Cut Pro, acquired by Apple from Macromedia in 1998, was released for $1,000—an order of magnitude less expensive than the cheapest comparable product from Avid.[13] Now that they could afford it, would consumers actually want professional editing tools?

In just a few years, Apple eroded a significant proportion of Avid's position in the professional editing realm. Walter Murch, ever the artist-technologist-pioneer, made headlines when he used Apple's Final Cut Pro to cut the major motion picture, *Cold Mountain* (2004).[14]

The Tech Building was finally alive with editing workstations, digital high-definition film, and sound moving through the pipelines of the Ranch. And the Avid in George's private office, connected to the servers downstairs, represented post-production in much the way he had always imagined it could be. In spite of his criticisms of the Avid, Lucas continued to use the product for the *Star Wars* prequels, with Ben Burtt handling much of the picture and sound editing.[15]

Seventeen years after George Lucas and Francis Coppola committed themselves to changing filmmaking by introducing new technology—editing tools in particular—the methods they embraced had become the status quo in Hollywood.

The Sound Project

The SoundDroid fared less well. The Droid Works closed before the production-ready version of the device was completed, before any products were delivered. Still, the audio research that went into it lived on. In the last months of 1986, Lucasfilm tried to find an industry leader to purchase the technologies that had been created there, with no success.

A few years earlier, a consortium of manufacturers, including Phillips and Sony, introduced the CD digital audio format, which was released to the public in 1983. Soon, new recordings were being made digitally, with high fidelity tools, and transferred to CD. But what of the old recordings? Every record album, movie soundtrack, and radio program ever made (by some calculations, millions of hours of audio), would need to find their way to disc.

The recordings were pretty badly beaten up; all the artifacts of the analog equipment—the hiss, the pops and clicks, the hum of wires—could be removed using previously unknown techniques.

At the same time, former Droid Works CEO Bob Doris was establishing a new company to start afresh. Doris stewed for a few months after being unceremoniously dismissed from Lucasfilm. Now he narrowed his focus from

[13] Refined by Ubillos and a small team of engineers, including the EditDroid's Ken Carson.

[14] Murch shared his experience in a book, *Behind the Seen: How Walter Murch Edited* Cold Mountain *Using Apple's Final Cut Pro and What This Means for Cinema*, by Charles Koppelman (2004).

[15] Ben Burtt, working at Lucasfilm throughout the years, moved from sound design and mixing to picture editing, and even directing on occasion. He is the credited editor on the films in the second *Star Wars* trilogy.

all-editing and all-sound post-production, to just one facet of sound post-production, the "de-noising" of analog recordings.

In the spirit of Lucasfilm development, where the old versions were built and then thrown out, leaving a clean slate to improve, Doris planned to build a new version of one facet of the SoundDroid, the de-nosing algorithms.

After Mary Sauer left Lucasfilm, she joined Bob Doris. Bob and Mary and another ex-Droid worker, Jeff Borish, reassembled themselves with a SUN-3 computer in an upstairs apartment in San Francisco's Richmond district, raised a small amount of capital, and launched Sonic Solutions. They called their new process "NoNoise." Andy Moorer joined them when the Droid Works closed.

Bruce Botnik had been the engineer/producer for The Doors, and had worked with them at a fateful concert at the Hollywood Bowl on July 5, 1968. Recorded on four film cameras and with sixteen tracks of audio, Jim Morrison's audio track was completely unusable, with loud and random crackles and snaps caused by the faulty microphone cable. The more Morrison danced around the stage, the worse the audio was. Botnik had tried every conceivable technology, every new invention and every acoustical trick, to fix the track. He had traveled the world for almost twenty years with the recording he desperately wanted to repair. In 1987 Mary Sauer convinced him to try NoNoise.

> Noises both colored music and detracted from it. Digitally removing noise was a somewhat subjective process. An audio track could have a tiny bit, or a lot of noise, depending on the desired effect.
>
> Removing crackle and pops (called de-clicking) was manual: listening on headphones to music, often a fraction of a second at a time, removing unwanted audio spikes, verifying nothing else had been changed. De-hissing the track was different. It involved finding a small bit of the recording, maybe $1/5$ of a second, where there was pure hiss, no sound of any kind. Once armed with a "fingerprint" of the noise, the Sonic Solutions software could subtract it from the music.

The results were amazing. Botnik wept with joy. The album and the movie *The Doors Live at the Hollywood Bowl* was released later that year.

Between 1987 and 1989 Sonic Solutions refined the software tools, and moved them from SUN workstations to the new Apple Macintosh II, which was finally capable of managing the specialized audio hardware they had designed.[16]

Sonic went public in 1994 and began preparing for the eventual shift from digital audio to digital video. In 1996, working with key consumer electronics companies (mostly from Japan) as the DVD format was developed and

[16] The *mini*computer was finally able to be replaced by the *micro*computer.

introduced, Sonic offered the first comprehensive set of tools for professionals to prepare films for release on DVD.[17]

With Steven Jobs' return to Apple in 1997 there was new interest there in DVD-video burning.[18] As the price of DVD recorders began to fall dramatically in 1999, Sonic began to bring its PC-based software tools to consumers.[19] Apple's tools, though elegant, remained limited to the Macintosh platform, leaving the larger Windows universe as Sonic's demesne. In 2005 more than 80 percent of Hollywood DVDs were created on Sonic workstations. It licensed its DVD creation technology to other companies, including Adobe, Sony, and Yahoo!, and corporate reports state that it will be integrated into the Microsoft OS "Longhorn."

The Graphics Project

Pixar had a wildly different path. Although Ed and Alvy and David and the rest of the former Graphics Group were cut off from the body of Lucasfilm, they remained on Kerner. They were busy with the orders for the Image Computer that had stacked up during the transition. They also continued to refine their software tools.

Steven Jobs was busy with his new company, NeXT.

After Siggraph 1986, when they showed *Luxo Jr.*, the graphics community hailed them as the next great thing—not the next great *animation studio*, but providers of the next great technology. The films proved it. John Lasseter's virtuosity at bringing life to 3-D models was praised and everyone waited for the next year's film. *Luxo* was nominated for an Academy Award for Best Animated Short Film—the first computer generated film to be so honored.

P · I · X · A · R

As Lucasfilm's departments began moving to Skywalker Ranch, Pixar expanded from C Building into A Building and then E Building. To show off Pixar's sophisticated hardware, Catmull allowed Lasseter to maintain a tiny animation team to create short films.[20]

Perhaps the biggest purchaser of the Pixar Image Computer was Disney Studios. In 1986, after years of negotiating, Ed and Alvy (the top Pixar executives), signed a deal with Disney for their cel painting system CAPS (the Computer Animation Production System). Implicit in the terms was that no one ever find out that Disney was using computers.[21]

"They thought it would take away the magic," recalled Alvy.

Disney was a great client, but Pixar struggled financially. Sales of their expensive hardware, while brisk at first, slowed drastically in the following

[17] Called "pre-mastering," it involves all the steps to input an analog movie and other sources, build menus and navigation, and do the compression required to place everything on the disc.

[18] Recording data to a DVD disc is a separate kind of encoding from using a disc to play movies and video.

[19] In 2000, Apple purchased a DVD tools competitor of Sonic—the German company Astarte. In early 2001, Apple announced the "SuperDrive," one of the first DVD recorders to be integrated into a personal computer and including an innovative consumer DVD-Video authoring program called "iDVD." Later in 2001, Apple purchased another of Sonic's competitors, Spruce Technologies, and subsequently released a professional DVD creation tool: DVD Studio Pro.

[20] Their second short film, *Red's Dream*, premiered at Siggraph in '87.

[21] CAPS was tested on one shot from *The Little Mermaid* (1989), then brought fully online for *The Rescuers Down Under* (1990), and the following year's *Beauty and the Beast*. Disney had long been developing 3-D tools in its feature animation department, as far back as *Tron* and integrated into traditional animation in *The Great Mouse Detective* (1986). The transition to digital compositing with CAPS allowed Disney to incorporate more 3-D elements, and in more sophisticated ways. The most impressive example at the time was in *Beauty and the Beast* (backgrounds in the ballroom scene). The main characters were drawn, but the room was 3-D and all were merged digitally.

years. Lasseter's short *Tin Toy* premiered at Siggraph in '88, and *Knick Knack* in '89. The accolades for the little projects was all that kept Pixar from laying off the small group of animators.

Jobs had capitalized Pixar with a revolving line of credit. The debt service alone was brutal, and Jobs realized it would be cheaper to pay it off and start over "fresh." In order to do that, however, he insisted the employees, including Ed and Alvy, give up their stock. They did so without much complaint. Staying together was reason enough.

The company had been hemorrhaging cash from the start, and by 1989 it was clear Pixar couldn't continue supporting itself through computer sales.[22] After adding a user friendly front-end and some associated tools, Pixar began selling their updated REYES rendering software, calling it RenderMan.

Tin Toy won the Oscar for Best Animated Short, and fresh from that success, Lasseter and Ralph Guggenheim spearheaded a new effort: producing television commercials. This was designed to make the animators, long a fringe element at the hardware company, self-sufficient. It would also allow them to build their technical skills.[23]

In 1990 Pixar stopped selling the Pixar Image Computer altogether, left the Lucasfilm "campus" on Kerner Blvd., and moved into a one-story office building on Point Richmond, about ten minutes away. Their life as a hardware company was over. Pixar was now supported mostly by RenderMan sales and the production of fifteen lucrative television commercials.

In late 1990, Peter Schneider, the head of Disney Feature Animation, called Pixar and suggested they discuss the possibility of making a feature film. The following February, the team from Pixar met with Jeffrey Katzenberg[24] in his conference room, and John Lasseter pitched his idea: a buddy movie about two toys who get set on a collision course at "their boy's" birthday party and ultimately end up on a chase to catch up with their owner and become bonded as friends. Katzenberg loved buddy movies. The pitch was a success. By March, the deal was signed to deliver three full-length feature films.

But Alvy Ray Smith, who was executive vice president of Pixar, overstepped a line with Jobs—that fine line between speaking truth-to-power, and outright contempt, and sowed the seeds of what became his eventual resignation. In the negotiating process he retained the rights to refine work he had been doing with image editing software. Turning those ideas into a product, Alvy created a new company he called Altamira.[25]

After almost twenty years in the trenches together, Ed's and Alvy's paths were separated.

Steven Jobs, preoccupied with NeXT, considered Pixar a side project. NeXT had investors; Pixar was all his own. "While we went to see him at NeXT every

[22] Adding to their flow of revenue, Pixar licensed a number of its patents, in particular the stochastic sampling patent based on Rob Cook's work that allowed for motion blur. Microsoft paid more than $3 million; a few years alter, Silicon Graphics (SGI) paid $6 million.

[23] Their first project was a commercial for Tropicana orange juice. A year later they produced commercials for Trident gum, Lifesavers, Listerine, Pillsbury (the doughboy), and Volkswagen.

[24] Katzenberg was hired at Paramount in 1975 and eventually assigned to revive the *Star Trek* franchise. Later he ran film production under executive Michael Eisner. When Eisner moved to Disney in 1984, Katzenberg went with him and was charged with reviving Disney's feature animation division. He is credited with the string of new classics from Disney, including *The Little Mermaid* (1988), *Beauty and the Beast* (1991), *Aladdin* (1992), and *The Lion King* (1994). In 1994 Katzenberg left Disney and co-founded DreamWorks SKG with Steven Spielberg and David Geffen.

[25] In 1994, Alvy sold Altamira to Microsoft for an undisclosed amount of Microsoft stock (thought to be worth millions). Microsoft was attempting to aggregate technologies that would draw developers into its web design standards.

two or three months, he visited our offices in Point Richmond no more than five times between 1986 and 1992, said Ralph Guggenheim, "no exaggeration."

In 1993 the CAPS development team joined their Disney compatriots (and Alvy Ray Smith) to pick up a technical achievement Academy Award. Winning the award was tricky because Disney still hadn't let on that it was utilizing computers in its process. The next year the RenderMan development team also won an Academy Award.[26]

In the months prior to the completion of *Toy Story*, Jobs was struggling; NeXT and Pixar were both sucking cash. Word was circulating that he would accept $50 million for Pixar, the amount he had poured into it. But when he saw the first screening of the film—and realized the avalanche of excitement it was undoubtedly going to create—he recognized not only the advantage in hanging onto it, but also the opportunity to take the company public.

Almost overnight, the computer manufacturer (updated to software company) was reborn as an animation studio.

Pixar scheduled its initial public offering in November 1995, concurrent with the release of *Toy Story*; it sold about 10 percent of the company and raised $150 million, making Jobs, once again, an extraordinarily wealthy young man.[27]

Only 77 minutes long, *Toy Story* had required 800,000 hours of number crunching by 117 SUN workstations. The credits represented a team that had worked together for more than a decade; written and directed by John Lasseter, executive produced by Ed Catmull,[28] co-produced by Ralph Guggenheim, sound work by former Sprockets soundmen Gary Rydsrom and Gary Summers. "Visual Effects" were credited to dozens, including Loren Carpenter, Rob Cook, Tom Porter, Bill Reeves, and many from the old team. It grossed more than $350 million dollars worldwide.

In 1996, Pixar (Alvy Ray Smith, Ed Catmull, Tom Porter, Tom Duff) won another Academy Award for its technical contributions to digital image compositing. In 1998, Alvy Ray Smith and Tom Porter shared an award with Dick Shoup for their pioneering efforts in the development of digital paint systems.

In 2001, Rob Cook, Loren Carpenter and Ed Catmull shared the Academy's highest technical award, where it was declared that "their broad professional influence in the industry continues to inspire and contribute to the advancement of computer-generated imagery for motion pictures."[29]

[26] At the 65th Academy Awards, Loren Carpenter, Rob Cook, Ed Catmull, Tom Porter, Pat Hanrahan, Tony Apodaca and Darwyn Peachey took home a plaque for their software that "produces images used in motion pictures from 3-D computer descriptions of shape and appearance." Two years later, David DiFrancesco and Gary Starkweather shared a technical achievement award with Scott Squires of ILM and Gary Demos and Dan Cameron of Triple-I, for their work on their laserscanners (and film input scanning).

[27] About 20% of the stock went to employees, 10% to the public, and Jobs retained the balance, giving him a net worth of just over $1 billion—something Apple hadn't yet been able to provide him. In June, 2005, Pixar had a market cap of $5.9 billion. While four or five of the original team became millionaires after the IPO, Jobs' idiosyncratic awarding of stock caused some tension within the long tight-knit group.

[28] And, of course, Steven Jobs.

A Pixar promotional giveaway in 2002: a wind-up toy of Martin Newell's famous teapot—sporting the RenderMan logo.

Toy Story launched Pixar on the road to a string of blockbuster movies.[30] Today, Pixar Animation Studios is widely regarded as the intellectual inheritor of the animation kingdom created by Disney, once thought inviolable.

The three components of the Lucasfilm Computer Division that Lucas did not want to shepherd—graphics, digital audio, editing—all ended up in some manner on the desk of Steven Jobs. Directly, Pixar (as biggest shareholder). Indirectly, Sonic Solutions and Avid (as biggest competitor).

Lucasfilm may have divested itself of the computer research, but ultimately, the R&D era benefited the company. Lucasfilm's brand became inseparable from its reputation as a technologically savvy organization.

Industrial Light & Magic

[29] Today, many members of the graphics project (and a few of the SoundDroid team) are still at Pixar: Carpenter, DiFrancesco, Cook, Porter, Duff—as well as former DroidWorks staff Michael O'Brien, Michael Shantzis, Heidi Stetner, Kay Frankom.

[30] No studio has produced a comparable unbroken string of hits. Total U.S. grosses by June 2005: *Toy Story* ($192 million), *A Bugs Life* ($163 million), *Toy Story 2* ($246 million), *Monsters, Inc.* ($256 million), *Finding Nemo* ($340 million), and *The Incredibles* ($262 million).

[31] Wire removal was a big deal. Every time an actor flew across a set or stunt guy blasted off a platform, the thin wires that made it possible had to be taken out of the shot. It was challenging by hand, requiring the delicate smearing of Vaseline on a piece of glass integrated into the optical printer. Even though it wouldn't be semi-automated until years later, the computer, by comparison, made it easy.

After Pixar's departure, George Joblove and Doug Kay remained at ILM to develop native talent with the new digital tools. They wrote their own custom software for the Pixar computer, to execute specific special effects for each film that came through their department. At first, the use of digital effects in films was sporadic and specialized. The first use of the film scanners and paint software (LayerPaint) was to remove wires from a few shots in *Howard the Duck* (1986).[31] John Knoll, a young motion control assistant, got an opportunity to watch a bit of the wire removal using Mark Leather's paint software on the $100,000 computer.

"Man, I want to be able to do that on *my* computer," said Knoll. This is the future. That's where it's all going to go…."

John Knoll (with his brother, a grad student at the University of Michigan) developed new software for Apple's Mac Plus computer over the next few years while John continued his job at ILM, contributing to films like *Innerspace* and *Willow*. In 1987 and 1988 they started shopping their product throughout the industry, unable to find a buyer. Finally, in 1989 they licensed their software to Adobe; it was called Photoshop. Knoll remained at ILM.

ILM's use of computer graphics continued to be largely 2-D and paint oriented. Realistic film-resolution 3-D modeling still wasn't practical. They made a 2-D model of an airplane that flew in the skies for a few frames of Spielberg's *Empire of the Sun* (1987).

In 1988, Doug Smyth developed software to take a 2-D image and through the careful selecting of key points in the frame, transform ("map") it into a different 2-D image, causing an odd blending between two images. He named the software "Morf." It was tried first on a scene in Ron Howard's

Willow (1988). (When *Newsweek* wrote about the effect, they misspelled it—or actually spelled it properly—"morph," or "morphing," soon became widely used).

Morphing became all the rage in computer graphics, and the technique was widely imitated, with varying degrees of success, in movies, television, and commercials. ILM used the effect again the following year in *Indiana Jones and the Last Crusade* (1989), but it reached its peak of hipness in James Cameron's *Terminator 2* (1991).

Cameron's *The Abyss* (1989) and *Terminator 2* pushed ILM to the limits of what was possible with 3-D digital "creatures" co-mingling with live action. In both, the creatures were aliens, so they could look both realistic and unreal. It wasn't until 1994, when Steven Spielberg wanted realistic dinosaurs to inhabit *Jurassic Park*, that 3-D modeling and rendering came of age.

Like many technological leaps, the use of computer graphics (CG) in *Jurassic Park* was unplanned. Movies take so long to develop, and technology moves so quickly, that CG only became viable well into the start of the production. It was the failure of the animatronics dinosaurs to look realistic and move quickly that provided the opportunity for computers to fill in. Even as Spielberg and the producers fretted about the inadequacy of the giant dinosaur models, a radical fringe at ILM was trying to reproduce dinosaur movement on their PCs. When Spielberg and company saw what is now called "the walk cycle," they realized CG could help. It also could provide new scene opportunities.

Dennis Muren, the lead effects producer at ILM since Edlund left in 1983,[32] had spent years working with model makers and animatronics designers, trying to prepare to execute the dinosaurs. "Back before *T2*," recalled Muren, "[Spielberg] had mentioned that he wanted a stampede sequence in *Jurassic Park*, with herds of animals, but he didn't know how to go about it. Creating herds of animals with puppets would be very difficult, so I thought maybe that was something we might be able to do with computer graphics."

The CG effort at ILM grew during production and went on to fully replace the miniature and go-motion techniques that had been under development for more than a year, and most of the larger animatronics. *Jurassic Park* was the first film to completely integrate the use of CG characters with live action so that it was seamless to the audience. The use of CG exploded following the film, at ILM and throughout Hollywood.

[32] Edlund left to open Boss Film, an effects company in the vein of ILM. By 1997 Boss was closed. Many of ILM's competitors were created by former staff, including Dykstra's Apogee (later closed), Scott Ross' Digital Domain (with James Cameron). "It has been a quirky business; in fact it may not be a business at all," said Jim Morris, president of LucasDigital, in a 1997 *New York Times* article. "The effects industry grew up with owner-operators [i.e., George Lucas]. They paid their bills and they broke even because they got to do what they loved."

Computer graphics swept through the industry and began to make previously impossible to film scenes—maybe too dangerous or too enormous—suddenly feasible. Industrial Light & Magic spawned its own field of competitors, from James Cameron's Digital Domain to Sony's Imageworks.

A decade later, at Lucas' insistence, virtually every aspect of ILM moved to digital. Matte painting, model building, miniature animation, rotoscoping, compositing of effects—the entire organization was computerized. Only some aspects of puppetry remained in the classic style.

THX Sound

While THX was never part of the Computer Division, the era of research at LFL gave rise to its development. By the mid-'80s, Lucasfilm and Dolby Labs were ping-ponging developments—"technological leapfrog" Tom Holman called it. Dolby was pushing improvements for recording sound on film and playing it back with expanded frequency and dynamic ranges; Lucasfilm focused on the auditorium.

In 1987, a committee of audio engineers debated the number of channels for digital sound on film. It was a lively debate about a range between two and eight channels; Holman proposed 5.1—five main channels and a dedicated sub-woofer channel. (Technically speaking, the sub-woofer represented 0.005 of a channel in bandwidth. "I call that marketing rounding!" said Holman.) 5.1 Surround Sound became the industry standard.[33]

The Theater Alignment Program (TAP), the sister project to THX, was initially merged under the THX banner, effectively loosing its identity as a quality-control operation; it was eventually absorbed by Dolby Labs.[34] Jim Kessler, who had been running the THX Division, left LFL in 1990 to follow the growing interest in high-end home theaters.

THX continued to grow inside Lucasfilm. A division with excellent revenues and low overhead, the THX Sound System became the *de facto* standard of superior theatrical presentation, and it had a profound impact on the theater industry. As the Tech Building at the Ranch was completed in 1987, Holman started to develop Home THX, while beginning to teach at USC.

In 1994, at the end of a seven-year consulting contract, Lucasfilm began bitter negotiations with Holman, stripping him of many of the creative privileges and product control he had long enjoyed. Holman felt their position was untenable and terminated the dialogue. By 1995 there were thousands of THX-certified theaters worldwide, and Holman was on his own.[35]

THX remained part of Lucasfilm until 2002, when it was spun off as an independent company, owned partly by LFL, with other corporate and private investors. Among them was Creative Labs, a Singapore-based corporation,[36] who leveraged the THX identity to support the high end of their product offerings.

The Lucasfilm Sound System had a direct impact on its own licensed theaters. It also became a growing influence within the industry, as many of its innovations, such as bi-amplification, became commonly used. Home THX thrives, continuing to build products licensing Holman's original patents.

[33] Zoetrope had used what they referred to as "5.2 channels" in the 70mm mix of *Apocalypse Now*.

[34] Dolby Labs was founded in the '60s by Ray Dolby. The Dolby-Lucasfilm association went back to *Star Wars* and the development of stereo surround, and it evolved into a whole Northern California influence on film sound. "It wasn't always an easy partnership between Dolby, Zoetrope, and Lucasfilm," said Tom Scott. "Francis or George would push to do something new and Dolby would have to pick up the pieces and make it work, but that's not always a bad thing." Dolby Labs raised $495 million at its IPO in February 2005.

[35] Kessler returned to Lucasfilm in 1996, to manage the interior development of ILM's domain at the new Letterman Digital Center in San Francisco. In 2004, when the design was completed, Kessler retired. Tom Holman began working with Audyssey Labs in 2005, a start-up company whose first product was a device that could tune professional and home theater sound.

[36] Founded in 1981. Creative's press said it were founded "with the vision that multimedia would revolutionize the way people interact with their PCs." In 1993 Creative acquired E-MU Systems, and in 1997, Cambridge SoundWorks.

The Games Division

"Games was a good group," said Norby. "I think the value of that group more than justified the investment that went into the Computer Division." Games was never quite like the other projects. Everyone else was making tools, but games were more like movies.

Re-situated at Skywalker Ranch, the Games Division flourished. Ron Gilbert and Gary Winnick expanded on the concept of adventure games with the continued development of *Maniac Mansion*. At that time, adventure games were combinations of text commands and images. A player would type "walk to door" and the computer would look at that, "parse" the language, and find the verb (walk) and object (door), and decide if it could give you another bit of information based on the command. But it was hit or miss. If someone typed "pull knob" and it was looking for "grab knob" there would be a disconnect.

Gilbert changed the way the instructions were given. "Let's get rid of the parser," he said. "There's already a limited number of words anyway; let's just put them on the screen and let you click on them." Pointing at a palette of actions and objects radically improved the experience of playing that kind of game.

Gilbert also created a new language for designing his adventure game. It seemed so useful he gave it a name: "Scripting Command Unit for *Maniac Mansion*," or SCUMM. Aside from the games themselves, SCUMM would prove to be one of the most significant developments from the Games Division. *Maniac Mansion* was released by Epyx and became a cult-phenomenon and financial blockbuster in the game world. It even led to a short-lived television series in 1990, produced by a number of Second City alum, including Eugene Levy and Michael Short (Martin Short's brother).

A screen from *Maniac Mansion* (1986). It's difficult to recognize how sophisticated the graphics were without comparing them to other games of the day. But given the limited color space and processing power, *Maniac Mansion* was one of the most expressive gaming displays of the era.

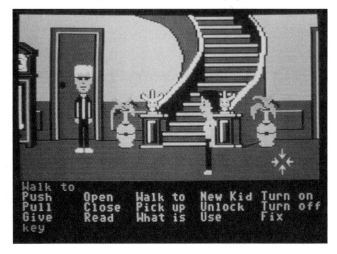

The success of Ron's SCUMM game engine lead to other LFL games based on the toolset, including David Fox's *Zak McKracken and the Alien Mindbenders* (1988) and Ron Gilbert's next effort, *The Secret of Monkey Island* (1990). All these adventures spawned legions of fans and years of sequels.

As Lucasfilm's confidence in the Games Division grew, it was agreed to test the waters with licensed characters, although it seemed risky to begin with *Star Wars* or *Indiana Jones* franchises. They chose *Labyrinth*.[37] Steve Arnold

[37] SCUMM wasn't ready, and so the *Labyrinth* adventure was a maze-filled navigation exercise executed with a pre-SCUMM "slot machine" text interface. Their follow-up to the licensed character games was *Indiana Jones and the Last Crusade* (1989).

and David Fox teamed up with Douglas Adams (author of *The Hitchhiker's Guide to the Galaxy*) to explore ways a videogame could have characters, themes and settings from a movie, but have its own plot.

Quantum finally rolled out *Habitat* in 1988, where it was quite successful for them, although the Commodore C64 computer was in decline by then and the market for the online community was ever shrinking. The game was rebranded *Club Caribe*, disabling many of its compelling attributes (the internal economy, the sex-change machine, weapons, magical items), but customer demand eventually saw that many of those features were returned in following years.

Said Morningstar, "In the end, it was *Habitat* in all but name."

Habitat was the prototype of the massively multi-player online role-playing game (MMORPG). A decade later, games like *EverQuest*[38] and eventually Lucasfilm's own *Star Wars Galaxies*, continued with that genre, leveraging the higher bandwidths on the Internet and 3-D graphical displays that were possible with modern computers.

After *Koronis Rift*, Noah Falstein began focusing on military simulations, which would begin a long line of successful war games. Falstein departed in 1992 to help launch The 3DO Company, a new venture from EA founder Trip Hawkins, and in 1995 became the third employee at Dreamworks Interactive. "Everything you do at Lucasfilm is under the shadow of George Lucas," Falstein said to the *San Francisco Chronicle* in 1998, "and sometimes you have to desire to go off and do something yourself."

Ron Gilbert left LFL Games in 1992 to start his own game company, Humongous Entertainment, specializing in kids software.[39] Ron negotiated with Lucasfilm to secure the rights to continue developing games with his SCUMM engine. Humongous became a game giant under Ron's leadership and spun off a division, Cavedog Entertainment (known for the *Total Annihilation* series of real-time strategy games).

Lucasfilm spent three years in litigation with Ron trying to undo their contract, but eventually reached a settlement that gave Ron rights to SCUMM. In 1995 Humongous Entertainment was sold to GT Interactive for $76 million in stock, leaving Ron to start a second company, Hulabee Entertainment, also in the children's game market.

Lucas never developed a personal interest in the videogames his company produced, but he did continue research into educational opportunities for games. In 1988 the Games Division cleaved into three distinct groups: Lucas Learning (for educational software), LucasArts Entertainment (the games

[38] *EverQuest,* released in 1999, hosts about half a billion subscribers, simultaneous users, who can explore a rich 3-D world and interact in the fantasy gaming environment.

[39] Best known for its children's adventure franchises, *Putt-Putt* and *Pajama Sam.*

developers), and Rebel Arts and Technology (developing location-based entertainment—"experiences" for theme parks and malls).[40] Lucas Learning and Rebel Arts remained at the Ranch, while LucasArts Entertainment—the largest group—moved back to A Building on Kerner, and then to a commercial property near Lucas Valley Road.

In 1988 Lucas established the George Lucas Educational Foundation (GLEF) a non-profit organization dedicated to "changing the face of public education, and sharing success stories of teaching and learning in the digital age." His creation of GLEF coincided with the early development of the *Young Indy* TV series, which integrated educational materials with *Indy*-style entertainment. Today they operate online (www.glef.org) and publish a magazine for educators called *Edutopia*.[41]

Nolan Bushnell, videogame pioneer and "serial entrepreneur" said in 2005 that education is a huge, untapped game market. "In three years, one third of revenue will be from game applications for education use."

The Games Division (renamed LucasArts Entertainment) steered away from the radical game innovation of its early years, and instead expanded their *Indiana Jones* and *Star Wars* franchise games, with relatively few non-film-related titles. Still, *Star Wars: Knights of the Old Republic* (a role-playing adventure) won Best Game at the 2004 Game Developers Conference.

The former Games Division, with 400 employees in 2005, remains one of the pillars of the Lucasfilm empire. In the summer of 2005, LucasArts joined Industrial Light & Magic and moved under one roof in the $350 million Letterman Digital Arts facility in San Francisco's Presidio. There, while the skills associated with game development are still unlike those required for film special effects, a workforce with experience in 3-D modeling and animation can circulate in both realms.

Francis Coppola

Coppola continued to make films under the Zoetrope banner throughout the years. The grapes begun in 1979 at his Napa estate were debuted in 1985: his Niebaum-Coppola Rubicon is now a classic. Coppola continued directing throughout the vagaries of his business: *The Cotton Club* (1984), *Peggy Sue Got Married* (1986), and *Gardens of Stone* (1987). In late 1986, Lucas urged Coppola to make *Tucker: The Man and His Dream*. According to Coppola's biography, "He would enjoy the benefits of Lucasfilm's state-of-the-art technology in San Rafael and [at the Ranch]. It would be like *American Graffiti* in reverse, with George supervising the production and Francis directing the show."

[40] David Fox managed Rebel Arts in its early years, before moving out on his own, starting Electric Eggplant game and entertainment consulting.

[41] Steve Arnold, former VP of the Games Division worked with Lucas to establish the organization and was GLEF vice chairman of the board. Steve left Lucasfilm in 1991 to work with Bill Gates; he later started a venture capital firm in Seattle, Polaris Venture Partners. In 2005 he was still serving as vice chairman of the GLEF.

Said Coppola, "Zoetrope failed because I was never realistic about finances. I never wanted to give up control to the money types who would come in and tell me, 'Well, you can't do *Napoleon*, you can't do *Koyaanisquatsi*, you can't do George Lucas' film.'"

But Coppola was always interested in the tools and the coming changes in the system. In 1988 Coppola told his biographer, "I am basically interested in a form of super television…I'm behaving now like a car speeding at 90mph…knowing that by the time I reach the junction, the bridge will be built. The bridge is not there right now, the new technology can't do the things that I imagined it could do, but I'm still committing myself in those directions knowing that in 1990, or 1992, it's going to be possible."

George Lucas

After *Star Wars*, Lucas was frustrated. "I was creatively very stifled," he said. "I had a lot of ideas that I wanted to do, and I was faced with trying to transform those ideas into puppets and people in rubber suits and very limited environments I could go to. And I was running out of environments—I had done all the deserts and jungles and snow planets that I could possible do, so I was running out of places I could shoot movies."

By 1989 Lucas was ready to get back into production. He wanted to do something small. He wanted to use digital technology. He even wanted to dovetail it with his educational initiatives. Lucas created a television series: *The Young Indiana Jones Chronicles,* based on the Indiana Jones character, but as a kid.

"I could see that George was looking for something else," said Rick McCallum, producer of the series. "He wanted to be in a different situation. He wanted to be in a world where things weren't taken that seriously, there wasn't the same protocol."

McCallum, an ex-pat making films in London, had met Lucas in 1984. "Even from that early time, I could see that [Lucas] yearned to do different, smaller stuff."

The series, which ran in 1992 and 1993, was a proving ground for a kind of filmmaking Lucas was attracted to: small budgets, one or two million dollars each; episodes shot quickly, sometimes in 16mm, sometimes on Super8; rehearsed in costume, edited fast on nonlinear editing systems; smart writers and many experimental directors, fully outside of the Hollywood system.[42] If one episode didn't work, the next one might.

McCallum and his teams used Skywalker Ranch as it had always been imagined, for the first time since it's creation.

"It was a *real* place where people could work together, party together, and try to write and come up with things. We'd be [at the Ranch] for a month at a time. We'd get drunk every night, and we'd be back in story meetings at eight

[42] It had a remarkable array of directors, including Terry Jones (of Monty Python fame), Nicolas Roeg (*Walkabout, The Man Who Fell to Earth, Bad Timing*), and writers David Hare (*The Hours*), Frank Darabont (*The Shawshank Redemption* and *The Green Mile*), Carrie Fisher (*Postcards from the Edge*) and others.

in the morning and wouldn't leave until eight at night…it was filmmaking camp."

The show was a period piece, like *Indiana Jones*, and it let Lucas begin to use digital tools for television in the way he understood would soon be able to do on film. With a high-end broadcasting tool called a Quantel Harry, they were able to produce a world that would have been impossible to find on location. They could shoot ten people and, with the Harry, create a believable crowd of thousands. They could build pyramids. They could recreate ancient empires.

In 1992 Lucas was honored by the Academy that seemed to have shunned him for years, presenting him with the Irving Thalberg Memorial Award.[43] The Thalberg statuette came home to a small display case at the entry to the Main House at Skywalker Ranch, alongside a tile from the Space Shuttle, Obi Wan Kenobi's light saber, and Indiana Jones' whip.

Like digital nonlinear editing, computer graphics and animation reached a new degree of maturity in 1994. As Pixar was finally able to make its animated feature film, *Toy Story*, ILM was impressing both Spielberg and Lucas with its use of similar 3-D graphical capabilities in *Jurassic Park* (and to a lesser degree, *Forrest Gump*).[44]

When George Lucas saw what ILM was doing on *Jurassic Park*, he realized that computer animation in film had reached the point he had loved in video. It would now be possible to realize his vision for another *Star Wars* trilogy. In 1994 Lucas announced on the front page of *Daily Variety* that he would start writing the prequel. He also said he was going to direct the film, which was tentatively scheduled for a 1998 release.

Though Lucas is often faulted (as much as he is lauded) for the advent of the blockbuster and the subsequent "ruination" of cinema, he must also share credit for the renaissance of independent filmmaking and the enjoyment the public gets from sounds and images on a screen. Lucasfilm contributed to the full spectrum of cinema today, from epics that would be unmakable without digital tools, to small personal digital films created by artists—or even kids.

Francis Coppola had long dreamed that the film in filmmaking would be replaced by a digital, high-resolution alternative that was neither film nor video. For different reasons, but particularly for special effects creation and ease of integration, Lucas wanted the same thing. After the success of *Young Indy*, he brought back his producing partner Rick McCallum, and they leveraged the unimaginable anticipation for his new *Star Wars* films, to coerce Sony into developing production-ready high definition cameras for the project.

[43] As an added treat, the crew of the orbiting space shuttle Atlantis participated in the award presentation and carried an Oscar statuette onboard.

[44] *Forrest Gump* (1994), directed by Robert Zemeckis, who co-wrote Speilberg's *1941*, and later went on to direct *Romancing the Stone* (1984), *Back to the Future* (1985), *Who Framed Roger Rabbit* (1988), *Contact* (1997), *Cast Away* (2000), *The Polar Express* (2004).

In 1996 Sony committed to creating a film-style digital camera (using a format called 24P) for Lucasfilm. Although legions of tests were done for *Episode I*, at production time the cameras were not ready. Still, *Episode I* had set the stage for filmmaking's move to high-def. And it became the first major studio release to be exhibited electronically (in selected theaters), using a high-definition projection system.[45]

Lucas said that "tests [of Sony and Panavision cameras] have convinced me that the familiar look and feel of motion picture film are fully present in this digital 24P system, and that the picture quality between the two is indistinguishable on the large screen."[46]

George Lucas revisited the first trilogy and fine-tuned it using his new digital tools. He added backgrounds, inserted some 3-D characters, fleshed out details, changed key events, and eventually updated the ending of *Return of the Jedi*.

"To me," said Lucas, "[the revised versions] are the films I wanted to make. Anybody who makes films knows the film is never finished. It's abandoned or it's ripped out of your hands and it's thrown into the marketplace, never finished. And even most artists, most painters, even composers, would want to come back and redo their work. They've got a new perspective on it, they've got more resources, better technology, and they can fix or finish the things that were never done…I wanted to actually finish the film the way it was meant to be when I was originally doing it."

Many fans considered his restoration blasphemous, as if the films belonged to the public and not the artisan. While Lucas never said it, his unrepentant adjustments represented little more than replacing the few minutes of film removed from *American Graffiti* by Universal—he was always uniquely committed to making films his own way, and he would let neither the studio system, the archaic technology, nor his adoring fans dictate the rules. The filmgoing public was only the last of the three to feel what it was like to have their power over the filmmaker dissolved.

Lucas announced at NAB 2000 that he would shoot most, if not all, of *Episode II* using the prototype tools.

While few recognized it as such, Lucas was generally as outrageous, pigheadedly independent, and risk-taking as Coppola. Similar motivations. Different methodologies.

George Lucas turned 60 in 2004 while working quietly on the sixth and final chapter in the two trilogies that comprised *The Star Wars*. *Episode III*: *Revenge of the Sith*, was released in 2005. While critics tended to pan the earlier episodes, the final chapter was well-received, and like it's predecessors, set new records in ticket sales.[47]

[45] The test in a handful of specially outfitted theaters utilized playback from a customized 360GB array. It was followed by other tests in 1999, from Disney (*Tarzan*) and Pixar (*Toy Story 2*).

[46] While there continues to be industry debate about whether Lucas bet on the right horse with regard to digital filmmaking standards, there is no argument that he played a role in moving everything a giant leap forward.

[47] The fastest film to gross $300 million domestically (17 days), and by the fall, one of the top 10 grossing films of all time.

The second trilogy not only closed the loop on the dramatic arc of the *Star Wars* saga, but it closed a different loop as well. As if to prove the concept, Lucas' second trilogy showed that it was possible for a gentlemanly Lucas to direct his own fantastical stories again, to the full extent of his imagination, in the kind of place he always dreamed he could make films.

The first film gave him the capital and set the plan in motion; by the sixth film, the "digital pipeline" was complete—all digital, from acquisition to distribution. He relocated much of his enormous company to the Presidio. Lucas told *Wired* magazine that he had finally bought himself the right to make small, personal films again. He told them that he bought himself the right to fail.

By late summer, 2005, all of Hollywood's top studios—including Disney, Paramount, Sony, Universal and Warner Bros.—finally came to an agreement about implementing digital cinema. The consortium they created in 2002, designed to unite studios, theater owners and technology manufacturers (the Digital Cinema Initiatives or DCI), announced the first version of their technical specifications. By not releasing movies on celluloid film, the distribution cost would drop dramatically and could mean an eventual annual saving of as much as $900 million to the industry.

USA Today reported that digital versions of films would be available to theaters before the end of the year. Said Lucas, "It's a giant leap forward for those of us who create movies and…for everyone who sees them. Digital cinema will increasingly become the standard and will change the way movies are made, seen and experienced around the world." Filmmakers who issued statements applauding the DCI announcement included Lucas, John Lasseter, Robert Zemeckis and Robert Rodriguez.

In spite of the *Star Wars* phenomenon, Lucasfilm was out of money in 1985. By 2004 (before *Revenge of the Sith*), *Forbes* estimated Lucas' personal worth to be more than $3 billion.

Haskell Wexler said that George Lucas lived his personal dream on a huge scale, without selling out to anybody.

"In his lifetime, he managed to beat Hollywood at its own game, on his terms, in making the kind of films that he gets pleasure from making. He has been able to become a total success in the capitalist system and maintain a level of artistic integrity, which has not happened in this business."

Because of new technology, anyone can be a filmmaker today. Every person with an Apple computer can edit video and mix multiple tracks of audio.

Any consumer can get a camcorder that can capture professional-quality digital video, even high-definition video. PCs routinely give users the ability to paint images in multiple layers, composite them in real time, and print them to film.

But the technology is not just about special effects or movies.

When Dr. Elliot Fishman, distinguished physician, made a presentation at a conference of 65,000 radiologists after Thanksgiving 2004, he began his slides with a frame from *Star Trek II: The Wrath of Kahn*; he showed the gathered doctors the Genesis Effect. He liked the image because it just seemed so implausible that the compelling special effect represented an important moment in *medical* history. Dr. Fishman explained the connection, from Lucasfilm's graphical research to the devices in clinical applications.

Today, doctors can use a computer and scanner to "snap" a photograph of a human heart, mid-beat, inside a breathing patient, and explore it in three-dimensions of such high resolution that vessels can be examined and tiny defects revealed. That cardiac snapshot is one of the more interesting legacies of the Computer Division.

On most days the only sounds that can be heard are black crows in the trees around Lake Ewok and the wind rolling down through the canyon and whistling through the grape vines. The metalwork archway leading to the Tech Building says "Viandante del Cielo"—*Walker of the Skies*—a name that adorned some special bottles of Chardonnay and Merlot harvested from Lucas' vineyards.[48]

[48] Initially planted for fun, Lucas contacted Coppola in 1992 to mention that the grapes were ready for picking. Coppola offered to make wine from them, and Lucas used the wine as holiday gifts. A decade later Lucas offered a small number of cases for sale to the general public.

The grapes that Coppola had gifted to Lucas were planted in the fields and hillsides around the Tech Building at the Ranch.

In 1992, Steven Spielberg wrote of his friend: "For two decades I've tried to figure out George's genius. I have tried to unearth it as though it were some archeological antiquity—George Lucas' crystal ball. After much thought, the only explanation I can offer is this: one day, in a brilliant flash of white light, he saw the future, and he has spent the last twenty years showing it to us."

As romantic as the quotation is, Lucas shrugs it off. He compares it to building a pyramid, as in Egypt. He says that just because it took decades to build a pyramid didn't necessarily mean that the guy who wanted it built could "see" decades into the future.

"All I did was pick a very big pyramid to build…I would rather we had been able to do the whole thing in five years and then move on to something else."

After another moment of conversation he adds, "Unfortunately the whole thing has moved so slowly that, as you realize, you sort of pick out what you're going to do, and then you're doing it the rest of your life, and it seems to whiz right by before you know what's happened."

Lucasfilm formed a bridge between the isolated world of Hollywood and the academic pursuits of computer science. By almost unanimous consent, all the people who made accomplishments at the Lucasfilm Computer Division are grateful to Lucas and give him credit for their work and the opportunity to do what they loved.

In the end one thing is clear: George Lucas deeply wanted to put a little technology into filmmaking. What he didn't realize was that in the process, he ended up putting a lot of filmmaking into technology.

Acknowledgements

THIS BOOK is primarily comprised of the aggregated recollections of the Lucas-film Computer Division, in its many incarnations over the years. I thank you all. This is less my story than yours, often in your words. It has been my honor to share in your history.

It's impossible to write a book about such independent spirits as Lucas and Coppola without becoming infected with their passions. Still, in spite of my demands for autonomy, a book like this would have been a far less complete work without the cooperation (and tolerance) of Lucasfilm, Zoetrope and Pixar. It was Lynne Hale at Lucasfilm who first believed I could tell the story with candor and accuracy. Steve Arnold was then, as always, a trusted advisor and true supporter. I also appreciate the confidence of Ed Catmull, who took the time to read drafts and give me notes.

Special appreciation to Jo Donaldson at the Lucasfilm Research Library, whose help was fundamental. Some of my favorite time on this project was spent at the Ranch (I can't adequately describe how pleasant it was to dig through files for hours then sit back in a leather chair and stare at that perfectly lit Maxfield Parrish painting). Also to Anahid Nazarian at the Zoetrope Research Library, thanks for your time and stories.

The photos were a late addition, and a bonus, but they have become an integral part of the book. To the archivists: Christine Freeman (Pixar), James Mockoski (Zoetrope), and especially Tina Mills (Lucasfilm)—thanks to you and your teams for the images and help. I also appreciate the kind donation of personal photos from Neftali Alvarez, Jim Blinn, Ben Burtt, Loren Carpenter, Ed Catmull, Gary Demos, Richard Edlund, Elliot Fishman, Walter Murch, Kent Reno, Tom Scott, Alvy Ray Smith, John Snell, John Whitney Jr., and Ken Yas; Also thank you to the organizations who made their image archives available to me, including Atari, Chyron, The Computer History Museum, Evans & Sutherland, JPL, Moviola Digital, NCSSM, Sun Microsystems, USC, University of Utah, and Xerox's Palo Alto Research Center.

I never really got the chance to thank Jane Bay for allowing me, back then a twenty-three year old, to wander alone through the hills and fields of Sky-walker Ranch, for days and months, with my camera; watching the moon rise each month over the Main House and feeling as much a part of the special place as the people who got to work there. It was a magical era and gave me the time to reflect on my film, technology and business experiences. It was the beginning, for me, of this work.

Also, thanks to my parents, who encourage these odd projects. In particular, my mother Lorna, who insisted on reviewing pass after pass of the book with sharpened pencil. I may need to go into therapy after completing a work like this with my mom's input, *but damn she's good*. I can't thank you enough.

My friends, for starting me on this path, especially Doug Abrams, Natasha Singer, and Paul Hoffman. I'm glad none of you told me how hard it would be. Richard Morse and the Petroglyph team whose interest and curiosity was a pleasant distraction during the long months of research and scribbling. You covered for me while my mind was on other things, and I appreciate the favor.

The unending patience and love of my wife Jennifer, who has heard these stories countless times over the past decade. She trusted me enough to lug my numerous boxes of "historical memorabilia" from L.A. back north, and store it for years while I assured her that some day I would have a use for the stuff. *Jen: What an epic this past year has been! I love you madly. Alina and Jonah, my team, my precious gems, this book is truly for you.*

And ultimately, none of this would have happened if it hadn't been for George Lucas. Thank you, George, for pursuing your vision and for your openness.

About the Research

THROUGHOUT THE BOOK, my overarching concern was to be true to the spirit of the people and events. Over the past three years I interviewed the majority of Lucasfilm employees whose stories are included here. While the view from the "generals" was crucial (I spoke with all three of the first CEOs of Lucasfilm, as well as George Lucas and the senior project leaders), so was the vantage point of the "privates" (I interviewed dozens of the computer scientists, the assistant film editors, administrative staff, and so on).

While I did not include myself in the narrative of this book, I was present at Lucasfilm for some of the period covered, and had first-hand knowledge and deep familiarity with the issues, locations, politics, and many personalities involved. [I was in marketing at The Droid Works, and was the principal demonstration expert on the EditDroid and SoundDroid. I moved into editing television and film after being one of the "babysitting" assistant editors on the Droid in Los Angeles. For most of my eighteen months, I commuted between Marin and Hollywood weekly. If I had been in this story, I would have showed up in chapter 25.]

The structure of the story was begun from a detailed timeline of the events at Lucasfilm and Zoetrope from the mid-'70s to the mid-'80s. It was constructed by referencing well-established nodal points (like film releases, conferences, and publication dates of papers) as well as Lucasfilm's internal company records (the annual yearbooks, in particular). On that latticework, I hung the interviews. In the end, I had about 160 hours of taped interviews and approximately 2,500 emails with 83 different "characters."

When quotations are used, they are either taken directly from those interviews, or from original sources (filmed documentaries, for instance). When conversations are dramatized, they are either attributed to one of the participants who was recalling events, or if unattributed, represent an exchange where the parties reviewed the reconstruction in the text and accepted it as accurate.

On some occasions quotations are from secondary sources—usually newspapers, magazines, books, memos, and very rarely, the Internet. Secondary sources were principally used for supporting information, history, or basic facts.

Worth noting, however, is that Act I is constructed mainly from facts and quotes from secondary sources (supplemented by a smaller-than-normal quantity of author interviews), and wholly unlike the remainder of the book. I found that very often "facts" from published books about Lucas contradicted my primary research, and I tended to disregard much of the information found in them. Of the data that I chose to include, I asked individuals close to the story to review those sections for accuracy. Ignoring most of the biographical books on Lucas made research slightly more challenging, but in the end, I believe, more accurate.

The Internet made it possible to sew together all the disparate information. The Internet Movie Database (IMDB, owned by Amazon) was my principle source for filmographies. (I can't imagine how research was done before Google.) In any given conversation there were sometimes a dozen references to outside topics or events, which required further exploration. Web-based sources were used for some facts and corroboration of information, but were rarely a final reference; its best use was only to start a path of more refined exploration.

After drafts of the work were crafted, key participants confirmed that the writing and editing process didn't augment or distort facts or remove important context. This back-and-forth with business leaders and computer scientists was not about polishing or censoring, but more like peer review.

This book represents a reconstruction of long-ago events, some of which have been colored by memory, distance, and sometimes various degrees of self-aggrandizement. Many of the people I spoke with were great storytellers, with lush recollections that I am sure have been refined over the years. After inquiry, I sometimes found factual errors in their statements, and I then returned to them for discussion. In general, the storytellers were excited to have their memories "clarified."

The greatest challenge was that often different people at the same event reported details in mutually exclusive ways. In those cases, I polled sources, weighing them based on my own experiences and filtering comments through my impressions of their individual agendas, to deduce something resembling "fair witness." My account may not be identical to any individual's telling, but in the end everyone involved tended to agree that the moments were accurately captured.

Both Lucasfilm and Zoetrope made their extensive clipping files available to me, providing virtually every print article that ever mentioned Lucas or Coppola, the Computer Division, and so on (thousands in all). This was invaluable. There was also a large quantity of internal company memos. Finally, there was a short stack of reference books that provided important supporting information on filmmaking, videogames, computer graphics, *Star Wars*, music, etc. All are cited in the bibliography.

Lucasfilm's only involvement in the text, in exchange for photo permissions, was simply to request I avoid personal and private information about George that clearly added no value to the story other than to be sensationalistic. When the company and the man are so intertwined, this is not always a clear line, but I tried to remain focused on the themes of filmmaking, business, and technology.

Because I insisted on maintaining final cut for this text, with no editorial control from Lucasfilm, Pixar, or Zoetrope, I also accept responsibility for any errors or inaccuracies that may be found here.

Bibliographic Notes

THE FULL BIBLIOGRAPHY is online at www.droidmaker.com/biblio.html. The web page is searchable, and contains attributions for all quotations as well as hyperlinks to web sources, only some of which are included below.

This story was largely gathered from oral histories (predominantly telephone interviews) all of which are listed below. Not listed here are countless follow up emails with most of the subjects. Following these interviews, published sources are grouped by topic. The topics overlap slightly, but seem to be a useful and concise way to introduce material to other investigators. Asterisks (*) denote reference sources that were particularly important to my research.

Author Interviews

Neftali Alvarez, 3/19/04
Steve Arnold, 3/27/04, 9/25/04, 5/05/05
Hal Barwood, 1/6/05
Andy Bechtolsheim, 10/28/04
Malcolm Blanchard, 5/04/04, 8/17/04
Les Blank, 8/23/04
Jim Blinn, 11/29/04
Bob Bralove, 6/10/04
Deborah Brown, 9/22/04
Thomas Brown, 6/21/02, 8/23/04,
    12/11/04
Ben Burtt, 10/28/04
Loren Carpenter, 3/18/04, 9/14/04
Ed Catmull, 3/12/04, 3/19/04, 8/31/04,
    1/4/05
Susan Anderson Catmull, 9/21/04
Jok Church, 4/14/04
Steve Cohen, 5/24/04
Pat Cole, 12/20/04
Rob Cook, 9/08/04, 12/10/04
Larry Cuba, 10/26/04
Robert Dalva, 6/22/05
David DiFrancesco, 3/19/04, 6/23/04
Gary Demos, 9/10/04, 3/16/05
Thomas Dolby, 5/13/04
Bob Doris, 6/14/02, 3/10/04, 3/12/04,
    3/22/04, 7/22/04, 9/1/04, 10/22/04
Bob Drebin, 11/30/04
Tom Duff, 8/18/04
Duwayne Dunham, 5/6/05

Richard Edlund, 3/14/05
Nick England, 11/29/04
Noah Falstein, 9/25/04, 9/30/04
Elliot Fishman, M.D., 12/3/04
David Fox, 06/30/04
Manny Gerard, 8/13/04
Doug Glenn, 3/12/04
Robert Greber, 5/14/04
Ralph Guggenheim, 6/12/02, 8/20/04,
    1/6/05
Pete Hammar, 11/29/04, 12/13/04,
    12/16/04
Mickey Hart, 3/17/05
Mike Hawley, 7/05/04
Augie Hess, 10/11/04
Clark Higgins, 6/19/02, 8/19/04, 8/23/04
Tom Holman, 11/22/04
George Joblove, 7/01/02, 7/03/02
Scott Johnston, 4/15/04
Howard Kazanjian, 10/28/04
Jim Kessler, 3/08/04, 4/07/04, 7/06/04
John Knoll, 4/13/04
Gary Kurtz, 3/14/05
Peter Langston, 6/20/02
John Lasseter, 9/08/04
Jim Lawsen, 8/27/04
Rob Lay, 6/18/02, 8/31/04
David Levine, 7/16/04
Evelyn Lincoln, 5/04/04
Michael Lowe, 3/09/04
George Lucas, 4/28/04

Rick McCallum, 6/3/05
John Meyer, 3/17/05
Andy Moorer, 06/24/02, 08/10/04, 10/04
Chip Morningstar, 9/25/04
Anahid Nazarian, 6/04/04
Doug Norby, 3/10/04, 8/27/04, 12/2/04
Tom Porter, 3/19/04, 7/23/04
Bill Reeves, 3/19/04
Owen Rubin, 7/26/04
David Salesin, 6 /27/02
Mary Sauer, 9/1/04
Chet Schuler, 10/20/04
Alexander Schure, 3/9/05
Steve Schwartz, 8/29/04
Tom Scott, 4/19/04, 5/4/04
John Seamons, 9/13/04
Michael Shantzis, 3/18/04
Leon Silverman, 12/8/04
Alvy Ray Smith, 1/23/02, 5/30/02,
    6/11/02, 6/21/04, 6/24/04, 8/24/04,
    9/4/04, 9/10/04, 9/15/04, 10/10/04
Lynne Smith, 3/10/04
John Snell, 11/19/04
Charles Solomon, 8/24/04
Howard Spielman, 9/9/04, 11/11/04
Rodney Stock, 11/26/04, 10/25/04
Andy van Dam, 5/26/04
Charlie Webber, 3/12/04
John Whitney, Jr., 9/27/04
Ken Yas, 6/12/02, 4/18/04, 10/9/04,
    10/22/04

Pre-1980: Lucas, Coppola, Murch, Filmmaking, Zoetrope

Books

Baxter, John. *George Lucas—A Biography*. Harper Collins, London, 1999.

Bergan, Ronald. *Francis Ford Coppola Close Up—The Making of His Movies*. Thunder's Mouth Press, New York, 1997.

Biskind, Peter. *Down and Dirty Pictures—Miramax, Sundance, and the Rise of Independent Film*. Simon and Schuster, New York, 2004.

*Biskind, Peter. *Easy Riders, Raging Bulls*. Bloomsbury, London, 1998.

*Cowie, Peter. *Coppola*. Andre Deutsch Ltd, London, 1989.

Crawley, Tony. *The Steven Spielberg Story—The Man Behind the Movies*. Quill, New York, 1983.

Hearn, Marcus. *The Cinema of George Lucas*. Harry N. Abrams Inc., New York, 2005.

Jenkins, Gary. *Empire Building—The Remarkable Real Life Story of Star Wars*. Citadel Press, New Jersey, 1997.

Kline, Sally (ed). *George Lucas Interviews*. University Press of Mississippi, 1999.

Lucas, George (Donald Glut, James Kahn et al). *Star Wars Trilogy*. Ballantine Books, New York, 1976.

Maxford, Howard. *George Lucas Companion—The Complete Guide to Hollywood's Most Influential Film-maker*. B.T. Bashford, London, 1999.

*Ondaatje, Michael. *The Conversations—Walter Murch and the Art of Editing Film*. Alfred A. Knopf, New York, 2002.

Pollock, Dale. *Skywalking: The Life and Films of George Lucas*. Da Capo Press, New York, 1999.

Pye, Michael and Miles, Linda. *The Movie Brats: How the film generation took over Hollywood*. Holt, Rinehart, and Winston, 1979

Salewicz, Chris. *George Lucas Close Up—The Making of His Movies*. Thunder's Mouth Press, New York, 1999.

Smith, Jim. *George Lucas*. Virgin Books, London, 2003.

Periodicals

Aigner, Hal. "The Viewers Revolution," *San Francisco Magazine*, July 1970.

American Zoetrope. "American Zoetrope Chronology," Internal Memo, Aug. 1979.

American Zoetrope. "AZ/ The Coppola Company Combined Financial Statements," Internal Memo, Jan. 31, 1970.

American Zoetrope. "Ed Kessler—Facility GM," Internal Memo.

American Zoetrope. "Pilgrimage—ABC Movie of the Week," correspondence to American Zoetrope, June 4, 1971.

American Zoetrope. "Statement of Operations- Feb 1, 1972-Aug 31, 1972," Internal Memo.

American Zoetrope. "Status Report/AZ Facility and Commercial Division," Internal Memo.

Arnold, Gary. "George Lucas—the Force that Matters," *The Washington Post*, June 25, 1978.

Blum, Walter. "A Director with New Directions," *San Francisco Sunday Examiner and Chronicle*, Feb. 1, 1970.

Caen, Herb. *San Francisco Chronicle*, Jan. 8, 1970.

Clark, Brian. "Hick Town?" *Modesto Bee*, April 1, 1979.

*Clouzot, Claire. "The Morning of the Magician: George Lucas and Star Wars," *Ercan*, Sept. 15, 1977 (Translated from French by Alisa Belanger).

"Columbus Tower," The Coppola Company, press release circa 1981.

Cook, Bruce. "Summing Up the Seventies' Talents," *American Film*, Dec. 1979.

"Coppola to Set Up Frisco Filmery," *Daily Variety*, Nov. 27, 1968.

"CVB Newsletter," San Francisco Convention and Visitors Bureau, Dec. 23, 1969.

*Eichelbaum, Stanley. "S.F.'s New Film-Making Co-op," *San Francisco Examiner*, June 1969.

*Eichelbaum, Stanley. "Debut of a Personal Film-Making Plant," *San Francisco Examiner*, December 12, 1969.

*Farber, Stephen. "George Lucas: The Stinky Kid Hits the Big Time," *Film Quarterly*, Vol 27, No. 3. Spring 1974.

"George Lucas—The Force that Matters," *Washington Post*, June 25, 1978.

Karman, Mal. "Francis Ford Coppola," *San Francisco Magazine*, May 1973.

Kilday, Greg. "Coppola Declares His Independence," *Los Angeles Times*, Aug. 31, 1974.

*Knapp, Dan. "A Visit with Francis Ford Coppola," *Performing Arts*, June 1970, Vol 4, No. 6.

*Knickerbocker, Paine. "A Lively New Movie-Making Project for the City," *San Francisco Chronicle*, Oct. 1969.

*Morrisoe, Patricia. "New Breed Takes Over the Movies," *Parade*, Dec. 2, 1979.

*Murch, Walter. "THX 1138: Made in San Francisco," *American Cinematographer*, Oct. 1971.

*Nachman, Gerald. "Coppola of Zoetrope—Older, Wiser and Poorer," *San Francisco Chronicle*, 1971.

"New Moves for Movies," *Newsweek*, Sept. 2, 1974.

"Novato—bedroom community of the stars," *Mill Valley/Marin News*, March 31, 1978.

"Of Francis Ford Coppola," *San Francisco Bay Guardian*, Aug. 16, 1972.

Olmstead, Marty. "What are Gene Kelly and George Lucas up to in Marin?" *San Francisco Magazine*, March 1979.

*Pearce, Christopher. "San Francisco's Own American Zoetrope," *American Cinematographer*, Oct. 1971.

Ryan, Desmond. "Lucas Buys Time with Dividends," *Star News*, April 25, 1978.

Silberman, Steve. "Life After Darth," *Wired*, May 2005.

"Star Wars—Lucas' fantasy," *Hamilton, Ohio Journal News*, Jan. 12, 1978.

*Stone, Judy. "George Lucas," *San Francisco Chronicle*, May 23, 1971.

"The Student Movie Makers," *Time*, Feb. 2, 1968.

*Sturhahn, Larry."The Filming of American Graffiti," *Filmmaker's Newsletter*, March 1974.

*Sweeney, Louise. "The Movie Business is Alive and Well and Living in San Francisco," *Show*, April 1970.

Warner Bros. correspondence to American Zoetrope, June 7, 1971.

"West Coast Hip Set Tries Moviemaking," UPI Press, May 5, 1970.

*Zito, Stephen. "George Lucas Goes Far Out," *American Film*, April 1977.

"Zoetrope is Francis Ford Coppola's Declaration of Semi-Independence," *Buffalo Evening News*, Sept. 18, 1970.

Documentaries

"Artifact from the Future—The Making of THX 1138," produced, directed and edited by Gary Leva. © 2004 Warner Bros. Entertainment, Inc.

*"Filmmaker: A Diary by George Lucas," 1970 (Lucas' personal account of his experiences with Coppola, making *The Rain People*.)

*"George Lucas, Maker of Films," PBS 1971 (an extended interview of George Lucas by Gene Youngblood).

*"Hearts of Darkness," by Eleanor Coppola, 1978 (Francis Coppola's wife's experiences with him, making *Apocalypse Now*.)

*"Legacy of Filmmakers: The Early Years of American Zoetrope," produced, written and directed by Gary Leva; © 2004 Warner Bros. Entertainment, Inc.

Selected Web-based References

Lumiere biographical: www.holonet.khm.de/visual_alchemy/lumiere.html and www.holonet.khm.de/visual_alchemy/lumiere-x.html

McQuarrie, Ralph. "Ralph McQuarrie: Illustrator Exclusive DVD Interview". www.ralphmcquarrie.com/interview/mcquarrie/interview.html

Nottingham, Stephen. "French New Wave." ourworld.compuserve.com/homepages/Stephen_Nottingham/cintxt2.htm

Peary, Gerald. "Verna Fields." *The Real Paper*—Oct. 23, 1980. www.geraldpeary.com/essays/def/fields-verna.html

"Undercurrents: Neglected Works from the French New Wave." www.harvardfilmarchive.org/calendars/02mayjune/newwave.html

Post-1980: Lucasfilm, Zoetrope

Books

*Champlin, Charles. *George Lucas—The Creative Impulse*. Harry N. Abrams Inc., USA, 1992.

Periodicals

"Another Close Encounter," *Newsweek*, Dec. 12, 1983.

"Cinema Alum Honored for 'Star Wars', 'Graffiti', 'THX", *Trojan Family USC*, Vol. 10, No. 5 .

"Conversation with Francis," *Videography*, Sept. 1982.

Foti, Laura. "Lucasfilm Enters Studio Market," *Billboard*, Oct. 8, 1983.

Grant, Lee. "Avco Cinema Digs In for 'Return' Onslaught," *Los Angeles Times*, May 25, 1983.

Haller, Scot. "Francis Coppola's Biggest Gamble," *Saturday Review*, July 1981.

*Harmetz, Aljean. "Burden of Dreams: George Lucas," *American Film*, June 1983.

Kelly, Kevin and Parisi, Paula. "Beyond Star Wars—What's Next for George Lucas," *Wired*, Feb. 1997.

Kilday, Gregg. "Francis Ford Coppola Forges a Bold New Moviemaking Experiment Around Video," *Home Video*, May 1981.

King, Thomas R. "Lucasvision," *The Wall Street Journal*, March 21, 1994.

Liberatore, Paul."Marin's Movie Emperor—George Lucas' Ranch Keeps Getting Bigger," *San Francisco Chronicle*, April 15, 1985.

Lucasfilm Ltd. Internal Memo, May 29, 1985.

Meisel, Myron. "Gearing Up for the Day of the Jedi," *Film Journal*, May 1983.

Meisel, Myron. "Letter from L.A.," *Film Journal*, June 30, 1983.

*O'Quinn, Kerry. "The George Lucas Saga," *Starlog*, July, Aug., Sept. 1981.

*Seabrook, John. "Letter from Skywalker Ranch: Why is the Force Still With Us?" *The New Yorker*, Jan. 6, 1997.

Sheff, David. "George Lucas," *Rolling Stone*, Nov. 5, 1987.

Sherman, Stratford P. "The Empire Pays Off", *Fortune*, Oct. 6, 1980.

Skywalker Development Company, "Stained Art Glass History," 12/1/80—3/1/85.

*Vallely, Jean. "*The Empire Strikes Back* and So Does Filmmaker George Lucas with his Sequel to Star Wars," *Rolling Stone*, June 12, 1980.

Vincenzi, Lisa. "A Short Time Ago, On a Ranch Not So Far Away…," *Millimeter*, April 1990.

Waggoner, Dianna. "In Homage to the Master—George Lucas and Francis Coppola Unleash their Clout for Kurosawa," *People*, Oct. 27, 1980.

Weiner, Rex. "Lucas the Loner Returns to Wars," *Weekly Variety*, June 5, 1995.

Weinraub, Bernard. "Luke Skywaker Goes Home," *Playboy*, July 1997.

*Williams, Joanne. "SunInterview—George Lucas," *Pacific Sun*, April 8, 1983.

Woods, Lynn. "The Skywalker Ranch and Skywalker Art Glass Studio," *The American Art Glass Quarterly*, Fall 1982.

Yarish, Alice. "George Lucas—hell-raiser to millionaire," *San Francisco Examiner*, Feb. 20, 1980.

Computers and Technology

Books

Linzmayer, Owen W. *Apple Confidential 2.0—The Definitive History of the World's Most Colorful Company*. No Starch Press, California, 2004.

Stork, David ed. *Hal's Legacy*. MIT Press, Cambridge, 1997.

Periodicals

Orth, Maureen. "High Noon in Hollywood," *California*, October 1981.

Videogames

Books

Cohen, Scott. *Zap! The Rise and Fall of Atari*. McGraw-Hill Companies Inc., USA, 1984.

Kent, Steven. *The Ultimate History of Video Games*. Three Rivers Press, New York, 2001.

Rubin, Michael. *Defending the Galaxy—The Complete Handbook of VideoGaming*. Triad Publishing, Florida, 1982.

Periodicals

Allen, Dennis. "Lucasfilm: Setting New Standards for Computer Games," *Popular Computing*, Oct. 1984.

"Atari/Lucasfilm's League of Giants Hints at New Medium," *Video Business*, New York, 1982.

"Atari Refuses to let Video Game Fad Die," *Business Week*, May 21, 1984.

"Atari's Struggle to Stay Ahead," *Business Week*, Sept. 13, 1982.

Ashley, Beth. "Playing Games on the Job," *Independent Journal*, San Rafael, CA, Aug. 31, 1985.

Blanchet, Michael. "Lucasfilm Teams Up with Epyx for 2 Computer Games," *Detroit Free Press*, Jan. 29, 1985.

Bloom, Steve. "The Empire Strikes Pay Dirt," *Computer Games*, Nov/Dec 1984.

"A Broader Range of Software Widens the Video Game Market," *Consumer Electronics*, Jan. 1989.

Daniell, Tina. "Lucasfilm, Atari Join in Video Game, Home Computer Effort," *Hollywood Reporter*, June 7, 1984

Eckhouse, John. "Atari Hopes to Put the Magic Back in Video Games," *San Francisco Chronicle*, May 9, 1984.

"Epyx, Lucasfilm ink 1-year Development Deal," *Computer + Software News*, New York, Feb. 18, 1985.

"Epyx Signs Pact with Lucasfilm for New SW Line," *Toy & Hobby World*, New York, March 1985.

"Epyx to Sell Games Developed by Lucasfilm," *HFD- Retailing Home Furnishings*, New York, Feb. 18, 1985.

"Exit—Vid-Games," *Star Busters*, England, Feb. 1985.

Graham, Jefferson. "All Time Attendance Records at Consumer Electronics Show," *The Hollywood Reporter*, June 10, 1982.

Graham, Jefferson. "New Entries in Video Market Stress Arcade-style Quality," *The Hollywood Reporter*, Aug. 23, 1982.

Greer, Jonathan. "Star Wars Creator Teams up with Atari," *San Jose Mercury News*, May 9, 1984.

Kneale, Dennis and Marcom, John Jr. "Warner Agrees to Sell Most of Atari Unit," *Electronic Games Hotline*, June 3, 1984.

Landro, Laura. "Atari and Lucasfilm Plan Joint Venture in Video Products," *Wall Street Journal*, June 7, 1982.

Langston, Peter. "The Way it Should Be Done," *Unix Review*, June 1985.

Leighty, John. "Lucasfilm Joins Atari to Enter Home Video Games Market," *Daily Commercial Record*, Dallas, TX, July 12, 1984.

"Lucas Looks Beyond Film," *Newsweek Access*, Fall 1984.

"Lucasfilm and Atari Join Forces," *Pro Sound News*, New York, Dec. 16, 1983.

Raskin, Robin. "The Lucasfilm Force," *K-Power*, Sept./Oct. 1984.

Schrage, Michael. "Raiders Meets Invaders," *American Film*, Sept. 1982.

Taylor, Chris. "You Ought to be in Pixels" , *Time*, April 12, 2004.

Walters, Donna. "A Leaner, Meaner Atari," *Tribune*, Oakland, CA, July 7, 1984.

Walters, Donna. "Atari/Lucasfilm Uncaps its Elixirs," *Oakland Tribune*, May 9, 1984.

Williams, Gregg. "Lucasfilm Enters Home Gaming," *Byte*, July 1985.

Williams, Stephen. "Merger Made in Hyperspace," *Garden City Newsday*, July 18, 1982.

Selected Web-based References

Ciraolo, Michael. Antic Vol. 3, No. 4 August 1984 www. atarimagazines.com/v3n4/lucasfilm.html

Powell, Jack. "Lucasfilm Games: Antic's Sneak Preview--The Eidolon and Koronis Rift," Antic Vol. 4, No. 8 Dec. 1985 www. atarimagazines.com/v4n8/Lucasfilm.html

"Atari's ET Game": members.fortunecity.co.uk/moviegames/et.htm And www.informationblast.com/E.T._%28Atari_2600%29. html

Baer, Ralph. "Once Uppon [sic] A Time The Video Game…" Sanders Associates; [Historical data extracted by permission from an upcoming book.] www.pong-story.com/sanders.htm

Covert, Colin. "Atari, Inc.—The Early Years (An Unauthorized History)," *Hi-Res* Vol. 1, No. 1. November 1983; Reprinted from *TWA Ambassador Magazine* with permission of the author and publisher; copyright 1982 by Trans World Airlines, Inc. www.atarimagazines.com/hi-res/v1n1/atarihistory.php

Detailed History of Atari VCS 2600 [Info from the Museum of Home Video Gaming]. www.old-computers.com/museum/ doc.asp?c=878&st=2

Dolan, Mike. "Behind the Screens: An insider's oral history of the videogame, from the birth of the Brown Box to the arrival of Xbox"; *Wired*, May 2001. www.wired.com/wired/archive/9.05/ history.html

"Games Department: Atari VCS," *Antic* Vol 2, No. 2, May 1983. www.atarimagazines.com/v2n2/atarivcs.html

Grubb, Bill and Koble, Dennis. "Video Games Interview: Bill Grubb and Dennis Koble," *Video Games Magazine*, Jan. 1983. www. atarihq.com/othersec/library/imagic.html

Morningstar, Chip and Farmer, Randy, "Lessons of Lucasfilm's Habitat." www.fudco.com/chip/lessons.html

Pitts, Bill. "The Galaxy Game," Oct 29, 1997. http://www-db. stanford.edu/pub/voy/museum/galaxy.html which references "SpaceWar!" in *Rolling Stone*, by Stewart Brand; Dec 7, 1972.

Editing and HDTV

Books

Dancyger, Ken. *The Technique of Film and Video Editing—History, Theory, and Practice*. Focal Press, USA, 2000.

Murch, Walter. *In the Blink of an Eye*. 2nd Edition. Silman-James Press, 2001.

Roberts, Kenneth H and Sharples, Win Jr. *A Primer for Film-Making; A Complete Guide to 16 and 35mm Film Production.* Bobbs-Merrill Company, USA, 1976.

Rubin, Michael. *Nonlinear v4—A Field Guide to Digital Video and Film Editing.* Triad Publishing, Florida, 2000.

Rubin, Michael. *Nonlinear v3—A Guide to Digital Film and Video Editing.* Triad Publishing, Florida, 1995.

Rubin, Michael. *Nonlinear v1– A Guide to Electronic Film and Video Editing.* Triad Publishing, Florida, 1991.

Schneider, Arthur. *Jump Cut! Memoirs of a Pioneer Television Editor.* McFarland & Company Inc., North Carolina, 1997.

Periodicals

Abbott, Denise. "George Lucas: His First Love is Editing," *American Cinemaeditor,* Spring 1991.

Amato, Mia. 'Editing Evolves," *VideoPro,* Sept. 1985.

"The Brave New World of HDTV," *Broadcasting,* Feb. 1, 1982.

Busch, Todd and Loschin, Andrew. "Avid's Script Integration," *Motion Picture Editor's Guild Newsletter,* July/Aug. 1999.

Carstensen, Toni Pace. "EditDroid—A Complete Experience," *On Location—The Film and Videotape Production Magazine,* June 1985.

Costello, Marjorie. "Hollywood Goes Video," *Videography,* Sept. 1982.

Daniels, William. "EditDroid: New Tool for Editors from Lucasfilm," *Variety,* June 11, 1984.

Droid Works Internal Memo, "EditDroid Customer List," May 1986.

"Francis Coppola's One From the Heart," *American Premiere,* Feb. 1982.

Griffin-Beale, Christopher. "Apocalypse Now for Celluloid?" *Montreux Technical Symposium Proceedings,* 1981.

Gross, Terry. "Francis Ford Has a Better Idea: Filming with Video," *International Herald Tribune,* July 4-5, 1981.

Hawthorne, David. "Droids shoot the works to post electronically—In latest George Lucas saga, its more science than fiction," *Millimeter,* April 1985.

Jenkins, C. Francis. "History of the Motion Picture" Transactions of the SMPE, Oct. 1920.

Lucasfilm Ltd. "Memorandum—Aspen Film Society Status," June 13, 1986.

"Lucasfilm Ltd. and convergence Corporation Form Company," Lucasfilm Ltd. press release Sept. 26, 1983.

Mannes, George. "The Inside Story on Off-line Editing," *Videography,* Aug. 1986.

Miranker, CW. "Lucasfilm Spins off High-tech Creations," *San Francisco Examiner,* March 24, 1985.

"Montage and EditDroid systems seen bringing video tape technique closer to that of film," *Television/Radio Age,* Oct. 1, 1984.

Reynolds, Mike. "Lucasfilm, Convergence unveil much-touted EditDroid System," *The Hollywood Reporter,* April 30, 1984.

Savage, Golda. "Coppola's Electronic Cinema Process," *Millimeter,* Oct. 1981.

Solomon, Charles. "Lucasfilm Introduces a High-tech Editing Tool," *Los Angeles Times,* Aug. 23, 1984.

Skywalker Ranch Internal Document, "Tech Building Task Force Meeting," July 1, 1986.

Vicenzi, Lisa. "A Short Time Ago, On a Ranch Not so Far Away…," *Millimeter,* April 1990.

"The Word on EDDROID," *Millimeter,* Dec. 1983.

*Zoetrope Studios. "Electronic Imagery Conference," Transcription, 1980.

Selected Web-based references

Bermingham, John. "Beta or VHS? When Good is Good Enough," *Drug Delivery Technology,* www.drugdeliverytech.com/cgi-bin/articles.cgi?idArticle=59

Flaherty, Joseph. "A World Of Change," HDTV News Online, www.hdtvmagazine.com/history/2005/06/a_world_of_chan.php

Jardin, Xeni, "Hollywood Plots End of Film Reels," Wired.com, July 28, 2005. www.wired.com/news/digiwood/0,1412,68332,00.html

Lieberman, David, "Top studios agree on standards for digital films," USA Today, July 28, 2005. www.usatoday.com

Mullin, Jack. "John (Jack) T. Mullin (1913-99) Recalls the American Development of the Tape Recorder." www.kcmetro.cc.mo.us/pennvalley/biology/lewis/crosby/mullin.htm

Spark, Nick, "A Conversation with Avid's Tom Ohanian" *The Motion Picture Editors Guild Newsletter,* Vol. 20, No. 2—March/April 1999. www.editorsguild.com/newsletter/MarApr99/ohanian.html

Turner, Bob. "A Reflection Eulogy—CMX calls it quits" SMPTE/New England http://www.v-site.net/smpte-ne/articles/eulogy.html

Computer Graphics, ILM, Pixar and Disney

Books

Shay, Don and Duncan, Jody. *The Making of Jurassic Park,* Ballantine Books, USA 1993.

*Smith, Thomas G. *Industrial Light & Magic: The Art of Special Effects.* Ballantine Books, New York, 1986.

Taylor, John. *Storming the Magic Kingdom—Wall Street, the Raiders, and the Battle for Disney.* Alfred A. Knopf, New York, 1987.

1984 PIXAR Brochure—"Lucasfilm Presents the Pixar Image Computer"

Periodicals

Clarke, Frederick S. "Return of the Jedi," *Cinefantastique,* April 1983.

"Computer Research and Development at Lucasfilm," *American Cinematographer,* Aug. 1982.

Cook, Carla Winslow. "Lucasfilm Enters the Fray," *Computer Graphics World.*

*Gabor, Andrea. "A Better Kind of Image from the Wizards of Hollywood," *Business Week,* April 1, 1985.

*Gannes, Stuart. "Lights, Cameras…Computers," *Discover,* August, 1984.

"George Lucas Moves his Sci-Fi Genius to the Production Room," *Business Week,* Dec. 5, 1983.

Hanauer, Gary. "The New Movie Makers—after the advent of computers, movies may never be the same," *Northwest Orient Passages*, Nov. 1982.

Lehrman, Paul. "Digicon 83," *Creative Computing,* April 1984.

"Lucasfilm Seeks New Markets for Graphics," *High Technology*, Jan. 1985.

Miller, Micheal W. "The Larger Market—Producers of computer graphics for Hollywood find new opportunities in science and industry," *Wall Street Journal* Sept. 16, 1985.

Smith, Alvy Ray. "The Adventures of Andre and Wally B.," Unpublished—Lucasfilm whitepaper.

Smith, Alvy Ray. "The Alpha Channel—A Simple Concept with Profound Implications," whitepaper, January 2, 1996.

Smith, Alvy Ray. "Alpha and the History of Digital Compositing" Technical Memo #7, Unpublished Aug. 15, 1995.

Smith, Alvy Ray. "Digital Paint Systems—Historical Overview," Technical Memo #14 , Unpublished May 31, 1997.

Smith, Alvy Ray. "The Genesis Demo—Special Effects for Star Trek II," *American Cinematographer,* Oct. 1982.

Sorensen, Peter. "Computer Imaging—An Apple for the Dreamsmiths," *Cinefx,* Oct. 1981.

Tucker, Jonathan B. "Computer Graphics Achieves New Realism," *High Technology*, June 1984.

West, Susan. "The New Realism—Creating an illusion on a computer screen, whether a figure or a cloud, means solving problems of light, form, and texture that every artist faces," *Science 84,* July/Aug. 1984.

Selected Web-based References

Blair, Cynthis. "It Happened on Long Island, 1963—New York Institute of Technology Opens at Vanderbilt Whitney Estate," www.Newsday.com

'The Early Days of Sun,' by Tom Lyon; www.lyon-about.com/sun.html

Falconer, Robert. "Of Galaxies Far, Far Away and Battlestars of Yesterday –Hollywood VFX maters, Richard Edlund, Talks about Work on the Original Battlestar Galactica," www. HollywoodNorthReport.com

Graphics info: www.alvyray.com

Jim Blinn's keynote address to Siggraph 1998; www.siggraph.org/ s98/conference/keynote/blinn.html

Lyons, Mike. "Toon Story: John Lasseter's Animated Life," *Animation World Magazine*, Issue 3.8, Nov. 1998: www.awn. com/mag/issue3.8/3.8pages/3.8lyonslasseter.html

Maxfield Parrish information: www.bpib.com/illustrat/parrish.htm

Perry. Tekla. S. "And the Oscar Goes to…." IEEE Spectrum, April 2001 Volume 38, No. 4, www.spectrum.ieee.org/careers/ careerstemplate.jsp?ArticleId=p040101

Pixar company info: www.pixar.com/companyinfo/history

Smith, Alvy Ray, and Heckbert, Paul. "Brief History of the New York Institute of Technology Computer Graphics Lab—excerpt from Terrance Masson's computer graphics history book," www-2.cs.cmu.edu/~ph/nyit/masson/nyit.html

Sound and THX

Periodicals

Bergren, Peter. "Sound Effects—New Tools and Techniques," *Mix,* Vol. 10, No 4.

Blake, Larry. "Digital Film Sound," *Recording Engineer/Producer,* Oct. 1985.

Blake, Larry. "Return of the Jedi—Sound Design for the Star Wars Trilogy by Ben Burtt," *Recording Engineer/Producer*, Oct. 1983.

Borish, Jeffrey. "The Future of Signal Processing in Professional Audio," *Mix,* May 1990.

Deal, Susan. "Star Wars Sound Effects Man Takes a Bow," *Christian Science Monitor,* Dec. 6, 1978.

Francis, Tony. "TV Sound vs. Theatre Sound," *Box Office,* Aug. 1984.

Horowitz, Marc. "Stereo Exchange: THX and a Unique Approach to the High End" *Audio Visual International,* Aug. 1991.

Hutchison, David. "Creating Science Fiction Sounds," *Starlog,* Feb. 1986.

Jones, Bill. "Thanks to George Lucas, the force is with movie dialogue," *The Phoenix Gazette,* May 29, 1984.

Lambert, Mel. "Tomlinson Holman," *Mix,* Oct. 1996.

Lander, David. "Laurie Fincham of THX," *Audio,* March 1999.

Lond, Harley. "Lucasfilm's Theatre Alignment Program," *Box Office*, June 1984.

London, Michael. "Looking Good—Indiana Jones resets standards for film industry," *Chicago Sun Times,* May 29, 1984.

Lucasfilm Ltd. "TAP Presentation," 1985.

"Lucasfilm Now Looks at Sound Installations," *Pro Sound News,* May 1983.

"Lucasfilm Reveals New Sound System in 'Jedi' Showcase," *The Hollywood Reporter,* May 18, 1983.

"Lucasfilm THX Audio Gaining," *Pro Sound News,* Nov. 9, 1984.

McKinney, Clyde & Pinkston, Bob. "Light! Projector! Action!," *Box Office,* Aug. 1987.

Meadow, James. "Century 21's New System Sounds Off," *Rocky Mountain Business Journal,* May 29, 1984.

Meisel, Myron. "THX Sound System—An All-around Effort," *Film Journal,* Aug. 1984.

Milano, Dominic. "Star Wars Sounds," *Contemporary Keyboard,* March 1978, Volume 4, Number 2.

"New Sound System for Theatres Introed," *Daily Variety,* May 19, 1983.

Palmer, Janet. "Three Generations of Birding," *Bird Watcher's Digest,* May/June 1989.

Pohlmann, Ken. "Tom Holman's New Experiment," *Stereo Review,* July 1996.

Pooley, Eric. "The Sound and the Movie," *New York Magazine,* Sept. 9 1991.

Rowand, Ken. "Interview—Ben Burtt," *Bantha Tracks,* Aug. 1982, No. 17.

Rumsey, Francis. "Digital Audio Editing."

"State of the Art Audio for Film and Video," *On Location—The Film and Videotape Production Magazine*, September, 1985.

"Theatres Getting Improved Audio," *Staten Island Advance*, June 5, 1983.

Warren, Scott. "How Sweet the Sound," *Premiere* Dec. 2004/Jan. 2005.

Selected Web-based References

Carlsson, Sven, "Sound Design of Star Wars," www.filmsound.org/starwars/

Kang, Peter. "Ben Burtt Interview," USC School of Cinema & Television

Burtt, Ben and Lauten, Erin. "Interview with Ben Burtt," Editor's Net. www.filmsound.org/starwars/editorsnet-interview.htm

Thomas Dolby and digital music: www.thomasdolby.com

Wendy Carlos biographical: www.wendycarlos.com

Other Background, Quotations, Etc.

Books

Aykroyd, Dan and Ramis, Harold. *Ghostbusters*. Screenplay. 1984

Boorstein, Daniel. *The Creators—A History of Heroes of the Imagination*. Random House, New York, 1992.

Brand, Stewart. *The Media Lab*. Viking, New York, 1987.

Bresman, Jonathan. *The Art of Star Wars—Episode I: The Phantom Menace*. Ballantine, USA, 1999.

Campbell, Joseph. *The Power of Myth*. Doubleday, New York, 1988.

Evans, Harold. *They Made America*. Little Brown and Company, Boston, 2004.

King, Ross. *Brunelleschi's Dome*. Penguin Books, New York, 2000.

LaRose, Robert and Straubhaar, Joseph. *Media Now— Understanding Media, Culture, and Technology*. Thomson Wadsworth, USA, 2004.

Titelman, Carol. *Star Wars—Episode IV: A New Hope*. Ballantine Books, New York, 1997.

Youngblood, Gene. *Expanded Cinema*. E.P. Dutton & Co. Inc., New York, 1970.

Periodicals

Coppola, Francis Ford. "Fantasy Life," *Time* Bonus Section, Feb. 2004.

Edwards, Gavin. "The Cult of Darth Vader," *Rolling Stone*, June 2, 2005.

Fisher, Carrie. "The Lucas Interview," *Sound and Vision*, Oct. 2004.

Brown, Patricia Leigh. "George Lucas at Skywalker Ranch," *Architectural Digest*, March 2004.

Hillner, Jennifer. "The Wall of Fame," *Wired*, Dec. 2003.

Mathews, Jack. "Saber Rattler," *Los Angeles Times*, Jan. 17, 1999.

Newman, Bruce. "Movie critic Bruce Newman talks to George Lucas," *San Jose Mercury News*, June 26, 2005.

Roston, Tom. "Holy Sith! It's the Last Star Wars," *Premiere*, May 2005.

Scanlon, Jesse. "The New Heart of the Empire," *Wired*, May 2005.

Windolf, Jim. "Star Wars: The Last Battle," *Vanity Fair*, Feb. 2005.

Photo Credits

Jacket
    Courtesy of Lucasfilm Ltd.

Author's Introduction
v   © Michael Rubin

Ch 1: The Mythology of George
4   Courtesy of Lucasfilm Ltd.
6   Courtesy of Lucasfilm Ltd.
7   Courtesy of Lucasfilm Ltd.
9   USC School of Cinema-Television
12   Courtesy of Moviola Digital
13   USC School of Cinema-Television (left and right)

Ch 2: Road Trip
26   Courtesy of Lucasfilm Ltd.
28   Reprinted from *American Cinematographer*, October 1971; Used with permission
29   © North Carolina School of Science and Mathematics
31   © San Francisco Architectural Heritage
32   Courtesy of Lucasfilm Ltd. (left and right)
33   Reprinted from *American Cinematographer*, October 1971; Used with permission
37   The Murch Family Collection
38   Reprinted from *American Cinematographer*, October 1971; Used with permission

Ch 3: The Restoration
45   © Michael Rubin.
48   Courtesy of Lucasfilm Ltd.
51   Courtesy of Lucasfilm Ltd.
53   The Murch Family Collection

Ch 4: The Star Wars
58   Courtesy of Lucasfilm Ltd.
61   © Ben and Peggy Burtt; Courtesy of Lucasfilm Ltd. (left and right)
63   Courtesy of Lucasfilm Ltd.
65   © Michael Rubin; Reprinted from *Nonlinear 4* (top)
65   Courtesy of Richard Edlund (bottom)
66   Courtesy of Lucasfilm Ltd.
67   Estate of John and James Whitney; All Rights Reserved
68   © Ben and Peggy Burtt; Courtesy of Lucasfilm Ltd.
70   Courtesy of Lucasfilm Ltd.
72   Courtesy of Lucasfilm Ltd.
73   Courtesy of Lucasfilm Ltd.

Ch 5: The Rebirth of Lucasfilm
76   Courtesy of Lucasfilm Ltd.
85   © Information International, Inc. Courtesy of Gary Demos
88   © Michael Rubin
89   © Michael Rubin

90   Courtesy of Lucasfilm Ltd.

Ch 6: The Godfather of Electronic Cinema
95   The Murch Family Collection
99   © Michael Rubin; Reprinted from *Nonlinear 4*

Ch 7: The Visionary of Long Island
106   Courtesy of Evans & Sutherland
109   Courtesy of Palo Alto Research Center
110   Courtesy of Palo Alto Research Center (top and bottom)
113   Courtesy of Lucasfilm Ltd.

Ch 8: The Train Wreck
115   Courtesy of Lucasfilm Ltd.
116   © Ed Catmull & Fred Parke. All Rights Reserved; Courtesy of Ed Catmull (top pair)
116   © Ed Catmull (bottom series)
117   Courtesy of Evans & Sutherland (pair)
117   © Fred Parke, University of Utah; Courtesy of Ed Catmull
118   Courtesy of Jim Blinn (top)
118   Courtesy of Alvy Ray Smith (bottom pair)
119   Courtesy of Lucasfilm Ltd. (top and bottom)
121   Courtesy of The Computer History Museum
125   Courtesy of Alvy Ray Smith
130   Courtesy of Alvy Ray Smith

Ch 9: Escape from New York
132   *Star Wars: Episode IV—A New Hope* ©1977 and 1997 Lucasfilm Ltd. &™. All rights reserved. Used under authorization. Unauthorized duplication is a violation of applicable law
136   Courtesy of Carol Emshwiller and Alvy Ray Smith
141   From the Jet Propulsion Laboratory; Courtesy of Jim Blinn

Ch 10: Inside Wonkaland
143   Courtesy of Lucasfilm Ltd.
145   © Michael Rubin
146   Courtesy of Lucasfilm Ltd.
148   From *Computer* magazine; Courtesy of Gary Demos
153   Courtesy of Lucasfilm Ltd.
154   Courtesy of Loren Carpenter
155   *Star Wars: Episode V—The Empire Strikes Back* ©1980 Lucasfilm Ltd. &™. All rights reserved. Used under authorization. Unauthorized duplication is a violation of applicable law.
157   Courtesy of Lucasfilm Ltd.
158   Courtesy of Chyron

Ch 11: Flying Free
165   © Zoetrope; Courtesy of Tom Scott and Alvy Ray Smith
167   Courtesy of Palo Alto Research Center
169   Courtesy of Lucasfilm Ltd.
170   Courtesy of Lucasfilm Ltd.
171   Courtesy of Lucasfilm Ltd.
174   Series courtesy of Loren Carpenter
176   Courtesy of Loren Carpenter
177   Courtesy of Lucasfilm Ltd.
177   Courtesy of Lucasfilm Ltd.

Ch 12: The Silverfish
185   Courtesy of Zoetrope (left and right)
186   Courtesy of Zoetrope
187   Courtesy of Zoetrope

Ch 13: Sound and Vision
192   © Capital Records
194   © Capital Records
194   © Capital Records
195   © Capital Records
196   Courtesy of Lucasfilm Ltd.
197   © Michael Rubin (left and right)
198   Courtesy of Lucasfilm Ltd.
202   Courtesy of Jim Blinn
204   © Information International, Inc. and Warner Studios; Courtesy of Gary Demos
205   © Michael Rubin (top/bottom)
207   © 2001 Michael Rubin; Reprinted from *Nonlinear 3*

Ch 14: Obnoxio
214   Courtesy of Lucasfilm Ltd.
215   Courtesy of Lucasfilm Ltd.
220   Courtesy of Lucasfilm Ltd.
228   Courtesy of Lucasfilm Ltd.

Ch 15: Double Suicide
234   Courtesy of Lucasfilm Ltd.
234   Jet Propulsion Laboratory; Courtesy of Jim Blinn
239   Reprinted from *American Cinematographer* magazine, October 1971; Used with permission
240   © Zoetrope; Courtesy of Thomas Brown

Ch 16: One thousand, six-hundred and twenty-one frames
252   © Kent Reno; All Rights Reserved
253   Courtesy of Lucasfilm Ltd.
255   Courtesy of Lucasfilm Ltd.

Ch 17: Queen's Rules
260   Courtesy of Lucasfilm Ltd. (all)
261   Courtesy of Lucasfilm Ltd.
262   Courtesy of Lucasfilm Ltd.
263   © Sun Microsystems (top)
263   Courtesy of Lucasfilm Ltd. (bottom)
264   Courtesy of Lucasfilm Ltd.
267   Courtesy of John Snell
268   Courtesy of Lucasfilm Ltd.

270 Courtesy of Lucasfilm Ltd.
272 Courtesy of Lucasfilm Ltd.
272 © Digital Productions. Courtesy of John Whitney, Jr.
274 Courtesy of Lucasfilm Ltd.
275 © Michael Rubin
277 Courtesy of Lucasfilm Ltd.
283 Courtesy of Lucasfilm Ltd.
284 © Pixar. Courtesy of Lucasfilm Ltd.
285 Courtesy of Lucasfilm Ltd.

Ch 18: A Hole in the Desert
294 © Activision; Courtesy of AtariAge.com
295 © Atari
299 © Atari
300 Courtesy of Lucasfilm Ltd.
303 Courtesy of Lucasfilm Ltd.
304 Courtesy of Lucasfilm Ltd.
305 Courtesy of Lucasfilm Ltd.
309 © Atari
311 Courtesy of Lucasfilm Ltd.
312 Courtesy of Lucasfilm Ltd.
313 Courtesy of Lucasfilm Ltd. (left and right)

Ch 19: Non-Stop Coffee Pots
316 *Star Wars: Episode VI—Return of the Jedi* ©1983 and 1997 Lucasfilm Ltd. &™. All rights reserved. Used under authorization. Unauthorized duplication is a violation of applicable law.
319 Courtesy of Lucasfilm Ltd./The Droid Works.
322 Courtesy of Chyron
324 Courtesy of Lucasfilm Ltd.
328 Courtesy of Lucasfilm Ltd.
329 Courtesy of Ken Yas
330 Courtesy of Lucasfilm Ltd.
333 Courtesy of Lucasfilm Ltd.
334 *Indiana Jones and the Temple of Doom* ©1984 Lucasfilm Ltd. &™. All rights reserved. Unauthorized duplication is a violation of applicable law. (left and right)

Ch 20: These Aren't the Droids You're Looking For
337 Courtesy of Lucasfilm Ltd.

338 Courtesy of Lucasfilm Ltd.
339 © Montage Group; Courtesy of Seth Haberman
340 Courtesy of Lucasfilm Ltd.
342 Courtesy of Lucasfilm Ltd.

Ch 21: My Breakfast with Andre
350 © Alvy Ray Smith
351 Adapted from an image courtesy of Loren Carpenter.
360 Courtesy of Lucasfilm Ltd.
361 © Pixar; Courtesy of the Pixar Archives (top)
361 © Pixar; Courtesy of Lucasfilm Ltd. (bottom)
362 Courtesy of Lucasfilm Ltd.
363 © Pixar; Courtesy of the Pixar Archives
364 Courtesy of Lucasfilm Ltd.
365 Courtesy of Lucasfilm Ltd. (top)
365 © Pixar; Courtesy of the Pixar Archives
366 Courtesy of Lucasfilm Ltd.
367 Courtesy of Lucasfilm Ltd.
368 Courtesy of Lucasfilm Ltd.
368 © Michael Rubin
369 Courtesy of Lucasfilm Ltd.
369 © Michael Rubin (bottom)
370 Courtesy of Lucasfilm Ltd.
371 Courtesy of Lucasfilm Ltd.
372 © Pixar; Courtesy of the Pixar Archives
374 © 1984 Lucasfilm Ltd. and Pixar; Courtesy of Lucasfilm Ltd.
377 Courtesy of the Pixar Archives

Ch 22: Playing Games
380 Courtesy of Lucasfilm Ltd.
380 Courtesy of Lucasfilm Ltd.
381 Courtesy of Lucasfilm Ltd.
382 Courtesy of Lucasfilm Ltd.
383 Courtesy of Lucasfilm Ltd. (top/bottom)
384 Courtesy of Lucasfilm Ltd.
386 Courtesy of Lucasfilm Ltd.
388 Courtesy of Lucasfilm Ltd. (left and right)
389 Courtesy of Lucasfilm Ltd. (all)
390 Courtesy of Lucasfilm Ltd./The Droid Works
391 Courtesy of Lucasfilm Ltd.

Ch 23: Rendezvous with Reality
400 Courtesy of Elliot Fishman
401 © Pixar; Courtesy of Lucasfilm Ltd., and Elliot Fishman
403 © Neftali Alvarez (left and right)
406 © Paramount Pictures; Courtesy of the Pixar Archives
407 Courtesy of Lucasfilm Ltd.
408 Courtesy of Lucasfilm Ltd.
409 © Paramount Pictures; Courtesy of the Pixar Archives
410 © Neftali Alvarez (left and right)
413 © Neftali Alvarez (top and bottom)
415 Courtesy of Lucasfilm Ltd.

Ch 24: Stay Small, Be the Best, Don't Loose Any Money
419 Courtesy of Lucasfilm Ltd.
422 Courtesy of Lucasfilm Ltd.
425 Courtesy of Lucasfilm Ltd.
427 Courtesy of Lucasfilm Ltd.
430 Courtesy of Lucasfilm Ltd.

Ch 25: Into the Twilight Zone
434 Courtesy of Lucasfilm Ltd.
435 © Michael Rubin
436 Courtesy of Lucasfilm Ltd.
445 Courtesy of Lucasfilm Ltd.

Ch 26: Esoteric Unto Occult
454 © Michael Rubin
457 Courtesy of Lucasfilm Ltd. (left and right)
458 © Pixar; Courtesy of the Pixar Archives
459 © Michael Rubin
460 © Michael Rubin
461 © Michael Rubin
462 © Michael Rubin (both)
463 © Michael Rubin

Epilogue
473 © Pixar; Courtesy of the Pixar Archives
475 © Michael Rubin
476 © Michael Rubin. Teapot and logo © Pixar
479 Courtesy of Lucasfilm Ltd.
486 © Michael Rubin
487 © Michael Rubin

The Lucasfilm Computer Division 1979–1986

	Name*	LFL Start	Project	Responsibility
1979	Ed Catmull	Jul-79		Director, Computer Division
	Susan Anderson	Nov-79		Admin/Computer Services Manager
1980	Alvy Ray Smith	Feb-80	Pixar	Graphics Project Leader
	David DiFrancesco	Feb-80	Pixar	Laser Project
	Malcolm Blanchard	Aug-80	EditDroid	Software
	John Seamons	Aug-80	Systems	Software
	Ralph Guggenheim	Sep-80	EditDroid	Editing Project Leader
	Bill Reeves	Sep-80	Pixar	Software
	Andy Moorer	Sep-80	SoundDroid	Sound Project Leader
	John Snell	Oct-80	SoundDroid	Hardware
	Tom Duff	Nov-80	Pixar	Software
	Clark Higgins	Nov-80	EditDroid	Video Engineer
	Dan Silva	Nov-80	EditDroid	Software
1981	Tom Porter	Jan-81	Pixar	Software
	Loren Carpenter	Jan-81	Pixar	Software
	Andy Neddermeyer	Jan-81	EditDroid	Video Technician
	Rob Poor	Jan-81	Pixar	Software
	Pat Cole	Feb-81	Pixar	Software
	Jim Blinn	Feb-81	Pixar	Software
	Jim Lawson	Mar-81	SoundDroid	Software
	Curtis Abbot	Mar-81	SoundDroid	Software
	Annie Arbogast	Mar-81	Systems	Technician
	Rodney Stock	May-81	Pixar	Hardware Engineer
	Gary Newman	May-81	Pixar	Hardware Engineer
	Rob Cook	Jun-81	Pixar	Software
	Lisa Ellis	Jun-81		Finance/HR
	Adam Levinthal	Nov-81	Pixar	Hardware Engineer
1982	Dorothy Land	Jan-82		Admin
	Shannon Collins	Jan-82		Admin
	Charlie Keagle	Feb-82	SoundDroid	Hardware Technician
	Jan Sweitzer	Feb-82	Systems	Technician
	Craig Good	May-82	Computer Services	Technician
	Muff Ryan	May-82	Systems	Admin
	Gabriel Stern	May-82	SoundDroid	Design Draftsman
	Glenn Sharp	May-82	Pixar	Technician
	Bob Doris	Jun-82		General Manager
	Peter Langston	Jul-82	Games	Games Project Leader
	Heidi Stettner	Jul-82	SoundDroid	Software
	Elizabeth Titherington	Jul-82	Systems	Technician
	Kay Frankcom	Aug-82		Admin
	Lane Molpus	Aug-82	Pixar	Design Engineer
	David Fox	Sep-82	Games	Games Designer
	Jed Rodriguey	Oct-82		Technician
	Dave Levine	Oct-82	Games	Games Designer
1983	Eben Ostby	Jan-83	Pixar	Software
	Thomas Noggle	Jan-83	Pixar	Laser Engineer
	Janice Diane	Jan-83		Budget Coordinator
	Alan Marr	Mar-83	SoundDroid	Software
	Thomas Heinz	Mar-83	Systems	Technician
	David Salesin	Mar-83	Pixar	Software
	Bruce Frederick	Mar-83	Pixar	Tech writer
	Charlie Kellner	April-83	Games	Games Designer
	Steve Schwartz	May-83	EditDroid	Video Engineer
	Sam Leffler	May-83	Pixar	Software
	Steven Baraniuk	Jul-83		Technician
	Leigh Yafa	*Mar-82*		Admin
	Michael Zentner	Aug-83	SoundDroid	Software
	Mark Leather	Aug-83	Pixar	Hardware

Name*	LFL Start	Project	Responsibility
David Blomgren	Sep-83	EditDroid	Tech writer
Bernard Mont-Reynaud	Sep-83	SoundDroid	Software Consultant
Michael O'Brien	Oct-83	CADDroid	Software
Rob Lay	Oct-83	EditDroid	Editing Project Leader
Andy Cohen	Nov-83	EditDroid	Software
John Lasseter	Nov-83	Pixar	Animator/Interface Designer
Julianne Keefe	Nov-83		Admin/Finance
Steve Arnold	Jan-84	Games	Games Project Leader
Gary Winnick	Jan-84	Games	Artist
Mary Paterno	*July-81*	Games	Admin
Matthew Martin	Jan-84	Pixar	Technician
Peter Nye	Feb-84	SoundDroid	Software
Noah Falstein	Feb-84	Games	Games Designer
Bob Drebin	Feb-84	Pixar	Software
Ronen Barzel	Feb-84	Pixar	Software
Noah Falstein	Feb-84	Games	Games Designer
Neftali Alvarez	Mar-84	Pixar	Technician
Dave Johansen	Mar-84		
Pamela Downey	Mar-84	Pixar	Technician
George Cagle	Mar-84	Computer Services	Technician
Sara Wright	Mar-84	Pixar	Admin
John Lynch	Mar-84	EditDroid	Software
Mary Sauer	Apr-84		Director of Marketing
Dennis "DJ" Jennings	Apr-84	Pixar	Purchasing
Mike Hawley	Apr-84	SoundDroid	Software
Carmen David	Apr-84	Droid	Admin
Chip Morningstar	May-84	Games	Games Designer
Craig Sexton	May-84	EditDroid	Sales
Jeff Borish	Jun-84	SoundDroid	Software
Kate Smith	Jul-84	EditDroid	Software
Ken Yas	Sep-84	EditDroid	Product Manager
Augie Hess	Oct-84	EditDroid	Field Service
Douglas Crockford	Nov-84	Games	Games Designer
Jim St.Louis	Nov-84	Games	Games Designer
Lola Gill	Dec-84	EditDroid	Admin
Ken Carson	Jan-85	EditDroid	Software
John Strawn	Jan-85	SoundDroid	Software
Keven Furry	Feb-85	Games	Games Designer
Aric Wilmunder	Feb-85	Games	Games Designer
Ron Gilbert	Mar-85	Games	Games Designer
Jeff Taylor	Apr-85	EditDroid	Field Service
John Newlander	Apr-85	EditDroid	Field Service
Michael Rubin	May-85	Droid	Marketing
Charles Ostman	May-85	Droid	Technical Designer
Merry Kaufman	May-85	Droid	Accounting
John Thompson	Jun-85	EditDroid	Software
Thom Blum	July-85	SoundDroid	Software
Cecil McGregor	Aug-85	EditDroid	Software
Lloyd Morgan	Aug-85	Droid	VP Manufacturing
F. Randall Farmer	Aug-85	Games	Games Designer
Ann Garcia	Sept-85	Droid	Buyer
Marie-Dominque Baudot	Sept-85	SoundDroid	Hardware
B. Morgan Martin	Jan-86	SoundDroid	Product Manager
Dennis Fahey	Mar-86	Droid	Hardware Engineer
Mark Puhalovitch	Mar-86	Droid	Finance
Mike Russell	Mar-86	Systems	Unix Engineer
Mike Shantzis	April-86	SoundDroid	Software

1984

1985

1986

•Isolated employees joined LFL prior to moving into the Computer Division; in those cases their start dates are in italics, and their position is the listing is roughly at the time they transferred in.

Index

Page numbers in italics indicate photographs.